D0500053

AMERICAN CONSTITUTIONAL ISSUES

McGRAW-HILL SERIES IN POLITICAL SCIENCE

Joseph P. Harris, *Consulting Editor*

ADRIAN · Governing Urban America: Structure, Politics, and Administration

ADRIAN · State and Local Governments

BONE · American Politics and the Party System

CHRISTENSON AND McWILLIAMS · Voice of the People: Readings in Public Opinion and Propaganda

EBENSTEIN · Political Thought in Perspective

FERGUSON AND McHENRY · American Federal Government

FERGUSON AND McHENRY · American System of Government

FERGUSON AND McHENRY · Elements of American Government

FIELD · Governments in Modern Society

FRANK · Cases on the Constitution

GOSNELL, LANCASTER, AND RANKIN · Fundamentals of American Government: National, State, and Local

GOSNELL, LANCASTER, AND RANKIN · Fundamentals of American National Government

GROSS · The Legislative Struggle

HAAS AND WHITING · Dynamics of International Relations

HARTMANN · Basic Documents of International Relations

HOLLOWAY · State and Local Government in the United States

McCLOSKY AND TURNER · The Soviet Dictatorship

MANGONE · A Short History of International Organization

MILLETT · Government and Public Administration

MILLETT · Management in the Public Service

NEUMANN · European and Comparative Government

PIERSON AND GIL · Governments of Latin America

PRITCHETT · The American Constitution

PRITCHETT · American Constitutional Issues

RIEMER · Problems of American Government

ROCHE AND STEDMAN · The Dynamics of Democratic Government

RODEE, ANDERSON, AND CHRISTOL · Introduction to Political Science

STRAUSZ-HUPÉ AND POSSONY · International Relations

SVARLIEN · An Introduction to the Law of Nations

TURNER · Politics in the United States: Readings in Political Parties and Pressure Groups

TURNER AND VIEG · The Government and Politics of California

VANDENBOSCH AND HOGAN · Toward World Order

WALDO · Ideas and Issues in Public Administration: A Book of Readings

WILSON · The American Political Mind

WILSON · Police Administration

AMERICAN CONSTITUTIONAL ISSUES

C. HERMAN PRITCHETT

Professor of Political Science
The University of Chicago

McGRAW-HILL BOOK COMPANY, INC.

New York · San Francisco · Toronto · London

AMERICAN CONSTITUTIONAL ISSUES

To the memory of

LEONARD D. WHITE

PREFACE

The Constitution of the United States, Charles Evans Hughes once remarked, means what the Supreme Court says it means. This is a book about the Constitution and what the Supreme Court has said that it means. For the most part, the Court is permitted to speak for itself in this volume, in which are reprinted some 50 of the Court's decisions on constitutional issues of great significance to present-day American government. However, to make these decisions fully meaningful, it has been necessary to supply a general introduction to each of the major sections of the book, as well as a commentary sketching in the background and development of each of the constitutional issues illustrated by the reprinted opinions.

While this emphasis on the role of the Supreme Court in constitutional interpretation is fully justified, it is important to understand that the Court has no monopoly in this field. Congress interprets the Constitution every time it passes a law or holds a hearing. The President construes the Constitution whenever he makes a decision, issues an order, or signs a bill into law. The Constitution of the United States is the body of practice built up during past decades by the executive departments. It is manifested in the historic crises that have been met—Lincoln facing the disintegration of the Union, Roosevelt facing the collapse of the national economy. It is discoverable equally at lower levels, in the routines and the customs of public life, in what Justice Holmes called the inarticulate major premises of a nation and a people.

Nevertheless, it is to the Supreme Court that we customarily defer as the ultimate arbiter of the Constitution. It is true that the Court has sometimes failed to live up to the standards of responsibility, wisdom, and statesmanship which its situation calls for. The political branches of the government may dispute or even, on occasion, override the judicial interpretation. But the Court has great resources of prestige and the life tenure of its members gives the Court a staying power which makes it a formidable opponent.

The Court has periodically been charged with making "political" decisions. The fact is that the Court cannot avoid political problems because the interpretation of the Constitution is a political task. But the issues of politics come to the Court in the form of a judicial case or controversy, from which at least some of the passion of politics has been drained. Moreover, the justices must present reasoned arguments for deciding cases the way they do. The quality of the Court's written opinions varies greatly, but at their best they may be gems of forensic skill and occasionally even noble literature. The fact that the Court is answering specific constitutional questions and doing so in the form of reasoned opinions which place the specific controversy against the whole context of prior constitutional thinking largely accounts for the fact that the Court's reputation as a constitutional interpreter is so much greater than that of the President or Congress.

A further factor which makes the Court's opinions ideal instruments for teaching purposes is the division of opinion among the justices in many of the most significant decisions. Justices who disagree with the Court's decision in a case are free to record their dissent and to state their reasons for disagreement. When this happens, the contrariety of views expressed offers the reader an unusual opportunity to appraise conflicting theories of constitutional interpretation. Some of the decisions included in this book have in fact been chosen because of the challenging character of the dissenting opinions.

Unfortunately, many of the Court's opinions are so long that for the purposes of this volume some editing is required. However, elimination of material has been kept to a minimum, in the belief that students will profit more from analyzing essentially the entire argument in a smaller number of cases than from reading snippets and disconnected paragraphs from a larger number of cases. Moreover, where dissenting opinions have been written, they are generally reproduced as fully as the majority views of the Court.

Finally, it should be noted that for the introductions and analytical material in this volume, the author has borrowed heavily from his treatise, *The American Constitution*, published by McGraw-Hill in 1959. The author also acknowledges substantial assistance rendered by Theodore M. Norton, now of San Jose State College.

C. Herman Pritchett

CONTENTS

PART THREE. THE PRESIDENT

PART FOUR. THE FEDERAL SYSTEM

PART FIVE. FIRST AMENDMENT FREEDOMS

PART ONE

The Judiciary

INTRODUCTION

The Constitution of the United States of America, drafted between May 14 and September 17, 1787, by fifty-five men meeting in the city of Philadelphia, and made effective on June 21, 1788, by the vote of nine state ratifying conventions, is now the oldest and preeminently the most successful written constitution in the modern history of man. The attention devoted to the American Constitution has been fully in proportion to the status it has achieved. It has attracted praise of outrageous extravagance—"The most wonderful work ever struck off at a given time by the brain and purpose of man," said William Gladstone—and has supplied a symbol of national unity sorely needed in a pageantless republic.

However, the document ratified in 1788—the parchment sheets preserved in a national shrine at the Archives in Washington—is not really the Constitution. Adding the twenty-three amendments which had been adopted up to 1961 does not markedly change the situation. All this language has had to be given life and meaning by the events that have occurred since 1788. In a real sense America's history is the American Constitution.

The process of constitutional adaptation is one which goes on at many levels and in many contexts. There are adaptations which develop on an entirely unplanned basis in the form of usages or customs or methods of procedure or institutions. Perhaps the most striking example in American history is the prompt development after 1789 of a party system, for which the framers had not planned, and which in fact they had taken some pains to try to prevent. The party system, with its tickets for President and Vice President, immediately required the remedial provisions of the Twelfth Amendment, but in no other respect has the written Constitution been changed to recognize the realities of party government. The development of committees in Congress, the tradition against a third term, the use of executive agreements instead of treaties, the custom that members of the House must be residents of the districts they represent in Congress—these and many other customs and usages represented evolutionary adjustments of the constitutional system to practical problems with which it was confronted.

The most highly rationalized type of constitutional interpretation is that engaged in by judges, and particularly by the Supreme Court of the United

States. Interpretation of the Constitution has been at issue in tens of thousands of the suits filed in American federal and state courts since 1789. A fraction of 1 per cent of this number has risen to the level of the United States Supreme Court for final decision, but in that handful are rulings of the most profound significance for the American nation. The great prestige of this Court is in fact based on its accepted position as ultimate judicial interpreter of the Constitution.

JUDICIAL ORGANIZATION

The judicial power of the United States, shall be vested in one Supreme Court, and in such inferior courts as the Congress may from time to time ordain and establish.   ART. III, SEC. I

The Supreme Court, the most distinguished and influential of the world's judicial tribunals, traces its position at the apex of the American judicial system directly to Article III of the Constitution. The members of the Constitutional Convention were clear that there had to be a top-level federal court, but they were less certain whether federal courts "inferior" to the Supreme Court were needed.

It was argued by some that the state courts could be authorized to try federal cases, subject to review by the federal Supreme Court. Others contended that the Constitution should provide for a full federal court system. The final decision was to hand this problem of federal organization over to Congress, and in the Judiciary Act of 1789 the advocates of a complete and separate system of federal courts were successful. However, these lower federal courts were given only a limited jurisdiction, and the plan of organization was faulty in several respects.

The Judiciary Act established a district court in each state, and grouped the districts into circuits with a circuit court for each. The district courts were given jurisdiction over admiralty proceedings and over lesser federal civil and criminal cases generally. District court decisions could be appealed to the circuit courts, which were also the courts of first instance for trial of all major civil and criminal cases coming within federal jurisdiction. Appointment of a United States attorney and marshal for each district was also authorized by the Judiciary Act.

The 1789 statute did not provide for any circuit court judges as such. The circuit courts were to be held by a Supreme Court justice and the district judge of the particular district, sitting together. This arrangement required Supreme Court justices to spend much of the year traveling by coach or on horseback, or perhaps by ship along the coast, from district to district and back to the capital. As the size of the country and the volume of litigation increased, it became less and less practicable for a Supreme Court justice to attend to his duties both on circuit and in Washington.

Eventually the district judges were authorized to hold the circuit courts alone —a practice which, incidentally, allowed them to rule on appeals from their own district court decisions. One permanent circuit judge was appointed for each circuit under an act of 1869, but circuit riding was not completely abandoned until the new circuit courts of appeal were established in 1891. Even today, each Supreme Court justice is assigned as "circuit justice" for one of the eleven circuits for purposes of certain paper work, and is entitled to sit on its court of appeals. The old circuit courts were finally combined with the district courts in 1911.

The federal judicial system consists of three levels. There are ninety-one district courts, at least one in each state, and more than three hundred district judges. Trials are held in the district courts before a single judge, except that when the constitutionality of a federal statute is questioned, and in certain other situations, three judges must sit in trial of a case. At the intermediate level are the courts of appeals for each of the ten circuits and the District of Columbia, with a total of some eighty judges. Each appeal is heard by a panel of three or more judges, and decisions of the courts of appeals go for review to the Supreme Court.

Outside the regular judicial establishment of district courts and courts of appeals are such specialized tribunals as the Court of Claims, the Customs Court, and the Court of Customs and Patent Appeals. The Court of Claims hears contract claims against the government; the Customs Court deals with questions arising in the administration of the tariff laws; and the Court of Customs and Patent Appeals reviews decisions of the Customs Court and the Patent Office.

On the edge of the federal judicial system are the so-called "legislative" courts. These are courts established by Congress under some constitutional authority other than Article III. Examples are the former territorial courts of Alaska and Hawaii and the courts of such insular possessions as Guam and the Virgin Islands. These tribunals were created under Article IV, section 3, which gives Congress power to make all needful rules and regulations respecting the territory or other property belonging to the United States. The judge of a legislative court can be appointed for a term of years rather than "during good behavior," his salary is not guaranteed, and he and his court can be required to perform duties not strictly judicial. He might also be subject to removal by the President for cause.

The notion of such legislative courts was sanctioned by John Marshall in *American Insurance Co. v. Canter,* 1 Pet. 511 (1828), who argued that such courts were not vested with any part of the "judicial power of the United States" under Article III. Since the Supreme Court is created by Article III and exercises only "judicial power," the question arises how it can review the decision of a legislative court. The Court of Claims was originally treated as a legislative court and the Supreme Court in *Gordon v. United States,* 117 U.S. 697 (1864), refused to review its decisions. Since that time, however, the Supreme Court has developed the doctrine that it will review the decisions even of legislative courts, if their proceedings are judicial in nature and admit of a final judgment, a conclusion which has been described as a "workable anomaly," illogical but practical. With respect to the Court of Claims, Customs Court, and Court of Customs and Patent Appeals, no such question can now arise, since Congress has declared by statute that each is a court created under Article III.

The courts of the District of Columbia are created under Article I, section 8, clause 17, giving Congress the power "to exercise exclusive legislation" over the District. These courts have been held to be both "legislative" and "constitutional"; thus the tenure and pay of their judges are protected by Article III but Congress can authorize them to exercise nonjudicial powers.

Other bodies called courts include the Tax Court and the Court of Military Appeals. The Tax Court is an administrative agency in the Treasury Department and legally not a court at all. The Court of Military Appeals is a part of the scheme of military justice established by Congress under its power (Art. I, sec. 8, clause 14) "To make rules for the government and regulation of the land and naval forces." The whole structure is outside the common-law system and there is no provision for review of court-martial decisions by the Supreme Court. By writ of habeas corpus, the civil courts will examine the claim of jurisdiction, whether the person and the offense are lawfully subject to trial by court-martial or military commission, but nothing beyond that point.

JURISDICTION OF THE FEDERAL COURTS

> The judicial power shall extend to all cases, in law and equity, arising under this Constitution, the laws of the United States, and treaties made, or which shall be made, under their authority;—to all cases affecting ambassadors, others public ministers and consuls;—to all cases of admiralty and maritime jurisdiction;—to controversies to which the United States shall be a party;—to controversies between two or more states;—between a state and citizens of another state;—between citizens of different states;—between citizens of the same state claiming lands under grants of different states, and between a state, or the citizens thereof, and foreign states, citizens or subjects.
>   ART. III, SEC. 2

The Constitution sets up a government of limited and delegated powers. The only powers Congress can exercise are those expressly granted in the Constitution or implied or resulting therefrom, and this axiom is as true of the federal courts as it is of Congress. The courts of the United States are courts of limited jurisdiction. If a case cannot be brought within one of the categories prescribed in Article III, no federal court can act, except to dismiss for want of jurisdiction.

The jurisdiction of the federal courts is defined by Article III on two different bases—subject matter and nature of the parties involved. The subject-matter classifications are (1) all cases in law and equity arising under the Constitution; (2) all cases in law and equity arising under the laws of the United States; (3) all cases in law and equity arising under treaties made under the authority of the United States; and (4) all cases of admiralty and maritime jurisdiction. Any case falling in these four fields can be brought in the federal courts, regardless of who the parties to the controversy may be.

Issues arising under the first three of these headings are referred to generally as "federal questions." Such a case arises wherever an interpretation or application of the Constitution or a federal statute or treaty is essential to a judicial decision. A plaintiff seeking to bring a case in the federal courts on one of these grounds must set forth on the face of his complaint a substantial claim as to the federal question involved. Cases appealed from state supreme courts are often refused review by the Supreme Court on the ground that no substantial federal question is involved.

The second basis for federal court jurisdiction is in terms of the parties involved. Article III extends federal jurisdiction to controversies (1) to which the United States is a party; (2) between two or more states; (3) between a state and citizens of another state; (4) between citizens of different states; (5) between a state, or the citizens thereof, and foreign states, citizens, or subjects; and (6) to all cases affecting ambassadors, other public ministers, and consuls. Matters involving these classes of parties can be brought in the federal courts, no matter what the subject matter.

Of these classes, the first and the fourth are by far the most important in the generation of litigation. The United States enters federal courts as a party plaintiff in a great number of civil and criminal suits every year, and it can also be haled into court as a defendant in situations where it has waived its sovereign immunity and given its consent to be sued. When no consent to sue the government has been given, it may be possible to sue officials acting for the government, particularly if they are alleged to be acting beyond their statutory authority or under an unconstitutional statute.

Suits between citizens of different states are commonly referred to as "diversity of citizenship" cases. The purpose of opening the federal courts to such cases was originally to provide a neutral forum for the determination of such disputes, since the state courts might be biased in favor of their own citizens and against "strangers" from other states. Today there is less likelihood of such bias, and many persons have urged the abolition of this class of federal jurisdiction. In 1958 Congress undertook to reduce the number of such cases in the federal courts by limiting them to disputes involving more than $10,000.

The provision extending federal jurisdiction to suits between a state and citizens of another state was the source of a controversy which resulted in adoption of the Eleventh Amendment. In *Chisholm* v. *Georgia*, 2 Dall. 419 (1793), the Supreme Court ruled that this language, which had been generally understood to be an authorization to each state to sue citizens of other states, also permitted citizens to sue a state other than their own. This judicial misreading of constitutional intent aroused a storm in the states, and Congress promptly responded by initiating the Eleventh Amendment to reverse this ruling.

Suits falling under federal jurisdiction can also be brought in state courts, except in those areas—such as federal criminal, admiralty, patent, and bankruptcy cases—where Congress has given the federal courts exclusive jurisdiction. In all other areas the state and federal courts enjoy concurrent jurisdiction over Article III cases. A suit meeting the tests of federal jurisdiction which is filed in a state court can by appropriate action be transferred to a federal court for trial. States have occasionally sought to place restrictions on the right of removal of civil suits from state to federal courts, particularly where out-of-state corporations are concerned, but such laws have usually been declared unconstitutional.

Where state courts do exercise federal jurisdiction, they are of course bound by the "supremacy clause" of the Constitution. Article VI, after making the Constitution, laws, and treaties of the United States "the supreme law of the land," continues: "and the judges in every state shall be bound thereby, any thing in the Constitution or laws of any state to the contrary notwithstanding."

The complication of a dual system of courts is one which other leading federal governments, such as Australia, Canada, and India, have avoided. In these countries there is only one federal court, superimposed on a complete system of state courts. By contrast the American system may often seem to be cumbersome and productive of confusion and delays. However, processes of cooperation and adjustment have largely solved the many potential conflicts in the dual system of courts.

THE FEDERAL JUDICIARY

The judges, both of the supreme and inferior courts, shall hold their offices during good behavior, and shall, at stated times, receive for their services, a compensation, which shall not be diminished during their continuance in office. ART. III, SEC. I

The appointment of federal judges is frankly and entirely a political process. With few exceptions the President limits his choice to members of his own party. From 1933 to 1961, for example, there were only two exceptions to this practice in Supreme Court appointments—President Truman's appointment of Republican Harold Burton, with whom he had been associated in the Senate, and President Eisenhower's naming of Democrat William Brennan, Jr. In the lower federal courts, during the present century over 90 per cent of all judicial appointments have gone to members of the President's party.

District judgeships are filled primarily on the recommendation of the state party organization and the senator from the state, if there is one of the President's party. The nominees thus suggested are given a thorough check by the Department of Justice, the FBI, and the American Bar Association's committee on the federal judiciary. Vacancies on the courts of appeals are sometimes filled by promotion of a district judge; the party organizations are still important, but not quite so dominant at this level.

For the Supreme Court, the President receives suggestions from many sources, and particularly from his Attorney General, but he makes his own decision, and often he has his own ideas on the subject, either as to specific persons or as to the qualifications he wants. Presidents usually concern themselves with the political viewpoint of a nominee, but predicting the future decisions of a potential justice is of course risky business. The Senate confirmation stage also affords an opportunity for the political views of the nominee to be considered. Perhaps the most famous instance was the violent fight on Justice Brandeis when he was nominated by President Wilson in 1916. He was attacked by conservatives because of his alleged lack of "judicial temperament," but won confirmation on a straight party vote. Charles Evans Hughes was also unsuccessfully opposed in 1931, some liberal Democrats and agrarian Republicans picturing him as a "corporation lawyer." The nomination of John J. Parker was actually defeated in 1930 because of unjustified allegations that he was antilabor and anti-Negro.

Appointment of federal judges for "good behavior" is one of the great pillars of judicial independence. A federal judge can be removed from office only by conviction on impeachment. Only one Supreme Court justice has ever been subjected to impeachment proceedings, Samuel Chase, whose judicial conduct was marked by gross and violent Federalist partisanship. In 1804 the triumphant Jeffersonians sought reprisal by way of impeachment, but failed to secure a conviction. Only eight lower federal court judges have been impeached in the entire history of the federal bench, four of whom were convicted.

The absence or inadequacy of retirement allowances has in the past been responsible for some judges retaining their posts long after they were physically or mentally incapacitated for the work. The age of Supreme Court justices was one of the key issues in President Roosevelt's 1937 "Court-packing" plan. As an aftermath of this controversy, Congress passed a liberalized retirement act which permits federal judges to retire after seventy on full pay without resigning, remaining thereafter subject to recall for further judicial duty in the lower courts.

THE SUPREME COURT AND ITS OPERATION

In all cases affecting ambassadors, other public ministers and consuls, and those in which a state shall be party, the Supreme Court shall have original jurisdiction. In all the other cases before mentioned, the Supreme Court shall have appellate jurisdiction, both as to law and fact, with such exceptions, and under such regulations as the Congress shall make.   ART. III, SEC. 2

The Supreme Court was originally composed of six judges, but its size was subsequently both reduced and increased by Congress, usually with political motives in mind. Since 1869 the size has been stable at nine members, and the effort of President Roosevelt to increase the number of justices in 1937 failed. The Court is headed by the Chief Justice of the United States. His formal authority consists primarily in his role as presiding officer in court and at the conferences and in his power to assign the writing of opinions.

There are some special problems of jurisdiction relating to the Supreme Court. It is primarily an appellate court, but the Constitution does define two categories of cases which can be heard in the Court's original jurisdiction, i.e., without prior consideration by any other court. These are cases in which a state is a party, and those affecting ambassadors, public ministers, and consuls. However, the Court generally does not have to accept a suit invoking its original jurisdiction unless it feels that there is a compelling reason of public policy.

All the remaining business of the Supreme Court comes to it in its appellate jurisdiction, which it exercises, as the Constitution says, "with such exceptions, and under such regulations as the Congress shall make." In the post-Civil War period Congress used this authority over the Court's appellate jurisdiction to withdraw from its consideration a politically embarrassing case in which the Court had already heard argument. The Supreme Court in *Ex parte McCardle*, 7 Wall. 506 (1869), agreed that such action was within congressional power. In 1957 Senator Jenner of Indiana unsuccessfully sought reprisal against the Court's decisions in certain national security cases by a bill withdrawing the Court's appellate jurisdiction in five specific kinds of cases.

Most of the cases the Supreme Court decides are brought before it by the writ of certiorari. This Latin word can be translated as "made more certain" or "better informed." It comes from the formal language of the old English writ of certiorari, by which a higher court ordered a lower court to send up the record of a case because the higher court wished to be better informed or more certain about the proceedings below.

Certiorari is a discretionary writ; that is, the Supreme Court does not have to grant a petition for certiorari and in most cases does not. Petitions are granted only in cases in which at least four of the nine justices agree that issues of special importance are presented.

Before a case can get to the Supreme Court it must have gone through whatever lower courts are proper for it. The role of the Supreme Court is then to correct errors of law—that is, mistakes in defining, interpreting, or applying the law—made by the courts below. But not all judicial errors are important enough to require correction by the Supreme Court. What are the "special and important" reasons the justices look for in considering a petition for certiorari? Rule 19 of the Rules of the Supreme Court provides as follows:

1. A review on writ of certiorari is not a matter of right, but of sound judicial discretion, and will be granted only where there are special and important reasons therefor. The following, while neither controlling nor fully measuring the court's discretion, indicate the character of reasons which will be considered:

(a) Where a state court has decided a federal question of substance not theretofore determined by this court, or has decided it in a way probably not in accordance with applicable decisions of this court.

(b) Where a court of appeals has rendered a decision in conflict with the decision of another court of appeals on the same matter; or has decided an important state or territorial question in a way in conflict with applicable state or territorial law; or has decided an important question of federal law which has not been, but should be, settled by this court; or has decided a federal question in a way in conflict with applicable decisions of this court; or has so far departed from the accepted and usual course of judicial proceedings, or so far sanctioned such a departure by a lower court, as to call for an exercise of this court's power of supervision.

In recent years the Supreme Court has granted less than 20 per cent of the petitions for certiorari filed annually. Even where reasons such as those mentioned in Rule 19 are shown, the Court may still decline to take up the case. The exercise of the Court's discretion in deciding whether to grant or deny certiorari may involve as much judicial statesmanship as the decision of a case on the merits. Justice Frankfurter once wrote: "Pertinent considerations of judicial policy here come into play. . . . Wise adjudication has its own time for ripening."

The bulk of the Supreme Court's cases come to it by certiorari, but there are several classes of cases in which an appeal has been provided for by act of Congress. Here the Court technically has no choice but to accept the case. Congress itself has determined that the matter is important enough to deserve Supreme Court attention. However, current procedure in appeals requires the appellant to file a preliminary "jurisdictional statement," and the Court tends to treat this statement as something like a petition for certiorari. If it decides to hear the case, probable jurisdiction is noted and the case set down for hearing. It may, however, consider a motion to dismiss or affirm at this stage, or simply refuse to review "for want of a substantial federal question."

Congress has provided for review by appeal of state court decisions denying a litigant's claim of federal right. A state court is said to have denied a claim of federal right (1) where it upholds a state law which one of the parties contends violates the federal Constitution, or (2) where one of the parties invokes a federal statute or treaty and the state court holds it invalid. Decisions of these types can be appealed from the highest state court "in which a decision could be had."

Appeals can also be taken from the lower federal courts. Appeals from the courts of appeals can be taken in cases where a state law has been held invalid as in conflict with a federal law, or where a federal statute has been held unconstitutional. An appeal can be taken from a federal district court directly to the Supreme Court (bypassing the court of appeals) where the district court has held either a state or a federal statute unconstitutional and issued an injunction forbidding its enforcement. Not only has Congress provided for a direct appeal in these cases, but they are considered so important that only a district court of three judges is permitted to issue such an injunction.

The Supreme Court meets for business in October of every year, and this "October Term" continues until the following June. The usual pattern of the Court's operation is to hear the arguments of counsel in cases before it for about two weeks at a time and then to recess for two weeks or so to study the cases and write opinions.

On Fridays during the term, the justices meet in conference to discuss and decide pending cases. At the conference the Chief Justice presents each case along with his views, and discussion then moves to the associate justices in order of seniority. When the vote is taken, the order is reversed, the most recent appointees to the Court voting first, and the Chief Justice last. Following the vote, the Chief Justice assigns the writing of the Court's opinion to himself or one of his colleagues. If the decision was not unanimous and the Chief Justice voted in the minority, the senior associate justice who voted in the majority controls the assignment of the decision. Drafts of opinions are circulated among the justices, and the author may revise the final opinion on the basis of comments by his colleagues.

In the Court's early days it was the custom for all justices to give their opinions seriatim in a case, and there was no single opinion "for the Court." However, when John Marshall became Chief Justice in 1801, he decided that the Court's prestige and power would be increased if a single opinion were prepared, and in fact he himself wrote the opinion in almost all important cases. Justices were still free to write concurring or dissenting opinions, but there was a tendency for them to go along with the Court in silence unless their disagreement was sharp. More recent practice permits dissents to be registered much more freely, and during many terms the nonunanimous decisions have outnumbered the unanimous ones.

It is a fundamental principle of American and English jurisprudence that a decision by the highest court in a jurisdiction is a binding precedent on the questions of law involved in the case. The court making the decision and all of the courts subordinate to it are expected to follow the precedent and to give similar answers to similar questions whenever they arise thereafter. The Latin label for this rule is *stare decisis*, "to stand by the things decided."

Although *stare decisis* is an ancient and fundamental principle, the Supreme Court does not always follow it. Particularly in constitutional cases, the Court may find it necessary to disregard or overrule its own prior decisions. If the Court will not change its interpretation of the Constitution, this can be accomplished only by a formal amendment. Justice Brandeis put the matter very well:

> Stare decisis is usually the wise policy, because in most matters it is more important that the applicable rule of law be settled than that it be settled right. . . . This is commonly true even where the error is a matter of serious concern, provided correction can be had by legislation. But in cases involving the Federal Constitution, where correction through legislative action is practically impossible, this Court has often overruled its earlier decisions. The Court bows to the lessons of experience and the force of better reasoning, recognizing that the process of trial and error, so fruitful in the physical sciences, is appropriate also in the judicial function.
> [*Burnet v. Coronado Oil & Gas Co.*, 285 U.S. 393 (1932).]

JUDICIAL MOTIVATION

Since only fourteen chief justices and eighty-two associate justices have sat on the Supreme Court since 1789, the impact of individual judicial minds upon constitutional development is interestingly visible. When we say that the Supreme Court has made a decision, we actually mean that the nine justices who compose the Court at a particular point in history have made the decision. Often, in fact, it is a decision made by only five members of the Court, with which the other four disagree. These justices are men—men of widely varying abilities, backgrounds, and political preferences. How the Constitution will be interpreted by them depends in part upon what kind of men they are and how the world looks to them.

This has not always been understood. During considerable periods of American history there has been a popular impression that when men were appointed to the Supreme Court, they somehow became depersonalized and disembodied of all ordinary prejudices and passions. In the rarefied atmosphere of their chambers they were presumed to be at work discovering the law by the exercise of pure reason. This myth has typically been strongest during periods when the Court was under conservative domination, and it served the purpose of convincing the public that judicial protection of property or the thwarting of regulatory legislation was not an expression of the personal preferences of the justices but a voicing of the authentic commands of the Constitution. The myth, however, was finally and irretrievably destroyed in the years from 1935 to 1937, when it became all too apparent that the doctrine which the Supreme Court majority was expounding was their personal laissez-faire economic beliefs. As Max Lerner said, the public learned then "that judicial decisions are not babies brought by constitutional storks."

It is an equally grave error, however, to jump to the conclusion that Supreme Court justices typically determine the meaning of the Constitution merely by consulting their personal preferences. There is an institutional ethos about the Court which cannot fail to have a restraining effect upon the most opinionated justice. One of these institutional factors, for example, is *stare decisis*, the rule of precedent. The individual judge may think that a particular precedent is wrong or outmoded. If so, he may follow his personal preference and state his reasons for voting to overrule the earlier holding. He is free to do that. But he is not free to ignore the precedents, to act as though they did not exist. He must dispose of them by rational arguments. He has free choice, but only among limited alternatives and after he has satisfied himself that he has met the obligations of consistency and respect for settled principles which his responsibility to the Court imposes upon him. His private views as an individual help to form and may be incorporated into his public views as a judge, but they are not the same thing.

The Supreme Court and its members have often been attacked for individual decisions or for the tendency of their decisions over a period of time. In the twentieth century, there have been two particularly severe periods of pressure on the Court. The first came between 1935 and 1937, when a Court composed entirely of members appointed before 1933 took issue with the New Deal and declared unconstitutional, often by a vote of five to four, a number of the key statutes in President Roosevelt's program for economic recovery from the Depression. After his smashing electoral victory in 1936, Roosevelt felt strong enough to tackle the Supreme Court with his "Court-packing" plan. While Congress defeated this proposal, in several key cases during the spring of 1937 the Court supported the administration by a five to four margin. At the end of the term one of the conservative justices, Van Devanter, resigned, and President Roosevelt had an opportunity to begin remaking the Court.

The other serious attack upon the Court was that which developed in Congress between 1956 and 1959. Primarily at issue here was the Court's 1954 decision declaring racial segregation in the public schools unconstitutional, as well as the decisions in certain national security matters, particularly congressional power to investigate Communist activities and the punishment of Communists under the Smith Act. Because the Court insisted on a serious consideration of equal protection and due process requirements and constitutional limitations on freedoms of speech and assembly, it was subjected to widespread attacks in Congress and in the country, and proposals were made to reverse some of the Court's decisions and even, as already noted, to strip it of some of its established appellate authority. However, again the Court survived with its powers unimpaired, though again it did withdraw from some of the positions it had taken.

Many efforts have been made to describe, analyze, and account for the views announced by individual members of the Supreme Court in its constitutional decisions. The Court can be regarded as a small legislature, and the voting behavior of the justices can be examined according to legislative patterns. A common method of analysis is to make a bloc analysis of the Court by recording the votes in nonunanimous decisions. The existence of blocs of opinion on the Court during various periods of its history is of course well established. During the New Deal period there was a conservative four-judge bloc composed of Justices McReynolds, Van Devanter, Sutherland, and Butler, and an equally cohesive liberal group of Justices Cardozo, Brandeis, and Stone. In that situation, the votes of the two remaining members of the Court, Chief Justice Hughes and Justice Roberts, determined how the decision would go in the controversial cases.

On the Court after 1937, Justices Black, Douglas, Murphy, and Rutledge were almost always together on civil liberties issues, so that they needed to get the vote of only one additional justice in order to control the Court. Later, on the Warren Court there was a slightly less firm bloc composed of the Chief Justice and Justices Brennan, Black, and Douglas.

It is possible to suggest only very broadly the issues on which Supreme Court justices have disagreed over the years. Inevitably the reader of the opinions reprinted here will undertake to label the justices who wrote them according to the positions they have taken on the issues. The labels which have been most commonly used in such analyses are the following:

1. Conservative versus liberal. These are such broad terms that they are often meaningless, but they can be sharpened somewhat if they are applied only in the area of economic policy. The divisions on the Court during the first third of the present century often reflected dispute between those justices who wished to keep the government from intervening in the economic field and those who were willing to allow government experimentation in regulating wages or prices or economic practices. The decision in *Lochner* v. *New York* (page 425) demonstrates this kind of split, which has become less important since 1937 with the disappearance of any real economic conservatives from the Court.

2. Nationalism versus states' rights. This division was particularly important during the nineteenth century. Chief Justice John Marshall took a strongly nationalist position in such decisions as *McCulloch* v. *Maryland* (page 79) and *Gibbons* v. *Ogden* (page 123), and it was largely due to his effective work that

the new government was armed with the constitutional powers it needed for vigorous development. On the other hand a later Chief Justice, Roger Taney, generally took a states' rights position.

3. Libertarian versus antilibertarian. Since the First World War the Supreme Court has increasingly been concerned with application of the Bill of Rights in federal and state cases. Considerable difference of opinion has been evident on the Court with respect to the importance of upholding libertarian claims, which always have to be balanced against other important community goals such as peace and order. The decision in *Near* v. *Minnesota* (page 235) is an early illustration of this division, particularly interesting since the antilibertarian minority of four justices also constituted the economic conservative bloc of that period. Later, on the Roosevelt Court the prolibertarians developed the so-called "preferred position" doctrine as a justification for the emphasis which they placed on safeguarding civil liberties.

4. Activism versus self-restraint. These labels have been widely used to suggest the difference between justices who are more willing to use their judicial powers to correct what they personally regard as injustices than are some of their colleagues. Justice Frankfurter has been by far the most persistent member of the Court in stating the case for judicial self-restraint, which he traces back to his mentor, Justice Holmes. Frankfurter's argument in *Poe* v. *Ullman* (page 27) against deciding the constitutionality of Connecticut's birth control law is a good demonstration of judicial self-restraint at work. Justices Black and Douglas have usually been regarded as the prototypes of judicial activism. However, this distinction is a very slippery one, and in *Southern Pacific Co.* v. *Arizona* (page 143) it was Justice Black who charged his majority colleagues with judicial activism by taking on the role of a "super-legislature."

Applying labels such as the above to justices is of course no real explanation of judicial motivation, but it is an inevitable part of the endlessly fascinating process of searching for the reasons which underlie the divisions of opinion revealed in these decisions.

GUIDE TO THE STUDY OF SUPREME COURT DECISIONS

Judicial decisions are identified by the names of the parties, as *Gibbons* v. *Ogden* or *Kent* v. *Dulles*. The "v." is an abbreviation of the Latin "versus," here translated as "against." Generally, the first name is that of the plaintiff, the one who started the proceedings, and the second is that of the defendant, of whom the plaintiff complains and against whom he seeks relief. On appeal, the party asking for review by a higher court is known as the appellant or petitioner, and his opponent as the appellee or respondent. If it is the defendant who appeals, the order of the names in the caption may be reversed and the defendant's, as appellant or petitioner, placed first.

The usual lawsuit has two parties of equal standing and opposed interests. In some proceedings, however, there will be only one party, at least in the initial stages. Anyone seeking a writ of habeas corpus directly from the Supreme Court must start by asking leave to file his petition. Since at this point no other party is or has been directly involved, the papers will be headed simply *Ex parte Jones*. "Ex parte" is lawyers' Latin meaning "on the part of" or "from the side of." The papers and decisions in many proceedings which do not necessarily have two adversary parties of the usual kind may also be entitled *In re Jones,* that is, "in the matter of Jones."

Supreme Court decisions can be identified by reference to the set of printed reports in which they are published. The citation for *Kent* v. *Dulles* is 357 U.S. 116. The first number indicates volume; the initials U.S. refer to the United States Reports, the official series published by the Government Printing Office; and the final number indicates the page where the decision begins.

Supreme Court decisions are also collected in two other sets of reports issued by commercial publishing houses. One is the Supreme Court Reporter, abbreviated S. Ct.; the citation for *Kent* v. *Dulles* in this source is 78 S. Ct. 1113. The other is known as Lawyers Edition, cited as L. Ed.; *Kent* v. *Dulles* is 2 L. Ed. 2d 1204.

Up to 1874, Supreme Court cases were identified not by the name of the series or set of volumes in which they were published, but by the name of the reporter who collected them. The citation for *Gibbons* v. *Ogden,* decided in 1824, is 9 Wheat. 1. "Wheat." is an abbreviation for Wheaton, whose twelve volumes of reports cover the years 1816–1827. The complete list of these early reporters, with the customary abbreviations, is as follows:

		U.S.
Dallas (Dall.)	1789–1800	1–4
Cranch (Cr.)	1801–1815	5–13
Wheaton (Wheat.)	1816–1827	14–25
Peters (Pet.)	1828–1842	26–41
Howard (How.)	1843–1860	42–65
Black (Bl.)	1861–1862	66–67
Wallace (Wall.)	1863–1874	68–90

These volumes, ninety in all, have also been assigned numbers in the U.S. series, as indicated.

Decisions of the United States Courts of Appeals are published in the Federal Reporter, now in its second series (F. 2d). District court judges do not always file formal written opinions, but may do so, and these are collected in the Federal Supplement (F. Supp.).

The process of summarizing or abstracting a court decision is referred to as "briefing" the opinion. A sample brief is given below:

McCULLOCH v. MARYLAND
4 Wheat. 316 (1819)

(1) *Character of the action.* From decision against him in Court of Appeals of state of Maryland, McCulloch appealed on writ of error to United States Supreme Court under section 25, Judiciary Act of 1789.

(2) *Facts.* Congress in 1816 passed act incorporating the Second Bank of the United States. Maryland in 1818 passed an act taxing all banks or branches not chartered by the state at prohibitory rates. Tax was on all notes issued by such banks or in lieu thereof a flat tax of $15,000 per year, with $500 penalty for each violation. McCulloch, cashier of Maryland branch of the Bank of the United States, issued notes and refused to pay the tax. Maryland brought suit against him to recover the penalties and obtained decision against McCulloch.

(3) *Issues.* (*a*) Has Congress power to incorporate the Bank of the United States? Yes. (*b*) Has Maryland the right to levy this tax against the bank chartered by Congress? No.

(4) *Decision.* Judgment of Court of Appeals of Maryland is reversed and annulled.

(5) *Opinion or reasons for the decision.* Marshall, C.J.: Has Congress power to charter bank? Constitution is not a mere compact of sovereign states, but established a supreme national government. Admittedly Congress is not expressly given power to issue charters of incorporation. But Tenth Amendment does not limit Congress's powers to those *expressly* granted. Congress is expressly granted power to lay and collect taxes, borrow money, regulate commerce, declare war, raise and support armies. Congress must have means to accomplish these ends. Power of issuing charters of incorporation only an incidental power. Congress expressly given power "to make all laws necessary and proper for carrying foregoing powers into execution." This is a grant of power, not a restriction. "Necessary and proper" does not limit Congress to those means which are indispensable but entitles it to use all those which are convenient and appropriate. Charter of bank is appropriate.

Can Maryland lay tax against the bank? Bank an instrument of the national government, which having power to create it also has power to preserve it. But state power to tax involves power to destroy it. National constitution and laws supreme and state laws repugnant thereto are void. No argument to say that we should assume Maryland will not use tax power to destroy. Therefore tax is unconstitutional.

(6) *Concurring or dissenting opinions.* None.

(7) *Comments.* This decision stems from Hamilton's opinion on constitutionality of the First Bank of the United States; cf. also Jefferson's opinion. It is the classic statement of the doctrines of implied powers of the national government, national supremacy over the states, and the function of the Court as umpire of the federal system. Cf. the Virginia and Kentucky Resolutions. Its influence on later statesmen such as Webster and Lincoln is incalculable.

Chapter 1

THE POWER OF JUDICIAL REVIEW

The most important responsibility of the Supreme Court is to interpret the Constitution of the United States. In carrying out that high duty the Court may find it necessary to nullify state statutes or even acts of Congress as violative of the Constitution. Naturally this is not something the Court does every day, but it happens often enough to serve as a constant reminder that the American system is one of "judicial supremacy."

It is a characteristic of judicial action that it comes last in the process of government. The legislature enacts new programs or regulations and the executive takes the steps to make them effective, but it often happens that some aspects of the enforcement program lead to disagreement or even to resistance. It is only by resort to the courts that these disagreements can be resolved or the resistance dispelled. Where government action proposes to take away a man's property or liberty, only a court decision can ratify such action.

So the courts have the last word. If they have the power to pass on questions of constitutionality, judicial review almost automatically becomes judicial supremacy. A Supreme Court decision on a constitutional issue can be overruled only by the Court itself or by a constitutional amendment.

The basic theory on which the American practice of judicial review is based may be summarized as follows. The written Constitution is a superior law, subject to change only by an extraordinary legislative process, and as such it is superior to common and statutory laws. The powers of the several departments of government are limited by the terms of the Constitution. The judges are expected to enforce the provisions of the Constitution as the higher law and to refuse to give effect to any legislative act or executive order in conflict therewith.

Now the curious thing is that there is nothing about this in the Constitution itself. The immediate source of the doctrine is the decision of Chief Justice John Marshall in the case of *Marbury* v. *Madison*, 1 Cranch 137 (1803). The facts in this case were simple enough. In the background, however, were the partisan struggles of the times. The Democrats, led by Jefferson, had decisively defeated the Federalists in 1800. Party feeling ran high on both sides. It was the rule, prior to the ratification of the Twentieth Amendment in 1933, that the winners in the elections in November did not take office until the following March. Although defeated, John Adams and the Federalists remained in control as "lame ducks" for this four-month interim.

The Democrats were hostile to the federal judiciary, because it stood for a

15

strong centralized government and because it supported a jurisprudence founded on the English law, which shared the unpopularity of all things English. Furthermore, the federal judges, all appointed by Washington or Adams, were overwhelmingly Federalists, and some of them rather violently so. The Democrats had even threatened wholesale impeachment of these Federalist judges.

The Federalists of course favored the federal judiciary for the same reasons that the Democrats opposed it. The "lame-duck" session of Congress in 1801 offered the Federalists a last chance to improve and strengthen the organization of the federal courts and also to provide for a few more Federalist appointments. A bill was passed to provide full-time judges for the circuit courts (thus relieving the Supreme Court justices of their circuit-riding duties), and President Adams was careful to fill these positions and all other judicial vacancies before leaving office. The men he appointed were called the "midnight judges" by the Democrats, who said that Adams, on March 3, had stayed up until his term expired at midnight signing the commissions.

The Federalist act establishing new circuit courts was without effect; the Democrats promptly repealed it. But two of Adams's last-minute appointments turned out to be of considerable importance. One was the naming of John Marshall as Chief Justice of the Supreme Court; the other was that of William Marbury as a justice of the peace for the District of Columbia.

In 1801, the situation of the Federalists and of the federal judiciary as an independent and equal (and Federalist) branch of the national government was dark indeed. As a political party, the Federalists were never to recover from their defeat in 1800. The judiciary was under Democratic attack, and even the Supreme Court had been temporarily immobilized. The new Democratic Congress, in an attempt to keep the Court from passing on the repeal of the Federalist judiciary act, had rearranged the Court's terms and postponed its next session by fourteen months. Pending before the Court was Marbury's petition for a writ of mandamus to Secretary of State James Madison.

What had happened was that after President Adams had signed and sealed the commission of Marbury as justice of the peace, the outgoing Federalist Secretary of State, none other than John Marshall, had failed to deliver it before going out of office, and Jefferson had instructed Madison not to deliver it. Marbury filed his petition for mandamus in the Supreme Court directly without any prior court proceedings, thus invoking the Court's original jurisdiction. Marbury's authority was a section of the Judiciary Act of 1789 providing that "the Supreme Court . . . shall have power to issue . . . writs of mandamus, in cases warranted by the principles and usages of law, to any courts appointed, or persons holding office, under the authority of the United States."

A writ of mandamus (Latin for "we command") is an order to a court or a public official to perform some act required by law. In this case, Marbury asked only that Madison be ordered to give him his commission or a certified copy thereof. The Supreme Court could grant the petition or deny it. At first glance, it seemed that the Court was bound to lose the contest for power and prestige whichever it did. If the writ were issued, Madison, with Jefferson's support, would refuse to obey it, and the Court would have no practical means of compelling him to do so. If the Court refused relief to Marbury, it would be admitting officially that it lacked any authority to control the executive. In either case, the judiciary and the Federalists would be humiliated and the triumph of Jefferson and the Democrats would be complete and obvious.

Marshall's decision was a masterful stroke. The Court declined to issue the writ, and consequently Madison and Jefferson had nothing to defy or resist. But the writ was refused not because the Court lacked power to give relief against executive officers, but because the Court asserted that the provision of the Judiciary Act quoted above was an unconstitutional attempt to add to the Supreme Court's original jurisdiction.

Legally, the decision is subject to considerable criticism. If the Court lacked jurisdiction, as Marshall held, there was no occasion to consider anything else, but such a course would have deprived Marshall of the opportunity to lecture the Democratic administration on its behavior. Moreover, the section of the Judiciary Act in question could have been interpreted in a way to make it constitutional. As we shall see, the Court has subsequently developed the rule that statutes should always be interpreted so as to avoid constitutional difficulties. The section on mandamus could have been held to apply only to cases within the Supreme Court's original jurisdiction on other grounds, that is, because a state or an ambassador was a party. But this interpretation would not have served Marshall's purpose.

The power asserted by Marshall has been the subject of endless discussion. Is a decision on the constitutionality of a statute simply a question of law and therefore clearly within the power of the courts as a part of their ordinary judicial duties? Or is it a question of a distinct and higher order, a question of politics and policy? This is the fundamental problem.

The draftsmen of the Constitution left the question unanswered. Such evidence as there is of contemporary opinion and practice tends to support Marshall. The notion of a higher law, the Bible, natural law, political compacts, and the old colonial charters were certainly familiar to the Americans of that day, and in case of a conflict between higher law and lower, the higher should of course prevail. That these matters were discussed in terms of "law" suggests that there was some conception that the courts were qualified to deal with them. What the revolutionary generation called the law of nature, we might be more likely to treat as ethics or political philosophy today, but this does not weaken the argument that the Constitution is a higher law, and by its own terms "the supreme law of the land."

Furthermore, though Marshall cited no precedents, state courts had already found occasion to strike down state statutes because they were in violation of state constitutions. Alexander Hamilton in No. 78 of *The Federalist* had argued strongly in favor of judicial review, an argument from which Marshall borrowed. And even the Democrats voiced no strong objections to the doctrine at the time, though they denounced Marshall's attempt to instruct Jefferson and Madison in the performance of their official duties. The Chief Justice's arguments may not have been unanswerable, but his conclusion that passing on the constitutionality of acts of Congress is one of the normal functions of the judiciary seems to have been pretty well accepted in 1803. It is, of course, unshakably established today.

In more modern times, judicial review has been criticized as undemocratic, in that it turns basic policy decisions over to a lifetime judiciary responsible to no popular will. That there is room for judicial discretion in decisions on constitutionality cannot be doubted. Seldom is a statute so plainly and obviously in violation of the Constitution that there is not room for two opinions about it. The fact is that decisions on constitutional issues are likely to be as much a matter of social and economic philosophy as of logical deduction and immutable principles of law, and the fact that these decisions are made by nine men called judges sitting in a marble palace does not change the situation.

One method of countering the undemocratic charge is to admit it and then go on to point out that democratic nature or quality is not the sole test of an institution in the American system. The Constitution does not provide for a simple democratic regime, always directly responsive to majority will, but for a federal representative republic equipped with a number of built-in checks and balances, of which judicial review is one.

Another answer also admits that the Supreme Court is undemocratic, but asserts that it is not dangerously so. The Court, it is said, is inherently so weak that it cannot long defy the settled determination of a substantial majority. When it has tried to do so, as in the battle against the New Deal in the thirties, it has not been able to maintain its position long. Congress controls most of its jurisdiction, many of its powers, and even the number of justices. The execution of its judgments and the appointment of its members depend on the President. It is consequently by no means immune from popular and political pressures.

Logically, of course, these two answers tend to cancel each other out. This is some indication of the Court's delicate and paradoxical position as a politically significant, formally nondemocratic, institution in a nation that thinks of itself as a democracy.

MARBURY v. MADISON
1 Cranch 137, 2 L. Ed. 60 (1803)

Opinion of the Court [by the CHIEF JUSTICE].

At the last term on the affidavits then read and filed with the clerk, a rule was granted in this case, requiring the secretary of state to show cause why a *mandamus* should not issue, directing him to deliver to William Marbury his commission as a justice of the peace for . . . the district of Columbia.

No cause has been shown, and the present motion is for a *mandamus*. The peculiar delicacy of this case, the novelty of some of its circumstances, and the real difficulty attending the points which occur in it, require a complete exposition of the principles on which the opinion to be given by the court is founded. . . .

In the order in which the court has viewed this subject, the following questions have been considered and decided.

1st. Has the applicant a right to the commission he demands? [The Court concluded that he did, and that withholding of the commission was "violative of a vested legal right."]

2dly. If he has a right, and that right has been violated, do the laws of his country afford him a remedy? [The Court concluded that they did.]

It remains to be inquired whether,

3dly. He is entitled to the remedy for which he applies. . . .

This . . . is a plain case for a *mandamus* . . . to deliver the commission . . . and it only remains to be inquired,

Whether it can issue from this court.

The act to establish the judicial courts of the United States authorizes the supreme court "to issue writs of *mandamus,* in cases warranted by the principles and usages of law, to any courts appointed, or persons holding office, under the authority of the United States."

The secretary of state, being a person holding an office under the authority of the United States, is precisely within the letter of the description; and if this court is not authorized to issue a writ of *mandamus* to such an officer, it must be because the law is unconstitutional, and therefore absolutely incapable of conferring the authority, and assigning the duties which its words purport to confer and assign.

The constitution vests the whole judicial power of the United States in one supreme court, and such inferior courts as congress shall, from time to time, ordain and establish. . . .

In the distribution of this power it is declared that "the supreme court shall have original jurisdiction in all cases affecting ambassadors, other public ministers and consuls, and those in which a state shall be a party. In all other cases, the supreme court shall have appellate jurisdiction." . . .

If it had been intended to leave it in the discretion of the legislature to apportion the judicial power between the supreme and inferior courts according to the will of that body, it would certainly have been useless to have proceeded further than to have defined the judicial power, and the tribunals in which it should be vested. The subsequent part of the section is mere surplusage, is entirely without meaning, if such is to be the construction. If congress remains at liberty to give this court appellate jurisdiction, where the constitution has declared their jurisdiction shall be original; and original jurisdiction where the constitution has declared it shall be appellate; the distribution of jurisdiction, made in the constitution, is form without substance. . . .

It cannot be presumed that any clause in the constitution is intended to be without effect; and, therefore, such a construction is inadmissible. . . .

To enable this court, then, to issue a *mandamus,* it must be shown to be an exercise of appellate jurisdiction, or to be necessary to enable them to exercise appellate jurisdiction. . . .

It is the essential criterion of appellate jurisdiction, that it revises and corrects the proceedings in a cause already instituted, and does not create that cause. Although, therefore, a *mandamus* may be directed to courts, yet to issue such a writ to an officer for the delivery of a paper, is in effect the same as to sustain an original action for that paper, and, therefore, seems not to belong to appellate, but to original jurisdiction. Neither is it necessary in such a case as this, to enable the court to exercise its appellate jurisdiction.

The authority, therefore, given to the supreme court, by the act establishing the judicial courts of the United States, to issue writs of *mandamus* to public officers, appears not to be warranted by the constitution; and it becomes necessary to inquire whether a jurisdiction so conferred can be exercised.

The question, whether an act, repugnant to the constitution, can become the law of the land, is a question deeply interesting to the United States; but, happily, not of an intricacy proportioned to its interest. It seems only necessary to recognise certain principles, supposed to have been long and well established, to decide it.

That the people have an original right to establish, for their future government, such principles as, in their opinion, shall most conduce to their own happiness is the basis on which the whole American fabric has been erected. The exercise of this original right is a very great exertion; nor can it, nor ought it, to be frequently repeated. The principles, therefore, so established, are deemed fundamental. And as the authority from which they proceed is supreme, and can seldom act, they are designed to be permanent.

This original and supreme will organizes the government, and assigns to different departments their respective powers. It may either stop here, or establish certain limits not to be transcended by those departments.

The government of the United States is of the latter description. The powers of the legislature are defined and limited; and that those limits may not be mistaken, or forgotten, the constitution is written. To what purpose are powers limited, and to what purpose is that limitation committed to writing, if these limits may, at any time, be passed by those intended to be restrained? The distinction between a government with limited and unlimited powers is abolished, if those limits do not confine the persons on whom they are imposed, and if acts prohibited and acts allowed, are of equal obligation. It is a proposition too plain to be contested, that the constitution controls any legislative act repugnant to it; or, that the legislature may alter the constitution by an ordinary act.

Between these alternatives there is no middle ground. The constitution is either a superior paramount law, unchangeable by ordinary means, or it is on a level with ordinary legislative acts, and, like other acts, is alterable when the legislature shall please to alter it.

If the former part of the alternative be true, then a legislative act contrary to the constitution is not law: if the latter part be true, then written constitutions are absurd attempts, on the part of the people, to limit a power in its own nature illimitable.

Certainly all those who have framed written constitutions contemplate them as forming the fundamental and paramount law of the nation, and, consequently, the theory of every such government must be, that an act of the legislature, repugnant to the constitution, is void.

This theory is essentially attached to a written constitution, and, is consequently, to be considered, by this court, as one of the fundamental principles of our society. It is not therefore to be lost sight of in the further consideration of this subject.

If an act of the legislature, repugnant to the constitution, is void, does it, notwithstanding its invalidity, bind the courts, and oblige them to give it effect? Or, in other words, though it be not law, does it constitute a rule as operative as if it was a law? This would be to overthrow in fact what was established in theory; and would seem, at first view, an absurdity too gross to be insisted on. It shall, however, receive a more attentive consideration.

It is emphatically the province and duty of the judicial department to say what the law is. Those who apply the rule to particular cases, must of necessity expound and interpret that rule. If two laws conflict with each other, the courts must decide on the operation of each.

So if a law be in opposition to the constitution; if both the law and the constitution apply to a particular case, so that the court must either decide that case conformably to the law, disregarding the constitution; or conformably to the constitution, disregarding the law; the court must determine which of these conflicting rules governs the case. This is of the very essence of judicial duty.

If, then, the courts are to regard the constitution, and the constitution is superior to any ordinary act of the legislature, the constitution, and not such ordinary act, must govern the case to which they both apply.

Those, then, who controvert the principle that the constitution is to be considered, in court, as a paramount law, are reduced to the necessity of maintaining that courts must close their eyes on the constitution, and see only the law.

This doctrine would subvert the very foundation of all written constitutions. It would declare that an act which, according to the principles and theory of our government, is entirely void, is yet, in practice, completely obligatory. It would declare that if the legislature shall do what is expressly forbidden, such act, notwithstanding the express prohibition, is in reality effectual. It would be giving to the legislature a practical and real omnipotence, with the same breath which professes to restrict their powers within narrow limits. It is prescribing limits, and declaring that those limits may be passed at pleasure.

That it thus reduces to nothing what we have deemed the greatest improvement on political institutions, a written constitution, would of itself be sufficient, in America, where written constitutions have been viewed with so much reverence, for rejecting the construction. But the peculiar expressions of the constitution of the United States furnish additional arguments in favour of its rejection.

The judicial power of the United States is extended to all cases arising under the constitution.

Could it be the intention of those who gave this power, to say that in using it the constitution should not be looked into? That a case arising under the constitution should be decided without examining the instrument under which it arises?

This is too extravagant to be maintained.

In some cases, then, the constitution must be looked into by the judges. And if they can open it at all, what part of it are they forbidden to read or to obey?

There are many other parts of the constitution which serve to illustrate this subject.

It is declared that "no tax or duty shall be laid on articles exported from any state." Suppose a duty on the export of cotton, of tobacco, or of flour; and a suit instituted to recover it. Ought judgment to be rendered in such a case? ought the judges to close their eyes on the constitution, and only see the law?

The constitution declares "that no bill of attainder or *ex post facto* law shall be passed."

If, however, such a bill should be passed, and a person should be prosecuted under it; must the court condemn to death those victims whom the constitution endeavours to preserve?

"No person," says the constitution, "shall be convicted of treason unless on the testimony of two witnesses to the same overt act, or on confession in open court."

Here the language of the constitution is addressed especially to the courts. It prescribes, directly for them, a rule of evidence not to be departed from. If the legislature should change that rule, and declare *one* witness, or a confession *out* of court, sufficient for conviction, must the constitutional principle yield to the legislative act?

From these, and many other selections which might be made, it is apparent, that the framers of the constitution contemplated that instrument as a rule for the government of *courts,* as well as of the legislature.

Why otherwise does it direct the judges to take an oath to support it? This oath certainly applies in an especial manner, to their conduct in their official character. How immoral to impose it on them, if they were to be used as the instruments, and the knowing instruments, for violating what they swear to support!

The oath of office, too, imposed by the legislature, is completely demonstrative of the legislative opinion on this subject. It is in these words: "I do solemnly swear that I will administer justice without respect to persons, and do equal right to the poor and to the rich; and that I will faithfully and impartially discharge all the duties incumbent on me as   , according to the best of my abilities and understanding, agreeably to *the constitution* and laws of the United States."

Why does a judge swear to discharge his duties agreeably to the constitution of the United States, if that constitution forms no rule for his government? if it is closed upon him, and cannot be inspected by him?

If such be the real state of things, this is worse than solemn mockery. To prescribe, or to take this oath, becomes equally a crime.

It is also not entirely unworthy of observation, that in declaring what shall be the *supreme* law of the land, the *constitution* itself is first mentioned; and not the laws of the United States generally, but those only which shall be made in *pursuance* of the constitution, have that rank.

Thus, the particular phraseology of the constitution of the United States confirms and strengthens the principle, supposed to be essential to all written constitutions, that a law repugnant to the constitution is void; and that *courts,* as well as other departments, are bound by that instrument.

The rule must be discharged.

EAKIN v. RAUB
12 Sergeant & Rawle 330 (1825)

There was no dissent on the Supreme Court against Chief Justice Marshall's reasoning in *Marbury v. Madison.* But in an otherwise unimportant decision by the Pennsylvania supreme court in 1825, Justice Gibson countered the Marshall arguments. While this is a state decision, Gibson's statement that the Pennsylvania constitution does not specifically mention judicial review is equally true of the federal Constitution.

GIBSON, J. . . .

. . . I begin, then, by observing that in this country, the powers of the judiciary are divisible into those that are POLITICAL and those that are purely CIVIL. Every power by which one organ of the government is enabled to control another, or to exert an influence over its acts, is a political power. . . . [The judiciary's] civil, are its *ordinary* and *appropriate* powers; being part of its essence, and existing independently of any supposed grant in the constitution. But where the government exists by virtue of a *written* constitution, the judiciary does not necessarily derive from that circumstance, any other than its ordinary and appropriate powers. Our judiciary is constructed on the principles of the common law, which enters so essentially into the composition of our social institutions as to be inseparable from them, and to be, in fact, the basis of the whole scheme of our civil and political liberty. In adopting any organ or instrument of the common law, we take it with just such powers and capacities as were incident to it as the common law, except where these are expressly, or by necessary implication, abridged or enlarged in the act of adoption; and, that such act is a written instrument, cannot vary its consequences or construction. . . . Now, what are the powers of the judiciary at the common law? They are those that necessarily arise out of its immediate business; and they are therefore commensurate only with the judicial execution of the municipal law, or, in other words, with the administration of distributive justice, without extending to anything of a politcal cast whatever. . . . With us, although the legislature be the depository of only so much of the sovereignty as the people have thought fit to impart, it is nevertheless sovereign within the limit of its powers, and may relatively claim the same pre-eminence here that it may claim elsewhere. It will be conceded, then, that the ordinary and essential powers of the judiciary do not extend to the annulling of an act of the legislature. . . .

The constitution of *Pennsylvania* contains no express grant of political powers to the judiciary. But, to establish a grant by implication, the constitution is said to be a law of superior obligation; and, consequently, that if it were to come into collision with an act of the legislature, the latter would have to give way. This is conceded. But it is a fallacy, to suppose that they can come into collision *before the judiciary.* . . .

The constitution and the right of the legislature to pass the act, may be in collision. But is that a legitimate subject for judicial determination? If it be, the judiciary must be a peculiar organ, to revise the proceedings of the legislature, and to correct its mistakes; and in what part of the constitution are we to look for this proud pre-eminence? Viewing the matter in the opposite direction, what would be thought of an act of assembly in which it should be declared that the Supreme Court had, in a particular case, put a wrong construction on the constitution of the United States, and that the judgment should therefore be reversed? It would doubtless be thought a usurpation of judicial power. But it is by no means clear, that to declare a law void which has been enacted according to the forms prescribed in the constitution, is not a usurpation of legislative power. . . .

But it has been said to be emphatically the business of the judiciary, to ascertain and pronounce what the law is; and that this necessarily involves a consideration of the constitution. It does so: but how far? If the judiciary will inquire into anything besides the form of enactment, where shall it stop? There must be some point of limitation to such an inquiry; for no one will pretend that a judge would be justifiable in calling for the election returns, or scrutinizing the qualifications of those who composed the legislature. . . .

. . . In theory, all the organs of the government are of equal capacity; or, if not equal, each must be supposed to have superior capacity only for those things which peculiarly belong to it; and, as legislation peculiarly involves the consideration of those limitations which are put on the law-making power, and the interpretation of the laws when made, involves only the construction of the laws themselves, it follows that the construction of the constitution in this particular belongs to the legislature, which ought therefore to be taken to have superior capacity to judge of the constitutionality of its own acts. But suppose all to be of equal capacity in every respect, why should one exercise a controlling power over the rest? That the judiciary is of superior rank, has never been pretended, although it has been said to be co-ordinate. It is not easy, however, to comprehend how the power which gives law to all the rest, can be of no more than equal rank with one which receives it, and is answerable to the former for the observance of its statutes. Legislation is essentially an act of sovereign power; but the execution of the laws by instruments that are governed by prescribed rules and exercise no power of volition, is essentially otherwise. . . . It may be said, the power of the legislature, also, is limited by prescribed rules. It is so. But it is, nevertheless, the power of the people, and sovereign as far as it extends. It cannot be said, that the judiciary is co-ordinate merely because it is established by the constitution. If that were sufficient, sheriffs, registers of wills, and recorders of deeds, would be so too. Within the pale of their authority, the acts of these officers will have the power of the people for their support; but no one will pretend, they are of equal dignity with the acts of the legislature. Inequality of rank arises not from the manner in which the organ has been constituted, but from its essence and the nature of its functions; and the legislative organ is superior to every other, inasmuch as the power to will and to command, is essentially superior to the power to act and to obey. . . .

. . . [H]ad it been intended to interpose the judiciary as an additional barrier, the matter would surely not have been left in doubt. The judges would not have been left to stand on the insecure and ever shifting ground of public opinion as to constructive powers; they would have been placed on the impregnable ground of an express grant. They would not have been compelled to resort to the debates in the convention, or the opinion that was generally entertained at the time. . . . The grant of a power so extraordinary ought to appear so plain, that he who should run might read. . . .

What I have in view in this inquiry, is the supposed right of the judiciary to interfere, in cases where the constitution is to be carried into effect through the instrumentality of the legislature, and where that organ must necessarily first decide on the constitutionality of its own act. The oath to support the constitution is not peculiar to the judges, but is taken indiscriminately by every officer of the government, and is designed rather as a test of the political principles of the man, than to bind the officer in the discharge of his duty: otherwise it is difficult to determine what operation it is to have in the case of a recorder of deeds, for instance, who, in the execution of his office, has nothing to do with the constitution. But granting it to relate to the official conduct of the judge, as well as every other officer, and not to his political principles, still it must be understood in reference to supporting the constitution, *only as far as that may be involved in his official duty;* and, consequently, if his official duty does not comprehend an inquiry into the authority of the legislature, neither does his oath. . . .

But do not the judges do a positive act in violation of the constitution, when they give effect to an unconstitutional law? Not if the law has been passed according to the forms established in the constitution. The fallacy of the question is, in supposing that the judiciary adopts the acts of the legislature as its own; whereas the enactment of a law and the interpretation of it are not concurrent acts, and as the judiciary is not required to concur in the enactment, neither is it in the breach of the constitution which may be the consequence of the enactment. The fault is imputable to the legislature, and on it the responsibility exclusively rests. . . .

But it has been said, that this construction would deprive the citizen of the advantages which are peculiar to a written constitution, by at once declaring the power of the legislature in practice to be illimitable. . . . But there is no magic or inherent power in parchment and ink, to command respect and protect principles from violation. In the business of government a recurrence to first principles answers the end of an observation at sea with a view to correct the dead reckoning; and for this purpose, a written constitution is an instrument of inestimable value. It is of inestimable value, also, in rendering its first principles familiar to the mass of people; for, after all, there is no effectual guard against legislative usurpation but public opinion, the force of which, in this country is inconceivably great. . . . Once let public opinion be so corrupt as to sanction every misconstruction of the constitution and abuse of power which the temptation of the moment may dictate, and the party which may happen to be predominant, will laugh at the puny efforts of a dependent power to arrest it in its course.

For these reasons, I am of opinion that it rests with the people, in whom full and absolute sovereign power resides, to correct abuses in legislation, by instructing their representatives to repeal the obnoxious act. . . . On the other hand, the judiciary is not infallible; and an error by it would admit of no remedy but a more distinct expression of the public will, through the extraordinary medium of a convention; whereas, an error by the legislature admits of a remedy by an exertion of the same will, in the ordinary exercise of the right of suffrage,—a mode better calculated to attain the end, without popular excitement. . . .

But in regard to an act of [a state] assembly, which is found to be in collision with the constitution, laws, or treaties of the *United States,* I take the duty of the judiciary to be exactly the reverse. By becoming parties to the federal constitution, the states have agreed to several limitations of their individual sovereignty, to enforce which, it was thought to be absolutely necessary to prevent them from giving effect to laws in violation of those limitations, through the instrumentality of their own judges. Accordingly, it is declared in the sixth article and second section of the federal constitution, that "This constitution, and the laws of the *United States* which shall be made in pursuance thereof, and all treaties made, or which shall be made under the authority of the *United States,* shall be the *supreme* law of the land; and the *judges* in every *state* shall be BOUND thereby: anything in the *laws* or *constitution* of any *state* to the contrary notwithstanding."

This is an express grant of a political power, and it is conclusive to show that no law of inferior obligation, as every state law must necessarily be, can be executed at the expense of the constitution, laws, or treaties of the *United States.* . . .

Chapter 2

JUSTICIABLE QUESTIONS

The Supreme Court recognizes, in principle, that its power to construe the Constitution, and particularly its power to declare acts of Congress unconstitutional, must be exercised with great restraint. Consequently it approaches constitutional questions with reluctance, and will normally decide cases on a constitutional issue only when there seems to be no feasible alternative.

The easiest means of avoiding constitutional questions is, of course, to deny certiorari in cases where such an issue is present, and this the Court sometimes does. Again, in a case which the Court has agreed to hear, decision may be delayed until the heat has gone out of a constitutional question. Several wartime civil liberties cases have not been decided until after the war was over.

The Supreme Court has, furthermore, imposed upon itself a comprehensive body of rules aimed at encouraging judicial self-restraint and avoiding constitutional decisions. As summarized by Justice Brandeis in his concurring opinion in *Ashwander* v. *Tennessee Valley Authority*, 297 U.S. 288 (1936), these include the following: (1) The Court will not anticipate a question of constitutionality in advance of the necessity of deciding that question, nor is it the habit of the Court to decide questions of a constitutional nature unless absolutely necessary to a decision of the case in hand. (2) The Court will not formulate a rule of constitutional law broader than is required by the precise facts to which it is to be applied. (3) The Court will not pass upon a constitutional question, although properly presented by the record, if there is also present some other ground upon which the case may be disposed of. (4) When the validity of an act of Congress is drawn into question, and even if a serious doubt of constitutionality is raised, it is a cardinal principle that the Court will first ascertain whether a construction of the statute is fairly possible by which the question may be avoided.

Whether or not the Court always follows these rules, they do reflect the general principles of its approach to judicial review. Beyond these maxims of judicial self-restraint, there are certain more technical rules applied to limit the breadth and freedom of the Supreme Court's approach to constitutional issues. One of these is the rule that the question must be "justiciable."

The judicial power that the Constitution gives the federal courts is the power to determine "cases" and "controversies" of the types specified in Article III. What is a case or controversy? Not every argument or dispute presented in the form of a lawsuit will qualify. To have a case or controversy in the constitutional sense there must be (1) adverse parties (2) who have a substantial legal interest (3) in a dispute arising out of facts, not hypothetical but real (4) in which there can be an enforceable determination of the rights of the parties. These conditions are so well understood that they customarily raise no difficulties, but they do relieve the Court of passing on some broad public issues which cannot be fitted into the context of a traditional lawsuit.

The Supreme Court will examine very closely any case in which a constitutional issue seems to be presented to determine whether it involves a genuine contest over substantial rights and interests. All courts rely on the litigants and their lawyers to inform the court fully, to explore all the issues of law and fact, and to explain and justify the result they wish the court to reach. The fact that the parties are in opposition and that opposing counsel can be relied on to point out each other's errors and omissions protects the court from acting without full understanding and consideration.

One reason the Supreme Court has always refused to give advisory opinions is that it would not have the benefit of this complete exploration of all the issues and implications in passing on a hypothetical question. For the same reason, it is usually quick to detect and to refuse to rule on made-up cases which are in reality nothing but attempts to obtain a Supreme Court ruling on abstract questions of law. Such a proceeding was once expressly authorized by Congress to settle the legal status of certain Indian lands, but the Court declined to act. *Muskrat* v. *United States*, 219 U.S. 346 (1911).

An additional danger formerly involved in "friendly" lawsuits has now been eliminated by statute. Generally only the parties of record have a right to be heard in a case. Constitutional cases usually present important questions of policy in which the public has an interest, but prior to 1937 if a case started out as one between private persons, there was no provision for participation by any public agency. If the suit was a friendly one, both parties might in fact be seeking the same result—for instance, to get a statute declared unconstitutional. In such a situation, there would be no one before the Court presenting the case for the statute.

In 1895, for example, the federal income tax was declared unconstitutional in a suit brought by a corporate stockholder against the corporation to prevent it from paying the tax: *Pollock* v. *Farmers' Loan & Trust Co.*, 157 U.S. 429. It seems unlikely that the corporation fought very hard to uphold its obligation to pay the tax. This particular decision was, in effect, overruled by the adoption of the Sixteenth Amendment, but the problem of representation of the public interest in constitutional litigation was not dealt with until 1937, when Congress provided that the United States must be joined as a party in any case in which the constitutionality of a federal statute was questioned.

An important element of justiciability is "standing to sue." Not everyone with money enough to bring a lawsuit is entitled to litigate the constitutionality or legality of government action in the federal courts. To have the standing necessary to maintain such an action, the plaintiff must establish the sufficiency of his interest in the controversy, and this means satisfying the courts on two main issues: (1) that his interest is one that is peculiar and personal to him and not one he shares with all other citizens generally, and (2) that the interest he is defending is a legally recognized and protected right immediately threatened by some government action.

The first of the above principles is well demonstrated by the case of *Massachu-*

setts v. *Mellon,* 262 U.S. 447 (1923). In 1921 Congress passed a maternity act providing grants-in-aid for states which would cooperate in a federal program to reduce maternal and infant mortality and protect the health of mothers and infants. Suit to enjoin the operation of the statute on grounds of unconstitutionality was brought in the District of Columbia by a Mrs. Frothingham, who sought to sustain her standing in court by alleging that she was a taxpayer of the United States and that the effect of the appropriations authorized by this act would be to increase the burden of future taxation and thereby take her property without due process of law.

The Supreme Court unanimously denied her standing to bring the suit. Although taxpayers' suits are rather common in local and state courts, Justice Sutherland pointed out that:

. . . the relation of a taxpayer of the United States to the Federal Government is very different. His interest in the moneys of the Treasury—partly realized from taxation and partly from other sources—is shared with millions of others; is comparatively minute and indeterminable; and the effect upon future taxation, of any payment out of the funds, so remote, fluctuating and uncertain, that no basis is afforded for an appeal to the preventive powers of a court of equity.

The courts are generally concerned with the rights and wrongs of past actions, but in some situations it is recognized that "anticipatory relief" may be justified. By means of a "declaratory judgment," federal courts, as well as those in most states, are authorized to declare rights and other legal relations in cases of actual controversy. A declaratory judgment permits parties who are in disagreement about their legal rights to secure a judicial decision without requiring that they place themselves in jeopardy by taking action based on their conflicting legal interpretations. A declaratory judgment is not an advisory opinion, but a court may decline to render a declaratory judgment where it feels that a decision would be premature, as in *Poe* v. *Ullman,* 367 U.S. 497 (1961). The same general position denying judicial review because the issues involved were prematurely raised was asserted by the Court majority under different circumstances in *Communist Party* v. *Subversive Activities Control Board,* 367 U.S. 1 (1961).

POE v. ULLMAN
367 U.S. 497, 81 S. Ct. 1752, 6 L. Ed. 2d 989 (1961)

MR. JUSTICE FRANKFURTER announced the judgment of the Court in an opinion which THE CHIEF JUSTICE, MR. JUSTICE CLARK and MR. JUSTICE WHITTAKER join.

These appeals challenge the constitutionality, under the Fourteenth Amendment, of Connecticut statutes which, as authoritatively construed by the Connecticut Supreme Court of Errors, prohibit the use of contraceptive devices and the giving of medical advice in the use of such devices. In proceedings seeking declarations of law, not on review of convictions for violation of the statutes, that court has ruled that these statutes would be applicable in the case of married couples and even under claim that conception would constitute a serious threat to the health or life of the female spouse.

No. 60 combines two actions brought in a Connecticut Superior Court for declaratory relief. The complaint in the first alleges that the plaintiffs Paul and Pauline Poe [fictitious names] are a husband and wife, thirty and twenty-six years old respectively, who live together and have no children. Mrs. Poe has had three consecutive pregnancies terminating in infants with multiple congenital abnormalities from which each died shortly after birth. Plaintiffs have consulted Dr. Buxton, an obstetrician and gynecologist of eminence, and it is Dr. Buxton's opinion that the cause of the infants' abnormalities is genetic. . . . In view of the great emotional stress already suffered by plaintiffs, the probable consequence of another pregnancy is psychological strain extremely disturbing to the physical and mental health of both husband and wife. Plaintiffs know that it is Dr. Buxton's opinion that the best and safest medical treatment which could be prescribed for their situation is advice in methods of preventing conception. Dr. Buxton knows of drugs, medicinal articles and instruments which can be safely used to effect contraception. Medically, the use of these devices is indicated as the best and safest preventive measure necessary for the protection of plaintiffs' health. Plaintiffs, however, have been unable to obtain this information for the sole reason that its delivery and use may or will be claimed by the defendant State's attorney . . . to constitute offenses against Connecticut law. The State's attorney intends to prosecute offenses against the State's laws, and claims that the giving of contraceptive advice and the use of contraceptive devices would be offenses forbidden by Conn. Gen. Stat. Rev. 1958, §§ 53–32 and 54–196. Alleging irreparable injury and a substantial uncertainty of legal relations . . . plaintiffs ask a declaratory judgment that §§ 53–32 and 54–196 are unconstitutional, in that they deprive the plaintiffs of life and liberty without due process of law.

The second action in No. 60 is brought by Jane Doe, a twenty-five-year-old housewife. Mrs. Doe, it is alleged, lives with her husband, they have no children; Mrs. Doe recently underwent a pregnancy which induced in her a critical physical illness—two weeks' unconsciousness and a total of nine weeks' acute sickness which left her with partial paralysis, marked impairment of speech, and emotional instability. Another pregnancy would be exceedingly perilous to her life. She, too, has consulted Dr. Buxton, who believes that the best and safest treatment for her is contraceptive advice. . . .

In No. 61, also a declaratory judgment action, Dr. Buxton is the plaintiff. Setting forth facts identical to those alleged by Jane Doe, he asks that the Connecticut statutes prohibiting his giving of contraceptive advice to Mrs. Doe be adjudged unconstitutional, as depriving him of liberty and property without due process. . . .

Appellants' complaints in these declaratory proceedings do not clearly, and certainly do not in terms, allege that appellee Ullman threatens to prosecute them for use of, or for giving advice concerning, contraceptive devices. The allegations are merely that, in the course of his public duty, he intends to prosecute any offenses against Connecticut law, and that he claims that use of and advice concerning contraceptives would constitute offenses. The lack of immediacy of the threat described by these allegations might alone raise serious questions of non-justiciability of appellants' claims. . . . But even were we to read the allegations to convey a clear threat of imminent prosecutions, we are not bound to accept as true all that is alleged on the face of the complaint and admitted, technically, by demurrer. . . . Formal agreement between parties that collides with plausibility is too fragile a foundation for indulging in constitutional adjudication.

The Connecticut law prohibiting the use of contraceptives has been on the State's books since 1879. . . . During the more than three quarters of a century since its enactment, a prosecution for its violation seems never to have been initiated, save in State v. Nelson, 126 Conn. 412, 11 A. 2d 856. The circumstances of that case, decided in 1940, only prove the abstract character of what is before us. There, a test case was brought to determine the constitutionality of the act as applied against two doctors and a nurse who had allegedly disseminated contraceptive information. After the Supreme Court of Errors sustained the legislation on appeal from a demurrer to the information, the State moved to dismiss the information. Neither counsel nor our own researches have discovered any other attempt to enforce the prohibition of distribution or use of contraceptive devices by criminal process. The unreality of these law suits is illumined by another circumstance. We were advised by counsel for appellant that contraceptives are commonly and notoriously sold in Connecticut drug stores. Yet no prosecutions are recorded; and certainly such ubiquitous, open, public sales would more quickly invite the attention of enforcement officials than the conduct in which the present appellants wish to engage—the giving of private medical advice by a doctor to his individual patients, and their private use of the devices prescribed. The undeviating policy of nullification by Connecticut of its anti-contraceptive laws throughout all the long years that they have been on the statute books bespeaks more than prosecutorial paralysis. . . .

The restriction of our jurisdiction to cases and controversies within the meaning of Article III of the Constitution . . . is not the sole limitation on the exercise of our appellate powers, especially in cases raising constitutional questions. The policy reflected in numerous cases and over a long period was thus summarized in the oft-quoted statement of Mr. Justice Brandeis: "The Court [has] developed, for its own governance in the cases confessedly within its jurisdiction, a series of rules under which it has avoided passing upon a large part of all the constitutional questions pressed upon it for decision." *Ashwander* v. *Tennessee Valley Authority,* 297 U.S. 288 (concurring opinion). In part the rules summarized in the *Ashwander* opinion have derived from the historically defined, limited nature and function of courts and from the recognition that, within the framework of our adversary system, the adjudicatory process is most securely founded when it is exercised under the impact of a lively conflict between antagonistic demands, actively pressed, which make resolution of the controverted issue a practical necessity. . . . In part they derive from the fundamental federal and tripartite character of our national government and from the role —restricted by its very responsibility—of the federal courts, and particularly this Court, within that structure. . . .

These considerations press with special urgency in cases challenging legislative action or state judicial action as repugnant to the Constitution. . . . The various doctrines of "standing," "ripeness," and "mootness," which this Court has evolved with particular, though not exclusive, reference to such cases are but several manifestations . . . of the primary conception that federal judicial power is to be exercised to strike down legislation, whether state or federal, only at the instance of one who is himself immediately harmed, or immediately threatened with harm, by the challenged action. . . .

The fact that Connecticut has not chosen to press the enforcement of this statute deprives these controversies of the immediacy which is an indispensable condition of constitutional adjudication. This Court cannot be umpire to debates concerning harmless, empty shadows. To find it necessary to pass on these statutes now, in order to protect appellants from the hazards of prosecution, would be to close our eyes to reality.

. . . It is true that this Court has several times passed upon criminal statutes challenged by persons who claimed that the effects of the statutes were to deter others from maintaining profitable or advantageous relations with the complainants. See, e.g., *Truax* v. *Raich,* 239 U.S. 33; *Pierce* v. *Society of Sisters,* 268 U.S. 510. But in these cases the deterrent effect complained of was one which was grounded in a realistic fear of prosecution. We cannot agree that if Dr. Buxton's compliance with these statutes is uncoerced by the risk of their enforcement, his patients are entitled to a declaratory judgment concerning the statutes' validity. And, with due regard to

Dr. Buxton's standing as a physician and to his personal sensitiveness, we cannot accept, as the basis of constitutional adjudication, other than as chimerical the fear of enforcement of provisions that have during so many years gone uniformly and without exception unenforced. . . .

Dismissed.

MR. JUSTICE BLACK dissents because he believes that the constitutional questions should be reached and decided.

MR. JUSTICE BRENNAN, concurring in the judgment.

. . . The true controversy in this case is over the opening of birth-control clinics on a large scale; it is that which the State has prevented in the past, not the use of contraceptives by isolated and individual married couples. It will be time enough to decide the constitutional questions urged upon us when, if ever, that real controversy flares up again. . . .

MR. JUSTICE DOUGLAS, dissenting.

These cases are dismissed because a majority of the members of this Court conclude, for varying reasons, that this controversy does not present a justiciable question. That conclusion is too transparent to require an extended reply. . . . Plaintiffs in No. 60 are two sets of husband and wife. One wife is pathetically ill, having delivered a stillborn fetus. If she becomes pregnant again, her life will be gravely jeopardized. This couple have been unable to get medical advice concerning the "best and safest" means to avoid pregnancy from their physician, plaintiff in No. 61, because if he gave it he would commit a crime. And it is alleged—and admitted by the State—that the State's Attorney intends to enforce the law by prosecuting offenses under the laws.

A public clinic dispensing birth control information has indeed been closed by the State. Doctors and a nurse working in that clinic were arrested by the police and charged with advising married women on the use of contraceptives. That litigation produced *State* v. *Nelson* . . . which upheld these statutes. . . .

The Court refers to the *Nelson* prosecution as a "test case" and implies that it had little impact. Yet its impact was described differently by a contemporary observer who concluded his comment with this sentence: "This serious setback to the birth control movement [the *Nelson* case] led to the closing of all the clinics in the state, just as they had been previously closed in the state of Massachusetts." At oral argument, counsel for appellants confirmed that the clinics are still closed. In response to a question from the bench he affirmed that "no public or private clinic" has dared give birth control advice since the decision in the *Nelson* case.

These, then, are the circumstances in which the Court feels that it can, contrary to every principle of American or English common law, go outside the record to conclude that there exists a "tacit agreement" that these statutes will not be enforced. No lawyer, I think, would advise his clients to rely on that "tacit agreement." No police official, I think, would feel himself bound by that "tacit agreement." . . .

When the Court goes outside the record to determine that Connecticut has adopted "an undeviating policy of nullification . . . of its anti-contraceptive laws," it selects a particularly poor case in which to exercise such a novel power. This is not a law which is a dead-letter. Twice since 1940, Connecticut has reenacted these laws as part of general statutory revisions. Consistently, bills to remove the statutes from the books have been rejected by the legislature. In short, the statutes—far from being the accidental left-overs of another era are the center of a continuing controversy in the State. . . .

Again, the Court relies on the inability of counsel to show any attempts, other than the *Nelson* case, "to enforce the prohibition of distribution or use of contraceptive devices by criminal process." Yet, or oral argument, counsel for the appellee stated on his own knowledge that several proprietors had been prosecuted in the "minor police courts of Connecticut" after they had been "picked up" for selling contraceptives. The enforcement of criminal laws in minor courts has just as much impact as in those cases where appellate courts are resorted to. . . .

What are these people—doctor and patients—to do? Flout the law and go to prison? Violate the law surreptitiously and hope they will not get caught? By today's decision we leave them no other alternatives. It is not the choice they need have under the regime of the declaratory judgment and our constitutional system. It is not the choice worthy of a civilized society. . . .

MR. JUSTICE HARLAN, dissenting.

I am compelled, with all respect, to dissent from the dismissal of these appeals. In my view the course which the Court has taken does violence to established concepts of "justiciability," and unjustifiably leaves these appellants under the threat of unconstitutional prosecution. . . .

The plurality opinion of the Court gives, as the basis for dismissing the appeals, the reason that, as to the two married appellants, the lack of demonstrated enforcement of the Connecticut statute bespeaks an absence of exigent adversity which is posited as the condition for evoking adjudication from us, and, as to the doctor, that his compliance with the State statute is uncoerced by any "realistic fear of prosecution," giving due recognition to "his standing as a physician and to his personal sensitiveness." . . .

The policy [against premature constitutional decision] is one to which I unreservedly subscribe. Without undertaking to be definitive, I would suppose it is a policy the wisdom of which is woven of several strands: (1) Due regard for the fact that the source of the Court's power lies ultimately in its duty to decide, in conformity with the Constitution, the particular controversies which come to it, and does not arise from some generalized power of supervision over state and national legislatures; (2) therefore it should insist that litigants bring to the Court interests and rights which require present recognition and controversies demanding immediate resolution; (3) also it follows that the controversy must be one which is in truth and fact the litigant's own, so that the clash of adversary contest which is needed to sharpen and illuminate issues is present and gives that aid on which our adjudicatory system has come to rely; (4) finally, it is required that other means of redress for the particular right claimed be unavailable, so that the process of the Court may not become overburdened and conflicts with other courts or departments of government may not needlessly be created, which might come about if either those truly affected are not the ones demanding relief, or if the relief we can give is not truly needed. . . .

. . . the precise failing in these proceedings which is said to justify refusal to exercise our mandatory appellate jurisdiction [is] that there has been but one recorded Connecticut case dealing with a *prosecution* under the statute. The significance of this lack of recorded evidence of prosecutions is said to make the presentation of appellants' rights too remote, too contingent, too hypothetical for adjudication in the light of the policies already considered. . . . In my view it is only as a result of misconceptions both about the purport of the record before us and about the nature of the rights appellants put forward that this conclusion can be reached.

As far as the record is concerned, I think it is pure conjecture, and indeed conjecture which to me seems contrary to realities, that an open violation of the statute by a doctor (or more obviously still by a birth control clinic) would not result in a substantial threat of prosecution. Crucial to the opposite conclusion is the description of the 1940 prosecution instituted in *State* v. *Nelson* . . . as a "test case" which, as it is viewed, scarcely even punctuates the uniform State practice of nonenforcement of this statute. I read the history of Connecticut enforcement in a very different light. The *Nelson* case, as appears from the state court's opinion, was a prosecution of two doctors and a nurse for aiding and abetting violations of this statute by married women in prescribing and advising in the use of contraceptive materials by them. It is true that there is evidence of a customary unwillingness to enforce the statute prior to *Nelson,* for in that case the prosecutor stated to the trial court . . . that "when this . . . clinic . . . was opened there were in operation elsewhere in the State at least eight other contraceptive clinics which had been in existence for a long period of time and no question as to their right to operate has been raised. . . ."

What must be noted is that the prosecutor followed this statement with an explanation that the primary purpose of the prosecution was to provide clear warning to all those who, like Nelson, might rely on this practice of nonenforcement. He stated that the purpose of the prosecution was:

> "the establishment of the constitutional validity and efficacy of the statutes under which these accused are informed against. Henceforth any person, whether a physician or layman, who violates the provisions of these statutes, must expect to be prosecuted and punished in accordance with the literal provisions of the law."

Thus the respect in which *Nelson* was a test case is only that it was brought for the purpose of making entirely clear the State's power and willingness to enforce against "*any* person, whether physician or layman" . . . the statute and to eliminate from future cases the very doubt about the existence of these elements which had resulted in eight open birth control clinics, and which would have made unfair the conviction of Nelson.

The plurality opinion now finds . . . that the only explanation of the absence of recorded prosecutions subsequent to the *Nelson* case is that Connecticut has renounced that intention . . . which it announced in *Nelson.* But if renunciation of the purposes of the *Nelson* prosecution is consistent with a lack of subsequent prosecutions, success of that purpose is no less consistent with this lack. I find it difficult to believe that doctors generally—and not just those operating specialized clinics—would continue openly to disseminate advice about contraceptives after *Nelson* in reliance on the State's supposed unwillingness to prosecute, or to consider that high-minded members of the profession would in consequence of such inaction deem themselves warranted in disrespecting this law so long as it is on the books. . . . In short, I fear that the Court has indulged in a bit of sleight-of-hand to be rid of this case. . . .

The Court's disposition assumes that to decide the case now, in the absence of any consummated prosecutions, is unwise because it forces a difficult decision in advance of any exigent necessity therefor. Of course it is abundantly clear that this requisite necessity can exist prior to any actual prosecution, for that is the theory of anticipatory relief, and is by now familiar law. What must be relied on, therefore, is that the historical absence of prosecutions in some way leaves these appellants free to violate the statute without fear of prosecution, whether or not the law is Constitutional, and thus absolves us from the duty of deciding if it is. . . . What is meant is simply that the appellants are more or less free to act without fear of prosecution because the prosecuting authorities of the State, in their discretion and at their whim, are, as a matter of prediction, unlikely to decide to prosecute.

Here is the core of my disagreement with the present disposition. As I will develop later in this opinion, the most substantial claim which these married persons press is their right to enjoy the privacy of their marital relations free of the enquiry of the criminal law, whether it be in a prosecution of them or of a doctor whom they have consulted. And I cannot agree that their enjoyment of this privacy is not substantially impinged upon, when they are told that if they use contraceptives, indeed whether they do so or not, the only thing which stands between them and being forced to render criminal account of their marital privacy is the whim of the prosecutor. . . . All that stands between the appellants and jail is the legally unfettered whim of the prosecutor and the Constitutional issue this Court today refuses to decide. . . .

[Discussion of the constitutional issue is omitted.]

MR. JUSTICE STEWART, dissenting. . . .

Following the Supreme Court's opinion in *Poe* v. *Ullman,* the Planned Parenthood League of Connecticut opened a birth control clinic in New Haven, with Dr. Buxton as its medical director. Dr. Buxton and another official of the clinic were arrested after the clinic had been in operation for only ten days, and the clinic was closed. The two officials were tried in a state court and in January, 1962, were found guilty of violating the Connecticut law which according to Justice Frankfurter had been nullified by "undeviating" state policy.

COMMUNIST PARTY v. SUBVERSIVE ACTIVITIES CONTROL BOARD
367 U.S. 1, 81 S. Ct. 1357, 6 L. Ed. 2d 625 (1961)

The Subversive Activities Control Act of 1950 required all Communist-action organizations to register with the Subversive Activities Control Board. Following registration, the organization and its members became liable under the act to a great many penalties and sanctions which are specified in the opinion below. The Communist Party challenged the constitutionality of the registration requirement, in large part because of these consequences. There was a "severability clause" in the act which provided that if any provision should be held invalid, the remaining provisions would not be affected thereby.

MR. JUSTICE FRANKFURTER delivered the opinion of the Court. . . .

The Party's constitutional attack on the Subversive Activities Control Act of 1950 assails virtually every provision of this extended and intricate regulatory statute. The registration requirement of § 7, by demanding self-subjection to what may be deemed a defamatory characterization and, in addition, disclosure of the identity of all rank-and-file members, is said to abridge the First Amendment rights of free expression and association of the Communist Party and its adherents. . . . The Party's officers, it is asserted, who by filing a registration statement in its behalf evidence their status as active members of the Party, are required to incriminate themselves in violation of the Fifth Amendment, as are the individual members who must register themselves under § 8 if the Party fails to register or fails to list them. . . . The provision that Communist organizations label their publications is attacked as a prior restraint on, and such sanctions as denial of tax exemption are attacked as a penalty on the exercise of, the Party's constitutionally protected freedom of speech. . . . The various consequences of the Party's registration for its individual members—prohibition of application for and use of passports, disqualification from government or defense-facility employment, disqualification from naturalization, subjection to denaturalization, proscription of officership or employment in labor organizations—are said to deny those members due process of law by, in effect, attainting them by association. . . . It is said that the establishment of an agency, the Subversive Activities Control Board, whose continued existence depends upon its finding the Communist Party a Communist-action organization within the meaning of the Act, necessarily biases the agency and deprives the Party of a fair hearing. In fact, the Party asserts, the statute as written so particularly designates the Communist Party as the organization at which it is aimed, that it constitutes an abolition of the Party by legislative fiat, in the nature of a bill of attainder. The provisions must be read as a whole, it is said; and when so read, they are seen to envisage not the registration and regulation of the Party, but the imposition of impossible requirements whose only purpose is to lay the foundation for criminal prosecution of the Party and its officers and members, in effect "outlawing" the Party.

Many of these questions are prematurely raised in this litigation. Merely potential impairment of constitutional rights under a statute does not of itself create a justiciable controversy in which the nature and extent of those rights may be litigated. . . . Even where some of the provisions of a comprehensive legislative enactment are ripe for adjudication, portions of the enactment not immediately involved are not thereby thrown open for a judicial determination of constitutionality. . . . No rule of practice of this Court is better settled than "never to anticipate a question of constitutional law in advance of the necessity of deciding it." . . . In part, this principle is based upon the realization that, by the very nature of the judicial process, courts can most wisely determine issues precisely defined by the confining circumstances of particular situations. . . . In part it represents a conception of the role of the judiciary in a government premised upon a separation of powers, a role which precludes interference by courts with legislative and executive functions which have not yet proceeded so far as to affect individual interests adversely. . . . These considerations, crucial as they are to this Court's power and obligation in constitutional cases, require that we delimit at the outset the issues which are properly before us in the present litigation.

This proceeding was brought by the Attorney General under § 13 (a) of the Subversive Activities Control Act, seeking an order of the Board that the Communist Party register as a Communist-action organization. . . . The Board has issued such an order. . . . The effect of that order is to require the Party to register and to file a registration statement within thirty days after the order becomes final . . . upon pain of fine up to $10,000 for each day of failure to register. When the order becomes final, other consequences also ensue, for the Party, for its members and for other persons. Certain acts of the Party—distributing its publications through the mails or through the instrumentalities of interstate or foreign commerce, or causing matter to be broadcast by radio or television, without the required identification—are prohibited, . . . and tax exemption is denied it. . . . Specified acts of its members—e.g., applying for or using a United States passport, holding government or defense-facility employment, holding labor union office or employment—are forbidden, . . . and those members are definitively subject to certain disqualifications—if aliens, they may not enter the United States, may be deported, may not be naturalized, may in some circumstances be denaturalized, with qualifications. . . . All of these consequences depend upon action taken subsequent to the time when the registration order becomes final. Some depend upon action which is, at best, highly contingent. The question is which, if any, of these consequences are now before us for constitutional adjudication, as necessarily involved in the determination of the constitutionality of the Board's registration order. . . .

The authoritative legislative history clearly demonstrates that a major purpose of the enactment was to regulate Communist-action organizations by means of the public disclosure effected by registration, apart from the other regulatory provisions of the Act. . . . This being so, our consideration of any other provisions than those of § 7, requiring Communist-action organizations to register and file a registration statement, could in no way affect our decision in the present case. Were every portion of the Act purporting to regulate or prohibit the conduct of registered organizations . . . and of their members, as such, unconstitutional, we would still have to affirm the judgment below. Expatiation on the validity of those portions would remain mere pronouncements, addressed to future and hypothetical controversies. This is true with regard to those sections of the Act which prescribe consequences legally enforceable against the Communist Party once a final registration order is in effect against it. . . . Although they become operative as soon as a registration order is made final, their application remains in a very real sense problematical. We cannot now foresee what effect, if any, upon the Party the denial of tax exemption will have. We do not know whether the Party now has, or whether it will have at any time after a Board order goes into effect, any taxable income, or, indeed, any income whatever. We do not know that, after such an order is in effect, the Party will wish to utilize the mails or any instrumentality of interstate commerce for the circulation of its publications. We cannot guess the nature of whatever publications it may wish to circulate, or their relation to the purposes and functions of the Party. These circumstances may be critical for constitutional determination. It will not do to discount their significance by saying, now, that no difference in circumstances will effect a different constitutional result—that the principles relevant to a determination of the validity of these statutory provisions do not depend upon the variations in circumstances in which they are potentially applicable. For this analysis presupposes that we now understand what are the relevant constitutional principles, whereas the reason of postponing decision until a constitutional issue is more clearly focused by, and receives the impact from, occurrence in particular circumstances is precisely that those circumstances may reveal relevancies that abstract, prospective supposition may not see or adequately assess.

These considerations are equally appropriate in the case of those sections of the Act which proscribe specified conduct by members of an organization concerning which a final registration order is in effect, or which impose obligations upon them, or which subject them to described disabilities under certain circumstances. It is wholly speculative now to foreshadow whether, or under what conditions, a member of the Party may in the future apply for a passport, or seek government or defense-facility or labor-union employment, or, being an alien, become a party to a naturalization or a denaturalization proceeding. None of these things may happen. If they do, appropriate administrative and judicial procedures will be available to test the constitutionality of applications of particular sections of the Act to particular persons in particular situations. Nothing justifies previsioning those issues now.

But the Party argues that the threat, however indefinite, of future application of these provisions to penalize individuals who are or become its members, affiliates or contributors, will effectively deter persons from associating with it or from aiding and supporting it. Thus, the provisions exercise a present effect upon the Party sufficiently prejudicial to justify its challenging them in this proceeding. . . . [But] the record here does not show that any present members, affiliates, or contributors of the Party have withdrawn because of the threatened consequences to them of its registration under the Subversive Activities Control Act, or that any prospective members . . . have been deterred from joining the Party or giving it their support. We cannot know how many, if any, members or prospective members of the Party are also employees or prospective employees of the Government or of defense facilities or labor unions, or how many, if any, contributors to the Party hold government or defense-facility employment. It is thus impossible to say now what effect the provisions of the Act affecting members of a registered organization will have on the Party. . . . To pass upon the validity of those provisions would be to make abstract assertions of possible future injury, indefinite in nature and degree, the occasion for constitutional decision. If we did so, we would be straying beyond our judicial bounds. . . .

Affirmed.

MR. CHIEF JUSTICE WARREN, dissenting. . . .

. . . the Court concludes that the resolution of some of the constitutional issues raised by the parties should be left for another day. However, in a surprising turnabout, the Court then proceeds to decide other constitutional questions, and it reaches these questions only by first brushing aside, on the basis of a procedural technicality or a strained analysis, many important non-constitutional issues. I do not think that the Court's action can be justified. . . .

MR. JUSTICE BLACK, dissenting. . . .

The Court's opinion is devoted chiefly to the task of explaining why it will not decide any of the substantial issues raised by this attack upon the constitutionality of the Act as it is actually written and will actually operate and why it must decide the case just as though none of these other burdens existed and we were dealing with an Act that required nothing more than the registration of an organization. I cannot agree to decide the case on any such hypothetical basis. If registration were the only issue in the case, I would agree at once that Congress has power to require every "person" acting as an agent of a foreign principal to file registration statements comprehensively showing his agency activities as is required, for example, by the Foreign Agents Registration Act. That Act requires the registration of any "person"—including an individual, partnership, association, corporation, organization, or other combination of individuals—"who acts or agrees to act, within the United States, as . . . a public-relations counsel, publicity agent, information-service employee, servant, agent, representative, or attorney for a foreign principal. . . ." Referring to that Act, I said in *Viereck v. United States*

> "Resting on the fundamental constitutional principle that our people, adequately informed, may be trusted to distinguish between the true and the false, the bill is intended to label information of foreign origin so that hearers and readers may not be deceived by the belief that the information comes from a disinterested source. Such legislation implements rather than detracts from the prized freedoms guaranteed by the First Amendment." [318 U.S. 236, 251]

The Act before us now, however, [is] unlike the Foreign Agents Registration Act. . . . The difference between the [two] is strikingly illustrated by the reasons Congress has itself given for the enactment of the statute now before us. When Viereck registered under the earlier and genuine registration statute, he was not thereby branded as being engaged in an evil, despicable undertaking bent on destroying this Nation. But that is precisely the effect of the present Act. . . .

The plan of the Act is to make it impossible for an organization to continue to function once a registration order is issued against it. To this end, the Act first provides crushing penalties to insure complete compliance with the disclosure requirements of registration within the time required by the Act, or if they fail to make annual reports as required, or to keep records as required, each individual guilty of such failure can be punished by a fine of $10,000, by imprisonment for five years, or both, for each offense—and each offense means "each day of failure to register" or "each listing of the name or address of any one individual" either by the organization or by an individual. Thus, for a delay of thirty days in filing required reports, a fine of $300,000 and imprisonment for 150 years could be imposed by a trial judge.

Having thus made it mandatory that Communist organizations and individual Communists make a full disclosure of their identities and activities, the Act then proceeds to heap burden after burden upon those so exposed. Certain tax deductions allowed to others are denied to a registered organization. Mail matter must be stamped before the organization sends it out to show that it was disseminated by a "Communist action" organization, with all the treasonable connotations given that term by the recitals of "fact" in the Act. Members of a registered organization cannot hold certain jobs with the Government, or any jobs with private business engaged in doing certain work for the Government. Members cannot use or attempt to use a passport and cannot even make application for a passport without being subject to a penalty of five years in the penitentiary. The Act thus makes it extremely difficult for a member of the Communist Party to live in this country and, at the same time, makes it a crime for him to try to get a passport to get out.

In addition to these burdens imposed directly by the Act itself, the registration requirement must also be considered in the context of the other laws now existing which affect the Communist Party. The Act requires that the information obtained upon registration be given wide publicity thus insuring that those identified as members of the Party will be subjected to all the civil disabilities, criminal prosecutions and public harassments that have become common in recent years. . . .

All of these enormous burdens, which are necessarily imposed upon the Party and its members by the act of registration, are dismissed by the Court on the basis of an alleged conflict with the Court-created rule that constitutional questions should be avoided whenever possible. Thus, the Court engages in extended discussions as to whether the people involved will ever want to do the things the Act says they cannot do and whether they will ever object to doing the things the Act says they must do, suggesting, among other things, that the members of the Communist Party may never object to providing the evidence needed to send them to prison for violating the Smith Act; that they may never protest because they are forced to give up tax deductions that other people receive; that they may be willing to stamp all the Party's mail as coming from an evil organization; that they may never want to hold the jobs from which the Act disqualifies them; and that they may never want to get a passport to get out of the country. On the basis of all these "uncertainties" the Court seems to consider its hands tied because, it says, these are as yet only potential impairments of constitutional rights. In its view, there is no "justiciable" issue at all between the United States and the Communist Party except the bare requirement of registration.

In the context of this case, I can find no justification for the Court's refusal to pass upon the serious constitutional questions raised. The Court of Appeals met its responsibility by deciding the questions. The Government has not asked that the Court refrain from giving a full decision on these important matters. Assuming that the Act is wholly valid aside from registration and that Congress does have the power to outlaw groups advocating dangerous ideas, it seems to me unfair to Congress for this Court to refuse to decide whether its Act can be fully enforced. And assuming that the Act is not wholly valid because of some limitation upon that power, it seems to me that we should say so now. By refusing to do so, the Court in effect allows this serious question to be decided by default. For the Party can no more continue to function with all of these tremendous burdens of undetermined constitutional validity overhanging it and its members than it could if the burdens were considered and upheld. The only sense in which the Court has avoided a constitutional issue is by permitting the destruction of a group seeking to raise the issue of the constitutionality of its destruction. . . .

Mr. Justice Douglas, dissenting. . . .

. . . the Act is unconstitutional and void as conflicting with the provision against self-incrimination accorded by the Fifth Amendment. . . .

Mr. Justice Brennan with whom the Chief Justice joins, dissenting in part. . . .

Chapter 3

POLITICAL QUESTIONS

Controversies which meet the test of justiciability are nevertheless occasionally refused adjudication by the Supreme Court on the ground that they involve "political questions." Like justiciability, the political questions doctrine is a manifestation of the general principle of judicial self-restraint. It is based in part on constitutional doubts about the scope of judicial power and in part on a prudent awareness of the practical limitations of courts and judges. The constitutional element in determining justiciability is the extent of judicial power under Article III; the constitutional element in the political questions doctrine is the separation of powers. Consideration is given, in other words, not only to the proper scope of the judicial power but also to the powers and duties assigned to the legislative and executive branches. A political question may also be nonjusticiable, but not necessarily.

Where the authority to make a certain decision appears to have been assigned by the Constitution exclusively to the Congress or the President, the courts will refuse to interfere, although the case may be otherwise justiciable. The conclusion that the Constitution assigns authority to solve a particular problem to the two political branches of the government is usually supported by practical considerations. Either the matter is not one suitable for handling by the judicial methods of taking evidence and hearing legal arguments, or enforcement of a court order would require an undesirable degree of interference in the affairs of other government agencies or for other reasons be unusually difficult. Sometimes, it must be admitted, these two factors, the theoretical and the practical, appear to be two different ways of saying the same thing—that judicial review in a particular case is simply not wise.

It is generally agreed that the Constitution gives the President almost exclusive authority over American relations with foreign governments. It follows, and the courts agree, that a question related to the conduct of foreign affairs is likely to be a political question with which the judiciary should not meddle. The rationale of judicial self-limitation in this field was well stated by Justice Jackson in *Chicago & Southern Air Lines v. Waterman S. S. Corp.*, 333 U.S. 103 (1948):

The President, both as Commander-in-Chief and as the Nation's organ for foreign affairs, has available intelligence services whose reports are not and ought not to be published to the world. It would be intolerable that courts, without the relevant information, should review and perhaps nullify actions of the Executive taken on information properly held secret. Nor can courts sit *in camera* in order to be taken

39

into executive confidences. But even if courts could require full disclosure, the very nature of executive decisions as to foreign policy is political, not judicial. Such decisions are wholly confided by our Constitution to the political departments of the government, Executive and Legislative. They are delicate, complex, and involve large elements of prophecy. They are and should be undertaken only by those directly responsible to the people whose welfare they advance or imperil. They are decisions of a kind for which the Judiciary has neither aptitude, facilities, nor responsibility and have long been held to belong in the domain of political power not subject to judicial intrusion or inquiry.

Foreign affairs of course do not constitute the only kind of political question. Whether or not a state has a "republican form of government," such as the Constitution guarantees to every state in Article IV, section 4, has been held to be a political question. In *Luther v. Borden,* 7 How. 1 (1849), the Supreme Court refused to decide which of two rival groups constituted the legal government of Rhode Island. This was a political decision to be made by Congress when seating legislators from that state, or by the President if the state authorities asked for protection against "domestic violence" under Article IV, section 4. *Pacific States Telephone & Telegraph Co.* v. *Oregon,* 223 U.S. 118 (1912), refused to decide whether a provision for the initiative and referendum in the Oregon constitution deprived that state of a republican form of government. The Court confirmed its refusal to enforce the republican guaranty in the famous Tennessee legislative apportionment case, *Baker* v. *Carr,* 369 U.S. 186 (1962).

The Supreme Court has had great difficulty in deciding whether state apportionment of seats in state legislatures or the national House of Representatives constitutes a political question. For sixteen years the rule was that stated in *Colegrove* v. *Green,* 328 U.S. 549 (1946), where the Court held itself unable to act against Illinois congressional districts grossly unequal in population due to failure to redistrict the state since 1901. However, in the 1962 case of *Baker* v. *Carr* (see Chapter 5), the Court reversed this position and directed a federal court in Tennessee, where the state legislature had not been reapportioned since 1901, to hear a case challenging the unequal districts as unconstitutional under the equal protection clause of the Fourteenth Amendment.

In the following case the Supreme Court expressed its views on whether the process of constitutional amendment is a political question.

COLEMAN v. MILLER
307 U.S. 433, 59 S. Ct. 972, 83 L. Ed. 1385 (1939)

In 1937 the Kansas Senate divided equally on a resolution ratifying an amendment to the Constitution authorizing federal regulation of child labor, and the resolution was passed only by the casting vote of the lieutenant governor. The resolution then passed the Kansas House, and a group of legislators, including all of the senators who had voted against it, asked the Kansas supreme court to compel the secretary of the Senate, by mandamus, to endorse the resolution as "not passed," and to prevent other state officials from signing it. The Kansas court held that the ratifying resolution had been duly adopted and denied mandamus. The amendment had been originally proposed by Congress in 1924, but had never been ratified by the required three-fourths of the states, and one contention was that it was no longer open to ratification because it had failed to be ratified within a reasonable time.

Opinion of the Court by MR. CHIEF JUSTICE HUGHES, announced by MR. JUSTICE STONE. . . .

First. The jurisdiction of this Court.—Our authority to issue the writ of certiorari is challenged upon the ground that petitioners have no standing to seek to have the judgment of the state court reviewed, and hence it is urged that the writ of certiorari should be dismissed. We are unable to accept that view. . . .

The plaintiffs include twenty senators, whose votes against ratification have been overridden and virtually held for naught although if they are right in their contentions their votes would have been sufficient to defeat ratification. We think that these senators have a plain, direct and adequate interest in maintaining the effectiveness of their votes. Petitioners come directly within the provisions of the statute governing our appellate jurisdiction. They have set up and claimed a right and privilege under the Constitution of the United States to have their votes given effect and the state court has denied that right and privilege. . . .

Second. The participation of the Lieutenant Governor.—Petitioners contend that, in the light of the powers and duties of the Lieutenant Governor and his relation to the Senate under the state constitution, as construed by the supreme court of the state, the Lieutenant Governor was not a part of the "legislature" so that under Article V of the Federal Constitution, he could be permitted to have a deciding vote on the ratification of the proposed amendment, when the senate was equally divided.

Whether this contention presents a justiciable controversy, or a question which is political in its nature and hence not justiciable, is a question upon which the Court is equally divided and therefore the Court expresses no opinion upon that point.

Third. The effect of the previous rejection of the amendment and of the lapse of time since its submission.

1. The state court adopted the view expressed by textwriters that a state legislature which has rejected an amendment proposed by the Congress may later ratify.

Historic instances are cited. In 1865, the Thirteenth Amendment was rejected by the legislature of New Jersey which subsequently ratified it, but the question did not become important as ratification by the requisite number of States had already been proclaimed. The question did arise in connection with the adoption of the Fourteenth Amendment. The legislatures of Georgia, North Carolina and South Carolina had rejected the amendment in November and December, 1866. New governments were erected in those States (and in others) under the direction of Congress. The new legislatures ratified the amendment, that of North Carolina on July 4, 1868, that of South Carolina on July 9, 1868, and that of Georgia on July 21, 1868. Ohio and New Jersey first ratified and then passed resolutions withdrawing their consent. As there were then thirty-seven States, twenty-eight were needed to constitute the requisite three-fourths. On July 9, 1868, the Congress adopted a resolution requesting the Secretary of State to communicate "a list of the States of the Union whose legislatures have ratified the fourteenth article of amendment," and in Secretary Seward's report attention was called to the action of Ohio and New Jersey. On July 20th Secretary Seward issued a proclamation reciting the ratification by twenty-eight States, including North Carolina, South Carolina, Ohio and New Jersey, and stating that it appeared that Ohio and New Jersey had since passed resolutions withdrawing their consent and that "it is deemed a matter of doubt and uncertainty whether such resolutions are not irregular, invalid and therefore ineffectual." The Secretary certified that if the ratifying resolutions of Ohio and New Jersey were still in full force and effect, notwithstanding the attempted withdrawal, the amendment had become a part of the Constitution. On the following day the Congress adopted a concurrent resolution which, reciting that three-fourths of the States having ratified (the list including North Carolina, South Carolina, Ohio and New Jersey), declared the Fourteenth Amendment to be a part of the Constitution and that it should be duly promulgated as such by the Secretary of State. Accordingly, Secretary Seward, on July 28th, issued his proclamation embracing the States mentioned in the congressional resolution and adding Georgia.

Thus the political departments of the Government dealt with the effect both of previous rejection and of attempted withdrawal and determined that both were ineffectual in the presence of an actual ratification. . . . This decision by the political departments of the Government as to the validity of the adoption of the Fourteenth Amendment has been accepted.

We think that in accordance with this historic precedent the question of the efficacy of ratifications by state legislatures, in the light of previous rejection or attempted withdrawal, should be regarded as a political question pertaining to the political departments, with the ultimate authority in the Congress in the exercise of its control over the promulgation of the adoption of the amendment. . . .

2. The more serious question is whether the proposal by the Congress of the amendment had lost its vitality through lapse of time and hence it could not be ratified by the Kansas legislature in 1937. The argument of petitioners stresses the fact that nearly thirteen years elapsed between the proposal in 1924 and the ratification in question. It is said that when the amendment was proposed there was a definitely adverse popular sentiment and that at the end of 1925 there had been rejection by both houses of the legislatures of sixteen States and ratification by only four States, and that it was not until about 1933 that an aggressive campaign was started in favor of the amendment. In reply, it is urged that Congress did not fix a limit of time for ratification and that an unreasonably long time had not elapsed since the submission; that the conditions which gave rise to the amendment had not been eliminated; that the prevalence of child labor, the diversity of state laws and the disparity in their administration, with the resulting competitive inequalities, continued to exist. Reference is also made to the fact that a number of the States have treated the amendment as still pending and that in the proceedings of the national government there have been indications of the same view. It is said that there were fourteen ratifications in 1933, four in 1935, one in 1936, and three in 1937.

We have held that the Congress in proposing an amendment may fix a reasonable time for ratification. *Dillon* v. *Gloss,* 256 U.S. 368. There we sustained the action of the Congress in providing in the proposed Eighteenth Amendment that it should be inoperative unless ratified within seven years. No limitation of time for ratification is provided in the instant case either in the proposed amendment or in the resolution of submission. But petitioners contend that, in the absence of a limitation by the Congress, the Court can and should decide what is a reasonable period within which ratification may be had. We are unable to agree with that contention.

It is true that in *Dillon* v. *Gloss* the Court said that nothing was found in Article V which suggested that an amendment once proposed was to be open to ratification for all time, or that ratification in some States might be separated from that in others by many years and yet be effective; that there was a strong suggestion to the contrary in that proposal and ratification were but succeeding steps in a single endeavor; that as amendments were deemed to be prompted by necessity, they should be considered and disposed of presently; and that there is a fair implication that ratification must be sufficiently contemporaneous in the required number of States to reflect the will of the people in all sections at relatively the same period; and hence that ratification must be within some reasonable time after the proposal. These considerations were cogent reasons for the decision in *Dillon* v. *Gloss* that the Congress had the power to fix a reasonable time for ratification. But it does not follow that, whenever Congress has not exercised that power, the Court should take upon itself the responsibility of deciding what constitutes a reasonable time and determine accordingly the validity of ratifications. That question was not involved in *Dillon* v. *Gloss* and, in accordance with familiar principle, what was there said must be read in the light of the point decided.

Where are to be found the criteria for such a judicial determination? None are to be found in Constitution or statute. In their endeavor to answer this question petitioners' counsel have suggested that at least two years should be allowed; that six years would not seem to be unreasonably long; that seven years had been used by the Congress as a reasonable period; that one year, six months and thirteen days was the average time used in passing upon amendments which have been ratified since the first ten amendments; that three years, six months and twenty-five days has been the longest time used in ratifying. To this list of variables, counsel add that "the nature and extent of publicity and the activity of the public and of the legislatures of the several States in relation to any particular proposal should be taken into consideration." That statement is pertinent, but there are additional matters to be examined and weighed. When a proposed amendment springs from a conception of economic needs, it would be necessary, in determining whether a reasonable time had elapsed since its submission, to consider the economic conditions prevailing in the country, whether these had so far changed since the submission as to make the proposal no longer responsive to the conception which inspired it or whether conditions were such as to intensify the feeling of need and the appropriateness of the proposed remedial action. In short, the question of a reasonable time in many cases would involve, as in this case it does involve, an appraisal of a great variety of relevant conditions, political, social and economic, which can hardly be said to be within the appropriate range of evidence receivable in a court of justice and as to which it would be an extravagant extension of judicial authority to assert judicial notice as the basis of deciding a controversy with respect to the validity of an amendment actually ratified. On the other hand, these conditions are appropriate for the consideration of the political departments of the Government. The questions they involve are essentially political and not justiciable. They can be decided by the Congress with the full knowledge and appreciation ascribed to the national legislature of the political, social and economic conditions which have prevailed during the period since the submission of the amendment.

Our decision that the Congress has the power under Article V to fix a reasonable limit of time for ratification in proposing an amendment proceeds upon the assumption that the question, what is a reasonable time, lies within the congressional province. If it be deemed that such a question is an open one when the limit has not been fixed in advance, we think that it should also be regarded as an open one for the consideration of the Congress when, in the presence of certified ratifications by three-fourths of the States, the time arrives for the promulgation of the adoption of the amendment. The decision by the Congress, in its control of the action of the Secretary of State, of the question whether the amendment had been adopted within a reasonable time would not be subject to review by the courts. . . .

For the reasons we have stated . . . we think that the Congress in controlling the promulgation of the adoption of a constitutional amendment has the final determination of the question whether by lapse of time its proposal of the amendment has lost its vitality prior to the required ratifications. The state officials should not be restrained from certifying to the Secretary of State the adoption by the legislature of Kansas of the resolution of ratification. . . .

Affirmed.

Concurring opinion by MR. JUSTICE BLACK, in which MR. JUSTICE ROBERTS, MR. JUSTICE FRANKFURTER and MR. JUSTICE DOUGLAS join.

The Constitution grants Congress exclusive power to control submission of constitutional amendments. Final determination by Congress that ratification by three-fourths of the States has taken place "is conclusive upon the courts." In the exercise of that power, Congress, of course, is governed by the Constitution. However, whether submission, intervening procedure or Congressional determination of ratification conforms to the commands of the Constitution, calls for decisions by a "political department" of questions of a type which this Court has frequently designated "political." And decision of a "political question" by the "political department" to which the Constitution has committed it "conclusively binds the judges, as well as all other officers, citizens and subjects of . . . government." Proclamation under authority of Congress that an amendment has been ratified will carry with it a solemn assurance by the Congress that ratification has taken place as the Constitution commands. Upon this assurance a proclaimed amendment must be accepted as a part of the Constitution, leaving to the judiciary its traditional authority of interpretation. To the extent that the Court's opinion in the present case even impliedly assumes a power to make judicial interpretation of the exclusive constitutional authority of Congress over submission and ratification of amendments, we are unable to agree. . . .

The Court here treats the amending process of the Constitution in some respects as subject to judicial construction, in others as subject to the final authority of the Congress. There is no disapproval of the conclusion arrived at in *Dillon* v. *Gloss,* that the Constitution impliedly requires that a properly submitted amendment must die unless ratified within a "reasonable time." Nor does the Court now disapprove its prior assumption of power to make such a pronouncement. And it is not made clear that only Congress has constitutional power to determine if there is any such implication in Article V of the Constitution. On the other hand, the Court's opinion declares that Congress has the exclusive power to decide the "political questions" of whether a State whose legislature has once acted upon a proposed amendment may subsequently reverse its position, and whether, in the circumstances of such a case as this, an amendment is dead because an "unreasonable" time has elapsed. No such division between the political and judicial branches of the government is made by Article V which grants power over the amending of the Constitution to Congress alone. Undivided control of that process has been given by the Article exclusively and completely to Congress. The process itself is "political" in its entirety, from submission until an amendment becomes part of the Constitution, and is not subject to judicial guidance, control or interference at any point. . . .

Congress, possessing exclusive power over the amending process, cannot be bound by and is under no duty to accept the pronouncements upon that exclusive power by this Court or by the Kansas courts. Neither state nor federal courts can review that power. Therefore, any judicial expression amounting to more than mere acknowledgment of exclusive Congressional power over the political process of amendment is a mere admonition to the Congress in the nature of an advisory opinion, given wholly without constitutional authority.

Opinion of MR. JUSTICE FRANKFURTER.

It is the view of MR. JUSTICE ROBERTS, MR. JUSTICE BLACK, MR. JUSTICE DOUGLAS and myself that the petitioners have no standing in this Court.

In endowing this Court with "judicial Power" the Constitution presupposed an historic content for that phrase and relied on assumption by the judiciary of authority only over issues which are appropriate for disposition by judges. The Constitution further explicitly indicated the limited area within which judicial action was to move —however far-reaching the consequences of action within that area—by extending "judicial Power" only to "Cases" and "Controversies." Both by what they said and by what they implied, the framers of the Judiciary Article gave merely the outlines of what were to them the familiar operations of the English judicial system and its manifestations on this side of the ocean before the Union. Judicial power could come into play only in matters that were the traditional concern of the courts at Westminster and only if they arose in ways that to the expert feel of lawyers constituted "Cases" or "Controversies." It was not for courts to meddle with matters that required no subtlety to be identified as political issues. And even as to the kinds of questions which were the staple of judicial business, it was not for courts to pass upon them as abstract, intellectual problems but only if a concrete, living contest between adversaries called for the arbitrament of law. . . .

It is not our function, and it is beyond our power, to write legal essays or to give legal opinions, however solemnly requested and however great the national emergency. See the correspondence between Secretary of State Jefferson and Chief Justice Jay, 3 Johnson, Correspondence and Public Papers of John Jay, 486–89. Unlike the rôle allowed to judges in a few state courts and to the Supreme Court of Canada, our exclusive business is litigation. The requisites of litigation are not satisfied when questions of constitutionality though conveyed through the outward forms of a conventional court proceeding do not bear special relation to a particular litigant. The scope and consequences of our doctrine of judicial review over executive and legislative action should make us observe fastidiously the bounds of the litigious process within which we are confined. No matter how seriously infringement of the Constitution may be called into question, this is not the tribunal for its challenge except by those who have some specialized interest of their own to vindicate, apart from a political concern which belongs to all. . . .

We can only adjudicate an issue as to which there is a claimant before us who has a special, individualized stake in it. One who is merely the self-constituted spokesman of a constitutional point of view can not ask us to pass on it. The Kansas legislators could not bring suit explicitly on behalf of the people of the United States to determine whether Kansas could still vote for the Child Labor Amendment. They can not gain standing here by having brought such a suit in their own names. Therefore, none of the petitioners can here raise questions concerning the power of the Kansas legislature to ratify the Amendment. . . .

[Mr. Justice Butler and Mr. Justice McReynolds dissented.]

Chapter 4

THE CONTEMPT POWER

The power of the federal courts to enforce their decisions is normally taken for granted, but in fact the courts have no enforcement machinery at their direct disposal except for a few marshals. The judiciary must look to the President and to Congress for help in case of any real resistance to its orders. Andrew Jackson's purported comment, "John Marshall has made his decision, now let him enforce it," reveals the need of the Supreme Court for support by its governmental colleagues and the backing of public opinion.

Within the framework of the Constitution and congressional statutes, the federal courts are vested with most of the traditional powers and functions of the courts of England. The power to punish for "contempt of court" is one of these. This authority is only incidental to the judiciary's primary function of making binding decisions. But it is so important a part of the machinery of justice that it is generally considered an inherent judicial power. In other words, the federal courts might claim to exercise such power simply because they are courts, even if Congress had not expressly authorized them to do so.

Contempts may be either civil or criminal. A civil contempt is committed when someone refuses to obey a court order affecting the rights of another. Here the power to punish contempts is employed to preserve and enforce the rights of the parties in the proceeding. Civil contempt can be purged by obedience to the order; if the person in contempt has been imprisoned, he is said to have the key to the jail in his pocket.

In criminal contempt, however, the purpose of the punishment is to vindicate the authority of the court. The act of contempt has been completed, and the guilty party cannot purge himself by any subsequent compliance. The same conduct may amount to both civil and criminal contempt, and a court may impose both coercive and punitive sanctions in the same proceeding.

Some criminal contempts can be punished summarily. If the judge can certify that he heard or saw the contemptuous conduct, neither notice, nor hearing, nor counsel, nor jury is required. Disorder in the courtroom obstructing the administration of justice would be an example. In other cases, due notice must be given, the accused is entitled to counsel, and if the alleged contempt involved disrespect to or criticism of a judge, the case must be tried before another judge according to federal law.

Trial of contempts by jury, however, is required in the federal courts only where Congress has so provided. Under the 1957 Civil Rights Act, for instance, the person accused in a criminal contempt proceeding of violating an injunction issued to protect voting rights is entitled to a trial—or, rather, a retrial—by jury if the penalty imposed on conviction by the judge alone is a fine in excess of $300 or imprisonment for more than forty-five days.

Obviously a criminal contempt proceeding closely resembles an ordinary criminal case. The argument has been made that it is so close to a prosecution for crime that the accused should be entitled, under the Sixth Amendment, to a jury trial in all cases, and even that indictment by a grand jury, under the Fifth Amendment, should be required. In his dissenting opinion in *Green and Winston v. United States*, 356 U.S. 165 (1958), Justice Black makes a strong argument for these propositions.

GREEN and WINSTON v. UNITED STATES
356 U.S. 165, 78 S. Ct. 632, 2 L. Ed. 2d 672 (1958)

Green and Winston were two of the eleven Communist Party leaders convicted under the Smith Act in 1949. All eleven were released on bail while their appeal was pending. When the conviction was affirmed in 1951, *Dennis v. United States*, 341 U.S. 494, defendants' counsel were notified that a formal order for the surrender of their clients to the federal marshal would be signed in the district court four days later, and counsel told their clients, including Green and Winston, to be in court on that day. Green and Winston did not appear, however, and in fact remained in hiding until 1956, when they voluntarily surrendered. They were then charged with criminal contempt for violation of the surrender order, tried without a jury, convicted, and sentenced to three years' imprisonment in addition to their Smith Act sentences.

Mr. Justice Harlan delivered the opinion of the Court. . . .

The contempt judgments rest on 18 U. S. C. § 401, which in pertinent part provides that a federal court:

". . . shall have power to punish by fine or imprisonment, at its discretion, such contempt of its authority, and none other, as—
"(3) Disobedience or resistance to its lawful . . . order. . . ."

. . . The first statute bearing on the contempt powers of federal courts was enacted as § 17 of the Judiciary Act of 1789, 1 Stat. 73, 83. It stated that federal courts "shall have power to . . . punish by fine or imprisonment, at the discretion of said courts, all contempts of authority in any cause or hearing before the same. . . ." The generality of this language suggests that § 17 was intended to do no more than expressly attribute to the federal judiciary those powers to punish for contempt possessed by English courts at common law. . . .

. . . At early English law courts dealt with absconding defendants not by way of contempt, but under the ancient doctrine of outlawry, a practice whereby the defendant was summoned by proclamation to five successive county courts and, for failure to appear, was declared forfeited of all his goods and chattels. . . . In view of this distinct method at English common law of punishing refusal to respond to this summons, which was the equivalent of the present surrender order, petitioners argue that § 17 of the Judiciary Act of 1789, incorporating English practice, did not reach to a surrender order. . . .

We find these arguments unconvincing. . . . It is significant that, so far as we know, the severe remedy of outlawry, which fell into early disuse in the state courts, was never known to the federal law. . . . Its unavailability to federal courts, and the absence of any other sanctions for the disobedience of surrender orders, are in themselves factors which point away from the conclusion that the kind of power traditionally used to assure respect for a court's process should be found wanting in this one instance. . . .

Entirely apart from the historical argument, there are no reasons of policy suggesting a need for limitation of the contempt power in this situation. As the present cases evidence, the issuance of a bench warrant and the forfeiture of bail following flight have generally proved inadequate to dissuade defendants from defying court orders. . . . At the time these contempts were committed bail-jumping itself was not a criminal offense, and considerations in past decisions limiting the scope of the contempt power where the conduct deemed to constitute a contempt was also punishable as a substantive crime are not here relevant. . . . There is small justification for permitting a defendant the assurance that his only risk in disobeying a surrender order is the forfeiture of a known sum of money, particularly when such forfeiture may result in injury only to a bail surety.

It may be true, as petitioners state, that this case and those of the other absconding *Dennis* defendants . . . provide the first instances where a federal court has exercised the contempt power for disobedience of a surrender order. But the power to punish for willful disobedience of a court order, once found to exist, cannot be said to have atrophied by disuse in this particular instance. Indeed, when Congress in 1954 made bail-jumping a crime in 18 U. S. C. § 3146, it expressly preserved the contempt power in this very situation. We find support in neither history nor policy to carve out so singular an exception from the clear meaning of § 401 (3). . . .

We deal [now] with petitioners' claim that the District Court was without power to sentence them to imprisonment for more than one year. . . . The claim is that proceedings for criminal contempts, if contempts are subject to prison terms of more than one year, must be based on grand jury indictments under the clause of the Fifth Amendment providing: "No person shall be held to answer for a capital, or otherwise *infamous crime,* unless on a presentment or indictment of a Grand Jury. . . ." (Italics added.) Since an "infamous crime" within the meaning of the Amendment is one punishable by imprisonment in a penitentiary, . . . and since imprisonment in a penitentiary can be imposed only if a crime is subject to imprisonment exceeding one year . . . petitioners assert that criminal contempts if subject to such punishment are infamous crimes under the Amendment.

But this assertion cannot be considered in isolation from the general status of contempts under the Constitution, whether subject to "infamous" punishment or not. The statements of this Court in a long and unbroken line of decisions involving contempts ranging from misbehavior in court to disobedience of court orders establish beyond peradventure that criminal contempts are not subject to jury trial as a matter of constitutional right. Although appearing to recognize this, petitioners nevertheless point out that punishment for criminal contempts cannot in any practical sense be distinguished from punishment for substantive crimes, see *Gompers* v. *United States,* 233 U.S. 604, 610, and that contempt proceedings have traditionally been surrounded with many of the protections available in a criminal trial. But this Court has never suggested that such protections included the right to grand jury indictment. . . . And of course the summary procedures followed by English courts prior to adoption of the Constitution in dealing with many contempts of court did not embrace the use of either grand or petit jury. . . .

We are told however that the decisions of this Court denying the right to jury trial in criminal contempt proceedings are based upon an "historical error" reflecting a misunderstanding as to the scope of the power of English courts at the early common law to try summarily for contempts, and that this error should not here be extended to a denial of the right to grand jury. But the more recent historical research into English contempt practices predating the adoption of our Constitution reveals no such clear error and indicates if anything that the precise nature of those practices is shrouded in much obscurity. And whatever the breadth of the historical error said by contemporary scholarship to have been committed by English courts of the late-Seventeenth and Eighteenth Centuries in their interpretation of English precedents involving the trials of contempts of court, it at least seems clear that English practice by the early Eighteenth Century comprehended the use of summary powers of conviction by courts to punish for a variety of contempts committed within and outside court. . . . Against this historical background, this Court has never deviated from the view that the constitutional guarantee of trial by jury for "crimes" and "criminal prosecutions" was not intended to reach to criminal contempts. And indeed beginning with the Judiciary Act of 1789, Congress has consistently preserved the summary nature of the contempt power in the Act of 1831 and its statutory successors, departing from this traditional notion only in specific instances where it has provided for jury trial for certain categories of contempt.

We do not write upon a clean slate. The principle that criminal contempts of court are not required to be tried by a jury under Article III or the Sixth Amendment is firmly rooted in our traditions. Indeed, the petitioners themselves have not contended that they were entitled to a jury trial. By the same token it is clear that criminal contempts, although subject, as we have held, to sentences of imprisonment exceeding one year, need not be prosecuted by indictment under the Fifth Amendment. In various respects, such as the absence of a statutory limitation of the amount of a fine or the length of a prison sentence which may be imposed for their commission, criminal contempts have always differed from the usual statutory crime under federal law. As to trial by jury and indictment by grand jury, they possess a unique character under the Constitution.

Affirmed.

MR. JUSTICE FRANKFURTER, concurring.

In joining the Court's opinion I deem it appropriate to add a few observations. Law is a social organism, and evolution operates in the sociological domain no less than in the biological. The vitality and therefore validity of law is not arrested by the circumstances of its orign. What Magna Carta has become is very different indeed from the immediate objects of the barons at Runnymede. The fact that scholarship has shown that historical assumptions regarding the procedure for punishment of contempt of court were ill-founded, hardly wipes out a century and a half of the legislative and judicial history of federal law based on such assumptions. . . .

Whatever the conflicting views of scholars in construing more or less dubious manuscripts of the Fourteenth Century, what is indisputable is that from the foundation of the United States the constitutionality of the power to punish for contempt without the intervention of a jury has not been doubted.

To be sure, it is never too late for this Court to correct a misconception in an occasional decision, even on a rare occasion to change a rule of law that may have long persisted but also have long been questioned and only fluctuatingly applied. To say that everybody on the Court has been wrong for 150 years and that that which has been deemed part of the bone and sinew of the law should now be extirpated is quite another thing. Decision-making is not a mechanical process, but neither is this Court an originating lawmaker. The admonition of Mr. Justice Brandeis that we are not a third branch of the legislature should never be disregarded. Congress has seen fit from time to time to qualify the power of summary punishment for contempt that it gave the federal courts in 1789 by requiring in explicitly defined situations that a jury be associated with the court in determining whether there has been a contempt. See, e.g., . . . Civil Rights Act of 1957, 71 Stat. 634, 638. . . . It is for Congress to extend this participation of the jury, whenever it sees fit to do so, to other instances of the exercise of the power to punish for contempt. It is not for this Court to fashion a wholly novel constitutional doctrine that would require such participation whatever Congress may think on the matter, and in the teeth of an unbroken legislative and judicial history from the foundation of the Nation.

MR. JUSTICE BLACK, with whom THE CHIEF JUSTICE and MR. JUSTICE DOUGLAS concur, dissenting.

The power of a judge to inflict punishment for criminal contempt by means of a summary proceeding stands as an anomaly in the law. In my judgment the time has come for a fundamental and searching reconsideration of the validity of this power which has aptly been characterized by a State Supreme Court as, "perhaps, nearest akin to despotic power of any power existing under our form of government." Even though this extraordinary authority first slipped into the law as a very limited and insignificant thing, it has relentlessly swollen, at the hands of not unwilling judges, until it has become a drastic and pervasive mode of administering criminal justice usurping our regular constitutional methods of trying those charged with offenses against society. Therefore to me this case involves basic questions of the highest importance far transcending its particular facts. But the specific facts do provide a striking example of how the great procedural safeguards erected by the Bill of Rights are now easily evaded by the ever-ready and boundless expedients of a judicial decree and a summary contempt proceeding.

I would reject those precedents which have held that the federal courts can punish an alleged violation outside the courtroom of their decrees by means of a summary trial, at least as long as they can punish by severe prison sentences or fines as they now can and do. I would hold that the defendants here were entitled to be tried by a jury after indictment by a grand jury and in full accordance with all the procedural safeguards required by the Constitution for "all criminal prosecutions." I am convinced that the previous cases to the contrary are wrong—wholly wrong for reasons which I shall set out in this opinion.

Ordinarily it is sound policy to adhere to prior decisions but this practice has quite properly never been a blind, inflexible rule. Courts are not omniscient. Like every other human agency, they too can profit from trial and error, from experience and reflection. As others have demonstrated, the principle commonly referred to as *stare decisis* has never been thought to extend so far as to prevent the courts from correcting their own errors. Accordingly, this Court has time and time again from the very beginning reconsidered the merits of its earlier decisions even though they claimed great longevity and repeated reaffirmation. . . . Indeed, the Court has a special responsibility where questions of constitutional law are involved to review its decisions from time to time and where compelling reasons present themselves to refuse to follow erroneous precedents; otherwise its mistakes in interpreting the Constitution are extremely difficult to alleviate and needlessly so. . . .

Before going any further, perhaps it should be emphasized that we are not at all concerned with the power of courts to impose conditional imprisonment for the purpose of compelling a person to obey a valid order. Such coercion, where the defendant carries the keys to freedom in his willingness to comply with the court's directive, is essentially a civil remedy designed for the benefit of other parties and has quite properly been exercised for centuries to secure compliance with judicial decrees. . . . Instead, at stake here is the validity of a criminal conviction for disobedience of a court order punished by a long, fixed term of imprisonment. In my judgment the distinction between conditional confinement to compel future performance and unconditional imprisonment designed to punish past transgressions is crucial, analytically as well as historically, in determining the permissible mode of trial under the Constitution.

Summary trial of criminal contempt, as now practiced, allows a single functionary of the state, a judge, to lay down the law, to prosecute those whom he believes have violated his command (as interpreted by him), to sit in "judgment" on his own charges, and then within the broadest kind of bounds to punish as he sees fit. It seems inconsistent with the most rudimentary principles of our system of criminal justice, a system carefully developed and preserved throughout the centuries to prevent oppressive enforcement of oppressive laws, to concentrate this much power in the hands of any officer of the state. No official, regardless of his position or the purity and nobleness of his character, should be granted such autocratic omnipotence. Indeed if any other officer were presumptuous enough to claim such power I cannot believe the courts would tolerate it for an instant under the Constitution. Judges are not essentially different from other government officials. Fortunately they remain human even after assuming their judicial duties. Like all the rest of mankind they may be affected from time to time by pride and passion, by pettiness and bruised feelings, by improper understanding or by excessive zeal. Frank recognition of these common human characteristics, as well as others which need not be mentioned, undoubtedly led to the determination of those who formed our Constitution to fragment power, especially the power to define and enforce the criminal law, among different departments and institutions of government in the hope that each would tend to operate as a check on the activities of the others and a shield against their excesses thereby securing the people's liberty.

When the responsibilities of lawmaker, prosecutor, judge, jury and disciplinarian are thrust upon a judge he is obviously incapable of holding the scales of justice perfectly fair and true and reflecting impartially on the guilt or innocence of the accused. He truly becomes the judge of his own cause. The defendant charged with criminal contempt is thus denied what I had always thought to be an indispensable element of due process of law—an objective, scrupulously impartial tribunal to determine whether he is guilty or innocent of the charges filed against him. . . .

The Constitution and Bill of Rights declare in sweeping unequivocal terms that "The Trial of all Crimes . . . shall be by Jury," that "In all criminal prosecutions, the accused shall enjoy the right to a speedy and public trial, by an impartial jury," and that "No person shall be held to answer for a capital, or otherwise infamous crime, unless on a presentment or indictment of a Grand Jury." As it may now be punished criminal contempt is manifestly a crime by every relevant test of reason or history. It was always a crime at common law punishable as such in the regular course of the criminal law. It possesses all of the earmarks commonly attributed to a crime. A mandate of the government has allegedly been violated for which severe punishment, including long prison sentences, may be exacted—punishment aimed at chastising the violator for his disobedience. . . .

I cannot help but believe that this arbitrary power to punish by summary process, as now used, is utterly irreconcilable with first principles underlying our Constitution and the system of government it created—principles which were uppermost in the minds of the generation that adopted the Constitution. Above all that generation deeply feared and bitterly abhorred the existence of arbitrary, unchecked power in the hands of any government official, particularly when it came to punishing alleged offenses against the state. A great concern for protecting individual liberty from even the possibility of irresponsible official action was one of the momentous forces which led to the Bill of Rights. And the Fifth, Sixth, Seventh and Eighth Amendments were directly and purposefully designed to confine the power of courts and judges, especially with regard to the procedures used for the trial of crimes. . . .

Apologists for summary trial of the crime of contempt also endeavor to justify it as a "necessity" if judicial orders are to be observed and the needful authority of the courts maintained. . . .

When examined in closer detail the argument from "necessity" appears to rest on the assumption that the regular criminal processes, including trial by petit jury and indictment by grand jury, will not result in conviction and punishment of a fair share of those guilty of violating court orders, are unduly slow and cumbersome, and by intervening between the court and punishment for those who disobey its mandate somehow detract from its dignity and prestige. Obviously this argument reflects substantial disrespect for the institution of trial by jury, although this method of trial is —and has been for centuries—an integral and highly esteemed part of our system of criminal justice enshrined in the Constitution itself. Nothing concrete is ever offered to support the innuendo that juries will not convict the same proportion of those guilty of contempt as would judges. Such evidence as is available plus my own experience convinces me that by and large juries are fully as responsible in meting out justice in criminal cases as are the judiciary. At the same time, and immeasurably more important, trial before a jury and in full compliance with all of the other protections of the Bill of Rights is much less likely to result in a miscarriage of justice than summary trial by the same judge who issued the order allegedly violated. . . .

I am confident that in the long run due respect for the courts and their mandates would be much more likely if they faithfully observed the procedures laid down by our nationally acclaimed charter of liberty, the Bill of Rights. Respect and obedience in this country are not engendered—and rightly not—by arbitrary and autocratic procedures. In the end such methods only yield real contempt for the courts and the law. . . .

In the last analysis there is no justification in history, in necessity, or most important in the Constitution for trying those charged with violating a court's decree in a manner wholly different from those accused of disobeying any other mandate of the state. It is significant that neither the Court nor the Government makes any serious effort to justify such differentiation except that it has been sanctioned by prior decisions. Under the Constitution courts are merely one of the coordinate agencies which hold and exercise governmental power. Their decrees are simply another form of sovereign directive aimed at guiding the citizen's activity. I can perceive nothing which places these decrees on any higher or different plane than the laws of Congress or the regulations of the Executive insofar as punishment for their violation is concerned. There is no valid reason why they should be singled out for an extraordinary and essentially arbitrary mode of enforcement. Unfortunately judges and lawyers have told each other the contrary so often that they have come to accept it as the gospel truth. In my judgment trial by the same procedures, constitutional and otherwise, which are extended to criminal defendants in all other instances is also wholly sufficient for the crime of contempt.

Mr. Justice Brennan, with whom The Chief Justice and Mr. Justice Douglas join, dissenting.

I dissent because I do not believe that the evidence was sufficient to establish beyond a reasonable doubt the petitioners' guilt of the criminal contempt charged. . . .

SELECTED REFERENCES

Black, Charles L., Jr., *The People and the Court*. New York: The Macmillan Company, 1960.

Cahn, Edmond (ed.), *Supreme Court and Supreme Law*. Bloomington, Ind.: Indiana University Press, 1954.

Carr, Robert K., *The Supreme Court and Judicial Review*. New York: Holt, Rinehart and Winston, Inc., 1942.

Corwin, Edward S. (ed.), *The Constitution of the United States of America: Analysis and Interpretation*, pp. 505–646. Washington: Government Printing Office, 1953.

Dunham, Allison, and Philip B. Kurland, *Mr. Justice*. Chicago: University of Chicago Press, 1956.

Frank, John P., *Marble Palace: The Supreme Court in American Life*. New York: Alfred A. Knopf, Inc., 1958.

Frankfurter, Felix, and James M. Landis, *The Business of the Supreme Court*. New York: The Macmillan Company, 1928.

Freund, Paul A., *On Understanding the Supreme Court*. Boston: Little, Brown & Company, 1949.

Hart, Henry M., Jr., and Herbert Wechsler, *The Federal Courts and the Federal System*. Brooklyn, N.Y.: The Foundation Press, 1953.

Hughes, Charles Evans, *The Supreme Court of the United States*. New York: Columbia University Press, 1928.

Hurst, Willard, *The Growth of American Law: The Law Makers*. Boston: Little, Brown & Company, 1950.

Jackson, Robert H., *The Supreme Court in the American System of Government*. Cambridge, Mass.: Harvard University Press, 1955.

McCloskey, Robert G., *The American Supreme Court*. Chicago: University of Chicago Press, 1960.

Mason, Alpheus T., *Harlan Fiske Stone: Pillar of the Law*. New York: The Viking Press, Inc., 1956.

Mendelson, Wallace, *Justices Black and Frankfurter*. Chicago: University of Chicago Press, 1961.

Murphy, Walter F., and C. Herman Pritchett, *Courts, Judges, and Politics: An Introduction to the Judicial Process*. New York: Random House, Inc., 1961.

Peltason, Jack, *58 Lonely Men*. New York: Harcourt, Brace & World, Inc., 1961.

Pritchett, C. Herman, *The American Constitution*, part 3. New York: McGraw-Hill Book Company, Inc., 1959.

——— *The Roosevelt Court: A Study in Judicial Politics and Values, 1937–1947*. New York: The Macmillan Company, 1948.

Rodell, Fred, *Nine Men: A Political History of the Supreme Court from 1790 to 1955*. New York: Random House, Inc., 1955.

Schubert, Glendon A., *Constitutional Politics*. New York: Holt, Rinehart and Winston, Inc., 1960.

Warren, Charles, *The Supreme Court in United States History*, 2 vols. Boston: Little, Brown & Company, 1947 (revised edition).

Westin, Allan, *The Supreme Court: Views from Inside*. New York: W. W. Norton & Company, Inc., 1961.

Wright, Benjamin F., *The Growth of American Constitutional Law*. Boston: Houghton Mifflin Company, 1942.

PART TWO

The Congress

INTRODUCTION

The legislative powers and institutions of the United States government are provided for in the first Article of the Constitution. Section 1 is a grant of general legislative power to the Congress. Sections 2 and 3 deal with the election of members to and the officers of the House and Senate respectively, and also contain the provisions on impeachment. Sections 4 to 6 are an assorted group of paragraphs relating to internal procedures and rights and privileges of members of Congress. Here is found the prohibition against congressmen being appointed to civil offices, which bars any approaches toward the parliamentary form of government; also the allocation of responsibility as between the states and Congress for holding elections. Section 7 regulates the procedure of adopting legislation. Section 8 is a long listing of powers specifically delegated to Congress, winding up with the catch-all "necessary and proper" clause. Sections 9 and 10 contain a somewhat shorter list of things which Congress and the states are forbidden to do.

To review briefly the legislative institutions, the Senate is composed of two senators for each state, elected for six-year terms. Originally they were chosen by the state legislatures, but the Seventeenth Amendment, adopted in 1913, provided for their election by direct popular vote.

Membership in the House of Representatives is based on population. After each decennial census Congress has the obligation to allocate to each state the number of seats proportional to its population. As the country grew, Congress increased the number of seats in the House every ten years until in the 1911 statute a size of 435 was reached. At that point it was decided that a ceiling had been reached, and in subsequent statutes the House has been frozen at 435 members (except that the admission of Alaska and Hawaii temporarily increased the membership to 437 pending adoption of a new allocation after the 1960 census). By an act of 1929 Congress delegated the task of making the allocation to the Census Bureau, and its plan goes into effect automatically unless modified by Congress. The term of representatives is two years.

A senator must be thirty years of age, nine years a citizen of the United States, and an inhabitant of the state from which he is elected. A representative need be only twenty-five years of age and a citizen for seven years, but the residence requirement is the same. By custom a representative must reside not only in the state but in the district from which he is elected. Each house is authorized by Article I, section 5, to "be the judge of the elections, returns and qualifications of its own members. . . ."

Congressmen are not subject to impeachment, but the Constitution does provide that each house may expel its members by a two-thirds vote, or punish them for "disorderly behavior." Congress is the sole judge of the reasons for expulsion. Formal censure proceedings have been brought against three of its members in Senate history. The most recent case was that of Senator Joseph McCarthy, who was censured in 1954 for conduct "contrary to Senatorial traditions."

Vacancies in the House are required to be filled by special elections. For senators, the Seventeenth Amendment provides for special elections but also authorizes each state legislature to empower the governor to make temporary appointments pending an election. Practically all states have taken advantage of this provision, with the result that Senate vacancies are usually filled immediately by appointment, while House vacancies often remain unfilled for months.

Senators and representatives, according to Article I, section 6, "shall in all cases, except treason, felony and breach of the peace, be privileged from arrest during their attendance at the session of their respective houses, and in going to and returning from the same; and for any speech or debate in either house, they shall not be questioned in any other place." This latter provision means that congressmen cannot be sued for libel or slander, or in any other way held legally accountable for statements made in their official capacity except by the House or Senate itself. Not only remarks on the floor of Congress, but written reports, resolutions offered, the act of voting, and all things done in a session by one of its members relating to the business before it, are covered.

Chapter 5

REGULATION OF ELECTIONS

The House of Representatives shall be composed of members chosen every second year by the people of the several States, and the electors in each State shall have the qualifications requisite for electors of the most numerous branch of the State legislature. ART. I, SEC. 2

The times, places and manner of holding elections for Senators and Representatives, shall be prescribed in each State by the legislature thereof; but the Congress may at any time by law make or alter such regulations, except as to the places of choosing Senators. ART. I, SEC. 4

The drafters of the Constitution had to deal with the problem of prescribing a national electorate only in connection with the selection of members of the House, since senators were elected by the state legislatures, and presidential electors were appointed in such manner as the state legislatures might direct. Eventually, of course, the responsibility for electing the President and members of both houses of Congress devolved upon the same electorate. By the provision in Article I, section 2, the Constitution assured election of the House on a popular base but avoided creation of a national electorate separate from the state electorates, which were defined by legal provisions varying widely from state to state.

Congress first took action under the "times, places and manner" clause in 1842, when it required that the members of the House be elected by districts rather than on a general state ticket. The first comprehensive federal statute on elections came in 1870, motivated by the political problems of the Reconstruction period. The Enforcement Act of 1870 and subsequent measures made federal offenses of false registration, bribery, voting without legal right, making false returns of votes cast, interference in any manner with officers of elections, or the neglect by any such officer of any duty required of him by state or federal law.

In addition to these two provisions of Article I, three of the amendments to the Constitution have a bearing on elections and the electorate. The equal protection clause of the Fourteenth Amendment has been applied to forbid discriminatory practices by state election officials. The Fourteenth Amendment also contains the threat of reduction of representation for denial of the right to vote. When it appeared that this provision would not achieve its purpose of securing the suffrage for Negroes, the Fifteenth Amendment was adopted in 1870, specifically guaranteeing that "the right of citizens of the United States to vote shall not be denied or abridged by the United States or by any state on account of race, color, or previous condition of servitude." The Nineteenth Amendment, adopted in

1920, uses the same formula to guarantee women the right to vote. The Fourteenth, Fifteenth, and Nineteenth Amendments all authorize Congress to enforce their provisions by appropriate legislation.

The Right to Vote. Because Article I, section 2, makes the right to vote in federal elections depend upon state laws prescribing the electorate, it is strictly true, as the Supreme Court held in the early case of *Minor* v. *Happersett,* 21 Wall. 162 (1875), that "the Constitution of the United States does not confer the right of suffrage upon anyone." Mrs. Minor had sought to compel election officials in Missouri, where suffrage was limited to male citizens, to accept her vote on the ground that she had a right to vote as a citizen of the United States under the Fourteenth Amendment, but the Court decisively rejected this contention.

The doctrine of the *Minor* case was not as absolute a bar to federal authority in the field of elections as it appeared on the surface, however. A decade later the Court in *Ex parte Yarbrough,* 110 U.S. 651 (1884), affirmed the conviction of several Klansmen for conspiring to intimidate a Negro from voting for a member of Congress, in violation of the Enforcement Act of 1870 which protected citizens in the exercise of any federal right. In spite of *Minor* v. *Happersett,* there was a *right* involved in this case. The earlier decision, the Court explained, merely meant that state law, not the federal Constitution, determined what classes of citizens could exercise the franchise. But once state law had determined who was eligible to vote by statutory provisions covering state elections, then the federal Constitution through Article I, section 2, stepped in to guarantee the right of those citizens to vote for members of Congress.

The close relationship of federal and state interests, moreover, meant that Congress could make violation of state election laws a federal offense. As the Court said in *Ex parte Siebold,* 100 U.S. 371 (1880), this was a method of providing additional sanctions and more effective supervision over the enforcement of state regulations on a matter of "vital importance to the United States" which had been "in effect adopted by Congress."

The Regulation of Party Primaries. These early interpretations confirmed an important measure of federal control over congressional elections, but the coming of the direct primary presented a new challenge to federal regulation. In the Corrupt Practices Act of 1910 Congress restricted campaign expenditures in securing nomination as well as in the elections. Truman H. Newberry was convicted of violating this statute in winning nomination and election to the Senate from Michigan in 1918. In *Newberry* v. *United States,* 256 U.S. 232 (1921), the Supreme Court set aside the conviction, five justices holding that when the Constitution referred to election it meant "the final choice of an officer by the duly qualified electors," and that the primary was "in no real sense part of the manner of holding the election."

This ruling was weakened because one of the majority, Justice McKenna, thought that the constitutional situation would be different if Congress had passed the statute in question *after* the adoption of the Seventeenth Amendment providing for the direct election of senators. The four-judge minority was clear that the primary was part of the election process, and also argued that Congress had the inherent power, entirely apart from Article I, section 4, to safeguard the purity of the process by which its members were elected.

In spite of the dubious majority in this case, Congress seemingly accepted this check on its powers and expressly excluded primary elections from the purview of the new Corrupt Practices Act passed in 1925. It took eventual action by the Court itself to reverse the presumed holding of the *Newberry* case. *United States v. Classic,* 313 U.S. 299 (1941), involved a prosecution brought by the Civil Rights Section of the U.S. Department of Justice against election officials in Louisiana who had tampered with the ballots in a primary where candidates for representative in Congress were chosen. The Court pointed out that Louisiana election laws made the primary "an integral part" of the process of electing congressmen, and that in fact the Democratic primary in Louisiana was "the only stage of the election procedure" where the voter's choice was of significance. The Court was thus taking a highly realistic view in its conclusion that the authority of Congress under Article I, section 4, "includes the authority to regulate primary elections when, as in this case, they are a step in the exercise by the people of their choice of representatives in Congress."

Negro Disfranchisement and the "Private Club" Theory. In spite of the Fifteenth Amendment, Negro disfranchisement was the general practice in most of the Southern states. While exclusion from the polls was often accomplished by extralegal methods, there was a constant search for constitutional procedures for achieving these ends. Success was achieved by a Mississippi law requiring voters to be able to read, understand, or interpret any section of the Constitution, which was upheld in *Williams* v. *Mississippi,* 170 U.S. 213 (1898), because on its face it did not discriminate against Negroes, whatever might be the practice in its administration.

The so-called "grandfather clause" type of restriction, however, was less successful. An Oklahoma law imposed a literacy test for voting, but gave exemption for persons whose ancestors had been entitled to vote in 1866. *Guinn* v. *United States,* 238 U.S. 347 (1915), held this provision to be an obvious effort to evade the Fifteenth Amendment, and so unconstitutional. Oklahoma rejoined with a new election registration law which permitted only a twelve-day registration period, but exempted from the registration requirement those who had voted in the 1914 election under the unconstitutional grandfather clause. The Court held this law invalid in *Lane* v. *Wilson,* 307 U.S. 268 (1939).

That the Fifteenth Amendment was not the only constitutional protection against racial discrimination in voting was demonstrated by the Texas "white primary" cases. Encouraged by the *Newberry* decision in 1921 to believe that primary elections were not subject to federal control, the Texas Legislature in 1923 flatly prohibited Negroes from voting in that state's Democratic primaries. When this statute was tested in the case of *Nixon* v. *Herndon,* 273 U.S. 536 (1927), the Supreme Court avoided a reconsideration of the constitutional status of primaries and the application to them of the Fifteenth Amendment; instead it invalidated the statute on the ground that it was a "direct and obvious infringement" of the equal protection of the laws clause in the Fourteenth Amendment.

The Texas Legislature then came back with another law authorizing political parties in the state, through their state executive committees, to prescribe the qualifications for voting in their primaries. The theory of this statute was that what the state could not do directly because of the Fourteenth Amendment, it could authorize political parties to do. The Democratic state executive committee then excluded Negroes from primary elections, but in *Nixon* v. *Condon,* 286 U.S. 73 (1932), the Court held that the party committee had acted as the agent of the state, which made the action equivalent to that by the state itself and so unconstitutional as state denial of equal protection.

In neither of these decisions did the Court question the *Newberry* assertion that party primaries were outside the protection of the Constitution; it was only the fact that state legislation was the basis for party action in these cases which made the Fourteenth Amendment applicable. Taking advantage of this situation, the Texas Democratic party convention, immediately after the *Condon* decision, on its own authority and without any state legislation on the subject, adopted a resolution confining party membership to white citizens. By unanimous vote the Court in *Grovey* v. *Townsend,* 295 U.S. 45 (1935), concluded that the Fourteenth Amendment had not been infringed since the action was taken by the party and not by the state.

The Supreme Court thus endorsed the view that political parties were private clubs uncontrolled by constitutional limitations on official action, and that the primaries they held were constitutionally no part of the election process. Both of these propositions were so directly contrary to the obvious facts of party operation that they were bound to fall sooner or later of their own weight. As already noted, the *Classic* decision in 1941 disposed of the fallacy that primaries were not part of the election process. Interestingly enough, the *Classic* opinion did not even mention *Grovey* v. *Townsend* (a stratagem to win the vote of Justice Roberts, who was the author of *Grovey*), but clearly its authority had been undermined and the private club theory had been left on very shaky legal ground.

Consequently a new test case from Texas was begun, which resulted in a direct reversal of the *Grovey* decision by the Court in *Smith* v. *Allwright,* 321 U.S. 649 (1914). The Court held that as a result of the *Classic* ruling, party primaries could no longer be regarded as private affairs nor the parties conducting them as unaffected by public responsibilities. Noting that parties and party primaries in Texas were in fact regulated at many points by state statutes, the Court reasoned that a party required to follow these directions was "an agency of the state," and if it practiced discrimination against Negroes, that was "state action within the meaning of the Fifteenth Amendment."

Inasmuch as the *Smith* decision stressed the extensive statutory regulations of parties and party primaries in Texas as proof that a party so regulated was "an agency of the state," South Carolina immediately resorted to the device of repealing all its statutes pertaining to party primaries, hoping thus to pass off the Democratic party in that state as a "private voluntary association of individuals," which could then exclude Negroes constitutionally by "club rules." The Supreme Court, by refusing in *Rice* v. *Elmore,* 333 U.S. 875 (1948), to review a lower court decision unfavorable to this contention, definitely liquidated the private club theory and brought political parties finally and fully within the ambit of constitutional protections and limitations.

In *Terry* v. *Adams,* 345 U.S. 461 (1953), the Court, with only one justice dissenting, applied the principle of *Smith* v. *Allwright* to invalidate the unofficial primaries conducted in a Texas county by the Jaybird party, a Democratic political organization which excluded Negroes. The winners in the Jaybird primaries then entered the regular Democratic party primaries, where over a sixty-year period they were never defeated for county office. In fact, other candidates seldom filed. The Court ruled that the "Jaybird primary has become an integral part, indeed the only effective part, of the elective process that determines who shall rule and govern in the county," and consequently that the Fifteenth Amendment was applicable and must be observed.

Supreme Court decisions alone, however, were not enough to break the widespread practice of Negro exclusion from the polls. In 1957 Congress passed a new Civil Rights Act, the first since Reconstruction days. The statute authorized federal prosecuting officers to secure injunctions against actual or threatened interference with the right to vote in the states, whereas it had previously been necessary for the individual voter to take the initiative in bringing suit to protect his rights of suffrage. The statute also created a Civil Rights Commission to gather information on denial of voting and other protected rights and to make recommendations to Congress on needed legislation. In *Hannah* v. *Larche,* 363 U.S. 420 (1960), the Supreme Court ruled that in hearings on denial of voting rights the commission could subpoena voting registrars and compel them to testify without giving them the names of Negroes who had filed complaints against them.

In 1960 Congress passed another Civil Rights Act intended to assist Negroes in securing registration. Referees appointed by federal judges were empowered to register, for voting in federal and state elections, qualified Negroes who had been refused registration in areas where a pattern of discrimination had been established by suits under the 1957 statute. The 1960 measure was a compromise which was not expected to prove very effective.

The Responsibility for Redistricting. In 1842 Congress required every state entitled to more than one representative to be divided by its legislature into districts "composed of contiguous territory," each returning one member. The reapportionment acts of 1901 and 1911 added a "compact" qualification in an effort to limit the practice of gerrymandering. But the 1929 act omitted any requirement for contiguous, compact, or even equal districts. In fact, the statute did not even require election of House members by districts. A few states had ignored this requirement, and it had not been enforced. In *Wood* v. *Broom,* 287 U.S. 1 (1932), the Supreme Court held that these omissions in the 1929 act were intentional, and that consequently it would take no action to correct state redistricting acts setting up gerrymandered districts.

In *Colegrove* v. *Green,* 328 U.S. 549 (1946), the Court by a vote of four to three held itself powerless to remedy a state's failure to redistrict. After the census of 1901 the Illinois Legislature divided the state into twenty-five congressional districts. Following the next four decennial censuses, the legislature failed to redistrict, though the shifts in population made the 1901 districts increasingly unequal. By 1940 one district had a population of 914,000 while another had only 112,000. The reason for the legislature's failure to act was that it was dominated by rural downstaters, and any redistricting plan would have increased the number of seats in Congress awarded to Chicago.

Colegrove and other qualified voters, living in districts of large population in the Chicago region, brought suit against the election officials to restrain them from conducting an election in November, 1946, under the 1901 law. Justice Frankfurter's opinion for the Court held that the fair representation of the states in the House of Representatives was a matter for the "exclusive authority" of Congress. If the Supreme Court sought to intervene, it would be entering into a "political thicket." Moreover, any relief the Court could give would be negative; it could declare the existing system invalid, but could not draw new district lines, with the result that Illinois might be thrown into the forthcoming congressional election, then only a few months away, with the necessity of electing all its House members at large.

The fourth vote on the majority side was cast by Justice Rutledge, who did not agree with Frankfurter's general view that the courts had no responsibility on such matters, but who did favor judicial abstention in this case because he thought that intervention just preceding the election would do more harm than good. The three dissenters, Justices Black, Douglas, and Murphy, contended that the failure to redistrict was "willful legislative discrimination" amounting to a denial of equal protection of the laws.

While judicial power to handle legislative districting issues was thus denied by only three members of the Court, the *Colegrove* decision was generally understood as establishing the principle of judicial nonintervention with legislative apportionments or electoral systems, and was cited as a precedent by the Court in several subsequent state election cases. One such case was *South v. Peters,* 339 U.S. 276 (1950), where the issue was a county unit system of voting in Georgia primary elections which clearly discriminated against the large city populations in favor of sparsely settled rural areas. Another was *MacDougall v. Green,* 335 U.S. 281 (1948), refusing to invalidate an Illinois law requiring that nominees for state-wide elections secure a minimum number of signatures on petitions in at least 50 of the state's 102 counties.

Speculation that the Court might be weakening on the *Colegrove* rule was aroused by the decision in *Gomillion v. Lightfoot,* 364 U.S. 339 (1960). Here the Court unanimously declared unconstitutional an Alabama state law redefining the city boundaries of Tuskegee so as to place all but four or five of the city's Negro voters outside the city limits, without removing a single white voter or resident. The statute altered the shape of the city from a square to a twenty-eight-sided figure.

Justice Frankfurter, author of the *Colegrove* opinion, also spoke for the Court in *Gomillion* and distinguished the two situations. In *Colegrove* there had been a "dilution" of the strength of the appellants' votes as a result of legislative inaction (failure to redistrict), whereas in Tuskegee petitioners had been deprived of their votes in the city by affirmative legislative action. "When a legislature thus singles out a readily isolated segment of a racial minority for special discriminatory treatment, it violates the Fifteenth Amendment."

While the two decisions could be thus differentiated, the Court's willingness to act in the Tuskegee case did suggest that the Court might reconsider the *Colegrove* principle, and in fact it soon did so in the 1962 case of *Baker v. Carr.*

BAKER v. CARR
369 U.S. 186, 82 S. Ct. 691, 7 L. Ed. 2d 633 (1962)

The constitution of Tennessee provides for ninety-nine members of the House of Representatives and thirty-three members of the Senate, and directs the legislature to allocate, at least every ten years, the senators and representatives among the several counties or districts "according to the number of qualified voters in each." Despite these mandatory requirements, no reapportionment had been made since 1901. During the period between 1901 and 1950, the population grew from 2,021,000 to 3,292,000, but the growth was very uneven between counties. Thus 37 per cent of the voting population could control twenty of the thirty-three members of the Senate, while 40 per cent of the voters could control sixty-three of the ninety-nine members of the House.

In 1959 suit was brought in federal district court by certain citizens of Tennessee against state election officials under the Civil Rights Act of 1871, alleging deprivation of federal constitutional rights under color of state authority. A three-judge court, relying on the *Colegrove* decision, dismissed the complaint in 1960.

MR. JUSTICE BRENNAN delivered the opinion of the Court.

This civil action was brought under 42 U.S.C. §§ 1983 and 1988 to redress the alleged deprivation of federal constitutional rights. The complaint, alleging that by means of a 1901 statute of Tennessee apportioning the members of the General Assembly among the State's 95 counties, "these plaintiffs and others similarly situated, are denied the equal protection of the laws accorded them by the Fourteenth Amendment to the Constitution of the United States by virtue' of the debasement of their votes," was dismissed by a three-judge court convened under 28 U.S.C. § 2281 in the Middle District of Tennessee. The court held that it lacked jurisdiction of the subject matter and also that no claim was stated upon which relief could be granted. 179 F. Supp. 824. . . . We hold that the dismissal was error, and remand the cause to the District Court for trial and further proceedings consistent with this opinion.

The General Assembly of Tennessee consists of the Senate with 33 members and the House of Representatives with 99 members. . . . Tennessee's standard for allocating legislative representation among her counties is the total number of qualified voters resident in the respective counties, subject only to minor qualifications. Decennial reapportionment in compliance with the constitutional scheme was effected by the General Assembly each decade from 1871 to 1901. . . . In 1901 the General Assembly . . . passed the Apportionment Act here in controversy. In the more than 60 years since that action, all proposals in both Houses of the General Assembly for reapportionment have failed to pass.

Between 1901 and 1961, Tennessee has experienced substantial growth and redistribution of her population. In 1901 the population was 2,020,616, of whom 487,380 were eligible to vote. The 1960 Federal Census reports the State's population at 3,567,089, of whom 2,092,891 are eligible to vote. The relative standings of the counties in terms of qualified voters have changed significantly. It is primarily the continued application of the 1901 Apportionment Act to this shifted and enlarged voting population which gives rise to the present controversy.

. . . It is alleged that "because of the population changes since 1900, and the failure of the legislature to reapportion itself since 1901," the 1901 statute became "unconstitutional and obsolete." Appellants also argue that, because of the composition of the legislature effected by the 1901 apportionment act, redress in the form of a state constitutional amendment to change the entire mechanism for reapportioning, or any other change short of that, is difficult or impossible. The complaint concludes that "these plaintiffs and others similarly situated, are denied the equal protection of the laws accorded them by the Fourteenth Amendment to the Constitution of the

United States by virtue of the debasement of their votes." They seek a declaration that the 1901 statute is unconstitutional and an injunction restraining the appellees from acting to conduct any further elections under it. They also pray that unless and until the General Assembly enacts a valid reapportionment, the District Court should either decree a reapportionment by mathematical application of the Tennessee constitutional formulae to the most recent Federal Census figures, or direct the appellees to conduct legislative elections, primary and general, at large. . . .

THE DISTRICT COURT'S OPINION AND ORDER OF DISMISSAL.

Because we deal with this case on appeal from an order of dismissal granted on appellees' motions, precise identification of the issues presently confronting us demands clear exposition of the grounds upon which the District Court rested in dismissing the case. . . .

The District Court's dismissal order . . . rested . . . upon lack of subject-matter jurisdiction and lack of a justiciable cause of action without attempting to distinguish between these grounds. . . . The court proceeded to explain its action as turning on the case's presenting a "question of the distribution of political strength for legislative purposes." For,

"from a review of [numerous Supreme Court] . . . decisions there can be no doubt that the federal rule, as enunciated and applied by the Supreme Court, is that the federal courts, whether from a lack of jurisdiction or from the inappropriateness of the subject matter for judicial consideration, will not intervene in cases of this type to compel legislative reapportionment." . . .

The court went on to express doubts as to the feasibility of the various possible remedies sought by the plaintiffs. . . . Then it made clear that its dismissal reflected a view not of doubt that violation of constitutional rights was alleged, but of a court's impotence to correct that violation:

"With the plaintiffs' argument that the legislature of Tennessee is guilty of a clear violation of the state constitution and of the rights of the plaintiffs the Court entirely agrees. It also agrees that the evil is a serious one which should be corrected without further delay. But even so the remedy in this situation clearly does not lie with the courts. It has long been recognized and is accepted doctrine that there are indeed some rights guaranteed by the Constitution for the violation of which the courts cannot give redress." . . .

In light of the District Court's treatment of the case, we hold today only (a) that the court possessed jurisdiction of the subject matter; (b) that a justiciable cause of action is stated upon which appellants would be entitled to appropriate relief; and (c) because appellees raise the issue before this Court, that the appellants have standing to challenge the Tennessee apportionment statutes. Beyond noting that we have no cause at this stage to doubt the District Court will be able to fashion relief if violations of constitutional rights are found, it is improper now to consider what remedy would be most appropriate if appellants prevail at the trial.

JURISDICTION OF THE SUBJECT MATTER.

The District Court was uncertain whether our cases withholding federal judicial relief rested upon a lack of federal jurisdiction or upon the inappropriateness of the subject matter for judicial consideration—what we have designated "nonjusticiability." The distinction between the two grounds is significant. In the instance of nonjusticiability, consideration of the cause is not wholly and immediately foreclosed; rather, the Court's inquiry necessarily proceeds to the point of deciding whether the duty asserted can be judicially identified and its breach judicially determined, and whether protection for the right asserted can be judicially molded. In the instance of lack of jurisdiction the cause either does not "arise under" the Federal Constitution, laws or treaties (or fall within one of the other enumerated categories of Art. III, § 2), or is not a "case or controversy" within the meaning of that section; or the cause is not one described by any jurisdictional statute. . . .

An unbroken line of our precedents sustains the federal courts' jurisdiction of the subject matter of federal constitutional claims of this nature. The first cases involved the redistricting of States for the purpose of electing Representatives to the Federal Congress. . . . When the Minnesota Supreme Court affirmed the dismissal of a suit to enjoin the Secretary of State of Minnesota from acting under Minnesota redistricting legislation, we reviewed the constitutional merits of the legislation and reversed the State Supreme Court. *Smiley* v. *Holm,* 285 U.S. 355. . . . When a three-judge District Court . . . permanently enjoined officers of the State of Mississippi from conducting an election of Representatives under a Mississippi redistricting act, we reviewed the federal questions on the merits and reversed the District Court. *Wood* v. *Broom,* 287 U.S. 1. . . .

The appellees refer to *Colegrove* v. *Green,* 328 U.S. 549, as authority that the District Court lacked jurisdiction of the subject matter. Appellees misconceive the holding of that case. The holding was precisely contrary to their reading of it. Seven members of the Court participated in the decision. Unlike many other cases in this field which have assumed without discussion that there was jurisdiction, all three opinions filed in *Colegrove* discussed the question. Two of the opinions expressing the views of four of the Justices, a majority, flatly held that there was jurisdiction of the subject matter. MR. JUSTICE BLACK joined by MR. JUSTICE DOUGLAS and Mr. Justice Murphy stated: "It is my judgment that the District Court had jurisdiction. . . ." Mr. Justice Rutledge, writing separately, expressed agreement with this conclusion. . . . Indeed, it is even questionable that the opinion of MR. JUSTICE FRANKFURTER, joined by Justices Reed and Burton, doubted jurisdiction of the subject matter. . . .

Several subsequent cases similar to *Colegrove* have been decided by the Court in summary *per curiam* statements. None was dismissed for want of jurisdiction of the subject matter. . . .

Two cases decided with opinions after *Colegrove* likewise plainly imply that the subject matter of this suit is within District Court jurisdiction. In *MacDougall* v. *Green,* 335 U.S. 281, the District Court dismissed for want of jurisdiction . . . a suit to enjoin enforcement of the requirement that nominees for state-wide elections be supported by a petition signed by a minimum number of persons from at least 50 of the State's 102 counties. This Court's disagreement with that action is clear since the Court affirmed the judgment after a review of the merits and concluded that the particular claim there was without merit. In *South* v. *Peters,* 339 U.S. 276, we affirmed the dismissal of an attack on the Georgia "county unit" system but founded our action on a ground that plainly would not have been reached if the lower court lacked jurisdiction of the subject matter. . . . The express words of our holding were that "federal courts consistently refuse to exercise their equity powers in cases posing political issues arising from a state's geographical distribution of electoral strength among its political subdivisions." 339 U.S., at 277.

We hold that the District Court has jurisdiction of the subject matter of the federal constitutional claim asserted in the complaint. . . .

JUSTICIABILITY.

In holding that the subject matter of this suit was not justiciable, the District Court relied on *Colegrove* v. *Green, supra,* and subsequent *per curiam* cases. . . . We understand the District Court to have read the cited cases as compelling the conclusion that since the appellants sought to have a legislative apportionment held unconstitutional, their suit presented a "political question" and was therefore non-justiciable. We hold that this challenge to an apportionment presents no nonjusticiable "political question." The cited cases do not hold the contrary.

Of course the mere fact that the suit seeks protection of a political right does not mean it presents a political question. Such an objection "is little more than a play upon words." . . . Rather, it is argued that apportionment cases, whatever the actual wording of the complaint, can involve no federal constitutional right except one resting on the guaranty of a republican form of government, and that complaints based on that clause have been held to present political questions which are nonjusticiable.

We hold that the claim pleaded here neither rests upon nor implicates the Guaranty Clause and that its justiciability is therefore not foreclosed by our decisions of cases involving that clause. The District Court misinterpreted *Colegrove* v. *Green* and other decisions of this Court on which it relied. Appellants' claim that they are being denied equal protection is justiciable, and if "discrimination is sufficiently shown, the right to relief under the equal protection clause is not diminished by the fact that the discrimination relates to political rights." *Snowden* v. *Hughes*, 321 U.S. 1, 11. To show why we reject the argument based on the Guaranty Clause . . . we deem it necessary first to consider the contours of the "political question" doctrine.

Our discussion . . . requires review of a number of political question cases, in order to expose the attributes of the doctrine. . . . That review reveals that in the Guaranty Clause cases and in the other "political question" cases, it is the relationship between the judiciary and the coordinate branches of the Federal Government, and not the federal judiciary's relationship to the States, which gives rise to the "political question." . . .

The nonjusticiability of a political question is primarily a function of the separation of powers. . . . Prominent on the surface of any case held to involve a political question is found a textually demonstrable constitutional commitment of the issue to a coordinate political department; or a lack of judicially discoverable and manageable standards for resolving it; or the impossibility of deciding without an initial policy determination of a kind clearly for nonjudicial discretion; or the impossibility of a court's undertaking independent resolution without expressing lack of the respect due coordinate branches of government; or an unusual need for unquestioning adherence to a political decision already made; or the potentiality of embarrassment from multifarious pronouncements by various departments on one question.

Unless one of these formulations is inextricable from the case at bar, there should be no dismissal for nonjusticiability on the ground of a political question's presence. The doctrine of which we treat is one of "political questions," not one of "political cases." The courts cannot reject as "no law suit" a bona fide controversy as to whether some action denominated "political" exceeds constitutional authority. . . .

But it is argued that this case shares the characteristics of decisions that constitute a category not yet considered, cases concerning the Constitution's guaranty, in Art. IV, § 4, of a republican form of government. . . .

[The Court then discusses at length *Luther* v. *Borden*, 7 How. 1 (1849), and other cases holding the republican guaranty provision judicially unenforceable.]

We conclude that the nonjusticiability of claims resting on the Guaranty Clause which arises from their embodiment of questions that were thought "political," can have no bearing upon the justiciability of the equal protection claim presented in this case. . . . We emphasize that it is the involvement in Guaranty Clause claims of the elements thought to define "political questions," and no other feature, which could render them nonjusticiable. Specifically, we have said that such claims are not held nonjusticiable because they touch matters of state governmental organization. . . . Only last Term, in *Gomillion* v. *Lightfoot*, 364 U.S. 339, we applied the

Fifteenth Amendment to strike down a redrafting of municipal boundaries which effected a discriminatory impairment of voting rights, in the face of what a majority of the Court of Appeals thought to be a sweeping commitment to state legislatures of the power to draw and redraw such boundaries. . . .

We conclude that the complaint's allegations of a denial of equal protection present a justiciable constitutional cause of action upon which appellants are entitled to a trial and a decision. The right asserted is within the reach of judicial protection under the Fourteenth Amendment.

The judgment of the District Court is reversed and the cause is remanded for further proceedings consistent with this opinion.

Reversed and remanded.

MR. JUSTICE WHITTAKER did not participate in the decision of this case.

MR. JUSTICE DOUGLAS, concurring.

While I join the opinion of the Court and, like the Court, do not reach the merits, a word of explanation is necessary. I put to one side the problems of "political" questions involving the distribution of power between this Court, the Congress, and the Chief Executive. We have here a phase of the recurring problem of the relation of the federal courts to state agencies. More particularly, the question is the extent to which a State may weight one person's vote more heavily than it does another's. . . .

The traditional test under the Equal Protection Clause has been whether a State has made "an invidious discrimination," as it does when it selects "a particular race or nationality for oppressive treatment." See *Skinner* v. *Oklahoma,* 316 U.S. 535, 541. Universal equality is not the test; there is room for weighting. As we stated in *Williamson* v. *Lee Optical Co.,* 348 U.S. 483, 489, "The prohibition of the Equal Protection Clause goes no further than the invidious discrimination."

I agree with my Brother CLARK that if the allegations in the complaint can be sustained a case for relief is established. We are told that a single vote in Moore County, Tennessee, is worth 19 votes in Hamilton County, that one vote in Stewart or in Chester County is worth nearly eight times a single vote in Shelby or Knox County. The opportunity to prove that an "invidious discrimination" exists should therefore be given the appellants. . . .

With the exceptions of *Colegrove* v. *Green,* 328 U.S. 549; *MacDougall* v. *Green,* 335 U.S. 281; *South* v. *Peters,* 339 U.S. 276, and the decisions they spawned, the Court has never thought that protection of voting rights was beyond judicial cognizance. Today's treatment of those cases removes the only impediment to judicial cognizance of the claims stated in the present complaint.

The justiciability of the present claims being established, any relief accorded can be fashioned in the light of well-known principles of equity.

MR. JUSTICE CLARK, concurring. . . .

I believe it can be shown that this case is distinguishable from earlier cases dealing with the distribution of political power by a State, that a patent violation of the Equal Protection Clause of the United States Constitution has been shown, and that an appropriate remedy may be formulated.

I.

I take the law of the case from *MacDougall* v. *Green,* 335 U.S. 281 (1948), which involved an attack under the Equal Protection Clause upon an Illinois election statute. The Court decided that case on its merits without hindrance from the "political question" doctrine. Although the statute under attack was upheld, it is clear that the Court based its decision upon the determination that the statute represented a rational state policy. It stated:

> "It would be strange indeed, and doctrinaire, for this Court, applying such broad constitutional concepts as due process and equal protection of the laws, to deny a State the power to assure a *proper* diffusion of political initiative as between its thinly populated counties and those having concentrated masses, *in view of the fact that the latter have practical opportunities for exerting their political weight at the polls not available to the former.*" Id., at 284. (Emphasis supplied.)

The other cases upon which my Brethren dwell are all distinguishable or inapposite. The widely heralded case of *Colegrove* v. *Green* . . . was one not only in which the Court was bob-tailed but in which there was no majority opinion. Indeed, even the "political question" point in Mr. Justice Frankfurter's opinion was no more than an alternative ground. Moreover, the appellants did not present an equal protection argument. While it has served as a Mother Hubbard to most of the subsequent cases, I feel it was in that respect ill-cast and for all of these reasons put it to one side. Likewise, I do not consider the Guaranty Clause cases based on Art. I, § 4, of the Constitution, because it is not invoked here and it involves different criteria, as the Court's opinion indicates. . . . Finally, the Georgia county unit system cases, such as *South* v. *Peters* . . . reflect the viewpoint of *MacDougall, i. e.,* to refrain from intervening where there is some rational policy behind the State's system.

II.

The controlling facts cannot be disputed. It appears from the record that 37% of the voters of Tennessee elect 20 of the 33 Senators while 40% of the voters elect 63 of the 99 members of the House. But this might not on its face be an "invidious discrimination," . . . for a "statutory discrimination will not be set aside if any state of facts reasonably may be conceived to justify it." *McGowan* v. *Maryland,* 366 U.S. 420, 426 (1961).

It is true that the apportionment policy incorporated in Tennessee's Constitution, *i. e.,* state-wide numerical equality of representation with certain minor qualifications, is a rational one. . . . However, the root of the trouble is not in Tennessee's Constitution, for admittedly its policy has not been followed. The discrimination lies in the action of Tennessee's Assembly in allocating legislative seats to counties or districts created by it. Try as one may, Tennessee's apportionment just cannot be made to fit the pattern cut by its Constitution. This was the finding of the District Court. The policy of the Constitution referred to by the dissenters, therefore, is of no relevance here. We must examine what the Assembly has done. The frequency and magnitude of the inequalities in the present districting admit of no policy whatever. . . . The apportionment picture in Tennessee is a topsy-turvical of gigantic proportions. . . . Tennessee's apportionment is a crazy quilt without rational basis. . . .

No one contends that mathematical equality among voters is required by the Equal Protection Clause. But certainly there must be some rational design to a State's districting. The discrimination here does not fit any pattern. . . . My Brother Harlan contends that other proposed apportionment plans contain disparities. Instead of chasing those rabbits he should first pause long enough to meet appellants' proof of discrimination by showing that in fact the present plan follows a rational policy. Not being able to do this, he merely counters with such generalities as "classic legislative judgment," no "significant discrepancy," and "de minimis departures." I submit that even a casual glance at the present apportionment picture shows these conclusions to be entirely fanciful. If present representation has a policy at all, it is to maintain the *status quo* of invidious discrimination at any cost. . . .

III.

Although I find the Tennessee apportionment statute offends the Equal Protection Clause, I would not consider intervention by this Court into so delicate a field if there were any other relief available to the people of Tennessee. But the majority of the people of Tennessee have no "practical opportunities of exerting their political weight at the polls" to correct the existing "invidious discrimination." Tennessee has no initiative and referendum. I have searched diligently for other "practical opportunities" present under the law. I find none other than through the federal courts. The majority of the voters have been caught up in a legislative strait jacket. Tennessee has an "informed, civically militant electorate" and "an aroused popular conscience," but it does not sear "the conscience of the people's representatives." This is because the legislative policy has riveted the present seats in the Assembly to their respective constituencies, and by the votes of their incumbents a reapportionment of any kind is prevented. The people have been rebuffed at the hands of the Assembly; they have tried the constitutional convention route, but since the call must originate in the Assembly it, too, has been fruitless. They have tried Tennessee courts with the same result, and Governors have fought the tide only to flounder. It is said that there is recourse in Congress and perhaps that may be, but from a practical standpoint this is without substance. To date Congress has never undertaken such a task in any State. We therefore must conclude that the people of Tennessee are stymied and without judicial intervention will be saddled with the present discrimination in the affairs of their state government.

IV.

Finally, we must consider if there are any appropriate modes of effective judicial relief. The federal courts are, of course, not forums for political debate, nor should they resolve themselves into state constitutional conventions or legislative assemblies. Nor should their jurisdiction be exercised in the hope that such a declaration, as is made today, may have the direct effect of bringing on legislative action and relieving the courts of the problem of fashioning relief. To my mind this would be nothing less than blackjacking the Assembly into reapportioning the State. If judicial competence were lacking to fashion an effective decree, I would dismiss this appeal. However . . . I see no such difficulty in the position of this case. One plan might be to start with the existing assembly districts, consolidate some of them, and award the seats thus released to those counties suffering the most egregious discrimination. Other possibilities are present and might be more effective. But the plan here suggested would at least release the strangle hold now on the Assembly and permit it to redistrict itself. . . .

MR. JUSTICE STEWART, concurring.

The separate writings of my dissenting and concurring Brothers stray so far from the subject of today's decision as to convey, I think, a distressingly inaccurate impression of what the Court decides. For that reason, I think it appropriate, in joining the opinion of the Court, to emphasize in a few words what the opinion does and does not say. . . .

The complaint in this case asserts that Tennessee's system of apportionment is utterly arbitrary—without any possible justification in rationality. The District Court did not reach the merits of that claim, and this Court quite properly expresses no view on the subject. Contrary to the suggestion of my Brother HARLAN, the Court does not say or imply that "state legislatures must be so structured as to reflect with approximate equality the voice of every voter." . . . The Court does not say or imply that there is anything in the Federal Constitution "to prevent a State, acting not irrationally, from choosing any electoral legislative structure it thinks best suited to the interests, temper, and customs of its people." . . . And contrary to the suggestion of my Brother Douglas, the Court most assuredly does not decide the question, "may a State weight the vote of one county or one district more heavily than it weights the vote in another?" . . .

My Brother CLARK has made a convincing prima facie showing that Tennessee's system of apportionment is in fact utterly arbitrary—without any possible justification in rationality. My Brother HARLAN has, with imagination and ingenuity, hypothesized possibly rational bases for Tennessee's system. But the merits of this case are not before us now. The defendants have not yet had an opportunity to be heard in defense of the State's system of apportionment; indeed, they have not yet even filed an answer to the complaint. As in other cases, the proper place for the trial is in the trial court, not here.

MR. JUSTICE FRANKFURTER, whom MR. JUSTICE HARLAN joins, dissenting.

The Court today reverses a uniform course of decision established by a dozen cases, including one by which the very claim now sustained was unanimously rejected only five years ago. The impressive body of rulings thus cast aside reflected the equally uniform course of our political history regarding the relationship between population and legislative representation—a wholly different matter from denial of the franchise to individuals because of race, color, religion or sex. Such a massive repudiation of the experience of our whole past in asserting destructively novel judicial power demands a detailed analysis of the role of this Court in our constitutional scheme. Disregard of inherent limits in the effective exercise of the Court's "judicial Power" not only presages the futility of judicial intervention in the essentially political conflict of forces by which the relation between population and representation has time out of mind been and now is determined. It may well impair the Court's position as the ultimate organ of "the supreme Law of the Land" in that vast range of legal problems, often strongly entangled in popular feeling, on which this Court must pronounce. The Court's authority—possessed neither of the purse nor the sword —ultimately rests on sustained public confidence in its moral sanction. Such feeling must be nourished by the Court's complete detachment, in fact and in appearance, from political entanglements and by abstention from injecting itself into the clash of political forces in political settlements.

A hypothetical claim resting on abstract assumptions is now for the first time made the basis for affording illusory relief for a particular evil even though it foreshadows deeper and more pervasive difficulties in consequence. The claim is hypothetical and the assumptions are abstract because the Court does not vouchsafe the lower courts —state and federal—guide-lines for formulating specific, definite, wholly unprecedented remedies for the inevitable litigations that today's umbrageous disposition is bound to stimulate in connection with politically motivated reapportionments in so many States. In such a setting, to promulgate jurisdiction in the abstract is meaningless. It is devoid of reality as "a brooding omnipresence in the sky" for it conveys no intimation what relief, if any, a District Court is capable of affording that would not invite legislatures to play ducks and drakes with the judiciary. For this Court to direct the District Court to enforce a claim to which the Court has over the years consistently found itself required to deny legal enforcement and at the same time to find it necessary to withhold any guidance to the lower court how to enforce this turnabout, new legal claim, manifests an odd—indeed an esoteric—conception of judicial propriety. One of the Court's supporting opinions, as elucidated by commentary, unwittingly affords a disheartening preview of the mathematical quagmire (apart from divers judicially inappropriate and elusive determinants), into which this

Court today catapults the lower courts of the country without so much as adumbrating the basis for a legal calculus as a means of extrication. Even assuming the indispensable intellectual disinterestedness on the part of judges in such matters, they do not have accepted legal standards or criteria or even reliable analogies to draw upon for making judicial judgments. To charge courts with the task of accommodating the incommensurable factors of policy that underlie these mathematical puzzles is to attribute, however flatteringly, omnicompetence to judges. The Framers of the Constitution persistently rejected a proposal that embodied this assumption and Thomas Jefferson never entertained it.

Recent legislation, creating a district appropriately described as "an atrocity of ingenuity," is not unique. Considering the gross inequality among legislative electoral units within almost every State, the Court naturally shrinks from asserting that in districting at least substantial equality is a constitutional requirement enforceable by courts. Room continues to be allowed for weighting. This of course implies that geography, economics, urban-rural conflict, and all the other non-legal factors which have throughout our history entered into political districting are to some extent not to be ruled out in the undefined vista now opened up by review in the federal courts of state reapportionments. To some extent—aye, there's the rub. In effect, today's decision empowers the courts of the country to devise what should constitute the proper composition of the legislatures of the fifty States. If state courts should for one reason or another find themselves unable to discharge this task, the duty of doing so is put on the federal courts or on this Court, if State views do not satisfy this Court's notion of what is proper districting.

We were soothingly told at the bar of this Court that we need not worry about the kind of remedy a court could effectively fashion once the abstract constitutional right to have courts pass on a state-wide system of electoral districting is recognized as a matter of judicial rhetoric, because legislatures would heed the Court's admonition. This is not only an euphoric hope. It implies a sorry confession of judicial impotence in place of a frank acknowledgment that there is not under our Constitution a judicial remedy for every political mischief, for every undesirable exercise of legislative power. The Framers carefully and with deliberate forethought refused so to enthrone the judiciary. In this situation, as in others of like nature, appeal for relief does not belong here. Appeal must be to an informed, civically militant electorate. In a democratic society like ours, relief must come through an aroused popular conscience that sears the conscience of the people's representatives. In any event there is nothing judicially more unseemly nor more self-defeating than for this Court to make *in terrorem* pronouncements, to indulge in merely empty rhetoric, sounding a word of promise to the ear, sure to be disappointing to the hope. . . .

I.

In sustaining appellants' claim, based on the Fourteenth Amendment, that the District Court may entertain this suit, this Court's uniform course of decision over the years is overruled or disregarded. Explicitly it begins with *Colegrove* v. *Green, supra*, decided in 1946, but its roots run deep in the Court's historic adjudicatory process.

Colegrove held that a federal court should not entertain an action for declaratory and injunctive relief to adjudicate the constitutionality, under the Equal Protection Clause and other federal constitutional and statutory provisions, of a state statute establishing the respective districts for the State's election of Representatives to the Congress. Two opinions were written by the four Justices who composed the majority of the seven sitting members of the Court. Both opinions joining in the result in *Colegrove* v. *Green* agreed that considerations were controlling which dictated denial of jurisdiction though not in the strict sense of want of power. While the two opinions show a divergence of view regarding some of these considerations, there are important points of concurrence. Both opinions demonstrate a predominant concern, first, with avoiding federal judicial involvement in matters traditionally left to legislative policy-making; second, with respect to the difficulty—in view of the nature of the problems of apportionment and its history in this country—of drawing on or devising judicial standards for judgment, as opposed to legislative determinations, of the part which mere numerical equality among voters should play as a criterion for the allocation of political power; and, third, with problems of finding appropriate modes of relief—particularly, the problem of resolving the essentially political issue of the relative merits of at-large elections and elections held in districts of unequal population. . . .

II.

The *Colegrove* doctrine, in the form in which repeated decisions have settled it, was not an innovation. It represents long judicial thought and experience. From its earliest opinions this Court has consistently recognized a class of controversies which do not lend themselves to judicial standards and judicial remedies. . . .

[Justice Frankfurter then discusses decisions involving the "political question" doctrine under the following headings: (1) war and foreign affairs; (2) structure and organization of state political institutions; (3) Negro disfranchisement; and (4) abstract questions of political power.]

5. The influence of these converging considerations—the caution not to undertake decision where standards meet for judicial judgment are lacking, the reluctance to interfere with matters of state government in the absence of an unquestionable and effectively enforceable mandate, the unwillingness to make courts arbiters of the broad issues of political organization historically committed to other institutions and for whose adjustment the judicial process is ill-adapted—has been decisive of the settled line of cases, reaching back more than a century, which holds that Art. IV, § 4, of the Constitution, guaranteeing to the States "a Republican Form of Government," is not enforceable through the courts. . . .

[A discussion follows of cases denying judicial responsibility for enforcing the republican form of government guaranty, particularly *Luther* v. *Borden,* 7 How. 1 (1849), and *Pacific States Telephone & Telegraph Co.* v. *Oregon,* 223 U.S. 118 (1912).]

III.

The present case involves all of the elements that have made the Guarantee Clause cases non-justiciable. It is, in effect, a Guarantee Clause claim masquerading under a different label. But it cannot make the case more fit for judicial action that appellants invoke the Fourteenth Amendment rather than Art. IV, § 4, where, in fact, the gist of their complaint is the same. . . .

What, then, is this question of legislative apportionment? Appellants invoke the right to vote and to have their votes counted. But they are permitted to vote and their votes are counted. They go to the polls, they cast their ballots, they send their representatives to the state councils. Their complaint is simply that the representatives are not sufficiently numerous or powerful—in short, that Tennessee has adopted a basis of representation with which they are dissatisfied. Talk of "debasement" or "dilution" is circular talk. One cannot speak of "debasement" or "dilution" of the value of a vote until there is first defined a standard of reference as to what a vote should be worth. What is actually asked of the Court in this case is to choose among competing bases of representation—ultimately, really, among competing theories of political philosophy—in order to establish an appropriate frame of government for the State of Tennessee and thereby for all the States of the Union.

In such a matter, abstract analogies which ignore the facts of history deal in unrealities; they betray reason. This is not a case in which a State has, through a device however oblique and sophisticated, denied Negroes or Jews or redheaded persons a vote, or given them only a third or a sixth of a vote. That was *Gomillion* v. *Lightfoot*. . . . What Tennessee illustrates is an old and still widespread method of representation—representation by local geographical division, only in part respective of population—in preference to others, others, forsooth, more appealing. Appellants contest this choice and seek to make this Court the arbiter of the disagreement. They would make the Equal Protection Clause the charter of adjudication, asserting that the equality which it guarantees comports, if not the assurance of equal weight to every voter's vote, at least the basic conception that representation ought to be proportionate to population, a standard by reference to which the reasonableness of apportionment plans may be judged.

To find such a political conception legally enforceable in the broad and unspecific guarantee of equal protection is to rewrite the Constitution. . . . Certainly, "equal protection" is no more secure a foundation for judicial judgment of the permissibility of varying forms of representative government than is "Republican Form." Indeed since "equal protection of the laws" can only mean an equality of persons standing in the same relation to whatever governmental action is challenged, the determination whether treatment is equal presupposes a determination concerning the nature of the relationship. This, with respect to apportionment, means an inquiry into the theoretic base of representation in an acceptably republican state. For a court could not determine the equal-protection issue without in fact first determining the Republican-Form issue, simply because what is reasonable for equal protection purposes will depend upon what frame of government, basically, is allowed. To divorce "equal protection" from "Republican Form" is to talk about half a question.

The notion that representation proportioned to the geographic spread of population is so universally accepted as a necessary element of equality between man and man that it must be taken to be the standard of a political equality preserved by the Fourteenth Amendment—that it is, in appellants' words "the basic principle of representative government"—is, to put it bluntly, not true. However desirable and however desired by some among the great political thinkers and framers of our government, it has never been generally practiced, today or in the past. It was not the English system, it was not the colonial system, it was not the system chosen for the national government by the Constitution, it was not the system exclusively or even predominantly practiced by the States at the time of adoption of the Fourteenth Amendment, it is not predominantly practiced by the States today. Unless judges, the judges of this Court, are to make their private views of political wisdom the measure of the Constitution—views which in all honesty cannot but give the appearance, if not reflect the reality, of involvement with the business of partisan politics so inescapably a part of apportionment controversies—the Fourteenth Amendment provides no guide for judicial oversight of the representation problem. . . .

[At this point Justice Frankfurter has a long discussion of representation and apportionment practices in Great Britain, the Colonies and the Union, the states at the time of the Fourteenth Amendment, and the contemporary period.]

Manifestly, the Equal Protection Clause supplies no clearer guide for judicial examination of apportionment methods than would the Guarantee Clause itself. Apportionment, by its character, is a subject of extraordinary complexity, involving— even after the fundamental theoretical issues concerning what is to be represented in a representative legislature have been fought out or compromised—considerations of geography, demography, electoral convenience, economic and social cohesions or divergencies among particular local groups, communications, the practical effects of political institutions like the lobby and the city machine, ancient traditions and ties of settled usage, respect for proven incumbents of long experience and senior status, mathematical mechanics, censuses compiling relevant data, and a host of others. Legislative responses throughout the country to the reapportionment demands of the 1960 Census have glaringly confirmed that these are not factors that lend themselves to evaluations of a nature that are the staple of judicial determinations or for which judges are equipped to adjudicate by legal training or experience or native wit. And this is the more so true because in every strand of this complicated, intricate web of values meet the contending forces of partisan politics. The practical significance of apportionment is that the next election results may differ because of it. Apportionment battles are overwhelmingly party or intra-party contests. It will add a virulent source of friction and tension in federal-state relations to embroil the federal judiciary in them.

IV.

Appellants, however, contend that the federal courts may provide the standard which the Fourteenth Amendment lacks by reference to the provisions of the constitution of Tennessee. The argument is that although the same or greater disparities of electoral strength may be suffered to exist immune from federal judicial review in States where they result from apportionment legislation consistent with state constitutions, the Tennessee legislature may not abridge the rights which, on its face, its own constitution appears to give, without by that act denying equal protection of the laws. It is said that the law of Tennessee, as expressed by the words of its written constitution, has made the basic choice among policies in favor of representation proportioned to population, and that it is no longer open to the State to allot its voting power on other principles.

This reasoning does not bear analysis. Like claims invoking state constitutional requirement have been rejected here and for good reason. It is settled that whatever federal consequences may derive from a discrimination worked by a state statute must be the same as if the same discrimination were written into the State's fundamental law. . . . Appellants complain of a practice which, by their own allegations, has been the law of Tennessee for sixty years. They allege that the apportionment act of 1901 created unequal districts when passed and still maintains unequal districts. They allege that the Legislature has since 1901 purposefully retained unequal districts. And the Supreme Court of Tennessee has refused to invalidate the law establishing these unequal districts. . . . Tennessee's law and its policy respecting apportionment are what 60 years of practice show them to be, not what appellants cull from the unenforced and, according to its own judiciary, unenforceable words of its Constitution.

A factor peculiar to this litigation emphasizes the duty of declining the exercise of federal judicial jurisdiction. In all of the apportionment cases which have come before the Court, a consideration which has been weighty in determining their non-justiciability has been the difficulty or impossibility of devising effective judicial remedies in this class of case. An injunction restraining a general election unless the legislature reapports would paralyze the critical centers of a State's political system and threaten political dislocation whose consequences are not foreseeable. A declaration devoid of implied compulsion of injunctive or other relief would be an idle threat. Surely a Federal District Court could not itself remap the State: the same complexities which impede effective judicial review of apportionment *a fortiori* make impossible a court's consideration of these imponderables as an original matter. And the choice of elections at large as opposed to elections by district, however unequal the districts, is a matter of sweeping political judgment having enormous political implications, the nature and reach of which are certainly beyond the informed understanding of, and capacity for appraisal by, courts. . . .

Although the District Court had jurisdiction in the very restricted sense of power to determine whether it could adjudicate the claim, the case is of that class of political controversy which, by the nature of its subject is unfit for federal judicial action. The judgment of the District Court, in dismissing the complaint for failure to state a claim on which relief can be granted, should therefore be affirmed.

Dissenting opinion of MR. JUSTICE HARLAN, whom MR. JUSTICE FRANKFURTER joins. . . .

It is at once essential to recognize this case for what it is. The issue here relates not to a method of state electoral apportionment by which seats in the *federal* House of Representatives are allocated, but solely to the right of a State to fix the basis of representation in its *own* legislature. Until it is first decided to what extent that right is limited by the Federal Constitution, and whether what Tennessee has done or failed to do in this instance runs afoul of any such limitation, we need not reach the issues of "justiciability" or "political question" or any of the other considerations which in such cases as *Colegrove* v. *Green* . . . led the Court to decline to adjudicate a challenge to a state apportionment affecting seats in the federal House of Representatives, in the absence of a controlling Act of Congress. . . .

The appellants' claim in this case ultimately rests entirely on the Equal Protection Clause of the Fourteenth Amendment. It is asserted that Tennessee has violated the Equal Protection Clause by maintaining in effect a system of apportionment that grossly favors in legislative representation the rural sections of the State as against its urban communities. Stripped to its essentials the complaint purports to set forth three constitutional claims of varying breadth:

(1) The Equal Protection Clause requires that each vote cast in state legislative elections be given approximately equal weight.

(2) Short of this, the existing apportionment of state legislators is so unreasonable as to amount to an arbitrary and capricious act of classification on the part of Tennessee Legislature, which is offensive to the Equal Protection Clause.

(3) In any event, the existing apportionment is rendered invalid under the Fourteenth Amendment because it flies in the face of the Tennessee Constitution. . . .

I.

I can find nothing in the Equal Protection Clause or elsewhere in the Federal Constitution which expressly or impliedly supports the view that state legislatures must be so structured as to reflect with approximate equality the voice of every voter. Not only is that proposition refuted by history . . . but it strikes deep into the heart of our federal system.

In the last analysis, what lies at the core of this controversy is a difference of opinion as to the function of representative government. It is surely beyond argument that those who have the responsibility for devising a system of representation may permissibly consider that factors other than bare numbers should be taken into account. The existence of the United States Senate is proof enough of that. . . . We must accept the present form of the Tennessee Legislature as the embodiment of the State's choice, or, more realistically, its compromise, between competing political philosophies. The federal courts have not been empowered by the Equal Protection Clause to judge whether this resolution to the State's internal political conflict is desirable or undesirable, wise or unwise. . . .

There is nothing in the Federal Constitution to prevent a State, acting not irrationally, from choosing any electoral legislative structure it thinks best suited to the interests, temper, and customs of its people. . . . A State's choice to distribute electoral strength among geographical units, rather than according to a census of population, is certainly no less a rational decision of policy than would be its choice to levy a tax on property rather than a tax on income. Both are legislative judgments entitled to equal respect from this Court.

II.

The claim that Tennessee's system of apportionment is so unreasonable as to amount to a capricious classification of voting strength stands up no better under dispassionate analysis.

The Court has said time and again that the Equal Protection Clause does not demand of state enactments either mathematical identity or rigid equality. . . . All that is prohibited is "invidious discrimination" bearing no rational relation to any permissible policy of the State. . . .

What then is the basis for the claim made in this case that the distribution of state senators and representatives is the product of capriciousness or of some constitutionally prohibited policy? It is not that Tennessee has arranged its electoral districts with a deliberate purpose to dilute the voting strength of one race, cf. *Gomillion* v. *Lightfoot* . . . or that some religious group is intentionally underrepresented. . . . Rather, the claim is that the State Legislature has unreasonably retained substantially the same allocation of senators and representatives as was established by statute in 1901, refusing to recognize the great shift in the population balance between urban and rural communities that has occurred in the meantime. . . .

A Federal District Court is asked to say that the passage of time has rendered the 1901 apportionment obsolete to the point where its continuance becomes vulnerable under the Fourteenth Amendment. But is not this matter one that involves a classic legislative judgment? Surely it lies within the province of a state legislature to conclude that an existing allocation of senators and representatives constitutes a desirable balance of geographical and demographical representation, or that in the interest of stability of government it would be best to defer for some further time the redistribution of seats in the state legislature.

Indeed, I would hardly think it unconstitutional if a state legislature's expressed reason for establishing or maintaining an electoral imbalance between its rural and urban population were to protect the State's agricultural interests from the sheer weight of numbers of those residing in its cities. . . . These are matters of local policy, on the wisdom of which the federal judiciary is neither permitted nor qualified to sit in judgment. . . .

From a reading of the majority and concurring opinions one will not find it difficult to catch the premises that underlie this decision. The fact that the appellants have been unable to obtain political redress of their asserted grievances appears to be regarded as a matter which should lead the Court to stretch to find some basis for judicial intervention. . . . The majority seems to have accepted the argument, pressed at the bar, that if this Court merely asserts authority in this field, Tennessee and other "malapportioning" States will quickly respond with appropriate political action, so that this Court need not be greatly concerned about the federal courts becoming further involved in these matters. At the same time the majority has wholly failed to reckon with what the future may hold in store if this optimistic prediction is not fulfilled. Thus, what the Court is doing reflects more an adventure in judicial experimentation than a solid piece of constitutional adjudication. . . .

Chapter 6

SOURCES OF LEGISLATIVE POWER

The Congress shall have power . . . To make all laws which shall be necessary and proper for carrying into execution the foregoing powers, and all other powers vested by this Constitution in the government of the United States, or in any department or officer thereof.

ART. I, SEC. 8, CLAUSE 18

The powers not delegated to the United States by the Constitution, nor prohibited by it to the states, are reserved to the states respectively, or to the people.

TENTH AMENDMENT

The first words in the Constitution, following the Preamble, are: "All legislative powers herein granted shall be vested in a Congress of the United States. . . ." As the legislative organ of a government of delegated powers, Congress must be able to support any exercise of legislative authority as both authorized and not forbidden by the Constitution. There are two types of authorization in Article I, section 8. The first seventeen clauses specifically enumerate a series of powers, ranging all the way from punishment of counterfeiting to the declaration of war. Then clause 18 is a general authorization, referred to in the ratification debates as "the sweeping clause."

The relationship of clause 18 to the enumerated powers preceding it quickly became the subject of controversy between Federalists and Jeffersonians, between broad and strict constructionists. The issue was joined over Hamilton's plan for a national bank, as presented to the First Congress. There was no authorization in the Constitution for Congress to create a bank; in fact, the Convention had specifically refused to grant to Congress even a restricted power to create corporations. On the invitation of President Washington, Hamilton and Jefferson submitted their respective views on whether he should sign the bill; they are classical expositions of divergent theories of constitutional interpretation.

Jefferson emphasized the "necessary" in the necessary and proper clause. Since all the enumerated powers could be carried out without a bank, it was not necessary and consequently not authorized. Hamilton, on the other hand, argued that the powers granted to Congress included the right to employ "all the *means* requisite and fairly applicable to the attainment of the *ends* of such power," unless they were specifically forbidden or immoral or contrary to the "essential ends of political society." The Hamiltonian theory of a broad and liberal interpretation of congressional power was successful in persuading Washington to sign the bank bill, and it has generally predominated in subsequent constitutional development.

77

In 1819 Marshall gave the definitive statement of this view in the great case of *McCulloch v. Maryland,* 4 Wheat. 316, where congressional authority to create a bank—the Bank of the United States, incorporated by statute in 1816—was again the issue.

Perhaps the principal doctrinal challenge of a general character which federal legislative power has had to meet since *McCulloch v. Maryland* is the contention that the powers reserved to the states under the Tenth Amendment constitute a limitation on expressly granted congressional authority. This theory, which is commonly called "dual federalism," grew out of the states' rights views of the Supreme Court under Chief Justice Taney. Its basic assumption was that the two levels of government were coequal sovereignties, each supreme in its own sphere.

The concept of dual federalism received its clearest statement in *Hammer v. Dagenhart,* 247 U.S. 251 (1918). By a five to four vote, the Court here invalidated a congressional statute restricting the transportation in interstate commerce of goods produced by child labor. For the majority, Justice Day wrote: "The grant of authority over a purely federal matter was not intended to destroy the local power always existing and carefully reserved to the States in the Tenth Amendment." He went on to say that in interpreting the Constitution it should never be forgotten that "the powers not expressly delegated to the National Government are reserved" to the states and the people by the Tenth Amendment.

To arrive at this conclusion Justice Day had to misquote the amendment; the term "expressly" does not appear in its text. He had to ignore judicial precedent; Marshall in *McCulloch v. Maryland* had held that the omission of "expressly" had left the question whether a particular power had been delegated to the national government to be answered by a "fair construction of the whole instrument." Justice Day had also to assume a position which was historically inaccurate; when the Tenth Amendment was under consideration in the First Congress the anti-Federalists had tried to insert the word "expressly," but had been voted down. In any case, the commerce power had been expressly delegated to Congress. These errors did not go unchallenged. Speaking for the four dissenters Justice Holmes said: "I should have thought that the most conspicuous decisions of this Court had made it clear that the power to regulate commerce and other constitutional powers could not be cut down or qualified by the fact that it might interfere with the carrying out of the domestic policy of any State."

Much of the struggle in the middle 1930s between the conservative members of the Supreme Court and President Roosevelt may be seen as a clash between Taney's dual federalism and the older national supremacy of Marshall. In the end it was the interpretation of Marshall and Roosevelt which prevailed. In a series of cases culminating in *United States v. Darby Lumber Co.,* 312 U.S. 100 (1941), the reconstituted Supreme Court upheld a number of federal laws which directly affected local policies. In the *Darby* opinion Justice Stone wrote that the Tenth Amendment "states but a truism that all is retained which has not been surrendered. There is nothing in the history of its adoption to suggest that it was more than declaratory of the relationship between the national and state governments as it had been established by the Constitution before the amendment." The *Darby* decision specifically overruled *Hammer v. Dagenhart.*

A view which is at the opposite extreme from dual federalism has been rejected with equal firmness by the Supreme Court. This is the theory put forward by James Wilson of Pennsylvania during the Convention period that "whenever an object occurs, to the direction of which no particular state is competent, the management of it must, of necessity, belong to the United States in Congress assembled." This contention of sovereign and inherent power in Congress was repeated by counsel in the case of *Kansas* v. *Colorado*, 206 U.S. 46 (1907). The steps in the argument were that complete legislative power must be vested either in state or in national government; that the states are limited to internal affairs; and that "consequently all powers which are national in their scope must be found vested in Congress." The Court rejected this position as in violation of the Tenth Amendment, and held that powers of a national character not delegated to Congress were "reserved to the people of the United States."

In constitutional theory, then, Congress does not derive its authority from any doctrine of sovereign and inherent power. Delegation by the Constitution is the source of federal legislative authority, but a broad doctrine of implied power, based on the necessary and proper clause, has been a supplemental source of great significance in equipping Congress with authority commensurate with its responsibilities.

McCULLOCH v. MARYLAND
4 Wheat. 316, 4 L. Ed. 579 (1819)

The First Bank of the United States was chartered by Congress in 1791 to carry out Hamilton's financial policies. The power of Congress to create the bank was not tested in the courts, and the charter expired in 1811. The Second Bank of the United States was chartered in 1816. It was highly unpopular, and many states sought to restrict its operations or levied heavy taxes upon it. Maryland forbade banks not chartered by the state to issue bank notes except upon special stamped paper which was heavily taxed, or alternatively required payment of an annual tax of $15,000. McCulloch, cashier of the Baltimore branch of the bank, issued notes without complying with the law or paying the tax.

Mr. Chief Justice MARSHALL delivered the opinion of the Court.

In the case now to be determined, the defendant, a sovereign State, denies the obligation of a law enacted by the legislature of the Union, and the plaintiff, on his part, contests the validity of an act which has been passed by the legislature of that State. The constitution of our country, in its most interesting and vital parts, is to be considered; the conflicting powers of the government of the Union and of its members, as marked in that constitution, are to be discussed; and an opinion given, which may essentially influence the great operations of the government. No tribunal can approach such a question without a deep sense of its importance, and of the awful responsibility involved in its decision. But it must be decided peacefully, or remain a source of hostile legislation, perhaps of hostility of a still more serious nature; and if it is to be so decided, by this tribunal alone can the decision be made. On the Supreme Court of the United States has the constitution of our country devolved this important duty.

The first question made in the cause is, has Congress power to incorporate a bank?

It has been truly said, that this can scarcely be considered as an open question, entirely unprejudiced by the former proceedings of the nation respecting it. The principle now contested was introduced at a very early period of our history, has been recognized by many successive legislatures, and has been acted upon by the judicial department, in cases of peculiar delicacy, as a law of undoubted obligation. . . .

The power now contested was exercised by the first Congress elected under the present constitution. The bill for incorporating the bank of the United States did not steal upon an unsuspecting legislature, and pass unobserved. Its principle was completely understood, and was opposed with equal zeal and ability. After being resisted, first in the fair and open field of debate, and afterwards in the executive cabinet, with as much persevering talent as any measure has ever experienced, and being supported by arguments which convinced minds as pure and as intelligent as this country can boast, it became a law. The original act was permitted to expire; but a short experience of the embarrassments to which the refusal to revive it exposed the government, convinced those who were most prejudiced against the measure of its necessity, and induced the passage of the present law. It would require no ordinary share of intrepidity to assert that a measure adopted under these circumstances was a bold and plain usurpation, to which the constitution gave no countenance.

These observations belong to the cause; but they are not made under the impression that, were the question entirely new, the law would be found irreconcilable with the constitution.

In discussing this question, the counsel for the State of Maryland have deemed it of some importance, in the construction of the constitution, to consider that instrument not as emanating from the people, but as the act of sovereign and independent States. The powers of the general government, it has been said, are delegated by the States, who alone are truly sovereign; and must be exercised in subordination to the States, who alone possess supreme dominion.

It would be difficult to sustain this proposition. The Convention which framed the constitution was indeed elected by the State legislatures. But the instrument, when it came from their hands, was a mere proposal, without obligation, or pretentions to it. It was reported to the then existing Congress of the United States, with a request that it might "be submitted to a Convention of Delegates, chosen in each State by the people thereof, under the recommendation of its Legislature, for their assent and ratification." This mode of proceeding was adopted; and by the Convention, by Congress, and by the State Legislatures, the instrument was submitted to the people. They acted upon it in the only manner in which they can act safely, effectively, and wisely, on such a subject, by assembling in Convention. It is true, they assembled in their several States—and where else should they have assembled? No political dreamer was ever wild enough to think of breaking down the lines which separate the States, and of compounding the American people into one common mass. Of consequence, when they act, they act in their States. But the measures they adopt do not, on that account, cease to be the measures of the people themselves, or become the measures of the State governments.

From these Conventions the constitution derives its whole authority. The government proceeds directly from the people; is "ordained and established" in the name of the people; and is declared to be ordained, "in order to form a more perfect union, establish justice, ensure domestic tranquillity, and secure the blessings of liberty to themselves and to their posterity." The assent of the States, in their sovereign capacity, is implied in calling a Convention, and thus submitting that instrument to the people. But the people were at perfect liberty to accept or reject it; and their act was final. It required not the affirmance, and could not be negatived, by the State governments. The constitution, when thus adopted, was of complete obligation, and bound the State sovereignties. . . .

The government of the Union, then, (whatever may be the influence of this fact on the case,) is, emphatically, and truly, a government of the people. In form and in substance it emanates from them. Its powers are granted by them, and are to be exercised directly on them, and for their benefit.

This government is acknowledged by all to be one of enumerated powers. The principle, that it can exercise only the powers granted to it, would seem too apparent to have required to be enforced by all those arguments which its enlightened friends, while it was depending before the people, found it necessary to urge. That principle is now universally admitted. But the question respecting the extent of the powers actually granted, is perpetually arising, and will probably continue to arise, as long as our system shall exist.

In discussing these questions, the conflicting powers of the general and State governments must be brought into view, and the supremacy of their respective laws, when they are in opposition, must be settled.

If any one proposition could command the universal assent of mankind, we might expect it would be this—that the government of the Union, though limited in its powers, is supreme within its sphere of action. This would seem to result necessarily from its nature. It is the government of all; its powers are delegated by all; it represents all, and acts for all. Though any one State may be willing to control its operations, no State is willing to allow others to control them. The nation, on those subjects on which it can act, must necessarily bind its component parts. But this question is not left to mere reason: the people have, in express terms, decided it, by saying, "this constitution, and the laws of the United States, which shall be made in pursuance thereof," "shall be the supreme law of the land," and by requiring that the members of the State legislatures, and the officers of the executive and judicial departments of the States, shall take the oath of fidelity to it.

The government of the United States, then, though limited in its powers, is supreme; and its laws, when made in pursuance of the constitution, form the supreme law of the land, "any thing in the constitution or laws of any State to the contrary notwithstanding."

Among the enumerated powers, we do not find that of establishing a bank or creating a corporation. But there is no phrase in the instrument which, like the articles of confederation, excludes incidental or implied powers; and which requires that everything granted shall be expressly and minutely described. Even the 10th amendment, which was framed for the purpose of quieting the excessive jealousies which had been excited, omits the word "expressly," and declares only that the powers "not delegated to the United States, nor prohibited to the States, are reserved to the States or to the people"; thus leaving the question, whether the particular power which may become the subject of contest has been delegated to the one government, or prohibited to the other, to depend on a fair construction of the whole instrument. The men who drew and adopted this amendment had experienced the embarrassments resulting from the insertion of this word in the articles of confederation, and probably omitted it to avoid those embarrassments. A constitution, to contain an accurate detail of all the subdivisions of which its great powers will admit, and of all the means by which they may be carried into execution, would partake of the prolixity of a legal code, and could scarcely be embraced by the human mind. It would probably never be understood by the public. Its nature, therefore, requires, that only its great outlines should be marked, its important objects designated, and the minor ingredients which compose those objects be deduced from the nature of the objects themselves. That this idea was entertained by the framers of the American constitution, is not only to be inferred from the nature of the instrument, but from the language. Why else were some of the limitations, found in the ninth section of the 1st article, introduced? It is also, in some degree, warranted by their having omitted to use any restrictive term which might prevent its receiving a fair and just interpretation. In considering this question, then, we must never forget, that it is *a constitution* we are expounding.

Although, among the enumerated powers of government, we do not find the word "bank" or "incorporation," we find the great powers to lay and collect taxes; to borrow money; to regulate commerce; to declare and conduct a war; and to raise and support armies and navies. The sword and the purse, all the external relations, and no inconsiderable portion of the industry of the nation, are entrusted to its government. It can never be pretended that these vast powers draw after them others of inferior importance, merely because they are inferior. Such an idea can never be advanced. But it may with great reason be contended, that a government, entrusted with such ample powers, on the due execution of which the happiness and prosperity of the nation so vitally depends, must also be entrusted with ample means for their execution. The power being given, it is the interest of the nation to facilitate its execution. It can never be their interest, and cannot be presumed to have been their intention, to clog and embarrass its execution by withholding the most appropriate means. Throughout this vast republic, from the St. Croix to the Gulph of Mexico, from the Atlantic to the Pacific, revenue is to be collected and expended, armies are to be marched and supported. The exigencies of the nation may require that the treasure raised in the north should be transported to the south, *that* raised in the east conveyed to the west, or that this order should be reversed. Is that construction of the constitution to be preferred which would render these operations difficult, hazardous, and expensive? Can we adopt that construction, (unless the words imperiously require it,) which would impute to the framers of that instrument, when granting these powers for the public good, the intention of impeding their exercise by withholding a choice of means? If, indeed, such be the mandate of the constitution, we have only to obey; but that instrument does not profess to enumerate the means by which the powers it confers may be executed; nor does it prohibit the creation of a corporation, if the existence of such a being be essential to the beneficial exercise of those powers. It is, then, the subject of fair inquiry, how far such means may be employed.

It is not denied, that the powers given to the government imply the ordinary means of execution. That, for example, of raising revenue, and applying it to national purposes, is admitted to imply the power of conveying money from place to place, as the exigencies of the nation may require, and of employing the usual means of conveyance. But it is denied that the government has its choice of means; or, that it may employ the most convenient means, if, to employ them, it be necessary to erect a corporation. . . .

. . . The power of creating a corporation, though appertaining to sovereignty, is not, like the power of making war, or levying taxes, or of regulating commerce, a great substantive and independent power, which cannot be implied as incidental to other powers, or used as a means of executing them. It is never the end for which other powers are exercised, but a means by which other objects are accomplished. No contributions are made to charity for the sake of an incorporation, but a corporation is created to administer the charity; no seminary of learning is instituted in order to be incorporated, but the corporate character is conferred to subserve the purposes of education. No city was ever built with the sole object of being incorporated, but is incorporated as affording the best means of being well governed. The power of creating a corporation is never used for its own sake, but for the purpose of effecting something else. No sufficient reason is, therefore, perceived, why it may not pass as incidental to those powers which are expressly given, if it be a direct mode of executing them.

But the constitution of the United States has not left the right of Congress to employ the necessary means, for the execution of the powers conferred on the government, to general reasoning. To its enumeration of powers is added that of making "all laws which shall be necessary and proper, for carrying into execution the foregoing powers, and all other powers vested by this constitution, in the government of the United States, or in any department thereof."

The counsel for the State of Maryland have urged various arguments, to prove that this clause, though in terms a grant of power, is not so in effect; but is really restrictive of the general right, which might otherwise be implied, of selecting means for executing the enumerated powers.

In support of this proposition, they have found it necessary to contend, that this clause was inserted for the purpose of conferring on Congress the power of making laws. That, without it, doubts might be entertained, whether Congress could exercise its powers in the form of legislation.

But could this be the object for which it was inserted? . . . That a legislature, endowed with legislative powers, can legislate, is a proposition too self-evident to have been questioned.

But the argument on which most reliance is placed, is drawn from the peculiar language of this clause. Congress is not empowered by it to make all laws, which may have relation to the powers conferred on the government, but such only as may be *"necessary and proper,"* for carrying them into execution. The word *"necessary,"* is considered as controlling the whole sentence, and as limiting the right to pass laws for the execution of the granted powers, to such as are indispensable, and without which the power would be nugatory. That it excludes the choice of means, and leaves to Congress, in each case, that only which is most direct and simple.

Is it true, that this is the sense in which the word "necessary" is always used? Does it always import an absolute physical necessity, so strong, that one thing, to which another may be termed necessary, cannot exist without that other? We think it does not. If reference be had to its use, in the common affairs of the world, or in approved authors, we find that it frequently imports no more than that one thing is convenient, or useful, or essential to another. To employ the means necessary to an end, is generally understood as employing any means calculated to produce the end, and not as being confined to those single means, without which the end would be entirely unattainable. Such is the character of human language, that no word conveys to the mind, in all situations, one single definite idea; and nothing is more common than to use words in a figurative sense. Almost all compositions contain words, which, taken in their rigorous sense, would convey a meaning different from that which is obviously intended. It is essential to just construction, that many words which import something excessive, should be understood in a more mitigated sense—in that sense which common usage justifies. The word "necessary" is of this description. It has not a fixed character peculiar to itself. It admits of all degrees of comparison; and is often connected with other words, which increase or diminish the impression the mind receives of the urgency it imports. A thing may be necessary, very necessary, absolutely or indispensably necessary. To no mind would the same idea be conveyed, by these several phrases. . . . This word, then, like others, is used in various senses; and, in its construction, the subject, the context, the intention of the person using them, are all to be taken into view.

Let this be done in the case under consideration. The subject is the execution of those great powers on which the welfare of a nation essentially depends. It must have been the intention of those who gave these powers, to insure, as far as human prudence could insure, their beneficial execution. This could not be done by confiding the choice of means to such narrow limits as not to leave it in the power of Congress to adopt any which might be appropriate, and which were conducive to the end. This provision is made in a constitution intended to endure for ages to come, and, consequently, to be adapted to the various *crises* of human affairs. To have prescribed the means by which government should, in all future time, execute its powers, would have been to change, entirely, the character of the instrument, and give it the properties of a legal code. It would have been an unwise attempt to provide, by immutable rules, for exigencies which, if foreseen at all, must have been seen dimly, and which can be best provided for as they occur. To have declared that the best means shall not be used, but those alone without which the power given would be nugatory, would have been to deprive the legislature of the capacity to avail itself of experience, to exercise its reason, and to accommodate its legislation to circumstances. If we apply this principle of construction to any of the powers of the government, we shall find it so pernicious in its operation that we shall be compelled to discard it. . . .

Take, for example, the power "to establish post offices and post roads." This power is executed by the single act of making the establishment. But, from this has been inferred the power and duty of carrying the mail along the post road, from one post office to another. And, from this implied power, has again been inferred the right to punish those who steal letters from the post office, or rob the mail. It may be said, with some plausibility, that the right to carry the mail, and to punish those who rob it, is not indispensably necessary to the establishment of a post office and post road. This right is indeed essential to the beneficial exercise of the power, but not indispensably necessary to its existence. . . .

But the argument which most conclusively demonstrates the error of the construction contended for by the counsel for the State of Maryland, is founded on the intention of the Convention, as manifested in the whole clause. To waste time and argument in proving that, without it, Congress might carry its powers into execution, would be not much less idle than to hold a lighted taper to the sun. As little can it be required to prove, that in the absence of this clause, Congress would have some choice of means. That it might employ those which, in its judgment, would most advantageously effect the object to be accomplished. That any means adapted to the end, any means which tended directly to the execution of the constitutional powers of the government, were in themselves constitutional. This clause, as construed by the State of Maryland, would abridge, and almost annihilate this useful and necessary right of the legislature to select its means. That this could not be intended, is, we should think, had it not been already controverted, too apparent for controversy. We think so for the following reasons:

1st. The clause is placed among the powers of Congress, not among the limitations on those powers.

2nd. Its terms purport to enlarge, not to diminish the powers vested in the government. It purports to be an additional power, not a restriction on those already granted. No reason has been, or can be assigned for thus concealing an intention to narrow the discretion of the national legislature under words which purport to enlarge it. The framers of the constitution wished its adoption, and well knew that it would be endangered by its strength, not by its weakness. Had they been capable of using language which would convey to the eye one idea, and, after deep reflection, impress on the mind another, they would rather have disguised the grant of power, than its limitation. If, then, their intention had been, by this clause, to restrain the free use of means which might otherwise have been implied, that intention would have been inserted in another place, and would have been expressed in terms resembling these. "In carrying into execution the foregoing powers, and all others," &c. "no laws shall be passed but such as are necessary and proper." Had the intention been to make this clause restrictive, it would unquestionably have been so in form as well as in effect.

The result of the most careful and attentive consideration bestowed upon this clause is, that if it does not enlarge, it cannot be construed to restrain the powers of

Congress, or to impair the right of the legislature to exercise its best judgment in the selection of measures to carry into execution the constitutional powers of the government. If no other motive for its insertion can be suggested, a sufficient one is found in the desire to remove all doubts respecting the right to legislate on that vast mass of incidental powers which must be involved in the constitution, if that instrument be not a splendid bauble.

We admit, as all must admit, that the powers of the government are limited, and that its limits are not to be transcended. But we think the sound construction of the constitution must allow to the national legislature that discretion, with respect to the means by which the powers it confers are to be carried into execution, which will enable that body to perform the high duties assigned to it, in the manner most beneficial to the people. Let the end be legitimate, let it be within the scope of the constitution, and all means which are appropriate, which are plainly adapted to that end, which are not prohibited, but consist with the letter and spirit of the constitution, are constitutional. . . .

After the most deliberate consideration, it is the unanimous and decided opinion of this Court, that the act to incorporate the Bank of the United States is a law made in pursuance of the constitution, and is a part of the supreme law of the land. . . .

Chapter 7

DELEGATION OF LEGISLATIVE POWER

All legislative powers herein granted shall be vested in a Congress of the
United States. . . .   ART. I, SEC. 1

The principle has been generally recognized that, though Congress cannot
shift its essential legislative responsibility, it may within limits ask other branches
of the government to exercise powers which it might have exercised itself. The
reasons why Congress must indulge in extensive delegation of legislative power
are well known. The legislative machinery is ponderous. Congressmen may succeed well enough in the task of formulating general policies, but they generally
lack the time and expert information needed to prescribe the specific methods for
carrying out those policies. Moreover, a piece of legislation once enacted is
extremely hard to amend, whereas the problems with which the legislation aims
to deal may be constantly changing. These legislative limitations have become
increasingly obvious with the expansion of governmental intervention into the
management of the economy, and in emergency or wartime periods the pressure
on Congress to authorize broad delegations of its powers to the executive is especially great.

In consequence of such legislative grants, an enormous volume of administrative rules and regulations has been issued. Much of this quasi-legislative output
simply governs the form and procedure of government action, but a large proportion is actually elaboration, definition, or amplification of the substantive provisions of federal statutes. Of course, delegation is not always to the executive
branch; for example, an act of 1934 delegated to the Supreme Court the power to
prescribe rules of civil procedure for the federal courts.

Chief Justice Marshall was the first to rationalize a legislative delegation. In
Wayman v. *Southard,* 10 Wheat. 1 (1825), he distinguished "important subjects,
which must be entirely regulated by the legislature itself, from those of less
interest, in which a general provision may be made, and power given to those who
are to act under such general provisions to fill up the details." This suggestion
that delegation may be employed only in dealing with less important subjects has
proved completely untenable. On the other hand, the legal fiction that delegation
is merely a "filling up the details" of a statute has been a perennially useful one.

Thus in *United States* v. *Grimaud,* 220 U.S. 506 (1911), the Court was confronted with a statute authorizing the Secretary of Agriculture to make rules and
regulations with respect to grazing on national forest reservations, which it upheld
on the ground that it was impracticable for Congress itself to adopt such regulations, covering as they did "local conditions." In empowering the Secretary of

86

Agriculture to act, "Congress was merely conferring administrative functions upon an agent, and not delegating to him legislative power." The fact that the statute provided penalties for violation of the grazing rules did not elevate the regulations "from an administrative to a legislative character."

Marshall's conception of "filling up the details" of course demands that there be an announced general legislative plan into which the details fit. Consequently the Court has consistently demanded that Congress supply standards to guide. and control the acts of delegatees. But the Court has normally been willing to accept rather broad and general standards as meeting constitutional requirements —such as the standard that the Interstate Commerce Commission shall fix rates that are just and reasonable, or the standard that the Federal Communications Commission shall grant licenses to radio stations when it is in the public convenience, interest, or necessity to do so.

Attention should be given to a special type of delegation, that made in so-called "contingent legislation." Here the delegation is not of power to make rules or fill in details; it is delegation of authority to determine facts which are to have the effect of suspending legislation, or alternatively, of bringing it into effect. For example, in 1809 Congress passed an act which prohibited the importation of goods from certain foreign countries but permitted the prohibition to lapse in case the President ascertained and proclaimed that those countries were no longer molesting the sea-borne commerce of the United States. The McKinley Tariff of 1890 illustrates the alternative type of contingent legislation. It authorized the admission of certain articles free of duty, but added that if a foreign country producing any of these commodities should impose upon American products duties found by the President to be "reciprocally unequal and unreasonable," then the President would have power to suspend the duty-free status of the foreign commodities, and duties set out in the act would become payable.

The Supreme Court in a series of cases has ruled that contingent delegation of legislative power, like the delegation of power to fill in details, does not violate constitutional standards. The 1809 Embargo Act was cleared of this charge in the case of *The Brig Aurora,* 7 Cranch 383 (1813). Upholding the flexible tariff arrangements of the McKinley Tariff, the Court in *Field v. Clark,* 143 U.S. 649 (1892), denied that the President had been endowed with any real legislative power. The only legislative action taken was "when Congress declared that the suspension should take effect upon a named contingency." The President's role was not that of legislator, but "mere agent of the law-making department to ascertain and declare the event upon which its expressed will was to take effect."

After well over a century of judicial failure to find any merit in allegations of unconstitutional delegation, there was a widespread feeling that this area was one of the dead letters of American constitutional law. Consequently there was considerable amazement when the Court ruled in *Panama Refining Co. v. Ryan,* 293 U.S. 388 (1935), that in giving the President authority to exclude from interstate commerce oil produced in excess of state regulations, Congress had not met constitutional tests by supplying an adequate standard to guide or control the President in the use of this power.

Justice Cardozo dissented from this holding, but four months later when *Schechter Poultry Corp. v. United States,* 295 U.S. 495 (1935), was decided, even he was convinced that the National Industrial Recovery Act, in giving the President authority to promulgate industrial codes of fair competition, had gone too far and delegated lawmaking power which was "unconfined and vagrant . . . not canalized within banks to keep it from overflowing." The following year, in Carter v. Carter Coal Co., 298 U.S. 238 (1936), the Guffey Coal Act was invalidated, partly because it was held to delegate legislative power to set up a code of mandatory regulations for the coal industry. This time the delegation was doubly condemned since it was not even to government officials, but to representatives of the coal industry.

These three decisions were handed down in the heat of the Supreme Court's battle with the New Deal. After the smoke of that controversy cleared away, there was no further serious difficulty with delegation charges. In 1939 the Federal Tobacco Inspection Act (Currin v. Wallace, 306 U.S. 1) and the Agricultural Marketing Agreement Act (United States v. Rock Royal Cooperative, 307 U.S. 533, and Hood & Sons v. United States, 307 U.S. 588) were upheld, though Justice Roberts in the latter case charged that the standards set up to govern the Secretary of Agriculture were "so vague as in effect to invest him with uncontrolled power of legislation." The Fair Labor Standards Act was similarly cleared in Opp Cotton Mills v. Administrator of Wage and Hours Division, 312 U.S. 126 (1941).

World War II brought even greater pressure for legislative delegation. In Yakus v. United States, 321 U.S. 414 (1944), legislative authority given the Office of Price Administration to fix maximum prices under the Emergency Price Control Act of 1942 was upheld, and in Bowles v. Willingham, 321 U.S. 503 (1944), a similar function was performed for rent controls. In both decisions the Court majority took a firmly practical tone, based on their conclusion that controls were a wartime necessity. As Chief Justice Stone said in the Yakus case: "The Constitution as a continually operative charter of government does not demand the impossible or the impracticable." Later the act for renegotiation of wartime profits was acquitted of the charge of unconstitutional delegation in Lichter v. United States, 334 U.S. 742 (1948). That the Court's attitude on subsequent peacetime delegation issues continued to be extremely permissive was demonstrated in United States v. Sharpnack, 355 U.S. 286 (1958), which was unusual in that it involved a charge of unconstitutional legislative delegation to a state.

UNITED STATES v. SHARPNACK
355 U.S. 286, 78 S. Ct. 291, 2 L. Ed. 2d 282 (1958)

Sharpnack was charged in federal court with sex crimes committed at Randolph Air Force Base, a federal enclave in Texas. In the Federal Assimilative Crimes Act of 1948 Congress had provided that within federal enclaves acts not punishable by any enactment of Congress were punishable by the then effective laws of the state in which the enclave was situated. The state law invoked here had not been adopted by the Texas Legislature until 1950. The federal district court dismissed the indictment, holding that Congress was unconstitutionally delegating its legislative power to the states by passing a law which made future state criminal statutes applicable to federal enclaves.

Mr. Justice Burton delivered the opinion of the Court.

The issue in this case is whether the Assimilative Crimes Act of 1948, 18 U.S.C. § 13, is constitutional insofar as it makes applicable to a federal enclave a subsequently enacted criminal law of the State in which the enclave is situated. For the reasons hereafter stated, we hold that it is constitutional. . . .

The 1948 Assimilative Crimes Act was enacted as part of the Revised Criminal Code of the United States and reads as follows:

"§ 13. Laws of States adopted for areas within Federal jurisdiction.

"Whoever within or upon any of the places now existing or hereafter reserved or acquired as provided in section 7 of this title, is guilty of any act or omission which, although not made punishable by any enactment of Congress, would be punishable if committed or omitted within the jurisdiction of the State, Territory, Possession, or District in which such place is situated, by the laws thereof in force at the time of such act or omission, shall be guilty of a like offense and subject to a like punishment." 18 U.S.C.

In the absence of restriction in the cessions of the respective enclaves to the United States, the power of Congress to exercise legislative jurisdiction over them is clearly stated in Article I, § 8, cl. 17, and Article IV, § 3, cl. 2, of the Constitution. . . . The first Federal Crimes Act, enacted in 1790, 1 Stat. 112, defined a number of federal crimes and referred to federal enclaves. The need for dealing more extensively with criminal offenses in the enclaves was evident, and one natural solution was to adopt for each enclave the offenses made punishable by the State in which it was situated. . . . Initially there was room for a difference of opinion as to the desirability of doing this by blanket legislation, rather than by a code enumerating and defining specific offenses applicable to the enclaves. Congress made its initial decision on this point in 1825 by adopting for otherwise undefined offenses the policy of general conformity to local law. On repeated occasions thereafter Congress has confirmed that policy by enacting an unbroken series of Assimilative Crimes Acts. During the same period, Congress has recognized a slowly increasing number of federal crimes in the field of major offenses by enacting for the enclaves specific criminal statutes which have defined those crimes and, to that extent, have excluded the state laws from that field.

In the Act of 1825, sponsored by Daniel Webster in the House of Representatives, Congress expressly adopted the fundamental policy of conformity to local law. That Act provided the basis from which has grown the Assimilative Crimes Act now before us. Congress thereby made it clear that, with the exception of the enlarged list of offenses specifically proscribed by it, the federal offenses in each enclave were to be identical with those proscribed by the State in which the enclave was situated. That Act made no specific reference to subsequent repeals or amendments by the State of any assimilated laws. It also made no specific reference to new offenses that might be added by the State after the enactment of the Assimilated Crimes Act. . . .

Due to the limitation of the Assimilative Crimes Act of 1825 to state laws in force at the time of its own enactment, the Act gradually lost much of its effectiveness in maintaining current conformity with state criminal laws. This result has been well called one of static conformity. To renew such conformity, Congress has enacted comparable Assimilative Crimes Acts in 1866, 14 Stat. 13; in 1874 as R.S. § 5391; in 1898, 30 Stat. 717; in 1909 as § 289 of the Criminal Code, 35 Stat. 1145; in 1933, 48 Stat. 152; in 1935, 49 Stat. 394; in 1940, 54 Stat. 234; and finally in 1948 in the Revised Criminal Code as 18 U.S.C. § 13.

The above series of substantial re-enactments demonstrates a consistent congressional purpose to apply the principle of conformity to state criminal laws in punishing most minor offenses committed within federal enclaves. In the re-enactments of 1866, 1874, 1898 and 1909, [Congress] expressly limit[ed] the assimilation to the state laws "now in force," or as the "laws of the State . . . now provide. . . ." In the Acts of 1933, 1935 and 1940, Congress continued to prescribe assimilation to the state laws "in force" on specified recent dates, and these three re-enactments also made the assimilation conditional upon the state laws "remaining in force at the time of the doing or omitting the doing of the prohibited act or thing. . . ." This helped to keep the federal law current with the state law by reflecting future deletions from the state laws as soon as made.

In 1948, coincidentally with its revision of the Criminal Code of the United States, Congress finally adopted the present language. This expressly limits the assimilation to acts or omissions committed within a federal enclave and "not made punishable by any enactment of Congress. . . ." It further specifies that "Whoever . . . is guilty of any act or omission which . . . would be punishable if committed or omitted within the jurisdiction of the State . . . in which such place is situated, *by the laws thereof in force at the time of such act or omission,* shall be guilty of a like [federal] offense and subject to a like punishment." (Emphasis supplied.) This assimilation applies whether the state laws are enacted before or after the Federal Assimilative Crimes Act and at once reflects every addition, repeal or amendment of a state law. Recognizing its underlying policy of 123 years' standing, Congress has thus at last provided that within each federal enclave, to the extent that offenses are not pre-empted by congressional enactments, there shall be complete current conformity with the criminal laws of the respective States in which the enclaves are situated.

There is no doubt that Congress may validly adopt a criminal code for each federal enclave. It certainly may do so by drafting new laws or by copying laws defining the criminal offenses in force throughout the State in which the enclave is situated. As a practical matter, it has to proceed largely on a wholesale basis. Its reason for adopting local laws is not so much because Congress has examined them individually as it is because the laws are already in force throughout the State in which the enclave is situated. The basic legislative decision made by Congress is its decision to conform the laws in the enclaves to the local laws as to all offenses not punishable by any enactment of Congress. Whether Congress sets forth the assimilated laws in full or assimilates them by reference, the result is as definite and as ascertainable as are the state laws themselves.

Having the power to assimilate the state laws, Congress obviously has like power to renew such assimilation annually or daily in order to keep the laws in the enclaves current with those in the States. That being so, we conclude that Congress is within its constitutional powers and legislative discretion when, after 123 years of experience with the policy of conformity, it enacts that policy in its most complete and accurate form. Rather than being a delegation by Congress of its legislative authority to the States, it is a deliberate continuing adoption by Congress for federal enclaves of such unpre-empted offenses and punishments as shall have been already put in effect by the respective States for their own government. Congress retains power to exclude a particular state law from the assimilative effect of the Act. This procedure is a practical accommodation of the mechanics of the legislative functions of State and Nation in the field of police power where it is especially appropriate to make the federal regulation of local conduct conform to that already established by the State. . . .

The application of the Assimilative Crimes Act to subsequently adopted state legislation, under the limitations here prescribed, is a reasonable exercise of congressional legislative power and discretion. Accordingly, the judgment of the District

Court is reversed and the case is remanded to it for further action consistent with this opinion.

Reversed and remanded.

Mr. Justice Douglas, with whom Mr. Justice Black concurs, dissenting.

There are two provisions of the Constitution involved in the present controversy. Article I, § 1 provides: "All legislative Powers herein granted shall be vested in a Congress of the United States, which shall consist of a Senate and House of Representatives." A supplementary provision is that contained in Art. IV, § 3: "The Congress shall have Power to dispose of and make all needful Rules and Regulations respecting the Territory or other Property belonging to the United States. . . ."

It is, therefore, the Congress, and the Congress alone, that has the power to make rules governing federal enclaves. I suppose there would be no doubt, at least after *Youngstown Sheet & Tube Co.* v. *Sawyer*, 343 U.S. 579, that this rule-making power could not be done by the President, let alone some federal agency such as the Department of the Interior. The power to make laws under which men are punished for crimes calls for as serious a deliberation as the fashioning of rules for the seizure of the industrial plants involved in the *Youngstown* case. Both call for the exercise of legislative judgment; and I do not see how that requirement can be satisfied by delegating the authority to the President, the Department of the Interior, or, as in this case, to the States. The Court held in *Schechter Poultry Corp.* v. *United States*, 295 U.S. 495, that the determination of what constitutes "fair competition" may not be left with the industry affected, subject to approval by the President. For the codes promulgated would have the standing of federal statutes. "But Congress cannot delegate legislative power to the President to exercise an unfettered discretion to make whatever laws he thinks may be needed or advisable for the rehabilitation and expansion of trade or industry." . . . The code-making authority was held to be an unconstitutional delegation of legislative power. . . . "The Congress is not permitted to abdicate or to transfer to others the essential legislative functions with which it is . . . vested." . . .

The vice in the *Schechter* case was not that the President was the one who received the delegated authority, but that the Congress had abdicated the lawmaking function. The result should be the same whether the lawmaking authority, constituted by Congress, is the President or a State.

Of course Congress can adopt as federal laws the laws of a State; and it has often done so. Even when it does so without any enumeration of the laws it "has acted as definitely as if it had repeated the words" used by the State, as Mr. Justice Holmes said in *Knickerbocker Ice Co.* v. *Stewart*, 253 U.S. 149, 167. Also Congress could, I think, adopt as federal law, governing an enclave, the state law governing speeding as it may from time to time be enacted. The Congress there determines what the basic policy is. Leaving the details to be filled in by a State is analogous to the scheme of delegated implementation of congressionally adopted policies with which we are familiar in the field of administrative law. But it is Congress that must determine the policy, for that is the essence of lawmaking. Under the scheme now approved a State makes such federal law, applicable to the enclave, as it likes, and that law becomes federal law, for the violation of which the citizen is sent to prison.

Here it is a sex crime on which Congress has never legislated. Tomorrow it may be a Blue Law, a law governing usury, or even a law requiring segregation of the races on buses and in restaurants. It may be a law that could never command a majority in the Congress or that in no sense reflected its will. It is no answer to say that the citizen would have a defense under the Fifth and Sixth Amendments to unconstitutional applications of these federal laws or the procedures under them. He is entitled to the considered judgment of Congress whether the law applied to him fits the federal policy. That is what federal lawmaking is. It is that policy which has led the Court heretofore to limit these Assimilative Crimes Acts to those state laws in force at the time of enactment of the Federal Act. . . .

There is some convenience in doing what the Court allows today. Congress is saved the bother of enacting new Assimilative Crimes Acts from time to time. Federal laws grow like mushrooms without Congress passing a bill. But convenience is not material to the constitutional problem. With all due deference to those who are convinced the other way, I am forced to conclude that under this Assimilative Crimes Act it is a State not the Congress that is exercising the legislative power under Art. I, § 1 of the Constitution and that is making the "needful Rules and Regulations" envisioned by Art. IV, § 3. That may not constitutionally be done.

Chapter 8

THE INVESTIGATORY POWER

The power of Congress to investigate is an implied power, supplementary to its specifically assigned functions to legislate, to appropriate, to pass on the elections and returns of members, and so on. The Supreme Court took a rather narrow view of the extent of investigatory powers when the issue was first raised. *Kilbourn* v. *Thompson*, 103 U.S. 168 (1881), held invalid a House investigation into a bankrupt firm, of which the United States government was one of the creditors. The Court pointed out that the matter was not one on which Congress could validly legislate. Moreover, the controversy was then pending in the courts, so that Congress was precluded from intervening by the principle of separation of powers.

Following the *Kilbourn* case the judicial attitude toward congressional investigatory power gradually became more favorable. The case of *In re Chapman*, 166 U.S. 661 (1897), arose out of a Senate investigation of charges that senators were yielding to corrupt influences in considering a tariff bill, and Chapman got involved by refusing to answer questions pertinent to the inquiry. The Court, taking note of the constitutional authority of both houses to punish or expel members, held that the inquiry related to the integrity and fidelity of senators in the discharge of their duties, and so was "within the range of constitutional powers of the Senate."

These two nineteenth-century precedents were the principal guides for the Court when in 1927 it came to decide *McGrain* v. *Daugherty*, 273 U.S. 135. This important case arose out of the Senate inquiry into Harry M. Daugherty's conduct of the Department of Justice under President Harding. The Senate resolution specifically directed a select committee to look into Daugherty's failure to prosecute the key figures of the Teapot Dome scandal as well as violators of the antitrust acts and other federal statutes. In the course of its work the committee had occasion to subpoena Mally S. Daugherty, brother of the Attorney General. He failed to honor the subpoena and the Senate ordered his arrest and appearance before the bar of the Senate. Daugherty then secured a writ of habeas corpus from a federal district judge, who ruled that the Senate was exceeding its proper legislative powers in making this investigation, and was really conducting a trial of the Attorney General.

The Supreme Court, however, concluded that the committee was investigating the administration of the Justice Department, which was a subject "on which legislation could be had and would be materially aided by the information which the investigation was calculated to elicit." The Court agreed that Congress had no "general" power to inquire into private affairs and compel disclosures, and that a witness "rightfully" might refuse to answer where the bounds of congressional power were exceeded or "the questions are not pertinent to the matter under inquiry."

The instrument through which Congress brings pressure on witnesses before its committees is the power to punish refusal to testify as contempt of Congress. In *Anderson* v. *Dunn,* 6 Wheat. 204 (1821), the Supreme Court upheld use of the contempt power as essential to the effective exertion of the expressly granted powers of Congress. While Congress can itself try persons for contempt of its authority and imprison those found guilty, it has preferred to act through the courts. By an 1857 statute Congress provided that persons refusing to appear before a legislative committee or to answer questions pertinent to an inquiry should be deemed guilty of a misdemeanor and be subject to indictment and judicial punishment. Under this act there is full opportunity for reviewing courts to determine whether the legislative conclusion that contempt had been committed was justified.

The more recent problems concerning congressional investigatory powers have been raised by the Communist-hunting activities of the House Committee on Un-American Activities, which was established in 1938, and by Senator Joseph McCarthy's operations in the Committee on Government Operations between 1950 and 1954. Many persons refused to answer inquiries by these committees on grounds of self-incrimination under the Fifth Amendment. This course guaranteed against a contempt citation, but laid that witness open to loss of employment and reputation, as witness Senator McCarthy's charges about "Fifth Amendment Communists." Other witnesses refused to take refuge in the Fifth Amendment, and refused to answer on the claim that their First Amendment rights were being infringed.

For a considerable period the Supreme Court avoided passing on the serious constitutional issues raised by these inquiries, even though some interesting and important cases were decided in the lower federal courts. Finally, in *Watkins* v. *United States,* 354 U.S. 178 (1957), the Court did uphold a witness who had declined to testify before the Un-American Activities Committee, and indicated some intention to assume a measure of responsibility for determining whether congressional committees were operating within their constitutional authority.

Watkins was a labor union official who refused to answer questions as to whether certain individuals were members of the Communist Party. He agreed to testify concerning persons whom he believed to be active current Communists, but refused to answer questions concerning former members who to his best knowledge had long since removed themselves from the movement. He contended that such questions were not authorized by law or relevant to the work of the committee; answers would accomplish no purpose except exposure of past activities.

The basic proposition in Chief Justice Warren's opinion was a reiteration of the well-established doctrine that the power of Congress to investigate, while broad, is not unlimited. What this means, Warren said, is that "there is no general authority to expose the private affairs of individuals without justification in terms of the functions of Congress." Moreover, no committee can act as a law-enforcement or trial agency. Under our system of separation of powers those are functions of the executive and judicial departments. In short, "no inquiry is an end in itself; it must be related to and in furtherance of a legitimate task of Congress."

Having reasserted this general principle, the Chief Justice nevertheless found it unnecessary to examine the legitimacy of the committee's purposes in questioning Watkins. While he had no doubt "that there is no congressional power to expose for the sake of exposure," Warren was understandably reluctant to get involved in "testing the motives of committee members." Instead, Watkins was upheld on the ground that the committee's investigatory authorization was unconstitutionally broad. The Court ruled that in setting up committees or specifying their jurisdiction, the House or Senate must instruct the committee members "on what they are to do with the power delegated to them." The instructions to the committee must "spell out that group's jurisdiction and purpose with sufficient particularity" so that a witness and a reviewing court may have some basis for judging whether the questions asked were pertinent to the committee's legislative purpose.

In the *Watkins* case the Court held that the Un-American Activities Committee had failed this test. Its jurisdiction was stated by the House so broadly as to cover any subject it might conceivably wish to examine. The Court was particularly concerned with the resulting threat to the First Amendment rights of witnesses. Chief Justice Warren wrote: "Clearly, an investigation is subject to the command that the Congress shall make no law abridging freedom of speech or press or assembly. . . . And investigation is part of lawmaking. . . ." Unrestrained inquiries such as those of this committee challenged the First Amendment, Warren thought. "The mere summoning of a witness and compelling him to testify, against his will, about his beliefs, expressions or associations is a measure of governmental interference. And when those forced revelations concern matters that are unorthodox, unpopular, or even hateful to the general public, the reaction in the life of the witness may be disastrous."

A companion decision to *Watkins* was *Sweezy* v. *New Hampshire,* 354 U.S. 234 (1957), in which the Court invalidated a state legislative inquiry by a six to two vote. The New Hampshire Legislature had constituted the attorney general of the state as a one-man legislative committee and directed him to determine whether there were in the state any "subversive persons" as defined in the state subversive activities act. Sweezy was twice subjected to broad inquiries into his activities and beliefs by the attorney general. Sweezy answered many questions, specifically denying that he had ever been a member of the Communist Party, but he refused to answer questions which he regarded as not pertinent to the subject under inquiry as well as any questions about his opinions or beliefs. As in *Watkins,* the Chief Justice used some broad condemnatory language, but ultimately based his decision on the narrower ground of absence of legislative control over the use of the investigatory power.

The *Watkins* decision was quite unexpected and was subjected to bitter attacks in many quarters. Senator Jenner immediately introduced a bill to withdraw the Supreme Court's appellate jurisdiction in prosecutions for contempt of Congress. In 1958 Senator Butler proposed a bill giving finality to legislative decisions on the pertinency of questions asked of witnesses. However, the Supreme Court largely terminated this criticism by its decision in *Barenblatt* v. *United States,*

360 U.S. 109 (1959), which substantially retreated from the *Watkins* holding. The vote in the *Barenblatt* case was five to four. The six-judge *Watkins* majority was reduced to a four-judge minority by the defection of Justices Harlan and Frankfurter. Joining these two in the new majority were Clark, who had been the sole dissenter in *Watkins,* Whittaker, who had not participated in *Watkins,* and Stewart, appointed after the *Watkins* decision.

On the same day, the *Sweezy* opinion was practically liquidated by *Uphaus* v. *Wyman,* 360 U.S. 72 (1959), which upheld the contempt conviction of a pacifist minister who had refused to supply to the New Hampshire attorney general, acting as a one-man legislative committee, the names of persons who had attended a summer camp he operated. As in the *Sweezy* case, the attorney general had legislative authorization to look for "subversive persons," and the Court majority thought the state was protecting its legitimate interest in self-preservation by these activities. Justice Brennan, dissenting, and speaking also for Warren, Black, and Douglas, asserted that the attorney general was not pursuing any general legislative goal, but rather matters of individual behavior and guilt; "the investigatory objective was the impermissible one of exposure for exposure's sake."

Thus the *Watkins* and *Sweezy* decisions were largely canceled out by *Barenblatt* and *Uphaus,* leaving federal and state legislative bodies free to inquire very broadly into individual conduct on the ground that legitimate legislative purposes are being served. The Supreme Court went even further in two 1961 decisions, *Wilkinson* v. *United States,* 365 U.S. 399, and *Braden* v. *United States,* 365 U.S. 431. Wilkinson had gone to Atlanta to organize opposition sentiment against the Un-American Activities Committee which was holding hearings there, and was subpoenaed to appear before the committee within one hour after he arrived in town. Braden had circulated a petition, which had been signed by 200 Negroes, asking the House not to permit the committee to conduct hearings in the South. He was required to go from Rhode Island to Atlanta for questioning about the petition. A five-judge majority upheld the inquiry in both cases. The four-judge minority charged that the committee in each case was merely seeking to harass its opponents and to expose them for the sake of exposure, not for the purpose of securing information for legislative purposes.

BARENBLATT v. UNITED STATES
360 U.S. 109, 79 S. Ct. 1081, 3 L. Ed. 2d 1115 (1959)

Lloyd Barenblatt, formerly an instructor in psychology at Vassar College, refused to tell a subcommittee of the House Committee on Un-American Activities whether he was or had ever been a member of the Communist Party. He did not claim the Fifth Amendment privilege against self-incrimination; instead he argued that the First Amendment bars congressional inquiry into matters of beliefs and associations.

MR. JUSTICE HARLAN delivered the opinion of the Court.

Once more the Court is required to resolve the conflicting constitutional claims of congressional power and of an individual's right to resist its exercise. The congressional power in question concerns the internal process of Congress in moving within its legislative domain; it involves the utilization of its committees to secure "testimony needed to enable it efficiently to exercise a legislative function belonging to it under the Constitution." *McGrain* v. *Daugherty,* 273 U.S. 135, 160. The power of inquiry has been employed by Congress throughout our history, over the whole range of the national interests concerning which Congress might legislate or decide upon due investigation not to legislate; it has similarly been utilized in determining what to appropriate from the national purse, or whether to appropriate. The scope of the power of inquiry, in short, is as penetrating and far-reaching as the potential power to enact and appropriate under the Constitution.

Broad as it is, the power is not, however, without limitations. Since Congress may only investigate into those areas in which it may potentially legislate or appropriate, it cannot inquire into matters which are within the exclusive province of one or the other branch of the Government. Lacking the judicial power given to the Judiciary, it cannot inquire into matters that are exclusively the concern of the Judiciary. Neither can it supplant the Executive in what exclusively belongs to the Executive. And the Congress, in common with all branches of the Government, must exercise its powers subject to the limitations placed by the Constitution on governmental action, more particularly in the context of this case the relevant limitations of the Bill of Rights.

The congressional power of inquiry, its range and scope, and an individual's duty in relation to it, must be viewed in proper perspective. . . . The power and the right of resistance to it are to be judged in the concrete, not on the basis of abstractions. In the present case congressional efforts to learn the extent of a nationwide, indeed worldwide, problem have brought one of its investigating committees into the field of education. Of course, broadly viewed, inquiries cannot be made into the teaching that is pursued in any of our educational institutions. When academic teaching-freedom and its corollary learning-freedom, so essential to the well-being of the Nation, are claimed, this Court will always be on the alert against intrusion by Congress into this constitutionally protected domain. But this does not mean that the Congress is precluded from interrogating a witness merely because he is a teacher. An educational institution is not a constitutional sanctuary from inquiry into matters that may otherwise be within the constitutional legislative domain merely for the reason that inquiry is made of someone within its walls. . . .

We here review petitioner's conviction under 2 U.S.C. § 192 for contempt of Congress, arising from his refusal to answer certain questions put to him by a Subcommittee of the House Committee on Un-American Activities during the course of an inquiry concerning alleged Communist infiltration into the field of education. . . .

Our function, at this point, is purely one of constitutional adjudication in the particular case and upon the particular record before us, not to pass judgment upon the general wisdom or efficacy of the activities of this Committee in a vexing and complicated field.

The precise constitutional issue confronting us is whether the Subcommittee's inquiry into petitioner's past or present membership in the Communist Party transgressed the provisions of the First Amendment, which of course reach and limit congressional investigations. . . .

The Court's past cases establish sure guides to decision. Undeniably, the First Amendment in some circumstances protects an individual from being compelled to disclose his associational relationships. However, the protections of the First Amendment, unlike a proper claim of the privilege against self-incrimination under the Fifth Amendment, do not afford a witness the right to resist inquiry in all circumstances. Where First Amendment rights are asserted to bar governmental interrogation resolution of the issue always involves a balancing by the courts of the competing private and public interests at stake in the particular circumstances shown. These principles were recognized in the *Watkins* case, where, in speaking of the First Amendment in relation to congressional inquiries, we said (at p. 198): "It is manifest that despite the adverse effects which follow upon compelled disclosure of private matters, not all such inquiries are barred. . . . The critical element is the existence of, and the weight to be ascribed to, the interest of the Congress in demanding disclosures from an unwilling witness." . . .

The first question is whether this investigation was related to a valid legislative purpose, for Congress may not constitutionally require an individual to disclose his political relationships or other private affairs except in relation to such a purpose. . . .

That Congress has wide power to legislate in the field of Communist activity in this Country, and to conduct appropriate investigations in aid thereof, is hardly debatable. The existence of such power has never been questioned by this Court, and it is sufficient to say, without particularization, that Congress has enacted or considered in this field a wide range of legislative measures, not a few of which have stemmed from recommendations of the very Committee whose actions have been drawn in question here. In the last analysis this power rests on the right of self-preservation, "the ultimate value of any society," *Dennis* v. *United States,* 341 U.S. 494, 509. Justification for its exercise in turn rests on the long and widely accepted view that the tenets of the Communist Party include the ultimate overthrow of the Government of the United States by force and violence, a view which has been given formal expression by the Congress.

On these premises, this Court in its constitutional adjudications has consistently refused to view the Communist Party as an ordinary political party, and has upheld federal legislation aimed at the Communist problem which in a different context would certainly have raised constitutional issues of the gravest character. . . . To suggest that because the Communist Party may also sponsor peaceable political reforms the constitutional issues before us should now be judged as if that Party were just an ordinary political party from the standpoint of national security, is to ask this Court to blind itself to world affairs which have determined the whole course of our national policy since the close of World War II, affairs to which Judge Learned Hand gave vivid expression in his opinion in *United States* v. *Dennis,* 183 F. 2d 201, 213, and to the vast burdens which these conditions have entailed for the entire Nation.

We think that investigatory power in this domain is not to be denied Congress solely because the field of education is involved. . . . Indeed we do not understand petitioner here to suggest that Congress in no circumstances may inquire into Communist activity in the field of education. Rather, his position is in effect that this particular investigation was aimed not at the revolutionary aspects but at the theoretical classroom discussion of communism.

In our opinion this position rests on a too constricted view of the nature of the investigatory process, and is not supported by a fair assessment of the record before us. An investigation of advocacy of or preparation for overthrow certainly embraces the right to identify a witness as a member of the Communist Party, see *Barsky* v. *United States,* 167 F. 2d 241, and to inquire into the various manifestations of the Party's tenets. The strict requirements of a prosecution under the Smith Act . . . are not the measure of the permissible scope of a congressional investigation into "overthrow," for of necessity the investigatory process must proceed step by step. Nor can it fairly be concluded that this investigation was directed at controlling what is being taught at our universities rather than at overthrow. . . . The record discloses considerable testimony concerning the foreign domination and revolutionary purposes and efforts of the Communist Party. That there was also testimony on the abstract philosophical level does not detract from the dominant theme of this investigation—Communist infiltration furthering the alleged ultimate purpose of overthrow. . . .

Nor can we accept the further contention that this investigation should not be deemed to have been in furtherance of a legislative purpose because the true objective of the Committee and of the Congress was purely "exposure." So long as Congress acts in pursuance of its constitutional power, the judiciary lacks authority to intervene on the basis of the motives which spurred the exercise of that power. . . . In stating in the *Watkins* case . . . that "there is no congressional power to expose for the sake of exposure," we at the same time declined to inquire into the "motives of committee members," and recognized that their "motives alone would not vitiate an investigation which had been instituted by a House of Congress if that assembly's legislative purpose is being served." Having scrutinized this record we cannot say that the unanimous panel of the Court of Appeals which first considered this case was wrong in concluding that "the primary purposes of the inquiry were in aid of legislative processes." . . . Certainly this is not a case like *Kilbourn* v. *Thompson,* 103 U.S. 168, 192, where "the House of Representatives not only exceeded the limit of its own authority, but assumed a power which could only be properly exercised by another branch of the government, because it was in its nature clearly judicial." . . . The constitutional legislative power of Congress in this instance is beyond question.

Finally, the record is barren of other factors which in themselves might sometimes lead to the conclusion that the individual interests at stake were not subordinate to those of the state. There is no indication in this record that the Subcommittee was attempting to pillory witnesses. Nor did petitioner's appearance as a witness follow from indiscriminate dragnet procedures, lacking in probable cause for belief that he possessed information which might be helpful to the Subcommittee. And the relevancy of the questions put to him by the Subcommittee is not open to doubt.

We conclude that the balance between the individual and the governmental interests here at stake must be struck in favor of the latter, and that therefore the provisions of the First Amendment have not been offended. . . .

Affirmed.

Mr. Justice Black, with whom The Chief Justice, and Mr. Justice Douglas concur, dissenting. . . .

The First Amendment says in no equivocal language that Congress shall pass no law abridging freedom of speech, press, assembly or petition. The activities of this Committee, authorized by Congress, do precisely that, through exposure, obloquy and public scorn. . . . The Court does not really deny this fact but relies on a combination of three reasons for permitting the infringement: (A) The notion that despite the First Amendment's command Congress can abridge speech and association if this Court decides that the governmental interest in abridging speech is greater than an individual's interest in exercising that freedom, (B) the Government's right to "preserve itself," (C) the fact that the Committee is only after Communists or suspected Communists in this investigation.

(A) I do not agree that laws directly abridging First Amendment freedoms can be justified by a congressional or judicial balancing process. . . .

To apply the Court's balancing test under such circumstances is to read the First Amendment to say "Congress shall pass no law abridging freedom of speech, press, assembly and petition, unless Congress and the Supreme Court reach the joint conclusion that on balance the interests of the Government in stifling these freedoms is greater than the interest of the people in having them exercised." This is closely akin to the notion that neither the First Amendment nor any other provision of the Bill of Rights should be enforced unless the Court believes it is *reasonable* to do so. . . .

But even assuming what I cannot assume, that some balancing is proper in this case, I feel that the Court after stating the test ignores it completely. At most it balances the right of the Government to preserve itself, against Barenblatt's right to refrain from revealing Communist affiliations. Such a balance, however, mistakes the factors to be weighed. In the first place, it completely leaves out the real interest in Barenblatt's silence, the interest of the people as a whole in being able to join organizations, advocate causes and make political "mistakes" without later being subjected to governmental penalties for having dared to think for themselves. It is this right, the right to err politically, which keeps us strong as a Nation. For no number of laws against communism can have as much effect as the personal conviction which comes from having heard its arguments and rejected them, or from having once accepted its tenets and later recognized their worthlessness. Instead, the obloquy which results from investigations such as this not only stifles "mistakes" but prevents all but the most courageous from hazarding any views which might at some later time become disfavored. This result, whose importance cannot be overestimated, is doubly crucial when it affects the universities, on which we must largely rely for the experimentation and development of new ideas essential to our country's welfare. It is these interests of society, rather than Barenblatt's own right to silence, which I think the Court should put on balance against the demands of the Government, if any balancing process is to be tolerated. . . .

(B) Moreover, I cannot agree with the Court's notion that First Amendment freedoms must be abridged in order to "preserve" our country. That notion rests on the unarticulated premise that this Nation's security hangs upon its power to punish people because of what they think, speak or write about, or because of those with whom they associate for political purposes. The Government, in its brief, virtually admits this position when it speaks of the "communication of unlawful ideas." I challenge this premise, and deny that ideas can be proscribed under our Constitution. I agree that despotic governments cannot exist without stifling the voice of opposition to their oppressive practices. The First Amendment means to me, however, that the only constitutional way our Government can preserve itself is to leave its people the fullest possible freedom to praise, criticize or discuss, as they see fit, all governmental policies and to suggest, if they desire, that even its most fundamental postulates are bad and should be changed; "Therein lies the security of the Republic, the very foundation of constitutional government." On that premise this land was created, and on that premise it has grown to greatness. Our Constitution assumes that the common sense of the people and their attachment to our country will enable them, after free discussion, to withstand ideas that are wrong. . . .

(C) The Court implies, however, that the ordinary rules and requirements of the Constitution do not apply because the Committee is merely after Communists and they do not constitute a political party but only a criminal gang. "[T]he long and widely accepted view," the Court says, is "that the tenets of the Communist Party include the ultimate overthrow of the Government of the United States by force and violence." This justifies the investigation undertaken. By accepting this charge and allowing it to support treatment of the Communist Party and its members which would violate the Constitution if applied to other groups, the Court, in effect, declares that Party outlawed. It has been only a few years since there was a practically unanimous feeling throughout the country and in our courts that this could not be done in our free land. Of course it has always been recognized that members of the Party who, either individually or in combination, commit acts in violation of valid laws can be prosecuted. But the Party as a whole and innocent members of it could not be attainted merely because it had some illegal aims and because some of its members were lawbreakers. . . .

No matter how often or how quickly we repeat the claim that the Communist Party is not a political party, we cannot outlaw it, as a group, without endangering the liberty of all of us. The reason is not hard to find, for mixed among those aims of communism which are illegal are perfectly normal political and social goals. And muddled with its revolutionary tenets is a drive to achieve power through the ballot, if it can be done. These things necessarily make it a political party whatever other, illegal, aims it may have. . . .

The fact is that once we allow any group which has some political aims or ideas to be driven from the ballot and from the battle for men's minds because some of its members are bad and some of its tenets are illegal, no group is safe. Today we deal with Communists or suspected Communists. In 1920, instead, the New York Assembly suspended duly elected legislators on the ground that, being Socialists, they were disloyal to the country's principles. In the 1830's the Masons were hunted as outlaws and subversives, and abolitionists were considered revolutionaries of the most dangerous kind in both North and South. Earlier still, at the time of the universally unlamented alien and sedition laws, Thomas Jefferson's party was attacked and its members were derisively called "Jacobins." Fisher Ames described the party as a "French faction" guilty of "subversion" and "officered, regimented and formed to subordination." Its members, he claimed, intended to "take arms against the laws as soon as they dare." History should teach us then, that in times of high emotional excitement minority parties and groups which advocate extremely unpopular social or governmental innovations will always be typed as criminal gangs and attempts will always be made to drive them out. It was knowledge of this fact, and of its great dangers, that caused the Founders of our land to enact the First Amendment as a guarantee that neither Congress nor the people would do anything to hinder or destroy the capacity of individuals and groups to seek converts and votes for any cause, however radical or unpalatable their principles might seem under the accepted notions of the time. Whatever the States were left free to do, the First Amendment sought to leave Congress devoid of any kind or quality of power to direct any type of national laws against the freedom of individuals to think what they please, advocate whatever policy they choose, and join with others to bring about the social, religious, political and governmental changes which seem best to them. Today's holding, in my judgment, marks another major step in the progressively increasing retreat from the safeguards of the First Amendment. . . .

Finally, I think Barenblatt's conviction violates the Constitution because the chief aim, purpose and practice of the House Un-American Activities Committee, as disclosed by its many reports, is to try witnesses and punish them because they are or have been Communists or because they refuse to admit or deny Communist affiliations. The punishment imposed is generally punishment by humiliation and public shame. There is nothing strange or novel about this kind of punishment. It is in fact one of the oldest forms of governmental punishment known to mankind; branding, the pillory, ostracism and subjection to public hatred being but a few examples of it. . . .

I do not question the Committee's patriotism and sincerity in doing all this. I merely feel that it cannot be done by Congress under our Constitution. For, even assuming that the Federal Government can compel witnesses to testify as to Communist affiliations in order to subject them to ridicule and social and economic retaliation, I cannot agree that this is a legislative function. Such publicity is clearly punishment, and the Constitution allows only one way in which people can be convicted and punished. . . . If communism is to be made a crime, and Communists are to be subjected to "pains and penalties," I would still hold this conviction bad, for the crime of communism, like all others, can be punished only by court and jury after a trial with all judicial safeguards. . . .

Mr. Justice Brennan, dissenting.

I would reverse this conviction. It is sufficient that I state my complete agreement with my Brother Black that no purpose for the investigation of Barenblatt is revealed by the record except exposure purely for the sake of exposure. This is not a purpose to which Barenblatt's rights under the First Amendment can validly be subordinated. An investigation in which the processes of law-making and law-evaluating are submerged entirely in exposure of individual behavior—in adjudication, of a sort, through the exposure process—is outside the constitutional pale of congressional inquiry. . . .

Chapter 9

THE TAXING POWER

The Congress shall have power [1.] To lay and collect taxes, duties, imposts and excises, to pay the debts and provide for the common defense and general welfare of the United States. . . .   ART. I, SEC. 8

The possession of adequate sources of revenue and broad authority to use public funds for public purposes are essential conditions for carrying on an effective government. Consequently the first rule for judicial review of tax statutes is that a heavy burden of proof lies on anyone who would challenge any congressional exercise of fiscal power. In almost every decision touching on the constitutionality of federal taxation, the Supreme Court has stressed the breadth of congressional power and the limits of its own reviewing powers. "The power to tax involves the power to destroy," said Marshall in *McCulloch* v. *Maryland*, 4 Wheat. 316 (1819). The authorization of the Constitution "reaches every subject," *License Tax Cases*, 5 Wall. 462 (1867); it embraces "every conceivable power of taxation," *Brushaber* v. *Union Pacific R.R.*, 240 U.S. 1 (1916). Yet in spite of such statements, the taxing power of Congress is not unlimited.

Specific Limits on the Taxing Power. One specific limitation is found in Article I, section 9: "No capitation, or other direct, tax shall be laid, unless in proportion to the census or enumeration herein before directed to be taken." In *Hylton* v. *United States*, 3 Dall. 171 (1796), the Supreme Court held that a specific tax on carriages was not a direct tax and so did not need to be apportioned among the states. The judges expressed the view that the only direct taxes were capitation and land taxes. An unapportioned Civil War income tax was upheld as not a direct tax in *Springer* v. *United States*, 102 U.S. 586 (1881).

Thus Congress had every reason to be confident of its authority when in 1894 it levied a tax of 2 per cent on incomes in excess of $4,000. However, the Supreme Court yielded to the clamor from the propertied interests of the country that this was a "communist" measure, and by a vote of five to four ruled that an income tax was a direct tax, and consequently unconstitutional unless apportioned on the basis of population. A campaign to "repeal" the Court's decision got under way immediately, and was finally successful when the Sixteenth Amendment was adopted in 1913.

The federal taxing power is also limited by the proviso in Article I, section 8, that "all duties, imposts and excises shall be uniform throughout the United States." The Court held in *Knowlton* v. *Moore*, 178 U.S. 41 (1900), that this requirement referred to geographical uniformity and did not invalidate the use of progressive rates in inheritance taxation.

Intergovernmental Tax Immunity. In addition to these specifically stated limits on the federal taxing power, the Supreme Court has found certain implied restrictions which derive from the inherent nature of the federal system. One group deals with the immunity to federal taxation of state governments, their property and activities.

The immunity doctrine was first developed by the Court in *McCulloch* v. *Maryland,* 4 Wheat. 316 (1819), and applied to protect the Bank of the United States from state taxation. It was not until 1871, in *Collector* v. *Day,* 11 Wall. 113, that this doctrine was applied in reverse to hold the salary of a state judge immune from the federal Civil War income tax. The Court saw no reason why immunity should not operate in both directions, though in fact there was an obvious flaw in this reasoning. State taxation falling on the federal government, as Justice Bradley pointed out, "involves an interference with the powers of a government in which other States and their citizens are equally interested with the State which imposes the taxation." But when Congress levies a tax affecting the states, every state has a voice in the decision through its representatives, and so the states are actually consenting to their own taxation. There is thus a political check on possible abuse of the federal taxing power against the states, whereas a state legislature is under no such sense of restraint in levying a tax which will fall primarily on the residents of other states.

The immunity doctrine was continued and enlarged when *Pollock* v. *Farmers' Loan & Trust Co.,* 157 U.S. 429, 158 U.S. 601 (1895), exempted from federal taxation the interest on state and local bonds. However, in *South Carolina* v. *United States,* 199 U.S. 437 (1905), the Court ruled that state-owned and state-operated liquor stores would have to pay the regular federal internal revenue taxes. Tax exemption, the Court said, would be limited to state functions of a "strictly governmental character."

During the 1920s an economically conservative Court carried the immunity principle into a number of new areas, extending both federal and state immunity. For example, in *Long* v. *Rockwood,* 277 U.S. 142 (1928), the Court by a five to four vote ruled that a state could not tax royalties received from a patent granted by the United States. On the other side of the coin, a similar five to four vote in *Burnet* v. *Coronado Oil & Gas Co.,* 285 U.S. 393 (1932), invalidated a federal tax imposed on the income which private persons derived from leasing state-owned oil lands.

Throughout this period there was a strong protest, particularly by Justices Holmes, Brandeis, and Stone, against the expansion of the immunity principle, and by 1938 this view had won control of the Court. *Helvering* v. *Mountain Producers Corp.,* 303 U.S. 376 (1938), reversed the *Burnet* and other oil-lands leasing cases. In *Helvering* v. *Gerhardt,* 304 U.S. 405 (1938), and *Graves* v. *O'Keefe,* 306 U.S. 466 (1939), the Court demolished intergovernmental tax immunity for the salaries of state and federal employees, overruling *Collector* v. *Day* and the other cases in that line. *New York* v. *United States,* 326 U.S. 572 (1946), upheld federal taxes on the sale of mineral waters bottled by the state of New York, thus standing by the limiting principle of the *South Carolina* decision that immunity would be granted only to a state's "sovereign functions."

After the 1930s, then, the immunity doctrine was no longer a substantial limitation on congressional taxing power. Of course Congress cannot levy a property tax on a state capitol building, or a stamp tax on writs served by a state court, or any other tax which falls directly on an essential state activity. But of the taxes thus prohibited, the only one of practical importance is the tax on income from state and municipal bonds. The same principles confine federal exemption from state taxation to the possessions, institutions, and activities of the federal government itself.

Taxation for Nonrevenue Purposes. Some constitutional questions have been raised by congressional efforts to use the taxing power for purposes which are primarily regulatory, and which result in the raising of comparatively little revenue, or sometimes none at all. Does this mixture of motives invalidate a tax statute? The Supreme Court has not thought so, except in a few instances and under quite unusual circumstances.

The protective tariff is of course a clear case of using taxation for goals other than the raising of revenue, and it has been regarded as constitutional ever since 1789, though the Supreme Court did not actually have an occasion to so hold until *J. W. Hampton, Jr. & Co. v. United States,* 276 U.S. 394 (1928). Other regulatory or prohibitory taxes have been no less firmly upheld. *Veazie Bank v. Fenno,* 8 Wall. 533 (1869), validated a 10 per cent tax on the circulation of state bank notes which Congress had adopted as a means of driving them out of use in favor of the notes of national banks. The Court considered that the taxing power in this situation was being used only as an auxiliary means for enforcing the federal government's admitted power to provide a sound and uniform national currency.

But even when there was no discernible relation between the regulatory tax and some specific authority of Congress, the Court seldom objected. The classic case is *McCray v. United States,* 195 U.S. 27 (1904), which involved an act of Congress levying a tax of 10 cents per pound on oleomargarine artificially colored yellow to look like butter, and only ¼ cent per pound on uncolored oleomargarine. There could be no doubt that the statute was adopted at the behest of the dairy industry to handicap the sale of a competitive product. But the Court denied that "the motives or purposes of Congress are open to judicial inquiry in considering the power of that body" to enact legislation. The statute was on its face an excise tax, and so it followed that it was within the power of Congress.

The principle of the *McCray* case was again endorsed in *United States v. Doremus,* 249 U.S. 86 (1919), where Congress used a small tax requirement to compel the registration of persons engaged in the narcotics trade. "The act may not be declared unconstitutional because its effect may be to accomplish another purpose as well as the raising of revenue," said the Court, but four justices dissented on the ground that the statute was a bold attempt to exercise police power reserved to the states.

The principal case in which a federal tax was invalidated by the Court on the ground that it was not truly a revenue measure was the child labor tax act, passed in 1919 to replace the 1916 child labor act based on the commerce clause, which the Court had held unconstitutional in *Hammer v. Dagenhart,* 247 U.S. 251 (1918). The Court, while denying that it had any right or desire to inquire into congressional motives, concluded that this "so-called tax" revealed on its face that it was not a revenue measure, but rather a penalty to regulate child labor. The justices particularly noted the provision that the tax was not to be imposed unless the employer knowingly hired children under the age limit, and pointed out: "*Scienter* is associated with penalties, not with taxes." Similarly in *United States v. Constantine*, 296 U.S. 287 (1935), a grossly disproportional federal excise tax, amounting to $1,000, imposed only on retail liquor dealers carrying on business in violation of local law, was declared unconstitutional.

It is not easy for the Court to arrive at such conclusions, for they necessarily involve a finding that Congress has been guilty of improper motives and has used a legislative subterfuge to accomplish ends which the Constitution forbids. Consequently it is not surprising that the *Bailey* and *Constantine* precedents have not been followed in subsequent cases, even in situations such as *Sonzinsky v. United States*, 300 U.S. 506 (1937), and *United States v. Kahriger*, 345 U.S. 22 (1953), in both of which the motivation of tax statutes was clearly not revenue.

UNITED STATES v. KAHRIGER
345 U.S. 22, 73 S. Ct. 510, 97 L. Ed. 754 (1953)

Following the sensational revelations of the Kefauver Crime Committee in 1950, Congress adopted the Gamblers' Occupational Tax Act in 1951, which levied a tax on persons engaged in the business of accepting wagers, and required them to register with the Collector of Internal Revenue. Kahriger was prosecuted for failure to register or to pay the tax.

Mr. Justice Reed delivered the opinion of the Court. . . .

The case comes here on appeal . . . from the United States District Court for the Eastern District of Pennsylvania, where an information was filed against appellee alleging that he was in the business of accepting wagers and that he willfully failed to register for and pay the occupational tax in question. Appellee moved to dismiss on the ground that the sections upon which the information was based were unconstitutional. The District Court sustained the motion on the authority of our opinion in *United States v. Constantine*, 296 U.S. 287. The court reasoned that while "the subject matter of this legislation so far as revenue purposes is concerned is within the scope of Federal authorities," the tax was unconstitutional in that the information called for by the registration provisions was "peculiarly applicable to the applicant from the standpoint of law enforcement and vice control," and therefore the whole of the legislation was an infringement by the Federal Government on the police power reserved to the states by the Tenth Amendment. . . .

The result below is at odds with the position of the seven other district courts which have considered the matter, and, in our opinion, is erroneous.

In the term following the *Constantine* opinion, this Court pointed out in *Sonzinsky v. United States*, 300 U.S. 506, at 513 (a case involving a tax on a "limited class" of objectionable firearms alleged to be prohibitory in effect and "to disclose unmistakably the legislative purpose to regulate rather than to tax"), that the subject of the tax in *Constantine* was "described or treated as criminal by the taxing statute." The tax in the *Constantine* case was a special additional excise tax of $1,000, placed only on persons who carried on a liquor business in violation of state law. The wagering tax with which we are here concerned applies to all persons engaged in the business of receiving wagers, regardless of whether such activity violates state law.

The substance of respondent's position with respect to the Tenth Amendment is that Congress has chosen to tax a specified business which is not within its power to regulate. The precedents are many upholding taxes similar to this wagering tax as a proper exercise of the federal taxing power. In the *License Tax Cases*, 5 Wall. 462, the controversy arose out of indictments for selling lottery tickets and retailing liquor in various states without having first obtained and paid for a license under the Internal Revenue Act of Congress. The objecting taxpayers urged that Congress could not constitutionally tax or regulate activities carried on within a state. . . .

Appellee would have us say that, because there is legislative history indicating a congressional motive to suppress wagering, this tax is not a proper exercise of such taxing power. In the *License Tax Cases, supra,* it was admitted that the federal license "discouraged" the activities. The intent to curtail and hinder, as well as tax, was also manifest in the following cases, and in each of them the tax was upheld: *Veazie Bank v. Fenno*, 8 Wall. 533 (tax on paper money issued by state banks); *McCray v. United States*, 195 U.S. 27, 59 (tax on colored oleomargarine); *United States v. Doremus*, 249 U.S. 86, and *Nigro v. United States*, 276 U.S. 332 (tax on narcotics); *Sonzinsky v. United States*, 300 U.S. 506 (tax on firearms); *United States v. Sanchez*, 340 U.S. 42 (tax on marihuana).

It is conceded that a federal excise tax does not cease to be valid merely because it discourages or deters the activities taxed. Nor is the tax invalid because the revenue obtained is negligible. Appellee, however, argues that the sole purpose of the statute is to penalize only illegal gambling in the states through the guise of a tax measure. As with the above excise taxes which we have held to be valid, the instant tax has a regulatory effect. But regardless of its regulatory effect, the wagering tax produces revenue. As such it surpasses both the narcotics and firearms taxes which we have found valid.

It is axiomatic that the power of Congress to tax is extensive and sometimes falls with crushing effect on businesses deemed unessential or inimical to the public welfare, or where, as in dealings with narcotics, the collection of the tax also is difficult. As is well known, the constitutional restraints on taxing are few. . . . The remedy for excessive taxation is in the hands of Congress, not the courts. . . .

The difficulty of saying when the power to lay uniform taxes is curtailed, because its use brings a result beyond the direct legislative power of Congress, has given rise to diverse decisions. In that area of abstract ideas, a final definition of the line between state and federal power has baffled judges and legislators.

. . . Where federal legislation has rested on other congressional powers, such as the Necessary and Proper Clause or the Commerce Clause, this Court has generally sustained the statutes, despite their effect on matters ordinarily considered state concern. When federal power to regulate is found, its exercise is a matter for Congress. Where Congress has employed the taxing clause a greater variation in the decisions has resulted. The division in this Court has been more acute. Without any specific differentiation between the power to tax and other federal powers, the indirect results from the exercise of the power to tax have raised more doubts. . . . It is hard to understand why the power to tax should raise more doubts because of indirect effects than other federal powers.

. . . Unless there are provisions extraneous to any tax need, courts are without authority to limit the exercise of the taxing power. All the provisions of this excise are adapted to the collection of a valid tax.

Nor do we find the registration requirements of the wagering tax offensive. All that is required is the filing of names, addresses, and places of business. This is quite general in tax returns. Such data are directly and intimately related to the collection of the tax and . . . make the tax simpler to collect.

Appellee's second assertion is that the wagering tax is unconstitutional because it is a denial of the privilege against self-incrimination as guaranteed by the Fifth Amendment.

Since appellee failed to register for the wagering tax, it is difficult to see how he can now claim the privilege even assuming that the disclosure of violations of law is called for. . . .

Assuming that respondent can raise the self-incrimination issue, that privilege has relation only to past acts, not to future acts that may or may not be committed. . . . If respondent wishes to take wagers subject to excise taxes under § 3285 . . . he must pay an occupational tax and register. Under the registration provisions of the wagering tax, appellee is not compelled to confess to acts already committed, he is merely informed by the statute that in order to engage in the business of wagering in the future he must fulfill certain conditions.

Mr. Justice Jackson, concurring.

I concur in the judgment and opinion of the Court, but with such doubt that if the minority agreed upon an opinion which did not impair legitimate use of the taxing power I probably would join it. But we deal here with important and contrasting values in our scheme of government, and it is important that neither be allowed to destroy the other. . . .

. . . here is a purported tax law which requires no reports and lays no tax except on specified gamblers whose calling in most states is illegal. It requires this group to step forward and identify themselves, not because they, like others, have income, but because of its source. This is difficult to regard as a rational or good-faith revenue measure, despite the deference that is due Congress. On the contrary, it seems to be a plan to tax out of existence the professional gambler whom it has been found impossible to prosecute out of existence. . . .

The United States has a system of taxation by confession. That a people so numerous, scattered and individualistic annually assesses itself with a tax liability, often in highly burdensome amounts, is a reassuring sign of the stability and vitality of our system of self-government. . . . It will be a sad day for the revenues if the good will of the people toward their taxing system is frittered away in efforts to accomplish by taxation moral reforms that cannot be accomplished by direct legislation. But the evil that can come from this statute will probably soon make itself manifest to Congress. The evil of a judicial decision impairing the legitimate taxing power by extreme constitutional interpretations might not be transient. Even though this statute approaches the fair limits of constitutionality, I join the decision of the Court.

Mr. Justice Black, with whom Mr. Justice Douglas concurs, dissenting.

The Fifth Amendment declares that no person "shall be compelled in any criminal case to be a witness against himself." The Court nevertheless here sustains an Act which requires a man to register and confess that he is engaged in the business of gambling. I think this confession can provide a basis to convict him of a federal crime for having gambled before registration without paying a federal tax. . . . Whether or not the Act has this effect, I am sure that it creates a squeezing device contrived to put a man in federal prison if he refuses to confess himself into a state prison as a violator of state gambling laws. . . . we have a Bill of Rights that condemns coerced confessions, however refined or legalistic may be the technique of extortion. I would hold that this Act violates the Fifth Amendment. . . .

Mr. Justice Frankfurter, dissenting.

The Court's opinion manifests a natural difficulty in reaching its conclusion. Constitutional issues are likely to arise whenever Congress draws on the taxing power not to raise revenue but to regulate conduct. This is so, of course, because of the distribution of legislative power as between the Congress and the State Legislatures in the regulation of conduct.

To review in detail the decisions of this Court, beginning with *Veazie Bank* v. *Fenno,* 8 Wall. 533, dealing with this ambivalent type of revenue enactment, would be to rehash the familiar. Two generalizations may, however, safely be drawn from this series of cases. Congress may make an oblique use of the taxing power in relation to activities with which Congress may deal directly, as for instance, commerce between the States. . . . However, when oblique use is made of the taxing power as to matters which substantively are not within the powers delegated to Congress, the Court cannot shut its eyes to what is obviously, because designedly, an attempt to control conduct which the Constitution left to the responsibility of the States, merely because Congress wrapped the legislation in the verbal cellophane of a revenue measure.

Concededly the constitutional questions presented by such legislation are difficult. On the one hand, courts should scrupulously abstain from hobbling congressional choice of policies, particularly when the vast reach of the taxing power is concerned. On the other hand, to allow what otherwise is excluded from congressional authority to be brought within it by casting legislation in the form of a revenue measure could, as so significantly expounded in the *Child Labor Tax Case* . . . offer an easy way for the legislative imagination to control "any one of the great number of subjects of public interest, jurisdiction of which the States have never parted with. . . ." . . . Issues of such gravity affecting the balance of powers within our federal system are not susceptible of comprehensive statement by smooth formulas such as that a tax is nonetheless a tax although it discourages the activities taxed, or that a tax may be imposed although it may effect ulterior ends. No such phrase, however fine and well-worn, enables one to decide the concrete case.

What is relevant to judgment here is that, even if the history of this legislation as it went through Congress did not give one the libretto to the song, the context of the circumstances which brought forth this enactment—sensationally exploited disclosures regarding gambling in big cities and small, the relation of this gambling to corrupt politics, the impatient public response to these disclosures, the feeling of ineptitude or paralysis on the part of local law-enforcing agencies—emphatically supports what was revealed on the floor of Congress, namely, that what was formally a means of raising revenue for the Federal Government was essentially an effort to check if not to stamp out professional gambling.

A nominal taxing measure must be found an inadmissible intrusion into a domain of legislation reserved for the States not merely when Congress requires that such a measure is to be enforced through a detailed scheme of administration beyond the obvious fiscal needs, as in the *Child Labor Tax Case.* . . . That is one ground for holding that Congress was constitutionally disrespectful of what is reserved to the States. Another basis for deeming such a formal revenue measure inadmissible is presented by this case. In addition to the fact that Congress was concerned with activity beyond the authority of the Federal Government, the enforcing provision of this enactment is designed for the systematic confession of crimes with a view to prosecution for such crimes under State law. . . .

. . . Congress, which cannot constitutionally grapple directly with gambling in the States, may [not] compel self-incriminating disclosures for the enforcement of State gambling laws, merely because it does so under the guise of a revenue measure obviously passed not for revenue purposes. The motive of congressional legislation is not for our scrutiny, provided only that the ulterior purpose is not expressed in ways which negative what the revenue words on their face express and which do not seek enforcement of the formal revenue purpose through means that offend those stand-ards of decency in our civilization against which due process is a barrier.

I would affirm this judgment.

Mr. Justice Douglas, while not joining in the entire opinion, agrees with the views expressed herein that this tax is an attempt by the Congress to control conduct which the Constitution has left to the responsibility of the States.

Chapter 10

THE SPENDING POWER

No money shall be drawn from the Treasury, but in consequence of appropriations made by law. . . .   ART. I, SEC. 9

The basic principle of legislative control over the purse, established by the
British Parliament after a long struggle with the crown, is safeguarded by the
provision quoted above. But are there any constitutional limits upon the purposes
for which Congress may appropriate federal funds? Clearly Congress can spend
money to achieve any of the purposes delegated to it by the Constitution, such as
regulating commerce or taking the census. But can reliance also be placed upon
the rather enigmatic language of the taxing clause which speaks of paying the
debts and providing for "the common defense and general welfare"?

On occasions it has been urged that the general welfare clause is an independent grant of power to the federal government, quite unrelated to the preceding
clause of the same sentence which deals with taxation. In other words, this argument treats the comma after "excises" as though it were a semicolon. This view,
which would empower the federal government to do anything the "general welfare" required, has never been authoritatively accepted. As Story pointed out in
his *Commentaries*, this simple sleight of hand with punctuation would have the
tremendous result of transforming the federal government from one of delegated
powers into one "of general and unlimited powers."

Even though the comma remains a comma, the general welfare clause offers
other perplexities. Madison asserted that it was nothing more than a reference
to the specifically enumerated powers in the subsequent clauses of the same section. Hamilton, on the other hand, contended that the clause conferred a power
separate and distinct from the enumerated powers, and that Congress consequently had a substantive power to tax and to appropriate, limited only by the
requirement of furthering the general welfare of the United States.

Up to 1936 the Supreme Court had never had an opportunity to settle this
argument, principally because a suit attacking federal spending could be prosecuted only by a litigant who had a sufficient legal interest in federal expenditures
to give him standing to sue. As already noted, *Massachusetts v. Mellon*, 262 U.S.
447 (1923), held that neither the state of Massachusetts nor a private taxpayer
had any standing in court to raise the question whether Congress had authorized
the spending of money under the Maternity Act of 1921 for an unconstitutional
purpose. A similar result was reached during the New Deal period when the
Alabama Power Company sought to enjoin Public Works Administrator Ickes

from making loans and grants to Alabama cities for the construction of public power systems. Since the company had been granted no exclusive franchise, it had no legal right to be free from municipal competition, the Court held, and so had no standing in court to contest the constitutionality of the statute. *Alabama Power Co. v. Ickes,* 302 U.S. 464 (1938).

Shortly afterward a group of electric companies was denied the opportunity to question the constitutionality of the Tennessee Valley Authority program, the Court holding in *Tennessee Electric Power Co. v. Tennessee Valley Authority,* 306 U.S. 118 (1939), that TVA competition resulted in no legal wrong against the companies. Because of this inability to secure a Supreme Court ruling on the TVA's constitutionality, Senator Ferguson in 1949 sought to attach an amendment to an appropriation for a TVA steam power plant, authorizing "any Federal taxpayer or any consumer of electric energy" to bring a suit against the TVA to enjoin construction of steam plants. "It is the intention of this provision," ran the amendment, "to vest in such Federal taxpayers and consumers of electric energy the private substantive right to be protected against unlawful expenditures of Federal funds and the unlawful construction of steam plants by the TVA." The Senate, after hearing arguments that this provision was an attempt to secure an advisory opinion from the courts, and unconstitutional under the doctrine of *Muskrat v. United States,* 219 U.S. 346 (1911), rejected the amendment.

To the rule that it is normally impossible to secure a court test of federal spending power, the case of *United States v. Butler,* 297 U.S. 1 (1936), stands as an important exception. The Agricultural Adjustment Act of 1933 had provided for federal payments to farmers who would cooperate in the government's program of price stabilization through production control. The money paid the farmers was to come from processing taxes on agricultural commodities which were authorized by the same statute. This statutory joinder of a spending program with the tax arrangements for financing it was quite unusual, and gave the Court, which was at that time in a bitterly anti-New Deal mood, an opening which it quickly exploited.

Butler, as receiver for the Hoosac Mills, resisted the collection of taxes on cotton processed at that plant. He was clearly entitled to raise this issue in court, but he was bound to lose on it, since the processing tax was obviously a bona fide exercise of the federal taxing power. It was how the tax money was being spent that Butler objected to, but under the doctrine of *Massachusetts v. Mellon* no taxpayer could be heard in court on the constitutionality of federal spending. Butler solved this dilemma by challenging the tax, not as a tax, but as a means of providing money for a program of agricultural production control which he alleged to be an unconstitutional invasion of the powers of the states—in short, "as a step in an unauthorized plan." The Court agreed with him that the tax and the spending were in fact "parts of a single scheme."

Thus it was that Butler gave the Court an opportunity to settle the argument that Madison and Hamilton had begun. The justices settled it in Hamilton's favor. This was an important victory for the spending power, but the Court immediately proceeded to make it a hollow one, so far as this case was concerned, by transferring the argument to an entirely new issue. Whether the spending was for national rather than local welfare was of no importance, the Court majority ruled, since as a statutory plan to regulate and control agricultural production, the act invaded the reserved rights of the states and was consequently invalid under the Tenth Amendment.

The *Butler* decision was little more than a nine-day wonder. As a barrier to federal agricultural regulation it was soon bypassed as the type of program it condemned was reenacted by Congress under the commerce power and upheld by a less antagonistic Court in *Mulford* v. *Smith,* 307 U.S. 38 (1939), and *Wickard* v. *Filburn,* 317 U.S. 111 (1942). As a general threat to the spending power, it was dispelled in 1937 when the Court upheld the tax provisions of the Social Security Act. *Steward Machine Co.* v. *Davis,* 301 U.S. 548 (1937), involved the unemployment compensation section of the act, which provided for a federal tax on employers of a certain percentage of the wages they paid to employees. The proceeds of the tax went into the general federal treasury. If employers paid into an unemployment fund set up under a satisfactory state law, they could credit such payments against the federal tax up to 90 per cent.

The Supreme Court denied by a five to four vote that these tax provisions were an attempt to coerce the states or to invade their reserved powers. The states were given, true enough, a compelling inducement to provide unemployment compensation, but the Court viewed this not as coercion but as freedom to adopt such social legislation without putting the employers of some states at a disadvantage compared with employers in states without unemployment compensation. The *Butler* case was specifically distinguished in the *Steward* decision on the grounds that here the proceeds of the tax were not earmarked for a special group; that the state itself had passed, and could at its pleasure repeal, the unemployment compensation law which was a condition of the credit; and that the relief of unemployment was an end for which nation and state could lawfully cooperate.

On the same day that the *Steward* case was decided, a second decision, *Helvering* v. *Davis,* 301 U.S. 619 (1937), sustained the Social Security Act system of old-age benefits. The argument here had been that the taxing power was being used to benefit a particular class of persons, but the Court believed that Congress might reasonably conclude that provision for old-age security would promote the general welfare.

Because the legislative power to appropriate is so broad and so difficult to question, Congress has sometimes been tempted to use it to achieve purposes which it lacks more direct constitutional power to accomplish. In *United States* v. *Lovett,* 328 U.S. 303 (1946), the Court was asked to pass on a rider to an appropriation act which Congress had adopted forbidding the use of money appropriated by the statute to pay the salaries of three named federal officials. The Court declared the legislation unconstitutional as a bill of attainder, without reaching such possible objections as that it violated the separation of powers by usurping the executive removal power or amounted to an unconstitutional substitute for the impeachment process.

UNITED STATES v. BUTLER
297 U.S. 1, 56 S. Ct. 312, 80 L. Ed. 477 (1936)

MR. JUSTICE ROBERTS delivered the opinion of the Court.

In this case we must determine whether certain provisions of the Agricultural Adjustment Act, 1933, conflict with the Federal Constitution. . . .

First. At the outset the United States contends that the respondents have no standing to question the validity of the tax. The position is that the act is merely a revenue measure levying an excise upon the activity of processing cotton,—a proper subject for the imposition of such a tax,—the proceeds of which go into the federal treasury and thus become available for appropriation for any purpose. It is said that what the respondents are endeavoring to do is to challenge the intended use of the money pursuant to Congressional appropriation when, by confession, that money will have become the property of the Government and the taxpayer will no longer have any interest in it. *Massachusetts* v. *Mellon,* 262 U.S. 447, is claimed to foreclose litigation by the respondents or other taxpayers, as such, looking to restraint of the expenditure of government funds. That case might be an authority in the petitioners' favor if we were here concerned merely with a suit by a taxpayer to restrain the expenditure of the public moneys. It was there held that a taxpayer of the United States may not question expenditures from its treasury on the ground that the alleged unlawful diversion will deplete the public funds and thus increase the burden of future taxation. Obviously the asserted interest of a taxpayer in the federal government's funds and the supposed increase of the future burden of taxation is minute and indeterminable. But here the respondents who are called upon to pay moneys as taxes, resist the exaction as a step in an unauthorized plan. . . .

The tax can only be sustained by ignoring the avowed purpose and operation of the act, and holding it a measure merely laying an excise upon processors to raise revenue for the support of government. Beyond cavil the sole object of the legislation is to restore the purchasing power of agricultural products to a parity with that prevailing in an earlier day; to take money from the processor and bestow it upon farmers who will reduce their acreage for the accomplishment of the proposed end, and, meanwhile to aid these farmers during the period required to bring the prices of their crops to the desired level.

The tax plays an indispensable part in the plan of regulation. . . . The whole revenue from the levy is appropriated in aid of crop control; none of it is made available for general governmental use. . . .

The statute not only avows an aim foreign to the procurement of revenue for the support of government, but by its operation shows the exaction laid upon processors to be the necessary means for the intended control of agricultural production. . . .

It is inaccurate and misleading to speak of the exaction from processors prescribed by the challenged act as a tax, or to say that as a tax it is subject to no infirmity. A tax, in the general understanding of the term, and as used in the Constitution, signifies an exaction for the support of the Government. The word has never been thought to connote the expropriation of money from one group for the benefit of another. We may concede that the latter sort of imposition is constitutional when imposed to effectuate regulation of a matter in which both groups are interested and in respect of which there is a power of legislative regulation. But manifestly no justification for it can be found unless as an integral part of such regulation. The exaction cannot be wrested out of its setting, denominated an excise for raising revenue and legalized by ignoring its purpose as a mere instrumentality for bringing about a desired end. To do this would be to shut our eyes to what all others than we can see and understand. *Child Labor Tax Case,* 259 U.S. 20, 37.

We conclude that the act is one regulating agricultural production; that the tax is a mere incident of such regulation and that the respondents have standing to challenge the legality of the exaction. . . .

Second. The Government asserts that even if the respondents may question the propriety of the appropriation embodied in the statute their attack must fail because Article I, § 8 of the Constitution authorizes the contemplated expenditure of the funds raised by the tax. This contention presents the great and the controlling question in the case. We approach its decision with a sense of our grave responsibility to render judgment in accordance with the principles established for the governance of all three branches of the Government.

There should be no misunderstanding as to the function of this court in such a case. It is sometimes said that the court assumes a power to overrule or control the action of the people's representatives. This is a misconception. The Constitution is the supreme law of the land ordained and established by the people. All legislation must conform to the principles it lays down. When an act of Congress is appropriately challenged in the courts as not conforming to the constitutional mandate the judicial branch of the Government has only one duty,—to lay the article of the Constitution which is invoked beside the statute which is challenged and to decide whether the latter squares with the former. All the court does, or can do, is to announce its considered judgment upon the question. The only power it has, if such it may be called, is the power of judgment. This court neither approves nor condemns any legislative policy. Its delicate and difficult office is to ascertain and declare whether the legislation is in accordance with, or in contravention of, the provisions of the Constitution; and, having done that, its duty ends. . . .

. . . [T]he Government does not attempt to uphold the validity of the act on the basis of the commerce clause, which, for the purpose of the present case, may be put aside as irrelevant.

The clause thought to authorize the legislation . . . confers upon the Congress power "to lay and collect Taxes, Duties, Imposts and Excises, to pay the Debts and provide for the common Defence and general Welfare of the United States. . . ." It is not contended that this provision grants power to regulate agricultural production upon the theory that such legislation would promote the general welfare. The Government concedes that the phrase "to provide for the general welfare" qualifies the power "to lay and collect taxes." The view that the clause grants power to provide for the general welfare, independently of the taxing power, has never been authoritatively accepted. Mr. Justice Story points out that if it were adopted "it is obvious that under color of the generality of the words, to 'provide for the common defence and general welfare,' the government of the United States is, in reality, a government of general and unlimited powers, notwithstanding the subsequent enumeration of specific powers." The true construction undoubtedly is that the only thing granted is the power to tax for the purpose of providing funds for payment of the nation's debts and making provision for the general welfare.

Nevertheless the Government asserts that warrant is found in this clause for the adoption of the Agricultural Adjustment Act. The argument is that Congress may appropriate and authorize the spending of moneys for the "general welfare"; that the phrase should be liberally construed to cover anything conducive to national welfare; that decision as to what will promote such welfare rests with Congress alone, and the courts may not review its determination; and finally that the appropriation under attack was in fact for the general welfare of the United States.

The Congress is expressly empowered to lay taxes to provide for the general welfare. Funds in the Treasury as a result of taxation may be expended only through appropriation. . . . They can never accomplish the objects for which they were collected unless the power to appropriate is as broad as the power to tax. The necessary implication from the terms of the grant is that the public funds may be appropriated "to provide for the general welfare of the United States." These words cannot be meaningless, else they would not have been used. The conclusion must be that they were intended to limit and define the granted power to raise and to expend money. How shall they be construed to effectuate the intent of the instrument?

Since the foundation of the Nation sharp differences of opinion have persisted as to the true interpretation of the phrase. Madison asserted it amounted to no more than a reference to the other powers enumerated in the subsequent clauses of the same section; that, as the United Sates is a government of limited and enumerated powers, the grant of power to tax and spend for the general national welfare must be confined to the enumerated legislative fields committed to the Congress. In this view the phrase is mere tautology, for taxation and appropriation are or may be necessary incidents of the exercise of any of the enumerated legislative powers. Hamilton, on the other hand, maintained the clause confers a power separate and distinct from those later enumerated, is not restricted in meaning by the grant of them, and Congress consequently has a substantive power to tax and to appropriate, limited only by the requirement that it shall be exercised to provide for the general welfare of the United States. Each contention has had the support of those whose views are entitled to weight. This court has noticed the question, but has never found it necessary to decide which is the true construction. Mr. Justice Story, in his Commentaries, espouses the Hamiltonian position. We shall not review the writings of public men and commentators or discuss the legislative practice. Study of all these leads us to conclude that the reading advocated by Mr. Justice Story is the correct one. While, therefore, the power to tax is not unlimited, its confines are set in the clause which confers it, and not in those of § 8 which bestow and define the legislative powers of the Congress. It results that the power of Congress to authorize expenditure of public moneys for public purposes is not limited by the direct grants of legislative power found in the Constitution.

But the adoption of the broader construction leaves the power to spend subject to limitations. . . . Story says that if the tax be not proposed for the common defence or general welfare, but for other objects wholly extraneous, it would be wholly indefensible upon constitutional principles. And he makes it clear that the powers of taxation and appropriation extend only to matters of national, as distinguished from local welfare. . . .

We are not now required to ascertain the scope of the phrase "general welfare of the United States" or to determine whether an appropriation in aid of agriculture falls within it. Wholly apart from that question, another principle embedded in our Constitution prohibits the enforcement of the Agricultural Adjustment Act. The act invades the reserved rights of the states. It is a statutory plan to regulate and control agricultural production, a matter beyond the powers delegated to the federal government. The tax, the appropriation of the funds raised, and the direction for their disbursement, are but parts of the plan. They are but means to an unconstitutional end.

From the accepted doctrine that the United States is a government of delegated powers, it follows that those not expressly granted, or reasonably to be implied from such as are conferred, are reserved to the states or to the people. To forestall any suggestion to the contrary, the Tenth Amendment was adopted. The same proposition, otherwise stated, is that powers not granted are prohibited. None to regulate agricultural production is given, and therefore legislation by Congress for that purpose is forbidden. . . .

Third. If the taxing power may not be used as the instrument to enforce a regulation of matters of state concern with respect to which the Congress has no authority to interfere, may it, as in the present case, be employed to raise the money necessary to purchase a compliance which the Congress is powerless to command? The Government asserts that whatever might be said against the validity of the plan if compulsory, it is constitutionally sound because the end is accomplished by voluntary co-operation. There are two sufficient answers to the contention. The regulation is not in fact voluntary. The farmer, of course, may refuse to comply, but the price of such refusal is the loss of benefits. The amount offered is intended to be sufficient to exert pressure on him to agree to the proposed regulation. The power to confer or withhold un-limited benefits is the power to coerce or destroy. If the cotton grower elects not to accept the benefits, he will receive less for his crops; those who receive payments will be able to undersell him. The result may well be financial ruin. . . .

But if the plan were one for purely voluntary co-operation it would stand no better so far as federal power is concerned. At best it is a scheme for purchasing with federal funds submission to federal regulation of a subject reserved to the states. . . .

Congress has no power to enforce its commands on the farmer to the ends sought by the Agricultural Adjustment Act. It must follow that it may not indirectly accom-plish those ends by taxing and spending to purchase compliance. The Constitution and the entire plan of our government negative any such use of the power to tax and to spend as the act undertakes to authorize. It does not help to declare that local conditions throughout the nation have created a situation of national concern; for this is but to say that whenever there is a widespread similarity of local conditions, Con-gress may ignore constitutional limitations upon its own powers and usurp those reserved to the states. If, in lieu of compulsory regulation of subjects within the states' reserved jurisdiction, which is prohibited, the Congress could invoke the taxing and spending power as a means to accomplish the same end, clause 1 of § 8 of Article I would become the instrument for total subversion of the governmental powers reserved to the individual states. . . .

Until recently no suggestion of the existence of any such power in the Federal Government has been advanced. The expressions of the framers of the Constitution, the decisions of this court interpreting that instrument, and the writings of great commentators will be searched in vain for any suggestion that there exists in the clause under discussion or elsewhere in the Constitution, the authority whereby every provision and every fair implication from that instrument may be subverted, the inde-pendence of the individual states obliterated, and the United States converted into a central government exercising uncontrolled police power in every state of the Union, superseding all local control or regulation of the affairs or concerns of the states. . . .

The judgment is

Affirmed.

Mr. Justice Stone, dissenting.

I think the judgment should be reversed.

The present stress of widely held and strongly expressed differences of opinion of the wisdom of the Agricultural Adjustment Act makes it important, in the interest of clear thinking and sound result, to emphasize at the outset certain propositions which should have controlling influence in determining the validity of the Act. They are:

1. The power of courts to declare a statute unconstitutional is subject to two guid-ing principles of decision which ought never to be absent from judicial consciousness. One is that courts are concerned only with the power to enact statutes, not with their wisdom. The other is that while unconstitutional exercise of power by the executive and legislative branches of the government is subject to judicial restraint, the only check upon our own exercise of power is our own sense of self-restraint. For the removal of unwise laws from the statute books appeal lies not to the courts but to the ballot and to the processes of democratic government.

2. The constitutional power of Congress to levy an excise tax upon the processing of agricultural products is not questioned. The present levy is held invalid, not for any want of power in Congress to lay such a tax to defray public expenditures, includ-ing those for the general welfare, but because the use to which its proceeds are put is disapproved.

3. As the present depressed state of agriculture is nation wide in its extent and effects, there is no basis for saying that the expenditure of public money in aid of farmers is not within the specifically granted power of Congress to levy taxes to "provide for the . . . general welfare." The opinion of the Court does not declare otherwise. . . .

It is upon the contention that state power is infringed by purchased regulation of agricultural production that chief reliance is placed. It is insisted that, while the Constitution gives to Congress, in specific and unambiguous terms, the power to tax and spend, the power is subject to limitations which do not find their origin in any express provision of the Constitution and to which other expressly delegated powers are not subject.

The Constitution requires that public funds shall be spent for a defined purpose, the promotion of the general welfare. Their expenditure usually involves payment on terms which will insure use by the selected recipients within the limits of the constitutional purpose. Expenditures would fail of their purpose and thus lose their constitutional sanction if the terms of payment were not such that by their influence on the action of the recipients the permitted end would be attained. The power of Congress to spend is inseparable from persuasion to action over which Congress has no legislative control. Congress may not command that the science of agriculture be taught in state universities. But if it would aid the teaching of that science by grants to state institutions, it is appropriate, if not necessary, that the grant be on the condition, incorporated in the Morrill Act, 12 Stat. 503, 26 Stat. 417, that it be used for the intended purpose. Similarly it would seem to be compliance with the Constitution, not violation of it, for the government to take and the university to give a contract that the grant would be so used. It makes no difference that there is a promise to do an act which the condition is calculated to induce. Condition and promise are alike valid since both are in furtherance of the national purpose for which the money is appropriated.

These effects upon individual action, which are but incidents of the authorized expenditure of government money, are pronounced to be themselves a limitation upon the granted power, and so the time-honored principle of constitutional interpretation that the granted power includes all those which are incident to it is reversed. . . .

Such a limitation is contradictory and destructive of the power to appropriate for the public welfare, and is incapable of practical application. The spending power of Congress is in addition to the legislative power and not subordinate to it. This independent grant of the power of the purse, and its very nature, involving in its exercise the duty to insure expenditure within the granted power, presuppose freedom of selection among divers ends and aims, and the capacity to impose such conditions as will render the choice effective. It is a contradiction in terms to say that there is power to spend for the national welfare, while rejecting any power to impose conditions reasonably adapted to the attainment of the end which alone would justify the expenditure.

The limitation now sanctioned must lead to absurd consequences. The government may give seeds to farmers, but may not condition the gift upon their being planted in places where they are most needed or even planted at all. The government may give money to the unemployed, but may not ask that those who get it shall give labor in return, or even use it to support their families. It may give money to sufferers from earthquake, fire, tornado, pestilence or flood, but may not impose conditions—health precautions designed to prevent the spread of disease, or induce the movement of population to safer or more sanitary areas. All that, because it is purchased regulation infringing state powers, must be left for the states, who are unable or unwilling to supply the necessary relief. . . . It may appropriate moneys to be expended by the

Reconstruction Finance Corporation "to aid in financing agriculture, commerce and industry," and to facilitate "the exportation of agricultural and other products." Do all its activities collapse because, in order to effect the permissible purpose, in myriad ways the money is paid out upon terms and conditions which influence action of the recipients within the states, which Congress cannot command? The answer would seem plain. If the expenditure is for a national public purpose, that purpose will not be thwarted because payment is on condition which will advance that purpose. The action which Congress induces by payments of money to promote the general welfare, but which it does not command or coerce, is but an incident to a specifically granted power, but a permissible means to a legitimate end. If appropriation in aid of a program of curtailment of agricultural production is constitutional, and it is not denied that it is, payment to farmers on condition that they reduce their crop acreage is constitutional. It is not any the less so because the farmer at his own option promises to fulfill the condition.

That the governmental power of the purse is a great one is not now for the first time announced. Every student of the history of government and economics is aware of its magnitude and of its existence in every civilized government. Both were well understood by the framers of the Constitution when they sanctioned the grant of the spending power to the federal government, and both were recognized by Hamilton and Story, whose views of the spending power as standing on a parity with the other powers specifically granted, have hitherto been generally accepted. . . .

A tortured construction of the Constitution is not to be justified by recourse to extreme examples of reckless congressional spending which might occur if courts could not prevent—expenditures which, even if they could be thought to effect any national purpose, would be possible only by action of a legislature lost to all sense of public responsibility. Such suppositions are addressed to the mind accustomed to believe that it is the business of courts to sit in judgment on the wisdom of legislative action. Courts are not the only agency of government that must be assumed to have capacity to govern. Congress and the courts both unhappily may falter or be mistaken in the performance of their constitutional duty. But interpretation of our great charter of government which proceeds on any assumption that the responsibility for the preservation of our institutions is the exclusive concern of any one of the three branches of government, or that it alone can save them from destruction is far more likely, in the long run, "to obliterate the constituent members" of "an indestructible union of indestructible states" than the frank recognition that language, even of a constitution, may mean what it says: that the power to tax and spend includes the power to relieve a nationwide economic maladjustment by conditional gifts of money.

Mr. Justice Brandeis and Mr. Justice Cardozo join in this opinion.

Chapter 11

THE COMMERCE POWER

The Congress shall have power . . . to regulate commerce with foreign nations, and among the several states, and with the Indian tribes. . . .
ART. I, SEC. 8, CLAUSE 3

The commerce clause has a deceptive simplicity. It is written in terms of a positive grant of power to Congress, and it does not say what power to regulate commerce, if any, is left to the states. Nor is any definition given for the key words in the clause. Its meaning has had to be derived by experience and judicial interpretation.

Congress was slow to utilize its power under the commerce clause, and for the first century of national existence commerce power problems turned primarily on how far the states could go in regulating commerce without invading the congressional sphere. This was the issue presented in *Gibbons* v. *Ogden,* 9 Wheat. 1 (1824), the first commerce clause decision and one in which Chief Justice Marshall laid down principles that have affected all subsequent interpretation of the constitutional language.

New York State had given a steamboat monopoly to Robert Fulton, the inventor, and his partner, and they had licensed Ogden to engage in navigation in New York. Gibbons was operating a steamboat between New York and New Jersey under a license granted by the federal government. Ogden sought to enjoin Gibbons from using vessels in New York waters. The principles which Marshall developed in his opinion were in fact largely irrelevant to the actual decision, for the Court finally struck down the New York monopoly on a finding of conflict between the state and federal statutes.

The long-run importance of the decision, however, lay in the ruling by Marshall that the congressional power over commerce "may very properly be restricted to that commerce which concerns more States than one." Before long this distinction which Marshall had drawn in flexible form was translated into a rather more dogmatic division between "interstate" and "intrastate" commerce, with federal power limited to the former category.

The clearest case for congressional control over commerce thus occurs where state lines are crossed in a commercial operation. Interstate railroad, motor, aviation, pipeline, navigation, electric, or communications services are obviously subject to congressional control. The Supreme Court has emphasized the unity of interstate transportation. An interstate journey cannot be broken up into the component parts which occur in each state for purposes of avoiding federal control.

Conversely, commercial operations which do not cross state lines have a prima facie claim to escape congressional regulation. This constitutional position came to be of great practical importance toward the end of the nineteenth century when Congress began to make greater use of its regulatory powers. A prosecution of the sugar trust under the Sherman Act of 1890 was defeated in *United States v. E. C. Knight Co.*, 156 U.S. 1 (1895), on the ground that the refining of sugar took place in one state and was a completely separate process from its distribution in interstate commerce. "Commerce succeeds to manufacture, and is not a part of it," the Court said.

Because of this production-distribution distinction, much litigation has been concerned with the precise point at which the local activity ends and interstate transportation begins. In general the rule is that local movement of goods preparatory to their delivery to a common carrier is not part of the interstate journey. In 1947 the Court held that taxi service between Chicago railroad stations was a local activity and not an integral part of interstate commerce. *United States v. Yellow Cab Co.*, 332 U.S. 218.

The point at which commerce loses its interstate or foreign character and comes under state regulatory control has been an equally difficult problem. In *Brown v. Maryland*, 12 Wheat. 419 (1827), Marshall held that goods imported from abroad retained their character as imports as long as they remained unsold in the original package. The effect of the "original package" doctrine has been to prevent states from exerting their police power on goods brought in from other states until after the first sale. However, with liquor and convict-made goods, Congress has waived the protection which interstate commerce status would provide, and has permitted states to adopt police power regulations effective as soon as the goods enter the state, thus making possible state prohibition of the sale of such materials. *Kentucky Whip & Collar Co. v. Illinois Central R.R. Co.*, 299 U.S. 334 (1937).

Congressional power to "regulate" commerce has been construed very broadly to cover not only protection and promotion but also restriction and even complete prohibition. In fact, Congress has on occasions used the commerce power as a kind of national police power. An 1895 statute making it unlawful to transport lottery tickets from state to state was upheld by the Court in *Champion v. Ames*, 188 U.S. 321 (1903), and the same method of exclusion from interstate commerce was successfully used against impure food and drugs, *Hipolite Egg Co. v. United States*, 220 U.S. 45 (1911), and the white slave traffic, *Hoke v. United States*, 227 U.S. 308 (1913).

However, by a five to four vote in *Hammer v. Dagenhart*, 247 U.S. 251 (1918), the Court declared the federal child labor act unconstitutional for its use of the same tactic. The Court sought to explain the inconsistency by arguing that lottery tickets and impure foods were harmful in and of themselves, while goods produced by child labor "are of themselves harmless." The weakness of this argument was obvious from the start, and eventually the *Hammer* decision was overruled.

Congressional power of regulation does not depend entirely upon the test of crossing a state line, however. Commercial transactions taking place within a state may have such an effect on commerce among the states as to justify or require their regulation. The Supreme Court has applied the "effect" doctrine in many situations. For example, where there is a "stream of commerce" moving across state lines, as in the raising of cattle and sending them off to stockyards to be slaughtered for meat, or in the growing, transportation, and distribution of grain, the sales in the stockyards or on the grain exchanges are integral parts of a stream of commerce which are subject to congressional regulation. *Swift & Co. v. United States,* 196 U.S. 375 (1905); *Chicago Board of Trade v. Olsen,* 262 U.S. 1 (1923). Where intrastate freight rates have the effect of burdening commerce moving under interstate rates, then Congress can control the intrastate rates, *Shreveport Rate Case,* 234 U.S. 342 (1914).

The Supreme Court, having once accepted "effect" on commerce as a justification for congressional regulation, was concerned lest this test be carried so far as to wipe out all areas of state control. Consequently it endeavored to find some method for keeping the effect test within bounds. The device developed for this purpose was the "direct-indirect" distinction. A direct effect on commerce could be the basis for federal control, but an indirect effect could not. It was up to the Supreme Court, of course, to decide which effects were direct and which indirect.

Perhaps the two most famous cases in which the Court denied congressional power to regulate because of this test were *Schechter Poultry Corp.* v. *United States,* 295 U.S. 495 (1935), and *Carter* v. *Carter Coal Co.,* 298 U.S. 238 (1936). The *Schechter* decision invalidated the National Recovery Administration, which was a major reliance of the New Deal in its attack on the Depression. Under the statute, codes of fair practice had been promulgated by the President for most of the industries of the country, large and small, fixing minimum wages and maximum hours, and regulating unfair or destructive competitive practices.

In the *Schechter* case the live poultry code had been applied to a Brooklyn slaughtering plant which sold chickens to retail dealers in the vicinity. The Court unanimously held that these activities were not transactions in interstate commerce, nor could it find that they directly affected commerce. Chief Justice Hughes, who wrote the opinion, was not able to define the difference between direct and indirect effects, but he was sure that the distinction was "a fundamental one, essential to the maintenance of our constitutional system."

In the *Carter* case Justice Sutherland attempted to do what Hughes had refrained from doing:

> The word "direct" implies that the activity or condition invoked or blamed shall operate proximately—not mediately, remotely, or collaterally—to produce the effect. It connotes the absence of an efficient intervening agency or condition. And the extent of the effect bears no logical relation to its character. The distinction between a direct and an indirect effect turns, not upon the magnitude of either the cause or the effect, but entirely upon the manner in which the effect has been brought about. If the production by one man of a single ton of coal intended for interstate sale and shipment . . . affects interstate commerce indirectly, the effect does not become direct by multiplying the tonnage, or increasing the number of men employed, or adding to the expense or complexities of the business, or by all combined.

Sutherland's conclusion from this analysis was that, while interstate commerce might be "greatly" affected by the ills which the coal codes were attempting to remedy, it could never be "directly" affected. Coal production was a local activity.

A production crisis in every part of the country simultaneously could never add up to a national problem, with which Congress could deal. Justices Cardozo, Brandeis, and Stone, dissenting, protested against such dogmatic formalism. The commerce power, summed up Cardozo, must be "as broad as the need that evokes it."

A constitutional doctrine which denied Congress the power to deal with national economic emergencies could not long be maintained. In 1937, in the famous case of *National Labor Relations Board* v. *Jones & Laughlin Corp.*, 301 U.S. 1 (1937), the Court upheld the Wagner Act and in the process effectively liquidated directness of effect on commerce as a test of congressional power. In restoring what he called a "practical conception" of interstate commerce, Chief Justice Hughes did not overrule the *Schechter* and *Carter* opinions, but he said as little about them as was feasible.

The *Jones & Laughlin* decision stated such a broad basis for the commerce power that few serious commerce clause questions have subsequently arisen. The Fair Labor Standards Act, legislating minimum wages and maximum hours as conditions for the shipment of goods in interstate commerce, was upheld unanimously in *United States* v. *Darby Lumber Co.*, 312 U.S. 100 (1941). This decision was the occasion for overruling the notorious case of *Hammer* v. *Dagenhart*.

Drastic agricultural regulations were accepted by the Court in *Wickard* v. *Filburn*, 317 U.S. 111 (1942). Here a farmer raising 23 acres of wheat, none of it intended for interstate commerce since all was to be consumed on the farm or fed to stock, was held to have such an effect on interstate commerce as to be liable to marketing quotas fixed under the Agricultural Adjustment Act of 1938. The Sherman Act was held applicable to the insurance business in *United States* v. *South-Eastern Underwriters Assn.*, 322 U.S. 533 (1944), ending an immunity from federal control which had been founded on an 1869 decision. Professional baseball was given an obviously temporary exemption from congressional powers of regulation in *Toolson* v. *New York Yankees*, 346 U.S. 356 (1953), but professional football, professional boxing, and the Schubert theatrical booking interests were all held subsequently to be interstate commerce and subject to the Sherman Act. As a result of the decisions since 1937, it is now clear that, as Cardozo had argued, the commerce power of Congress is "as broad as the need that evokes it."

GIBBONS v. OGDEN
9 Wheat. 1, 6 L. Ed. 23 (1824)

MR. CHIEF JUSTICE MARSHALL delivered the opinion of the court . . . :

The appellant contends that this decree is erroneous, because the laws which purport to give the exclusive privilege it sustains, are repugnant to the constitution and laws of the United States.

They are said to be repugnant—

1st. To that clause in the constitution which authorizes Congress to regulate commerce.

2d. To that which authorizes Congress to promote the progress of science and useful arts. . . .

As preliminary to the very able discussions of the constitution, which we have heard from the bar, and as having some influence on its construction, reference has been made to the political situation of these States, anterior to its formation. It has been said, that they were sovereign, were completely independent, and were connected with each other only by a league. This is true. But, when these allied sovereigns converted their league into a government, when they converted their Congress of Ambassadors, deputed to deliberate on their common concerns, and to recommend measures of general utility, into a Legislature, empowered to enact laws on the most interesting subjects, the whole character in which the States appear, underwent a change, the extent of which must be determined by a fair consideration of the instrument by which that change was effected.

This instrument contains an enumeration of powers expressly granted by the people to their government. It has been said, that these powers ought to be construed strictly. But why ought they to be so construed? Is there one sentence in the constitution which gives countenance to this rule? In the last of the enumerated powers, that which grants, expressly, the means for carrying all others into execution, Congress is authorized "to make all laws which shall be necessary and proper" for the purpose. But this limitation on the means which may be used, is not extended to the powers which are conferred; nor is there one sentence in the constitution, which has been pointed out by the gentlemen of the bar, or which we have been able to discern, that prescribes this rule. We do not, therefore, think ourselves justified in adopting it. What do gentlemen mean, by a strict construction? If they contend only against that enlarged construction, which would extend words beyond their natural and obvious import, we might question the application of the term, but should not controvert the principle. If they contend for that narrow construction which, in support of some theory not to be found in the constitution, would deny to the government those powers which the words of the grant, as usually understood, import, and which are consistent with the general views and objects of the instrument; for that narrow construction, which would cripple the government, and render it unequal to the objects for which it is declared to be instituted, and to which the powers given, as fairly understood, render it competent; then we cannot perceive the propriety of this strict construction, nor adopt it as the rule by which the constitution is to be expounded. As men, whose intentions require no concealment, generally employ the words which most directly and aptly express the ideas they intend to convey, the enlightened patriots who framed our constitution, and the people who adopted it, must be understood to have employed words in their natural sense, and to have intended what they have said. If, from the imperfection of human language, there should be serious doubts respecting the extent of any given power, it is a well settled rule, that the objects for which it was given, especially when those objects are expressed in the instrument itself, should have great influence in the construction. We know of no reason for excluding this rule from the present case. The grant does not convey power which might be beneficial to the grantor, if retained by himself, or which can enure solely to the benefit of the grantee; but is an investment of power for the general advantage, in the hands of agents selected for that purpose; which power can never be exercised by the people themselves, but must be placed in the hands of agents, or lie dormant. We know of no rule for construing the extent of such powers, other than is given by the language of the instrument which confers them, taken in connexion with the purposes for which they were conferred.

The words are, "Congress shall have power to regulate commerce with foreign nations, and among the several States, and with the Indian tribes."

The subject to be regulated is commerce; and our constitution being, as was aptly said at the bar, one of enumeration, and not of definition, to ascertain the extent of the power, it becomes necessary to settle the meaning of the word. The counsel for the appellee would limit it to traffic, to buying and selling, or the interchange of commodities, and do not admit that it comprehends navigation. This would restrict a general term, applicable to many objects, to one of its significations. Commerce, undoubtedly, is traffic, but it is something more: it is intercourse. It describes the commercial intercourse between nations, and parts of nations, in all its branches, and is regulated by prescribing rules for carrying on that intercourse. The mind can scarcely conceive a system for regulating commerce between nations, which shall exclude all laws concerning navigation, which shall be silent on the admission of the vessels of the one nation into the ports of the other, and be confined to prescribing rules for the conduct of individuals, in the actual employment of buying and selling, or of barter.

If commerce does not include navigation, the government of the Union has no direct power over that subject, and can make no law prescribing what shall constitute American vessels, or requiring that they shall be navigated by American seamen. Yet this power has been exercised from the commencement of the government, has been exercised with the consent of all, and has been understood by all to be a commercial regulation. All America understands, and has uniformly understood, the word "commerce," to comprehend navigation. It was so understood, and must have been so understood, when the constitution was framed. The power over commerce, including navigation, was one of the primary objects for which the people of America adopted their government, and must have been contemplated in forming it. The convention must have used the word in that sense, because all have understood it in that sense; and the attempt to restrict it comes too late. . . .

The word used in the constitution, then, comprehends, and has been always understood to comprehend, navigation within its meaning; and a power to regulate navigation, is as expressly granted, as if that term had been added to the word "commerce."

To what commerce does this power extend? The constitution informs us, to commerce "with foreign nations, and among the several States, and with the Indian tribes."

It has, we believe, been universally admitted, that these words comprehend every species of commercial intercourse between the United States and foreign nations. No sort of trade can be carried on between this country and any other, to which this power does not extend. It has been truly said, that commerce, as the word is used in the constitution, is a unit, every part of which is indicated by the term.

If this be the admitted meaning of the word, in its application to foreign nations, it must carry the same meaning throughout the sentence, and remain a unit, unless there be some plain intelligible cause which alters it.

The subject to which the power is next applied, is to commerce "among the several States." The word "among" means intermingled with. A thing which is among others, is intermingled with them. Commerce among the States, cannot stop at the external boundary line of each State, but may be introduced into the interior.

It is not intended to say that these words comprehend that commerce, which is completely internal, which is carried on between man and man in a State, or between different parts of the same State, and which does not extend to or affect other States. Such a power would be inconvenient, and is certainly unnecessary.

Comprehensive as the word "among" is, it may very properly be restricted to that commerce which concerns more States than one. The phrase is not one which would probably have been selected to indicate the completely interior traffic of a State, because it is not an apt phrase for that purpose; and the enumeration of the particular classes of commerce to which the power was to be extended, would not have been made, had the intention been to extend the power to every description. The enumeration presupposes something not enumerated; and that something, if we regard the language or the subject of the sentence, must be the exclusively internal commerce of a State. The genius and character of the whole government seem to be, that its action is to be applied to all the external concerns of the nation, and to those internal concerns which affect the States generally; but not to those which are completely within a particular State, which do not affect other States, and with which it is not necessary to interfere, for the purpose of executing some of the general powers of the government. The completely internal commerce of a State, then, may be considered as reserved for the State itself.

But, in regulating commerce with foreign nations, the power of Congress does not stop at the jurisdictional lines of the several States. It would be a very useless power, if it could not pass those lines. The commerce of the United States with foreign nations, is that of the whole United States. Every district has a right to participate in it. The deep streams which penetrate our country in every direction, pass through the interior of almost every State in the Union, and furnish the means of exercising this right. If Congress has the power to regulate it, that power must be exercised whenever the subject exists. If it exists within the States, if a foreign voyage may commence or terminate at a port within a State, then the power of Congress may be exercised within a State.

This principle is, if possible, still more clear, when applied to commerce "among the several States." They either join each other, in which case they are separated by a mathematical line, or they are remote from each other, in which case other States lie between them. What is commerce "among" them; and how is it to be conducted? Can a trading expedition between two adjoining States, commence and terminate outside of each? And if the trading intercourse be between two States remote from each other, must it not commence in one, terminate in the other, and probably pass through a third? Commerce among the States must, of necessity, be commerce with the States. In the regulation of trade with the Indian tribes, the action of the law, especially when the constitution was made, was chiefly within a State. The power of Congress, then, whatever it may be, must be exercised within the territorial jurisdiction of the several States. . . .

We are now arrived at the inquiry—What is this power?

It is the power to regulate; that is, to prescribe the rule by which commerce is to be governed. This power, like all others vested in Congress, is complete in itself, may be exercised to its utmost extent, and acknowledges no limitations, other than are prescribed in the constitution. These are expressed in plain terms, and do not affect the questions which arise in this case, or which have been discussed at the bar. . . .

The power of Congress, then, comprehends navigation, within the limits of every State in the Union; so far as that navigation may be, in any manner, connected with "commerce with foreign nations, or among the several States, or with the Indian tribes." It may, of consequence, pass the jurisdictional line of New-York, and act upon the very waters to which the prohibition now under consideration applies.

But it has been urged with great earnestness, that, although the power of Congress to regulate commerce with foreign nations, and among the several States, be coextensive with the subject itself, and have no other limits than are prescribed in the constitution, yet the States may severally exercise the same power, within their respective jurisdictions. In support of this argument, it is said, that they possessed it as an inseparable attribute of sovereignty, before the formation of the constitution, and still retain it, except so far as they have surrendered it by that instrument; that this principle results from the nature of the government, and is secured by the tenth amendment; that an affirmative grant of power is not exclusive, unless in its own nature it be such that the continued exercise of it by the former possessor is inconsistent with the grant, and that this is not of that description.

The appellant, conceding these postulates, except the last, contends, that full power to regulate a particular subject implies the whole power, and leaves no residuum; that a grant of the whole is incompatible with the existence of a right in another to any part of it. . . .

Both parties have appealed to the constitution, to legislative acts, and judicial decisions; and have drawn arguments from all these sources, to support and illustrate the propositions they respectively maintain.

The grant of the power to lay and collect taxes is, like the power to regulate commerce, made in general terms, and has never been understood to interfere with the exercise of the same power by the States; and hence has been drawn an argument which has been applied to the question under consideration. But the two grants are not, it is conceived, similar in their terms or their nature. Although many of the powers formerly exercised by the States, are transferred to the government of the Union, yet the State governments remain, and constitute a most important part of our system. The power of taxation is indispensable to their existence, and is a power which, in its own nature, is capable of residing in, and being exercised by, different authorities at the same time. We are accustomed to see it placed, for different purposes, in different hands. Taxation is the simple operation of taking small portions from a perpetually accumulating mass, susceptible of almost infinite division; and a power in one to take what is necessary for certain purposes, is not, in its nature, incompatible with a power in another to take what is necessary for other purposes. Congress is authorized to lay and collect taxes, &c. to pay the debts, and provide for the common defence and general welfare of the United States. This does not interfere with the power of the States to tax for the support of their own governments; nor is the exercise of that power by the States, an exercise of any portion of the power that is granted to the United States. In imposing taxes for State purposes, they are not doing what Congress is empowered to do. Congress is not empowered to tax for those purposes which are within the exclusive province of the States. When, then, each government exercises the power of taxation, neither is exercising the power of the other. But, when a State proceeds to regulate commerce with foreign nations, or among the several States, it is exercising the very power that is granted to Congress, and is doing the very thing which Congress is authorized to do. There is no analogy, then, between the power of taxation and the power of regulating commerce.

In discussing the question, whether this power is still in the States, in the case under consideration, we may dismiss from it the inquiry, whether it is surrendered by the mere grant to Congress, or is retained until Congress shall exercise the power. We may dismiss that inquiry, because it has been exercised, and the regulations which Congress deemed it proper to make, are now in full operation. The sole question is, can a State regulate commerce with foreign nations and among the States, while Congress is regulating it? . . .

The act passed in 1803, prohibiting the importation of slaves into any State which shall itself prohibit their importation, implies, it is said, an admission that the States possessed the power to exclude or admit them; from which it is inferred, that they possess the same power with respect to other articles.

If this inference were correct; if this power was exercised, not under any particular clause in the constitution, but in virtue of a general right over the subject of commerce, to exist as long as the constitution itself, it might now be exercised. Any State might now import African slaves into its own territory. But it is obvious, that the power of the States over this subject, previous to the year 1808, constitutes an exception to the power of Congress to regulate commerce, and the exception is expressed in such words, as to manifest clearly the intention to continue the pre-existing right of the States to admit or exclude, for a limited period. The words are, "the migration or importation of such persons as any of the States, now existing, *shall* think proper to admit, shall not be prohibited by the Congress prior to the year 1808." The whole object of the exception is, to preserve the power to those States which might be disposed to exercise it; and its language seems to the Court to convey this idea unequivocally. The possession of this particular power, then, during the time limited in the constitution, cannot be admitted to prove the possession of any other similar power.

It has been said, that the act of August 7, 1789, acknowledges a concurrent power in the States to regulate the conduct of pilots, and hence is inferred an admission of their concurrent right with Congress to regulate commerce with foreign nations, and amongst the States. But this inference is not, we think, justified by the fact.

Although Congress cannot enable a State to legislate, Congress may adopt the provisions of a State on any subject. When the government of the Union was brought into existence, it found a system for the regulation of its pilots in full force in every State. The act which has been mentioned, adopts this system, and gives it the same validity as if its provisions had been specially made by Congress. But the act, it may be said, is prospective also, and the adoption of laws to be made in future, presupposes the right in the maker to legislate on the subject.

The act unquestionably manifests an intention to leave this subject entirely to the States, until Congress should think proper to interpose; but the very enactment of such a law indicates an opinion that it was necessary; that the existing system would not be applicable to the new state of things, unless expressly applied to it by Congress. . . .

These acts were cited at the bar for the purpose of showing an opinion in Congress, that the States possess, concurrently with the Legislature of the Union, the power to regulate commerce with foreign nations and among the States. Upon reviewing them, we think they do not establish the proposition they were intended to prove. They show the opinion, that the States retain powers enabling them to pass the laws to which allusion has been made, not that those laws proceed from the particular power which has been delegated to Congress.

It has been contended by the counsel for the appellant, that, as the word "to regulate" implies in its nature, full power over the thing to be regulated, it excludes, necessarily, the action of all others that would perform the same operation on the same thing. That regulation is designed for the entire result, applying to those parts which remain as they were, as well as to those which are altered. It produces a uniform whole, which is as much disturbed and deranged by changing what the regulating power designs to leave untouched, as that on which it has operated.

There is great force in this argument, and the Court is not satisfied that it has been refuted.

Since, however, in exercising the power of regulating their own purely internal affairs, whether of trading or police, the States may sometimes enact laws, the validity of which depends on their interfering with, and being contrary to, an act of Congress passed in pursuance of the constitution, the Court will enter upon the inquiry, whether the laws of New-York, as expounded by the highest tribunal of that State, have, in their application to this case, come into collision with an act of Congress, and deprived a citizen of a right to which that act entitles him. Should this collision exist, it will be immaterial whether those laws were passed in virtue of a concurrent power "to regulate commerce with foreign nations and among the several States," or, in virtue of a power to regulate their domestic trade and police. In one case and the other, the acts of New-York must yield to the law of Congress; and the decision sustaining the privilege they confer, against a right given by a law of the Union, must be erroneous. . . .

The questions . . . whether the conveyance of passengers be a part of the coasting trade, and whether a vessel can be protected in that occupation by a coasting license, are not, and cannot be, raised in this case. The real and sole question seems to be, whether a steam machine, in actual use, deprives a vessel of the privileges conferred by a license.

In considering this question, the first idea which presents itself, is, that the laws of Congress for the regulation of commerce, do not look to the principle by which vessels are moved. That subject is left entirely to individual discretion; and, in that vast and complex system of legislative enactment concerning it, which embraces every thing that the Legislature thought it necessary to notice, there is not, we believe, one word respecting the peculiar principle by which vessels are propelled through the water, except what may be found in a single act, granting a particular privilege to steam boats. With this exception, every act, either prescribing duties, or granting privileges, applies to every vessel, whether navigated by the instrumentality of wind or fire, of sails or machinery. The whole weight of proof, then, is thrown upon him who would introduce a distinction to which the words of the law give no countenance.

If a real difference could be admitted to exist between vessels carrying passengers and others, it has already been observed, that there is no fact in this case which can bring up that question. And, if the occupation of steam boats be a matter of such general notoriety, that the Court may be presumed to know it, although not specially informed by the record, then we deny that the transportation of passengers is their exclusive occupation. It is a matter of general history, that, in our western waters, their principal employment is the transportation of merchandise; and all know, that in the waters of the Atlantic they are frequently so employed.

But all inquiry into this subject seems to the Court to be put completely at rest, by the act already mentioned, entitled, "An act for the enrolling and licensing of steam boats."

This act authorizes a steam boat employed, or intended to be employed, only in a river or bay of the United States, owned wholly or in part by an alien, resident within the United States, to be enrolled and licensed as if the same belonged to a citizen of the United States.

This act demonstrates the opinion of Congress, that steam boats may be enrolled and licensed, in common with vessels using sails. They are, of course, entitled to the same privileges, and can no more be restrained from navigating waters, and entering ports which are free to such vessels, than if they were wafted on their voyage by the winds, instead of being propelled by the agency of fire. The one element may be as legitimately used as the other, for every commercial purpose authorized by the laws of the Union; and the act of a State inhibiting the use of either to any vessel having a license under the act of Congress, comes, we think, in direct collision with that act.

As this decides the cause, it is unnecessary to enter in an examination of that part of the constitution which empowers Congress to promote the progress of science and the useful arts. . . .

MR. JUSTICE JOHNSON. The judgment entered by the Court in this cause, has my entire approbation; but having adopted my conclusions on views of the subject materially different from those of my brethren, I feel it incumbent on me to exhibit those views. I have, also, another inducement: in questions of great importance and great delicacy, I feel my duty to the public best discharged, by an effort to maintain my opinions in my own way. . . .

. . . The power of a sovereign state over commerce . . . amounts to nothing more than a power to limit and restrain it at pleasure. And since the power to prescribe the limits to its freedom, necessarily implies the power to determine what shall remain unrestrained, it follows, that the power must be exclusive; it can reside but in one potentate; and hence, the grant of this power carries with it the whole subject, leaving nothing for the State to act upon. . . .

It is impossible, with the views which I entertain of the principle on which the commercial privileges of the people of the United States, among themselves, rests, to concur in the view which this Court takes of the effect of the coasting license in this cause. I do not regard it as the foundation of the right set up in behalf of the appellant. If there was any one object riding over every other in the adoption of the constitution, it was to keep the commercial intercourse among the States free from all invidious and partial restraints. And I cannot overcome the conviction, that if the licensing act was repealed to-morrow, the rights of the appellant to a reversal of the decision complained of, would be as strong as it is under this license. . . .

NATIONAL LABOR RELATIONS BOARD v. JONES & LAUGHLIN STEEL CORP.
301 U.S. 1, 57 S. Ct. 615, 81 L. Ed. 893 (1937)

The National Labor Relations Act of 1935, better known as the Wagner Act, sought to protect the rights of employees to organize into labor unions, and to bargain collectively with their employers. The statute defined certain types of interference with these rights as unfair labor practices and set up the National Labor Relations Board with authority to compel employers to cease and desist from such practices. The Jones & Laughlin Steel Corporation was charged with unfair labor practices involving discrimination against members of the union in hiring and tenure of employment, and coercion and intimidation of employees in order to interfere with their self-organization. The NLRB sustained the charges and ordered the company to cease and desist from such practices, to reinstate ten discharged employees with back pay, and to post notices that the company would not discharge these union members or discriminate against them. The company failed to comply and the board applied to the courts for enforcement of its order.

Along with the *Jones & Laughlin* decision, the Court also upheld the Wagner Act in two other cases on the same day, *NLRB v. Fruehauf Trailer Co.,* 301 U.S. 49, and *NLRB v. Friedman-Harry Marks Clothing Co.,* 301 U.S. 58. The dissent discusses all three cases.

Mr. Chief Justice Hughes delivered the opinion of the Court.

In a proceeding under the National Labor Relations Act of 1935, the National Labor Relations Board found that the respondent, Jones & Laughlin Steel Corporation, had violated the Act by engaging in unfair labor practices affecting commerce. . . .

Contesting the ruling of the Board, the respondent argues (1) that the Act is in reality a regulation of labor relations and not of interstate commerce; (2) that the Act can have no application to the respondent's relations with its production employees because they are not subject to regulation by the federal government; and (3) that the provisions of the Act violate § 2 of Article III and the Fifth and Seventh Amendments of the Constitution of the United States.

The facts as to the nature and scope of the business of the Jones & Laughlin Steel Corporation have been found by the Labor Board and, so far as they are essential to the determination of this controversy, they are not in dispute. The Labor Board has found: The corporation is organized under the laws of Pennsylvania and has its principal office at Pittsburgh. It is engaged in the business of manufacturing iron and steel in plants situated in Pittsburgh and nearby Aliquippa, Pennsylvania. It manufactures and distributes a widely diversified line of steel and pig iron, being the fourth largest producer of steel in the United States. With its subsidiaries—nineteen in number—it is a completely integrated enterprise, owning and operating ore, coal and limestone properties, lake and river transportation facilities and terminal railroads located at its manufacturing plants. It owns or controls mines in Michigan and Minnesota. It operates four ore steamships on the Great Lakes, used in the transportation of ore to its factories. It owns coal mines in Pennsylvania. It operates towboats and steam barges used in carrying coal to its factories. It owns limestone properties in various places in Pennsylvania and West Virginia. It owns the Monongahela connecting railroad which connects the plants of the Pittsburgh works and forms an interconnection with the Pennsylvania, New York Central and Baltimore and Ohio Railroad systems. It owns the Aliquippa and Southern Railroad Company which connects the Aliquippa works with the Pittsburgh and Lake Erie, part of the New York Central system. Much of its product is shipped to its warehouses in Chicago, Detroit, Cincinnati and Memphis,—to the last two places by means of its own barges and transportation equipment. In Long Island City, New York, and in New Orleans it operates structural steel fabricating shops in connection with the warehousing of semi-finished materials sent from its works. Through one of its wholly-owned subsidiaries it owns, leases and operates stores, warehouses and yards for the distribution of equipment and supplies for drilling and operating oil and gas wells and for pipe lines, refineries and pumping stations. It has sales offices in twenty cities in the United States and a wholly-owned subsidiary which is devoted exclusively to distributing its product in Canada. Approximately 75 per cent. of its product is shipped out of Pennsylvania.

Summarizing these operations, the Labor Board concluded that the works in Pittsburgh and Aliquippa "might be likened to the heart of a self-contained, highly integrated body. They draw in the raw materials from Michigan, Minnesota, West Virginia, Pennsylvania in part through arteries and by means controlled by the respondent; they transform the materials and then pump them out to all parts of the nation through the vast mechanism which the respondent has elaborated." . . .

First. The scope of the Act.—The Act is challenged in its entirety as an attempt to regulate all industry, thus invading the reserved powers of the States over their local concerns. It is asserted that the references in the Act to interstate and foreign commerce are colorable at best; that the Act is not a true regulation of such commerce or of matters which directly affect it but on the contrary has the fundamental object of placing under the compulsory supervision of the federal government all industrial labor relations within the nation. The argument seeks support in the broad words of the preamble (section one) and in the sweep of the provisions of the Act, and it is further insisted that its legislative history shows an essential universal purpose in the light of which its scope cannot be limited by either construction or by the application of the separability clause.

If this conception of terms, intent and consequent inseparability were sound, the Act would necessarily fall by reason of the limitation upon the federal power which inheres in the constitutional grant, as well as because of the explicit reservation of the Tenth Amendment. *Schechter Corp.* v. *United States.* . . . The authority of the federal government may not be pushed to such an extreme as to destroy the distinction, which the commerce clause itself establishes, between commerce "among the several States" and the internal concerns of a State. That distinction between what is national and what is local in the activities of commerce is vital to the maintenance of our federal system. . . .

The critical words of this provision, prescribing the limits of the Board's authority in dealing with the labor practices, are "affecting commerce." . . . The Act defines the term "affecting commerce" (§ 2 (7)):

"The term 'affecting commerce' means in commerce, or burdening or obstructing commerce or the free flow of commerce, or having led or tending to lead to a labor dispute burdening or obstructing commerce or the free flow of commerce."

This definition is one of exclusion as well as inclusion. The grant of authority to the Board does not purport to extend to the relationship between all industrial employees and employers. Its terms do not impose collective bargaining upon all industry regardless of effects upon interstate or foreign commerce. It purports to reach only what may be deemed to burden or obstruct that commerce and, thus qualified, it must be construed as contemplating the exercise of control within constitutional bounds. It is a familiar principle that acts which directly burden or obstruct interstate or foreign commerce, or its free flow, are within the reach of the congressional power. . . . Whether or not particular action does affect commerce in such a close and intimate fashion as to be subject to federal control, and hence to lie within the authority conferred upon the Board, is left by the statute to be determined as individual cases arise. We are thus to inquire whether in the instant case the constitutional boundary has been passed.

Second. The unfair labor practices in question.—The unfair labor practices found by the Board are those defined in § 8, subdivisions (1) and (3). These provide:

Sec. 8. It shall be an unfair labor practice for an employer—

"(1) To interfere with, restrain, or coerce employees in the exercise of the rights guaranteed in section 7."

"(3) By discrimination in regard to hire or tenure of employment or any term or condition of employment to encourage or discourage membership in any labor organization: . . ."

Section 8, subdivision (1), refers to § 7, which is as follows:

"Sec. 7. Employees shall have the right to self-organization, to form, join, or assist labor organizations, to bargain collectively through representatives of their own choosing, and to engage in concerted activities, for the purpose of collective bargaining or other mutual aid or protection."

Thus, in its present application, the statute goes no further than to safeguard the right of employees to self-organization and to select representatives of their own choosing for collective bargaining or other mutual protection without restraint or coercion by their employer.

That is a fundamental right. Employees have as clear a right to organize and select their representatives for lawful purposes as the respondent has to organize its business and select its own officers and agents. Discrimination and coercion to prevent the free exercise of the right of employees to self-organization and representation is a proper subject for condemnation by competent legislative authority. Long ago we stated the reason for labor organizations. We said that they were organized out of the necessities of the situation; that a single employee was helpless in dealing with an employer; that he was dependent ordinarily on his daily wage for the maintenance of himself and family; that if the employer refused to pay him the wages that he thought fair, he was nevertheless unable to leave the employ and resist arbitrary and unfair treatment; that union was essential to give laborers opportunity to deal on an equality with their employer. . . . Fully recognizing the legality of collective action on the part of employees in order to safeguard their proper interests, we said that Congress was not required to ignore this right but could safeguard it. Congress could seek to make appropriate collective action of employees an instrument of peace rather than of strife.

We said that such collective action would be a mockery if representation were made futile by interference with freedom of choice. Hence the prohibition by Congress of interference with the selection of representatives for the purpose of negotiation and conference between employers and employees, "instead of being an invasion of the constitutional right of either, was based on the recognition of the rights of both." . . .

Third. The application of the Act to employees engaged in production.—The principle involved.—Respondent says that whatever may be said of employees engaged in interstate commerce, the industrial relations and activities in the manufacturing department of respondent's enterprise are not subject to federal regulation. The argument rests upon the proposition that manufacturing in itself is not commerce. [Citing cases.]

The Government distinguishes these cases. The various parts of respondent's enterprise are described as interdependent and as thus involving "a great movement of iron ore, coal and limestone along well-defined paths to the steel mills, thence through them, and thence in the form of steel products into the consuming centers of the country—a definite and well-understood course of business." It is urged that these activities constitute a "stream" or "flow" of commerce, of which the Aliquippa manufacturing plant is the focal point, and that industrial strife at that point would cripple the entire movement. Reference is made to our decision sustaining the Packers and Stockyards Act. *Stafford* v. *Wallace, 258* U.S. *495.* The Court found that the stockyards were but a "throat" through which the current of commerce flowed and the transactions which there occurred could not be separated from that movement. . . . Applying the doctrine of *Stafford* v. *Wallace* . . . the Court sustained the Grain Futures Act of 1922 with respect to transactions on the Chicago Board of Trade, although these transactions were "not in and of themselves interstate commerce." Congress had found that they had become "a constantly recurring burden and obstruction to that commerce." *Chicago Board of Trade* v. *Olsen, 262* U.S. *1, 32.* . . .

Respondent contends that the instant case presents material distinctions. Respondent says that the Aliquippa plan is extensive in size and represents a large investment in buildings, machinery and equipment. The raw materials which are brought to the plant are delayed for long periods and, after being subjected to manufacturing processes, "are changed substantially as to character, utility and value." . . .

We do not find it necessary to determine whether these features of defendant's business dispose of the asserted analogy to the "stream of commerce" cases. The instances in which that metaphor has been used are but particular, and not exclusive, illustrations of the protective power which the Government invokes in support of the present Act. The congressional authority to protect interstate commerce from burdens and obstructions is not limited to transactions which can be deemed to be an essential part of a "flow" of interstate or foreign commerce. Burdens and obstructions may be due to injurious action springing from other sources. The fundamental principle is that the power to regulate commerce is the power to enact "all appropriate legislation" for "its protection and advancement" . . . ; to adopt measures "to promote its growth and insure its safety" . . . ; "to foster, protect, control and restrain." . . . That power is plenary and may be exerted to protect interstate commerce "no matter what the source of the dangers which threaten it." . . . Although activities may be intrastate in character when separately considered, if they have such a close and substantial relation to interstate commerce that their control is essential or appropriate to protect that commerce from burdens and obstructions, Congress cannot be denied the power to exercise that control. . . . Undoubtedly the scope of this power must be considered in the light of our dual system of government and may not be extended so as to embrace effects upon interstate commerce so indirect and remote that to embrace them, in view of our complex society, would effectually obliterate the distinction between what is national and what is local and create a completely centralized government. . . . The question is necessarily one of degree. . . .

The close and intimate effect which brings the subject within the reach of federal power may be due to activities in relation to productive industry although the industry when separately viewed is local. . . .

It is thus apparent that the fact that the employees here concerned were engaged in production is not determinative. The question remains as to the effect upon interstate commerce of the labor practice involved. In the *Schechter* case, *supra*, we found that the effect there was so remote as to be beyond the federal power. To find "immediacy or directness" there was to find it "almost everywhere," a result inconsistent with the maintenance of our federal system. In the *Carter* case . . . the Court was of the opinion that the provisions of the statute relating to production were invalid upon several grounds,—that there was improper delegation of legislative power, and that the requirements not only went beyond any sustainable measure of protection of interstate commerce but were also inconsistent with due process. These cases are not controlling here.

Fourth. Effects of the unfair labor practice in respondent's enterprise.—Giving full weight to respondent's contention with respect to a break in the complete continuity of the "stream of commerce" by reason of respondent's manufacturing operations, the fact remains that the stoppage of those operations by industrial strife would have a most serious effect upon interstate commerce. In view of respondent's far-flung activities, it is idle to say that the effect would be indirect or remote. It is obvious that it would be immediate and might be catastrophic. We are asked to shut our eyes to the plainest facts of our national life and to deal with the question of direct and indirect effects in an intellectual vacuum. Because there may be but indirect and remote effects upon interstate commerce in connection with a host of local enterprises throughout the country, it does not follow that other industrial activities do not have such a close and intimate relation to interstate commerce as to make the presence of industrial strife a matter of the most urgent national concern. When industries organize themselves on a national scale, making their relation to interstate commerce the dominant factor in their activities, how can it be maintained that their industrial labor relations constitute a forbidden field into which Congress may not enter when it is necessary to protect interstate commerce from the paralyzing consequences of industrial war? We have often said that interstate commerce itself is a practical conception. It is equally true that interferences with that commerce must be appraised by a judgment that does not ignore actual experience.

Experience has abundantly demonstrated that the recognition of the right of employees to self-organization and to have representatives of their own choosing for the purpose of collective bargaining is often an essential condition of industrial peace. Refusal to confer and negotiate has been one of the most prolific causes of strife. This is such an outstanding fact in the history of labor disturbances that it is a proper subject of judicial notice and requires no citation of instances. . . .

. . . The steel industry is one of the great basic industries of the United States, with ramifying activities affecting interstate commerce at every point. The Government aptly refers to the steel strike of 1919–1920 with its far-reaching consequences. The fact that there appears to have been no major disturbance in that industry in the more recent period did not dispose of the possibilities of future and like dangers to interstate commerce which Congress was entitled to foresee and to exercise its protective power to forestall. It is not necessary again to detail the facts as to respondent's enterprise. Instead of being beyond the pale, we think that it presents in a most striking way the close and intimate relation which a manufacturing industry may have to interstate commerce and we have no doubt that Congress had constitutional authority to safeguard the right of respondent's employees to self-organization and freedom in the choice of representatives for collective bargaining.

Fifth. The means which the Act employs.—Questions under the due process clause and other constitutional restrictions.—Respondent asserts its right to conduct its business in an orderly manner without being subjected to arbitrary restraints. What we have said points to the fallacy in the argument. Employees have their correlative right to organize for the purpose of securing the redress of grievances and to promote agreements with employers relating to rates of pay and conditions of work. . . . Restraint for the purpose of preventing an unjust interference with that right cannot be considered arbitrary or capricious. . . .

The Act does not compel agreements between employers and employees. It does not compel any agreement whatever. It does not prevent the employer "from refusing to make a collective contract and hiring individuals on whatever terms" the employer "may by unilateral action determine." The Act expressly provides in § 9 (a) that any individual employee or a group of employees shall have the right at any time to present grievances to their employer. The theory of the Act is that free opportunity for negotiation with accredited representatives of employees is likely to promote industrial peace and may bring about the adjustments and agreements which the Act in itself does not attempt to compel. . . . The Act does not interfere with the normal exercise of the right of the employer to select its employees or to discharge them. The employer may not, under cover of that right, intimidate or coerce its employees with respect to their self-organization and representation, and, on the other hand, the Board is not entitled to make its authority a pretext for interference with the right of discharge when that right is exercised for other reasons than such intimidation and coercion. The true purpose is the subject of investigation with full opportunity to show the facts. It would seem that when employers freely recognize the right of their employees to their own organizations and their unrestricted right of representation there will be much less occasion for controversy in respect to the free and appropriate exercise of the right of selection and discharge.

The Act has been criticised as one-sided in its application; that it subjects the employer to supervision and restraint and leaves untouched the abuses for which employees may be responsible; that it fails to provide a more comprehensive plan,— with better assurances of fairness to both sides and with increased chances of success in bringing about, if not compelling, equitable solutions of industrial disputes affecting interstate commerce. But we are dealing with the power of Congress, not with a particular policy or with the extent to which policy should go. We have frequently said that the legislative authority, exerted within its proper field, need not embrace all the evils within its reach. The Constitution does not forbid "cautious advance, step by step," in dealing with the evils which are exhibited in activities within the range of legislative power. . . . The question in such cases is whether the legislature, in what it does prescribe, has gone beyond constitutional limits. . . .

Our conclusion is that the order of the Board was within its competency and that the Act is valid as here applied. . . .

Reversed.

Mr. Justice McReynolds delivered the following dissenting opinion in the cases preceding:

Mr. Justice Van Devanter, Mr. Justice Sutherland, Mr. Justice Butler and I are unable to agree with the decisions just announced. . . .

Considering the far-reaching import of these decisions, the departure from what we understand has been consistently ruled here, and the extraordinary power confirmed to a Board of three, the obligation to present our views becomes plain.

The Court, as we think, departs from well-established principles followed in *Schechter Corp.* v. *United States* . . . and *Carter* v. *Carter Coal Co.* . . . Upon the authority of these decisions, the Circuit Courts of Appeals of the Fifth, Sixth and Second Circuits in the causes now before us have held the power of Congress under the commerce clause does not extend to relations between employers and their employees engaged in manufacture, and therefore the Act conferred upon the National Labor Relations Board no authority in respect of matters covered by the questioned orders. . . . The Circuit Court of Appeals, Fourth Circuit, held the Act inapplicable to manufacture and expressed the view that if so extended it would be invalid. Six district courts, on the authority of *Schechter's* and *Carter's* cases, have held that the Board has no authority to regulate relations between employers and employees engaged in local production. No decision or judicial opinion to the contrary has been cited, and we find none. Every consideration brought forward to uphold the Act before us was applicable to support the Acts held unconstitutional in causes decided within two years. And the lower courts rightly deemed them controlling. . . .

Respondent in No. 419 is a large, integrated manufacturer of iron and steel products—the fourth largest in the United States. . . . So far as they relate to essential principles presently important, the activities of this Corporation, while large, do not differ materially from those of the other respondents and very many small producers and distributors. It has attained great size; occupies an important place in business; owns and operates mines of ore, coal, and lime-stone outside Pennsylvania, the output of which, with other raw material, moves to the production plants. At the plants this movement ends. Having come to rest this material remains in warehouses, storage yards, etc., often for months, until the process of manufacture begins. After this has been completed, the finished products go into interstate commerce. The discharged employees labored only in the manufacturing department. They took no part in the transportation to or away from the plant; nor did they participate in any activity which preceded or followed manufacture.

Our concern is with those activities which are common to the three enterprises. Such circumstances as are merely fortuitous—size, character of products, etc.—may be put on one side. The wide sweep of the statute will more readily appear if consideration be given to the Board's proceedings against the smallest and relatively least important—the Clothing Company. If the Act applies to the relations of that Company to employees in production, of course it applies to the larger respondents with like business elements although the affairs of the latter may present other characteristics. Though differing in some respects, all respondents procure raw materials outside the state where they manufacture, fabricate within and then ship beyond the state.

In Nos. 420–21 the respondent, Michigan corporation, manufactures commercial trailers for automobiles from raw materials brought from outside that state, and thereafter sells these in many states. It has a single manufacturing plant at Detroit and annual receipts around $3,000,000; 900 people are employed.

In Nos. 422–23 the respondent is a Virginia corporation engaged in manufacturing and distributing men's clothing. It has a single plant and chief office at Richmond, annual business amounting perhaps to $2,000,000, employs 800, brings in almost all raw material from other states and ships the output in interstate commerce. There are some 3,300 similar plants for manufacturing clothing in the United States, which together employ 150,000 persons and annually put out products worth $800,000,000.

The Clothing Company is a typical small manufacturing concern which produces less than one-half of one per cent of the men's clothing produced in the United States and employs 800 of the 150,000 workmen engaged therein. If closed today, the ultimate effect on commerce in clothing obviously would be negligible. It stands alone, is not seeking to acquire a monopoly or to restrain trade. There is no evidence of a strike by its employees at any time or that one is now threatened, and nothing to indicate the probable result if one should occur. . . .

The precise question for us to determine is whether in the circumstances disclosed Congress has power to authorize what the Labor Board commanded the respondents to do. Stated otherwise, in the circumstances here existing could Congress by statute direct what the Board has ordered? . . .

A relatively small concern caused raw material to be shipped to its plant at Richmond, Virginia, converted this into clothing, and thereafter shipped the product to points outside the state. A labor union sought members among the employees at the plant and obtained some. The Company's management opposed this effort, and in order to discourage it discharged eight who had become members. The business of the Company is so small that to close its factory would have no direct or material effect upon the volume of interstate commerce in clothing. The number of operatives who joined the union is not disclosed; the wishes of other employees are not shown; probability of a strike is not found.

The argument in support of the Board affirms: "Thus the validity of any specific application of the preventive measures of this Act depends upon whether industrial strife resulting from the practices in the particular enterprise under consideration would be of the character which Federal power could control if it occurred. If strife in that enterprise could be controlled, certainly it could be prevented."

Manifestly that view of Congressional power would extend it into almost every field of human industry. . . .

We are told that Congress may protect the "stream of commerce" and that one who buys raw material without the state, manufactures it therein, and ships the output to another state is in that stream. Therefore it is said he may be prevented from doing anything which may interfere with its flow.

This, too, goes beyond the constitutional limitations heretofore enforced. If a man raises cattle and regularly delivers them to a carrier for interstate shipment, may Congress prescribe the conditions under which he may employ or discharge helpers on the ranch? The products of a mine pass daily into interstate commerce; many things are brought to it from other states. Are the owners and the miners within the power of Congress in respect of the miners' tenure and discharge? May a mill owner be prohibited from closing his factory or discontinuing his business because so to do would stop the flow of products to and from his plant in interstate commerce? May employees in a factory be restrained from quitting work in a body because this will close the factory and thereby stop the flow of commerce? May arson of a factory be made a Federal offense whenever this would interfere with such flow? If the business cannot continue with the existing wage scale, may Congress command a reduction? If the ruling of the Court just announced is adhered to these questions suggest some of the problems certain to arise. . . .

There is no ground on which reasonably to hold that refusal by a manufacturer, whose raw materials come from states other than that of his factory and whose products are regularly carried to other states, to bargain collectively with employees in his manufacturing plant, directly affects interstate commerce. In such business, there is not one but two distinct movements or streams in interstate transportation. The first brings in raw material and there ends. Then follows manufacture, a separate and local activity. Upon completion of this, and not before, the second distinct movement or stream in interstate commerce begins and the products go to other states. Such is the common course for small as well as large industries. It is unreasonable and unprecedented to say the commerce clause confers upon Congress power to govern relations between employers and employees in these local activities. . . .

The right to contract is fundamental and includes the privilege of selecting those with whom one is willing to assume contractual relations. This right is unduly abridged by the Act now upheld. A private owner is deprived of power to manage his own property by freely selecting those to whom his manufacturing operations are to be entrusted. We think this cannot lawfully be done in circumstances like those here disclosed.

It seems clear to us that Congress has transcended the powers granted.

Chapter 12

THE STATES AND COMMERCE

The legislatures of the states are continually passing statutes which, intentionally or not, assert regulatory powers over commerce among the states. Ever since *Gibbons* v. *Ogden* was decided in 1824, the Supreme Court has been deciding whether such state laws are in unconstitutional conflict with the congressional commerce power. In addition to *Gibbons*, Marshall decided two other cases where this issue was present. In *Brown* v. *Maryland*, 12 Wheat. 419 (1827), the state had levied a rather heavy license tax on importers of foreign articles and had forbidden them to sell the goods they imported until they paid the tax. In *Willson* v. *Black-Bird Creek Marsh Co.*, 2 Pet. 245 (1829), a dam built across a navigable creek under authority of a Delaware law had been broken by a vessel. When the owners of the dam brought an action of trespass against the owner of the vessel, he defended on the ground that the creek was a navigable highway which had been unlawfully obstructed by the dam.

In deciding these and the hundreds of similar conflicts that have subsequently arisen, the Court has a dual problem. It has to make a decision in each case which in the light of the particular circumstances will constitute a practical adjustment of the competing interests at stake. But, second, it has to make these practical adjustments on the basis of some consistent constitutional theory about the nature of federal-state relations under the commerce clause. The Court has on various occasions considered four such theories, ultimately rejecting all but one.

One theory was discussed and decisively rejected by Marshall in the *Gibbons* case. This was the notion of "concurrent power," which held that both federal and state governments had the power to regulate commerce, just as they both had the power to tax. Marshall had no trouble in demonstrating that any such arrangement would be completely unworkable, since dual regulations in the same fields were bound to conflict.

In *Gibbons* Marshall also considered a second theory, that of "dormant power," which would have protected and magnified federal power by holding that the mere grant of commerce power to Congress, even though unexercised and dormant, prevented the states from any regulation of commerce. Marshall avoided any consideration of this drastic position in *Gibbons* as pointless, since federal regulations had in fact been adopted there. In the *Black-Bird* case there were no federal regulations, but again Marshall avoided the issue by quibbling that the state power under which the creek had been dammed was the police power rather than the commerce power. The validity of the dormant power theory was finally, but temporarily, asserted by a Court majority in *The Passenger Cases,* 7 How. 283 (1849), and then abandoned three years later.

A third theory was the one which Marshall had seemed to favor in *Gibbons,* that of "mutual exclusiveness." According to this view, Congress and the states each had areas which they could regulate and from which the other was excluded. The states, for example, had responsibility for inspection, quarantine or health laws, and over turnpikes, ferries, and "internal commerce" generally. But Marshall failed to make the division in any rigorous way, and the decision in *Gibbons* did not actually turn on this distinction.

It was not until 1852, in the great case of *Cooley v. Port Wardens of Phila-delphia,* 12 How. 299, that the Court was able to settle on what proved to be a viable theoretical foundation, "selective exclusiveness." A state act of 1803 had provided that ships coming into the port of Philadelphia from abroad or leaving for foreign ports must engage a local pilot. Failure to do so would result in a fine equal to half the cost of pilotage, payable to the board of wardens of the port for a fund for superannuated pilots. By statute of 1789 Congress had in effect adopted all then existing state harbor regulations, and provided that pilots should continue to be regulated in conformity with state laws subsequently enacted, pending further legislation by Congress.

The Supreme Court upheld the state law, grounding its decision on the very practical observation that the subjects of regulation under the commerce power were "exceedingly various" and "quite unlike in their nature." Consequently the rules by which they were regulated had to be similarly adaptable. Whereas "some imperatively demand . . . a single uniform rule, operating equally on the commerce of the United States in every port," others "as imperatively demand . . . that diversity, which alone can meet the local necessities."

This analysis clearly doomed the rigidities of the dormant power theory. Congressional power over commerce would be exclusive in some circumstances, but it depended on the circumstances. As Justice Curtis said, in the key sentences of the decision:

> Either absolutely to affirm, or deny that the nature of this power requires exclusive legislation by congress, is to lose sight of the nature of the subjects of this power, and to assert concerning all of them, what is really applicable but to a part. Whatever subjects of this power are in their nature national, or admit only of one uniform system, or plan of regulation, may justly be said to be of such a nature as to require exclusive legislation by congress.

Subjects lacking in these characteristics, by the same token, were not within the exclusive power of Congress. Pilotage laws, Curtis concluded, were in this latter category.

> The Act of 1789 contains a clear and authoritative declaration by the first congress, that the nature of this subject is such, that until congress should find it necessary to exert its power, it should be left to the legislation of the States; that it is local and not national; that it is likely to be best provided for, not by one system, or plan of regulations, but by as many as the legislative discretion of the several States should deem applicable to the local peculiarities of the ports within their limits.

The pragmatism of the *Cooley* decision has characterized most subsequent Court thinking in this field. The decisions are complicated and admittedly often seem contradictory. It is hard to derive understandable principles out of the welter of factual situations with which the Court has dealt. Certainly not logic alone, but judicial views on the essential operating conditions of a federal system have been instrumental in the decisions arrived at.

Understanding of the cases may be facilitated by dividing them into two categories. First are those in which state legislation impinges on commerce and there is no conflicting federal legislation. Here the alleged conflict is directly with the commerce clause, and the Court must decide whether state regulation is consistent with the area of free trade carved out by the Constitution itself.

In such situations the Court may conclude that the state regulation is either valid or invalid. A holding of validity will be basically on the grounds stated in *Cooley,* namely, that the problem is essentially a local one in which there is no necessity for a national uniform rule. For example, in *Bob-Lo Excursion Co.* v. *Michigan,* 333 U.S. 28 (1948), a state civil rights act had been invoked against a Detroit amusement park company which operated an excursion steamer to an island on the Canadian side of the Detroit River. The company had refused to transport a Negro girl to the island, and in court the defense was that the state law could have no applicability to foreign commerce. The Court majority, however, held that this commerce was only technically foreign, and was in fact "highly local," the island being "economically and socially, though not politically, an amusement adjunct of the city of Detroit." No national interest would be adversely affected by enforcing the state statute. This was a local problem which could be subjected to local regulation.

For the Court to uphold state regulation of commerce, it is also necessary that the state law be found to constitute no burden on commerce, or at least that the burden be distributed evenly on interstate and intrastate commerce. In *South Carolina Highway Department* v. *Barnwell Brothers,* 303 U.S. 177 (1938), the state had adopted regulations covering the width and weight of motor trucks which were substantially stricter than in adjacent states. A general federal statute regulated interstate truck transportation, but did not cover size and weight. In these circumstances the Court permitted the state law to stand. The "essentially local" requirement of the *Cooley* case was met, since "few subjects of state regulation are so peculiarly of local concern as is the use of state highways." Moreover, any burden on commerce fell on all truckers equally. If there had been any evidence that the state was seeking to favor local companies, the result would probably have been different.

But where the Court does find that a single national rule is needed, or that a heavy or discriminatory burden on interstate commerce results from state regulation, then it will invalidate the state law. The case of *Southern Pacific Co.* v. *Arizona* (1945) saw the Court majority reach such a result, which is in interesting contrast with the conclusion in the *Barnwell Brothers* case.

Again, in *Morgan* v. *Virginia,* 328 U.S. 373 (1946), the Virginia law requiring the separation of white and colored passengers on all motor carriers within the state was invalidated so far as it affected buses in interstate travel. A "single, uniform rule to promote and protect national travel" was believed essential. Enforcement of local rules on interstate buses would result in real disturbance to the comfort of passengers.

Bibb v. *Navajo Freight Lines,* 359 U.S. 520 (1959), saw the Court strike down an Illinois statute requiring contour rear-fender mudguards on trucks operating in the state, and making the conventional mudflap, which is legal in forty-five states, illegal in Illinois. The Court regarded this as a "nondiscriminatory" but nevertheless unconstitutionally severe burden on commerce.

Where a burden takes the form of a complete obstruction to commerce, then the case against the state regulation is very strong indeed. In *Edwards* v. *California*, 314 U.S. 160 (1941), the Court held unconstitutional a state statute making it a misdemeanor for anyone knowingly to bring or assist in bringing into the state a nonresident "indigent" person.

When we turn to situations where state action is alleged to conflict with congressional legislation regulating interstate commerce, then the Court's problem is somewhat simpler. The issue to be decided is whether Congress has completely occupied the field, or whether it has left some room for nonconflicting state legislation.

A whole series of such problems has been raised by state labor laws which have been attacked as in conflict with the national labor relations acts. In *Allen-Bradley Local No. 1111* v. *Wisconsin Employment Relations Board*, 315 U.S. 740 (1942), the Court ruled that the federal Wagner Act was not intended to impair a state's powers to punish or in some instances to prevent offensive conduct relating to "such traditionally local matters as public safety and order and the use of streets and highways." In this case state action was upheld as applied against mass picketing, threats of physical violence against workers, and obstruction of access to a plant by strikers.

On the other hand, the Court has not permitted the states to fetter the exercise of rights protected by federal statute. In *Hill* v. *Florida*, 325 U.S. 538 (1945), a state statute providing for compulsory licensing of labor union business agents was held to conflict with the purposes of the Wagner Act. State restrictions on the right to strike were invalidated in *Interstate Union of United Automobile Workers* v. *O'Brien*, 339 U.S. 454 (1950), and *Amalgamated Assn.* v. *Wisconsin Employment Relations Board*, 340 U.S. 383 (1951).

The issue of federal-state statutory conflict has of course been faced in many fields other than labor relations. In *Huron Portland Cement Co.* v. *Detroit*, 362 U.S. 440 (1960), the conflict was between the federal steamship licensing and inspection laws, as administered by the United States Coast Guard, and a municipal smoke-abatement ordinance.

Perhaps the best recent effort to summarize the Court's rulings on congressional "occupation of the field" came in *Pennsylvania* v. *Nelson*, 350 U.S. 497 (1956). Here a conviction for violation of the Pennsylvania sedition act had been reversed by the state supreme court on the ground that the federal sedition law, the Smith Act, had occupied the field and superseded the state law. The Supreme Court agreed, on the basis of three criteria which Chief Justice Warren suggested as controlling in such controversies. First, is the plan of federal regulation so pervasive as to make it a reasonable inference that Congress had left no room for the states? Second, do the federal statutes touch a field in which the interest of the national government is so dominant that it must be assumed to preclude state action on the same subject? Third, does enforcement of the state act present a serious danger of conflict with the administration of the federal program?

SOUTHERN PACIFIC CO. *v.* ARIZONA
325 U.S. 761, 65 S. Ct. 1515, 89 L. Ed. 1915 (1945)

The Arizona Train Limit Law of 1912 made it unlawful to operate within the state a railroad train of more than fourteen passenger or seventy freight cars, and authorized the state to recover a money penalty for each violation. In 1940 Arizona brought suit against the Southern Pacific Company to recover the statutory penalties for two violations of the law. The trial court gave judgment for the company, but the state supreme court reversed the judgment. It held that the power of the state to regulate the length of interstate trains had not been restricted by congressional action. The act was sustained as a safety measure adopted by the state under its police power to reduce the number of accidents. A statute bearing some reasonable relation to the health, safety, and well-being of the people of the state, of which the state legislature is the judge, was not to be judicially overturned, notwithstanding the admittedly adverse effect on the operation of interstate trains.

Mr. Chief Justice Stone delivered the opinion of the Court.

. . . Appellant's principal contention [is] that the state statute contravenes the commerce clause of the Federal Constitution.

Although the commerce clause conferred on the national government power to regulate commerce, its possession of the power does not exclude all state power of regulation. Ever since *Willson* v. *Black-Bird Creek Marsh Co.,* 2 Pet. 245, and *Cooley* v. *Board of Wardens,* 12 How. 299, it has been recognized that, in the absence of conflicting legislation by Congress, there is a residuum of power in the state to make laws governing matters of local concern which nevertheless in some measure affect interstate commerce or even, to some extent, regulate it. . . . Thus the states may regulate matters which, because of their number and diversity, may never be adequately dealt with by Congress. . . . When the regulation of matters of local concern is local in character and effect, and its impact on the national commerce does not seriously interfere with its operation, and the consequent incentive to deal with them nationally is slight, such regulation has been generally held to be within state authority. . . .

But ever since *Gibbons* v. *Ogden,* 9 Wheat. 1, the states have not been deemed to have authority to impede substantially the free flow of commerce from state to state, or to regulate those phases of the national commerce which, because of the need of national uniformity, demand that their regulation, if any, be prescribed by a single authority. . . .

In the application of these principles some enactments may be found to be plainly within and others plainly without state power. But between these extremes lies the infinite variety of cases, in which regulation of local matters may also operate as a regulation of commerce, in which reconciliation of the conflicting claims of state and national power is to be attained only by some appraisal and accommodation of the competing demands of the state and national interests involved. . . .

For a hundred years it has been accepted constitutional doctrine that the commerce clause, without the aid of Congressional legislation, thus affords some protection from state legislation inimical to the national commerce, and that in such cases, where Congress has not acted, this Court, and not the state legislature, is under the commerce clause the final arbiter of the competing demands of state and national interests. . . .

Congress has undoubted power to redefine the distribution of power over interstate commerce. It may either permit the states to regulate the commerce in a manner which would otherwise not be permissible, . . . or exclude state regulation even of matters of peculiarly local concern which nevertheless affect interstate commerce. . . .

But in general Congress has left it to the courts to formulate the rules thus interpreting the commerce clause in its application, doubtless because it has appreciated the destructive consequences to the commerce of the nation if their protection were withdrawn, . . . and has been aware that in their application state laws will not be invalidated without the support of relevant factual material which will "afford a sure basis" for an informed judgment. . . . Meanwhile, Congress has accommodated its legislation, as have the states, to these rules as an established feature of our constitutional system. There has thus been left to the states wide scope for the regulation of matters of local state concern, even though it in some measure affects the commerce, provided it does not materially restrict the free flow of commerce across state lines, or interfere with it in matters with respect to which uniformity of regulation is of predominant national concern.

Hence the matters for ultimate determination here are the nature and extent of the burden which the state regulation of interstate trains, adopted as a safety measure, imposes on interstate commerce, and whether the relative weights of the state and national interests involved are such as to make inapplicable the rule, generally observed, that the free flow of interstate commerce and its freedom from local restraints in matters requiring uniformity of regulation are interests safeguarded by the commerce clause from state interference. . . .

The findings show that the operation of long trains, that is trains of more than fourteen passenger and more than seventy freight cars, is standard practice over the main lines of the railroads of the United States, and that, if the length of trains is to be regulated at all, national uniformity in the regulation adopted, such as only Congress can prescribe, is practically indispensable to the operation of an efficient and economical national railway system. . . .

In Arizona, approximately 93% of the freight traffic and 95% of the passenger traffic is interstate. Because of the Train Limit Law appellant is required to haul over 30% more trains in Arizona than would otherwise have been necessary. The record shows a definite relationship between operating costs and the length of trains, the increase in length resulting in a reduction of operating costs per car. The additional cost of operation of trains complying with the Train Limit Law in Arizona amounts for the two railroads traversing that state to about $1,000,000 a year. The reduction in train lengths also impedes efficient operation. More locomotives and more manpower are required; the necessary conversion and reconversion of train lengths at terminals and the delay caused by breaking up and remaking long trains upon entering and leaving the state in order to comply with the law, delays the traffic and diminishes its volume moved in a given time, especially when traffic is heavy. . . .

The unchallenged findings leave no doubt that the Arizona Train Limit Law imposes a serious burden on the interstate commerce conducted by appellant. It materially impedes the movement of appellant's interstate trains through that state and interposes a substantial obstruction to the national policy proclaimed by Congress, to promote adequate, economical and efficient railway transportation service. Interstate Commerce Act, preceding § 1, 54 Stat. 899. Enforcement of the law in Arizona, while train lengths remain unregulated or are regulated by varying standards in other states, must inevitably result in an impairment of uniformity of efficient railroad operation because the railroads are subjected to regulation which is not uniform in its application. Compliance with a state statute limiting train lengths requires interstate trains of a length lawful in other states to be broken up and reconstituted as they enter each state according as it may impose varying limitations upon train lengths. The alternative is for the carrier to conform to the lowest train limit restriction of any of the states through which its trains pass, whose laws thus control the carriers' operations both within and without the regulating state. . . .

If one state may regulate train lengths, so may all the others, and they need not prescribe the same maximum limitation. The practical effect of such regulation is to control train operations beyond the boundaries of the state exacting it because of the necessity of breaking up and reassembling long trains at the nearest terminal points before entering and after leaving the regulating state. The serious impediment to the free flow of commerce by the local regulation of train lengths and the practical necessity that such regulation, if any, must be prescribed by a single body having a nation-wide authority are apparent.

The trial court found that the Arizona law had no reasonable relation to safety, and made train operation more dangerous. Examination of the evidence and the detailed findings makes it clear that this conclusion was rested on facts found which indicate that such increased danger of accident and personal injury as may result from the greater length of trains is more than offset by the increase in the number of accidents resulting from the larger number of trains when train lengths are reduced. In considering the effect of the statute as a safety measure, therefore, the factor of controlling significance for present purposes is not whether there is basis for the conclusion of the Arizona Supreme Court that the increase in length of trains beyond the statutory maximum has an adverse effect upon safety of operation. The decisive question is whether in the circumstances the total effect of the law as a safety measure in reducing accidents and casualties is so slight or problematical as not to outweigh the national interest in keeping interstate commerce free from interferences which seriously impede it and subject it to local regulation which does not have a uniform effect on the interstate train journey which it interrupts.

The principal source of danger of accident from increased length of trains is the resulting increase of "slack action" of the train. Slack action is the amount of free movement of one car before its transmits its motion to an adjoining coupled car. This free movement results from the fact that in railroad practice cars are loosely coupled, and the coupling is often combined with a shock-absorbing device, a "draft gear," which, under stress, substantially increases the free movement as the train is started or stopped. Loose coupling is necessary to enable the train to proceed freely around curves and is an aid in starting heavy trains, since the application of the locomotive power to the train operates on each car in the train successively, and the power is thus utilized to start only one car at a time.

. . . The length of the train increases the slack since the slack action of a train is the total of the free movement between its several cars. The amount of slack action has some effect on the severity of the shock of train movements, and on freight trains sometimes results in injuries to operatives, which most frequently occur to occupants of the caboose. The amount and severity of slack action, however, are not wholly dependent upon the length of train, as they may be affected by the mode and conditions of operation as to grades, speed, and load. And accidents due to slack action also occur in the operation of short trains. . . .

As the trial court found, reduction of the length of trains also tends to increase the number of accidents because of the increase in the number of trains. The application of the Arizona law compelled appellant to operate 30.08%, or 4,304, more freight trains in 1938 than would otherwise have been necessary. And the record amply supports the trial court's conclusion that the frequency of accidents is closely related to the number of trains run. . . . The accident rate in Arizona is much higher than on comparable lines elsewhere, where there is no regulation of length of trains. The record lends support to the trial court's conclusion that the train length limitation increased rather than diminished the number of accidents. . . .

We think, as the trial court found, that the Arizona Train Limit Law, viewed as a safety measure, affords at most slight and dubious advantage, if any, over unregulated train lengths, because it results in an increase in the number of trains and train operations and the consequent increase in train accidents of a character generally more severe than those due to slack action. Its undoubted effect on the commerce is the regulation, without securing uniformity, of the length of trains operated in interstate commerce, which lack is itself a primary cause of preventing the free flow of commerce by delaying it and by substantially increasing its cost and impairing its efficiency. In these respects the case differs from those where a state, by regulatory measures affecting the commerce, has removed or reduced safety hazards without substantial interference with the interstate movement of trains. . . .

Here we conclude that the state [goes] too far. Its regulation of train lengths, admittedly obstructive to interstate train operation, and having a seriously adverse effect on transportation efficiency and economy, passes beyond what is plainly essential for safety since it does not appear that it will lessen rather than increase the danger of accident. Its attempted regulation of the operation of interstate trains cannot establish nation-wide control such as is essential to the maintenance of an efficient transportation system, which Congress alone can prescribe. The state interest cannot be preserved at the expense of the national interest by an enactment which regulates interstate train lengths without securing such control, which is a matter of national concern. To this the interest of the state here asserted is subordinate.

Appellees especially rely on the full train crew cases, *Chicago, R. I. & P. R. Co.* v. *Arkansas* [219 U.S. 453] . . . and also on *South Carolina Highway Dept.* v. *Barnwell Bros.* [303 U.S. 177], as supporting the state's authority to regulate the length of interstate trains. While the full train crew laws undoubtedly placed an added financial burden on the railroads in order to serve a local interest, they did not obstruct interstate transportation or seriously impede it. They had no effects outside the state beyond those of picking up and setting down the extra employees at the state boundaries; they involved no wasted use of facilities or serious impairment of transportation efficiency, which are among the factors of controlling weight here. In sustaining those laws the Court considered the restriction a minimal burden on the commerce comparable to the law requiring the licensing of engineers as a safeguard against those of reckless and intemperate habits, sustained in *Smith* v. *Alabama*, 124 U.S. 465, or those afflicted with color blindness, upheld in *Nashville, C. & St. L. R. Co.* v. *Alabama*, 128 U.S. 96, and other similar regulations. . . .

South Carolina Highway Dept. v. *Barnwell Bros., supra*, was concerned with the power of the state to regulate the weight and width of motor cars passing interstate over its highways, a legislative field over which the state has a far more extensive control than over interstate railroads. In that case, . . . we were at pains to point out that there are few subjects of state regulation affecting interstate commerce which are so peculiarly of local concern as is the use of the state's highways. Unlike the railroads local highways are built, owned and maintained by the state or its municipal subdivisions. The state is responsible for their safe and economical administration. Regulations affecting the safety of their use must be applied alike to intrastate and interstate traffic. The fact that they affect alike shippers in interstate and intrastate commerce in great numbers, within as well as without the state, is a safeguard against regulatory abuses. Their regulation is akin to quarantine measures, game laws, and like local regulations of rivers, harbors, piers, and docks, with respect to which the state has exceptional scope for the exercise of its regulatory power, and which, Con-gress not acting, have been sustained even though they materially interfere with interstate commerce. . . .

The contrast between the present regulation and the full train crew laws in point of their effects on the commerce, and the like contrast with the highway safety regula-tions, in point of the nature of the subject of regulation and the state's interest in it, illustrate and emphasize the considerations which enter into a determination of the relative weights of state and national interests where state regulation affecting inter-state commerce is attempted. Here examination of all the relevant factors makes it plain that the state interest is outweighed by the interest of the nation in an adequate, economical and efficient railway transportation service, which must prevail.

Reversed.

MR. JUSTICE RUTLEDGE concurs in the result.

MR. JUSTICE BLACK, dissenting.

In *Hennington* v. *Georgia*, 163 U.S. 299, 304, a case which involved the power of a state to regulate interstate traffic, this Court said, "The whole theory of our govern-ment, federal and state, is hostile to the idea that questions of legislative authority may depend . . . upon opinions of judges as to the wisdom or want of wisdom in the enactment of laws under powers clearly conferred upon the legislature." What the Court decides today is that it is unwise governmental policy to regulate the length of trains. I am therefore constrained to note my dissent. . . .

In the state court a rather extraordinary "trial" took place. Charged with violating the law, the railroad admitted the charge. It alleged that the law was unconstitutional, however, and sought a trial of facts on that issue. The essence of its charge of uncon-stitutionality rested on one of these two grounds: (1) the legislature and people of Arizona erred in 1912 in determining that the running of long trains was dangerous; or (2) railroad conditions had so improved since 1912 that previous dangers did not exist to the same extent, and that the statute should be stricken down either because it cast an undue burden on interstate commerce by reason of the added cost, or because the changed conditions had rendered the Act "arbitrary and unreasonable." Thus, the issue which the court "tried" was not whether the railroad was guilty of violating the law, but whether the law was unconstitutional either because the legislature had been guilty of misjudging the facts concerning the degree of the danger of long trains, or because the 1912 conditions of danger no longer existed.

Before the state trial court finally determined that the dangers found by the legis-lature in 1912 no longer existed, it heard evidence over a period of 5½ months which appears in about 3,000 pages of the printed record before us. It then adopted findings of fact submitted to it by the railroad, which cover 148 printed pages, and conclu-sions of law which cover 5 pages. We can best understand the nature of this "trial" by analogizing the same procedure to a defendant charged with violating a state or national safety appliance act, where the defendant comes into court and admits viola-tion of the act. In such cases, the ordinary procedure would be for the court to pass upon the constitutionality of the act; and either discharge or convict the defendants. The procedure here, however, would justify quite a different trial method. Under it, a defendant is permitted to offer voluminous evidence to show that a legislative body has erroneously resolved disputed facts in finding a danger great enough to justify the passage of the law. This new pattern of trial procedure makes it necessary for a judge to hear all the evidence offered as to why a legislature passed a law and to make findings of fact as to the validity of those reasons. If under today's ruling a court does make findings, as to a danger contrary to the findings of the legislature, and the evidence heard "lends support" to those findings, a court can then invalidate the law. In this respect, the Arizona County Court acted, and this Court today is acting, as a "super-legislature." . . .

. . . The determination of whether it is in the interest of society for the length of trains to be governmentally regulated is a matter of public policy. Someone must fix that policy—either the Congress, or the state, or the courts. A century and a half of constitutional history and government admonishes this Court to leave that choice to the elected legislative representatives of the people themselves, where it properly belongs both on democratic principles and the requirements of efficient government.

I think that legislatures, to the exclusion of courts, have the constitutional power to enact laws limiting train lengths, for the purpose of reducing injuries brought about by "slack movements." Their power is not less because a requirement of short trains might increase grade crossing accidents. This latter fact raises an entirely different element of danger which is itself subject to legislative regulation. For legislatures may, if necessary, require railroads to take appropriate steps to reduce the likelihood of injuries at grade crossings. . . . And the fact that grade-crossing improvements may be expensive is no sufficient reason to say that an unconstitutional "burden" is put upon a railroad even though it be an interstate road. . . .

The Supreme Court of Arizona did not discuss the County Court's so-called findings of fact. It properly designated the Arizona statute as a safety measure, and finding that it bore a reasonable relation to its purpose declined to review the judgment of the legislature as to the necessity for the passage of the act. In so doing it was well fortified by a long line of decisions of this Court. Today's decision marks an abrupt departure from that line of cases.

There have been many sharp divisions of this Court concerning its authority, in the absence of congressional enactment, to invalidate state laws as violating the Commerce Clause. . . . That discussion need not be renewed here, because even the broadest exponents of judicial power in this field have not heretofore expressed doubt as to a state's power, absent a paramount congressional declaration, to regulate interstate trains in the interest of safety. For as early as 1913, this Court, speaking through Mr. Justice Hughes, later Chief Justice, referred to "the settled principle that, in the absence of legislation by Congress, the states are not denied the exercise of their power to secure safety in the physical operation of railroad trains within their territory, even though such trains are used in interstate commerce. That has been the law since the beginning of railroad transportation." . . .

. . . Congress knew about the Arizona law. It is common knowledge that the Interstate Commerce Committees of the House and the Senate keep in close and intimate touch with the affairs of railroads and other national means of transportation. Every year brings forth new legislation which goes through those Committees, much of it relating to safety. The attention of the members of Congress and of the Senate have been focused on the particular problem of the length of railroad trains. We cannot assume that they were ignorant of the commonly known fact that a long train might be more dangerous in some territories and on some particular types of railroad. The history of congressional consideration of this problem leaves little if any room to doubt that the choice of Congress to leave the state free in this field was a deliberate choice, which was taken with a full knowledge of the complexities of the problems and the probable need for diverse regulations in different localities. I am therefore compelled to reach the conclusion that today's decision is the result of the belief of a majority of this Court that both the legislature of Arizona and the Congress made wrong policy decisions in permitting a law to stand which limits the length of railroad trains. . . .

We are not left in doubt as to why, as against the potential peril of injuries to employees, the Court tips the scales on the side of "uniformity." For the evil it finds in a lack of uniformity is that it (1) delays interstate commerce, (2) increases its cost and (3) impairs its efficiency. All three of these boil down to the same thing, and that is that running shorter trains would increase the cost of railroad operations. The "burden" on commerce reduces itself to mere cost because there was no finding, and no evidence to support a finding, that by the expenditure of sufficient sums of money, the railroads could not enable themselves to carry goods and passengers just as quickly and efficiently with short trains as with long trains. Thus the conclusion that a requirement for long trains will "burden interstate commerce" is a mere euphemism for the statement that a requirement for long trains will increase the cost of railroad operations. . . .

This record in its entirety leaves me with no doubt whatever that many employees have been seriously injured and killed in the past, and that many more are likely to be so in the future, because of "slack movement" in trains. Everyday knowledge as well as direct evidence presented at the various hearings, substantiates the report of the Senate Committee that the danger from slack movement is greater in long trains than in short trains. It may be that offsetting dangers are possible in the operation of short trains. The balancing of these probabilities, however, is not in my judgment a matter for judicial determination, but one which calls for legislative consideration. Representatives elected by the people to make their laws, rather than judges appointed to interpret those laws, can best determine the policies which govern the people. That at least is the basic principle on which our democratic society rests. I would affirm the judgment of the Supreme Court of Arizona.

Mr. Justice Douglas, dissenting. . . .

HURON PORTLAND CEMENT CO. v. DETROIT
362 U.S. 440, 80 S. Ct. 813, 4 L. Ed. 2d 852 (1960)

Mr. Justice Stewart delivered the opinion of the Court.

This appeal from a judgment of the Supreme Court of Michigan draws in question the constitutional validity of certain provisions of Detroit's Smoke Abatement Code as applied to ships owned by the appellant and operated in interstate commerce.

The appellant is a Michigan corporation. . . . It maintains a fleet of five vessels which it uses to transport cement from its mill in Alpena, Michigan, to distributing plants located in various states bordering the Great Lakes. Two of the ships . . . are equipped with hand-fired scotch marine boilers. While these vessels are docked for loading and unloading it is necessary, in order to operate deck machinery, to keep the boilers fired and to clean the fires periodically. When the fires are cleaned, the ship's boiler stacks emit smoke which in density and duration exceeds the maximum standards allowable under the Detroit Smoke Abatement Code. Structural alterations would be required in order to insure compliance with the Code. . . .

In support of the claim that the ordinance cannot constitutionally be applied to appellant's ships, two basic arguments are advanced. First, it is asserted that since the vessels and their equipment, including their boilers, have been inspected, approved and licensed to operate in interstate commerce in accordance with a comprehensive system of regulation enacted by Congress, the City of Detroit may not legislate in such a way as, in effect, to impose additional or inconsistent standards. Secondly, the argument is made that even if Congress has not expressly pre-empted the field, the municipal ordinance "materially affects interstate commerce in matters where uniformity is necessary." We have concluded that neither of these contentions can prevail, and that the Federal Constitution does not prohibit application to the appellant's vessels of the criminal provisions of the Detroit ordinance.

The ordinance was enacted for the manifest purpose of promoting the health and welfare of the city's inhabitants. Legislation designed to free from pollution the very air that people breathe falls clearly within the exercise of even the most traditional concept of what is compendiously known as the police power. In the exercise of that power, the states and their instrumentalities may act, in many areas of interstate commerce and maritime activities, concurrently with the federal government. . . .

The basic limitations upon local legislative power in this area are clear enough. . . . Evenhanded local regulation to effectuate a legitimate local public interest is valid unless pre-empted by federal action . . . or unduly burdensome on maritime activities or interstate commerce. . . .

In determining whether state regulation has been pre-empted by federal action, "the intent to supersede the exercise by the state of its police power as to matters not covered by the Federal legislation is not to be inferred from the mere fact that Congress has seen fit to circumscribe its regulation and to occupy a limited field. In other words, such intent is not to be implied unless the act of Congress, fairly interpreted, is in actual conflict with the law of the state." . . .

In determining whether the state has imposed an undue burden on interstate commerce, it must be borne in mind that the Constitution when "conferring upon Congress the regulation of commerce, . . . never intended to cut the States off from legislating on all subjects relating to the health, life, and safety of their citizens, though the legislation might indirectly affect the commerce of the country. Legislation, in a great variety of ways, may affect commerce and persons engaged in it without constituting a regulation of it, within the meaning of the Constitution." . . . But a state may not impose a burden which materially affects interstate commerce in an area where uniformity of regulation is necessary. . . .

For many years Congress has maintained an extensive and comprehensive set of controls over ships and shipping. Federal inspection of steam vessels was first required in 1838 . . . and the requirement has been continued ever since. . . . Steam vessels which carry passengers must pass inspections annually . . . and those which do not every two years. . . . Failure to meet the standards invoked by law results in revocation of the inspection certificate, or refusal to issue a new one. . . . It is unlawful for a vessel to operate without such a certificate. . . .

These inspections are broad in nature. . . . As is apparent on the face of the legislation, however, the purpose of the federal inspection statutes is to insure the seagoing safety of vessels subject to inspection. . . . The thrust of the federal inspection laws is clearly limited to affording protection from the perils of maritime navigation. . . .

By contrast, the sole aim of the Detroit ordinance is the elimination of air pollution to protect the health and enhance the cleanliness of the local community. Congress recently recognized the importance and legitimacy of such a purpose, when in 1955 it provided:

"In recognition of the dangers to the public health and welfare, injury to agricultural crops and livestock, damage to and deterioration of property, and hazards to air and ground transportation, from air pollution, it is hereby declared to be the policy of Congress to preserve and protect the primary responsibilities and rights of the States and local governments in controlling air pollution, to support and aid technical research to devise and develop methods of abating such pollution, and to provide Federal technical services and financial aid to State and local government air pollution control agencies and other public or private agencies and institutions in the formulation and execution of their air pollution abatement research programs." 69 Stat. 322.

We conclude that there is no overlap between the scope of the federal ship inspection laws and that of the municipal ordinance here involved. For this reason we cannot find that the federal inspection legislation has pre-empted local action. To hold otherwise would be to ignore the teaching of this Court's decisions which enjoin seeking out conflicts between state and federal regulation where none clearly exists. . . .

An additional argument is advanced, however, based not upon the mere existence of the federal inspection standards, but upon the fact that the appellant's vessels were actually licensed. . . . It is asserted that the vessels have thus been given a dominant federal right to the use of the navigable waters of the United States, free from the local impediment that would be imposed by the Detroit ordinance. . . .

The mere possession of a federal license, however, does not immunize a ship from the operation of the normal incidents of local police power, not constituting a direct regulation of commerce. . . . The Detroit ordinance requires no more than compliance with an orderly and reasonable scheme of community regulation. The ordinance does not exclude a licensed vessel from the Port of Detroit, nor does it destroy the right of free passage. We cannot hold that the local regulation so burdens the federal license as to be constitutionally invalid.

The claim that the Detroit ordinance, quite apart from the effect of federal legislation, imposes as to the appellant's ships an undue burden on interstate commerce needs no extended discussion. State regulation, based on the police power, which does not discriminate against interstate commerce or operate to disrupt its required uniformity, may constitutionally stand. . . .

It has not been suggested that the local ordinance, applicable alike to "any person, firm or corporation" within the city, discriminates against interstate commerce as such. It is a regulation of general application, designed to better the health and welfare of the community. And while the appellant argues that other local governments might impose differing requirements as to air pollution, it has pointed to none. . . . We conclude that no impermissible burden on commerce has been shown.

The judgment is

Affirmed.

MR. JUSTICE DOUGLAS, with whom MR. JUSTICE FRANKFURTER concurs, dissenting. . . .

Here we have a criminal prosecution against a shipowner and officers of two of its vessels for using the very equipment on these vessels which the Federal Government says may be used. At stake are a possible fine of $100 on the owner and both a fine and a 30-day jail sentence on the officers.

Appellant has a federal certificate for each of its vessels. . . . The certificate states "The said vessel is permitted to be navigated for one year on the Great Lakes." The certificate specifies the boilers which are and may be used. . . . It also specifies the fuel which is used and is to be used in those boilers. . . .

Appellant, operating the vessel in waters at the Detroit dock, is about to be fined criminally for using the precise equipment covered by the federal certificate because, it is said, the use of that equipment will violate a smoke ordinance of the City of Detroit.

The federal statutes give the Coast Guard the power to inspect "the boilers" of freight vessels every two years, and provide that when the Coast Guard approves the vessel and her equipment throughout, a certificate to that effect shall be made.

The requirements of the Detroit smoke ordinance are squarely in conflict with the federal statute. . . . The ordinance requires not only the inspection and approval of equipment which has been inspected and approved by the Coast Guard, but also the sealing of equipment, even though it has been approved by the Coast Guard. . . . In other words, this equipment approved and licensed by the Federal Government for use on navigable waters cannot pass muster under local law. . . .

The boats of appellant . . . have credentials good for any port; and I would not allow this local smoke ordinance to work in derogation of them. The fact that the Federal Government in certifying equipment applies standards of safety for seagoing vessels, while Detroit applies standards of air pollution seems immaterial. Federal pre-emption occurs when the boilers and fuel to be used in the vessels are specified in the certificate. No state authority can, in my view, change those specifications. Yet that is in effect what is allowed here. . . .

By what authority can a local government fine people or send them to jail for using in interstate commerce the precise equipment which the federal regulatory agency has certified and approved? . . . Never before, I believe, have we recognized the right of local law to make the use of an unquestionably legal federal license a criminal offense.

SELECTED REFERENCES

Bailey, Stephen K., *Congress Makes A Law*. New York: Columbia University Press, 1950.

Barth, Alan, *Government by Investigation*. New York: The Viking Press, Inc., 1955.

Beck, Carl, *Contempt of Congress*. New Orleans, La.: Hauser, 1959.

Binkley, Wilfred E., *President and Congress*. New York: Alfred A. Knopf, Inc., 1947.

Burns, James M., *Congress on Trial*. New York: Harper & Brothers, 1949.

Carr, Robert K., *The House Committee on Un-American Activities, 1945–1950*. Ithaca, N.Y.: Cornell University Press, 1952.

Corwin, Edward S. (ed.), *The Constitution of the United States of America: Analysis and Interpretation*, pp. 61–370. Washington: Government Printing Office, 1953.

Crosskey, W. W., *Politics and the Constitution in the History of the United States*. Chicago: University of Chicago Press, 1953.

Douglas, William O., *We the Judges*, chaps. 4, 6, 7. New York: Doubleday & Company, Inc., 1956.

Frankfurter, Felix, *The Commerce Clause under Marshall, Taney and Waite*. Chapel Hill, N.C.: The University of North Carolina Press, 1937.

Galloway, George B., *The Legislative Process in Congress*. New York: Thomas Y. Crowell Company, 1953.

Griffith, Ernest S., *Congress: Its Contemporary Role*. New York: New York University Press, 1951.

Griswold, Erwin N., *The Fifth Amendment Today*. Cambridge, Mass.: Harvard University Press, 1955.

Harris, Joseph P., *The Advice and Consent of the Senate*. Berkeley, Calif.: University of California Press, 1953.

Haynes, George H., *The Senate of the United States: Its History and Practice*. Boston: Houghton Mifflin Company, 1938.

Pritchett, C. Herman, *The American Constitution,* part 4. New York: McGraw-Hill Book Company, Inc., 1959.

Schmeckebier, Laurence F., *Congressional Apportionment.* Washington, D.C.: The Brookings Institution, 1941.

Taylor, Telford, *Grand Inquest: The Story of Congressional Investigations.* New York: Simon and Schuster, Inc., 1955.

White, William S., *Citadel: The Story of the United States Senate.* New York: Harper & Brothers, 1957.

Wilson, Woodrow, *Congressional Government.* Boston: Houghton Mifflin Company, 1885.

Young, Roland, *The American Congress.* New York: Harper & Brothers, 1957.

PART THREE

The President

INTRODUCTION

The establishment of a strong single-headed executive was one of the surprises of the Constitutional Convention. During the period immediately preceding the Revolution, the executive power, represented by royal governors, had been far from popular, and when control passed into the hands of the states the first impulse was to slash away at the executive and exalt the legislatures. This distrust of the executive was also present at Philadelphia in 1787, and proposals were heard that the executive branch be headed by a committee of three, for fear that a single official might develop monarchical powers. Again, it was argued that if a single executive were set up, he should be encumbered by a council. But these views were defeated by those who had seen the fumbling and the weakness of a headless government under the Articles of Confederation. They were defeated by those who had come to see through experience in the states that an unchecked legislature could be as dangerous as a tyrannical executive ("The legislative department is everywhere extending the sphere of its activity," said Madison in 1787, "and drawing all power into its impetuous vortex") and who consequently favored a strong executive to checkmate possible legislative usurpation.

The ultimate decision to create the office of President was the occasion for bitter attacks on the new Constitution when it was presented for ratification. As Hamilton wrote in No. 67 of *The Federalist*: "The authorities of a magistrate, in few instances greater, in some instances less, than those of a governor of New York, have been magnified into more than royal prerogatives." The office has of course turned out to have considerably more stature than this modest estimate; the Presidency has become, in fact, the most important responsible executive office on the globe.

This growth of presidential power has for the most part occurred quite independently of judicial aid or assistance. The Supreme Court has only infrequently been called on to resolve the constitutional issues of the Presidency. When executive action has impinged on private rights, or occasionally in cases of conflict between the President and Congress, judicial intervention to define the

155

constitutional situation has been successfully invoked. But over the broad reaches of presidential power the judicial influence has been minor.

On the basic problem of filling the presidential office, none of the issues has been suitable for judicial consideration. The initial plan of Article II called for each state to "appoint, in such manner as the legislature thereof may direct, a number of electors, equal to the whole number of Senators and Representatives to which the State may be entitled in the Congress." . . . The electors were to "meet in their respective States, and vote by ballot for two persons, of whom one at least shall not be an inhabitant of the same State with themselves."

The results of the vote were to be transmitted to the president of the Senate, who would open the sealed certificates in the presence of both houses, and the votes would then be counted. The person with the greatest number of votes was to be the President, provided he had a majority of the whole number of electors. If two candidates were tied, and both had more than a majority, the House was immediately to choose between them. If no candidate had a majority, then the House would choose from the five highest on the list. In either event the House was to vote by states, "the representation from each State having one vote," with a majority required to elect. After the choice of President, the person having the next greatest number of votes was to be Vice President, and in the event of a tie, the Senate was to choose between the contenders.

This arrangement proved faulty very quickly. After Washington's two terms, the electors were selected by the parties and ceased to have any will of their own. The 1796 balloting gave the Presidency and Vice Presidency to different parties, with John Adams and Thomas Jefferson ranking first and second in the electoral voting. In 1800 a tie resulted because Jefferson and Aaron Burr, the Republican candidates for President and Vice President, were voted for by each Republican elector. Everyone understood that Jefferson was the presidential choice, but the tie threw the election into the House, where it took all of Hamilton's efforts to dissuade the lame-duck Federalists from giving the post to Burr.

This experience led to adoption of the Twelfth Amendment in 1804, and it still controls the electoral process. It made the following changes: (1) The electors were to ballot separately for President and Vice President; (2) if no candidate for President received a majority, the House, voting as before by states, was to choose "from the persons having the highest numbers not exceeding three on the list"; (3) the Vice President also had to receive a majority of the electoral votes, and if no one achieved a majority, the Senate was to choose between the two highest candidates; and (4) if the choice of President fell to the House, and it had not made a choice by March 4, the Vice President was to act as President.

This system has weathered two great crises, has three times been responsible for electing a President who had fewer popular votes than his leading opponent, and has been the cause of constant criticism. In 1824 there was no majority in the electoral college, and the House chose John Quincy Adams, though Andrew Jackson had a larger electoral and popular vote. In 1876 there was a dispute over twenty electoral votes, and Congress ultimately set up a completely extraconstitutional Electoral Commission to decide which votes to accept. This body, with an eight to seven Republican majority, decided in favor of the Republican electors and Hayes, with a popular vote minority, was elected by one electoral vote.

In 1888 Harrison was the winner in the electoral college, though receiving 100,000 fewer popular votes than Cleveland.

Normally the electoral vote magnifies the popular vote margin of the winning candidate, largely because each state casts its entire block of electoral votes for the winner in that state. Other factors in distortion of the popular vote by the electoral result are the overweighting of the less populous states in the electoral college, and the varying rate of voter turnout in different states.

Another defect of the present system is that electors may refuse to cast their ballots in accordance with the results of the balloting in their state. In the elections of 1948, 1956, and 1960, one elector on each occasion failed to vote for the candidates of the party which he represented. Moreover, in 1960 eight "unpledged" electors from Mississippi and six from Alabama were elected in a throwback to the original electoral plan which challenged the principle of direct election.

Three principal types of proposals for reform of the electoral system have been made. The first, simplest and most drastic, would require the President to be chosen in a direct nationwide popular election. This plan would terminate the advantages in overweighting of electoral votes which the smaller states now possess; consequently the chance of securing ratification by three-fourths of the states of a constitutional amendment making this change appears remote.

A second proposal would retain the existing electoral vote distribution, but have electors chosen from the congressional districts. However, the two electors to which each state is entitled by reason of its two senators would continue to be chosen on the basis of the statewide popular vote.

The third proposal would also continue to assign electoral votes as at present (though the electors would be abolished), but the electoral vote of each state would be divided exactly proportional to the popular vote each candidate received in the state, percentages being carried three places beyond the decimal point.

The language of Article II, section 1, on succession to the Presidency was not entirely clear, but constitutional practice has now determined its meaning. The provision is: "In case of the removal of the President from office, or of his death, resignation, or inability to discharge the powers and duties of the said office, the same shall devolve on the Vice President. . . ." It is not clear from this wording whether it is the "office" of President which devolves on the Vice President, or only the "powers and duties" of the office. If the latter is the intention, then the Vice President would become only an acting President. However, John Tyler, the first Vice President to face this problem, asserted his claim to full presidential status after the death of President Harrison in 1841, and this precedent has been fully accepted.

The Constitution contemplates the necessity of carrying on the work of the Presidency in event of the incumbent's "inability to discharge the powers and duties" of the office through illness or for any other reason. It seems clear that the Constitution intended to permit the Vice President to act as President temporarily in such emergencies, with the actual President resuming his post when the emergency was terminated. However, in the past there has been enough fear of constitutional complications from having two Presidents at the same time to prevent any use of this authorization on occasions when it might have been appropriate. As a partial solution to this dilemma, both Presidents Eisenhower and Kennedy entered into written agreements with their respective Vice Presidents that the Vice President would be authorized to serve as Acting President in the event of the President's incapacity; when the President determined that his inability had ended, he would resume the full powers of his office.

Chapter 13

THEORIES OF EXECUTIVE POWER

The executive power shall be vested in a President of the United States of
America.   ART. II, SEC. 1

[The President] shall take care that the laws be faithfully executed. . . .
                                                            ART. II, SEC. 3

Article II begins with the statement about executive power quoted above, and
then continues with a number of more or less specific authorizations, such as the
power to grant pardons, to receive ambassadors, to make appointments, and to
see that the laws are faithfully executed. The executive power of the President
is grounded in these provisions, but it may also derive on occasion from the very
character of the executive function, which John Locke referred to as "residual."
The executive is always in session, always capable of moving quickly and so
available to fill in gaps and meet emergencies. In contrast, as Locke notes, "the
law making power is not always in being, and is usually too numerous and so
too slow for the dispatch requisite to execution." . . .

The great controversies about executive power have consequently tended to
be concerned with the latitude which the President may claim in meeting crises
calling for the use of powers not specified in the law or the Constitution. In
general, there have been two views on this subject. One is well summarized in
the "stewardship" conception of the presidential office asserted by Theodore
Roosevelt. In his *Autobiography* he set forth his belief that:

The executive power was limited only by specific restrictions and prohibitions
appearing in the Constitution or imposed by the Congress under its Constitutional
powers. . . . I declined to adopt the view that what was imperatively necessary for
the Nation could not be done by the President unless he could find some specific
authorization to do it. My belief was that it was not only his right but his duty to do
anything that the needs of the Nation demanded unless such action was forbidden
by the Constitution or by the laws.

On the other hand, William Howard Taft took a much more cautious and
limited view of the President's powers. In lectures which he gave in 1916 after
his presidential term, he said:

The true view of the Executive functions is, as I conceive it, that the President can
exercise no power which cannot be fairly and reasonably traced to some specific grant
of power or justly implied and included within such express grant as proper and
necessary to its exercise. Such specific grant must be either in the Federal Constitution

or in an act of Congress passed in pursuance thereof. There is no undefined residuum of power which he can exercise because it seems to him to be in the public interest.

The issue that emerges from these conflicting statements is whether the President must always be able to cite a "law" of the United States or a specific constitutional authorization in support of his actions, or whether the broad "executive power" with which he is vested justifies any actions he conceives as being in the public interest, so long as there is no conflict with existing legislation or constitutional provisions. Locke put this issue in its classical form. Pointing to the relative characteristics of executive and legislature already quoted, he concluded that the executive must always be equipped with discretionary and prerogative powers:

For the legislators not being able to foresee and provide by laws for all that may be useful to the community, the executor of the laws, having the power in his hands, has by the common law of Nature a right to make use of it for the good of society, in many cases where the municipal law has given no direction, till the legislative can conveniently be assembled to provide for it. Many things there are which the law can by no means provide for, and those must necessarily be left to the discretion of him that has the executive power in his hands, to be ordered by him as the public good and advantage shall require; nay, it is fit that the laws themselves should in some cases give way to the executive power, or rather to this fundamental law of Nature and government—viz., that, as much as may be, all the members of the society are to be preserved.

The Supreme Court found it necessary to take a position on this issue in the case of *In re Neagle,* 135 U.S. 1 (1890), and it agreed with Locke. Supreme Court Justice Field, whose judicial circuit included California, had had his life threatened by a disappointed litigant named Terry, and the Attorney General assigned a United States marshal to protect Field while he was riding circuit in that state. When Terry attempted to make a physical attack on Field, the marshal, Neagle, killed him. There was some local feeling favorable to Terry, and Neagle was arrested and held by state authorities on a charge of murder. The United States sought Neagle's release on habeas corpus under a provision of the federal statutes making the writ available to one "in custody for an act done or omitted in pursuance of a law of the United States."

The problem was that Congress had enacted no *law* authorizing the President or the Attorney General to assign marshals as bodyguards to federal justices. But the Supreme Court did not propose to interpret "law" so narrowly. "In the view we take of the Constitution . . . any obligation fairly and properly inferrible from that instrument, or any duty of the marshal to be derived from the general scope of his duties under the laws of the United States, is a 'law,' within the meaning of this phrase." It would be unthinkable, said the Court, for a sovereign government to have "within the domain of its powers no means of protecting . . . judges" in the discharge of their duties. The power must exist somewhere, and the Court found the President to be admirably equipped for performing such a function.

There is "a peace of the United States," the Court went on, and by necessity and design the President is the principal conservator of that peace. The President's duty to see that the laws are faithfully executed is consequently not "limited to the enforcement of acts of Congress . . . according to their *express terms"* but includes also "the rights, duties and obligations growing out of the Constitution itself, our international relations, and all the protection implied by the nature of the government under the Constitution."

This broad interpretation of the laws which the President was obliged faithfully to execute was underlined five years later in the case of *In re Debs,* 158 U.S. 564 (1895). President Cleveland had sent troops to Chicago to deal with a railway strike, and had his Attorney General secure a federal court injunction against the strikers. There was no explicit statutory basis for the injunction, but the Supreme Court sustained it on the broad ground that "Every government, entrusted, by the very terms of its being, with powers and duties to be exercised and discharged for the general welfare, has a right to apply to its own courts for any proper assistance in the exercise of the one and the discharge of the other." . . . Here again the theme was that the right of self-preservation must belong to a government, whether claimed by statute or not, and that the executive was constitutionally entitled to act in such cases.

In contrast to these strong supports for the doctrine of inherent or implied presidential powers, stands the decision in *Youngstown Sheet & Tube Co.* v. *Sawyer,* 343 U.S. 579 (1952). In the latter part of 1951, a dispute arose between the steel companies and their employees over terms and conditions of employment. On December 18, the steelworkers' union gave notice of intention to strike when existing agreements terminated on December 31. On December 22, President Truman referred the dispute to the Federal Wage Stabilization Board, and the strike was called off, but the board's subsequent report produced no settlement. On April 4, 1952, notice of a strike on April 9 was issued. A few hours before the strike was to begin, the President issued an executive order directing the Secretary of Commerce to take possession of and operate the steel mills of the country. The President based his action on a contention that the work stoppage would jeopardize national defense, particularly in Korea. The next morning he sent a message to Congress reporting his action, and a second message on April 21.

The steel companies obeyed the Secretary's orders under protest, and brought suit for injunction against him in the District of Columbia district court. On April 31, Judge Pine granted a preliminary injunction restraining the Secretary from continuing the seizure. In his opinion he denied that the President had any inherent powers not traceable to an express grant in the Constitution, citing Taft's statement as proof. Judge Pine dismissed Roosevelt's stewardship theory as one which does not "comport with our recognized theory of government." The case went to the Supreme Court with almost unprecedented speed, and on June 2, the Court held by a vote of six to three that the President had exceeded his constitutional powers. Extremely important to the majority justices was the fact that Congress in the 1947 Labor-Management Relations (Taft-Hartley) Act had authorized the President to deal with any strike periling "the national health or safety" by securing an injunction delaying the strike for eighty days. While debating this bill, Congress considered giving seizure power to the President, but decided against including such an authorization in the act. President Truman thus had ignored the injunction remedy which the Taft-Hartley Act (passed over Truman's veto) had given him, and had used the seizure power which Congress had not authorized.

YOUNGSTOWN SHEET & TUBE CO. v. SAWYER
343 U.S. 579, 72 S. Ct. 863, 96 L. Ed. 1153 (1952)

MR. JUSTICE BLACK delivered the opinion of the Court.

We are asked to decide whether the President was acting within his constitutional power when he issued an order directing the Secretary of Commerce to take possession of and operate most of the Nation's steel mills. The mill owners argue that the President's order amounts to lawmaking, a legislative function which the Constitution has expressly confided to the Congress and not to the President. The Government's position is that the order was made on findings of the President that his action was necessary to avert a national catastrophe which would inevitably result from a stoppage of steel production, and that in meeting this grave emergency the President was acting within the aggregate of his constitutional powers as the Nation's Chief Executive and the Commander in Chief of the Armed Forces of the United States. . . .

The President's power, if any, to issue the order must stem either from an act of Congress or from the Constitution itself. There is no statute that expressly authorizes the President to take possession of property as he did here. Nor is there any act of Congress to which our attention has been directed from which such a power can fairly be implied. Indeed, we do not understand the Government to rely on statutory authorization for this seizure. . . .

Moreover, the use of the seizure technique to solve labor disputes in order to prevent work stoppages was not only unauthorized by any congressional enactment; prior to this controversy, Congress had refused to adopt that method of settling labor disputes. When the Taft-Hartley Act was under consideration in 1947, Congress rejected an amendment which would have authorized such governmental seizures in cases of emergency. . . .

It is clear that if the President had authority to issue the order he did, it must be found in some provisions of the Constitution. And it is not claimed that express constitutional language grants this power to the President. The contention is that presidential power should be implied from the aggregate of his powers under the Constitution. Particular reliance is placed on provisions in Article II which say that "the executive Power shall be vested in a President . . ."; that "he shall take Care that the Laws be faithfully executed"; and that he "shall be Commander in Chief of the Army and Navy of the United States."

The order cannot properly be sustained as an exercise of the President's military power as Commander in Chief of the Armed Forces. The Government attempts to do so by citing a number of cases upholding broad powers in military commanders engaged in day-to-day fighting in a theater of war. Such cases need not concern us here. Even though "theater of war" be an expanding concept, we cannot with faithfulness to our constitutional system hold that the Commander in Chief of the Armed Forces has the ultimate power as such to take possession of private property in order to keep labor disputes from stopping production. This is a job for the Nation's lawmakers, not for its military authorities.

Nor can the seizure order be sustained because of the several constitutional provisions that grant executive power to the President. In the framework of our Constitution, the President's power to see that the laws are faithfully executed refutes the idea that he is to be a lawmaker. The Constitution limits his functions in the lawmaking process to the recommending of laws he thinks wise and the vetoing of laws he thinks bad. . . .

It is said that other Presidents without congressional authority have taken possession of private business enterprises in order to settle labor disputes. But even if this be true, Congress has not thereby lost its exclusive constitutional authority to make laws necessary and proper to carry out the powers vested by the Constitution "in the Government of the United States, or any Department or Officer thereof."

The Founders of this Nation entrusted the lawmaking power to the Congress alone in both good and bad times. It would do no good to recall the historical events, the fears of power and the hopes for freedom that lay behind their choice. Such a review would but confirm our holding that this seizure order cannot stand.

The judgment of the District Court is

Affirmed.

MR. JUSTICE FRANKFURTER, concurring.

Although the considerations relevant to the legal enforcement of the principle of separation of powers seem to me more complicated and flexible than may appear from what MR. JUSTICE BLACK has written, I join his opinion because I thoroughly agree with the application of the principle to the circumstances of this case. . . .

The issue before us can be met, and therefore should be, without attempting to define the President's powers comprehensively. . . .

We must . . . put to one side consideration of what powers the President would have had if there had been no legislation whatever bearing on the authority asserted by the seizure, or if the seizure had been only for a short, explicitly temporary period, to be determined automatically unless Congressional approval were given. These and other questions, like or unlike, are not now here. I would exceed my authority were I to say anything about them. . . .

In adopting the provisions which it did, by the Labor Management Relations Act of 1947, for dealing with a "national emergency" arising out of a breakdown in peaceful industrial relations, Congress was very familiar with Government seizure as a protective measure. On a balance of considerations Congress chose not to lodge this power in the President. . . .

It cannot be contended that the President would have had power to issue this order had Congress explicitly negated such authority in formal legislation. Congress has expressed its will to withhold this power from the President as though it had said so in so many words. The authoritatively expressed purpose of Congress to disallow such power to the President and to require him, when in his mind the occasion arose for such a seizure, to put the matter to Congress and ask for specific authority from it, could not be more decisive if it had been written into §§ 206–210 of the Labor Management Relations Act of 1947. . . .

Apart from his vast share of responsibility for the conduct of our foreign relations, the embracing function of the President is that "he shall take Care that the Laws be faithfully executed." . . . Art. II, § 3. The nature of that authority has for me been comprehensively indicated by Mr. Justice Holmes. "The duty of the President to see that the laws be executed is a duty that does not go beyond the laws or require him to achieve more than Congress sees fit to leave within his power." *Myers v. United States,* 272 U.S. 52, 177. The powers of the President are not as particularized as are those of Congress. But unenumerated powers do not mean undefined powers. The separation of powers built into our Constitution gives essential content to undefined provisions in the frame of our government. . . .

A scheme of government like ours no doubt at times feels the lack of power to act with complete, all-embracing, swiftly moving authority. No doubt a government with distributed authority, subject to be challenged in the courts of law, at least long enough to consider and adjudicate the challenge, labors under restrictions from which other governments are free. It has not been our tradition to envy such governments. In any event our government was designed to have such restrictions. The price was deemed not too high in view of the safeguards which these restrictions afford. . . .

MR. JUSTICE DOUGLAS, concurring.

There can be no doubt that the emergency which caused the President to seize these steel plants was one that bore heavily on the country. But the emergency did not create power; it merely marked an occasion when power should be exercised. And the fact that it was necessary that measures be taken to keep steel in production does not mean that the President, rather than the Congress, had the constitutional authority to act. The Congress, as well as the President, is trustee of the national welfare. The President can act more quickly than the Congress. The President with the armed services at his disposal can move with force as well as with speed. All executive power —from the reign of ancient kings to the rule of modern dictators—has the outward appearance of efficiency.

Legislative power, by contrast, is slower to exercise. There must be delay while the ponderous machinery of committees, hearings, and debates is put into motion. That takes time; and while the Congress slowly moves into action, the emergency may take its toll in wages, consumer goods, war production, the standard of living of the people, and perhaps even lives. . . .

We therefore cannot decide this case by determining which branch of government can deal most expeditiously with the present crisis. The answer must depend on the allocation of powers under the Constitution. . . .

. . . The language of the Constitution is not ambiguous or qualified. It places not *some* legislative power in the Congress; Article I, Section 1 says "All legislative Powers herein granted shall be vested in a Congress of the United States, which shall consist of a Senate and House of Representatives."

The legislative nature of the action taken by the President seems to me to be clear. . . .

If we sanctioned the present exercise of power by the President, we would be expanding Article II of the Constitution and rewriting it to suit the political conveniences of the present emergency. Article II which vests the "executive Power" in the President defines that power with particularity. Article II, Section 2 makes the Chief Executive the Commander in Chief of the Army and Navy. But our history and tradition rebel at the thought that the grant of military power carries with it authority over civilian affairs. Article II, Section 3 provides that the President shall "from time to time give to the Congress Information of the State of the Union, and recommend to their Consideration such Measures as he shall judge necessary and expedient." The power to recommend legislation, granted to the President, serves only to emphasize that it is his function to recommend and that it is the function of the Congress to legislate. Article II, Section 3 also provides that the President "shall take Care that the Laws be faithfully executed." But as MR. JUSTICE BLACK and MR. JUSTICE FRANKFURTER point out the power to execute the laws starts and ends with the laws Congress has enacted. . . .

We pay a price for our system of checks and balances, for the distribution of power among the three branches of government. It is a price that today may seem exorbitant to many. Today a kindly President uses the seizure power to effect a wage increase and to keep the steel furnaces in production. Yet tomorrow another President might use the same power to prevent a wage increase, to curb trade unionists, to regiment labor as oppressively as industry thinks it has been regimented by this seizure.

MR. JUSTICE JACKSON, concurring in the judgment and opinion of the Court. . . .

We may well begin by a somewhat over-simplified grouping of practical situations in which a President may doubt, or others may challenge, his powers, and by distinguishing roughly the legal consequences of this factor of relativity.

1. When the President acts pursuant to an express or implied authorization of Congress, his authority is at its maximum, for it includes all that he possesses in his own right plus all that Congress can delegate. In these circumstances, and in these only, may he be said (for what it may be worth), to personify the federal sovereignty. If his act is held unconstitutional under these circumstances, it usually means that the Federal Government as an undivided whole lacks power. A seizure executed by the President pursuant to an Act of Congress would be supported by the strongest of presumptions and the widest latitude of judicial interpretation, and the burden of persuasion would rest heavily upon any who might attack it.

2. When the President acts in absence of either a congressional grant or denial of authority, he can only rely upon his own independent powers, but there is a zone of twilight in which he and Congress may have concurrent authority, or in which its distribution is uncertain. Therefore, congressional inertia, indifference or quiescence may sometimes, at least as a practical matter, enable, if not invite, measures on independent presidential responsibility. In this area, any actual test of power is likely to depend on the imperatives of events and contemporary imponderables rather than on abstract theories of law.

3. When the President takes measures incompatible with the expressed or implied will of Congress, his power is at its lowest ebb, for then he can rely only upon his own constitutional powers minus any constitutional powers of Congress over the matter. Courts can sustain exclusive Presidential control in such a case only by disabling the Congress from acting upon the subject. Presidential claim to a power at once so conclusive and preclusive must be scrutinized with caution, for what is at stake is the equilibrium established by our constitutional system.

Into which of these classifications does this executive seizure of the steel industry fit? It is eliminated from the first by admission, for it is conceded that no congressional authorization exists for this seizure. . . .

Can it then be defended upon flexible tests available to the second category? It seems clearly eliminated from that class because Congress has not left seizure of private property an open field but has covered it by three statutory policies inconsistent with this seizure. . . . None of these were invoked. In choosing a different and inconsistent way of his own, the President cannot claim that it is necessitated or invited by failure of Congress to legislate upon the occasions, grounds and methods for seizure of industrial properties.

This leaves the current seizure to be justified only by the severe tests under the third grouping, where it can be supported only by any remainder of executive power after subtraction of such powers as Congress may have over the subject. In short, we can sustain the President only by holding that seizure of such strike-bound industries is within his domain and beyond control by Congress. Thus, this Court's first review of such seizures occurs under circumstances which leave Presidential power most vulnerable to attack and in the least favorable of possible constitutional postures. . . .

The Solicitor General seeks the power of seizure in three clauses of the Executive Article, the first reading, "The executive Power shall be vested in a President of the United States of America." Lest I be thought to exaggerate, I quote the interpretation which his brief puts upon it: "In our view, this clause constitutes a grant of all the executive powers of which the Government is capable." If that be true, it is difficult to see why the forefathers bothered to add several specific items, including some trifling ones. . . . I cannot accept the view that this clause is a grant in bulk of all conceivable executive power but regard it as an allocation to the presidential office of the generic powers thereafter stated.

The clause on which the Government next relies is that "The President shall be Commander in Chief of the Army and Navy of the United States." . . . These cryptic words have given rise to some of the most persistent controversies in our constitutional history. Of course, they imply something more than an empty title. But just what authority goes with the name has plagued Presidential advisers who would not waiye or narrow it by nonassertion yet cannot say where it begins or ends. It undoubtedly puts the Nation's armed forces under Presidential command. Hence, this loose appellation is sometimes advanced as support for any Presidential action, internal or external, involving use of force, the idea being that it vests power to do anything, anywhere, that can be done with an army or navy. . . .

We should not use this occasion to circumscribe, much less to contract, the lawful role of the President as Commander-in-Chief. I should indulge the widest latitude of interpretation to sustain his exclusive function to command the instruments of national force, at least when turned against the outside world for the security of our society. But, when it is turned inward, not because of rebellion but because of a lawful economic struggle between industry and labor, it should have no such indulgence. His command power is not such an absolute as might be implied from that office in a militaristic system but is subject to limitations consistent with a constitutional Republic whose law and policy-making branch is a representative Congress. The purpose of lodging dual titles in one man was to insure that the civilian would control the military, not to enable the military to subordinate the presidential office. No penance would ever expiate the sin against free government of holding that a President can escape control of executive powers by law through assuming his military role. What the power of command may include I do not try to envision, but I think it is not a military prerogative, without support of law, to seize persons or property because they are important or even essential for the military and naval establishment.

The third clause in which the Solicitor General finds seizure powers is that "he shall take Care that the Laws be faithfully executed." . . . That authority must be matched against words of the Fifth Amendment that "No person shall be . . . deprived of life, liberty or property, without due process of law. . . ." One gives a governmental authority that reaches so far as there is law, the other gives a private right that authority shall go no farther. These signify about all there is of the principle that ours is a government of laws, not of men, and that we submit ourselves to rulers only if under rules.

The Solicitor General lastly grounds support of the seizure upon nebulous, inherent powers never expressly granted but said to have accrued to the office from the customs and claims of preceding administrations. The plea is for a resulting power to deal with a crisis or an emergency according to the necessities of the case, the unarticulated assumption being that necessity knows no law. . . .

The appeal . . . that we declare the existence of inherent powers *ex necessitate* to meet an emergency asks us to do what many think would be wise, although it is something the forefathers omitted. . . . I do not think we rightfully may so amend their work, and, if we could, I am not convinced it would be wise to do so, although many modern nations have forthrightly recognized that war and economic crises may upset the normal balance between liberty and authority. . . .

In the practical working of our Government we already have evolved a technique within the framework of the Constitution by which normal executive powers may be considerably expanded to meet an emergency. Congress may and has granted extraordinary authorities which lie dormant in normal times but may be called into play by the Executive in war or upon proclamation of a national emergency.

In view of the ease, expedition and safety with which Congress can grant and has granted large emergency powers, certainly ample to embrace this crisis, I am quite unimpressed with the argument that we should affirm possession of them without statute. . . .

Mr. Justice Burton, concurring in both the opinion and judgment of the Court. . . .

Does the President, in such a situation, have inherent constitutional power to seize private property which makes congressional action in relation thereto unnecessary? We find no such power available to him under the present circumstances. The present situation is not comparable to that of an imminent invasion or threatened attack. We do not face the issue of what might be the President's constitutional power to meet such catastrophic situations. Nor is it claimed that the current seizure is in the nature of a military command addressed by the President, as Commander-in-Chief, to a mobilized nation waging, or imminently threatened with, total war.

The controlling fact here is that Congress, within its constitutionally delegated power, has prescribed for the President specific procedures, exclusive of seizure, for his use in meeting the present type of emergency. Congress has reserved to itself the right to determine where and when to authorize the seizure of property in meeting such an emergency. Under these circumstances, the President's order of April 8 invaded the jurisdiction of Congress. It violated the essence of the principle of the separation of governmental powers. Accordingly, the injunction against its effectiveness should be sustained.

Mr. Justice Clark, concurring in the judgment of the Court. . . .

I conclude that where Congress has laid down specific procedures to deal with the type of crisis confronting the President, he must follow those procedures in meeting the crisis; but that in the absence of such action by Congress, the President's independent power to act depends upon the gravity of the situation confronting the nation. I cannot sustain the seizure in question because here . . . Congress had prescribed methods to be followed by the President in meeting the emergency at hand.

Mr. Chief Justice Vinson, with whom Mr. Justice Reed and Mr. Justice Minton join, dissenting. . . .

Those who suggest that this is a case involving extraordinary powers should be mindful that these are extraordinary times. A world not yet recovered from the devastation of World War II has been forced to face the threat of another and more terrifying global conflict. . . .

One is not here called upon even to consider the possibility of executive seizure of a farm, a corner grocery store or even a single industrial plant. Such considerations arise only when one ignores the central fact of this case—that the Nation's entire basic steel production would have shut down completely if there had been no Government seizure. Even ignoring for the moment whatever confidential information the President may possess as "the Nation's organ for foreign affairs," the uncontroverted affidavits in this record amply support the finding that "a work stoppage would immediately jeopardize and imperil our national defense."

Plaintiffs do not remotely suggest any basis for rejecting the President's finding that *any* stoppage of steel production would immediately place the Nation in peril. More-over, even self-generated doubts that *any* stoppage of steel production constitutes an emergency are of little comfort here. The Union and the plaintiffs bargained for 6 months with over 100 issues in dispute—issues not limited to wage demands but including the union shop and other matters of principle between the parties. At the time of seizure there was not, and there is not now, the slightest evidence to justify the belief that any strike will be of short duration. The Union and the steel companies may well engage in a lengthy struggle. Plaintiff's counsel tells us that "sooner or later" the mills will operate again. That may satisfy the steel companies and, perhaps, the Union. But our soldiers and our allies will hardly be cheered with the assurance that the ammunition upon which their lives depend will be forthcoming—"sooner or later," or, in other words, "too little and too late."

Accordingly, if the President has any power under the Constitution to meet a critical situation in the absence of express statutory authorization, there is no basis whatever for criticizing the exercise of such power in this case. . . .

A review of executive action demonstrates that our Presidents have on many occa-sions exhibited the leadership contemplated by the Framers when they made the President Commander in Chief, and imposed upon him the trust to "take Care that the Laws be faithfully executed." With or without explicit statutory authorization, Presidents have at such times dealt with national emergencies by acting promptly and resolutely to enforce legislative programs, at least to save those programs until Con-gress could act. Congress and the courts have responded to such executive initiative with consistent approval. . . .

The President reported to Congress the morning after the seizure that he acted because a work stoppage in steel production would immediately imperil the safety of the Nation by preventing execution of the legislative programs for procurement of military equipment. And, while a shutdown could be averted by granting the price concessions requested by plaintiffs, granting such concessions would disrupt the price stabilization program also enacted by Congress. Rather than fail to execute either legis-lative program, the President acted to execute both. . . .

The absence of a specific statute authorizing seizure of the steel mills as a mode of executing the laws—both the military procurement program and the anti-inflation pro-gram—has not until today been thought to prevent the President from executing the laws. Unlike an administrative commission confined to the enforcement of the statute under which it was created, or the head of a department when administering a par-ticular statute, the President is a constitutional officer charged with taking care that a "mass of legislation" be executed. Flexibility as to mode of execution to meet critical situations is a matter of practical necessity. . . .

There is no statute prohibiting seizure as a method of enforcing legislative pro-grams. Congress has in no wise indicated that its legislation is not to be executed by the taking of private property (subject of course to the payment of just compensa-tion) if its legislation cannot otherwise be executed. . . .

Whatever the extent of Presidential power on more tranquil occasions, and what-ever the right of the President to execute legislative programs as he sees fit without reporting the mode of execution to Congress, the single Presidential purpose disclosed on this record is to faithfully execute the laws by acting in an emergency to maintain the status quo, thereby preventing collapse of the legislative programs until Congress could act. The President's action served the same purposes as a judicial stay entered to maintain the status quo in order to preserve the jurisdiction of a court. In his Message to Congress immediately following the seizure, the President explained the necessity of his action in executing the military procurement and anti-inflation legis-lative programs and expressed his desire to cooperate with any legislative proposals approving, regulating or rejecting the seizure of the steel mills. Consequently, there is no evidence whatever of any Presidential purpose to defy Congress or act in any way inconsistent with the legislative will. . . .

Plaintiffs admit that the emergency procedures of Taft-Hartley are not mandatory. Nevertheless, plaintiffs apparently argue that, since Congress did provide the 80-day injuction method for dealing with emergency strikes, the President cannot claim that an emergency exists until the procedures of Taft-Hartley have been exhausted. This argument was not the basis of the District Court's opinion and, whatever merit the argument might have had following the enactment of Taft-Hartley, it loses all force when viewed in light of the statutory pattern confronting the President in this case. . . .

When the President acted on April 8, he had exhausted the procedures for settlement available to him. Taft-Hartley was a route parallel to, not connected with, the WSB procedure. The strike had been delayed 99 days as contrasted with the maximum delay of 80 days under Taft-Hartley. There had been a hearing on the issues in dispute and bargaining which promised settlement up to the very hour before seizure had broken down. Faced with immediate national peril through stoppage in steel production on the one hand and faced with destruction of the wage and price legislative programs on the other, the President took temporary possession of the steel mills as the only course open to him consistent with his duty to take care that the laws be faithfully executed. . . .

The broad executive power granted by Article II to an officer on duty 365 days a year cannot, it is said, be invoked to avert disaster. Instead, the President must confine himself to sending a message to Congress recommending action. Under this messenger-boy concept of the Office, the President cannot even act to preserve legislative programs from destruction so that Congress will have something left to act upon. There is no judicial finding that the executive action was unwarranted because there was in fact no basis for the President's finding of the existence of an emergency for, under this view, the gravity of the emergency and the immediacy of the threatened disaster are considered irrelevant as a matter of law. . . .

Faced with the duty of executing the defense programs which Congress had enacted and the disastrous effects that any stoppage in steel production would have on those programs, the President acted to preserve those programs by seizing the steel mills. There is no question that the possession was other than temporary in character and subject to congressional direction—either approving, disapproving or regulating the manner in which the mills were to be administered and returned to the owners. The President immediately informed Congress of his action and clearly stated his intention to abide by the legislative will. No basis for claims of arbitrary action, unlimited powers or dictatorial usurpation of congressional power appears from the facts of this case. On the contrary, judicial, legislative and executive precedents throughout our history demonstrate that in this case the President acted in full conformity with his duties under the Constitution. Accordingly, we would reverse the order of the District Court.

Chapter 14

APPOINTMENT AND REMOVAL

[The President] shall . . . nominate, and by and with the advice and consent of the Senate, shall appoint ambassadors, other public ministers and consuls, judges of the Supreme Court, and all other officers of the United States, whose appointments are not herein otherwise provided for, and which shall be established by law: but the Congress may by law vest the appointment of such inferior officers, as they think proper, in the President alone, in the courts of law, or in the heads of departments.   ART. II, SEC. 2

The President shall have power to fill up all vacancies that may happen during the recess of the Senate, by granting commissions which shall expire at the end of their next session.   ART. II, SEC. 2

The President, Vice President and all civil officers of the United States, shall be removed from office on impeachment for, and conviction of, treason, bribery, or other high crimes and misdemeanors.   ART. II, SEC. 4

Generally speaking, the President's nominating power has occasioned little constitutional litigation. Standing as one of the most important executive prerogatives, it is firmly grounded in the provisions of Article II, section 2. It is vulnerable, however, to a certain degree in two respects.

First, there is the requirement of senatorial confirmation for all appointees except "inferior officers." Determination of officers falling in this class is within the discretion of Congress, which has shown a marked tendency to expand the role of the Senate by extending the requirement of confirmation into additional brackets of the public service. The Senate, moreover, has made its confirmation power into a very effective weapon against the President by the practice of "senatorial courtesy," which demands that appointees be personally acceptable to the administration senator or senators of the state from which the appointee comes.

A second way in which Congress can limit the President's discretion in appointment is by statutory specification of the qualifications of appointees. Normally Congress uses this power only to indicate the general qualities it conceives as desirable for the position, such as that in selecting members of the Federal Reserve Board the President "shall have due regard to a fair representation of the financial, agricultural, and geographical divisions of the country." But at the other extreme there is the classic case where a 1916 Army reorganization act creating certain vacancies in the Judge Advocate's Department provided that "one such vacancy, not below the rank of Major, shall be filled by the appointment of a person from civil life, not less than forty-five nor more than fifty years of age, who shall have been for ten years a Judge of the Supreme Court of the Philippine Islands, shall have served for two years as a Captain in the regular or volunteer army, and shall be proficient in the Spanish language and laws." Naturally there was only one man in the country who fitted these specifications, and he was a friend of the principal congressional draftsman of the legislation.

The President's authority to "fill up all vacancies that may happen during the recess of the Senate" does offer the President some opportunity of evading the confirmation requirement, since such appointments run until the end of the next session of the Senate. By the use of recess appointments President Jefferson kept a Secretary of the Navy for four years without Senate confirmation. Congress has made this practice less likely by prohibiting payment of salary to persons given recess appointments, if the vacancy existed while the Senate was in session, until the appointment has been confirmed by the Senate. This prohibition does not apply if the vacancy occurred within the last thirty days of the session of the Senate, or if the nomination was pending in the Senate at the end of a session.

Impeachment is the only method of removal from office specified in the Constitution. There is no language pertaining to the President's power to remove, or declaring whether officers appointed with the confirmation of the Senate can be removed by the President without Senate approval. Widely varying opinions have been held on this question.

In No. 77 of *The Federalist*, Alexander Hamilton argued that the Senate was associated with the President in exercise of the removal power. However, in the debate on establishment of the State Department in the First Congress, Madison contended successfully for the theory that the Secretary of State was removable by the President alone. The original statutory language proposed on this subject making the Secretary "removable by the President" was questioned because it might be interpreted as conferring on the President powers he would not otherwise have had. Consequently the act as finally passed merely provided that the Department's chief clerk should act as Secretary if the latter was "removed from office by the President." This important decision, which seemed to confirm the proposition that the President's removal power was conferred on him directly by the Constitution, and in which many of the drafters of the Constitution participated, has been called "the decision of 1789."

In accordance with this view, the President's sole control of the removal power was practically unquestioned until the Civil War, even with respect to appointments for which Congress had specified a fixed term of years. It is true that Marshall expressed the opinion in *Marbury* v. *Madison* that since the statute had provided for a five-year term for justices of the peace in the District of Columbia, "the appointment was not revocable" by the President. However, this statement was discounted as dictum in a partisan opinion. A dramatic illustration of the effectiveness of the President's removal power came in 1833 when President Jackson removed Secretary of the Treasury Duane who had refused to withdraw government funds from the Bank of the United States without first consulting Congress.

In the bitter feud between President Johnson and Congress after the Civil War, Congress sought to recapture a share in the removal power. The tenure of office act passed in 1867 denied the President power to remove the heads of executive departments without the advice and consent of the Senate. A violation of this act, which Johnson contended was unconstitutional, was one of the charges on which he was impeached. The act was repealed in 1887 without ever having been subjected to a definitive constitutional test.

In 1876 Congress passed an act providing for Senate participation in the removal of postmasters. Litigation arising under this statute resulted in 1926 in a long-delayed vindication of Johnson's position. The case was *Myers v. United States*, 272 U.S. 52, involving a postmaster in Portland, Oregon, who was removed by President Wilson before the expiration of his four-year term without securing Senate consent. Myers brought suit in the Court of Claims for salary for the remainder of his term. The Supreme Court ruled against the claim (Myers had died by the time the case was decided) on the ground that the act of 1876 was unconstitutional.

Chief Justice Taft, who knew what the Presidency looked like from the inside, and how important the removal power was, wrote the Court's opinion. He relied in part on the "decision of 1789" and the consistent practice of presidential removal which had been challenged only in the heat of the battle against Johnson. But Taft also based his conclusions directly upon the constitutional provisions vesting "executive power" in the President and charging him with faithful execution of the laws. From these responsibilities, Taft concluded:

> The reasonable implication, even in the absence of express words, was that as part of his executive power he should select those who were to act for him under his direction in the execution of the laws. The further implication must be, in the absence of any express limitation respecting removals, that as his selection of administrative officers is essential to the execution of the laws by him, so must be his power of removing those for whom he cannot continue to be responsible.

Three justices—Holmes, Brandeis, and McReynolds—dissented, Holmes contending that Taft's constitutional arguments were "spiders' webs inadequate to control the dominant facts," and Brandeis pointing out that a postmaster was clearly an inferior officer whose appointment Congress might have taken away from the President entirely and given to the head of a department.

Though this decision could be determinative only for the type of position actually involved, Taft matched Marshall's earlier overassertiveness by a dictum to the effect that the principle laid down in this case would apply generally, even in the case of executive officers to whom Congress had given "duties of a quasi judicial character . . . and members of executive tribunals. . . ." Nine years later the Supreme Court had to pass on a case of precisely this character involving a member of the Federal Trade Commission who had been removed by President Franklin D. Roosevelt without any showing of cause, although the statute specified "inefficiency, neglect of duty, or malfeasance in office" as grounds for presidential removal. In *Humphrey's Executor v. United States*, 295 U.S. 602 (1935)—Humphrey, like Myers, died before the case was decided— the Court unanimously held this language to be a valid restriction on the removal power, thus reversing Taft's dictum as Taft had reversed Marshall's dictum.

Justice Sutherland pointed out that the officer involved in the *Myers* case, a postmaster, was "restricted to the performance of executive functions," and rather lowly ones at that. In contrast, Humphrey was a member of "an administrative body created by Congress to carry into effect legislative policies embodied in the statute," performing its duties "without executive leave." In fact, Sutherland continued, a Federal Trade Commissioner "occupies no place in the executive department and . . . exercises no part of the executive power vested by the Constitution in the President." The Federal Trade Commission is a "quasi-legislative or quasi-judicial" agency, which Congress intended to discharge its duties "independently of executive control." Forbidding the President to remove its commissioners except for cause is a legitimate way of implementing that policy, "for it is quite evident that one who holds his office only during the pleasure of another, cannot be depended upon to maintain an attitude of independence against the latter's will."

Sutherland challenged not only the dicta of Taft's opinion, but also its basic constitutional theory. He ignored Taft's interpretation of the "executive power" clause as a grant of authority. He appeared to whittle presidential power down to two categories. First, there were the prerogatives explicitly granted to the President in the Constitution. The impact of the "decision of 1789," Sutherland said, was limited to this category, since it concerned the Secretary of State, an officer who was "purely executive . . . responsible to the President, and to him alone, in a very definite sense." The second category of presidential responsibility was for those officials who exercised only nondiscretionary or ministerial powers, such as a postmaster. Apart from these two classes of officials, it appeared that Congress was free to impose such limitations as it chose upon the removal power.

It was rather generally thought from the *Humphrey* decision that the Court would require Congress actually to express by legislation its intention to limit the President's removal power before any such limitation would be judicially recognized. However, in *Wiener v. United States*, 357 U.S. 349 (1958), the Court extended the *Humphrey* principle to cover a quasi-judicial officer where there had been no specific statutory language protecting against removal. Under the *Wiener* decision, then, the President's power of removal, which normally can be exercised at his discretion, may be used against quasi-judicial officers only for cause, regardless of whether Congress has so provided.

WIENER v. UNITED STATES
357 U.S. 349, 78 S. Ct. 1275, 2 L. Ed. 2d 1377 (1958)

Mr. Justice Frankfurter delivered the opinion of the Court.

This is a suit for back pay, based on petitioner's alleged illegal removal as a member of the War Claims Commission. The facts are not in dispute. By the War Claims Act of 1948, 62 Stat. 1240, Congress established that Commission with "jurisdiction to receive and adjudicate according to law," § 3, claims for compensating internees, prisoners of war, and religious organizations, §§ 5, 6 and 7, who suffered personal injury or property damage at the hands of the enemy in connection with World War II. The Commission was to be composed of three persons, at least two of whom were to be members of the bar, to be appointed by the President, by and with the advice and consent of the Senate. The Commission was to wind up its affairs not later than three years after the expiration of the time for filing claims, originally limited to two years but extended by successive legislation first to March 1, 1951, 63 Stat. 112, and later to March 31, 1952, 65 Stat. 28. This limit on the Commission's life was the mode by which the tenure of the Commissioners was defined, and Congress made no provision for removal of a Commissioner.

Having been duly nominated by President Truman, the petitioner was confirmed on June 2, 1950, and took office on June 8, following. On his refusal to heed a request for his resignation, he was, on December 10, 1953, removed by President Eisenhower in the following terms: "I regard it as in the national interest to complete the administration of the War Claims Act of 1948, as amended, with personnel of my own selection." The following day, the President made recess appointments to the Commission, including petitioner's post. After Congress assembled, the President, on February 15, 1954, sent the names of the new appointees to the Senate. The Senate had not confirmed these nominations when the Commission was abolished, July 1, 1954. . . . Thereupon, petitioner brought this proceeding in the Court of Claims for recovery of his salary as a War Claims Commissioner from December 10, 1953, the day of his removal by the President, to June 30, 1954, the last day of the Commission's existence. A divided Court of Claims dismissed the petition, 135 Ct. Cl. 827, 142 F. Supp. 910. We brought the case here, 352 U. S. 980, because it presents a variant of the constitutional issue decided in *Humphrey's Executor* v. *United States,* 295 U. S. 602.

Controversy pertaining to the scope and limits of the President's power of removal fills a thick chapter of our political and judicial history. The long stretches of its history, beginning with the very first Congress, with early echoes in the Reports of this Court, were laboriously traversed in *Myers* v. *United States,* 272 U. S. 52, and need not be retraced. President Roosevelt's reliance upon the pronouncements of the Court in that case in removing a member of the Federal Trade Commission on the ground that "the aims and purposes of the Administration with respect to the work of the Commission can be carried out most effectively with personnel of my own selection" reflected contemporaneous professional opinion regarding the significance of the *Myers* decision. Speaking through a Chief Justice who himself had been President, the Court did not restrict itself to the immediate issue before it, the President's inherent power to remove a postmaster, obviously an executive official. As of set purpose and not by way of parenthetic casualness, the Court announced that the President had inherent constitutional power of removal also of officials who have "duties of a quasi-judicial character . . . whose decisions after hearing affect interests of individuals, the discharge of which the President can not in a particular case properly influence or control." . . . This view of presidential power was deemed to flow from his "constitutional duty of seeing that the laws be faithfully executed." . . .

The assumption was short-lived that the *Myers* case recognized the President's inherent constitutional power to remove officials, no matter what the relation of the executive to the discharge of their duties and no matter what restrictions Congress may have imposed regarding the nature of their tenure. The versatility of circumstances often mocks a natural desire for definitiveness. Within less than ten years a unanimous Court, in *Humphrey's Executor* v. *United States,* 295 U. S. 602, narrowly confined the scope of the *Myers* decision to include only "all purely executive officers." . . . The Court explicitly "disapproved" the expressions in *Myers* supporting the President's inherent constitutional power to remove members of quasi-judicial bodies. . . . Congress had given members of the Federal Trade Commission a seven-year term and also provided for the removal of a Commissioner by the President for inefficiency, neglect of duty or malfeasance in office. In the present case, Congress provided for a tenure defined by the relatively short period of time during which the

War Claims Commission was to operate—that is, it was to wind up not later than three years after the expiration of the time for filing of claims. But nothing was said in the Act about removal.

This is another instance in which the most appropriate legal significance must be drawn from congressional failure of explicitness. Necessarily this is a problem in probabilities. We start with one certainty. The problem of the President's power to remove members of agencies entrusted with duties of the kind with which the War Claims Commission was charged was within the lively knowledge of Congress. Few contests between Congress and the President have so recurringly had the attention of Congress as that pertaining to the power of removal. Not the least significant aspect of the *Myers* case is that on the Court's special invitation Senator George Wharton Pepper, of Pennsylvania, presented the position of Congress at the bar of this Court.

Humphrey's case was a *cause célèbre*—and not least in the halls of Congress. And what is the essence of the decision in Humphrey's case? It drew a sharp line of cleavage between officials who were part of the Executive establishment and were thus removable by virtue of the President's constitutional powers, and those who are members of a body "to exercise its judgment without the leave or hindrance of any other official or any department of the government," . . . as to whom a power of removal exists only if Congress may fairly be said to have conferred it. This sharp differentiation derives from the difference in functions between those who are part of the Executive establishment and those whose tasks require absolute freedom from Executive interference. "For it is quite evident," again to quote *Humphrey's Executor*, "that one who holds his office only during the pleasure of another, cannot be depended upon to maintain an attitude of independence against the latter's will." . . .

Thus, the most reliable factor for drawing an inference regarding the President's power of removal in our case is the nature of the function that Congress vested in the War Claims Commission. What were the duties that Congress confided to this Commission? And can the inference fairly be drawn from the failure of Congress to provide for removal that these Commissioners were to remain in office at the will of the President? For such is the assertion of power on which petitioner's removal must rest. The ground of President Eisenhower's removal of petitioner was precisely the same as President Roosevelt's removal of Humphrey. Both Presidents desired to have Commissioners, one on the Federal Trade Commission, the other on the War Claims Commission, "of my own selection." They wanted these Commissioners to be their men. The terms of removal in the two cases are identic and express the assumption that the agencies of which the two Commissioners were members were subject in the discharge of their duties to the control of the Executive. An analysis of the Federal Trade Commission Act left this Court in no doubt that such was not the conception of Congress in creating the Federal Trade Commission. The terms of the War Claims Act of 1948 leave no doubt that such was not the conception of Congress regarding the War Claims Commission.

The history of this legislation emphatically underlines this fact. The short of it is that the origin of the Act was a bill, H.R. 4044, 80th Cong., 1st Sess., passed by the House that placed the administration of a very limited class of claims by Americans against Japan in the hands of the Federal Security Administrator and provided for a Commission to inquire into and report upon other types of claims. . . . The Federal Security Administrator was indubitably an arm of the President. When the House bill reached the Senate, it struck out all but the enacting clause, rewrote the bill, and established a Commission with "jurisdiction to receive and adjudicate according to law" three classes of claims, as defined by §§ 5, 6 and 7. The Commission was established as an adjudicating body with all the paraphernalia by which legal claims are put to the test of proof, with finality of determination "not subject to review by any other official of the United States or by any court, by mandamus or otherwise," § 11. Awards were to be paid out of a War Claims Fund in the hands of the Secretary of the Treasury, whereby such claims were given even more assured collectability than adheres to judgments rendered in the Court of Claims. . . . With minor amendment . . . this Senate bill became law.

When Congress has for distribution among American claimants funds derived from foreign sources, it may proceed in different ways. Congress may appropriate directly; it may utilize the Executive; it may resort to the adjudicatory process. . . . For Congress itself to have made appropriations for the claims with which it dealt under the War Claims Act was not practical in view of the large number of claimants and the diversity in the specific circumstances giving rise to the claims. The House bill in effect put the distribution of the narrow class of claims that it acknowledged into Executive hands, by vesting the procedure in the Federal Security Administrator. The final form of the legislation, as we have seen, left the widened range of claims to be determined by adjudication. Congress could, of course, have given jurisdiction over these claims to the District Courts or to the Court of Claims. The fact that it chose to establish a Commission to "adjudicate according to law" the classes of claims defined in the statute did not alter the intrinsic judicial character of the task with which the Commission was charged. The claims were to be "adjudicated according to law," that is, on the merits of each claim, supported by evidence and governing legal considerations, by a body that was "entirely free from the control or coercive influence, direct or indirect," . . . of either the Executive or the Congress. If, as one must take for granted, the War Claims Act precluded the President from influencing the Commission in passing on a particular claim, *a fortiori* must it be inferred that Congress did not wish to have hang over the Commission the Damocles' sword of removal by the President for no reason other than that he preferred to have on that Commission men of his own choosing.

For such is this case. We have not a removal for cause involving the rectitude of a member of an adjudicatory body, nor even a suspensory removal until the Senate could act upon it by confirming the appointment of a new Commissioner or otherwise dealing with the matter. Judging the matter in all the nakedness in which it is presented, namely, the claim that the President could remove a member of an adjudicatory body like the War Claims Commission merely because he wanted his own appointees on such a Commission, we are compelled to conclude that no such power is given to the President directly by the Constitution, and none is impliedly conferred upon him by statute simply because Congress said nothing about it. The philosophy of *Humphrey's Executor,* in its explicit language as well as its implication, precludes such a claim.

The judgment is

Reversed.

Chapter 15

FOREIGN RELATIONS

The Congress shall have power . . . to declare war, grant letters of marque and reprisal, and make rules concerning captures on land and water. . . .
ART. I, SEC. 8

No state shall enter into any treaty, alliance or confederation. . . . No state shall, without the consent of Congress, . . . keep troops, or ships of war in time of peace, enter into any agreement or compact with another state, or with a foreign power, or engage in war, unless actually invaded, or in such imminent danger as will not admit of delay.   ART. I, SEC. 10

[The President] shall have power, by and with the advice and consent of the Senate, to make treaties, provided two thirds of the senators present concur; and he shall nominate, and by and with the advice and consent of the Senate, shall appoint ambassadors, other public ministers and consuls. . . .   ART. II, SEC. 2

This Constitution, and the laws of the United States which shall be made in pursuance thereof; and all treaties made, or which shall be made, under the authority of the United States, shall be the supreme law of the land.
ART. VI

The provisions of the Constitution pertaining to foreign relations take the form of assignments of particular functions to the various branches of the government. They do not by any means cover the whole range of foreign affairs, and there is no grant of authority over foreign relations in broad terms comparable to the authorization to regulate commerce among the states and with foreign nations. However, such a grant is not necessary. Authority over foreign affairs is an inherent power, which attaches automatically to the federal government as a sovereign entity, and derives from the Constitution only as the Constitution is the creator of that sovereign entity.

The constitutional difference between the source of the federal government's power over external and internal affairs was examined by the Supreme Court in *United States* v. *Curtiss-Wright Export Corp.*, 299 U.S. 304 (1936). Justice Sutherland endeavored, perhaps not too convincingly, to trace this difference to the historical situation prevailing when the Constitution was adopted. In the field of internal affairs, he said, "the primary purpose of the Constitution was to carve from the general mass of legislative powers *then possessed by the states* such portions as it was thought desirable to vest in the federal government, leaving those not included in the enumeration still in the states."

But the Constitution could not transfer power over external affairs in this way from the states to the Union because "the states severally never possessed international powers." Rather, on the separation of the Colonies "acting as a unit" from Great Britain, "the powers of external sovereignty passed from the Crown not to the colonies severally, but to the colonies in their collective and corporate capacity as the United States of America." Even before the Declaration of Independence, the Colonies were acting through a common agency, the Continental Congress, and when "the external sovereignty of Great Britain in respect of the colonies ceased, it immediately passed to the Union." Thus the Union, existing before the Constitution, "was the sole possessor of external sovereignty and in the Union it remained without change save in so far as the Constitution in express terms qualified its exercise."

As for the location of the power to carry on the foreign relations of the United States, the principal theoretical writers on whom the Founders relied—Blackstone, Locke, Montesquieu—were unanimous in contending that the responsibility must rest with the executive. Nevertheless, the Constitution allocated the power to declare war to Congress. It made the Senate's consent necessary to the ratification of treaties, and by a two-thirds vote. It made the Senate's advice and consent a condition to the appointment of ambassadors. When account is taken of the general lawmaking and appropriating powers of Congress, the exercise of which is often essential to the formulation and execution of foreign policy decisions, it is clear that "the Constitution, considered only for its affirmative grants of powers capable of affecting the issue, is an invitation to struggle for the privilege of directing American foreign policy."[1]

For this struggle the President is powerfully equipped by the general characteristics of executive power already noted, by his constitutional authority as Commander in Chief, and by his recognized position as "the Nation's organ for foreign affairs." The Supreme Court has repeatedly recognized the President's primacy and special position in this area, as it did in the *Curtiss-Wright* case.

That controversy involved a joint resolution adopted by Congress in 1934 authorizing the President by proclamation to prohibit the sale of arms within the United States to certain South American belligerent states. The President issued such a proclamation. A conviction for violation of the proclamation and joint resolution was attacked on the ground that the statute constituted an unlawful delegation of legislative power to the President. The Court replied that, whatever might have been the merits of such a charge if internal affairs had been involved, it could not be upheld where "the very delicate, plenary and exclusive power of the President as the sole organ of the federal government in the field of international relations" was at issue. Justice Sutherland went on:

It is quite apparent that if, in the maintenance of our international relations, embarrassment . . . is to be avoided and success for our aims achieved, congressional legislation which is to be made effective through negotiation and inquiry within the international field must often accord to the President a degree of discretion and freedom from statutory restriction which would not be admissible were domestic affairs alone involved. Moreover, he, not Congress, has the better opportunity of knowing the conditions which prevail in foreign countries. . . . He has his confidential

[1] Edward S. Corwin, *The President: Office and Powers* (New York: New York University Press, 1957), p. 171.

sources of information. He has his agents in the form of diplomatic, consular and other officials.

The powers which the President exercises as "sole organ" of foreign relations for the nation can be briefly indicated. He is the channel for communications to and from other nations, and conducts negotiations directly or through his appointed representatives. He has the power of recognizing foreign governments. He can use his control of the armed forces to implement his policies and to protect American rights or interests abroad. To a considerable degree these powers cancel out the most important grant of external authority to Congress, the power to declare war. For the President can, by his management of foreign affairs and his use of the armed forces, so shape the nation's policy and the development of events that he leaves Congress no choice other than to declare war.

On the other hand, the necessity of securing Senate consent by a two-thirds vote for the ratification of treaties has proved in practice to be a real limitation on executive policy making. The shambles which Senate obduracy has often made of United States foreign policy has led many students to conclude that consent to treaty ratification by a majority vote of the two houses of Congress would be preferable to the present arrangement.

Partly because of the hazards of Senate treaty approval, the President has made extensive use of "executive agreements" with foreign countries, which do not require Senate assent. They may be employed for minor matters which it would be inappropriate to embody in a treaty, but often they deal with matters of major importance. Unless such agreements are based on acts of Congress authorizing them, they are usually said to find their constitutional authority in the President's power as Commander in Chief or in his position as the sole organ of international relations. Efforts to distinguish between the legal effects of treaties and executive agreements have generally been unsuccessful.

Article VI sets up treaties and acts of Congress on a par—both are "the supreme law of the land." In case of conflict between a treaty and a statute, the later in point of time generally supersedes the earlier. However, a non-self-executing treaty (i.e., one which requires congressional legislation to put it into effect) does not supersede an earlier conflicting act of Congress.

According to Article VI, laws must be made "in pursuance" of the Constitution in order to have status as supreme law of the land, but treaties need only be made "under the authority of the United States." Considerable effort has been made to conjure up from this difference in wording the bogey of a treaty power unlimited by the Constitution. Some substance may seem to be given these fears by the fact that the Supreme Court has never held a treaty unconstitutional, and by the circumstances of the Court's decision in *Missouri v. Holland* 252 U.S. 416 (1920).

Admittedly there is something startling about the holding in that case whereby ratification of a treaty gives Congress constitutional powers it did not possess in the absence of the treaty. But this result is an inevitable consequence of the plenary nature of federal power over foreign affairs. The complete incapacity of the states for foreign relationships requires that the federal government have authority to deal with all matters which are of legitimate concern to American foreign relations. This does not mean, however, that the treaty power can be used to amend the Constitution, nor does it open up all constitutional rights to revision by treaties.

During the 1950s, American isolationists sought to raise doubt on these points as part of the campaign to secure adoption of the Bricker Amendment. The first section of the amendment, in its 1953 version, read: "A provision of a treaty which conflicts with this Constitution shall not be of any force or effect." However, this was clearly already the law on the subject. Any doubt on this score was removed in 1957 by the Court's decision in *Reid* v. *Covert*, 354 U.S. 1, which specifically held that Article VI did not permit the United States "to exercise power under an international agreement without observing constitutional prohibitions."

A second purpose of the Bricker Amendment was to reverse the holding in *Missouri* v. *Holland* and to render the national government incapable of assuming the regulation of subjects reserved to the states by entering into a treaty. The Bricker Amendment proposed this language: "A treaty shall become effective as internal law in the United States only through legislation which would be valid in the absence of a treaty." The purpose was to prevent the federal government from dealing with any internal problem on the basis of a treaty, where it lacked authority to legislate under its other constitutional powers. Yet the majority of American treaties have dealt with matters internally under the jurisdiction of the states. These include such matters as the right to own property, to inherit, to collect debts, to organize corporations, to escape discriminatory taxes, to have access to the courts, or to enter a profession. The United States enters into treaties guaranteeing such rights to aliens in the United States so that American citizens can have the benefit of reciprocal protection abroad. As the purpose and effect of the Bricker Amendment came to be understood, its support dwindled and it ceased to be a political issue.

At about the same time, however, another political issue arose over the issuance of passports. A passport is necessary for a citizen to leave or enter the United States, and consequently the power of the Secretary of State over the issuance of passports gives him the authority to control travel. During the 1950s the policy of the State Department to refuse passports to persons suspected of being Communists or engaged in activities which would advance the Communist cause, was subjected to attack in the courts. In *Kent* v. *Dulles*, 357 U.S. 116 (1958), the Supreme Court held that "the right to travel is a part of the 'liberty' of which the citizen cannot be deprived without the due process of law of the Fifth Amendment."

Having decided this much, the Court found it unnecessary to take up the more difficult question of how far this liberty might be curtailed without infringing on due process, because the majority concluded that Congress had not authorized the kinds of curtailment which the State Department had been practicing. Thus the Department was left with no discretionary power to refuse passports to individuals, and several well-known Communists were granted passports. Efforts to adopt new passport control legislation failed in Congress, but the Supreme Court's decision in *Communist Party* v. *Subversive Activities Control Board*, 367 U.S. 1 (1961), brought into effect the restrictions of the Internal Security Act on use of passports by Communists. Under this authority the

State Department in 1962 issued regulations barring passports to Communist Party members, but allowing anyone accused of party membership the right to confront and cross-examine his accusers.

MISSOURI v. HOLLAND
252 U.S. 416, 40 S. Ct. 382, 64 L. Ed. 641 (1920)

In 1913 Congress passed a law strictly regulating the killing of migratory birds. The Constitution does not specifically authorize Congress to legislate on this subject, and two lower federal courts held the act unconstitutional. In 1916 the United States entered into a treaty with Great Britain under which the United States and Canada agreed to protect migratory birds and to adopt legislation for that purpose. Congress passed such a law in 1918, giving the Secretary of Agriculture authority to adopt regulations carrying out the purposes of the treaty.

MR. JUSTICE HOLMES delivered the opinion of the court.

This is a bill in equity brought by the State of Missouri to prevent a game warden of the United States from attempting to enforce the Migratory Bird Treaty Act of July 3, 1918, c. 128, 40 Stat. 755, and the regulations made by the Secretary of Agriculture in pursuance of the same. The ground of the bill is that the statute is an unconstitutional interference with the rights reserved to the States by the Tenth Amendment, and that the acts of the defendant done and threatened under that authority invade the sovereign right of the State and contravene its will manifested in statutes. The State also alleges a pecuniary interest, as owner of the wild birds within its borders and otherwise, admitted by the Government to be sufficient, but it is enough that the bill is a reasonable and proper means to assert the alleged quasi sovereign rights of a State. . . . A motion to dismiss was sustained by the District Court on the ground that the act of Congress is constitutional. . . . The State appeals.

On December 8, 1916, a treaty between the United States and Great Britain was proclaimed by the President. It recited that many species of birds in their annual migrations traversed certain parts of the United States and of Canada, that they were of great value as a source of food and in destroying insects injurious to vegetation, but were in danger of extermination through lack of adequate protection. It therefore provided for specified closed seasons and protection in other forms, and agreed that the two powers would take or propose to their law-making bodies the necessary measures for carrying the treaty out. 39 Stat. 1702. The above mentioned Act of July 3, 1918, entitled an act to give effect to the convention, prohibited the killing, capturing or selling any of the migratory birds included in the terms of the treaty except as permitted by regulations compatible with those terms, to be made by the Secretary of Agriculture. Regulations were proclaimed on July 31, and October 25, 1918. 40 Stat. 1812; 1863. It is unnecessary to go into any details, because, as we have said, the question raised is the general one whether the treaty and statute are void as an interference with the rights reserved to the States.

To answer this question it is not enough to refer to the Tenth Amendment, reserving the powers not delegated to the United States, because by Article II, § 2, the power to make treaties is delegated expressly, and by Article VI treaties made under the authority of the United States, along with the Constitution and laws of the United States made in pursuance thereof, are declared the supreme law of the land. If the treaty is valid there can be no dispute about the validity of the statute under

Article I, § 8, as a necessary and proper means to execute the powers of the Government. The language of the Constitution as to the supremacy of treaties being general, the question before us is narrowed to an inquiry into the ground upon which the present supposed exception is placed.

It is said that a treaty cannot be valid if it infringes the Constitution, that there are limits, therefore, to the treaty-making power, and that one such limit is that what an act of Congress could not do unaided, in derogation of the powers reserved to the States, a treaty cannot do. An earlier act of Congress that attempted by itself and not in pursuance of a treaty to regulate the killing of migratory birds within the States had been held bad in the District Court. *United States* v. *Shauver,* 214 Fed. Rep. 154. *United States* v. *McCullagh,* 221 Fed. Rep. 288. Those decisions were supported by arguments that migratory birds were owned by the States in their sovereign capacity for the benefit of their people, and that under cases like *Geer* v. *Connecticut,* 161 U. S. 519, this control was one that Congress had no power to displace. The same argument is supposed to apply now with equal force.

Whether the two cases cited were decided rightly or not they cannot be accepted as a test of the treaty power. Acts of Congress are the supreme law of the land only when made in pursuance of the Constitution, while treaties are declared to be so when made under the authority of the United States. It is open to question whether the authority of the United States means more than the formal acts prescribed to make the convention. We do not mean to imply that there are no qualifications to the treaty-making power; but they must be ascertained in a different way. It is obvious that there may be matters of the sharpest exigency for the national well being that an act of Congress could not deal with but that a treaty followed by such an act could, and it is not lightly to be assumed that, in matters requiring national action, "a power which must belong to and somewhere reside in every civilized government" is not to be found. . . . We are not yet discussing the particular case before us but only are considering the validity of the test proposed. With regard to that we may add that when we are dealing with words that also are a constituent act, like the Constitution of the United States, we must realize that they have called into life a being the development of which could not have been foreseen completely by the most gifted of its begetters. It was enough for them to realize or to hope that they had created an organism; it has taken a century and has cost their successors much sweat and blood to prove that they created a nation. The case before us must be considered in the light of our whole experience and not merely in that of what was said a hundred years ago. The treaty in question does not contravene any prohibitory words to be found in the Constitution. The only question is whether it is forbidden by some invisible radiation from the general terms of the Tenth Amendment. We must consider what this country has become in deciding what that Amendment has reserved.

The State as we have intimated founds its claim of exclusive authority upon an assertion of title to migratory birds, an assertion that is embodied in statute. No doubt it is true that as between a State and its inhabitants the State may regulate the killing and sale of such birds, but it does not follow that its authority is exclusive of paramount powers. To put the claim of the State upon title is to lean upon a slender reed. Wild birds are not in the possession of anyone; and possession is the beginning of ownership. The whole foundation of the State's rights is the presence within their jurisdiction of birds that yesterday had not arrived, tomorrow may be in another State and in a week a thousand miles away. If we are to be accurate we cannot put the case of the State upon higher ground than that the treaty deals with creatures that for the moment are within the state borders, that it must be carried out by officers of the United States within the same territory, and that but for the treaty the State would be free to regulate this subject itself.

As most of the laws of the United States are carried out within the States and as many of them deal with matters which in the silence of such laws the State might regulate, such general grounds are not enough to support Missouri's claim. Valid treaties of course "are as binding within the territorial limits of the States as they are elsewhere throughout the dominion of the United States." . . . No doubt the great body of private relations usually fall within the control of the State, but a treaty may override its power. . . .

Here a national interest of very nearly the first magnitude is involved. It can be protected only by national action in concert with that of another power. The subject-matter is only transitorily within the State and has no permanent habitat therein. But for the treaty and the statute there soon might be no birds for any powers to deal with. We see nothing in the Constitution that compels the Government to sit by while a food supply is cut off and the protectors of our forests and our crops are destroyed. It is not sufficient to rely upon the States. The reliance is vain, and were it otherwise, the question is whether the United States is forbidden to act. We are of opinion that the treaty and statute must be upheld. . . .

Decree affirmed.

MR. JUSTICE VAN DEVANTER and MR. JUSTICE PITNEY dissent.

Chapter 16

WAR POWERS

The Congress shall have power . . .
To declare war, grant letters of marque and reprisal, and make rules concerning captures on land and water; To raise and support armies, but no appropriation of money to that use shall be for a longer term than two years; To provide and maintain a navy; To make rules for the government and regulation of the land and naval forces. . . .   ART. I, SEC. 8

The President shall be Commander in Chief of the Army and Navy of the United States, and of the militia of the several states, when called into the actual service of the United States. . . .   ART. II, SEC. 2

The war power of Congress has seldom been subjected to judicial criticism or limitation. The reason, of course, is that the power to wage war must be the power to wage war successfully, and judges are unlikely to set their opinions over against those of the legislature as to the steps necessary for success in combat. Conscription during the First World War was upheld in the *Selective Draft Law Cases*, 245 U.S. 366 (1918), against contentions that it amounted to involuntary servitude. Wartime legislation controlling economic freedom and the use of private property has with rare exceptions been supported. In upholding rent controls during World War II, Justice Douglas said in *Bowles* v. *Willingham*, 321 U.S. 503 (1944): "A nation which can demand the lives of its men and women in the waging of . . . war is under no constitutional necessity of providing a system of price control on the domestic front which will assure each landlord a 'fair return' on his property."

The war power does not require the existence of a state of war for its exercise. It can be a justification of preparatory action before war starts, and for ameliorating action after war is over. The so-called Wartime Prohibition Act was passed on November 22, 1918, eleven days after the armistice. The rent control statute passed in 1947 was upheld in *Woods* v. *Miller Co.*, 333 U.S. 138 (1948), the Court pointing out "that there has not yet been eliminated the deficit in housing which in considerable measure was caused by the heavy demobilization of veterans and by the cessation or reduction in residential construction during the period of hostilities."

The Constitution is clear on how wars are declared, but does not indicate how they are ended, and so the judicial response has been again to accept the political decisions. As for the actual cessation of hostilities by armistice or otherwise, that is a decision for the President to make. Termination of the legal state of war is effected normally by negotiation of a treaty, but there is American experience with other methods. The Civil War was ended by presidential proclamation, World War I by joint resolution of Congress. "Whatever the mode," said the Supreme Court in *Ludecke v. Watkins,* 335 U.S. 160 (1948), termination of a state of war "is a political act."

The difficult constitutional issues concerning the extent of the war power have been raised by actions of the President rather than by congressional legislation. The President's tremendous executive authority is buttressed here by his status as Commander in Chief. In No. 69 of *The Federalist,* Hamilton thought that the President's role as Commander in Chief would amount "to nothing more than the supreme command and direction of the military and naval forces, as first general and admiral of the Confederacy," while the more significant powers of declaring war and raising and regulating fleets and armies would be exercised by Congress. Actually this was an accurate enough forecast of the limited role of the Comamnder in Chief from 1789 to 1861. It was President Lincoln who, in his resolve to save the Union, linked together the presidential power to take care that the laws be faithfully executed with that of Commander in Chief to yield a result approaching constitutional dictatorship.

For ten weeks after the fall of Fort Sumter until he called Congress into special session, Lincoln met the emergency by a series of actions which were for the most part without statutory authorization, though they were subsequently ratified by Congress. He added 40,000 men to the Army and Navy, closed the Post Office to treasonable correspondence, paid out 2 million dollars from unappropriated funds in the Treasury, proclaimed a blockade of Southern ports, suspended the writ of habeas corpus in several areas, and caused the arrest and military detention of persons suspected of treasonable practices. World Wars I and II, with their progressively greater impact on the civilian economy of the country, saw a proportionate increase in the President's wartime powers, though the expansion was achieved in nearly all cases with greater regard for the constitutional proprieties than was characteristic of the Civil War.

Lincoln's suspension of the writ of habeas corpus led to one of the great decisions in this field, *Ex parte Milligan,* 4 Wall. 2 (1866). In a proclamation of September, 1862, Lincoln suspended the writ and ordered that all persons "guilty of any disloyal practice affording aid and comfort to rebels" should be liable to trial by military commissions. Milligan was arrested at his home in Indiana late in 1864, tried by a military commission, and sentenced to be hanged. In May, 1865, he secured a writ of habeas corpus from the federal court in Indianapolis, and a year later the Supreme Court ruled unanimously that the President had no power to order trial of civilians by military courts in areas where the regular courts were open and operating.

There was a considerable similarity between Lincoln's military commissions and the situation which prevailed in Hawaii during the greater part of World War II. Martial law was declared by the governor of Hawaii immediately after the Japanese attack on December 7, 1941, and the President approved his action two days later. Civil and criminal courts were forbidden to try cases, military tribunals being set up to replace them. In *Duncan v. Kahanamoku,* 327 U.S. 304 (1946), the Supreme Court held that when Congress in the Hawaii Organic Act had granted the governor power to declare martial law, it had not meant to supersede constitutional guarantees of a fair trial which apply elsewhere in the United States.

Justices Burton and Frankfurter dissented. Their position was that "the conduct of war under the Constitution is largely an executive function," in which "executive discretion to determine policy is . . . intended by the Constitution to be supreme," at least on the battlefield. The original declaration of martial law after Pearl Harbor was clearly justified, and the executive authorities should be allowed a reasonable period in which "to decide when and how to restore the battlefield to its peace time controls."

So far as military personnel are concerned, offenses are punished by a system of courts-martial under regulations prescribed by Congress. Articles of War were adopted for the Army by Congress in 1789, and for the Navy in 1800. In 1950 these two statutes, as amended, were replaced by the Uniform Code of Military Justice, setting up a single system for all the armed services.

In general, the courts-martial and the civilian courts constitute completely separate systems of justice. However, the writ of habeas corpus furnishes a method whereby detention as a result of a court-martial decision can be reviewed by the civil courts. Such review is strictly limited, however, to the issue of jurisdiction of the court-martial, as is illustrated by the case of *United States ex rel. Toth* v. *Quarles,* 350 U.S. 11 (1955). After service in Korea, Toth had been honorably discharged. He returned to his home in Pittsburgh and went to work in a steel plant. Five months later he was arrested by military authorities, charged with having committed murder while in Korea, and flown there to stand trial before a court-martial. This action was taken under a provision of the Uniform Code allowing courts-martial to try former members of the armed forces after their discharge for serious offenses, punishable under military regulations by as much as five years' imprisonment, committed while in the service. Toth's sister instituted habeas corpus proceedings against the Secretary of the Air Force in a District of Columbia court, which ordered Toth's return to the United States.

For the Supreme Court, Justice Black noted that no claim of presidential power as Commander in Chief was involved. The statute had to be justified solely by the power of Congress to "make rules for the government and regulation of the land and naval forces," as supplemented by the "necessary and proper" clause. The provision applied to over three million Americans who had become veterans since the act was passed (and the number would grow each year), threatening them with military trial, the characteristics of which Black compared quite unfavorably with trial by the civil courts. The Court found there was no sufficient justification for thus depriving so many Americans of their constitutional right to trial by jury and indictment by grand jury, particularly since there was an alternative and perfectly constitutional method which Congress could have used to deal with the problem of crimes committed by servicemen while in service but not discovered until later—namely, to confer on the regular federal courts jurisdiction over such crimes.

Whether military courts may assert jurisdiction over dependents accompanying American servicemen stationed abroad in occupied territory or at American military bases has given the Supreme Court some trouble. The question was considered in two 1956 cases, *Reid v. Covert,* 351 U.S. 487, and *Kinsella v. Krueger,* 351 U.S. 470. With three justices dissenting and one reserving his opinion, the Court upheld the jurisdiction of courts-martial in these circumstances. However, a petition for rehearing was subsequently granted, and one year later the Court by a vote of six to two reversed its previous holdings.

In both instances wives of military personnel, living on American bases in England and Japan, had killed their husbands. The Uniform Code of Military Justice makes subject to its provisions "all persons serving with, employed by, or accompanying the armed forces without the continental limits of the United States." In an opinion by Justice Black, the Court concluded that this attempt to subject civilians "accompanying" the armed forces to courts-martial was unconstitutional, on the ground that constitutional safeguards apply to United States government action against a citizen abroad. The minority position in the *Reid v. Covert* rehearing, 354 U.S. 1 (1957), stressed the practical problems encountered in maintaining armed forces in sixty-three foreign countries and contended that in effect wives of servicemen were as much a part of military installations as their husbands.

There was some disagreement on the Court as to whether the reasoning in this case was applicable only when capital crimes were involved. However, in *Kinsella v. United States ex rel. Singleton,* 361 U.S. 234 (1960), the Court majority ruled that military trial of service dependents for noncapital offenses was also unconstitutional. Moreover, American civilian employees of the armed forces abroad could not be tried by military courts for either capital or noncapital offenses, according to *McElroy v. United States ex rel. Guagliardo,* 361 U.S. 281 (1960), and *Grisham v. Hagan,* 361 U.S. 278 (1960).

Courts-martial or military commissions have occasionally been set up by the President, under statutory authorization or his inherent powers as Commander in Chief, to deal with military crimes committed by others than the armed forces of the United States. A military commission was created to try the assassins of President Lincoln. In 1942 President Roosevelt established a military commission to try eight German saboteurs who had been landed in this country by submarine with the assignment of blowing up factories and bridges. The Supreme Court unanimously upheld this military trial in *Ex parte Quirin,* 317 U.S. 1 (1942).

Following World War II certain Japanese generals who had commanded troops in the Pacific theater were placed on trial before an American military commission in the Philippines. *In re Yamashita,* 327 U.S. 1 (1946), upheld the authority of the commission and ruled that its somewhat irregular procedures were not reviewable by the courts. *Hirota v. MacArthur,* 338 U.S. 197 (1948), involved war crimes trials by a military tribunal acting for all the powers which had defeated Japan. The Supreme Court ruled that it had no jurisdiction at all over this tribunal because of its international character. *Johnson v. Eisentrager,* 339 U.S. 763 (1950), likewise denied the jurisdiction of American courts over Germans confined in Germany by order of military courts of the American occupation forces.

There are no significant judicial discussions of the President's wartime powers over the internal economy. President Truman's seizure of the steel mills in 1952 was not during a period of declared war, and the Supreme Court refused to give any consideration to claims that the action could be justified by his status as Commander in Chief.

However, a much more serious wartime infringement on personal rights, the compulsory evacuation of persons of Japanese descent—most of whom were American citizens—from the West Coast during World War II did secure Supreme Court approval. In *Hirabayashi v. United States,* 320 U.S. 81 (1943), the Court avoided the major evacuation issue and upheld a curfew regulation for all persons of Japanese ancestry as a temporary emergency war measure. But in *Korematsu v. United States,* 323 U.S. 214 (1944), the constitutionality of the evacuation program, then in effect for over 2½ years, could no longer be avoided, and the Court upheld it by a divided vote.

KOREMATSU v. UNITED STATES
323 U.S. 214, 65 S. Ct. 193, 89 L. Ed. 194 (1944)

On February 19, 1942, President Roosevelt issued an executive order empowering the Secretary of War to designate military areas from which any or all persons might be excluded in order to prevent espionage and sabotage. Under this authorization the three West Coast states and part of Arizona were proclaimed military areas and all persons of Japanese ancestry, 70,000 of whom were American citizens, were cleared from these areas and moved by the Army to evacuation camps inland. Congress on March 21, 1942, passed a law ratifying the executive order. Korematsu, an American citizen of Japanese descent, was convicted for remaining in California after the exclusion order had become effective.

MR. JUSTICE BLACK delivered the opinion of the Court.

The petitioner, an American citizen of Japanese descent, was convicted in a federal district court for remaining in San Leandro, California, a "Military Area," contrary to Civilian Exclusion Order No. 34 of the Commanding General of the Western Command, U.S. Army, which directed that after May 9, 1942, all persons of Japanese ancestry should be excluded from that area. No question was raised as to petitioner's loyalty to the United States. The Circuit Court of Appeals affirmed, and the importance of the constitutional question involved caused us to grant certiorari.

It should be noted, to begin with, that all legal restrictions which curtail the civil rights of a single racial group are immediately suspect. That is not to say that all such restrictions are unconstitutional. It is to say that courts must subject them to the most rigid scrutiny. Pressing public necessity may sometimes justify the existence of such restrictions; racial antagonism never can. . . .

The 1942 Act was attacked in the *Hirabayashi* case as an unconstitutional delegation of power; it was contended that the curfew order and other orders on which it rested were beyond the war powers of the Congress, the military authorities and of the President, as Commander in Chief of the Army; and finally that to apply the curfew order against none but citizens of Japanese ancestry amounted to a constitutionally prohibited discrimination solely on account of race. To these questions, we gave the serious consideration which their importance justified. We upheld the curfew order as an exercise of the power of the government to take steps necessary to prevent espionage and sabotage in an area threatened by Japanese attack.

In the light of the principles we announced in the *Hirabayashi* case, we are unable to conclude that it was beyond the war power of Congress and the Executive to exclude those of Japanese ancestry from the West Coast war area at the time they did. True, exclusion from the area in which one's home is located is a far greater deprivation than constant confinement to the home from 8 p.m. to 6 a.m. Nothing short of apprehension by the proper military authorities of the gravest imminent danger to the public safety can constitutionally justify either. But exclusion from a threatened area, no less than curfew, has a definite and close relationship to the prevention of espionage and sabotage. The military authorities, charged with the primary responsibility of defending our shores, concluded that curfew provided inadequate protection and ordered exclusion. They did so, as pointed out in our *Hirabayashi* opinion, in accordance with Congressional authority to the military to say who should, and who should not, remain in the threatened areas.

In this case the petitioner challenges the assumptions upon which we rested our conclusions in the *Hirabayashi* case. He also urges that by May 1942, when Order No. 34 was promulgated, all danger of Japanese invasion of the West Coast had disappeared. After careful consideration of these contentions we are compelled to reject them.

Here, as in the *Hirabayashi* case, *supra*, p. 99, ". . . we cannot reject as unfounded the judgment of the military authorities and of Congress that there were disloyal members of that population, whose number and strength could not be precisely and quickly ascertained. We cannot say that the war-making branches of the Government did not have ground for believing that in a critical hour such persons could not readily be isolated and separately dealt with, and constituted a menace to the national defense and safety, which demanded that prompt and adequate measures be taken to guard against it."

Like curfew, exclusion of those of Japanese origin was deemed necessary because of the presence of an unascertained number of disloyal members of the group, most of whom we have no doubt were loyal to this country. It was because we could not reject the finding of the military authorities that it was impossible to bring about an immediate segregation of the disloyal from the loyal that we sustained the validity of the curfew order as applying to the whole group. In the instant case, temporary exclusion of the entire group was rested by the military on the same ground. The judgment that exclusion of the whole group was for the same reason a military imperative answers the contention that the exclusion was in the nature of group punishment based on antagonism to those of Japanese origin. That there were members of the group who retained loyalties to Japan has been confirmed by investigations made subsequent to the exclusion. Approximately five thousand American citizens of Japanese ancestry refused to swear unqualified allegiance to the United States and to renounce allegiance to the Japanese Emperor, and several thousand evacuees requested repatriation to Japan.

We uphold the exclusion order as of the time it was made and when the petitioner violated it. . . . In doing so, we are not unmindful of the hardships imposed by it upon a large group of American citizens. . . . But hardships are part of war, and war is an aggregation of hardships. All citizens alike, both in and out of uniform, feel the impact of war in greater or lesser measure. Citizenship has its responsibilities as well as its privileges, and in time of war the burden is always heavier. Compulsory exclusion of large groups of citizens from their homes, except under circumstances of direst emergency and peril, is inconsistent with our basic governmental institutions. But when under conditions of modern warfare our shores are threatened by hostile forces, the power to protect must be commensurate with the threatened danger. . . .

It is said that we are dealing here with the case of imprisonment of a citizen in a concentration camp solely because of his ancestry, without evidence or inquiry concerning his loyalty and good disposition towards the United States. Our task would be simple, our duty clear, were this a case involving the imprisonment of a loyal citizen in a concentration camp because of racial prejudice. Regardless of the true nature of the assembly and relocation centers—and we deem it unjustifiable to call them concentration camps with all the ugly connotations that term implies—we are dealing specifically with nothing but an exclusion order. To cast this case into outlines of racial prejudice, without reference to the real military dangers which were presented, merely confuses the issue. Korematsu was not excluded from the Military Area because of hostility to him or his race. He *was* excluded because we are at war with the Japanese Empire, because the properly constituted military authorities feared an invasion of our West Coast and felt constrained to take proper security measures, because they decided that the military urgency of the situation demanded that all citizens of Japanese ancestry be segregated from the West Coast temporarily, and finally, because Congress, reposing its confidence in this time of war in our military leaders—as inevitably it must—determined that they should have the power to do just this. There was evidence of disloyalty on the part of some, the military authorities considered that the need for action was great, and time was short. We cannot—by availing ourselves of the calm perspective of hindsight—now say that at that time these actions were unjustified.

Affirmed.

Mr. Justice Frankfurter, concurring. . . .

The provisions of the Constitution which confer on the Congress and the President powers to enable this country to wage war are as much part of the Constitution as provisions looking to a nation of peace. And we have had recent occasion to quote approvingly the statement of former Chief Justice Hughes that the war power of the Government is "the power to wage war successfully." . . . Therefore, the validity of action under the war power must be judged wholly in the context of war. That action is not to be stigmatized as lawless because like action in times of peace would be lawless. To talk about a military order that expresses an allowable judgment of war needs by those entrusted with the duty of conducting war as "an unconstitutional order" is to suffuse a part of the Constitution with an atmosphere of unconstitutionality. The respective spheres of action of military authorities and of judges are of course very different. But within their sphere, military authorities are no more outside the bounds of obedience to the Constitution than are judges within theirs. "The war power of the United States, like its other powers . . . is subject to applicable constitutional limitations," *Hamilton* v. *Kentucky Distilleries Co.,* 251 U.S. 146, 156. To recognize that military orders are "reasonably expedient military precautions" in time of war and yet to deny them constitutional legitimacy makes of the Constitution an instrument for dialectic subtleties not reasonably to be attributed to the hard-headed Framers, of whom a majority had had actual participation in war. If a military order such as that under review does not transcend the means appropriate for conducting war, such action by the military is as constitutional as would be any authorized action by the Interstate Commerce Commission within the limits of the constitutional power to regulate commerce. And being an exercise of the war power explicitly granted by the Constitution for safeguarding the national life by prosecuting war effectively, I find nothing in the Constitution which denies to Congress the power to enforce such a valid military order by making its violation an offense triable in the civil courts. . . . To find that the Constitution does not forbid the military measures now complained of does not carry with it approval of that which Congress and the Executive did. That is their business, not ours.

Mr. Justice Roberts.

I dissent, because I think the indisputable facts exhibit a clear violation of Constitutional rights.

This is not a case of keeping people off the streets at night as was *Hirabayashi* v. *United States,* 320 U.S. 81, nor a case of temporary exclusion of a citizen from an area for his own safety or that of the community, nor a case of offering him an opportunity to go temporarily out of an area where his presence might cause danger to himself or to his fellows. On the contrary, it is the case of convicting a citizen as a punishment for not submitting to imprisonment in a concentration camp, based on his ancestry, and solely because of his ancestry, without evidence or inquiry concerning his loyalty and good disposition towards the United States. If this be a correct statement of the facts disclosed by this record, and facts of which we take judicial notice, I need hardly labor the conclusion that Constitutional rights have been violated. . . .

Mr. Justice Murphy, dissenting.

This exclusion of "all persons of Japanese ancestry, both alien and non-alien," from the Pacific Coast area on a plea of military necessity in the absence of martial law ought not to be approved. Such exclusion goes over "the very brink of constitutional power" and falls into the ugly abyss of racism.

In dealing with matters relating to the prosecution and progress of a war, we must accord great respect and consideration to the judgments of the military authorities who are on the scene and who have full knowledge of the military facts. The scope of their discretion must, as a matter of necessity and common sense, be wide. And their judgments ought not to be overruled lightly by those whose training and duties ill-equip them to deal intelligently with matters so vital to the physical security of the nation.

At the same time, however, it is essential that there be definite limits to military discretion, especially where martial law has not been declared. . . .

The judicial test of whether the Government, on a plea of military necessity, can validly deprive an individual of any of his constitutional rights is whether the deprivation is reasonably related to a public danger that is so "immediate, imminent, and impending" as not to admit of delay and not to permit the intervention of ordinary constitutional processes to alleviate the danger. . . . Civilian Exclusion Order No. 34, banishing from a prescribed area of the Pacific Coast "all persons of Japanese ancestry, both alien and non-alien," clearly does not meet that test. Being an obvious racial discrimination, the order deprives all those within its scope of the equal protection of the laws as guaranteed by the Fifth Amendment. It further deprives these individuals of their constitutional rights to live and work where they will, to establish a home where they choose and to move about freely. In excommunicating them without benefit of hearings, this order also deprives them of all their constitutional rights to procedural due process. Yet no reasonable relation to an "immediate, imminent, and impending" public danger is evident to support this racial restriction which is one of the most sweeping and complete deprivations of constitutional rights in the history of this nation in the absence of martial law.

It must be conceded that the military and naval situation in the spring of 1942 was such as to generate a very real fear of invasion of the Pacific Coast, accompanied by fears of sabotage and espionage in that area. The military command was therefore justified in adopting all reasonable means necessary to combat these dangers. In adjudging the military action taken in light of the then apparent dangers, we must not erect too high or too meticulous standards; it is necessary only that the action have some reasonable relation to the removal of the dangers of invasion, sabotage and espionage. But the exclusion, either temporarily or permanently, of all persons with Japanese blood in their veins has no such reasonable relation. And that relation is lacking because the exclusion order necessarily must rely for its reasonableness upon the assumption that *all* persons of Japanese ancestry may have a dangerous tendency to commit sabotage and espionage and to aid our Japanese enemy in other ways. It is difficult to believe that reason, logic or experience could be marshalled in support of such an assumption.

That this forced exclusion was the result in good measure of this erroneous assumption of racial guilt rather than bona fide military necessity is evidenced by the Commanding General's Final Report on the evacuation from the Pacific Coast area. In it he refers to all individuals of Japanese descent as "subversive," as belonging to "an enemy race" whose "racial strains are undiluted," and as constituting "over 112,000 potential enemies . . . at large today" along the Pacific Coast. In support of this blanket condemnation of all persons of Japanese descent, however, no reliable evidence is cited to show that such individuals were generally disloyal, or had generally so conducted themselves in this area as to constitute a special menace to defense installations or war industries, or had otherwise by their behavior furnished reasonable ground for their exclusion as a group.

Justification for the exclusion is sought, instead, mainly upon questionable racial and sociological grounds not ordinarily within the realm of expert military judgment, supplemented by certain semi-military conclusions drawn from an unwarranted use of circumstantial evidence. Individuals of Japanese ancestry are condemned because they are said to be "a large, unassimilated, tightly knit racial group, bound to an enemy nation by strong ties of race, culture, custom and religion." They are claimed to be given to "emperor worshipping ceremonies" and to "dual citizenship." Japanese language schools and allegedly pro-Japanese organizations are cited as evidence of possible group disloyalty, together with facts as to certain persons being educated and residing at length in Japan. It is intimated that many of these individuals deliberately resided "adjacent to strategic points," thus enabling them "to carry into execution a tremendous program of sabotage on a mass scale should any considerable number of them have been inclined to do so." . . . Finally, it is intimated, though not directly charged or proved, that persons of Japanese ancestry were responsible for three minor isolated shellings and bombings of the Pacific Coast area, as well as for unidentified radio transmissions and night signalling.

The main reasons relied upon by those responsible for the forced evacuation, therefore, do not prove a reasonable relation between the group characteristics of Japanese Americans and the dangers of invasion, sabotage and espionage. The reasons appear, instead, to be largely an accumulation of much of the misinformation, half-truths and insinuations that for years have been directed against Japanese Americans by people with racial and economic prejudices—the same people who have been among the foremost advocates of the evacuation. A military judgment based upon such racial and sociological considerations is not entitled to the great weight ordinarily given the judgments based upon strictly military considerations. Especially is this so when every charge relative to race, religion, culture, geographical location, and legal and economic status has been substantially discredited by independent studies made by experts in these matters. . . .

No adequate reason is given for the failure to treat these Japanese Americans on an individual basis by holding investigations and hearings to separate the loyal from the disloyal, as was done in the case of persons of German and Italian ancestry. . . . It is asserted merely that the loyalties of this group "were unknown and time was of the essence." Yet nearly four months elapsed after Pearl Harbor before the first exclusion order was issued; nearly eight months went by until the last order was issued; and the last of these "subversive" persons was not actually removed until almost eleven months had elapsed. Leisure and deliberation seem to have been more of the essence than speed. And the fact that conditions were not such as to warrant a declaration of martial law adds strength to the belief that the factors of time and military necessity were not as urgent as they have been represented to be.

Moreover, there was no adequate proof that the Federal Bureau of Investigation and the military and naval intelligence services did not have the espionage and sabotage situation well in hand during this long period. Nor is there any denial of the fact that not one person of Japanese ancestry was accused or convicted of espionage or sabotage after Pearl Harbor while they were still free, a fact which is some evidence of the loyalty of the vast majority of these individuals and of the effectiveness of the established methods of combatting these evils. It seems incredible that under these circumstances it would have been impossible to hold loyalty hearings for the mere 112,000 persons involved—or at least for the 70,000 American citizens—especially when a large part of this number represented children and elderly men and women. . . .

I dissent, therefore, from this legalization of racism. Racial discrimination in any form and in any degree has no justifiable part whatever in our democratic way of life. It is unattractive in any setting but it is utterly revolting among a free people who have embraced the principles set forth in the Constitution of the United States. All residents of this nation are kin in some way by blood or culture to a foreign land. Yet they are primarily and necessarily a part of the new and distinct civilization of the United States. They must accordingly be treated at all times as the heirs of the American experiment and as entitled to all the rights and freedoms guaranteed by the Constitution.

Mr. Justice Jackson, dissenting. . . .

It would be impracticable and dangerous idealism to expect or insist that each specific military command in an area of probable operations will conform to conventional tests of constitutionality. When an area is so beset that it must be put under military control at all, the paramount consideration is that its measures be successful, rather than legal. The armed services must protect a society, not merely its Constitution. The very essence of the military job is to marshal physical force, to remove every obstacle to its effectiveness, to give it every strategic advantage. Defense measures will not, and often should not, be held within the limits that bind civil authority in peace. No court can require such a commander in such circumstances to act as a reasonable man; he may be unreasonably cautious and exacting. Perhaps he should be. But a commander in temporarily focusing the life of a community on defense is carrying out a military program; he is not making law in the sense the courts know the term. He issues orders, and they may have a certain authority as military commands, although they may be very bad as constitutional law.

But if we cannot confine military expedients by the Constitution, neither would I distort the Constitution to approve all that the military may deem expedient. That is what the Court appears to be doing, whether consciously or not. I cannot say, from any evidence before me, that the orders of General DeWitt were not reasonably expedient military precautions, nor could I say that they were. But even if they were permissible military procedures, I deny that it follows that they are constitutional. If, as the Court holds, it does follow, then we may as well say that any military order will be constitutional and have done with it.

The limitations under which courts always will labor in examining the necessity for a military order are illustrated by this case. How does the Court know that these orders have a reasonable basis in necessity? No evidence whatever on that subject has been taken by this or any other court. There is sharp controversy as to the credibility of the DeWitt report. So the Court, having no real evidence before it, has no choice but to accept General DeWitt's own unsworn, self-serving statement, untested by any cross-examination, that what he did was reasonable. And thus it will always be when courts try to look into the reasonableness of a military order.

In the very nature of things, military decisions are not susceptible of intelligent judicial appraisal. They do not pretend to rest on evidence, but are made on information that often would not be admissible and on assumptions that could not be proved. Information in support of an order could not be disclosed to courts without danger that it would reach the enemy. Neither can courts act on communications made in confidence. Hence courts can never have any real alternative to accepting the mere declaration of the authority that issued the order that it was reasonably necessary from a military viewpoint.

Much is said of the danger to liberty from the Army program for deporting and detaining these citizens of Japanese extraction. But a judicial construction of the due process clause that will sustain this order is a far more subtle blow to liberty than the promulgation of the order itself. A military order, however unconstitutional, is not apt to last longer than the military emergency. Even during that period a succeeding commander may revoke it all. But once a judicial opinion rationalizes such an order to show that it conforms to the Constitution, or rather rationalizes the Constitution to show that the Constitution sanctions such an order, the Court for all time has validated the principle of racial discrimination in criminal procedure and of transplanting American citizens. The principle then lies about like a loaded weapon ready for the hand of any authority that can bring forward a plausible claim of an urgent need. Every repetition imbeds that principle more deeply in our law and thinking and expands it to new purposes. All who observe the work of courts are familiar with what Judge Cardozo described as "the tendency of a principle to expand itself to the limit of its logic." A military commander may overstep the bounds of constitutionality, and it is an incident. But if we review and approve, that passing incident becomes the doctrine of the Constitution. There it has a generative power of its own, and all that it creates will be in its own image. Nothing better illustrates this danger than does the Court's opinion in this case. . . .

I should hold that a civil court cannot be made to enforce an order which violates constitutional limitations even if it is a reasonable exercise of military authority. The courts can exercise only the judicial power, can apply only law, and must abide by the Constitution, or they cease to be civil courts and become instruments of military policy.

Of course the existence of a military power resting on force, so vagrant, so centralized, so necessarily heedless of the individual, is an inherent threat to liberty. But I would not lead people to rely on this Court for a review that seems to me wholly delusive. The military reasonableness of these orders can only be determined by military superiors. If the people ever let command of the war power fall into irresponsible and unscrupulous hands, the courts wield no power equal to its restraint. The chief restraint upon those who command the physical forces of the country, in the future as in the past, must be their responsibility to the political judgments of their contemporaries and to the moral judgments of history.

My duties as a justice as I see them do not require me to make a military judgment as to whether General DeWitt's evacuation and detention program was a reasonable military necessity. I do not suggest that the courts should have attempted to interfere with the Army in carrying out its task. But I do not think they may be asked to execute a military expedient that has no place in law under the Constitution. I would reverse the judgment and discharge the prisoner.

SELECTED REFERENCES

Binkley, Wilfred E., *The Man in the White House.* Baltimore: Johns Hopkins Press, 1958.

Corwin, Edward S., *The President: Office and Powers.* New York: New York University Press, 1957 (4th ed.).

——(ed.), *The Constitution of the United States of America: Analysis and Interpretation,* pp. 371–504. Washington: Government Printing Office, 1953.

——*Total War and the Constitution.* New York: Alfred A. Knopf, Inc., 1947.

——and Louis W. Koenig, *The Presidency Today.* New York: New York University Press, 1956.

Fenno, Richard F., Jr., *The President's Cabinet.* Cambridge, Mass.: Harvard University Press, 1959.

Finer, Herman, *The Presidency: Crisis and Regeneration.* Chicago: University of Chicago Press, 1960.

Hyman, Sidney, *The American President.* New York: Harper & Brothers, 1954.

Laski, Harold J., *The American Presidency.* New York: Harper & Brothers, 1940.

Longaker, Richard P., *The Presidency and Individual Liberties.* Ithaca, N.Y.: Cornell University Press, 1961.

May, Ernest R. (ed.), *The Ultimate Decision: The President as Commander in Chief.* New York: Braziller, 1960.

Neustadt, Richard E., *Presidential Power.* New York: John Wiley & Sons, Inc., 1960.

Rossiter, Clinton, *The American Presidency.* New York: Harcourt, Brace & World, Inc., 1956.

—— *The Supreme Court and the Commander in Chief.* Ithaca, N.Y.: Cornell University Press, 1951.

Schubert, Glendon A., *The Presidency in the Courts.* Minneapolis: University of Minnesota Press, 1957.

Silva, Ruth C., *Presidential Succession.* Ann Arbor, Mich.: University of Michigan Press, 1951.

ten Broek, Jacobus, Edward N. Barnhart, and Floyd W. Matson, *Prejudice, War and the Constitution.* Berkeley, Calif.: University of California Press, 1954.

Westin, Alan, *The Anatomy of a Constitutional Law Case.* New York: The Macmillan Company, 1958.

Williams, Irving G., *The Rise of the Vice-Presidency.* Washington, D.C.: Public Affairs Press, 1956.

Wilmerding, Lucius, Jr., *The Electoral College.* New Brunswick, N.J.: Rutgers University Press, 1958.

PART FOUR

The Federal System

INTRODUCTION

The nature of the federal Union created by the Constitution was a perennial matter of controversy until the issue was finally settled by the Civil War. The general political philosophy of the eighteenth century stressed contract as the basis of governmental authority. The Constitution was such a contract, but who were the parties to it—the states or the people of the United States? The language of the Constitution could be cited to support both views. Article VII provides that approval by conventions in nine states "shall be sufficient for the establishment of this Constitution between the states so ratifying the same." On the other hand, the Preamble declares that it is "the people of the United States" who "do ordain and establish this Constitution," and conventions rather than state legislatures were chosen as the instruments of ratification precisely to emphasize the popular base of the contract.

In the pre-Civil War period there were three significant efforts to assert state power as overriding national authority. The first came in the form of the Kentucky and Virginia Resolutions, drafted by Jefferson and Madison as a protest against the Alien and Sedition Acts passed by the Federalist Congress in 1798. In the Kentucky Resolutions, Jefferson asserted "that this government, created by this compact, was not made the exclusive or final judge of the extent of the powers delegated to itself, since that would have made its discretion, and not the Constitution, the measure of its powers; but that, as in all other cases of compact among parties having no common Judge, *each party has an equal right to judge for itself, as well of infractions as of the mode and measure of redress.*"

In a second set of resolutions passed in 1799, the Kentucky Legislature proclaimed: "That a Nullification, by those sovereignties, of all unauthorized acts done under color of that instrument, is the rightful remedy." Madison, who drafted the Virginia Resolutions, contributed the concept of "interposition" to American constitutional history in the third paragraph of those resolutions, when he concluded "that, in case of a deliberate, palpable, and dangerous exercise of other powers, not granted by the said compact, the states, who are parties thereto, have the right, and are in duty bound, to interpose, for arresting the progress of the evil, and for maintaining within their respective limits, the authorities, rights, and liberties, appertaining to them."

This language about nullification and interposition sounds more threatening than Jefferson and Madison probably intended. They were deadly serious in their belief that the Federalist Congress had passed legislation prohibited by the Constitution and in their desire to organize resistance to it. But both sets of resolutions were vague as to how such resistance was to be carried out. They certainly did not mean to assert that the Union was a system of fully sovereign states, a confederation from which each state could retire at any time.

The Kentucky and Virginia Resolutions were circulated among the other states, and they elicited responses from at least seven, mostly in the Federalist Northeast, upholding the concept of federal supremacy and denying the right of a state to nullify federal law. Jefferson's victory over the Federalists in the election of 1800, due in no small part to popular resentment over the Alien and Sedition Acts, terminated this episode.

The second attack on the theory of the Union saw an interesting reversal of roles. The New England states, driven by the pressure of severe economic hardship resulting from President Jefferson's embargo policy, came to assert an extreme states' rights doctrine. This sectional disaffection was increased by the strains of the War of 1812, during which the New England states sometimes refused to cooperate with the American military operations and considerable trade with Britain was continued. The Hartford Convention of 1814–1815, in which the movement culminated, recommended to the legislatures of the states represented that they pass measures to protect their citizens from the operation of unconstitutional national acts. But before the resolutions even got to Washington, the war was over, the complaints were forgotten, and the only result of the Convention was to annihilate the Federalist party.

The third and most clearly elaborated theory of nullification and resistance to national authority was stated in 1828 by John C. Calhoun, as a rationalization of Southern opposition to the continuous increase in tariff rates between 1816 and 1828. Calhoun was alarmed at the open talk of secession in the South, and offered the doctrine of nullification as a substitute, contending that his plan was a logical extension of the Virginia and Kentucky Resolutions.

Calhoun held that the Constitution was a compact formed by "sovereign and independent communities." The national government was not a party to the compact but an emanation from it, "a joint commission, appointed to superintend and administer the interests in which all are jointly concerned, but having, beyond its proper sphere, no more power than if it did not exist." He thought, however, that mere recognition of the right of interposition would probably "supersede the necessity of its exercise, by impressing on the movements of the Government that moderation and justice so essential to harmony and peace, in a country of such vast extent and diversity of interests as ours."

In 1832 South Carolina carried this theory to the point of action by passing a statute purporting to nullify the federal tariff acts of 1828 and 1832. President Jackson immediately challenged this action, saying that the power of nullification was "incompatible with the existence of the Union, contradicted expressly by the letter of the Constitution, unauthorized by its spirit, inconsistent with every principle on which it was founded, and destructive of the great object for which it was formed." He sent federal vessels into Charleston Harbor to enforce the tariff, but passage of a compromise tariff bill with lower rates made it possible for South Carolina to withdraw its nullification statute.

The final test remained. In the years preceding the Civil War, with the controversies over slavery and the tariff going on around them, Southern statesmen shifted their ground from the right of nullification to secession as a means to preserve their economic life and social institutions. For Calhoun, secession was justified as a final remedy to preserve states' rights. According to his theory, after a state had interposed its authority to prevent federal action, the federal government could appeal to the amending process. If three-fourths of the states upheld the federal claim, the matter was settled as far as those states were concerned. But the dissenting state was not obliged to acquiesce in all instances.

That a State, as a party to the constitutional compact, has the right to secede,—acting in the same capacity in which it ratified the constitution,—cannot, with any show of reason, be denied by any one who regards the constitution as a compact,—if a power should be inserted by the amending power, which would radically change the character of the constitution, or the nature of the system.

Lincoln's decision to use force to keep the Southern states in the Union and the victory of the North in the Civil War closed the debate over the legality of secession. After the war, the Supreme Court tidied up a bit in *Texas* v. *White*, 7 Wall. 700 (1869). The case hinged on the question whether or not Texas had ever left the Union, and the Court held:

When, therefore, Texas became one of the United States, she entered into an indissoluble relation. . . . The act which consummated her admission into the Union was something more than a compact; it was the incorporation of a new member into the political body. And it was final. The union between Texas and the other States was as complete, as perpetual, and as indissoluble as the union between the original States.

Chief Justice Chase summed up the principle involved: "The Constitution, in all its provisions, looks to an indestructible Union, composed of indestructible States."

Chapter 17

FEDERAL-STATE RELATIONS

This Constitution, and the laws of the United States which shall be made in pursuance thereof . . . shall be the supreme law of the land; and the judges in every state shall be bound thereby, any thing in the constitution or laws of any state to the contrary notwithstanding.   ART. VI

The powers not delegated to the United States by the Constitution, nor prohibited by it to the states, are reserved to the states respectively, or to the people.   TENTH AMENDMENT

In essence, American federalism is a form of political organization in which the exercise of power is divided between two levels of government, each having the use of those powers as a matter of right, and each acting on the same citizen body. The appropriate division of powers between these two levels was one of the major concerns of the Constitutional Convention, and the pattern of allocation which emerged was fairly complex, as the following summary indicates:

1. Exclusively national powers. Since a nation obviously must speak with one voice in foreign relations, the power to declare war and make treaties was allocated to the national government. For different but equally obvious reasons, a uniform monetary system was essential, which necessitated central control of the power to coin money.

2. Exclusively state powers. The Constitution did not undertake to state specifically what powers, if any, were exclusively reserved to the states. Rather than leave this matter to inference, the Tenth Amendment propounded a formula, but the intent and effect of this amendment have been the subject of great dispute. How much of a limitation it constitutes on federal authority depends upon the meaning of the words, "the powers not delegated to the United States." But clearly the amendment is not a source of *state* power, since the "nondelegated" and "nonprohibited" powers *may* belong to "the people" rather than to the states. In practice, however, the Tenth Amendment is generally regarded as protecting state control over such "inherently local" functions as regulation of marriage and divorce.

3. Concurrent powers. The Constitution specifically gives to the national government such important powers as levying taxes and regulating commerce, but it makes no effort to prohibit the states from also exercising such authority within their own borders.

4. Powers prohibited to the national government. According to the principle that the national government is one of delegated powers, the national government has no authority to exercise powers not authorized by the Constitution.

This argument was used at the Convention to deny the necessity for a protective bill of rights. However, the framers did include in the Constitution a few express prohibitions on federal power, such as those against the levying of direct taxes or suspending the writ of habeas corpus. When the Bill of Rights was added, the extensive prohibitions of the first eight amendments were incorporated in this group.

5. Powers prohibited to the states. In Article I, section 10, a whole group of activities is forbidden to the states. The purpose of these prohibitions is primarily to enforce the exclusive nature of national control over foreign relations, the monetary system, and foreign commerce. A further prohibition, which does not fall in any of these three categories, is against any law impairing the obligation of contracts.

6. Powers prohibited to both the nation and the states. Certain prohibitions on the states in Article I, section 10, are also imposed on the national government by the preceding section. These include the ban on passing bills of attainder and ex post facto laws, and granting titles of nobility.

With this rather elaborate division of functions and powers between the two levels of government, disputes are bound to occur. The Constitution supplies a principle for settling them in the "supremacy clause" of Article VI. The effectiveness of this section was demonstrated in *McCulloch* v. *Maryland* (1819), already discussed, in which John Marshall upheld the power of Congress to create a bank and warned that no state had any power "to retard, impede, burden, or in any manner control, the operations of the constitutional laws enacted by Congress."

Implementing the principle of national supremacy required that the Supreme Court have authority to review the decisions of state courts. The Judiciary Act of 1789, in section 25, provided for such review of final judgments or decrees in state courts in three classes of cases: (1) where the validity of a federal law or treaty was "drawn in question," and the decision was against its validity; (2) where a state statute was questioned as "repugnant to the constitution, treaties or laws of the United States," and the decision was in favor of its validity; and (3) where the construction of the federal Constitution, treaty, or statute was drawn in question, and the decision was against the title, right, privilege, or exemption claimed. These categories were all based on the principle that if the Constitution and laws of the United States were to be observed, the Supreme Court would have to have an opportunity to review decisions of state courts which ruled adversely on asserted federal rights.

The Supreme Court's power of review over state supreme court decisions was affirmed against state resistance in two great decisions, *Martin* v. *Hunter's Lessee*, 1 Wheat. 304 (1816), and *Cohens* v. *Virginia*, 6 Wheat. 264 (1821). There have also been a few historical incidents where states sought to nullify federal court decisions. One was *United States* v. *Peters*, 5 Cranch 115 (1809), when the Pennsylvania Legislature defied a federal judgment in a prize case and declared it to be in violation of the Eleventh Amendment. Another was *Ableman* v. *Booth*, 21 How. 506 (1859), in which Wisconsin authorities resisted efforts to enforce the federal Fugitive Slave Law in that state. The Supreme Court decisions in each case firmly spelled out the principles of federal judicial supremacy.

In 1956 the dust was blown off the doctrines of interposition and nullification, as they were invoked by several Southern states in protest against the Supreme Court's decision invalidating racial segregation in the schools. In its act of nullification the state of Alabama laid down the basic premise of its action:

Whereas the states, being the parties to the constitutional compact, it follows of necessity that there can be no tribunal above their authority to decide, in the last resort, whether the compact made by them be violated; and, consequently, they must decide themselves, in the last resort, such questions as may be of sufficient magnitude to require their interposition.

Such assertions are of course in the plainest possible defiance of the history and principles of the American federal system, but the Supreme Court had to take them seriously enough to answer them when comparable claims were made in the 1958 Little Rock case, *Cooper* v. *Aaron*, 358 U.S. 1. As though writing a constitutional primer, the Court pointed out that in 1803 *Marbury* v. *Madison* had "declared the basic principle that the federal judiciary is supreme in the exposition of the law of the Constitution, and that principle has ever since been respected by this Court and the Country as a permanent and indispensable feature of our constitutional system."

The Court seldom has to deal with such basic challenges to federal authority, but it does have the continuing task of adjudicating the conflicts which arise when federal and state legislation cover the same subject matter. Federal legislation voids all incompatible state regulation, but as already noted in the commerce field, federal regulation may leave room for nonconflicting state legislation. This is a problem which is of course much broader than commercial regulation, and the Supreme Court has endeavored to develop some general rules which will aid in passing on all federal-state legislative conflicts. One of the most useful discussions of these principles is found in *Pennsylvania* v. *Nelson*, 350 U.S. 497 (1956).

PENNSYLVANIA v. NELSON
350 U.S. 497, 76 S. Ct. 47, 100 L. Ed. 640 (1956)

Congress adopted the Smith Act in 1940, prohibiting the knowing advocacy of the overthrow of the government of the United States by force and violence. Steve Nelson and certain other admitted members of the Communist Party were convicted of conspiracy to violate the Smith Act by a federal court. While under this federal sentence, Nelson was convicted of a violation of the Pennsylvania sedition act. The state supreme court reversed the conviction on the ground that the state law had been superseded by the federal statute, and the United States Supreme Court agreed with this view. Seven months later, the Supreme Court reversed Nelson's federal conviction with direction to grant a new trial because the government had presented false testimony by paid informers at the trial. *Mesarosh* v. *United States*, 352 U.S. 1 (1956).

MR. CHIEF JUSTICE WARREN delivered the opinion of the Court.

The respondent Steve Nelson, an acknowledged member of the Communist Party, was convicted in the Court of Quarter Sessions of Allegheny County, Pennsylvania, of a violation of the Pennsylvania Sedition Act and sentenced to imprisonment for twenty years and to a fine of $10,000 and to costs of prosecution in the sum of $13,000. The Superior Court affirmed the conviction. . . . The Supreme Court of Pennsylvania, recognizing but not reaching many alleged serious trial errors and conduct of the trial court infringing upon respondent's right to due process of law, decided the case on the narrow issue of supersession of the state law by the Federal Smith Act. In its opinion, the court stated:

> "And, while the Pennsylvania statute proscribes sedition against either the Government of the United States or the Government of Pennsylvania, it is only alleged sedition against the United States with which the instant case is concerned. Out of all the voluminous testimony, we have not found, nor has anyone pointed to, a single word indicating a seditious act or even utterance directed against the Government of Pennsylvania."

The precise holding of the court, and all that is before us for review, is that the Smith Act of 1940, as amended in 1948, which prohibits the knowing advocacy of the overthrow of the Government of the United States by force and violence, supersedes the enforceability of the Pennsylvania Sedition Act which proscribes the same conduct. . . .

It should be said at the outset that the decision in this case does not affect the right of States to enforce their sedition laws at times when the Federal Government has not occupied the field and is not protecting the entire country from seditious conduct. . . . Nor does it limit the jurisdiction of the States where the Constitution and Congress have specifically given them concurrent jurisdiction, as was done under the Eighteenth Amendment and the Volstead Act. *United States* v. *Lanza,* 260 U.S. 377. Neither does it limit the right of the State to protect itself at any time against sabotage or attempted violence of all kinds. . . .

Where, as in the instant case, Congress has not stated specifically whether a federal statute has occupied a field in which the States are otherwise free to legislate, different criteria have furnished touchstones for decision. Thus,

> "[t]his Court, in considering the validity of state laws in the light of . . . federal laws touching the same subject, has made use of the following expressions: conflicting; contrary to; occupying the field; repugnance; difference; irreconcilability; inconsistency; violation; curtailment; and interference. But none of these expressions provides an infallible constitutional test or an exclusive constitutional yardstick. In the final analysis, there can be no one crystal clear distinctly marked formula." *Hines* v. *Davidowitz,* 312 U.S. 52, 67.

. . . In this case, we think that each of several tests of supersession is met.

First, "[t]he scheme of federal regulation [is] so pervasive as to make reasonable the inference that Congress left no room for the States to supplement it." *Rice* v. *Santa Fe Elevator Corp.,* 331 U.S., at 230. The Congress determined in 1940 that it was necessary for it to re-enter the field of antisubversive legislation, which had been abandoned by it in 1921. In that year, it enacted the Smith Act which proscribes advocacy of the overthrow of any government—federal, state or local—by force and violence and organization of and knowing membership in a group which so advocates. Conspiracy to commit any of these acts is punishable under the general criminal conspiracy provisions in 18 U.S.C. § 371. The Internal Security Act of 1950 is aimed more directly at Communist organizations. It distinguishes between "Communist-action organizations" and "Communist-front organizations," requiring such organizations to register and to file annual reports with the Attorney General giving complete details as to their officers and funds. Members of Communist-action organizations who have not been registered by their organization must register as individuals. Failure to register in accordance with the requirements of Sections 786–787 is punishable by a fine of not more than $10,000 for an offending organization and by a fine of not more than $10,000 or imprisonment for not more than five years or both for an individual offender—each day of failure to register constituting a separate offense. And the Act imposes certain sanctions upon both "action" and "front" organizations and their members. The Communist Control Act of 1954 declares "that the Communist Party of the United States, although purportedly a political party, is in fact an instrumentality of a conspiracy to overthrow the Government of the United States" and that "its role as the agency of a hostile foreign power renders its existence a clear present and continuing danger to the security of the United States." It also contains a legislative finding that the Communist Party is a "Communist-action organization" within the meaning of the Internal Security Act of 1950 and provides that "knowing" members of the Communist Party are "subject to all the provisions and penalties" of that Act. It furthermore sets up a new classification of "Communist-infiltrated organizations" and provides for the imposition of sanctions against them.

We examine these Acts only to determine the congressional plan. Looking to all of them in the aggregate, the conclusion is inescapable that Congress has intended to occupy the field of sedition. Taken as a whole, they evince a congressional plan which makes it reasonable to determine that no room has been left for the States to supplement it. Therefore, a state sedition statute is superseded regardless of whether it purports to supplement the federal law. . . .

Second, the federal statutes "touch a field in which the federal interest is so dominant that the federal system [must] be assumed to preclude enforcement of state laws on the same subject." *Rice* v. *Santa Fe Elevator Corp.*, 331 U.S., at 230, citing *Hines* v. *Davidowitz, supra*. Congress has devised an all-embracing program for resistance to the various forms of totalitarian aggression. Our external defenses have been strengthened, and a plan to protect against internal subversion has been made by it. It has appropriated vast sums, not only for our own protection, but also to strengthen freedom throughout the world. It has charged the Federal Bureau of Investigation and the Central Intelligence Agency with responsibility for intelligence concerning Communist seditious activities against our Government, and has denominated such activities as part of a world conspiracy. It accordingly proscribed sedition against all government in the nation—national, state and local. Congress declared that these steps were taken "to provide for the common defense, to preserve the sovereignty of the United States as an independent nation, and to guarantee to each State a republican form of government." . . . Congress having thus treated seditious conduct as a matter of vital national concern, it is in no sense a local enforcement problem. As was said in the court below:

> "Sedition against the United States is not a *local* offense. It is a crime against the *Nation*. As such, it should be prosecuted and punished in the Federal courts where this defendant has in fact been prosecuted and convicted and is now under sentence. It is not only important but vital that such prosecutions should be exclusively within the control of the Federal Government." . . .

Third, enforcement of state sedition acts presents a serious danger of conflict with the administration of the federal program. Since 1939, in order to avoid a hampering of uniform enforcement of its program by sporadic local prosecutions, the Federal Government has urged local authorities not to intervene in such matters, but to turn over to the federal authorities immediately and unevaluated all information concerning subversive activities. The President made such a request on September 6, 1939, when he placed the Federal Bureau of Investigation in charge of investigation in this field:

> "The Attorney General has been requested by me to instruct the Federal Bureau of Investigation of the Department of Justice to take charge of investigative work in matters relating to espionage, sabotage, and violations of the neutrality regulations.
>
> "This task must be conducted in a comprehensive and effective manner on a national basis, and all information must be carefully sifted out and correlated in order to avoid confusion and irresponsibility.
>
> "To this end I request all police officers, sheriffs, and all other law enforcement officers in the United States promptly to turn over to the nearest representative of the Federal Bureau of Investigation any information obtained by them relating to espionage, counterespionage, sabotage, subversive activities and violations of the neutrality laws."

And in addressing the Federal-State Conference on Law Enforcement Problems of National Defense, held on August 5 and 6, 1940, only a few weeks after the passage of the Smith Act, the Director of the Federal Bureau of Investigation said:

> "The fact must not be overlooked that meeting the spy, the saboteur and the subverter is a problem that must be handled on a nation-wide basis. An isolated incident in the middle west may be of little significance, but when fitted into a national pattern of similar incidents, it may lead to an important revelation of subversive activity. It is for this reason that the President requested all of our citizens and law enforcing agencies to report directly to the Federal Bureau of Investigation any complaints or information dealing with espionage, sabotage or subversive activities. In such matters, time is of the essence. It is unfortunate that in a few States efforts have been made by individuals not fully acquainted with the far-flung ramifications of this problem to interject superstructures of agencies between local law enforcement and the FBI to sift what might be vital information, thus delaying its immediate reference to the FBI. This cannot be, if our internal security is to be best served. This is no time for red tape or amateur handling of such vital matters. There must be a direct and free flow of contact between the local law enforcement agencies and the FBI. The job of meeting the spy or saboteur is one for experienced men of law enforcement."

Moreover, the Pennsylvania Statute presents a peculiar danger of interference with the federal program. For, as the court below observed:

> "Unlike the Smith Act, which can be administered only by federal officers acting in their official capacities, indictment for sedition under the Pennsylvania statute can be initiated upon an information made by a private individual. The opportunity thus present for the indulgence of personal spite and hatred or for furthering some selfish advantage or ambition need only be mentioned to be appreciated. Defense of the Nation by law, no less than by arms, should be a public and not a private undertaking. It is important that punitive sanctions for sedition *against the United States* be such as have been promulgated by the central governmental authority and administered under the supervision and review of that authority's judiciary. If that be done, sedition will be detected and punished, no less, wherever it may be found, and the right of the individual to speak freely and without fear, even in criticism of the government, will at the same time be protected."

In his brief, the Solicitor General states that forty-two States plus Alaska and Hawaii have statutes which in some form prohibit advocacy of the violent overthrow of established government. These statutes are entitled anti-sedition statutes, criminal anarchy laws, criminal syndicalist laws, etc. Although all of them are primarily directed against the overthrow of the United States Government, they are in no sense uniform. And our attention has not been called to any case where the prosecution has been successfully directed against an attempt to destroy state or local government. Some of these Acts are studiously drawn and purport to protect fundamental rights by appropriate definitions, standards of proof and orderly procedures in keeping with the avowed congressional purpose "to protect freedom from those who would destroy it, without infringing upon the freedom of all our people." Others are vague and are almost wholly without such safeguards. Some even purport to punish mere membership in subversive organizations which the federal statutes do not punish where federal registration requirements have been fulfilled. . . .

Since we find that Congress has occupied the field to the exclusion of parallel state legislation, that the dominant interest of the Federal Government precludes state intervention, and that administration of state Acts would conflict with the operation of the federal plan, we are convinced that the decision of the Supreme Court of Pennsylvania is unassailable. . . .

The judgment of the Supreme Court of Pennsylvania is

Affirmed.

MR. JUSTICE REED, with whom MR. JUSTICE BURTON and MR. JUSTICE MINTON join, dissenting.

The problems of governmental power may be approached in this case free from the varied viewpoints that focus on the problems of national security. This is a jurisdictional problem of general importance because it involves an asserted limitation on the police power of the States when it is applied to a crime that is punishable also by the Federal Government. As this is a recurring problem, it is appropriate to explain our dissent.

Congress has not, in any of its statutes relating to sedition, specifically barred the exercise of state power to punish the same Acts under state law. And, we read the majority opinion to assume for this case that, absent federal legislation, there is no constitutional bar to punishment of sedition against the United States by both a State and the Nation. The majority limits to the federal courts the power to try charges of sedition against the Federal Government.

First, the Court relies upon the pervasiveness of the antisubversive legislation embodied in the Smith Act of 1940, 18 U.S.C. § 2385, the Internal Security Act of 1950, 64 Stat. 987, and the Communist Control Act of 1954, 68 Stat. 775. It asserts that these Acts in the aggregate mean that Congress has occupied the "field of sedition" to the exclusion of the States. The "occupation of the field" argument has been developed by this Court for the Commerce Clause and legislation thereunder to prevent partitioning of this country by locally erected trade barriers. In those cases this Court has ruled that state legislation is superseded when it conflicts with the comprehensive regulatory scheme and purpose of a federal plan. . . .

But the federal sedition laws are distinct criminal statutes that punish willful advocacy of the use of force against "the government of the United States or the government of any State." These criminal laws proscribe certain local activity without creating any statutory or administrative regulation. There is, consequently, no question as to whether some general congressional regulatory scheme might be upset by a coinciding state plan. In these circumstances the conflict should be clear and direct before this Court reads a congressional intent to void state legislation into the federal sedition acts. . . . Moreover, it is quite apparent that since 1940 Congress has been keenly aware of the magnitude of existing state legislation proscribing sedition. It may be validly assumed that in these circumstances this Court should not void state legislation without a clear mandate from Congress.

We cannot agree that the federal criminal sanctions against sedition directed at the United States are of such a pervasive character as to indicate an intention to void state action.

Secondly, the Court states that the federal sedition statutes touch a field "in which the federal interest is so dominant" they must preclude state laws on the same subject. . . .

We look upon the Smith Act as a provision for controlling incitements to overthrow by force and violence the Nation, or any State, or any political subdivision of either. Such an exercise of federal police power carries, we think, no such dominancy over similar state powers as might be attributed to continuing federal regulations concerning foreign affairs or coinage, for example. In the responsibility of national and local governments to protect themselves against sedition, there is no "dominant interest."

We are citizens of the United States and of the State wherein we reside and are dependent upon the strength of both to preserve our rights and liberties. Both may enact criminal statutes for mutual protection unless Congress has otherwise provided. . . .

Thirdly, the Court finds ground for abrogating Pennsylvania's antisedition statute because, in the Court's view, the State's administration of the Act may hamper the enforcement of the federal law. Quotations are inserted from statements of President Roosevelt and Mr. Hoover, the Director of the Federal Bureau of Investigation, to support the Court's position. But a reading of the quotations leads us to conclude that their purpose was to gain prompt knowledge of evidence of subversive activities so that the federal agency could be fully advised. We find no suggestion from any official source that state officials should be less alert to ferret out or punish subversion. The Court's attitude as to interference seems to us quite contrary to that of the Legislative and Executive Departments. Congress was advised of the existing state sedition legislation when the Smith Act was enacted and has been kept current with its spread. No declaration of exclusiveness followed. In this very case the Executive appears by brief of the Department of Justice, *amicus curiae.* The brief summarizes this point:

> "The administration of the various state laws has not, in the course of the fifteen years that the federal and state sedition laws have existed side by side, in fact interfered with, embarrassed, or impeded the enforcement of the Smith Act. The significance of this absence of conflict in administration or enforcement of the federal and state sedition laws will be appreciated when it is realized that this period has included the stress of wartime security requirements and the federal investigation and prosecution under the Smith Act of the principal national and regional Communist leaders." . . .

Mere fear by courts of possible difficulties does not seem to us in these circumstances a valid reason for ousting a State from exercise of its police power. Those are matters for legislative determination. . . .

The law stands against any advocacy of violence to change established governments. Freedom of speech allows full play to the processes of reason. The state and national legislative bodies have legislated within constitutional limits so as to allow the widest participation by the law enforcement officers of the respective governments. The individual States were not told that they are powerless to punish local acts of sedition, nominally directed against the United States. Courts should not interfere. We would reverse the judgment of the Supreme Court of Pennsylvania.[1]

[1] In *Uphaus* v. *Wyman,* 360 U.S. 72 (1959), Justice Clark for the Court majority interpreted the decision in *Pennsylvania* v. *Nelson* as follows: "The basis of *Nelson* thus rejects the notion that it stripped the States of the right to protect themselves. All the opinion proscribed was a race between federal and state prosecutors to the courthouse door. The opinion made clear that a State could proceed with prosecutions for sedition against the State itself." . . .

Chapter 18

INTERSTATE RELATIONS

No state shall, without the consent of Congress . . . enter into any agreement or compact with another state. . . .   ART. I, sec. 10

Full faith and credit shall be given in each state to the public acts, records,
and judicial proceedings of every other state.   ART. IV, sec. 1

The citizens of each state shall be entitled to all privileges and immunities
of citizens in the several states.   ART. IV, sec. 2

A person charged in any state with treason, felony, or other crime, who
shall flee from justice, and be found in another state, shall on demand of
the executive authority of the state from which he fled, be delivered up, to
be removed to the state having jurisdiction of the crime.   ART. IV, sec. 2

These provisions of the Constitution represent the principal efforts of the
Founding Fathers to foresee the problems that might arise when quasi-sovereign
states with large areas for independent action and authority were associated in
a federal system. One thing was certain; they were bound to have disputes
among themselves over such matters as boundaries or use of water resources.
For settling such controversies the federal courts were available. By Article II,
section 2, federal judicial power was extended "to controversies between two
or more states." Moreover, the Supreme Court could assume original jurisdiction over any case in which a state was a party.

In adjudicating disputes between states, the Supreme Court makes considerable
use of the principles of international law, modified by the exigencies of a federal system. In *Kansas* v. *Colorado,* 206 U.S. 46 (1907), Justice Brewer suggested that in judging interstate conflicts the Court had been in effect "building
up what may not improperly be called interstate common law."

Some interesting problems in the enforcement of Supreme Court judgments
against a state were raised in the historic Virginia–West Virginia dispute. As
part of the terms of its becoming a separate state during the Civil War, West
Virginia had agreed to assume its just share of the Virginia state debt and the
compact had been duly ratified by Congress. In 1907, after four decades of
negotiation had yielded no monetary results, Virginia brought suit for collection.
The litigation continued to 1915, when the Supreme Court fixed the amount
of West Virginia's liability. However, the state still made no motion to pay.

The matter came to a head in *Virginia* v. *West Virginia,* 246 U.S. 565
(1918), where the Court warned that the federal government had the power
to enforce a court decision against a recalcitrant state. First, Congress could leg-

islate. Second, further judicial action was possible. The Court did not say what it had in mind, but undoubtedly some appropriate compulsory writ could have been granted, with federal executive assistance if necessary to secure its enforcement. Fortunately, however, before the Court held hearings on the judicial remedies that might be invoked, the West Virginia Legislature appropriated funds to meet the obligation.

Interstate Compacts. Of course states can agree as well as disagree. The Constitution authorizes compacts between states, through the rather negative device of forbidding such compacts unless Congress consents to them. In fact Congress has given its consent to a great number of compacts, covering such diverse matters as conservation of natural resources, mutual sharing of water power in interstate streams, flood and pollution control, and regulation of large river basins or harbors.

There is no set formula as to when and how congressional approval of compacts should be registered. The assent may be given before or after the agreement; it may be explicit, implicit, or tacit. Nor is there any form in which Congress must cast its approval. It may be done by specific statute, by a joint resolution, by ratification of a state constitution which contains such a compact, or by means of a compact between Congress and the states involved. Congress may even extend blanket approval to future agreements in certain specified fields.

No case has arisen in which a compact has been held unconstitutional. Once a state has formally ratified a compact and the approval of Congress has been obtained, the agreement is binding on the state and all its officers. In *West Virginia ex rel. Dyer* v. *Sims,* 341 U.S. 22 (1951), a state's effort unilaterally to declare a compact in violation of its constitution and to use this as a basis for withdrawal was condemned by the Supreme Court, which said: "A State cannot be its own judge in a controversy with a sister State."

Interstate Privileges and Immunities. The provision guaranteeing to the citizens of each state all privileges and immunities of citizens in the several states has been of only limited importance as an instrument of federalism. There is no definition of the privileges and immunities to which citizens in the several states are entitled. Neither is it made clear whether the citizen is entitled to these privileges in his own state, or when he is temporarily in other states, or both.

The earliest effort at interpretation was that of Justice Bushrod Washington, sitting in federal circuit court in the case of *Corfield* v. *Coryell,* 6 Fed. Cases 3230 (1823). A New Jersey statute prohibited any person who was not an actual inhabitant or resident of New Jersey from gathering oysters in the state. Was this statute in conflict with Article IV, section 2? Washington decided that it was not. The privileges and immunities which the Constitution protects, said Washington, are those "which are, in their nature, fundamental; which belong, of right, to the citizens of all free governments." . . . He suggested that these included the right of a citizen of one state to pass through, or reside in, other states for purposes of trade or profession; the right to institute and maintain court actions; exemption from higher taxes than are paid by other citizens of the state; and the elective franchise, as regulated by the laws of the state in which it is exercised.

However, Article IV, section 2, does not preclude a state from treating out-of-state citizens differently when there are acceptable reasons why the two groups should be placed on different footings. Technical requirements for access to the courts for out-of-state citizens may be somewhat different from those for local citizens. The right to engage in normal businesses is protected, but the practice of certain professions connected with the public interest, such as medicine and law, can be restricted by individual states, and persons who pursue these professions must prove to the state government competence in their fields. In addition, some public rights do not accrue to a citizen who moves across a state line. For example, a state can limit the right to vote to its own citizens.

Full Faith and Credit. Each state must accord full faith and credit to three types of official acts of sister states: public records, statutes, and court decisions. Even without this explicit requirement some obligation of the sort would have existed under the doctrine of comity in international law. The Constitution removes the matter of faith and credit from considerations of mutual courtesy and amity and makes it a legal duty enforceable in the federal courts.

Under authority of the full faith and credit clause, Congress passed legislation in 1790 and 1804, providing a simple method of authentication, and commanding that judicial proceedings and public records be given the same effect in every court that they had in the court which issued them. Because of these explicit provisions the matter of according full faith and credit to judicial acts is relatively uncomplicated, except in divorce cases. Because of the lenient divorce laws in some states, particularly Nevada and Florida, major problems have arisen as to whether other states are required to give full faith and credit to "quickie" divorces granted in those states.

Historically a divorce suit has been treated as an action *in rem,* that is, a proceeding against the marriage status. A court must have jurisdiction over the marriage status in order to grant a divorce decree, and the test of jurisdiction has been domicile. Where both parties were domiciled in the same state, there was no problem. The full faith and credit issue arose where the husband and wife were domiciled in different states, and where the plaintiff brought the divorce suit in the state of his or her domicile. What is the obligation of courts in the state of the defendant's domicile, or courts in states other than the two states of domicile, to recognize the validity of such a divorce?

Prior to 1906 a divorce granted in a state where the plaintiff was domiciled was valid in all states, even though the defendant had not been personally served with notice of the suit and was not represented in court. This system achieved certainty, but the objection was that it permitted ex parte divorces, that is, proceedings in which only one party to the marriage was in court. Then in *Haddock v. Haddock,* 201 U.S. 562 (1906), the Supreme Court held that a wife in New York, whose husband brought suit for divorce in Connecticut, was required to be given personal notice of the suit or to be present voluntarily in court. In this case neither had happened, and so the divorce was held not effective in New York. However, the Court did agree that a state had the inherent power to determine the marital status of its own citizens, and so ruled that the husband's divorce was effective in Connecticut. Thus the Haddocks, when both were in Connecticut, were divorced; when both were in New York, were married; and when the husband was in Connecticut and the wife in New

York, he was legally single and she was still married. Fortunately much of the confusion inherent in this new doctrine of the Court was eliminated by the sensible action of most of the states in recognizing out-of-state divorces as a matter of comity.

For a considerable period there appeared to be no disposition to question the power of each state to determine for itself what should constitute domicile for divorce purposes. In 1942, however, the lax Nevada domicile requirement of only six weeks was responsible for the case of *Williams* v. *North Carolina*, 317 U.S. 287. Two residents of North Carolina, which has relatively rigid divorce laws, went to Nevada, lived in a tourist court for six weeks, shed their respective spouses, married each other, and then returned to North Carolina. That state refused to recognize the validity of the Nevada divorce, and brought bigamy charges against the couple. They were convicted on the ground that the Nevada divorce had no effect in North Carolina because adequate notice of the proceedings had not been given to the North Carolina spouses, under the *Haddock* doctrine.

A divided Supreme Court reversed this finding by overruling the *Haddock* case. The majority was disturbed by the possibility that a person could be "a bigamist for living in one state with the only one with whom the other state would permit him lawfully to live." The *Williams* decision held that the "substituted service" here employed met the requirements of due process. The divorce decree was thus "wholly effective" in Nevada to change the marital status of the two couples, and the full faith and credit clause required other states to recognize this change, even though it might conflict with their public policy. "Such is part of the price of our federal system," said Justice Douglas.

The state court conviction had not been based on a contention that there was no bona fide domicile in Nevada, and consequently the Supreme Court had no occasion to examine this issue in the first *Williams* decision. However, North Carolina, rebuffed in its first attempt, brought another bigamy prosecution (in spite of the fact that one of the home-staying spouses had died and the other had remarried), this time alleging that the Nevada domicile was a sham, and that North Carolina was under no obligation to recognize the decrees. In *Williams* v. *North Carolina II*, 325 U.S. 226 (1945), the Supreme Court, still divided, upheld the right of North Carolina courts to decide for themselves, before recognizing the validity of an out-of-state divorce, whether residents of the state had established a bona fide domicile outside the state.

While *Williams II* did make it possible to challenge divorces on the ground of jurisdiction, it also had the effect of recognizing the right of any actual domiciliary state to grant ex parte divorces to which other states must afford full faith and credit. However, the Court subsequently drew back from some of the consequences of ex parte divorces, particularly as they affect the property rights of parties, alimony payments, or custody of children.

For example, in *Estin* v. *Estin*, 334 U.S. 541 (1948), the wife received a separation order on grounds of desertion and an alimony award in New York. The next year the husband moved to Nevada and brought suit for divorce. The wife was notified by constructive service, but entered no appearance, and Estin received an absolute divorce with no provision for alimony, though the Nevada court had been advised of the New York decree. When his ex-wife sued him in

New York for nonpayment of alimony, Estin appeared and set up his Nevada decree as a defense.

The Supreme Court held that the New York support order had survived the Nevada decree, on the ground that the divorce was "divisible"—effective as to marital status but ineffective on the issue of alimony. The New York judgment was a property interest created in a proceeding in which both parties participated. This property was an intangible, over which a court could have jurisdiction only by control over the owner. The debtor's state of domicile (Nevada) had no power to determine the personal rights of the creditor in the intangible unless the creditor had been personally served or appeared in the proceeding. As a matter of public policy, New York had a concern that the abandoned spouse not be left impoverished and perhaps become a public charge.

Justice Jackson, protesting this "Solomon-like conclusion," did not see how it could be *full* faith and credit to hold the Nevada decree half good and half bad. "It is good to free the husband from the marriage; it is not good to free him from its incidental obligations." However, the Court continued to apply the concept of "divisible" divorces in subsequent decisions.

Extradition. The full faith and credit clause does not not require a state to enforce the criminal laws of another state. The only obligation here is in the extradition provision of Article IV, section 2. Congress in 1793 passed a statute implementing this provision and affirming the obligation of a governor to surrender a fugitive from another state. However, in *Kentucky* v. *Dennison*, 24 How. 66 (1861), the Supreme Court held that Congress had not provided any means to compel the execution of this duty, and that the federal government could not constitutionally force a state official to take such action. Thus governors can, and occasionally do, refuse to honor a request for extradition. However, most of the states have adopted a uniform criminal extradition act.

WILLIAMS v. NORTH CAROLINA II
325 U.S. 226, 65 S. Ct. 1092, 89 L. Ed. 1577 (1945)

Mr. Justice Frankfurter delivered the opinion of the Court.

This case is here to review judgments of the Supreme Court of North Carolina, affirming convictions for bigamous cohabitation, assailed on the ground that full faith and credit, as required by the Constitution of the United States, was not accorded divorces decreed by one of the courts of Nevada. . . .

Under our system of law, judicial power to grant a divorce—jurisdiction, strictly speaking—is founded on domicil. . . . Domicil implies a nexus between person and place of such permanence as to control the creation of legal relations and responsibilities of the utmost significance. The domicil of one spouse within a State gives power to that State, we have held, to dissolve a marriage wheresoever contracted. . . . Divorce, like marriage, is of concern not merely to the immediate parties. It affects personal rights of the deepest significance. It also touches basic interests of society. Since divorce, like marriage, creates a new status, every consideration of policy makes it desirable that the effect should be the same wherever the question arises.

It is one thing to reopen an issue that has been settled after appropriate opportunity to present their contentions has been afforded to all who had an interest in its adjudication. This applies also to jurisdictional questions. After a contest these cannot be relitigated as between the parties. . . . But those not parties to a litigation ought not to be foreclosed by the interested actions of others; especially not a State which is concerned with the vindication of its own social policy and has no means, certainly no effective means, to protect that interest against the selfish action of those outside its borders. The State of domiciliary origin should not be bound by an unfounded, even if not collusive, recital in the record of a court of another State. As to the truth or existence of a fact, like that of domicil, upon which depends the power to exert judicial authority, a State not a party to the exertion of such judicial authority in another State but seriously affected by it has a right, when asserting its own unquestioned authority, to ascertain the truth or existence of that crucial fact. . . .

. . . In short, the decree of divorce is a conclusive adjudication of everything except the jurisdictional facts upon which it is founded, and domicil is a jurisdictional fact. To permit the necessary finding of domicil by one State to foreclose all States in the protection of their social institutions would be intolerable.

But to endow each State with controlling authority to nullify the power of a sister State to grant a divorce based upon a finding that one spouse had acquired a new domicil within the divorcing State would, in the proper functioning of our federal system, be equally indefensible. No State court can assume comprehensive attention to the various and potentially conflicting interests that several States may have in the institutional aspects of marriage. The necessary accommodation between the right of one State to safeguard its interest in the family relation of its own people and the power of another State to grant divorces can be left to neither State.

The problem is to reconcile the reciprocal respect to be accorded by the members of the Union to their adjudications with due regard for another most important aspect of our federalism whereby "the domestic relations of husband and wife . . . were matters reserved to the States," . . . and do not belong to the United States. . . . The rights that belong to all the States and the obligations which membership in the Union imposes upon all, are made effective because this Court is open to consider claims, such as this case presents, that the courts of one State have not given the full faith and credit to the judgment of a sister State that is required by Art. IV, § 1 of the Constitution.

But the discharge of this duty does not make of this Court a court of probate and divorce. Neither a rational system of law nor hard practicality calls for our independent determination, in reviewing the judgment of a State court, of that rather elusive relation between person and place which establishes domicil. . . . The challenged judgment must, however, satisfy our scrutiny that the reciprocal duty of respect owed by the States to one another's adjudications has been fairly discharged, and has not been evaded under the guise of finding an absence of domicil and therefore a want of power in the court rendering the judgment.

What is immediately before us is the judgment of the Supreme Court of North Carolina. We have authority to upset it only if there is want of foundation for the conclusion that that Court reached. The conclusion it reached turns on its finding that the spouses who obtained the Nevada decrees were not domiciled there. The fact that the Nevada court found that they were domiciled there is entitled to respect, and more. The burden of undermining the verity which the Nevada decrees import rests heavily upon the assailant. But simply because the Nevada court found that it had power to award a divorce decree cannot, we have seen, foreclose reexamination by another State. Otherwise, as was pointed out long ago, a court's record would establish its power and the power would be proved by the record. Such circular reasoning would give one State a control over all the other States which the Full Faith and Credit Clause certainly did not confer. . . .

When this case was first here, North Carolina did not challenge the finding of the Nevada court that petitioners had acquired domicils in Nevada. . . . Upon retrial, however, the existence of domicil in Nevada became the decisive issue. The judgments of conviction now under review bring before us a record which may be fairly summarized by saying that the petitioners left North Carolina for the purpose of getting divorces from their respective spouses in Nevada and as soon as each had done so and married one another they left Nevada and returned to North Carolina to live there together as man and wife. Against the charge of bigamous cohabitation under § 14-183 of the North Carolina General Statutes, petitioners stood on their Nevada divorces and offered exemplified copies of the Nevada proceedings. The trial judge charged that the State had the burden of proving beyond a reasonable doubt that (1) each petitioner was lawfully married to one person; (2) thereafter each petitioner contracted a second marriage with another person outside North Carolina; (3) the spouses of petitioners were living at the time of this second marriage; (4) petitioners cohabited with one another in North Carolina after the second marriage. The burden, it was charged, then devolved upon petitioners "to satisfy the trial jury, not beyond a reasonable doubt nor by the greater weight of the evidence, but simply to satisfy" the jury from all the evidence, that petitioners were domiciled in Nevada at the time they obtained their divorces. The court further charged that "the recitation" of *bona fide* domicil in the Nevada decree was "prima facie evidence" sufficient to warrant a finding of domicil in Nevada but not compelling "such an inference." If the jury found, as they were told, that petitioners had domicils in North Carolina and went to Nevada "simply and solely for the purpose of obtaining" divorces, intending to return to North Carolina on obtaining them, they never lost their North Carolina domicils nor acquired new domicils in Nevada. . . .

The scales of justice must not be unfairly weighted by a State when full faith and credit is claimed for a sister-State judgment. But North Carolina has not so dealt with the Nevada decrees. She has not raised unfair barriers to their recognition. North Carolina did not fail in appreciation or application of federal standards of full faith and credit. Appropriate weight was given to the finding of domicil in the Nevada decrees, and that finding was allowed to be overturned only by relevant standards of proof. There is nothing to suggest that the issue was not fairly submitted to the jury and that it was not fairly assessed on cogent evidence.

State courts cannot avoid review by this Court of their disposition of a constitutional claim by casting it in the form of an unreviewable finding of fact. *Norris* v. *Alabama*, 294 U.S. 587, 590. This record is barren of such attempted evasion. What it shows is that petitioners, long-time residents of North Carolina, came to Nevada, where they stayed in an auto-court for transients, filed suits for divorce as soon as the Nevada law permitted, married one another as soon as the divorces were obtained, and promptly returned to North Carolina to live. It cannot reasonably be claimed that one set of inferences rather than another regarding the acquisition by petitioners of new domicils in Nevada could not be drawn from the circumstances attending their Nevada divorces. . . . And so we cannot say that North Carolina was not entitled to draw the inference that petitioners never abandoned their domicils in North Carolina, particularly since we could not conscientiously prefer, were it our business to do so, the contrary finding of the Nevada court.

If a State cannot foreclose, on review here, all the other States by its finding that one spouse is domiciled within its bounds, persons may, no doubt, place themselves in situations that create unhappy consequences for them. This is merely one of those untoward results inevitable in a federal system in which regulation of domestic relations has been left with the States and not given to the national authority. But the occasional disregard by any one State of the reciprocal obligations of the forty-eight States to respect the constitutional power of each to deal with domestic relations of those domiciled within its borders is hardly an argument for allowing one State to deprive the other forty-seven States of their constitutional rights. Relevant statistics happily do not justify lurid forebodings that parents without number will disregard the fate of their offspring by being unmindful of the status of dignity to which they are entitled. But, in any event, to the extent that some one State may, for considerations of its own, improperly intrude into domestic relations subject to the authority of the other States, it suffices to suggest that any such indifference by a State to the bond of the Union should be discouraged, not encouraged.

In seeking a decree of divorce outside the State in which he has theretofore maintained his marriage, a person is necessarily involved in the legal situation created by our federal system whereby one State can grant a divorce of validity in other States only if the applicant has a *bona fide* domicil in the State of the court purporting to dissolve a prior legal marriage. The petitioners therefore assumed the risk that this Court would find that North Carolina justifiably concluded that they had not been domiciled in Nevada. Since the divorces which they sought and received in Nevada had no legal validity in North Carolina and their North Carolina spouses were still alive, they subjected themselves to prosecution for bigamous cohabitation under North Carolina law. . . . Mistaken notions about one's legal rights are not sufficient to bar prosecution for crime.

We conclude that North Carolina was not required to yield her State policy because a Nevada court found that petitioners were domiciled in Nevada when it granted them decrees of divorce. North Carolina was entitled to find, as she did, that they did not acquire domicils in Nevada and that the Nevada court was therefore without power to liberate the petitioners from amenability to the laws of North Carolina governing domestic relations. . . .

Affirmed.

Mr. Justice Murphy, concurring. . . .

Mr. Justice Rutledge, dissenting. . . .

Nevada's judgment has not been voided. It could not be, if the same test applies to sustain it as upholds the North Carolina convictions. It stands, with the marriages founded upon it, unimpeached. For all that has been determined or could be, unless another change is in the making, petitioners are lawful husband and wife in Nevada. . . . They may be such everywhere outside North Carolina. Lawfully wedded also, in North Carolina, are the divorced spouse of one and his wife, taken for all we know in reliance upon the Nevada decree. That is, unless another jury shall find they too are bigamists for their reliance. No such jury has been impanelled. But were one called, it could pronounce the Nevada decree valid upon the identical evidence from which the jury in this case drew the contrary conclusion. That jury or it and another, if petitioners had been tried separately, could have found one guilty, the other innocent, upon that evidence unvaried by a hair. And, by the Court's test, we could do nothing but sustain the contradictory findings in all these cases.

I do not believe the Constitution has thus confided to the caprice of juries the faith and credit due the laws and judgments of sister states. Nor has it thus made that question a local matter for the states themselves to decide. Were all judgments given the same infirmity, the full faith and credit clause would be only a dead constitutional letter. . . .

Mr. Justice Black, dissenting.

Anglo-American law has, until today, steadfastly maintained the principle that before an accused can be convicted of crime, he must be proven guilty beyond a reasonable doubt. These petitioners have been sentenced to prison because they were unable to prove their innocence to the satisfaction of the State of North Carolina. They have been convicted under a statute so uncertain in its application that not even the most learned member of the bar could have advised them in advance as to whether their conduct would violate the law. In reality the petitioners are being deprived of their freedom because the State of Nevada, through its legislature and courts, follows a liberal policy in granting divorces. They had Nevada divorce decrees which authorized them to remarry. Without charge or proof of fraud in obtaining these decrees, and without holding the decrees invalid under Nevada law, this Court affirms a conviction of petitioners, for living together as husband and wife. I cannot reconcile this with the Full Faith and Credit Clause and with Congressional legislation passed pursuant to it.

It is my firm conviction that these convictions cannot be harmonized with vital constitutional safeguards designed to safeguard individual liberty and to unite all the states of this whole country into one nation. The fact that two people will be deprived of their constitutional rights impels me to protest as vigorously as I can against affirmance of these convictions. Even more, the Court's opinion today will cast a cloud over the lives of countless numbers of the multitude of divorced persons in the United States. The importance of the issues prompts me to set out my views in some detail.

Statistics indicate that approximately five million divorced persons are scattered throughout the forty-eight states. More than 85% of these divorces were granted in uncontested proceedings. Not one of this latter group can now retain any feeling of security in his divorce decree. Ever present will be the danger of criminal prosecution and harassment. . . .

The petitioners were married in Nevada. North Carolina has sentenced them to prison for living together as husband and wife in North Carolina. This Court today affirms those sentences without a determination that the Nevada marriage was invalid under that state's laws. This holding can be supported, if at all, only on one of two grounds: (1) North Carolina has extra-territorial power to regulate marriages within Nevada's territorial boundaries, or, (2) North Carolina can punish people who live together in that state as husband and wife even though they have been validly married in Nevada. A holding based on either of these two grounds encroaches upon the general principle recognized by this Court that a marriage validly consummated under one state's laws is valid in every other state. If the Court is today abandoning that principle, it takes away from the states a large part of their hitherto plenary control over the institution of marriage. A further consequence is to subject people to criminal prosecutions for adultery and bigamy merely because they exercise their constitutional right to pass from a state in which they were validly married into another state which refuses to recognize their marriage. Such a consequence runs counter to the basic guarantees of our federal union. *Edwards v. California*, 314 U.S. 160. . . .

When the Nevada decrees were granted, the petitioners' former spouses lived in North Carolina. When petitioners were tried and convicted, one of their former spouses was dead and the other had remarried. Under the legal doctrine prevailing in Nevada and in most of the states, these facts would make both the decrees immune from attack unless, perhaps, by persons other than the North Carolina spouses, whose property rights might be adversely affected by the decrees. So far as appears from the record no person's property rights were adversely affected by the dissolution decrees. None of the parties to the marriage, although formally notified of the Nevada divorce proceedings, made any protest before or after the decrees were rendered. The state did not sue here to protect any North Carolinian's property rights or to obtain support for the families which had been deserted. The result of all this is that the right of the state to attack the validity of these decrees in a criminal proceeding is today sustained, although the state's citizens, on whose behalf it purports to act, could not have done so at the time of the conviction in a civil proceeding. Furthermore, all of the parties to the first two marriages were apparently satisfied that their happiness did not lie in continued marital cohabitation. North Carolina claims no interest in abridging their individual freedom by forcing them to live together against their own desires. The state's interest at the time these petitioners were convicted thus comes down to its concern in preserving a bare marital status for a spouse who had already married again. If the state's interest before that time be considered, it was to preserve a bare marital status as to two persons who had sought a divorce and two others who had not objected to it. It is an extraordinary thing for a state to procure a retroactive invalidation of a divorce decree, and then punish one of its citizens for conduct authorized by that decree, when it had never been challenged by either of the people most immediately interested in it. I would not permit such an attenuated state interest to override the Full Faith and Credit Clause of the Constitution and an Act of Congress pursuant to it. . . .

The Constitution provides that "Full Faith and Credit shall be given in each State to the public Acts, Records, and judicial Proceedings of every other State. And the Congress may by general Laws prescribe the Manner in which such Acts, Records and Proceedings shall be proved, and the *Effect thereof.*" (Emphasis added.) Acting pursuant to this constitutional authority, Congress in 1790 declared what law should govern and what "Effect" should be given the judgments of state courts. That statute is still the law. Its command is that they "shall have such faith and credit given to them . . . as they have by law or usage in the Courts of the state from which they are taken." 28 U.S.C. 687. If, as the Court today implies, divorce decrees should be given less effect than other court judgments, Congress alone has the constitutional power to say so. We should not attempt to solve the "divorce problem" by constitutional interpretation. At least, until Congress has commanded a different "Effect" for divorces granted on a short sojourn within a state, we should stay our hands. A proper respect for the Constitution and the Congress would seem to me to require that we leave this problem where the Constitution did. If we follow that course, North Carolina cannot be permitted to disregard the Nevada decrees without passing upon the "faith and credit" which Nevada itself would give to them under its own "law or usage." The Court has decided the matter as though it were a purely *federal* question; Congress and the Constitution declared it to be a *state* question. The logic of the Court does not persuade me that we should ignore these mandates of the Congress and the Constitution. . . .

MR. JUSTICE DOUGLAS joins in this dissent.

SELECTED REFERENCES

Anderson, William, *Intergovernmental Relations in Review*. Minneapolis: University of Minnesota Press, 1960.

———— *The Nation and States, Rivals or Partners?* Minneapolis: University of Minnesota Press, 1955.

Commission on Intergovernmental Relations, *Report to the President*. Washington: Government Printing Office, 1955.

Corwin, Edward S. (ed.), *The Constitution of the United States of America: Analysis and Interpretation*, pp. 647–705. Washington: Government Printing Office, 1953.

Hart, Henry M., Jr., and Herbert Wechsler, *The Federal Courts and the Federal System*. Brooklyn, N.Y.: The Foundation Press, 1953.

Jackson, Robert H., *Full Faith and Credit: The Lawyer's Clause of the Constitution*. New York: Columbia University Press, 1945.

Kilpatrick, James J., *The Sovereign States*. Chicago: Henry Regnery Company, 1957.

Macmahon, Arthur W. (ed.), *Federalism, Mature and Emergent*. New York: Doubleday & Company, Inc., 1955.

Pritchett, C. Herman, *The American Constitution*, part 2. New York: McGraw-Hill Book Company, Inc., 1959.

Schmidhauser, John R., *The Supreme Court as Final Arbiter in Federal-State Relations, 1789–1957*. Chapel Hill, N.C.: The University of North Carolina Press, 1958.

White, Leonard D., *The States and the Nation*. Baton Rouge, La.: Louisiana State University Press, 1953.

PART FIVE

First Amendment Freedoms

INTRODUCTION

The theory of the Constitutional Convention was that traditional American freedoms did not need much in the way of specific constitutional protection. The basic concept of limited national government was to be achieved by division of functions—separation of powers, checks and balances—calculated to frustrate any drive toward dictatorial power. The framers believed that the broad expanse of the Republic would encompass such a variety of interests as to make combination into a domineering majority difficult. Said Madison in No. 10 of *The Federalist:*

The smaller the society, the fewer probably will be the distinct parties and interests composing it . . . and . . . the more easily will they concert and execute their plans of oppression. Extend the sphere, and you take in a greater variety of parties and interests; you make it less probable that a majority of the whole will have a common motive to invade the rights of other citizens. . . .

Although the dominant theory of the Convention was that individual liberty did not need to be planned for or guaranteed by specific provisions, it was departed from in a few instances. There are in fact several provisions in the original Constitution which bear more or less closely on issues of civil liberty: protection against suspension of the writ of habeas corpus; prohibition of the passage of bills of attainder or ex post facto laws by either Congress or the state legislatures; the ban on religious tests as a qualification for public office; the requirement of trial by jury; the restrictions on conviction for treason; and the guarantee to citizens of each state of all privileges and immunities of citizens in the several states.

When the proposed Constitution went to the states for ratification, it quickly became apparent that the framers' view of civil liberties as needing little special protection in the new charter was not widely shared. In several of the important states, ratification was secured only on the understanding that amendments protecting individual rights would be immediately added to the Constitution. In his first inaugural address, Washington urged Congress to give careful attention to the demand for these amendments.

James Madison took the lead in bringing together the various suggestions for amendments, which he presented to the House on June 8, 1789. His proposals mainly dealt with protecting citizens from infringement of their rights by Congress, and in guaranteeing fair criminal trials. Madison originally proposed that these changes be incorporated in the body of the Constitution at the appropriate points, but Roger Sherman convinced the House that the amendments should be appended to the Constitution, each complete, independent, and understandable in itself. The House proposals went to the Senate on August 24, where additional changes were made.

Twelve amendments were ultimately approved by both houses, and were sent to the states for ratification on September 25, 1789. Two of these proposed amendments failed' of ratification. The first had to do with the ratio between population and the number of representatives in the House, and the second would have postponed the effect of any alteration in the compensation of congressmen until an election had intervened. The remaining ten amendments were ratified by the necessary states on December 15, 1791.

The ten amendments can be thought of as falling into four categories. The First, and justly the most famous of the amendments, covers freedom of speech, press, assembly, and religion. The Second and Third, which are of little contemporary significance, deal with the right of the people to keep and bear arms, and the quartering of soldiers in private homes. The Fourth through the Eighth are concerned primarily with procedural protections in criminal trials, but other matters are also covered, such as the prohibition on taking of private property for public use without just compensation. Finally, the Ninth and Tenth are simply declaratory of the existing constitutional situation, and have already been considered in this volume.

Only gradually did the conception grow that these ten amendments constituted a great Bill of Rights. About half the state constitutions at the time did not include a bill of rights in their provisions, and it could easily be argued that these ten amendments accomplished no substantial changes in the constitutional pattern. They took away from Congress few powers which it could reasonably have been thought to have had before the amendments were ratified, and the procedural limitations on criminal trials would no doubt have been carried over from the common law in any event. However, it cannot be denied that the Bill of Rights has had a tremendous impact on the development of American constitutional thinking and practice.

This section of the book is devoted to a consideration of the basic rights to freedom of speech, press, assembly, and religion which are guaranteed by the First Amendment. According to the general understanding of the time, and as specifically held by the Supreme Court in *Barron* v. *Baltimore,* 7 Pet. 243 (1833), the provisions of the First through the Eighth Amendments constituted limitations only on Congress, not on the states. It is only by reason of the Fourteenth Amendment that the guarantees of the First Amendment have become effective against state action.

For this reason it is necessary to look briefly here at the circumstances which were responsible for the addition of the Fourteenth Amendment to the Constitution and for the specific form which it took. The basic motivation in Congress, which drafted the amendment in 1866, was unquestionably to protect the rights of the newly freed Negroes and to establish constitutional guarantees which would be effective when military control was withdrawn from the Southern states. This purpose led to the writing into the Constitution, by way of the Fourteenth Amendment, of three important new standards for the protection of civil liberties against state action.

The first was the provision that "No state shall make or enforce any law which shall abridge the privileges or immunities of citizens of the United States. . . ." This language was drawn from Article IV, section 2, but in that form it had never been authoritatively construed and had never achieved any particular effectiveness. In the case of *Corfield* v. *Coryell* (1825), as noted in Chapter 18, Justice Washington had seemed to view it as guaranteeing those fundamental rights which belong to the citizens of all free governments. But there was another view which held that this language merely protected a citizen of one state who went into another state from being discriminated against because of his out-of-state origin. This narrow view was adopted by Chief Justice Taney in the case of *Dred Scott* v. *Sandford,* 19 How. 393 (1857), which also eliminated any possible application to Negroes by holding that they could not be citizens of the United States. Nevertheless, there was enough confusion about or faith in the effectiveness of this vague formulation to lead to its inclusion in the Fourteenth Amendment.

Second, the amendment forbade any state to "deprive any person of life, liberty, or property without due process of law. . . ." Here the drafters were picking up another earlier provision of the Constitution, the due process clause from the Fifth Amendment. This clause, like privileges and immunities, was vague and had been little construed by the Supreme Court, but it was supposed to have descended from the Magna Carta of 1215, and had been defined in the *Dartmouth College Case,* 4 Wheat. 518 (1819), as "the general law; a law, which hears before it condemns; which proceeds upon inquiry, and renders judgment only after trial," so that "every citizen shall hold his life, liberty, property, and immunities, under the protection of the general rules which govern society."

Finally, the Fourteenth Amendment adopted a new standard, equal protection of the laws, which was a general guarantee against state discrimination or unequal treatment for "any person within its jurisdiction. . . ." The equal protection clause was the most specific of the three provisions. Like the due process clause, it covered all "persons," whereas the privileges and immunities provision applied only to citizens. In actual application, the due process and the equal protection clauses have both been important guarantees of American civil liberties in the states.

The constitutional role and development of the due process concept will be examined in Part Six of this volume. However, at this point it is important to note how the due process provision in the Fourteenth Amendment brought the First Amendment protections into play against the states. The Supreme Court accomplished this constitutional expansion with no previous warning in the 1925 case of *Gitlow* v. *New York,* 268 U.S. 652, relying on the equivalence of the liberties mentioned in the First Amendment and the "liberty" protected against infringement without due process in the Fourteenth. Justice Sanford said in the *Gitlow* case: ". . . we may and do assume that freedom of speech and of the press . . . are among the fundamental personal rights and 'liberties' protected . . . from impairment by the States." Thus the principles of the First Amendment achieved universal applicability in American government.

Chapter 19

JUDICIAL STANDARDS

Congress shall make no law . . . abridging the freedom of speech, or of the press. . . . FIRST AMENDMENT

The First Amendment on its face is a clear and absolute barrier to any congressional abridgment of freedom of speech or press. It does not, to be sure, forbid the abridgment of speech, but only the *freedom* of speech. Certainly we are all familiar with situations where speech is abridged, with common consent. One may not talk freely in a library reading room, or during a church service, or during a theater performance, or while a court is in session. There are rules of order governing legislative assemblies or public meetings, which keep two people from talking at the same time, or which prevent speech irrelevant to the issue under discussion. One who talks another person into committing a crime is a guilty partner in that crime.

Clearly the "freedom" of speech is not involved in such restrictions. The freedom of speech refers to the right of discussion of public issues, free from governmental restraint, in the press or in the normal arenas of public contact. But is there an absolute freedom of public discussion through normal public channels? Alexander Meiklejohn contends that there is, and must be, if the democratic ideal is to be achieved.

Just so far as, at any point, the citizens who are to decide an issue are denied acquaintance with information or opinion or doubt or disbelief or criticism which is relevant to that issue, just so far the result must be ill-considered, ill-balanced planning for the general good. . . . When a question of policy is "before the house," free men choose to meet it not with their eyes shut, but with their eyes open. To be afraid of ideas, any idea, is to be unfit for self-government. Any such suppression of ideas about the common good, the First Amendment condemns with its absolute disapproval. The freedom of ideas shall not be abridged.[1]

Members of the Supreme Court have on occasion asserted freedom of speech in similarly unqualified terms. In *Beauharnais* v. *Illinois*, 343 U.S. 250 (1952), Justice Douglas pointed out that the Bill of Rights does in fact indicate which freedoms are absolute and which are not.

The First Amendment is couched in absolute terms—freedom of speech shall not be abridged. Speech has therefore a preferred position as contrasted to some other civil rights. For example, privacy, equally sacred to some, is protected by the Fourth

[1] *Free Speech and Its Relation to Self-Government* (New York: Harper & Brothers, 1948), pp. 17, 26–27.

Amendment only against unreasonable searches and seizures. There is room for regulation of the ways and means of invading privacy. No such leeway is granted the invasion of the right of free speech guaranteed by the First Amendment.

When the Supreme Court comes to decide First Amendment cases, however, it seldom finds such language about absolute protection to be much help. Justice Murphy, one of the most devoted civil libertarians ever to sit on the bench, said in *Chaplinsky* v. *New Hampshire,* 315 U.S. 568 (1942): "It is well understood that the right of free speech is not absolute at all times and under all circumstances." The judicial problem consequently becomes one of distinguishing between the times and circumstances permitting or justifying abridgment of the freedom of speech and those which do not.

The Supreme Court was first faced with these issues after the First World War. During the war the Espionage Act of 1917 and the Sedition Act of 1918 were used to jail a substantial number of persons for speech offenses, such as criticizing the war effort or hindering it in some way. These prosecutions raised the whole question of the relation between words and illegal acts. It is clear that words which directly incite to illegal acts are themselves tainted with the illegality. The common law recognized the crime of incitement to violence, and the First Amendment has never been understood as extending its sanctuary to speech criminal in purpose and intent. But it immediately becomes apparent that there are questions of degree involved here. How closely related must the speech be to the crime in order to taint the speech with illegality? How clear must the purpose be to incite to crime? What degree of immediacy must there be in the situation?

Justice Holmes was the spokesman for the Court in its initial First Amendment decisions, and he developed the famous "clear and present danger" test to measure the extent of the federal government's powers to punish the spoken or written word because of its connection with illegal action. In *Schenck* v. *United States,* 249 U.S. 47 (1919), the defendants had mailed circulars to men eligible for the draft, declaring conscription to be unconstitutional despotism and urging them to assert their rights. The Espionage Act prohibited the obstructing of recruitment or the causing of insubordination in the armed forces, and a unanimous Court held the mailing of these circulars to be in violation of the statute. Holmes wrote: "The question in every case is whether the words used are used in such circumstances and are of such a nature as to create a clear and present danger that they will bring about the substantive evils that Congress has a right to prevent. It is a question of proximity and degree." He then added, with particular reference to the problems of the *Schenck* case: "When a nation is at war many things that might be said in time of peace are such a hindrance to its effort that their utterance will not be endured so long as men fight and that no Court could regard them as protected by any constitutional right."

This decision was protective of the freedom of speech in that it required the relationship between speech and illegal acts to be proximate, not remote and indirect. Professor Zechariah Chafee, Jr., praised the *Schenck* ruling as supplying "for the first time an authoritative judicial interpretation in accord with the purposes of the framers of the Constitution." But nevertheless the test did approve the jailing of Schenck for using the freedom of speech.

A few months later, in *Abrams* v. *United States,* 250 U.S. 616 (1919), Holmes, along with his colleague, Justice Brandeis, found a situation where he endeavored to protect speech rights by use of the clear and present danger test, but the two justices were unable to carry the rest of the Court with them. The crime in *Abrams* was printing and circulating pamphlets attacking the government's action in sending American troops to Vladivostok and Murmansk in the summer of 1918 and calling for a general strike of munitions workers. Again, in *Gitlow* v. *New York,* 268 U.S. 652 (1925), Holmes thought that the clear and present danger test should nullify a conviction under the New York criminal anarchy statute for publication of a radical manifesto. But the Court majority denied that the test was even applicable. Finally, in *Whitney* v. *California,* 274 U.S. 357 (1927), involving the California syndicalism act, Brandeis and Holmes made one more effort to expound the clear and present danger test, but again with no effect on their colleagues.

The Court majority in both *Gitlow* and *Whitney* insisted that the standard the Court should apply was that of reasonableness, not clear and present danger. The New York and California Legislatures had concluded that communism or criminal syndicalism represented a threat to the state. The role of the Supreme Court, said the majority, was not to satisfy itself whether a danger existed from such sources; all it could do was to ask whether a "reasonable" man could have reached the conclusion that the legislatures did. Every presumption was to be indulged in favor of the validity of the statute, and legislatures were to be reversed only if they acted arbitrarily or unreasonably.

The reasonable man test was in fact one which Holmes himself had urged in dealing with state economic legislation. Why should it not apply also in the civil liberties field? One answer was supplied by an argument which the Court began to develop after Holmes had left the bench, namely, that civil liberties occupied a "preferred" constitutional position. Consequently, restrictions on these freedoms had to be subjected to stricter constitutional tests than would apply to legislative constraints in other fields. This position was set forth at various times by Stone, Douglas, Black, Jackson, and others, but perhaps the clearest statement was made by Justice Rutledge in *Thomas* v. *Collins,* 323 U.S. 516 (1945):

. . . any attempt to restrict those liberties must be justified by clear public interest, threatened not doubtfully or remotely, but by clear and present danger. The rational connection between the remedy provided and the evil to be curbed, which in other contexts might support legislation against attack on due process grounds, will not suffice. These rights rest on firmer foundation. Accordingly, whatever occasion would restrain orderly discussion and persuasion, at appropriate time and place, must have clear support in public danger, actual or impending. Only the gravest abuses, endangering paramount interests, give occasion for permissible limitation.

In summary, the reasonable man test presumes the validity of legislation limiting speech or press rights. The clear and present danger test does not necessarily presume the *invalidity* of such infringements, but it does require a strong affirmative showing in their behalf. The preferred position argument reinforces the clear and present danger test and supplies its reason for being.

ABRAMS *v.* UNITED STATES
250 U.S. 616, 40 S. Ct. 17, 63 L. Ed. 1173 (1919)

Late in World War I, after the Russian Revolution, the United States conducted a military expedition into Russia through its Pacific Ocean ports. The five defendants in this case were Russian immigrants and radicals who favored the Revolution. They were not opposed to the war with Germany, but violently attacked the expedition to Russia in pamphlets distributed in New York City which are described in the opinion. They were convicted for violation of the Espionage and Sedition Acts by having circulated "disloyal, scurrilous, and abusive language about the form of government of the United States"; by having published statements "to urge, incite, and advocate curtailment of production" of war materials; and by having committed related offenses.

MR. JUSTICE CLARKE delivered the opinion of the court. . . .

All of the five defendants were born in Russia. They were intelligent, had considerable schooling, and at the time they were arrested they had lived in the United States terms varying from five to ten years, but none of them had applied for naturalization. Four of them testified as witnesses in their own behalf and of these, three frankly avowed that they were "rebels," "revolutionists," "anarchists," that they did not believe in government in any form, and they declared that they had no interest whatever in the Government of the United States. The fourth defendant testified that he was a "socialist" and believed in "a proper kind of government, not capitalistic," but in his classification the Government of the United States was "capitalistic."

It was admitted on the trial that the defendants had united to print and distribute the described circulars and that five thousand of them had been printed and distributed about the 22d day of August, 1918. The group had a meeting place in New York City, in rooms rented by defendant Abrams, under an assumed name, and there the subject of printing the circulars was discussed about two weeks before the defendants were arrested. The defendant Abrams, although not a printer, on July 27, 1918, purchased the printing outfit with which the circulars were printed and installed it in a basement room where the work was done at night. The circulars were distributed some by throwing them from a window of a building where one of the defendants was employed and others secretly, in New York City.

The defendants pleaded "not guilty," and the case of the Government consisted in showing the facts we have stated, and in introducing in evidence copies of the two printed circulars attached to the indictment, a sheet entitled "Revolutionists Unite for Action," written by the defendant Lipman, and found on him when he was arrested, and another paper, found at the headquarters of the group, and for which Abrams assumed responsibility.

Thus the conspiracy and the doing of the overt acts charged were largely admitted and were fully established.

On the record thus described it is argued, somewhat faintly, that the acts charged against the defendants were not unlawful because within the protection of that freedom of speech and of the press which is guaranteed by the First Amendment to the Constitution of the United States, and that the entire Espionage Act is unconstitutional because in conflict with that Amendment.

This contention is sufficiently discussed and is definitely negatived in *Schenck v.*

United States and *Baer* v. *United States,* 249 U.S. 47; and in *Frohwerk* v. *United States,* 249 U.S. 204.

The claim chiefly elaborated upon by the defendants in the oral argument and in their brief is that there is no substantial evidence in the record to support the judgment upon the verdict of guilty and that the motion of the defendants for an instructed verdict in their favor was erroneously denied. A question of law is thus presented, which calls for an examination of the record, not for the purpose of weighing conflicting testimony, but only to determine whether there was some evidence, competent and substantial, before the jury, fairly tending to sustain the verdict. . . .

The first of the two articles attached to the indictment is conspicuously headed, "The Hypocrisy of the United States and Her Allies." After denouncing President Wilson as a hypocrite and a coward because troops were sent into Russia, it proceeds to assail our Government in general, saying:

"His [the President's] shameful, cowardly silence about the intervention in Russia reveals the hypocrisy of the plutocratic gang in Washington and vicinity."

It continues:

"He [the President] is too much of a coward to come out openly and say: 'We capitalistic nations cannot afford to have a proletarian republic in Russia.' "

Among the capitalistic nations Abrams testified the United States was included.

Growing more inflammatory as it proceeds, the circular culminates in:

"The Russian Revolution cries: Workers of the World! Awake! Rise! Put down your enemy and mine!

"Yes! friends, there is only one enemy of the workers of the world and that is CAPITALISM."

This is clearly an appeal to the "workers" of this country to arise and put down by force the Government of the United States which they characterize as their "hypocritical," "cowardly" and "capitalistic" enemy.

It concludes:

"Awake! Awake, you Workers of the World!

"REVOLUTIONISTS."

The second of the articles was printed in the Yiddish language and in the translation is headed, "Workers—Wake up." After referring to "his Majesty, Mr. Wilson, and the rest of the gang; dogs of all colors!", it continues:

"Workers, Russian emigrants, you who had the least belief in the honesty of *our* Government," which defendants admitted referred to the United States Government, "must now throw away all confidence, must spit in the face the false, hypocritic, military propaganda which has fooled you so relentlessly, calling forth your sympathy, your help, to the prosecution of the war."

The purpose of this obviously was to persuade the persons to whom it was addressed to turn a deaf ear to patriotic appeals in behalf of the Government of the United States, and to cease to render it assistance in the prosecution of the war.

It goes on:

"With the money which you have loaned, or are going to loan them, they will make bullets not only for the Germans, but also for the Workers Soviets of Russia. *Workers in the ammunition factories, you are producing bullets, bayonets, cannon, to murder not only the Germans, but also your dearest, best, who are in Russia and are fighting for freedom.*"

It will not do to say, as is now argued, that the only intent of these defendants was to prevent injury to the Russian cause. Men must be held to have intended, and to be accountable for, the effects which their acts were likely to produce. Even if their primary purpose and intent was to aid the cause of the Russian Revolution, the plan of action which they adopted necessarily involved, before it could be realized, defeat of the war program of the United States, for the obvious effect of this appeal, if it should become effective, as they hoped it might, would be to persuade persons of character such as those whom they regarded themselves as addressing, not to aid government loans and not to work in ammunition factories, where their work would produce "bullets, bayonets, cannon" and other munitions of war, the use of which would cause the "murder" of Germans and Russians. . . .

The remaining article, after denouncing the President for what is characterized as hostility to the Russian revolution, continues:

"We, the toilers of America, who believe in real liberty, shall *pledge ourselves*, in case the United States will participate in that bloody conspiracy against Russia, *to create so great a disturbance that the autocrats of America shall be compelled to keep their armies at home, and not be able to spare any for Russia.*"

It concludes with this definite threat of armed rebellion:

"If they will use arms against the Russian people to enforce their standard of order, *so will we use arms,* and they shall never see the ruin of the Russian Revolution."

These excerpts sufficiently show, that while the immediate occasion for this particular outbreak of lawlessness, on the part of the defendant alien anarchists, may have been resentment caused by our Government sending troops into Russia as a strategic operation against the Germans on the eastern battle front, yet the plain purpose of their propaganda was to excite, at the supreme crisis of the war, disaffection, sedition, riots, and, as they hoped, revolution, in this country for the purpose of embarrassing and if possible defeating the military plans of the Government in Europe. A technical distinction may perhaps be taken between disloyal and abusive language applied to the *form* of our government or language intended to bring the *form* of our government into contempt and disrepute, and language of like character and intended to produce like results directed against the President and Congress, the agencies through which that form of government must function in time of war. But it is not necessary to a decision of this case to consider whether such distinction is vital or merely formal, for the language of these circulars was obviously intended to provoke and to encourage resistance to the United States in the war, as the third count runs, and, the defendants, in terms, plainly urged and advocated a resort to a general strike of workers in ammunition factories for the purpose of curtailing the production of ordnance and munitions necessary and essential to the prosecution of the war as is charged in the fourth count. Thus it is clear not only that some evidence but that much persuasive evidence was before the jury tending to prove that the defendants were guilty as charged in both the third and fourth counts of the indictment and under the long established rule of law hereinbefore stated the judgment of the District Court must be

Affirmed.

Mr. JUSTICE HOLMES dissenting. . . .

I never have seen any reason to doubt that the questions of law that alone were before this Court in the cases of *Schenck, Frohwerk* and *Debs,* 249 U.S. 47, 204, 211, were rightly decided. I do not doubt for a moment that by the same reasoning that would justify punishing persuasion to murder, the United States constitutionally may punish speech that produces or is intended to produce a clear and imminent danger that it will bring about forthwith certain substantive evils that the United States constitutionally may seek to prevent. The power undoubtedly is greater in time of war than in time of peace because war opens dangers that do not exist at other times.

But as against dangers peculiar to war, as against others, the principle of the right to free speech is always the same. It is only the present danger of immediate evil or an intent to bring it about that warrants Congress in setting a limit to the expression of opinion where private rights are not concerned. Congress certainly cannot forbid all effort to change the mind of the country. Now nobody can suppose that the surreptitious publishing of a silly leaflet by an unknown man, without more, would present any immediate danger that its opinions would hinder the success of the government arms or have any appreciable tendency to do so. Publishing those opinions for the very purpose of obstructing however, might indicate a greater danger and at any rate would have the quality of an attempt. So I assume that the second leaflet if published for the purposes alleged in the fourth count might be punishable. . . .

I do not see how anyone can find the intent required by the statute in any of the defendants' words. The second leaflet is the only one that affords even a foundation for the charge, and there, without invoking the hatred of German militarism expressed in the former one, it is evident from the beginning to the end that the only object of the paper is to help Russia and stop American intervention there against the popular government—not to impede the United States in the war that it was carrying on. . . .

In this case sentences of twenty years imprisonment have been imposed for the publishing of two leaflets that I believe the defendants had as much right to publish as the Government has to publish the Constitution of the United States now vainly invoked by them. Even if I am technically wrong and enough can be squeezed from these poor and puny anonymities to turn the color of legal litmus paper; I will add, even if what I think the necessary intent were shown; the most nominal punishment seems to me all that possibly could be inflicted, unless the defendants are to be made to suffer not for what the indictment alleges, but for the creed that they avow—a creed that I believe to be the creed of ignorance and immaturity when honestly held, as I see no reason to doubt that it was held here, but which, although made the subject of examination at the trial, no one has a right even to consider in dealing with the charges before the Court.

Persecution for the expression of opinions seems to me perfectly logical. If you have no doubt of your premises or your power and want a certain result with all your heart you naturally express your wishes in law and sweep away all opposition. To allow opposition by speech seems to indicate that you think the speech impotent, as when a man says that he has squared the circle, or that you do not care wholeheartedly for the result, or that you doubt either your power or your premises. But when men have realized that time has upset many fighting faiths, they may come to believe even more than they believe the very foundations of their own conduct that the ultimate good desired is better reached by free trade in ideas—that the best test of truth is the power of the thought to get itself accepted in the competition of the market, and that truth is the only ground upon which their wishes safely can be carried out. That at any rate is the theory of our Constitution. It is an experiment, as all life is an experiment. Every year if not every day we have to wager our salvation upon some prophecy based upon imperfect knowledge. While that experiment is part of our system I think that we should be eternally vigilant against attempts to check the expression of opinions that we loathe and believe to be fraught with death, unless they so imminently threaten immediate interference with the lawful and pressing purposes of the law that an immediate check is required to save the country. I wholly disagree with the argument of the government that the First Amendment left the common law as to seditious libel in force. History seems to me against the notion. I had conceived that the United States through many years had shown its repentance for the Sedition Act of 1798, by repaying fines that it imposed. Only the emergency that makes it immediately dangerous to leave the correction of evil counsels to time warrants making any exception to the sweeping command, "Congress shall make no law . . . abridging the freedom of speech." Of course I am speaking only of expressions of opinion and exhortations, which were all that were uttered here, but I regret that I cannot put into more impressive words my belief that in their conviction upon this indictment the defendants were deprived of their rights under the Constitution of the United States.

MR. JUSTICE BRANDEIS concurs with the foregoing opinion.

Chapter 20

CENSORSHIP OF THE PRESS

There are, in general, two ways in which governments may deny freedom of speech, press, or assembly. One is by legal limitations imposed in advance which prohibit or otherwise effectively restrain speaking or publishing or assembling. The other is by legal proceedings to punish persons for speech or publication which is alleged to violate statutory standards. More simply, this is the distinction between censorship of speech and punishment for speech abuses. It is the difference between officials banning a meeting or silencing a newspaper, and prosecuting individuals after the event for allegedly unlawful speech or publication.

Prior restraint, or censorship, is generally regarded as more dangerous to freedom of expression than subsequent punishment. It is broader in its application to communication, since it aims at inspection of an entire field, rather than scrutiny of particular cases which are the subject of complaint. It is easier to impose prior restraint, for it requires only an administrative decision which can often be taken behind a screen of informality and partial concealment, whereas subsequent punishment is a time-consuming, expensive, and public process involving compliance with the protective safeguards of criminal prosecution. Finally, there is something about the nature of censorship—perhaps it is the psychology of persons who are attracted to this kind of work—which leads irresistibly to unintelligent and overzealous administration.

Freedom of the Press. The American tradition has been strongly against prior restraints on the press, and consequently there have been comparatively few opportunities for the Supreme Court to apply the First Amendment in censorship cases. The basic right of the publisher is that he shall not be required to have government permission to publish or be subjected to a governmental ban or tax on publication. In the Supreme Court's first great anticensorship decision, *Near v. Minnesota,* 283 U.S. 697 (1931), the state control attempted took the form of a statute providing for the abating, as a public nuisance, of "malicious, scandalous and defamatory" newspapers or periodicals and the enjoining of anyone maintaining such a nuisance. Under this statute public officials in Minneapolis secured an injunction closing down a low-level scandal-mongering weekly. The Supreme Court by a five to four vote held the statute unconstitutional as authorizing a prior restraint on publications.

Discriminatory taxation against newspapers was unanimously invalidated in *Grosjean v. American Press Co.,* 297 U.S. 233 (1936). In 1934 the Louisiana Legislature, under the control of Huey Long, enacted a 2 per cent tax on gross receipts from advertising on all firms publishing newspapers or periodicals having a circulation of over 20,000 copies per week. It was denominated as a license tax on the privilege of engaging in the business of selling advertising. The statute affected 13 of the 17 daily newspapers published in the state, but did not touch any of the 120 weekly newspapers. The measure was clearly aimed at the city papers, which on the whole were opposing the Long regime, whereas the country press was favorable to Long. The Court's position was not of course that newspapers were immune from taxation. This particular tax was unconstitutional because it was "a deliberate and calculated device in the guise of a tax to limit the circulation of information to which the public is entitled in virtue of the constitutional guaranties."

Newspapers are subject, not only to normal taxes, but to all regular commercial or industrial regulations of the business of publishing. The Wagner Act regulating labor relations was held applicable to the press by a five to four vote in *Associated Press* v. *NLRB,* 301 U.S. 103 (1937). The NLRB had ordered the Associated Press to reinstate one of its news editors allegedly discharged because of his activity in organizing and furthering the American Newspaper Guild. The AP contended that, although the statute could be applied to its mechanical employees, its responsibility of furnishing unbiased and impartial news reports required that it have complete freedom in determining for itself the qualifications of its news employees. Justice Roberts responded that the AP retained complete freedom to discharge any employee "save only as a punishment for, or discouragement of," union activities. Similarly the antitrust provisions of the Sherman Act and the wage and hour requirements of the Fair Labor Standards Act have been held applicable to the press. *Associated Press* v. *United States,* 326 U.S. 1 (1945); *Oklahoma Press Publishing Co.* v. *Walling,* 327 U.S. 186 (1946).

Circulation of Handbills. Anyone with a hand printing press is a publisher for purposes of the First Amendment, with full rights not to be hampered by government restrictions in the publishing and circulation of his printed product. This has been established by a series of Supreme Court decisions involving handbills.

The first was *Lovell* v. *Griffin,* 303 U.S. 444 (1938), which held unconstitutional "on its face" a municipal ordinance requiring permission of the city manager to distribute publications. The city argued that handbills distributed on the streets and thrown away by recipients created a litter problem, and also contended that the distributor of handbills in this case, a member of Jehovah's Witnesses, was not a member of the press and so not "entitled to invoke the constitutional provisions touching the freedom of the press."

The Court rejoined that pamphlets and leaflets had been "historic weapons in the defense of liberty, as the pamphlets of Thomas Paine and others in our own history abundantly attest. The press in its historic connotation comprehends every sort of publication which affords a vehicle of information and opinion." As for the littering objection, the Court noted that the ordinance was a blanket prohibition, "not limited to ways which might be regarded as inconsistent with the maintenance of public order or as involving disorderly conduct, the molestation of the inhabitants, or the misuse or littering of the streets."

During the year following the *Lovell* decision, four more handbill cases were considered by the Supreme Court in *Schneider* v. *State* (*Town of Irvington*),

308 U.S. 147 (1939). In all of them the states involved sought to show that the regulations were more carefully drawn than the ordinance in *Lovell* and aimed more specifically at handbill abuses, such as frauds, disorder, and littering. But the Court replied that there were other ways to accomplish these legitimate aims without abridging freedom of speech and press. Frauds, street littering, and disorderly conduct could be specifically denounced and punished as offenses.

In *Talley* v. *California*, 362 U.S. 60 (1960), the Court declared unconstitutional a Los Angeles ordinance prohibiting the distribution of handbills which did not have printed on them the names and addresses of the persons who prepared, distributed, or sponsored them. The argument was that such identification was necessary to prevent fraud, false advertising, and libel, but again the Court held that the ordinance was not carefully drawn to accomplish these ends, while the identification requirement was bound to restrict freedom to distribute information and thereby freedom of expression. A three-judge minority supported the right of free speech, but not the "freedom of anonymity. The Constitution says nothing about freedom of anonymous speech."

Circulation through the Mails. The Post Office has asserted in various ways a substantial degree of control over materials which can be sent through the mails. An act of 1872 closed the mail to lottery tickets, obscene or indecent publications, and instructions for preventing conception and procuring abortions. The lottery ban was the only one on which test cases got to the Supreme Court. It was upheld in *Ex parte Jackson*, 96 U.S. 727 (1878), the Court saying: "In excluding various articles from the mail, the object of Congress has not been to interfere with the freedom of the press, or with any other rights of the people; but to refuse its facilities for the distribution of matter deemed injurious to the public morals."

The nineteenth-century lottery decisions constituted, until 1957, the principal Supreme Court support for congressional regulation of the mails on the grounds of protecting the public morals. But the banning of literature from postal distribution because of alleged obscenity presents entirely different problems from those presented by a lottery. Lottery tickets are easily identified, but judgments as to what is obscene vary tremendously, and many literary classics have been treated as nonmailable by the Post Office. In addition to obscenity, which it has statutory authority to intercept, the Post Office has also undertaken on occasion to bar certain types of political opinions from the mail, in spite of the fact that its statutory authority to do so is dubious or nonexistent.

Three instrumentalities have been employed by the Post Office for prior restraint purposes. The first is confiscation and destruction, which have been primarily used against allegedly obscene matter and foreign political propaganda. Court decisions on obscene publications will be reviewed in Chapter 24. No court tests on confiscation of foreign political propaganda have reached the Supreme Court, primarily because the Post Office has mooted all the test cases by releasing the confiscated material when suit is brought. The Kennedy administration abandoned these confiscation practices in 1961.

A second Post Office instrument of prior restraint is the "stop order," first authorized by Congress against persons or firms found by the Post Office to be using the mails to defraud. All mail to such persons is intercepted, and postal money orders mailed to them will not be paid. Justices Holmes and Brandeis in a dissenting opinion in *Leach* v. *Carlile,* 258 U.S. 138 (1922), charged that this procedure was contrary to the First Amendment, but it has been continued, and in 1950 the Post Office secured from Congress the power to employ the stop order procedure against firms using the mails to deal in obscenity. Another act of 1956 authorizes the Post Office to impound mail suspected of promoting fraud, obscenity, and gambling, but books are exempted and some definite procedural protections are provided.

The third type of Post Office restraint relates to the granting of second-class mailing privileges. The circulation of publications carried at second-class rates is in effect subsidized by the government, for the rates are much below the cost of service, and the second-class privilege is essential if a periodical publication is to compete successfully in its field.

In *Milwaukee Publishing Co.* v. *Burleson,* 255 U.S. 407 (1921), the Court upheld the denial of second-class privileges to a Socialist newspaper, over the protest of Justices Brandeis and Holmes that such power could make the Postmaster General "the universal censor of publications." However, the Postmaster General was frustrated by the Court's decision in *Hannegan* v. *Esquire,* 327 U.S. 146 (1946), when he sought to withdraw second-class privileges from *Esquire* magazine. The claim was that *Esquire* did not meet the statutory test of being "published for the dissemination of information of a public character, or devoted to literature, the sciences, arts, or some special industry." The Postmaster General argued that the material in *Esquire,* while not obscene in a technical sense, was so close to it that it was "morally improper and not for the public welfare and the public good."

A unanimous Court held that Congress had not meant to grant the Postmaster General rights of censorship when it attached these conditions to the second-class privilege. The statute had not authorized him to make general findings based on "the public good or welfare." The Holmes-Brandeis dissent in *Milwaukee Publishing Co.* was noted, with the comment: "Grave constitutional questions are immediately raised once it is said that the use of the mails is a privilege which may be extended or withheld on any grounds whatsoever."

In spite of this language, Congress and the Post Office continue to operate on the theory that access to postal service is a privilege, not a right, and that it can be limited at will.

NEAR v. MINNESOTA
283 U.S. 697, 51 S. Ct. 625, 75 L. Ed. 1357 (1931)

Defendants were publishers of *The Saturday Press,* a Minneapolis paper which was anti-Semitic and made violent charges against the local law-enforcement officers. The county attorney brought an action for injunction against publication of the paper under a 1925 statute permitting injunctions against "a malicious, scandalous and defamatory newspaper." The trial court enjoined the defendants from publishing in an improper manner but not "restraining them from operating a newspaper in harmony with the public welfare." So construed, the decree was affirmed by the state supreme court, and Near appealed.

MR. CHIEF JUSTICE HUGHES delivered the opinion of the Court. . . .

The District Court made findings of fact, which followed the allegations of the complaint and found in general terms that the editions in question were "chiefly devoted to malicious, scandalous and defamatory articles," concerning the individuals named. The court further found that the defendants through these publications "did engage in the business of regularly and customarily producing, publishing and circulating a malicious, scandalous and defamatory newspaper," and that "the said publication" "under said name of The Saturday Press, or any other name, constitutes a public nuisance under the laws of the State." Judgment was thereupon entered adjudging that "the newspaper, magazine and periodical known as The Saturday Press," as a public nuisance, "be and is hereby abated." The judgment perpetually enjoined the defendants "from producing, editing, publishing, circulating, having in their possession, selling or giving away any publication whatsoever which is a malicious, scandalous or defamatory newspaper, as defined by law," and also "from further conducting said nuisance under the name and title of said The Saturday Press or any other name or title." . . .

This statute, for the suppression as a public nuisance of a newspaper or periodical, is unusual, if not unique, and raises questions of grave importance transcending the local interests involved in the particular action. It is no longer open to doubt that the liberty of the press, and of speech, is within the liberty safeguarded by the due process clause of the Fourteenth Amendment from invasion by state action. It was found impossible to conclude that this essential personal liberty of the citizen was left unprotected by the general guaranty of fundamental rights of person and property. *Gitlow* v. *New York,* 268, U.S. 652, 666; *Whitney* v. *California,* 274 U.S. 357, 362, 373; *Fiske* v. *Kansas,* 274 U.S. 380, 382; *Stromberg* v. *California,* 283 U.S. 359. In maintaining this guaranty, the authority of the State to enact laws to promote the health, safety, morals and general welfare of its people is necessarily admitted. The limits of this sovereign power must·always be determined with appropriate regard to the particular subject of its exercise. . . . Liberty of speech, and of the press, is . . . not an absolute right, and the State may punish its abuse. . . . Liberty, in each of its phases, has its history and connotation and, in the present instance, the inquiry is as to the historic conception of the liberty of the press and whether the statute under review violates the essential attributes of that liberty. . . .

First. The statute is not aimed at the redress of individual or private wrongs. Remedies for libel remain available and unaffected. The statute, said the state court, "is not directed at threatened libel but at an existing business which, generally speaking, involves more than libel." It is aimed at the distribution of scandalous matter as "detrimental to public morals and to the general welfare," tending "to disturb the peace of the community" and "to provoke assaults and the commission of crime." In order to obtain an injunction to suppress the future publication of the newspaper or periodical, it is not necessary to prove the falsity of the charges that have been made in the publication condemned. In the present action there was no allegation that the matter published was not true. It is alleged, and the statute requires the allegation, that the publication was "malicious." But, as in prosecutions for libel, there is no requirement of proof by the State of malice in fact as distinguished from malice inferred from the mere publication of the defamatory matter. The judgment in this case proceeded upon the mere proof of publication. The statute permits the defense, not of the truth alone, but only that the truth was published with good motives and for justifiable ends. It is apparent that under the statute the publication is to be regarded as defamatory if it injures reputation, and that it is scandalous if it circulates charges of reprehensible conduct, whether criminal or otherwise, and the publication is thus deemed to invite public reprobation and to constitute a public scandal. The court sharply defined the purpose of the statute, bringing out the precise point, in these words: "There is no constitutional right to publish a fact merely because it is true. It is a matter of common knowledge that prosecutions under the criminal libel statutes do not result in efficient repression or suppression of the evils of scandal. Men who are the victims of such assaults seldom resort to the courts. This is especially true if their sins are exposed and the only question relates to whether it was done with good motives and for justifiable ends. This law is not for the protection of the person attacked nor to punish the wrongdoer. It is for the protection of the public welfare."

Second. The statute is directed not simply at the circulation of scandalous and defamatory statements with regard to private citizens, but at the continued publication by newspapers and periodicals of charges against public officers of corruption, malfeasance in office, or serious neglect of duty. Such charges by their very nature create a public scandal. They are scandalous and defamatory within the meaning of the statute, which has its normal operation in relation to publications dealing prominently and chiefly with the alleged derelictions of public officers.

Third. The object of the statute is not punishment, in the ordinary sense, but suppression of the offending newspaper or periodical. The reason for the enactment, as the state court has said, is that prosecutions to enforce penal statutes for libel do not result in "efficient repression or suppression of the evils of scandal." Describing the business of publication as a public nuisance, does not obscure the substance of the proceeding which the statute authorizes. It is the continued publication of scandalous and defamatory matter that constitutes the business and the declared nuisance. In the case of public officers, it is the reiteration of charges of official misconduct, and the fact that the newspaper or periodical is principally devoted to that purpose, that exposes it to suppression. In the present instance, the proof was that nine editions of the newspaper or periodical in question were published on successive dates, and that they were chiefly devoted to charges against public officers and in relation to the prevalence and protection of crime. In such a case, these officers are not left to their ordinary remedy in a suit for libel, or the authorities to a prosecution for criminal libel. Under this statute, a publisher of a newspaper or periodical, undertaking to conduct a campaign to expose and to censure official derelictions, and devoting his publication principally to that purpose, must face not simply the possibility of a verdict against him in a suit or prosecution for libel, but a determination that his newspaper or periodical is a public nuisance to be abated, and that this abatement and suppression will follow unless he is prepared with legal evidence to prove the truth of the charges and also to satisfy the court that, in addition to being true, the matter was published with good motives and for justifiable ends.

This suppression is accomplished by enjoining publication and that restraint is the object and effect of the statute.

Fourth. The statute not only operates to suppress the offending newspaper or periodical but to put the publisher under an effective censorship. . . .

If we cut through mere details of procedure, the operation and effect of the statute in substance is that public authorities may bring the owner or publisher of a newspaper or periodical before a judge upon a charge of conducting a business of publishing scandalous and defamatory matter—in particular that the matter consists of charges against public officers of official dereliction—and unless the owner or publisher is able and disposed to bring competent evidence to satisfy the judge that the charges are true and are published with good motives and for justifiable ends, his newspaper or periodical is suppressed and further publication is made punishable as a contempt. This is of the essence of censorship.

The question is whether a statute authorizing such proceedings in restraint of publication is consistent with the conception of the liberty of the press as historically conceived and guaranteed. In determining the extent of the constitutional protection, it has been generally, if not universally, considered that it is the chief purpose of the guaranty to prevent previous restraints upon publication. The struggle in England, directed against the legislative power of the licenser, resulted in renunciation of the censorship of the press. The liberty deemed to be established was thus described by Blackstone: "The liberty of the press is indeed essential to the nature of a free state; but this consists in laying no *previous* restraints upon publications, and not in freedom from censure for criminal matter when published. Every freeman has an undoubted right to lay what sentiments he pleases before the public; to forbid this, is to destroy the freedom of the press; but if he publishes what is improper, mischievous or illegal, he must take the consequence of his own temerity." 4 Bl. Com. 151, 152. . . .

The criticism upon Blackstone's statement has not been because immunity from previous restraint upon publication has not been regarded as deserving of special emphasis, but chiefly because that immunity cannot be deemed to exhaust the conception of the liberty guaranteed by state and federal constitutions. The point of criticism has been "that the mere exemption from previous restraints cannot be all that is secured by the constitutional provisions"; and that "the liberty of the press might be rendered a mockery and a delusion, and the phrase itself a by-word, if, while every man was at liberty to publish what he pleased, the public authorities might nevertheless punish him for harmless publications." 2 Cooley, Const. Lim., 8th ed., p. 885. But it is recognized that punishment for the abuse of the liberty accorded to the press is essential to the protection of the public, and that the common law rules that subject the libeler to responsibility for the public offense, as well as for the private injury, are not abolished by the protection extended in our constitutions. . . . The law of criminal libel rests upon that secure foundation. There is also the conceded authority of courts to punish for contempt when publications directly tend to prevent the proper discharge of judicial functions. *Patterson* v. *Colorado, supra; Toledo Newspaper Co.* v. *United States,* 247 U.S. 402, 419. In the present case, we have no occasion to inquire as to the permissible scope of subsequent punishment. For whatever wrong the appellant has committed or may commit, by his publications, the State appropriately affords both public and private redress by its libel laws. . . .

The objection has also been made that the principle as to immunity from previous restraint is stated too broadly, if every such restraint is deemed to be prohibited. That is undoubtedly true; the protection even as to previous restraint is not absolutely unlimited. But the limitation has been recognized only in exceptional cases: "When a nation is at war many things that might be said in time of peace are such a hindrance to its effort that their utterance will not be endured so long as men fight and that no Court could regard them as protected by any constitutional right." *Schenck* v. *United States,* 249 U.S. 47, 52. No one would question but that a government might prevent actual obstruction to its recruiting service or the publication of the sailing dates of transports or the number and location of troops. On similar grounds, the primary requirements of decency may be enforced against obscene publications. The security of the community life may be protected against incitements to acts of violence and the overthrow by force of orderly government. . . . These limitations are not applicable here. . . .

The exceptional nature of its limitations places in a strong light the general conception that liberty of the press, historically considered and taken up by the Federal Constitution, has meant, principally although not exclusively, immunity from previous restraints or censorship. The conception of the liberty of the press in this country had broadened with the exigencies of the colonial period and with the efforts to secure freedom from oppressive administration. That liberty was especially cherished for the immunity it afforded from previous restraint of the publication of censure of public officers and charges of official misconduct. . . .

The fact that for approximately one hundred and fifty years there has been almost an entire absence of attempts to impose previous restraints upon publications relating to the malfeasance of public officers is significant of the deep-seated conviction that such restraints would violate constitutional right. Public officers, whose character and conduct remain open to debate and free discussion in the press, find their remedies for false accusations in actions under libel laws providing for redress and punishment, and not in proceedings to restrain the publication of newspapers and periodicals. The general principle that the constitutional guaranty of the liberty of the press gives immunity from previous restraints has been approved in many decisions under the provisions of state constitutions.

The importance of this immunity has not lessened. While reckless assaults upon public men, and efforts to bring obloquy upon those who are endeavoring faithfully to discharge official duties, exert a baleful influence and deserve the severest condemnation in public opinion, it cannot be said that this abuse is greater, and it is believed to be less, than that which characterized the period in which our institutions took shape. Meanwhile, the administration of government has become more complex, the opportunities for malfeasance and corruption have multiplied, crime has grown to most serious proportions, and the danger of its protection by unfaithful officials and of the impairment of the fundamental security of life and property by criminal alliances and official neglect, emphasizes the primary need of a vigilant and courageous press, especially in great cities. The fact that the liberty of the press may be abused by miscreant purveyors of scandal does not make any the less necessary the immunity of the press from previous restraint in dealing with official misconduct. Subsequent punishment for such abuses as may exist is the appropriate remedy, consistent with constitutional privilege. . . .

The statute in question cannot be justified by reason of the fact that the publisher is permitted to show, before injunction issues, that the matter published is true and is published with good motives and for justifiable ends. If such a statute, authorizing suppression and injunction on such a basis, is constitutionally valid, it would be equally permissible for the legislature to provide that at any time the publisher of any newspaper could be brought before a court, or even an administrative officer (as the constitutional protection may not be regarded as resting on mere procedural details) and required to produce proof of the truth of his publication, or of what he intended to publish, and of his motives, or stand enjoined. If this can be done, the legislature may provide machinery for determining in the complete exercise of its discretion what are justifiable ends and restrain publication accordingly. And it would be but a step to a complete system of censorship. The recognition of authority to impose previous restraint upon publication in order to protect the community against the circulation of charges of misconduct, and especially of official misconduct, necessarily would carry with it the admission of the authority of the censor against which the constitutional barrier was erected. . . .

Equally unavailing is the insistence that the statute is designed to prevent the circulation of scandal which tends to disturb the public peace and to provoke assaults and the commission of crime. Charges of reprehensible conduct, and in particular of official malfeasance, unquestionably create a public scandal, but the theory of the constitutional guaranty is that even a more serious public evil would be caused by authority to prevent publication. . . . There is nothing new in the fact that charges of reprehensible conduct may create resentment and the disposition to resort to violent means of redress, but this well-understood tendency did not alter the determination to protect the press against censorship and restraint upon publication. . . . The danger of violent reactions becomes greater with effective organization of defiant groups resenting exposure, and if this consideration warranted legislative interference with the initial freedom of publication, the constitutional protection would be reduced to a mere form of words.

For these reasons we hold the statute, so far as it authorized the proceedings in this action under clause (b) of section one, to be an infringement of the liberty of the press guaranteed by the Fourteenth Amendment. . . .

Judgment reversed.

Mr. Justice Butler, dissenting.

The decision of the Court in this case declares Minnesota and every other State powerless to restrain by injunction the business of publishing and circulating among the people malicious, scandalous and defamatory periodicals that in due course of judicial procedure has been adjudged to be a public nuisance. It gives to freedom of the press a meaning and a scope not heretofore recognized and construes "liberty" in the due process clause of the Fourteenth Amendment to put upon the States a federal restriction that is without precedent. . . .

The record shows, and it is conceded, that defendants' regular business was the publication of malicious, scandalous and defamatory articles concerning the principal public officers, leading newspapers of the city, many private persons and the Jewish race. It also shows that it was their purpose at all hazards to continue to carry on the business. In every edition slanderous and defamatory matter predominates to the practical exclusion of all else. Many of the statements are so highly improbable as to compel a finding that they are false. The articles themselves show malice. . . .

Defendant concedes that the editions of the newspaper complained of are "defamatory *per se*." And he says: "It has been asserted that the constitution was never intended to be a shield for malice, scandal, and defamation when untrue, or published with bad motives, or for unjustifiable ends. . . . The contrary is true; every person *does* have a constitutional right to publish malicious, scandalous, and defamatory matter though untrue, and with bad motives, and for unjustifiable ends, *in the first instance,* though he is subject to responsibility therefor *afterwards.*" The record, when the substance of the articles is regarded, requires that concession here. And this Court is required to pass on the validity of the state law on that basis. . . .

The Minnesota statute does not operate as a *previous* restraint on publication within the proper meaning of that phrase. It does not authorize administrative control in advance such as was formerly exercised by the licensers and censors but prescribes a remedy to be enforced by a suit in equity. In this case there was previous publication made in the course of the business of regularly producing malicious, scandalous and defamatory periodicals. The business and publications unquestionably constitute an abuse of the right of free press. The statute denounces the things done as a nuisance on the ground, as stated by the state supreme court, that they threaten morals, peace and good order. There is no question of the power of the State to denounce such transgressions. The restraint authorized is only in respect of continuing to do what has been duly adjudged to constitute a nuisance. . . .

It is well known, as found by the state supreme court, that existing libel laws are inadequate effectively to suppress evils resulting from the kind of business and publications that are shown in this case. The doctrine that measures such as the one before us are invalid because they operate as previous restraints to infringe freedom of press exposes the peace and good order of every community and the business and private affairs of every individual to the constant and protracted false and malicious assaults of any insolvent publisher who may have purpose and sufficient capacity to contrive and put into effect a scheme or program for oppression, blackmail or extortion.

The judgment should be affirmed.

MR. JUSTICE VAN DEVANTER, MR. JUSTICE McREYNOLDS, and MR. JUSTICE SUTHERLAND concur in this opinion.

Chapter 21

CENSORSHIP OF SPEECH

Because of its social setting, the process of communication by speech is likely to create more temptations and justifications for government intervention than is the process of communication by the printed word. People who are reading cause no trouble, and the government should have no concern about what they are reading. A possible exception to this rule is if the reading matter is outrageously obscene; the problems of obscenity are considered in Chapter 24. But communication through speech is by definition a social process, and often occurs in situations where public problems necessarily result. Speeches often draw crowds. They are often made on public property. They may be amplified by loudspeakers to the point of becoming a public nuisance. They may arouse animosities or inflame listeners to the point of physical violence. The public interest in peace and order may often be thought to require some prior restraints on speech, and the Supreme Court has adjudicated many conflicts of this sort.

Speech and Assembly in Public Places. One situation which seems to encourage public controls over speech is where public properties—parks, streets, meeting halls, schools—are being used by speakers. An 1895 opinion of the Massachusetts supreme court, written by Justice Holmes, upheld a Boston ordinance which required a permit for speeches on Boston Common. Holmes said that Boston had as much right to forbid speeches in public places as the owner of a private house had to forbid them in his house. *Commonwealth* v. *Davis,* 162 Mass. 510 (1895).

Clearly Holmes had not thought through the problem at that time, and the Supreme Court had to disregard this reasoning in *Hague* v. *C.I.O.,* 307 U.S. 496 (1939). A Jersey City ordinance prohibited assemblies in the public streets, parks, and buildings without a permit from the director of public safety. The Supreme Court held that these invasions of liberty could not be defended as valid police regulations. Streets and parks have immemorially been held in trust for benefit of the public and used for purposes of assembly and communication. Their use for these purposes may be regulated in the interests of all, but may not, in the guise of regulations, be abridged or denied.

On the other hand, *Cox* v. *New Hampshire,* 312 U.S. 569 (1941), presented a type of regulation of street meetings which the Court unanimously upheld. A group of Jehovah's Witnesses had marched single file along the downtown streets of a city, carrying placards to advertise a meeting, without securing the license required by state statute for "parades or processions" on the public streets.

The Court thought that the license requirement here was a valid traffic regulation, and that the conviction was not for conveying information or holding a meeting.

As the Supreme Court has balanced the equities in subsequent public meetings cases, its clear tendency has been to declare unconstitutional any permit or license requirements for speech in public places unless they are so restricted or minimal that they cannot be used for discriminatory purposes. The best example of this tendency is supplied by *Kunz* v. *New York,* 340 U.S. 290 (1951), where the Court denied the right of New York City to oust a bigoted preacher from the public streets by use of a permit requirement. The permit system for public speaking is constitutionally suspect.

Whether this same rule should apply to the amplified human voice has caused the Court greater trouble. *Saia* v. *New York,* 334 U.S. 558 (1948), involved a Jehovah's Witnesses minister who gave lectures in a public park on designated Sundays, using sound equipment mounted on top of his car to reach a wider audience. The city had an ordinance requiring permission of the chief of police for use of sound-amplifying devices. The minister had such a permit, but when it expired, renewal was refused on the ground that there had been "complaints." He went on preaching without a license, and was arrested. By a five to four vote the Supreme Court held the ordinance unconstitutional as a prior restraint on speech. There might be abuses in the use of loudspeakers, but if so they could only be controlled by "narrowly drawn" statutes aimed at those abuses, not by giving a police officer power to deny the use of loudspeakers entirely.

But the following year, in *Kovacs* v. *Cooper,* 336 U.S. 77 (1949), the Court withdrew from this position. The city ordinance here made it unlawful for sound trucks emitting "loud and raucous" noises to be operated on the streets, and it was applied against a sound truck engaged in commenting on a local labor dispute. The Court upheld this ordinance by another five to four vote, apparently on the ground that it was aimed only at "loud and raucous" sound trucks, though the state courts had interpreted the language as banning all sound trucks. Thus the law on this subject was left in a rather unclear condition.

The Right to Privacy. Persons in the privacy of their homes certainly have some rights to protect themselves from unwanted communications. The right to free speech may conflict with the right to privacy. Recognizing such conflicts, most states provide that householders who do not want to receive solicitors can post "no trespassing" signs, with violators subject to prosecution for trespass. But can the community on its own account endeavor to protect the privacy of its citizens?

The answer seems to be that, in so far as purely commercial visitors are concerned, a community can adopt any kind of antisolicitation regulation it likes without raising any First Amendment problems. But for noncommercial door-to-door canvassing, the situation is not so simple. In *Martin* v. *City of Struthers,* 319 U.S. 141 (1943), an ordinance made it unlawful to ring doorbells or otherwise summon the occupant of a dwelling to the door just to give him a circular or handbill. The ordinance had been adopted to protect the daytime sleep of industrial workers during the war, many of them being employed on night shifts. It was applied against a Jehovah's Witness who was distributing a dodger announcing a meeting and lecture.

By a six to three vote, the Supreme Court invalidated the ordinance. Justice Black noted that "for centuries it has been a common practice in this and other countries for persons not specifically invited to go from home to home and knock on doors or ring doorbells to communicate ideas to the occupants or to invite them to political, religious, or other kinds of public meetings." An ordinance which specifically controlled "the distribution of literature," and which substituted community judgment for the desires of individuals, many of whom might be glad to receive the literature, was invalid because in conflict with the freedom of speech and press.

In two 1946 decisions the Court again protected the right of Jehovah's Witnesses to go onto private property—a "company town" and a federal housing development—regardless of the wishes of the proprietors. *Marsh* v. *Alabama,* 326 U.S. 501 (1946); *Tucker* v. *Texas,* 326 U.S. 517 (1946). But *Breard* v. *Alexandria,* 341 U.S. 622 (1951), gave a different answer. Here an antisolicitation ordinance was applied against salesmen of magazine subscriptions. The Court majority felt that the case turned on "a balancing of the conveniences between some householders' desire for privacy and the publisher's right to distribute publications in the precise way that those soliciting for him think bring the best results." Communities which had found house-to-house canvassing obnoxious had a right to control it by ordinance. Magazines could be sold some other way. Justices Black and Douglas dissented on First Amendment grounds, saying: "The constitutional sanctuary for the press must necessarily include liberty to publish and circulate. In view of our economic system, it must also include freedom to solicit paying subscribers."

Limitations on the Political Process. Two federal statutes which have a clearly restrictive effect upon participation by speech in the national political process have nevertheless been upheld by the Supreme Court. The first is the Hatch Act of 1939, limiting the political activity of government employees, which was upheld in *United Public Workers* v. *Mitchell,* 330 U.S. 75 (1947), by a vote of four to three. The majority approved the power of Congress to decide that it would be in the best interests of an efficient public service for civil service employees to be prohibited from active participation in politics. "To declare that the present supposed evils of political activity are beyond the power of Congress to redress would leave the nation impotent to deal with what many sincere men believe is a material threat to the democratic system."

Justice Black, one of the dissenters, castigated a policy which muzzled several million citizens and deprived the body politic of their political participation and interest. "I think the Constitution prohibits legislation which prevents millions of citizens from contributing their arguments, complaints, and suggestions to the political debates which are the essence of our democracy." Moreover, the statute endowed the Civil Service Commission "with the awesome power to censor the thoughts, expressions, and activities of law-abiding citizens in the field of free expression. . . ."

The second statute is the Federal Regulation of Lobbying Act, adopted in 1946. The law had a very broad reach, requiring reports to Congress from all persons "receiving any contributions or expending any money" for the purpose of influencing any legislation by Congress. In *United States* v. *Harriss,* 347 U.S. 612 (1954), the Supreme Court was obviously worried about the impact of these provisions on free speech and the right to petition the government. However, by construing the law to cover only "lobbying in its commonly accepted sense," that is, direct communication with members of Congress, and not to apply to organizations seeking to propagandize the general public," the Court majority was able to hold the act constitutional.

Picketing and Free Speech. In *Thornhill* v. *Alabama,* 310 U.S. 88 (1940), the Supreme Court placed peaceful picketing in labor disputes under the protection of the free speech clause. The state statute, as applied in this case, made punishable a mere conversation between a picket on company property and a nonunion worker. The Court said that "in the circumstances of our times the dissemination of information concerning the facts of a labor dispute must be regarded as within that area of free discussion that is guaranteed by the Constitution." A statute precluding all practicable and effective methods of enlightening the public on the issues in a labor dispute was unconstitutional on its face.

However, subsequent cases have demonstrated that picketing can be forbidden, in spite of its communication role, when it damages other social values which are also protected by law. *Milk Wagon Drivers Union* v. *Meadowmoor Dairies,* 312 U.S. 287 (1941), held that Illinois courts were justified in enjoining all picketing in a labor dispute which had been so marred by past violence that it was believed impossible for future picketing to be maintained on a peaceful basis. In *Carpenters and Joiners Union* v. *Ritter's Cafe,* 315 U.S. 722 (1942), Ritter was having a residence built by nonunion labor, but the pickets were operating around his cafe, a mile away, where the pressure would hurt him more. By a five to four vote the Court ruled that Texas had the right to restrict picketing to the area within which a labor dispute arises.

A conflict between picketing rights and the Missouri antitrust law was decided in favor of the latter in *Giboney* v. *Empire Storage & Ice Co.,* 336 U.S. 490 (1949). A union of retail ice peddlers was picketing an ice company, trying to force an agreement not to sell ice to nonunion peddlers. Such an agreement, if made, would have violated the state law on restraint of trade. The picketing was thus "an essential and inseparable part of a grave offense against an important public law," and the Court ruled that the First Amendment would not immunize that unlawful conduct from state control.

A similar case was *International Brotherhood of Teamsters* v. *Hanke,* 339 U.S. 470 (1950), except that here the union was not making an unlawful demand. It was picketing to force used-car businesses to close on evenings and weekends. If such an agreement had been reached, it would have been quite legal. Nevertheless the state courts enjoined picketing for this purpose, saying that "the union's interest in the welfare of a mere handful of members . . . is far outweighed by the interests of individual proprietors and the people of the community as a whole. . . ." The Supreme Court agreed that the state, by either its legislature or its courts, was free to strike a balance between competing economic interests, and that the balance here achieved was not "so inconsistent with rooted traditions of a free people that it must be found an unconstitutional choice."

Thus it appears that in the area of communication by picketing, only flat restraints on all picketing are forbidden. In all other respects legislatures and judges are free to define public purposes which may override picketing rights.

KUNZ v. NEW YORK
340 U.S. 290, 71 S. Ct. 312, 95 L. Ed. 280 (1951)

MR. CHIEF JUSTICE VINSON delivered the opinion of the Court.

New York City has adopted an ordinance which makes it unlawful to hold public worship meetings on the streets without first obtaining a permit from the city police commissioner. Appellant, Carl Jacob Kunz, was convicted and fined $10 for violating this ordinance by holding a religious meeting without a permit. The conviction was affirmed by the Appellate Part of the Court of Special Sessions, and by the New York Court of Appeals, three judges dissenting, 300 N. Y. 273, 90 N. E. 2d 455 (1950). The case is here on appeal, it having been urged that the ordinance is invalid under the Fourteenth Amendment.

Appellant is an ordained Baptist minister who speaks under the auspices of the "Outdoor Gospel Work," of which he is the director. He has been preaching for about six years, and states that it is his conviction and duty to "go out on the highways and byways and preach the word of God." In 1946, he applied for and received a permit under the ordinance in question, there being no question that appellant comes within the classes of persons entitled to receive permits under the ordinance. This permit, like all others, was good only for the calendar year in which issued. In November, 1946, his permit was revoked after a hearing by the police commissioner. The revocation was based on evidence that he had ridiculed and denounced other religious beliefs in his meetings.

Although the penalties of the ordinance apply to anyone who "ridicules and denounces other religious beliefs," the ordinance does not specify this as a ground for permit revocation. Indeed, there is no mention in the ordinance of any power of revocation. However, appellant did not seek judicial or administrative review of the revocation proceedings, and any question as to the propriety of the revocation is not before us in this case. In any event, the revocation affected appellant's rights to speak in 1946 only. Appellant applied for another permit in 1947, and again in 1948, but was notified each time that his application was "disapproved," with no reason for the disapproval being given. On September 11, 1948, appellant was arrested for speaking at Columbus Circle in New York City wthout a permit. It is from the conviction which resulted that this appeal has been taken.

Appellant's conviction was thus based upon his failure to possess a permit for 1948. We are here concerned only with the propriety of the action of the police commissioner in refusing to issue that permit. Disapproval of the 1948 permit application by the police commissioner was justified by the New York courts on the ground that a permit had previously been revoked "for good reasons." It is noteworthy that there is no mention in the ordinance of reasons for which such a permit application can be refused. This interpretation allows the police commissioner, an administrative official, to exercise discretion in denying subsequent permit applications on the basis of his interpretation, at that time, of what is deemed to be conduct condemned by the ordinance. We have here, then, an ordinance which gives an administrative official discretionary power to control in advance the right of citizens to speak on religious matters on the streets of New York. As such, the ordinance is clearly invalid as a prior restraint on the exercise of First Amendment rights.

In considering the right of a municipality to control the use of public streets for the expression of religious views, we start with the words of Mr. Justice Roberts that "Wherever the title of streets and parks may rest, they have immemorially been held in trust for the use of the public and, time out of mind, have been used for purposes of assembly, communicating thoughts between citizens, and discussing public questions." *Hague* v. *C.I.O.*, 307 U.S. 496, 515 (1939). Although this Court has recognized that a statute may be enacted which prevents serious interference with normal usage of streets and parks, *Cox* v. *New Hampshire*, 312 U.S. 569 (1941), we have consistently condemned licensing systems which vest in an administrative official discretion to grant or withhold a permit upon broad criteria unrelated to proper regulation of public places. In *Cantwell* v. *Connecticut,* 310 U.S. 296 (1940), this Court held invalid an ordinance which required a license for soliciting money for religious causes. Speaking for a unanimous Court, Mr. Justice Roberts said: "But to condition the solicitation of aid for the perpetuation of religious views or systems upon a license, the grant of which rests in the exercise of a determination by state authority as to what is a religious cause, is to lay a forbidden burden upon the exercise of liberty protected by the Constitution." 310 U.S. at 307. To the same effect are *Lovell* v. *Griffin,* 303 U.S. 444 (1938); *Hague* v. *C.I.O.*, 307 U.S. 496 (1939); *Largent* v. *Texas,* 318 U.S. 418 (1943). In *Saia* v. *New York*, 334 U.S. 558 (1948), we reaffirmed the invalidity of such prior restraints upon the right to speak: "We hold that § 3 of this ordinance is unconstitutional on its face, for it establishes a previous restraint on the right of free speech in violation of the First Amendment which is protected by the Fourteenth Amendment against State action. To use a loudspeaker or amplifier one has to get a permit from the Chief of Police. There are no standards prescribed for the exercise of his discretion." 334 U.S. at 559–560.

The court below has mistakenly derived support for its conclusion from the evidence produced at the trial that appellant's religious meetings had, in the past, caused some disorder. There are appropriate public remedies to protect the peace and order of the community if appellant's speeches should result in disorder or violence. "In the present case, we have no occasion to inquire as to the permissible scope of subsequent punishment." *Near* v. *Minnesota*, 283 U.S. 697, 715 (1931). We do not express any opinion on the propriety of punitive remedies which the New York authorities may utilize. We are here concerned with suppression—not punishment. It is sufficient to say that New York cannot vest restraining control over the right to speak on religious subjects in an administrative official where there are no appropriate standards to guide his action.

Reversed.

Mr. Justice Black concurs in the result.

Mr. Justice Frankfurter, concurring in the result. . . .

We must be mindful of the enormous difficulties confronting those charged with the task of enabling the polyglot millions in the City of New York to live in peace and tolerance. Street-preaching in Columbus Circle is done in a milieu quite different from preaching on a New England village green. Again, religious polemic does not touch the merely ratiocinative nature of man, and the ugly facts disclosed by the record of this case show that Kunz was not reluctant to offend the deepest religious feelings of frequenters of Columbus Circle. . . .

I cannot make too explicit my conviction that the City of New York is not restrained by anything in the Constitution of the United States from protecting completely the community's interests in relation to its streets. But if a municipality conditions street meetings on the granting of a permit by the police, the basis which guides licensing officials in granting or denying a permit must not give them a free hand, or a hand effectively free when the actualities of police administration are taken into account. . . .

Administrative control over the right to speak must be based on appropriate standards. . . . The vice to be guarded against is arbitrary action by officials. The fact that in a particular instance an action appears not arbitrary does not save the validity of the authority under which the action was taken. . . .

MR. JUSTICE JACKSON, dissenting.

Essential freedoms are today threatened from without and within. It may become difficult to preserve here what a large part of the world has lost—the right to speak, even temperately, on matters vital to spirit and body. In such a setting, to blanket hateful and hate-stirring attacks on races and faiths under the protections for freedom of speech may be a noble innovation. On the other hand, it may be a quixotic tilt at windmills which belittles great principles of liberty. Only time can tell. But I incline to the latter view and cannot assent to the decision.

To know what we are doing, we must first locate the point at which rights asserted by Kunz conflict with powers asserted by the organized community. New York City has placed no limitation upon any speech Kunz may choose to make on private property, but it does require a permit to hold religious meetings in its streets. The ordinance, neither by its terms nor as it has been applied, prohibited Kunz, even in street meetings, from preaching his own religion or making any temperate criticism or refutation of other religions; indeed, for the year 1946, he was given a general permit to do so. His meetings, however, brought "a flood of complaints" to city authorities that he was engaging in scurrilous attacks on Catholics and Jews. On notice, he was given a hearing at which eighteen complainants appeared. The Commissioner revoked his permit and applications for 1947 and 1948 were refused. For a time he went on holding meetings without a permit in Columbus Circle, where in September, 1948, he was arrested for violation of the ordinance. He was convicted and fined ten dollars.

At these meetings, Kunz preached, among many other things of like tenor, that "The Catholic Church makes merchandise out of souls," that Catholicism is "a religion of the devil," and that the Pope is "the anti-Christ." The Jews he denounced as "Christ-killers," and he said of them, "All the garbage that didn't believe in Christ should have been burnt in the incinerators. It's a shame they all weren't."

These utterances, as one might expect, stirred strife and threatened violence. Testifying in his own behalf, Kunz stated that he "became acquainted with" one of the complaining witnesses, whom he thought to be a Jew, "when he happened to sock one of my Christian boys in the puss." Kunz himself complained to the authorities, charging a woman interrupter with disorderly conduct. He also testified that when an officer is not present at his meetings "I have trouble then," but "with an officer, no trouble."

The contention which Kunz brings here and which this Court sustains is that such speeches on the streets are within his constitutional freedom and therefore New York City has no power to require a permit. He does not deny that this has been and will continue to be his line of talk. He does not claim that he should have been granted a permit; he attacks the whole system of control of street meetings and says the Constitution gives him permission to speak and he needs none from the City.

The speeches which Kunz has made and which he asserts he has a *right* to make in the future were properly held by the courts below to be out of bounds for a street meeting and not constitutionally protected. This Court, without discussion, makes a contrary assumption which is basic to its whole opinion. It says New York has given "an administrative official discretionary power to control in advance *the right* of citizens to speak on religious matters on the streets." Again, it says that "prior restraint on the exercise of First Amendment *rights*" invalidates the ordinance. (Emphasis supplied.) This seems to take the last step first, assuming as a premise what is in question. Of course, if Kunz is only exercising his constitutional *rights*, then New York can neither restrain nor punish him. But I doubt that the Court's assumption will survive analysis.

This Court today initiates the doctrine that language such as this, in the environment of the street meeting, is immune from prior municipal control. We would have a very different question if New York had presumed to say that Kunz could not speak his piece in his own pulpit or hall. But it has undertaken to restrain him only if he chooses to speak at street meetings. There is a world of difference. The street preacher takes advantage of people's presence on the streets to impose his message upon what, in a sense, is a captive audience. A meeting on private property is made up of an audience that has volunteered to listen. The question, therefore, is not whether New York could, if it tried, silence Kunz, but whether it must place its streets at his service to hurl insults at the passer-by.

What Mr. Justice Holmes said for a unanimous Court in *Schenck* v. *United States,* 249 U.S. 47, 52, has become an axiom: "The most stringent protection of free speech would not protect a man in falsely shouting fire in a theatre and causing a panic." This concept was applied in one of its few unanimous decisions in recent years, when, through Mr. Justice Murphy, the Court said: "There are certain well-defined and narrowly limited classes of speech, *the prevention and punishment* of which *have never been thought to raise any Constitutional problem*. These include the lewd and obscene, the profane, the libelous, and *the insulting or 'fighting' words*—those which by their very utterance inflict injury or *tend to incite* an immediate breach of the peace. . . ." (Emphasis supplied.) *Chaplinsky* v. *New Hampshire*, 315 U.S. 568, 571–572.

There held to be "insulting or 'fighting' words" were calling one a "God damned racketeer" and a "damned Fascist." Equally inciting and more clearly "fighting words," when thrown at Catholics and Jews who are rightfully on the streets of New York, are statements that "The Pope is the anti-Christ" and the Jews are "Christ-killers." These terse epithets come down to our generation weighted with hatreds accumulated through centuries of bloodshed. They are recognized words of art in the profession of defamation. They are not the kind of insult that men bandy and laugh off when the spirits are high and the flagons are low. They are not in that class of epithets whose literal sting will be drawn if the speaker smiles when he uses them. They are always, and in every context, insults which do not spring from reason and can be answered by none. Their historical associations with violence are well understood, both by those who hurl and those who are struck by these missiles. Jews, many of whose families perished in extermination furnaces of Dachau and Auschwitz, are more than tolerant if they pass off lightly the suggestion that unbelievers in Christ should all have been burned. Of course, people might pass this speaker by as a mental case, and so they might file out of a theatre in good order at the cry of "fire." But in both cases there is genuine likelihood that someone will get hurt. . . .

It is peculiar that today's opinion makes no reference to the "clear and present danger" test which for years has played some part in free-speech cases. . . . If New York has benefit of the rule as Mr. Justice Holmes announced it, *Schenck* v. *United States, supra*, at 52, it would mean that it could punish or prevent speech if "the words used are used in such circumstances and are of such a nature as to create a clear and present danger that they will bring about the substantive evils" that the City has a right to prevent, among which I should suppose we would list street fighting or riots. As I have pointed out, the proof in this case leaves no doubt that Kunz's words, in the environment of the streets, have and will result in that, unless a police escort attends to awe the hearers into submission. . . .

We should weigh the value of insulting speech against its potentiality for harm. Is the Court, when declaring Kunz has the *right* he asserts, serving the great end for which the First Amendment stands?

The purpose of constitutional protection of speech is to foster peaceful interchange of all manner of thoughts, information and ideas. Its policy is rooted in faith in the force of reason. This Court wisely has said, "Resort to epithets or personal abuse is not in any proper sense communication of information or opinion safeguarded by the Constitution." *Cantwell* v. *Connecticut,* 310 U.S. 296, 309–310. "It has been well observed that such utterances are no essential part of any exposition of ideas, and are of such slight social value as a step to truth that any benefit that may be derived from them is clearly outweighed by the social interest in order and morality." So said we all in *Chaplinsky* v. *New Hampshire, supra,* at 572. It would be interesting if the Court would expose its reasons for thinking that Kunz's words are of more social value than those of Chaplinsky. . . .

The question remains whether the Constitution prohibits a city from control of its streets by a permit system which takes into account dangers to public peace and order. I am persuaded that it does not do so, provided, of course, that the city does not so discriminate as to deny equal protection of the law or undertake a censorship of utterances that are not so defamatory, insulting, inciting, or provocative as to be reasonably likely to cause disorder and violence.

The Court does not hold that New York has abused the permit system by discrimination or actual censorship, nor does it deny the abuses on Kunz's part. But neither, says the Court, matters, holding that any prior restraint is bad, regardless of how fairly administered or what abuses it seeks to prevent. . . .

Of course, as to the press, there are the best of reasons against any licensing or prior restraint. Decisions such as *Near* v. *Minnesota, supra,* hold any licensing or prior restraint of the press unconstitutional, and I heartily agree. But precedents from that field cannot reasonably be transposed to the street-meeting field. The impact of publishing on public order has no similarity with that of a street meeting. Publishing does not make private use of public property. It reaches only those who choose to read, and, in that way, is analogous to a meeting held in a hall where those who come do so by choice. Written words are less apt to incite or provoke to mass action than spoken words, speech being the primitive and direct communication with the emotions. Few are the riots caused by publication alone, few are the mobs that have not had their immediate origin in harangue. The vulnerability of various forms of communication to community control must be proportioned to their impact upon other community interests.

It is suggested that a permit for a street meeting could be required if the ordinance would prescribe precise standards for its grant or denial. . . .

Of course, standards for administrative action are always desirable, and the more exact the better. But I do not see how this Court can condemn municipal ordinances for not setting forth comprehensive First Amendment standards. This Court never has announced what those standards must be, it does not now say what they are, and it is not clear that any majority could agree on them. In no field are there more numerous individual opinions among the Justices. The Court as an institution not infrequently disagrees with its former self or relies on distinctions that are not very substantial. Compare *Jones* v. *Opelika* of 1942, 316 U.S. 584, with *Jones* v. *Opelika* of 1943, 319 U.S. 103; *Minersville School District* v. *Gobitis* of 1940, 310 U.S. 586, with *Board of Education* v. *Barnette* of 1943, 319 U.S. 624; *Saia* v. *New York* of 1948, *supra,* with *Kovacs* v. *Cooper* of 1949, *supra.* It seems hypercritical to strike down local laws on their faces for want of standards when we have no standards. And I do not find it required by existing authority. I think that where speech is outside of constitutional immunity the local community or the State is left a large measure of discretion as to the means for dealing with it.

If the Court is deciding that the permit system for street meetings is so unreasonable as to deny due process of law, it would seem appropriate to point out respects in which it is unreasonable. This I am unable to learn, from this or any former decision. . . .

The law of New York does not segregate, according to their diverse nationalities, races, religions, or political associations, the vast hordes of people living in its narrow confines. Every individual in this frightening aggregation is legally free to live, to labor, to travel, when and where he chooses. In streets and public places, all races and nationalities and all sorts and conditions of men walk, linger and mingle. Is it not reasonable that the City protect the dignity of these persons against fanatics who take possession of its streets to hurl into its crowds defamatory epithets that hurt like rocks?

If any two subjects are intrinsically incendiary and divisive, they are race and religion. Racial fears and hatreds have been at the root of the most terrible riots that have disgraced American civilization. They are ugly possibilities that overhang every great American city. The "consecrated hatreds of sect" account for more than a few of the world's bloody disorders. These are the explosives which the Court says Kunz may play with in the public streets, and the community must not only tolerate but aid him. I find no such doctrine in the Constitution.

In this case there is no evidence of a purpose to suppress speech, except to keep it in bounds that will not upset good order. If there are abuses of censorship or discrimination in administering the ordinance, as well there may be, they are not proved in this case. This Court should be particularly sure of its ground before it strikes down, in a time like this, the going, practical system by which New York has sought to control its street-meeting problem. . . .

Chapter 22

SPEECH AND BREACH OF THE PEACE

An essential part of the case for freedom of speech from prior restraint is, as we have seen, that speech abuses can be punished after the event. Censorship is aimed at what *may* be said; its justification must be based on probabilities and hypotheses, and it denies society the right to hear everything that can be said on issues of public policy. Subsequent punishment for a speech offense must be based on definite acts and real happenings, and must be established by proof in proper judicial proceedings.

All this helps to justify the constitutional preference for subsequent punishment over previous restraint. But it does not mean that subsequent punishment is no danger to constitutional liberties. Severe and certain sanctions against exercise of speech rights can be just as effective in discouraging their assertion as censorship. Moreover, by definition prior restraint gives advance warning of peril to a person who challenges the restraint, whereas subsequent punishment often turns on questions of degree, and a penalty may be imposed for acts which were thought to be entirely permissible when they were performed.

Punishment because of speech is probably most often attempted on grounds that the speaker had threatened the maintenance of public order. Clearly, preservation of the peace is a prime responsibility of a community's officials. In all states there are statutes defining such misdemeanors or crimes as breach of the peace, disorderly conduct, inciting to riot, and the like, in which speech may be involved. In their application against alleged speech abuses the problem is always one of balancing the gravity of the evil against the seriousness of the limits imposed on constitutional liberties.

A pair of practically contemporaneous decisions offers a convenient starting point. Both were unanimous decisions, one upholding and the other denying a free speech claim. In *Cantwell* v. *Connecticut,* 310 U.S. 296 (1940), a member of Jehovah's Witnesses was on a public street seeking converts. In accordance with the practice of his sect, he carried a phonograph and records, which he sought to play for anyone who would listen. He stopped two pedestrians and requested that they listen to a record. They agreed. The record was a violent attack on all organized religions and particularly the Catholic Church. The listeners, both Catholics, were offended, and felt like hitting him, but when they made known their displeasure, Cantwell packed up his phonograph and left. The incident did not draw a crowd or impede traffic, and no blows were struck. Nevertheless, Cantwell was charged with inciting a breach of the peace, and convicted.

The Supreme Court reversed the conviction. There had been "no assault or threatening of bodily harm, no truculent bearing, no intentional discourtesy, no personal abuse. On the contrary, we find only an effort to persuade a willing listener to buy a book or to contribute money in the interest of what Cantwell, however misguided others may think him, conceived to be true religion." Justice Roberts then went on to state the constitutional principles which should govern such a case:

In the realm of religious faith, and in that of political belief, sharp differences arise. In both fields the tenets of one man may seem the rankest error to his neighbor. To persuade others to his own point of view, the pleader, as we know, at times, resorts to exaggeration, to vilification of men who have been, or are, prominent in church or state, and even to false statement. But the people of this nation have ordained in the light of history, that, in spite of the probability of excesses and abuses, these liberties are, in the long view, essential to enlightened opinion and right conduct on the part of the citizens of a democracy.

The second case was *Chaplinsky* v. *New Hampshire*, 315 U.S. 568 (1942). Chaplinsky, threatened with arrest after creating a public disturbance by his open denunciation of all religion as a "racket," had told a city marshal that he was a "God damned racketeer" and a "damned Fascist." The Court upheld Chaplinsky's conviction of violating a state statute against calling anyone "offensive or derisive" names in public. Justice Murphy observed that insults and "fighting" words "are no essential part of any exposition of ideas, and are of such slight social value as a step to truth that any benefit that may be derived from them is clearly outweighed by the social interest in order and morality."

Comparing the two cases, the Court had regarded Cantwell's phonograph record as a legitimate attempt at communication, no matter how wrongheaded and provocative it might seem to most people. Consequently he could be punished only if the incident had resulted in a "clear and present menace to public peace and order." But in *Chaplinsky* the clear and present danger test was not mentioned, because the Court thought that abusive epithets are not "in any proper sense communication of information or opinion." The words are bad in and of themselves, and so can be punished without demonstrating any clear and present danger that they may cause violence.

Perhaps the Court's most significant case involving the relationship between free speech and the expectation of violence was *Terminiello* v. *Chicago*, 337 U.S. 1 (1949). However, the discussion was somewhat unsatisfactory since the majority upheld the speaking rights of a provocateur whose harangue had contributed to a riotous situation on the basis of some abstract theories, while only the minority really attempted to balance the relative community interest in free discussion and freedom from street battles.

After the absolutist liberalism of the *Terminiello* decision, the Court moved rather sharply toward the opposite position in *Feiner* v. *New York*, 340 U.S. 315 (1951). A university student had made a rather fiery speech on a Syracuse street corner, in which he attacked the American Legion and urged that Negroes fight for their rights. Police officers, attracted by the traffic problem which the crowd created, heard some "angry mutterings" among the listeners and arrested the youth, who was convicted of disorderly conduct.

The Supreme Court, by a six to three vote, upheld the conviction. The majority credited the opinion of the policemen, supported by the state courts, that a riot might have resulted if the speech had not been stopped. But Justice Douglas, dissenting, thought that the record indicated no likelihood of riot. "It shows an unsympathetic audience and the threat of one man to haul the speaker from the stage. It is against that kind of threat that speakers need police protection. If they do not receive it and instead the police throw their weight on the side of those who would break up the meetings, the police become the new censors of speech."

Justice Jackson agreed with the *Feiner* decision, but in his dissent to *Kunz* v. *New York*, decided the same day, he charged that the Court-approved *Feiner* type of police control was actually more dangerous than the permit system which the Court disapproved in *Kunz*:

City officials stopped the meetings of both Feiner and Kunz. The process by which Feiner was stopped was the order of patrolmen, put into immediate effect without hearing. Feiner may have believed there would be no interference but Kunz was duly warned by refusal of a permit. He was advised of charges, given a hearing, confronted by witnesses, and afforded a chance to deny the charges or to confess them and offer to amend his ways. The decision of revocation was made by a detached and responsible administrative official and Kunz could have had the decision reviewed in court. . . . It seems to me that this procedure better protects freedom of speech than to let everyone speak without leave, but subject to surveillance and to being ordered to stop in the discretion of the police.

TERMINIELLO v. CHICAGO
337 U.S. 1, 69 S. Ct. 894, 93 L. Ed. 1131 (1949)

Mr. Justice Douglas delivered the opinion of the Court.

Petitioner after jury trial was found guilty of disorderly conduct in violation of a city ordinance of Chicago and fined. The case grew out of an address he delivered in an auditorium in Chicago under the auspices of the Christian Veterans of America. The meeting commanded considerable public attention. The auditorium was filled to capacity with over eight hundred persons present. Others were turned away. Outside of the auditorium a crowd of about one thousand persons gathered to protest against the meeting. A cordon of policemen was assigned to the meeting to maintain order; but they were not able to prevent several disturbances. The crowd outside was angry and turbulent.

Petitioner in his speech condemned the conduct of the crowd outside and vigorously, if not viciously, criticized various political and racial groups whose activities he denounced as inimical to the nation's welfare.

The trial court charged that "breach of the peace" consists of any "misbehavior which violates the public peace and decorum"; and that the "misbehavior may constitute a breach of the peace if it stirs the public to anger, invites dispute, brings about a condition of unrest, or creates a disturbance, or if it molests the inhabitants in the enjoyment of peace and quiet by arousing alarm." Petitioner did not take exception to that instruction. But he maintained at all times that the ordinance as applied to his conduct violated his right to free speech under the Federal Constitution. . . .

The argument here has been focused on the issue of whether the content of petitioner's speech was composed of derisive, fighting words, which carried it outside the scope of the constitutional guarantees. See *Chaplinsky* v. *New Hampshire*, 315 U.S. 568; *Cantwell* v. *Connecticut,* 310 U.S. 296, 310. We do not reach that question, for there is a preliminary question that is dispositive of the case.

As we have noted, the statutory words "breach of the peace" were defined in instructions to the jury to include speech which "stirs the public to anger, invites dispute, brings about a condition of unrest, or creates a disturbance. . . ." That construction of the ordinance is a ruling on a question of state law that is as binding on us as though the precise words had been written into the ordinance. . . .

The vitality of civil and political institutions in our society depends on free discussion. As Chief Justice Hughes wrote in *De Jonge* v. *Oregon,* 299 U.S. 353, 365, it is only through free debate and free exchange of ideas that government remains responsive to the will of the people and peaceful change is effected. The right to speak freely and to promote diversity of ideas and programs is therefore one of the chief distinctions that sets us apart from totalitarian regimes.

Accordingly a function of free speech under our system of government is to invite dispute. It may indeed best serve its high purpose when it induces a condition of unrest, creates dissatisfaction with conditions as they are, or even stirs people to anger. Speech is often provocative and challenging. It may strike at prejudices and preconceptions and have profound unsettling effects as it presses for acceptance of an idea. That is why freedom of speech, though not absolute, *Chaplinsky* v. *New Hampshire, supra,* pp. 571–572, is nevertheless protected against censorship or punishment, unless shown likely to produce a clear and present danger of a serious substantive evil that rises far above public inconvenience, annoyance, or unrest. See *Bridges* v. *California,* 314 U.S. 25,262; *Craig* v. *Harney,* 331 U.S. 367, 373. There is no room under our Constitution for a more restrictive view. For the alternative would lead to standardization of ideas either by legislatures, courts, or dominant political or community groups.

The ordinance as construed by the trial court seriously invaded this province. It permitted conviction of petitioner if his speech stirred people to anger, invited public dispute, or brought about a condition of unrest. A conviction resting on any of those grounds may not stand.

The fact that petitioner took no exception to the instruction is immaterial. No exception to the instructions was taken in *Stromberg* v. *California,* 283 U.S. 359. But a judgment of conviction based on a general verdict under a state statute was set aside in that case, because one part of the statute was unconstitutional. The statute had been challenged as unconstitutional and the instruction was framed in its language. The Court held that the attack on the statute as a whole was equally an attack on each of its individual parts. Since the verdict was a general one and did not specify the ground upon which it rested, it could not be sustained. For one part of the statute was unconstitutional and it could not be determined that the defendant was not convicted under that part.

The principle of that case controls this one. As we have said, the gloss which Illinois placed on the ordinance gives it a meaning and application which are conclusive on us. We need not consider whether as construed it is defective in its entirety. As construed and applied it at least contains parts that are unconstitutional. The verdict was a general one; and we do not know on this record but what it may rest on the invalid clauses.

The statute as construed in the charge to the jury was passed on by the Illinois courts and sustained by them over the objection that as so read it violated the Fourteenth Amendment. The fact that the parties did not dispute its construction makes the adjudication no less ripe for our review, as the *Stromberg* decision indicates. We can only take the statute as the state courts read it. From our point of view it is immaterial whether the state law question as to its meaning was controverted or accepted.

The pinch of the statute is in its application. It is that question which the petitioner has brought here. To say therefore that the question on this phase of the case is whether the trial judge gave a wrong charge is wholly to misconceive the issue.

But it is said that throughout the appellate proceedings the Illinois courts assumed that the only conduct punishable and punished under the ordinance was conduct constituting "fighting words." That emphasizes, however, the importance of the rule of the *Stromberg* case. Petitioner was not convicted under a statute so narrowly construed. For all anyone knows he was convicted under the parts of the ordinance (as construed) which, for example, make it an offense merely to invite dispute or to bring about a condition of unrest. We cannot avoid that issue by saying that all Illinois did was to measure petitioner's conduct, not the ordinance, against the Constitution. Petitioner raised both points—that his speech was protected by the Constitution; that the inclusion of his speech within the ordinance was a violation of the Constitution. We would, therefore, strain at technicalities to conclude that the constitutionality of the ordinance as construed and applied to petitioner was not before the Illinois courts. The record makes clear that petitioner at all times challenged the constitutionality of the ordinance as construed and applied to him.

Reversed.

Mr. Chief Justice Vinson, dissenting.

I dissent. The Court today reverses the Supreme Court of Illinois because it discovers in the record one sentence in the trial court's instructions which permitted the jury to convict on an unconstitutional basis. The offending sentence had heretofore gone completely undetected. It apparently was not even noticed, much less excepted to, by the petitioner's counsel at the trial. No objection was made to it in the two Illinois appellate tribunals which reviewed the case. Nor was it mentioned in the petition for certiorari or the briefs in this Court. In short, the offending sentence in the charge to the jury was no part of the case until this Court's independent research ferreted it out of a lengthy and somewhat confused record. I think it too plain for argument that a reversal on such a basis does not accord with any principle governing review of state court decisions heretofore announced by this Court. . . .

Mr. Justice Frankfurter, dissenting.

For the first time in the course of the 130 years in which State prosecutions have come here for review, this Court is today reversing a sentence imposed by a State court on a ground that was urged neither here nor below and that was explicitly disclaimed on behalf of the petitioner at the bar of this Court.

The impropriety of that part of the charge which is now made the basis of reversal was not raised at the trial nor before the Appellate Court of Illinois. The fact that counsel for Terminiello wholly ignored it is emphasized by the objections that he did make in relation to other instructions given and not given. On appeal to the Supreme Court of Illinois, counsel still failed to claim as error that which this Court on its own motion now finds violative of the Constitution. It was not mentioned by the Illinois Supreme Court in its careful opinion disposing of other claims and it was not included in the elaborate petition for rehearing in that court. Thus an objection, not raised by counsel in the Illinois courts, not made the basis of the petition for certiorari here— not included in the "Questions Presented," nor in the "Reasons Relied On for the Allowance of the Writ"—and explicitly disavowed at the bar of this Court, is used to upset a conviction which has been sustained by three courts of Illinois.

Reliance on *Stromberg v. California*, 283 U.S. 359, for what is done today is wholly misplaced. Neither expressly nor by implication has that decision any bearing upon the issue which the Court's opinion in this case raises, namely, whether it is open for this Court to reverse the highest court of a State on a point which was not brought before that court, did not enter into the judgment rendered by that court, and at no stage of the proceedings in this Court was invoked as error by the State court whose reversal is here sought. . . .

Only the uninformed will deride as a merely technical point objection to what the Court is doing in this case. The matter touches the very basis of this Court's authority in reviewing the judgments of State courts. We have no authority to meddle with such a judgment unless some claim under the Constitution or the laws of the United States has been made before the State court whose judgment we are reviewing and unless the claim has been denied by that court. How could there have been a denial of a federal claim by the Illinois courts, *i.e.,* that the trial judge offended the Constitution of the United States in what he told the jury, when no such claim was made? The relation of the United States and the courts of the United States to the States and the courts of the States is a very delicate matter. It is too delicate to permit silence when a judgment of a State court is reversed in disregard of the duty of this Court to leave untouched an adjudication of a State unless that adjudication is based upon a claim of a federal right which the State has had an opportunity to meet and to recognize. If such a federal claim was neither before the State court nor presented to this Court, this Court unwarrantably strays from its province in looking through the record to find some federal claim that might have been brought to the attention of the State court and, if so brought, fronted, and that might have been, but was not, urged here. This is a court of review, not a tribunal unbounded by rules. We do not sit like a kadi under a tree dispensing justice according to considerations of individual expediency.

Freedom of speech undoubtedly means freedom to express views that challenge deep-seated, sacred beliefs and to utter sentiments that may provoke resentment. But those indulging in such stuff as that to which this proceeding gave rise are hardly so deserving as to lead this Court to single them out as beneficiaries of the first departure from the restrictions that bind this Court in reviewing judgments of State courts. Especially odd is it to bestow such favor not for the sake of life or liberty, but to save a small amount of property—$100, the amount of the fine imposed upon the petitioner in a proceeding which is civil, not criminal, under the laws of Illinois, and thus subject only to limited review. . . .

Mr. Justice Jackson and Mr. Justice Burton join this dissent.

Mr. Justice Jackson, dissenting.

The Court reverses this conviction by reiterating generalized approbations of freedom of speech with which, in the abstract, no one will disagree. Doubts as to their applicability are lulled by avoidance of more than passing reference to the circumstances of Terminiello's speech and judging it as if he had spoken to persons as dispassionate as empty benches, or like a modern Demosthenes practicing his Philippics on a lonely seashore.

But the local court that tried Terminiello was not indulging in theory. It was dealing with a riot and with a speech that provoked a hostile mob and incited a friendly one, and threatened violence between the two. When the trial judge instructed the jury that it might find Terminiello guilty of inducing a breach of the peace if his behavior stirred the public to anger, invited dispute, brought about unrest, created a disturbance or molested peace and quiet by arousing alarm, he was not speaking of these as harmless or abstract conditions. He was addressing his words to the concrete behavior and specific consequences disclosed by the evidence. He was saying to the jury, in effect, that if this particular speech added fuel to the situation already so inflamed as to threaten to get beyond police control, it could be punished as inducing a breach of peace. When the light of the evidence not recited by the Court is thrown upon the Court's opinion, it discloses that underneath a little issue of Terminiello and his hundred-dollar fine lurk some of the most far-reaching constitutional questions that can confront a people who value both liberty and order. This Court seems to regard these as enemies of each other and to be of the view that we must forego order to achieve liberty. So it fixes its eyes on a conception of freedom of speech so rigid as to tolerate no concession to society's need for public order.

An old proverb warns us to take heed lest we "walk into a well from looking at the stars." To show why I think the Court is in some danger of doing just that, I must bring these deliberations down to earth by a long recital of facts. [This recital is omitted.]

. . .

Such was the speech. Evidence showed that it stirred the audience not only to cheer and applaud but to expressions of immediate anger, unrest and alarm. One called the speaker a "God damned liar" and was taken out by the police. Another said that "Jews, niggers and Catholics would have to be gotten rid of." One response was, "Yes, the Jews are all killers, murderers. If we don't kill them first, they will kill us." The anti-Jewish stories elicited exclamations of "Oh!" and "Isn't that terrible!" and shouts of "Yes, send the Jews back to Russia," "Kill the Jews," "Dirty kikes," and much more of ugly tenor. This is the specific and concrete kind of anger, unrest and alarm, coupled with that of the mob outside, that the trial court charged the jury might find to be a breach of peace induced by Terminiello. It is difficult to believe that this Court is speaking of the same occasion, but it is the only one involved in this litigation.

Terminiello, of course, disclaims being a fascist. Doubtless many of the indoor audience were not consciously such. His speech, however, followed, with fidelity that is more than coincidental, the pattern of European fascist leaders.

The street mob, on the other hand, included some who deny being communists, but Terminiello testified and offered to prove that the demonstration was communist-organized and communist-led. He offered literature of left-wing organizations calling members to meet and "mobilize" for instruction as pickets and exhorting followers: "All out to fight Fascist Smith."

As this case declares a nation-wide rule that disables local and state authorities from punishing conduct which produces conflicts of this kind, it is unrealistic not to take account of the nature, methods and objectives of the forces involved. This was not an isolated, spontaneous and unintended collision of political, racial or ideological adversaries. It was a local manifestation of a world-wide and standing conflict between two organized groups of revolutionary fanatics, each of which has imported to this country the strong-arm technique developed in the struggle by which their kind has devastated Europe. Increasingly, American cities have to cope with it. One faction organizes a mass meeting, the other organizes pickets to harass it; each organizes squads to counteract the other's pickets; parade is met with counterparade. Each of these mass demonstrations has the potentiality, and more than a few the purpose, of disorder and violence. This technique appeals not to reason but to fears and mob spirit; each is a show of force designed to bully adversaries and to overawe the indifferent. We need not resort to speculation as to the purposes for which these tactics are calculated nor as to their consequences. Recent European history demonstrates both. . . .

The present obstacle to mastery of the streets by either radical or reactionary mob movements is not the opposing minority. It is the authority of local governments which represent the free choice of democratic and law-abiding elements of all shades of opinion, but who, whatever their differences, submit them to free elections which register the results of their free discussion. The fascist and communist groups, on the contrary, resort to these terror tactics to confuse, bully and discredit those freely chosen governments. Violent and noisy shows of strength discourage participation of moderates in discussions so fraught with violence, and real discussion dries up and disappears. And people lose faith in the democratic process when they see public authority flouted and impotent and begin to think the time has come when they must choose sides in a false and terrible dilemma such as was posed as being at hand by the call for the Terminiello meeting: "Christian Nationalism or World Communism— Which?"

This drive by totalitarian groups to undermine the prestige and effectiveness of local democratic governments is advanced whenever either of them can win from this Court a ruling which paralyzes the power of these officials. This is such a case. The group of which Terminiello is a part claims that his behavior, because it involved a speech, is above the reach of local authorities. If the mild action those authorities have taken is forbidden, it is plain that hereafter there is nothing effective left that they can do. If they can do nothing as to him, they are equally powerless as to rival totalitarian groups. Terminiello's victory today certainly fulfills the most extravagant hopes of both right and left totalitarian groups, who want nothing so much as to paralyze and discredit the only democratic authority that can curb them in their battle for the streets.

I am unable to see that the local authorities have transgressed the Federal Constitution. Illinois imposed no prior censorship or suppression upon Terminiello. On the contrary, its sufferance and protection was all that enabled him to speak. It does not appear that the motive in punishing him is to silence the ideology he expressed as offensive to the State's policy or as untrue, or has any purpose of controlling his thought or its peaceful communication to others. There is no claim that the proceedings against Terminiello are designed to discriminate against him or the faction he represents or the ideas that he bespeaks. There is no indication that the charge against him is a mere pretext to give the semblance of legality to a covert effort to silence him or to prevent his followers or the public from hearing any truth that is in him.

A trial court and jury has found only that in the context of violence and disorder in which it was made, this speech was a provocation to immediate breach of the peace and therefore cannot claim constitutional immunity from punishment. Under the Constitution as it has been understood and applied, at least until most recently, the State was within its powers in taking this action. . . .

I . . . think we should . . . adhere to the principles heretofore announced to safeguard our liberties against abuse as well as against invasion. It should not be necessary to recall these elementary principles, but it has been a long time since some of them were even mentioned in this Court's writing on the subject and results indicate they may have been overlooked.

I begin with the oft-forgotten principle which this case demonstrates, that freedom of speech exists only under law and not independently of it. What would Terminiello's theoretical freedom of speech have amounted to had he not been given active aid by the officers of the law? He could reach the hall only with their help, could talk only because they restrained the mob, and could make his getaway only under their protection. . . .

This case demonstrates also that this Court's service to free speech is essentially negative and can consist only of reviewing actions by local magistrates. But if free speech is to be a practical reality, affirmative and immediate protection is required; and it can come only from nonjudicial sources. It depends on local police, maintained by law-abiding taxpayers, and who, regardless of their own feelings, risk themselves to maintain supremacy of law. Terminiello's theoretical right to speak free from interference would have no reality if Chicago should withdraw its officers to some other section of the city, or if the men assigned to the task should look the other way when the crowd threatens Terminiello. Can society be expected to keep these men at Terminiello's service if it has nothing to say of his behavior which may force them into dangerous action? . . .

In considering abuse of freedom by provocative utterances it is necessary to observe that the law is more tolerant of discussion than are most individuals or communities. Law is so indifferent to subjects of talk that I think of none that it should close to discussion. Religious, social and political topics that in other times or countries have not been open to lawful debate may be freely discussed here.

Because a subject is legally arguable, however, does not mean that public sentiment will be patient of its advocacy at all times and in all manners. So it happens that, while peaceful advocacy of communism or fascism is tolerated by the law, both of these doctrines arouse passionate reactions. A great number of people do not agree that introduction to America of communism or fascism is even debatable. Hence many speeches, such as that of Terminiello, may be legally permissible but may neverthe-less in some surroundings be a menace to peace and order. When conditions show the speaker that this is the case, as it did here, there certainly comes a point beyond which he cannot indulge in provocations to violence without being answerable to society.

Determination of such an issue involves a heavy responsibility. Courts must beware lest they become mere organs of popular intolerance. Not every show of opposition can justify treating a speech as a breach of peace. Neither speakers nor courts are obliged always and in all circumstances to yield to prevailing opinion and feeling. As a people grow in capacity for civilization and liberty their tolerance will grow, and they will endure, if not welcome, discussion even on topics as to which they are committed. They regard convictions as tentative and know that time and events will make their own terms with theories, by whomever and by whatever majorities they are held, and many will be proved wrong. But on our way to this idealistic state of tolerance the police have to deal with men as they are. The crowd mind is never tolerant of any idea which does not conform to its herd opinion. It does not want a tolerant effort at meeting of minds. It does not know the futility of trying to mob an idea. Released from the sense of personal responsibility that would restrain even the worst individuals in it if alone and brave with the courage of numbers, both radical and reactionary mobs endanger liberty as well as order. The authorities must control them and they are entitled to place some checks upon those whose behavior or speech calls such mobs into being. When the right of society to freedom from probable violence should prevail over the right of an individual to defy opposing opinion, presents a problem that always tests wisdom and often calls for immediate and vigorous action to preserve public order and safety.

I do not think that the Constitution of the United States denies to the states and the municipalities power to solve that problem in the light of local conditions, at least so long as danger to public order is not invoked in bad faith, as a cover for censorship or suppression. The preamble declares domestic tranquility as well as liberty to be an object in founding a Federal Government and I do not think the Forefathers were naive in believing both can be fostered by the law. . . .

This Court has gone far toward accepting the doctrine that civil liberty means the removal of all restraints from those crowds and that all local attempts to maintain order are impairments of the liberty of the citizen. The choice is not between order and liberty. It is between liberty with order and anarchy without either. There is danger that, if the Court does not temper its doctrinaire logic with a little practical wisdom, it will convert the constitutional Bill of Rights into a suicide pact.

I would affirm the conviction.

MR. JUSTICE BURTON joins in this opinion.

Chapter 23

LIBEL

Freedom of speech does not justify libel or slander, and persons responsible for statements of this character can be prosecuted. A libel is any written or printed material defaming or reflecting on the character of a person, published maliciously and without justification. A slander is an oral statement of the same kind. American practice in the punishment of libel developed largely out of English law, which permitted a very wide range of libel prosecutions. The English law of seditious libel was particularly offensive. It permitted punishment for publications which tended to bring into hatred or contempt, or excite disaffection against, the king, the government, Parliament, or the administration of justice. The First Amendment was probably intended to wipe out the common law of seditious libel, but the adoption by Congress of the Sedition Act in 1798 revealed the persistence of these ideas.

Libel may be treated according to circumstances as either a tort or a crime. A libel punishable criminally is one which tends to excite a breach of the peace. The law of libel was initially developed largely by the Star Chamber, which made no use of a jury. After the Star Chamber was abolished in 1641, the King's Bench was influenced by its tradition and permitted juries only a limited role, such as finding facts as to authorship or publication, reserving for the bench the question whether these facts constituted a libel. A long line of oppressive political libel prosecutions finally led to Fox's Libel Act in 1792, which allowed the jury to find a general verdict in cases of criminal libel. American statutes have likewise generally entrusted the determination of criminality to the jury, and also have admitted truth as a defense. The Sedition Act of 1798 had both these features.

Litigation in the various states has firmly established that enactments imposing criminal liability for defamation are not violations of freedom of speech and press. Since the First Amendment was not regarded as applicable to state laws until 1925, the Supreme Court has had much less occasion to consider constitutional aspects of state libel laws. However, an important exception was *Beauharnais v. Illinois*, 343 U.S. 250 (1952), in which the Court upheld a "group libel" law.

BEAUHARNAIS v. ILLINOIS
343 U.S. 250, 72 S. Ct. 725, 96 L. Ed. 919 (1952)

Characteristically, criminal liability has been incurred by defamation of an individual. However, it has also been recognized as an offense to defame an identifiable class or group of persons, such as a family or a society, even though no individual member is specifically mentioned. Illinois has a statute of this sort, which makes it unlawful for persons or corporations to publish or exhibit any writing, picture, drama, or moving picture which portrays "depravity, criminality, unchastity, or lack of virtue of a class of citizens, of any race, color, creed or religion . . . [or] exposes the citizens of any race, color, creed or religion to contempt, derision, or obloquy or which is productive of breach of the peace or riots."

Joseph Beauharnais, head of an organization called the White Circle League, circulated on Chicago street corners anti-Negro leaflets which were in the form of petitions to the mayor and city council. The leaflets made defamatory and derogatory comments about Negroes and asked the use of the police power to protect the white race from their "rapes, robberies, knives, guns and marijuana." The leaflets also appealed for persons to join the White Circle League and asked for financial contributions. Beauharnais was convicted of violating the statute and was fined $200.

MR. JUSTICE FRANKFURTER delivered the opinion of the Court. . . .

The statute before us is not a catchall enactment left at large by the State court which applied it. . . . It is a law specifically directed at a defined evil, its language drawing from history and practice in Illinois and in more than a score of other jurisdictions a meaning confirmed by the Supreme Court of that State in upholding this conviction. We do not, therefore, parse the statute as grammarians or treat it as an abstract exercise in lexicography. We read it in the animating context of well-defined usage . . . and State court construction which determines its meaning for us. *Cox v. New Hampshire*, 312 U.S. 569; *Chaplinsky v. New Hampshire*, 315 U.S. 568.

The Illinois Supreme Court tells us that § 224a "is a form of criminal libel law." . . . The defendant, the trial court and the Supreme Court consistently treated it as such. The defendant offered evidence tending to prove the truth of parts of the utterance, and the courts below considered and disposed of this offer in terms of ordinary criminal libel precedents. Section 224a does not deal with the defense of truth, but by the Illinois Constitution, Art. II, § 4, "in all trials for libel, both civil and criminal, the truth, when published with good motives and for justifiable ends, shall be a sufficient defense." See also Ill. Rev. Stat., 1949, c. 38, § 404. Similarly, the action of the trial court in deciding as a matter of law the libelous character of the utterance, leaving to the jury only the question of publication, follows the settled rule in prosecutions for libel in Illinois and other States. Moreover, the Supreme Court's characterization of the words prohibited by the statute as those "liable to cause violence and disorder" paraphrases the traditional justification for punishing libels criminally, namely their "tendency to cause breach of the peace."

Libel of an individual was a common-law crime, and thus criminal in the colonies. Indeed, at common law, truth or good motives was no defense. In the first decades after the adoption of the Constitution, this was changed by judicial decision, statute or constitution in most States, but nowhere was there any suggestion that the crime of libel be abolished. Today, every American jurisdiction . . . punish[es] libels directed at individuals. "There are certain well-defined and narrowly limited classes of speech, the prevention and punishment of which have never been thought to raise any Constitutional problem. These include the lewd and obscene, the profane, the libelous, and the insulting or 'fighting' words—those which by their very utterance inflict injury or tend to incite an immediate breach of the peace. It has been well observed that such utterances are no essential part of any exposition of ideas, and are of such slight social value as a step to truth that any benefit that may be derived from them is clearly outweighed by the social interest in order and morality. 'Resort to epithets or personal abuse is not in any proper sense communication of information or opinion safeguarded by the Constitution, and its punishment as a criminal act would raise no question under that instrument.' *Cantwell v. Connecticut*, 310 U.S. 296, 309–310." Such were the views of a unanimous Court in *Chaplinsky v. New Hampshire, supra*, at 571–572.

No one will gainsay that it is libelous falsely to charge another with being a rapist, robber, carrier of knives and guns, and user of marijuana. The precise question before us, then, is whether the protection of "liberty" in the Due Process Clause of the Fourteenth Amendment prevents a State from punishing such libels—as criminal libel has been defined, limited and constitutionally recognized time out of mind—directed at designated collectivities and flagrantly disseminated. There is even authority, however dubious, that such utterances were also crimes at common law. It is certainly clear that some American jurisdictions have sanctioned their punishment under ordinary criminal libel statutes. We cannot say, however, that the question is concluded by history and practice. But if an utterance directed at an individual may be the object of criminal sanctions, we cannot deny to a State power to punish the same utterance directed at a defined group, unless we can say that this is a wilful and purposeless restriction unrelated to the peace and well-being of the State.

Illinois did not have to look beyond her own borders or await the tragic experience of the last three decades to conclude that wilful purveyors of falsehood concerning racial and religious groups promote strife and tend powerfully to obstruct the manifold adjustments required for free, ordered life in a metropolitan, polyglot community. From the murder of the abolitionist Lovejoy in 1837 to the Cicero riots of 1951, Illinois has been the scene of exacerbated tension between races, often flaring into violence and destruction. In many of these outbreaks, utterances of the character here in question, so the Illinois legislature could conclude, played a significant part. The law was passed on June 29, 1917, at a time when the State was struggling to assimilate vast numbers of new inhabitants, as yet concentrated in discrete racial or national or religious groups—foreign-born brought to it by the crest of the great wave of immigration, and Negroes attracted by jobs in war plants and the allurements of northern claims. Nine years earlier, in the very city where the legislature sat, what is said to be the first northern race riot had cost the lives of six people, left hundreds of Negroes homeless and shocked citizens into action far beyond the borders of the State. Less than a month before the bill was enacted, East St. Louis had seen a day's rioting, prelude to an outbreak, only four days after the bill became law, so bloody that it led to Congressional investigation. A series of bombings had begun which was to culminate two years later in the awful race riot which held Chicago in its grip for seven days in the summer of 1919. Nor has tension and violence between the groups defined in the statute been limited in Illinois to clashes between whites and Negroes.

In the face of this history and its frequent obligato of extreme racial and religious propaganda, we would deny experience to say that the Illinois legislature was without reason in seeking ways to curb false or malicious defamation of racial and religious groups, made in public places and by means calculated to have a powerful emotional impact on those to whom it was presented. . . .

It may be argued, and weightily, that this legislation will not help matters; that tension and on occasion violence between racial and religious groups must be traced to causes more deeply embedded in our society than the rantings of modern Know-Nothings. Only those lacking responsible humility will have a confident solution for problems as intractable as the frictions attributable to differences of race, color or religion. This being so, it would be out of bounds for the judiciary to deny the legislature a choice of policy, provided it is not unrelated to the problem and not forbidden by some explicit limitation on the State's power. That the legislative remedy might not in practice mitigate the evil, or might itself raise new problems, would only manifest once more the paradox of reform. It is the price to be paid for the trial-and-error inherent in legislative efforts to deal with obstinate social issues. . . . Certainly the Due Process Clause does not require the legislature to be in the vanguard of science— especially sciences as young as human ecology and cultural anthropology. . . .

. . . It is not within our competence to confirm or deny claims of social scientists as to the dependence of the individual on the position of his racial or religious group in the community. It would, however, be arrant dogmatism, quite outside the scope of our authority in passing on the powers of a State, for us to deny that the Illinois legislature may warrantably believe that a man's job and his educational opportunities and the dignity accorded him may depend as much on the reputation of the racial and religious group to which he willy-nilly belongs, as on his own merits. This being so, we are precluded from saying that speech concededly punishable when immediately directed at individuals cannot be outlawed if directed at groups with whose position and esteem in society the affiliated individual may be inextricably involved. . . .

It is suggested that while it was clearly within the constitutional power of Illinois to punish this utterance if the proceeding were properly safeguarded, in this particular case Illinois denied the defendant rights which the Due Process Clause commands. Specifically, it is argued that the defendant was not permitted to raise at the trial defenses constitutionally guaranteed in a criminal libel prosecution: (1) the defense of truth; (2) justification of the utterance as "fair comment"; and (3) its privilege as a means for redressing grievances.

Neither by proffer of evidence, requests for instructions, nor motion before or after verdict did the defendant seek to justify his utterance as "fair comment" or as privileged. Nor has the defendant urged as a ground for reversing his conviction in this Court that his opportunity to make those defenses was denied below. And so, whether a prosecution for libel of a racial or religious group is unconstitutionally invalid where the State did deny the defendant such opportunities is not before us. . . .

As to the defense of truth, Illinois in common with many States requires a showing not only that the utterance state the facts, but also that the publication be made "with good motives and for justifiable ends." Ill. Const., Art. II, § 4. Both elements are necessary if the defense is to prevail. What has been called "the common sense of American criminal law," as formulated, with regard to necessary safeguards in criminal libel prosecutions, in the New York Constitution of 1821, Art. VII, § 8, has been adopted in terms by Illinois. The teaching of a century and a half of criminal libel prosecutions in this country would go by the board if we were to hold that Illinois was not within her rights in making this combined requirement. Assuming that defendant's offer of proof directed to a part of the defense was adequate, it did not satisfy the entire requirement which Illinois could exact.

Libelous utterances not being within the area of constitutionally protected speech, it is unnecessary, either for us or for the State courts, to consider the issues behind the phrase "clear and present danger." Certainly no one would contend that obscene speech, for example, may be punished only upon a showing of such circumstances. Libel, as we have seen, is in the same class. . . .

[I]t bears repeating—although it should not—that our finding that the law is not constitutionally objectionable carries no implication of approval of the wisdom of the legislation or of its efficacy. These questions may raise doubts in our minds as well as in others. It is not for us, however, to make the legislative judgment. We are not at liberty to erect those doubts into fundamental law.

Affirmed.

MR. JUSTICE BLACK, with whom MR. JUSTICE DOUGLAS concurs, dissenting. . . .

That Beauharnais and his group were making a genuine effort to petition their elected representatives is not disputed. . . . After independence was won, Americans stated as the first unequivocal command of their Bill of Rights: "Congress shall make no law . . . abridging the freedom of speech, or of the press; or the right of the people peaceably to assemble, and to petition the Government for a redress of grievances." Without distortion, this First Amendment could not possibly be read so as to hold that Congress has power to punish Beauharnais and others for petitioning Congress as they have here sought to petition the Chicago authorities. See *e.g., Bridges v. California,* 314 U.S. 252, 277. And we have held in a number of prior cases that the Fourteenth Amendment makes the specific prohibitions of the First Amendment equally applicable to the states.

In view of these prior holdings, how does the Court justify its holding today that states can punish people for exercising the vital freedoms intended to be safeguarded from suppression by the First Amendment? The prior holdings are not referred to; the Court simply acts on the bland assumption that the First Amendment is wholly irrelevant. It is not even accorded the respect of a passing mention. . . .

. . . [W]e are cautioned that state legislatures must be left free to "experiment" and to make "legislative" judgments. We are told that mistakes may be made during the legislative process of curbing public opinion. In such event the Court fortunately does not leave those mistakenly curbed, or any of us for that matter, unadvised. Consolation can be sought and must be found in the philosophical reflection that state legislative error in stifling speech and press "is the price to be paid for the trial-and-error inherent in legislative efforts to deal with obstinate social issues." My own belief is that no legislature is charged with the duty or vested with the power to decide what public issues Americans can discuss. In a free country that is the individual's choice, not the state's. State experimentation in curbing freedom of expression is startling and frightening doctrine in a country dedicated to self-government by its people. I reject the holding that either state or nation can punish people for having their say in matters of public concern. . . .

This statute imposes state censorship over the theater, moving pictures, radio, television, leaflets, magazines, books and newspapers. . . .

The Court condones this expansive state censorship by painstakingly analogizing it to the law of criminal libel. As a result of this refined analysis, the Illinois statute emerges labeled a "group libel law." This label may make the Court's holding more palatable for those who sustain it, but the sugar-coating does not make the censorship less deadly. However tagged, the Illinois law is not that criminal libel which has been "defined, limited and constitutionally recognized time out of mind." For as "constitutionally recognized" that crime has provided for punishment of false, malicious, scurrilous charges against individuals, not against huge groups. This limited scope of the law of criminal libel is of no small importance. It has confined state punishment of speech and expression to the narrowest of areas involving nothing more than purely private feuds. Every expansion of the law of criminal libel so as to punish discussions of matters of public concern means a corresponding invasion of the area dedicated to free expression by the First Amendment.

Prior efforts to expand the scope of criminal libel beyond its traditional boundaries

have not usually met with widespread popular acclaim. "Seditious libel" was such an
expansion and it did have its day, particularly in the English Court of Star Chamber.
But the First Amendment repudiated seditious libel for this country. And one need
only glance through the parliamentary discussion of Fox's Libel Law passed in England
in 1792, to sense the bad odor of criminal libel in that country even when confined
to charges against individuals only. . . .

Unless I misread history the majority is giving libel a more expansive scope and
more respectable status than it was ever accorded even in the Star Chamber. For here
it is held to be punishable to give publicity to any picture, moving picture, play, drama
or sketch, or any printed matter which a judge may find unduly offensive to any race,
color, creed or religion. In other words, in arguing for or against the enactment of laws
that may differently affect huge groups, it is now very dangerous indeed to say something critical of one of the groups. And any "person, firm or corporation" can be tried
for this crime. "Person, firm or corporation" certainly includes a book publisher,
newspaper, radio or television station, candidate or even a preacher. . . .

No rationalization on a purely legal level can conceal the fact that state laws like
this one present a constant overhanging threat to freedom of speech, press and religion.
. . . I think the First Amendment, with the Fourteenth, "absolutely" forbids such
laws without any "ifs" or "buts" or "whereases." Whatever the danger, if any, in such
public discussions, it is a danger the Founders deemed outweighed by the danger
incident to the stifling of thought and speech. . . .

If there be minority groups who hail this holding as their victory, they might consider the possible relevancy of this ancient remark:
"Another such victory and I am undone."

Mr. Justice Reed, with whom Mr. Justice Douglas joins, dissenting. . . .

The Court speaks at length of the constitutional power of a state to pass group libel
laws to protect the public peace. This dissent assumes that power. What is under discussion is whether the conviction of Beauharnais on a general charge of violation of
the statute can stand when the statute contains without statutory or judicial definition
words of such ambiguous meaning and uncertain connotation as "virtue," "derision,"
or "obloquy." The Court does not attempt to speak specifically as to that contention. . . .

These words—"virtue," "derision," and "obloquy"—have neither general nor special
meanings well enough known to apprise those within their reach as to limitations on
speech. . . . Since this judgment may rest upon these vague and undefined words,
which permit within their scope the punishment of incidents secured by the guarantee
of free speech, the conviction should be reversed.

Mr. Justice Douglas, dissenting.

Hitler and his Nazis showed how evil a conspiracy could be which was aimed at
destroying a race by exposing it to contempt, derision, and obloquy. I would be willing
to concede that such conduct directed at a race or group in this country could be
made an indictable offense. For such a project would be more than the exercise of free
speech. Like picketing, it would be free speech plus.

I would also be willing to concede that even without the element of conspiracy
there might be times and occasions when the legislative or executive branch might
call a halt to inflammatory talk, such as the shouting of "fire" in a school or a theatre.

My view is that if in any case other public interests are to override the plain command of the First Amendment, the peril of speech must be clear and present, leaving no room for argument, raising no doubts as to the necessity of curbing speech in order to prevent disaster. . . .

MR. JUSTICE JACKSON, dissenting. . . .

The assumption of other dissents is that the "liberty" which the Due Process Clause of the Fourteenth Amendment protects against denial by the States is the literal and identical "freedom of speech or of the press" which the First Amendment forbids only Congress to abridge. The history of criminal libel in America convinces me that the Fourteenth Amendment did not "incorporate" the First, that the powers of Congress and of the States over this subject are not of the same dimensions, and that because Congress probably could not enact this law it does not follow that the States may not. . . .

More than forty State Constitutions, while extending broad protections to speech and press, reserve a responsibility for their abuse and implicitly or explicitly recognize validity of criminal libel laws. We are justified in assuming that the men who sponsored the Fourteenth Amendment in Congress, and those who ratified it in the State Legislatures, knew of such provisions then in many of their State Constitutions. Certainly they were not consciously canceling them or calling them into question, or we would have some evidence of it. Congresses, during the period while this Amendment was being considered or was but freshly adopted, approved Constitutions of "Reconstructed" States that expressly mentioned state libel laws, and also approved similar Constitutions for States erected out of the federal domain.

Certainly this tolerance of state libel laws by the very authors and partisans of the Fourteenth Amendment shows either that they were not intending to incorporate the First Amendment or that they believed it would not prevent federal libel laws. Adoption of the incorporation theory today would lead to the dilemma of either confining the States as closely as the Congress or giving the Federal Government the latitude appropriate to state governments. . . .

. . . Experience by Anglo-Saxon peoples with defamation and laws to punish it extends over centuries and the statute and case books exhibit its teachings. If one can claim to announce the judgment of legal history on any subject, it is that criminal libel laws are consistent with the concept of ordered liberty only when applied with safeguards evolved to prevent their invasion of freedom of expression. . . .

This Court, by construction of the Fourteenth Amendment, has imposed but one addition to the safeguards voluntarily taken upon the States by themselves. It is that where expression, oral or printed, is punished, although it has not actually caused injuries or disorders but is thought to have a tendency to do so, the likelihood of such consequence must not be remote or speculative. That is the "clear and present danger" test. . . .

In this case, neither the court nor jury found or were required to find any injury to any person, or group, or to the public peace, nor to find any probability, let alone any clear and present danger, of injury to any of these. . . . No actual violence and no specific injury was charged or proved. . . . The conviction rests on judicial attribution of a likelihood of evil results. . . .

Punishment of printed words, based on their *tendency* either to cause breach of the peace or injury to persons or groups, in my opinion, is justifiable only if the prosecution survives the "clear and present danger" test. It is the most just and workable standard yet evolved for determining criminality of words whose injurious or inciting tendencies are not demonstrated by the event but are ascribed to them on the basis of probabilities. . . .

No group interest in any particular prosecution should forget that the shoe may be on the other foot in some prosecution tomorrow. In these, as in other matters, our guiding spirit should be that each freedom is balanced with a responsibility, and every power of the State must be checked with safeguards. Such is the spirit of our American law of criminal libel, which concedes the power to the State, but only as a power restrained by recognition of individual rights. I cannot escape the conclusion that as the Act has been applied in this case it lost sight of the rights.

Chapter 24

OBSCENITY AND IMMORALITY

Obscenity, like libel, has long been punished under state laws and, as already noted, there is the federal obscenity statute applying to the United States mails. These statutes were generally assumed by reviewing courts, including the United States Supreme Court, to be constitutional. The judicial problem lay in finding and applying the standards for determining what is obscene. In 1868 Justice Cockburn in the English case of *Queen* v. *Hicklin* framed a legal definition of obscenity which came to be widely accepted. He said: "I think the test of obscenity is this, whether the tendency of the matter charged as obscenity is to deprave and corrupt those whose minds are open to such immoral influences, and into whose hands a publication of this sort may fall."

The *Hicklin* test ignored literary and other social values, judged a whole book by passages taken out of context, and tested for obscenity by the tendency of the passages alone to deprave the minds of those open to such influence and into whose hands the book might come. Nevertheless, this test became so thoroughly established in the United States that in 1913 Judge Learned Hand felt compelled to give it effect in a decision, even though he personally rejected it in the following memorable language:

I hope it is not improper for me to say that the rule as laid down, however consonant it may be with mid-Victorian morals, does not seem to me to answer to the understanding and morality of the present time. . . . I question whether in the end men will regard that as obscene which is honestly relevant to the adequate expression of innocent ideas, and whether they will not believe that truth and beauty are too precious to society at large to be mutilated in the interests of those most likely to pervert them to base uses. . . .

Yet, if the time is not yet when men think innocent all which is honestly germane to a pure subject, however little it may mince its words, still I scarcely think that they would forbid all which might corrupt the most corruptible, or that society is prepared to accept for its own limitations those which may perhaps be necessary to the weakest of its members. . . . To put thought in leash to the average conscience of the time is perhaps tolerable, but to fetter it by the necessities of the lowest and least capable seems a fatal policy. [*United States* v. *Kennerley*, 209 Fed. 119 (1913).]

It was not until the 1930s that this counsel began to be effective in American judicial decisions. In the celebrated *Ulysses* case, 72 F. 2d 705 (1934), Judge Augustus N. Hand in the court of appeals explicitly repudiated the *Hicklin* rule and replaced it with this new standard:

While any construction of the statute that will fit all cases is difficult, we believe that the proper test of whether a given book is obscene is its dominant effect. In applying this test, relevancy of the objectionable parts to the theme, the established reputation of the work in the estimation of approved critics, if the book is modern, and the verdict of the past, if it is ancient, are persuasive pieces of evidence; for works of art are not likely to sustain a high position with no better warrant for their existence than their obscene content.

The Supreme Court did not write an opinion in an obscene publication case until 1957. In *Roth v. United States* and its companion case, *Alberts v. California,* 354 U.S. 476 (1957), a divided Court sweepingly upheld both federal and state criminal obscenity laws. The federal statute involved was the postal act making "obscene, lewd, lascivious, or filthy" books or pictures nonmailable and providing criminal punishment for "knowingly" depositing nonmailable matter in the mails. Under the state law the proprietor of a mail-order business was convicted on a misdemeanor complaint charging him "with lewdly keeping for sale obscene and indecent books, and with . . . publishing an obscene advertisement of them." The defense in both cases was that the statutes violated First Amendment guaranties of freedom of speech and press. No claim of literary or artistic significance was made for the books involved.

In *Smith v. California,* 361 U.S. 147 (1959), the Supreme Court somewhat tempered the effect of the *Alberts* ruling by holding that a bookseller could not be convicted for possession of an "obscene" book unless he was aware of its obscenity. A Los Angeles city ordinance had been interpreted as imposing an absolute criminal liability for possessing obscene books, but the Court thought that such a rule would inevitably restrict the public's access to reading matter, because bookdealers would hesitate to stock books of which they had not made a personal inspection.

In addition to criminal punishment, the Supreme Court also approved in 1957 a limited form of prior restraint as a method of striking at obscene publications. *Kingsley Books, Inc. v. Brown,* 354 U.S. 436 (1957), involved a New York law which authorized the chief executive or legal officer of any city or town in the state to bring an injunction against the sale of any indecent books or other materials. The person whom it was sought to enjoin was entitled to a trial of the issues within one day and the court was to give its decision two days after the trial ended. If the injunction was granted, the material was to be surrendered to the sheriff or seized by him and destroyed.

The statute was attacked as violating the principle of *Near v. Minnesota,* but the Court upheld it by a five to four margin. Justice Frankfurter for the majority thought there was little resemblance between the two cases. In *Near* a court was enjoining future issues of a publication because its past issues had been found to be offensive and derogatory to a public official. In *Kingsley Books* a court was enjoining circulation of material already published, which had been found in a judicial proceeding to be obscene. This was prior restraint, to be sure, but Frankfurter thought it was no more restrictive an interference with freedom of publication than criminal punishment after the event would be.

Chief Justice Warren, dissenting, argued that book seizure "savors too much of book burning." The New York statute, totally ignoring the "manner of use" of the book, or the "setting in which it is placed," put the book itself on trial, not its seller. "It is the conduct of the individual that should be judged, not the quality of art or literature. To do otherwise is to impose a prior restraint and hence to violate the Constitution. Certainly in the absence of a prior judicial determination of illegal use, books, pictures, and other objects of expression should not be destroyed."

ROTH v. UNITED STATES
ALBERTS v. CALIFORNIA
354 U.S. 476, 77 S. Ct. 1304, 1 L. Ed. 2d 1498 (1957)

Roth was convicted of violating the federal statute making it a crime to mail any "obscene, lewd, lascivious, or filthy book, . . . picture, . . . or other publication of an indecent character" or any advertisement of such a work. Alberts was convicted under a California statute making it a crime to sell or keep for sale "any obscene or indecent writing, paper or book" or to publish an advertisement thereof. It was contended that both statutes violated First Amendment guarantees of freedom of speech and press. No claim of literary or artistic significance was made for the books involved here, nor was it denied on the appeal that they were obscene.

MR. JUSTICE BRENNAN delivered the opinion of the Court.

The constitutionality of a criminal obscenity statute is the question in each of these cases. In *Roth*, the primary constitutional question is whether the federal obscenity statute violates the provision of the First Amendment that "Congress shall make no law . . . abridging the freedom of speech, or of the press. . . ." In *Alberts*, the primary constitutional question is whether the obscenity provisions of the California Penal Code invade the freedoms of speech and press as they may be incorporated in the liberty protected from state action by the Due Process Clause of the Fourteenth Amendment. . . .

The dispositive question is whether obscenity is utterance within the area of protected speech and press. Although this is the first time the question has been squarely presented to this Court, either under the First Amendment or under the Fourteenth Amendment, expressions found in numerous opinions indicate that this Court has always assumed that obscenity is not protected by the freedoms of speech and press. . . .

The guaranties of freedom of expression in effect in 10 of the 14 States which by 1792 had ratified the Constitution, gave no absolute protection for every utterance. Thirteen of the 14 States provided for the prosecution of libel, and all of those States made either blasphemy or profanity, or both, statutory crimes. . . .

In light of this history, it is apparent that the unconditional phrasing of the First Amendment was not intended to protect every utterance. This phrasing did not prevent this Court from concluding that libelous utterances are not within the area of constitutionally protected speech. *Beauharnais* v. *Illinois,* 343 U.S. 250, 266. At the time of the adoption of the First Amendment, obscenity law was not as fully developed as libel law, but there is sufficiently contemporaneous evidence to show that obscenity, too, was outside the protection intended for speech and press. . . .

All ideas having even the slightest redeeming social importance—unorthodox ideas, controversial ideas, even ideas hateful to the prevailing climate of opinion—have the full protection of the guaranties, unless excludable because they encroach upon the limited area of more important interests. But implicit in the history of the First Amendment is the rejection of obscenity as utterly without redeeming social importance. This rejection for that reason is mirrored in the universal judgment that obscenity should be restrained, reflected in the international agreement of over 50 nations, in the obscenity laws of all of the 48 States, and in the 20 obscenity laws enacted by the Congress from 1842 to 1956. This is the same judgment expressed by this Court in *Chaplinsky* v. *New Hampshire*, 315 U.S. 568, 571–572:

> ". . . There are certain well-defined and narrowly limited classes of speech, the prevention and punishment of which have never been thought to raise any Constitutional problem. *These include the lewd and obscene. . . . It has been well observed that such utterances are no essential part of any exposition of ideas, and are of such slight social value as a step to truth that any benefit that may be derived from them is clearly outweighed by the social interest in order and morality. . . .*" (Emphasis added.)

We hold that obscenity is not within the area of constitutionally protected speech or press.

It is strenuously urged that these obscenity statutes offend the constitutional guaranties because they punish incitation to impure sexual *thoughts,* not shown to be related to any overt antisocial conduct which is or may be incited in the persons stimulated to such *thoughts.* . . . It is insisted that the constitutional guaranties are violated because convictions may be had without proof either that obscene material will perceptibly create a clear and present danger of antisocial conduct, or will probably induce its recipients to such conduct. But, in light of our holding that obscenity is not protected speech, the complete answer to this argument is in the holding of this Court in *Beauharnais* v. *Illinois, supra,* at 266:

> "Libelous utterances not being within the area of constitutionally protected speech, it is unnecessary, either for us or for the State courts, to consider the issues behind the phrase 'clear and present danger.' Certainly no one would contend that obscene speech, for example, may be punished only upon a showing of such circumstances. Libel, as we have seen, is in the same class."

However, sex and obscenity are not synonymous. Obscene material is material which deals with sex in a manner appealing to prurient interest. The portrayal of sex, *e.g.,* in art, literature and scientific works, is not itself sufficient reason to deny material the constitutional protection of freedom of speech and press. Sex, a great and mysterious motive force in human life, has indisputably been a subject of absorbing interest to mankind through the ages; it is one of the vital problems of human interest and public concern. As to all such problems, this Court said in *Thornhill* v. *Alabama,* 310 U.S. 88, 101–102:

> "The freedom of speech and of the press guaranteed by the Constitution embraces at the least the liberty to discuss publicly and truthfully *all matters of public concern* without previous restraint or fear of subsequent punishment. The exigencies of the colonial period and the efforts to secure freedom from oppressive administration developed a broadened conception of these liberties as adequate to supply the public need for *information and education with respect to the significant issues of the times. . . .* Freedom of discussion, if it would fulfill its historic function in this nation, must embrace *all issues about which information is needed or appropriate to enable the members of society to cope with the exigencies of their period.*" (Emphasis added.)

The fundamental freedoms of speech and press have contributed greatly to the development and well-being of our free society and are indispensable to its continued growth. Ceaseless vigilance is the watchword to prevent their erosion by Congress or by the States. The door barring federal and state intrusion into this area cannot be left ajar; it must be kept tightly closed and opened only the slightest crack necessary to prevent encroachment upon more important interests. It is therefore vital that the standards for judging obscenity safeguard the protection of freedom of speech and press for material which does not treat sex in a manner appealing to prurient interest.

The early leading standard of obscenity allowed material to be judged merely by the effect of an isolated excerpt upon particularly susceptible persons. *Regina* v. *Hicklin*, [1868] L. R. 3 Q. B. 360. Some American courts adopted this standard but later decisions have rejected it and substituted this test: whether to the average person, applying contemporary community standards, the dominant theme of the material taken as a whole appeals to prurient interest. The *Hicklin* test, judging obscenity by the effect of isolated passages upon the most susceptible persons, might well encompass material legitimately treating with sex, and so it must be rejected as unconstitutionally restrictive of the freedoms of speech and press. On the other hand, the substituted standard provides safeguards adequate to withstand the charge of constitutional infirmity.

Both trial courts below sufficiently followed the proper standard. Both courts used the proper definition of obscenity. . . .

The judgments are

Affirmed.

Mr. Chief Justice Warren, concurring in the result.

I agree with the result reached by the Court in these cases, but, because we are operating in a field of expression and because broad language used here may eventually be applied to the arts and sciences and freedom of communication generally, I would limit our decision to the facts before us and to the validity of the statutes in question as applied. . . .

The line dividing the salacious or pornographic from literature or science is not straight and unwavering. Present laws depend largely upon the effect that the materials may have upon those who receive them. It is manifest that the same object may have a different impact, varying according to the part of the community it reached. But there is more to these cases. It is not the book that is on trial; it is a person. The conduct of the defendant is the central issue, not the obscenity of a book or picture. The nature of the materials is, of course, relevant as an attribute of the defendant's conduct, but the materials are thus placed in context from which they draw color and character. A wholly different result might be reached in a different setting.

The personal element in these cases is seen most strongly in the requirement of *scienter*. Under the California law, the prohibited activity must be done "wilfully and lewdly." The federal statute limits the crime to acts done "knowingly." In his charge to the jury, the district judge stated that the matter must be "calculated" to corrupt or debauch. The defendants in both these cases were engaged in the business of purveying textual or graphic matter openly advertised to appeal to the erotic interest of their customers. They were plainly engaged in the commercial exploitation of the morbid and shameful craving for materials with prurient effect. I believe that the State and Federal Governments can constitutionally punish such conduct. That is all that these cases present to us, and that is all we need to decide.

Mr. Justice Harlan, concurring in the result in No. 61, and dissenting in No. 582.

I regret not to be able to join the Court's opinion. I cannot do so because I find lurking beneath its disarming generalizations a number of problems which not only leave me with serious misgivings as to the future effect of today's decisions, but which also, in my view, call for different results in these two cases. . . .

In final analysis, the problem presented by these cases is how far, and on what terms, the state and federal governments have power to punish individuals for disseminating books considered to be undesirable because of their nature or supposed deleterious effect upon human conduct. Proceeding from the premise that "no issue is presented in either case, concerning the obscenity of the material involved," the Court finds the "dispositive question" to be "whether obscenity is utterance within the area of protected speech and press," and then holds that "obscenity" is not so protected because it is "utterly without redeeming social importance." This sweeping formula appears to me to beg the very question before us. The Court seems to assume that "obscenity" is a peculiar *genus* of "speech and press," which is as distinct, recognizable, and classifiable as poison ivy is among other plants. On this basis the *constitutional* question before us simply becomes, as the Court says, whether "obscenity," as an abstraction, is protected by the First and Fourteenth Amendments, and the question whether a *particular* book may be suppressed becomes a mere matter of classification, of "fact," to be entrusted to a factfinder and insulated from independent constitutional judgment. But surely the problem cannot be solved in such a generalized fashion. Every communication has an individuality and "value" of its own. The suppression of a particular writing or other tangible form of expression is, therefore, an *individual* matter, and in the nature of things every such suppression raises an individual constitutional problem, in which a reviewing court must determine for *itself* whether the attacked expression is suppressable within constitutional standards. Since those standards do not readily lend themselves to generalized definitions, the constitutional problem in the last analysis becomes one of particularized judgments which appellate courts must make for themselves.

I do not think that reviewing courts can escape this responsibility by saying that the trier of the facts, be it a jury or a judge, has labeled the questioned matter as "obscene," for, if "obscenity" is to be suppressed, the question whether a particular work is of that character involves not really an issue of fact but a question of constitutional *judgment* of the most sensitive and delicate kind. Many juries might find that Joyce's "Ulysses" or Bocaccio's "Decameron" was obscene, and yet the conviction of a defendant for selling either book would raise, for me, the gravest constitutional problems, for no such verdict could convince me, without more, that these books are "utterly without redeeming social importance." In short, I do not understand how the Court can resolve the constitutional problems now before it without making its own independent judgment upon the character of the material upon which these convictions were based. I am very much afraid that the broad manner in which the Court has decided these cases will tend to obscure the peculiar responsibilities resting on state and federal courts in this field and encourage them to rely on easy labeling and jury verdicts as a substitute for facing up to the tough individual problems of constitutional judgment involved in every obscenity case. . . .

I concur in the judgment of the Court in No. 61, *Alberts* v. *California*. . . .

In judging the constitutionality of this conviction, we should remember that our function in reviewing state judgments under the Fourteenth Amendment is a narrow one. We do not decide whether the policy of the State is wise, or whether it is based on assumptions scientifically substantiated. We can inquire only whether the state action so subverts the fundamental liberties implicit in the Due Process Clause that it cannot be sustained as a rational exercise of power. . . .

What, then, is the purpose of this California statute? Clearly the state legislature has made the judgment that printed words *can* "deprave or corrupt" the reader—that words can incite to anti-social or immoral action. The assumption seems to be that the distribution of certain types of literature will induce criminal or immoral sexual conduct. It is well known, of course, that the validity of this assumption is a matter of dispute among critics, sociologists, psychiatrists, and penologists. There is a large school of thought, particularly in the scientific community, which denies any causal connection between the reading of pornography and immorality, crime, or delinquency. Others disagree. Clearly it is not our function to decide this question. That function belongs to the state legislature. . . .

Above all stands the realization that we deal here with an area where knowledge is small, data is insufficient, and experts are divided. Since the domain of sexual morality is pre-eminently a matter of state concern, this Court should be slow to interfere with state legislation calculated to protect that morality. It seems to me that nothing in the broad and flexible command of the Due Process Clause forbids California to prosecute one who sells books whose dominant tendency might be to "deprave or corrupt a reader." I agree with the Court, of course, that the books must be judged as a whole and in relation to the normal adult reader. . . .

I dissent in No. 582, *Roth* v. *United States.*

We are faced here with the question whether the federal obscenity statute, as construed and applied in this case, violates the First Amendment to the Constitution. To me, this question is of quite a different order than one where we are dealing with state legislation under the Fourteenth Amendment. . . . The substantive powers of the two governments, in many instances, are distinct. . . . Whether a particular limitation on speech or press is to be upheld because it subserves a paramount governmental interest must, to a large extent, I think, depend on whether that government has, under the Constitution, a direct substantive interest, that is, the power to act, in the particular area involved.

The Federal Government has, for example, power to restrict seditious speech directed against it, because that Government certainly has the substantive authority to protect itself against revolution. Cf. *Pennsylvania* v. *Nelson,* 350 U.S. 497. But in dealing with obscenity we are faced with the converse situation, for the interests which obscenity statutes purportedly protect are primarily entrusted to the care, not of the Federal Government, but of the States. Congress has no substantive power over sexual morality. Such powers as the Federal Government has in this field are but incidental to its other powers, here the postal power, and are not of the same nature as those possessed by the States, which bear direct responsibility for the protection of the local moral fabric. . . .

Not only is the federal interest in protecting the Nation against pornography attenuated, but the dangers of federal censorship in this field are far greater than anything the States may do. . . . The danger is perhaps not great if the people of one State, through their legislature, decide that "Lady Chatterley's Lover" goes so far beyond the acceptable standards of candor that it will be deemed offensive and non-sellable, for the State next door is still free to make its own choice. At least we do not have one uniform standard. But the dangers to free thought and expression are truly great if the Federal Government imposes a blanket ban over the Nation on such a book. The prerogative of the States to differ on their ideas of morality will be destroyed, the ability of States to experiment will be stunted. The fact that the people of one State cannot read some of the works of D. H. Lawrence seems to me, if not wise or desirable, at least acceptable. But that no person in the United States should be allowed to do so seems to me to be intolerable, and violative of both of the letter and spirit of the First Amendment.

I judge this case, then, in view of what I think is the attenuated federal interest in this field, in view of the very real danger of a deadening uniformity which can result from nation-wide federal censorship, and in view of the fact that the constitutionality of this conviction must be weighed against the First and not the Fourteenth Amendment. So viewed, I do not think that this conviction can be upheld. . . .

Mr. Justice Douglas, with whom Mr. Justice Black concurs, dissenting.

When we sustain these convictions, we make the legality of a publication turn on the purity of thought which a book or tract instills in the mind of the reader. I do not think we can approve that standard and be faithful to the command of the First Amendment which by its terms is a restraint on Congress and which by the Fourteenth is a restraint on the States.

In the *Roth* case the trial judge charged the jury that the statutory words "obscene, lewd and lascivious" describe "that form of immorality which has relation to sexual impurity and has a tendency to excite lustful thoughts." He stated that the term "filthy" in the statute pertaining "to that sort of treatment of sexual matters in such a vulgar and indecent way, so that it tends to arouse a feeling of disgust and revulsion." He went on to say that the material "must be calculated to corrupt and debauch the minds and morals" of "the average person in the community" not those of any particular class. "You judge the circulars, pictures and publications which have been put in evidence by present-day standards of the community. You may ask yourselves does it offend the common conscience of the community by present-day standards."

The trial judge who, sitting without a jury, heard the *Alberts* case and the appellate court that sustained the judgment of conviction, . . . held that a book is obscene "if it has a substantial tendency to deprave or corrupt its readers by inciting lascivious thoughts or arousing lustful desire."

By these standards punishment is inflicted for thoughts provoked, not for overt acts nor anti-social conduct. This test cannot be squared with our decisions under the First Amendment. Even the ill-starred *Dennis* case conceded that speech to be punishable must have some relation to action which could be penalized by government. *Dennis v. United States,* 341 U.S. 494, 502–511. . . .

The tests by which these convictions were obtained require only the arousing of sexual thoughts. Yet the arousing of sexual thoughts and desires happens every day in normal life in dozens of ways. Nearly 30 years ago a questionnaire sent to college and normal school women graduates asked what things were most stimulating sexually. Of 409 replies, 9 said "music"; 18 said "pictures"; 29 said "dancing"; 40 said "drama"; 95 said "books"; and 218 said "man." Alpert, Judicial Censorship of Obscene Literature, 52 Harv. L. Rev. 40, 73. . . .

If we were certain that impurity of sexual thoughts impelled to action, we would be on less dangerous ground in punishing the distributors of this sex literature. But it is by no means clear that obscene literature, as so defined, is a significant factor in influencing substantial deviations from the community standards. . . .

The absence of dependable information on the effect of obscene literature on human conduct should make us wary. It should put us on the side of protecting society's interest in literature, except and unless it can be said that the particular publication has an impact on action that the government can control. . . .

I assume there is nothing in the Constitution which forbids Congress from using its power over the mails to proscribe *conduct* on the grounds of good morals. No one would suggest that the First Amendment permits nudity in public places, adultery, and other phases of sexual misconduct. . . .

. . . Government should be concerned with anti-social conduct, not with utterances. Thus if the First Amendment guarantee of freedom of speech and press is to mean anything in this field, it must allow protests even against the moral code that the standard of the day sets for the community. In other words, literature should not be suppressed merely because it offends the moral code of the censor.

The legality of a publication in this country should never be allowed to turn either on the purity of thought which it instills in the mind of the reader or on the degree to which it offends the community conscience. By either test the role of the censor is exalted, and society's values in literary freedom are sacrificed. . . .

I do not think that the problem can be resolved by the Court's statement that "obscenity is not expression protected by the First Amendment." With the exception of *Beauharnais* v. *Illinois,* 343 U.S. 250, none of our cases have resolved problems of free speech and free press by placing any form of expression beyond the pale of the absolute prohibition of the First Amendment. Unlike the law of libel, wrongfully relied on in *Beauharnais,* there is no special historical evidence that literature dealing with sex was intended to be treated in a special manner by those who drafted the First Amendment. In fact, the first reported court decision in this country involving obscene literature was in 1821. . . . I reject too the implication that problems of freedom of speech and of the press are to be resolved by weighing against the values of free expression, the judgment of the Court that a particular form of that expression has "no redeeming social importance." The First Amendment, its prohibition in terms absolute, was designed to preclude courts as well as legislatures from weighing the values of speech against silence. The First Amendment puts free speech in the preferred position.

Freedom of expression can be suppressed if, and to the extent that, it is so closely brigaded with illegal action as to be an inseparable part of it. . . . As a people, we cannot afford to relax that standard. For the test that suppresses a cheap tract today can suppress a literary gem tomorrow. All it need do is to incite a lascivious thought or arouse a lustful desire. The list of books that judges or juries can place in that category is endless.

I would give the broad sweep of the First Amendment full support. I have the same confidence in the ability of our people to reject noxious literature as I have in their capacity to sort out the true from the false in theology, economics, politics, or any other field.

Chapter 25

MOTION PICTURE CENSORSHIP

State censorship of motion pictures was approved by the Supreme Court in *Mutual Film Corp. v. Industrial Commission of Ohio*, 236 U.S. 230 (1915). The motion picture of that era was of course only an entertaining novelty rather completely devoid of any ideational content, and it was readily assimilated to burlesque or other theatrical spectacles which were customarily subjected to control on moral grounds. Moreover, the 1915 decision antedated the Court's concern with civil liberties problems.

Over the years both motion pictures and the Court changed. The movies came somewhat closer to being commentaries on the social scene, and in documentary films and newsreels they rivaled the newspapers in reporting current events. Yet censorship continued to be practiced, and there were even some noteworthy instances of its application to newsreels. These developments were not lost on the Supreme Court, and during the 1940s several justices intimated that moving pictures were entitled to the protection of the First and Fourteenth Amendments.

It was not until 1952, however, that the 1915 censorship decision was overruled. *Burstyn v. Wilson*, 343 U.S. 495, concerned Rosselini's film *The Miracle*, which had been licensed for exhibition in New York and shown for about two months. After a Catholic campaign against the film, appropriate administrative review was undertaken, and the license was withdrawn on the ground that the picture was "sacrilegious." A state statute authorized denial of a license to a movie found to be "obscene, indecent, immoral, inhuman, sacrilegious, or . . . of such a character that its exhibition would tend to corrupt morals or incite to crime."

Justice Clark wrote the Court's opinion holding that states could not constitutionally censor motion pictures on the ground that they are sacrilegious. First, Clark definitely brought movies within the protection of the First Amendment, by way of the Fourteenth. Contrary to the view of the *Mutual Film* case that they were merely spectacles, Clark said: "It cannot be doubted that motion pictures are a significant medium for the communication of ideas."

Second, Clark condemned this example of censorship on the ground that sacrilege, the standard applied in the case, was too loose and meaningless. It set the censor "adrift upon a boundless sea amid a myriad of conflicting currents of religious views, with no charts but those provided by the most vocal and powerful orthodoxies." But the Court warned that it was expressing no opinion on "whether a state may censor motion pictures under a clearly drawn statute designed and applied to prevent the showing of obscene films."

In several subsequent decisions the Court invalidated censorship as applied to particular films, but in none of these cases was an opinion written for the Court. This method of handling the censorship issue made it uncertain whether the Court was invalidating motion picture censorship only because these films did not seem objectionable to the Court or because the legislative standards were too vague, or whether motion picture censorship was regarded by the Court as unconstitutional no matter what the standards. Several states redrafted their censorship laws on the assumption that a tightly drawn statute would be upheld by the Supreme Court.

The redrafted New York law came up for consideration in *Kingsley International Pictures* v. *New York*, 360 U.S. 684 (1959). In spite of the efforts of the New York Legislature, the Court held that the new law as applied in this case cut too close to the heart of constitutionally protected liberty. But again the Court refusesd to say whether or not the states were entirely without power to censor motion pictures, or whether there were any differences between movies and books or newspapers which would justify different control practices.

Times Film Corp. v. *Chicago*, 365 U.S. 43 (1961), sought to force the Court to answer this question, the tactic being to refuse to submit the film *Don Juan* for review by the Chicago censorship board. The Court, however, refused to be backed into a corner, and would not rule that movie censorship was necessarily unconstitutional. Thus the Court left open the possibility that motion pictures may be more subject to censorship than other forms of communication, though if they are, the Court has not yet explained why they are. It has assumed that a constitutional movie censorship law can be drafted, but in fact all those it has actually tested in operation have been held unconstitutional. Further decisions will be needed to clarify this situation.

KINGSLEY INTERNATIONAL PICTURES CORP. v. REGENTS OF THE UNIVERSITY OF THE STATE OF NEW YORK
360 U.S. 684, 79 S. Ct. 1362, 3 L. Ed. 2d 1512 (1959)

MR. JUSTICE STEWART delivered the opinion of the Court.

Once again the Court is required to consider the impact of New York's motion picture licensing law upon First Amendment liberties, protected by the Fourteenth Amendment from infringement by the States. Cf. *Joseph Burstyn, Inc.* v. *Wilson,* 343 U.S. 495.

The New York statute makes it unlawful "to exhibit, or to sell, lease or lend for exhibition at any place of amusement for pay or in connection with any business in the state of New York, any motion picture film or reel [with certain exceptions not relevant here], unless there is at the time in full force and effect a valid license or permit therefor of the education department. . . ." The law provides that a license shall issue "unless such film or a part thereof is obscene, indecent, immoral, inhuman, sacrilegious, or is of such a character that its exhibition would tend to corrupt morals or incite to crime. . . ." A recent statutory amendment provides that, "the term 'immoral' and the phrase 'of such a character that its exhibition would tend to corrupt morals' shall denote a motion picture film or part thereof, the dominant purpose or effect of which is erotic or pornographic; or which portrays acts of sexual immorality, perversion, or lewdness, or which expressly or impliedly presents such acts as desirable, acceptable or proper patterns of behavior."

As the distributor of a motion picture entitled "Lady Chatterley's Lover," the appellant Kingsley submitted that film to the Motion Picture Division of the New York Education Department for a license. Finding three isolated scenes in the film " 'immoral' within the intent of our Law," the Division refused to issue a license until the scenes in question were deleted. The distributor petitioned the Regents of the State of New York for a review of that ruling. The Regents upheld the denial of a license, but on the broader ground that "the whole theme of this motion picture is immoral under said law, for that theme is the presentation of adultery as a desirable, acceptable and proper pattern of behavior."

Kingsley sought judicial review of the Regents' determination. The Appellate Division unanimously annulled the action of the Regents and directed that a license be issued. . . . A sharply divided Court of Appeals, however, reversed the Appellate Division and upheld the Regents' refusal to license the film for exhibition.

The Court of Appeals unanimously and explicitly rejected any notion that the film is obscene. See *Roth* v. *United States,* 354 U.S. 476. Rather, the court found that the picture as a whole "alluringly portrays adultery as proper behavior." As Chief Judge Conway's prevailing opinion emphasized, therefore, the only portion of the statute involved in this case is that part of §§ 122 and 122 (a) of the Education Law requiring the denial of a license to motion pictures "which are immoral in that they portray 'acts of sexual immorality . . . as desirable, acceptable, or proper patterns of behavior.' " A majority of the Court of Appeals ascribed to that language a precise purpose of the New York Legislature to require the denial of a license to a motion picture "because its subject matter is adultery presented as being right and desirable for certain people under certain circumstances."

We accept the premise that the motion picture here in question can be so characterized. We accept too, as we must, the construction of the New York Legislature's language which the Court of Appeals has put upon it. *Albertson* v. *Millard,* 345 U.S. 242; *United States* v. *Burnison,* 339 U.S. 87; *Aero Mayflower Transit Co.* v. *Board of R. R. Comm'rs,* 332 U.S. 495. That construction, we emphasize, gives to the term "sexual immorality" a concept entirely different from the concept embraced in words like "obscenity" or "pornography." Moreover, it is not suggested that the film would itself operate as an incitement to illegal action. Rather, the New York Court of Appeals tells us that the relevant portion of the New York Education Law requires the denial of a license to any motion picture which approvingly portrays an adulterous relationship, quite without reference to the manner of its portrayal.

What New York has done, therefore, is to prevent the exhibition of a motion picture because that picture advocates an idea—that adultery under certain circumstances may be proper behavior. Yet the First Amendment's basic guarantee is of freedom to advocate ideas. The State, quite simply, has thus struck at the very heart of constitutionally protected liberty.

It is contended that the State's action was justified because the motion picture attractively portrays a relationship which is contrary to the moral standards, the religious precepts, and the legal code of its citizenry. This argument misconceives what it is that the Constitution protects. Its guarantee is not confined to the expression of ideas that are conventional or shared by a majority. It protects advocacy of the opinion that adultery may sometimes be proper, no less than advocacy of socialism or the single tax. And in the realm of ideas it protects expression which is eloquent no less than that which is unconvincing.

Advocacy of conduct proscribed by law is not, as Mr. Justice Brandeis long ago pointed out, "a justification for denying free speech where the advocacy falls short of incitement and there is nothing to indicate that the advocacy would be immediately acted on." *Whitney* v. *California,* 274 U.S. 357, at 376 (concurring opinion).

"Among free men, the deterrents ordinarily to be applied to prevent crime are education and punishment for violations of the law, not abridgment of the rights of free speech. . . ." *Id.*, at 378.

The inflexible command which the New York Court of Appeals has attributed to the State Legislature thus cuts so close to the core of constitutional freedom as to make it quite needless in this case to examine the periphery. Specifically, there is no occasion to consider the appellant's contention that the State is entirely without power to require films of any kind to be licensed prior to their exhibition. Nor need we here determine whether, despite problems peculiar to motion pictures, the controls which a State may impose upon this medium of expression are precisely coextensive with those allowable for newspapers, books, or individual speech. It is enough for the present case to reaffirm that motion pictures are within the First and Fourteenth Amendments' basic protection. *Joseph Burstyn, Inc. v. Wilson*, 343 U.S. 495.

Reversed.

Mr. Justice Black, concurring.

I concur in the Court's opinion and judgment but add a few words because of concurring opinions by several Justices who rely on their appraisal of the movie Lady Chatterley's Lover for holding that New York cannot constitutionally bar it. Unlike them, I have not seen the picture. My view is that stated by Mr. Justice Douglas, that prior censorship of moving pictures like prior censorship of newspapers and books violates the First and Fourteenth Amendments. If despite the Constitution, however, this Nation is to embark on the dangerous road of censorship, my belief is that this Court is about the most inappropriate Supreme Board of Censors that could be found. So far as I know, judges possess no special expertise providing exceptional competency to set standards and to supervise the private morals of the Nation. In addition, the Justices of this Court seem especially unsuited to make the kind of value judgments —as to what movies are good or bad for local communities—which the concurring opinions appear to require. We are told that the only way we can decide whether a State or municipality can constitutionally bar movies is for this Court to view and appraise each movie on a case-by-case basis. Under these circumstances, every member of the Court must exercise his own judgment as to how bad a picture is, a judgment which is ultimately based at least in large part on his own standard of what is immoral. The end result of such decisions seems to me to be a purely personal determination by individual Justices as to whether a particular picture viewed is too bad to allow it to be seen by the public. Such an individualized determination cannot be guided by reasonably fixed and certain standards. Accordingly, neither States nor moving picture makers can possibly know in advance, with any fair degree of certainty, what can or cannot be done in the field of movie making and exhibiting. This uncertainty cannot easily be reconciled with the rule of law which our Constitution envisages.

The different standards which different people may use to decide about the badness of pictures are well illustrated by the contrasting standards mentioned in the opinion of the New York Court of Appeals and the concurring opinion of Mr. Justice Frankfurter here. As I read the New York court's opinion this movie was held immoral and banned because it makes adultery too alluring. Mr. Justice Frankfurter quotes Mr. Lawrence, author of the book from which the movie was made, as believing censorship should be applied only to publications that make sex look ugly, that is, as I understand it, less alluring.

In my judgment, this Court should not permit itself to get into the very center of such policy controversies, which have so little in common with lawsuits.

MR. JUSTICE FRANKFURTER, concurring in the result.

As one whose taste in art and literature hardly qualifies him for the *avant-garde,* I am more than surprised, after viewing the picture, that the New York authorities should have banned "Lady Chatterley's Lover." To assume that this motion picture would have offended Victorian moral sensibilities is to rely only on the stuffiest of Victorian conventions. Whatever one's personal preferences may be about such matters, the refusal to license the exhibition of this picture, on the basis of the 1954 amendment to the New York State Education Law, can only mean that that enactment forbids the public showing of any film that deals with adultery except by way of sermonizing condemnation or depicts any physical manifestation of an illicit amorous relation. Since the denial of a license by the Board of Regents was confirmed by the highest court of the State, I have no choice but to agree with this Court's judgment in holding that the State exceeded the bounds of free expression protected by the "liberty" of the Fourteenth Amendment. But I also believe that the Court's opinion takes ground that exceeds the appropriate limits for decision. By way of reinforcing my brother HARLAN's objections to the scope of the Court's opinion, I add the following.

Even the author of "Lady Chatterley's Lover" did not altogether rule out censorship, nor was his passionate zeal on behalf of society's profound interest in the endeavors of true artists so doctrinaire as to be unmindful of the facts of life regarding the sordid exploitation of man's nature and impulses. He knew there was such a thing as pornography, dirt for dirt's sake, or, to be more accurate, dirt for money's sake. This is what D. H. Lawrence wrote:

"But even I would censor genuine pornography, rigorously. It would not be very difficult. In the first place, genuine pornography is almost always underworld, it doesn't come into the open. In the second, you can recognize it by the insult it offers invariably, to sex, and to the human spirit.

"Pornography is the attempt to insult sex, to do dirt on it. This is unpardonable. Take the very lowest instance, the picture post-card sold underhand, by the underworld, in most cities. What I have seen of them have been of an ugliness to make you cry. The insult to the human body, the insult to a vital human relationship! Ugly and cheap they make the human nudity, ugly and degraded they make the sexual act, trivial and cheap and nasty." (D. H. Lawrence, Pornography and Obscenity, p. 13.)

This traffic has not lessened since Lawrence wrote. Apparently it is on the increase. In the course of the recent debate in both Houses of Parliament on the Obscene Publications Bill, now on its way to passage, designed to free British authors from the hazards of too rigorous application in our day of Lord Cockburn's ruling, in 1868, in *Regina* v. *Hicklin,* L. R. 3 Q. B. 360, weighty experience was adduced regarding the extensive dissemination of pornographic materials. . . .

It is not surprising, therefore, that the pertinacious, eloquent and free-spirited promoters of the liberalizing legislation in Great Britain did not conceive the needs of a civilized society, in assuring the utmost freedom to those who make literature and art possible—authors, artists, publishers, producers, book sellers—easily attainable by sounding abstract and unqualified dogmas about freedom. They had a keen awareness that freedom of expression is no more an absolute than any other freedom, an awareness that is reflected in the opinions of Mr. Justice Holmes and Mr. Justice Brandeis, to whom we predominantly owe the present constitutional safeguards on behalf of freedom of expression. And see *Near* v. *Minnesota*, 283 U.S. 697, 715–716, for limitations on constitutionally protected freedom of speech.

In short, there is an evil against which a State may constitutionally protect itself, whatever we may think about the questions of policy involved. The real problem is the formulation of constitutionally allowable safeguards which society may take against evil without impinging upon the necessary dependence of a free society upon the fullest scope of free expression. One cannot read the debates in the House of Commons and the House of Lords and not realize the difficulty of reconciling these conflicting interests, in the framing of legislation on the ends of which there was agreement, even for those who most generously espouse that freedom of expression without which all freedom gradually withers. . . .

The New York legislation of 1954 was the product of careful lawyers who sought to meet decisions of this Court which had left no doubt that a motion-picture licensing law is not inherently outside the scope of the regulatory powers of a State under the Fourteenth Amendment. The Court does not strike the law down because of vagueness, as we struck down prior New York legislation. Nor does it reverse the judgment of the New York Court of Appeals, as I would, because in applying the New York law to "Lady Chatterley's Lover" it applied it to a picture to which it cannot constitutionally be applied without invading the area of constitutionally free expression. The difficulty which the Court finds seems to derive from some expressions culled here and there from the opinion of the Chief Judge of the New York Court of Appeals. This leads the Court to give the phrase "acts of sexual immorality . . . as desirable, acceptable or proper patterns of behavior" an innocent content, meaning, in effect, an allowable subject-matter for discussion. But, surely, to attribute that result to the decision of the Court of Appeals, on the basis of a few detached phrases of Chief Judge Conway, is to break a faggot into pieces, is to forget that the meaning of language is to be felt and its phrases not to be treated disjointedly. "Sexual immorality" is not a new phrase in this branch of law and its implications dominate the context. I hardly conceive it possible that the Court would strike down as unconstitutional the federal statute against mailing lewd, obscene and lascivious matter, which has been the law of the land for nearly a hundred years, see the Act of March 3, 1865, 13 Stat. 507, and March 3, 1873, 17 Stat. 599, whatever specific instances may be found not within its allowable prohibition. In sustaining this legislation this Court gave the words "lewd, obscene and lascivious" concreteness by saying that they concern "sexual immorality."

Unless I misread the opinion of the Court, it strikes down the New York legislation in order to escape the task of deciding whether a particular picture is entitled to the protection of expression under the Fourteenth Amendment. Such an exercise of the judicial function, however onerous or ungrateful, inheres in the very nature of the judicial enforcement of the Due Process Clause. We cannot escape such instance-by-instance, case-by-case application of that clause in all the variety of situations that come before this Court. . . . It is the nature of the concept of Due Process, and, I venture to believe, its high serviceability in our constitutional system, that the judicial enforcement of the Due Process Clause is the very antithesis of a Procrustean rule. This was recognized in the first full-dress discussion of the Due Process Clause of the Fourteenth Amendment, when the Court defined the nature of the problem as a "gradual process of judicial inclusion and exclusion, as the cases presented for decision shall require, with the reasons on which such decision may be founded." *Davidson* v. *New Orleans*, 96 U.S. 97, 104. The task is onerous and exacting, demanding as it does the utmost discipline in objectivity, the severest control of personal predilections. But it cannot be escaped, not even by disavowing that such is the nature of our task.

MR. JUSTICE DOUGLAS, with whom MR. JUSTICE BLACK joins, concurring.

While I join in the opinion of the Court, I adhere to the views I expressed in *Superior Films* v. *Department of Education*, 346 U.S. 587, 588–589, that censorship of movies is unconstitutional, since it is a form of "previous restraint" that is as much at war with the First Amendment, made applicable to the States through the Fourteenth, as the censorship struck down in *Near* v. *Minnesota*, 283 U.S. 697. If a particular movie violates a valid law, the exhibitor can be prosecuted in the usual way. I can find in the First Amendment no room for any censor whether he is scanning an editorial, reading a news broadcast, editing a novel or a play, or previewing a movie.

Reference is made to British law and British practice. But they have little relevance to our problem, since we live under a written Constitution. What is entrusted to the keeping of the legislature in England is protected from legislative interference or regulation here. As we stated in *Bridges* v. *California*, 314 U.S. 252, 265, "No purpose in ratifying the Bill of Rights was clearer than that of securing for the people of the United States much greater freedom of religion, expression, assembly, and petition than the people of Great Britain had ever enjoyed." If we had a provision in our Constitution for "reasonable" regulation of the press such as India has included in hers, there would be room for argument that censorship in the interests of morality would be permissible. Judges sometimes try to read the word "reasonable" into the First Amendment or make the rights it grants subject to reasonable regulation (see *Beauharnais* v. *Illinois*, 343 U.S. 250, 262; *Dennis* v. *United States*, 341 U.S. 494, 523–525), or apply to the States a watered-down version of the First Amendment. See *Roth* v. *United States*, 354 U.S. 476, 505–506. But its language, in terms that are absolute, is utterly at war with censorship. Different questions may arise as to censorship of some news when the Nation is actually at war. But any possible exceptions are extremely limited. That is why the tradition represented by *Near* v. *Minnesota, supra,* represents our constitutional ideal.

Happily government censorship has put down few roots in this country. . . . Deletion of the residual part of censorship that remains would constitute the elimination of an institution that intrudes on First Amendment rights.

MR. JUSTICE CLARK, concurring in the result. . . .

MR. JUSTICE HARLAN, whom MR. JUSTICE FRANKFURTER and MR. JUSTICE WHITTAKER join, concurring in the result.

I think the Court has moved too swiftly in striking down a statute which is the product of a deliberate and conscientious effort on the part of New York to meet constitutional objections raised by this Court's decisions respecting predecessor statutes in this field. But although I disagree with the Court that the parts of §§ 122 and 122-a of the New York Education Law . . . here particularly involved are unconstitutional on their face, I believe that in their application to this film constitutional bounds were exceeded. . . .

I do not understand that the Court would question the constitutionality of the particular portions of the statute with which we are here concerned if the Court read, as I do, the majority opinions in the Court of Appeals as construing these provisions to require obscenity or incitement, not just mere abstract expressions of opinion. It is difficult to understand why the Court should strain to read those opinions as it has. Our usual course in constitutional adjudication is precisely the opposite.

The application of the statute to this film is quite a different matter. I have heretofore ventured the view that in this field the States have wider constitutional latitude than the Federal Government. See the writer's separate opinion in *Roth* v. *United States* and *Alberts* v. *California,* 354 U.S. 476, 496. With that approach, I have viewed this film.

Giving descriptive expression to what in matters of this kind are in the last analysis bound to be but individual subjective impressions, objectively as one may try to discharge his duty as a judge, is not apt to be repaying. I shall therefore content myself with saying that, according full respect to, and with, I hope, sympathetic consideration for, the views and characterizations expressed by others, I cannot regard this film as depicting anything more than a somewhat unusual, and rather pathetic, "love triangle," lacking in anything that could properly be termed obscene or corruptive of the public morals by inciting the commission of adultery. I therefore think that in banning this film New York has exceeded constitutional limits.

I conclude with one further observation. It is sometimes said that this Court should shun considering the particularities of individual cases in this difficult field lest the Court become a final "board of censorship." But I cannot understand why it should be thought that the process of constitutional judgment in this realm somehow stands apart from that involved in other fields, particularly those presenting questions of due process. Nor can I see, short of holding that all state "censorship" laws are constitutionally impermissible, a course from which the Court is carefully abstaining, how the Court can hope ultimately to spare itself the necessity for individualized adjudication. . . .

TIMES FILM CORP. v. CHICAGO
365 U.S. 43, 81 S. Ct. 391, 5 L. Ed. 2d 403 (1961)

MR. JUSTICE CLARK delivered the opinion of the Court.

Petitioner challenges on constitutional grounds the validity on its face of that portion of § 155-4 of the Municipal Code of the City of Chicago which requires submission of all motion pictures for examination prior to their public exhibition. Petitioner is a New York corporation owning the exclusive right to publicly exhibit in Chicago the film known as "Don Juan." It applied for a permit as Chicago's ordinance required, and tendered the license fee but refused to submit the film for examination. The appropriate city official refused to issue the permit and his order was made final on appeal to the Mayor. The sole ground for denial was petitioner's refusal to submit the film for examination as required. Petitioner then brought this suit seeking injunctive relief ordering the issuance of the permit without submission of the film and restraining the city officials from interfering with the exhibition of the picture. Its sole ground is that the provision of the ordinance requiring submission of the film constitutes, on its face, a prior restraint within the prohibition of the First and Fourteenth Amendments. . . .

. . . In *Joseph Burstyn, Inc.,* v. *Wilson,* 343 U.S. 495, 502 (1952), we held that motion pictures are included "within the free speech and free press guaranty of the First and Fourteenth Amendments." Admittedly, the challenged section of the ordinance imposes a previous restraint, and the broad justiciable issue is therefore present as to whether the ambit of constitutional protection includes complete and absolute freedom to exhibit, at least once, any and every kind of motion picture. It is that question alone which we decide. We have concluded that § 155-4 of Chicago's ordinance requiring the submission of films prior to their public exhibition is not, on the grounds set forth, void on its face.

Petitioner's narrow attack upon the ordinance does not require that any consideration be given to the validity of the standards set out therein. They are not challenged and are not before us. Prior motion picture censorship cases which reached this Court involved questions of standards. The films had all been submitted to the authorities and permits for their exhibition were refused because of their content. Obviously, whether a particular statute is "clearly drawn," or "vague," or "indefinite," or whether a clear standard is in fact met by a film are different questions involving other constitutional challenges to be tested by considerations not here involved.

Moreover, there is not a word in the record as to the nature and content of "Don Juan." We are left entirely in the dark in this regard, as were the city officials and the other reviewing courts. Petitioner claims that the nature of the film is irrelevant, and that even if this film contains the basest type of pornography, or incitement to riot, or forceful overthrow of orderly government, it may nonetheless be shown without prior submission for examination. The challenge here is to the censor's basic authority; it does not go to any statutory standards employed by the censor or procedural requirements as to the submission of the film.

In this perspective we consider the prior decisions of this Court touching on the problem. Beginning over a third of a century ago in *Gitlow* v. *New York,* 268 U.S. 652 (1925), they have consistently reserved for future decision possible situations in which the claimed First Amendment privilege might have to give way to the necessities of the public welfare. It has never been held that liberty of speech is absolute. Nor has it been suggested that all previous restraints on speech are invalid. On the contrary, in *Near* v. *Minnesota,* 283 U.S. 697, 715-716 (1931), Chief Justice Hughes, in discussing the classic legal statements concerning the immunity of the press from censorship, observed that the principle forbidding previous restraint "is stated too broadly, if every such restraint is deemed to be prohibited. . . . [T]he protection even as to previous restraint is not absolutely unlimited. But the limitation has been recognized only in exceptional cases." These included, the Chief Justice found, utterances creating "a hindrance" to the Government's war effort, and "actual obstruction to its recruiting service or the publication of the sailing dates of transports or the number and location of troops." In addition, the Court said that "the primary requirements of decency may be enforced against obscene publications" and the "security of the community life may be protected against incitements to acts of violence and the overthrow by force of orderly government." Some years later a unanimous Court, speaking through Mr. Justice Murphy, in *Chaplinsky* v. *New Hampshire,* 315 U.S. 568, 571-572 (1942), held that there were "certain well-defined and narrowly limited classes of speech, the prevention and punishment of which have never been thought to raise any Constitutional problem. These include the lewd and obscene, the profane, the libelous, and the insulting or 'fighting' words—those which by their very utterance inflict injury or tend to incite an immediate breach of the peace." . . .

Petitioner would have us hold that the public exhibition of motion pictures must be allowed under any circumstances. The State's sole remedy, it says, is the invocation of criminal process under the Illinois pornography statute, Ill. Rev. Stat. (1959), c. 38, § 470, and then only after a transgression. But this position, as we have seen, is founded upon the claim of absolute privilege against prior restraint under the First Amendment—a claim without sanction in our cases. To illustrate its fallacy we need only point to one of the "exceptional cases" which Chief Justice Hughes enumerated in *Near* v. *Minnesota, supra,* namely, "the primary requirements of decency [that] may be enforced against obscene publications." Moreover, we later held specifically "that obscenity is not within the area of constitutionally protected speech or press." *Roth* v. *United States,* 354 U.S. 476, 485 (1957). Chicago emphasizes here its duty to protect its people against the dangers of obscenity in the public exhibition of motion pictures. To this argument petitioner's only answer is that regardless of **the** capacity for, or extent of such an evil, previous restraint cannot be justified. With this we cannot agree. We recognized in *Burstyn, supra,* that "capacity for evil . . . may be relevant in determining the permissible scope of community control," at p. 502, and that motion pictures were not "necessarily subject to the precise rules governing any other particular method of expression. Each method," we said, "tends to present its own peculiar problems." At p. 503. Certainly petitioner's broadside attack does not warrant, nor could it justify on the record here, our saying that—aside from any consideration of the other "exceptional cases" mentioned in our decisions—the State is stripped of all constitutional power to prevent, in the most effective fashion, the utterance of this class of speech. It is not for this Court to limit the State in its selection of the remedy it deems most effective to cope with such a problem, absent, of course, a showing of unreasonable strictures on individual liberty resulting from its application in particular circumstances. . . .

As to what may be decided when a concrete case involving a specific standard provided by this ordinance is presented, we intimate no opinion. The petitioner has not challenged all—or for that matter any—of the ordinance's standards. Naturally we could not say that every one of the standards, including those which Illinois' highest court has found sufficient, is so vague on its face that the entire ordinance is void. At this time we say no more than this—that we are dealing only with motion pictures and, even as to them, only in the context of the broadside attack presented on this record.

Affirmed.

MR. CHIEF JUSTICE WARREN, with whom MR. JUSTICE BLACK, MR. JUSTICE DOUGLAS and MR. JUSTICE BRENNAN join, dissenting.

I cannot agree with either the conclusion reached by the Court or with the reasons advanced for its support. To me, this case clearly presents the question of our approval of unlimited censorship of motion pictures before exhibition through a system of administrative licensing. Moreover, the decision presents a real danger of eventual censorship for every form of communication be it newspapers, journals, books, magazines, television, radio or public speeches. The Court purports to leave these questions for another day, but I am aware of no constitutional principle which permits us to hold that the communication of ideas through one medium may be censored while other media are immune. Of course each medium presents its own peculiar problems, but they are not of the kind which would authorize the censorship of one form of communication and not the others. I submit that in arriving at its decision the Court has interpreted our cases contrary to the intention at the time of their rendition and, in exalting the censor of motion pictures, has endangered the First and Fourteenth Amendment rights of all others engaged in the dissemination of ideas. . . .

I hesitate to disagree with the Court's formulation of the issue before us, but, with all deference, I must insist that the question presented in this case is *not* whether a motion picture exhibitor has a constitutionally protected, "complete and absolute freedom to exhibit, at least once, any and every kind of motion picture." . . . Surely, the Court is not bound by the petitioner's conception of the issue or by the more extreme positions that petitioner may have argued at one time in the case. The question here presented is whether the City of Chicago—or, for that matter, any city, any State or the Federal Government—may require all motion picture exhibitors to submit all films to a police chief, mayor or other administrative official, for licensing and censorship prior to public exhibition within the jurisdiction.

The Court does not even have before it an attempt by the city to restrain the exhibition of an allegedly "obscene" film, see *Roth v. United States,* 354 U.S. 476.

Nor does the city contend that it is seeking to prohibit the showing of a film which will impair the "security of community life" because it acts as an incitement to "violence and the overthrow by force of orderly government." See *Near* v. *Minnesota, supra,* at p. 716. The problem before us is not whether the city may forbid the exhibition of a motion picture, which, by its very showing, might in some way "inflict injury or tend to incite an immediate breach of the peace." See *Chaplinsky* v. *New Hampshire,* 315 U.S. 568, 572.

Let it be completely clear what the Court's decision does. It gives official license to the censor, approving a grant of power to city officials to prevent the showing of any moving picture these officials deem unworthy of a license. It thus gives formal sanction to censorship in its purest and most far-reaching form, to a classical plan of licensing that, in our country, most closely approaches the English licensing laws of the seventeenth century which were commonly used to suppress dissent in the mother country and in the colonies. . . . By its decision, the Court gives its assent to unlimited censorship of moving pictures through a licensing system, despite the fact that Chicago has chosen this most objectionable course to attain its goals without any apparent attempt to devise other means so as not to intrude on the constitutionally protected liberties of speech and press. . . .

Perhaps today's surrender was forecast by *Kingsley Books, Inc.,* v. *Brown, supra.* But, that was obviously not this case, and accepting *arguendo* the correctness of that decision, I believe that it leads to a result contrary to that reached today. The statute in *Kingsley* authorized "the chief executive, or legal officer, of a municipality to invoke a 'limited injunctive remedy,' under closely defined procedural safeguards, against the sale and distribution of written and printed matter found after due trial [by a court] to be obscene. . . ." The Chicago scheme has no procedural safeguards; there is no trial of the issue before the blanket injunction against exhibition becomes effective. In *Kingsley,* the grounds for the restraint were that the written or printed matter was "obscene, lewd, lascivious, filthy, indecent, or disgusting . . . or immoral. . . ." The Chicago objective is to capture much more. The *Kingsley* statute required the existence of some cause to believe that the publication was obscene before the publication was put on trial. The Chicago ordinance requires no such showing.

The booklets enjoined from distribution in *Kingsley* were concededly obscene. There is no indication that this is true of the moving picture here. This was treated as a particularly crucial distinction. Thus, the Court has suggested that, in times of national emergency, the Government might impose a prior restraint upon "the publication of the sailing dates of transports or the number and location of troops." *Near* v. *Minnesota, supra,* p. 716; cf. *Ex parte Milligan,* 71 U.S. 2. But, surely this is not to suggest that the Government might require that all newspapers be submitted to a censor in order to assist it in preventing such information from reaching print. Yet in this case the Court gives its blessing to the censorship of all motion pictures in order to prevent the exhibition of those it feels to be constitutionally unprotected.

The statute in *Kingsley* specified that the person sought to be enjoined was to be entitled to a trial of the issues within one day after joinder and a decision was to be rendered by the court within two days of the conclusion of the trial. The Chicago plan makes no provision for prompt judicial determination. In *Kingsley,* the person enjoined had available the defense that the written or printed matter was not obscene if an attempt was made to punish him for disobedience of the injunction. The Chicago ordinance admits no defense in a prosecution for failure to procure a license other than that the motion picture was submitted to the censor and a license was obtained.

Finally, the Court in *Kingsley* painstakingly attempted to establish that that statute, in its effective operation, was no more a previous restraint on, or interference with, the liberty of speech and press than a statute imposing criminal punishment for the publication of pornography. In each situation, it contended, the publication may have passed into the hands of the public. Of course, this argument is inadmissible in this case and the Court does not purport to advance it. . . .

A revelation of the extent to which censorship has recently been used in this country is indeed astonishing. The Chicago licensors have banned newsreel films of Chicago policemen shooting at labor pickets and have ordered the deletion of a scene depicting the birth of a buffalo in Walt Disney's *Vanishing Prairie*. . . . Recently, Chicago refused to issue a permit for the exhibition of the motion picture *Anatomy of a Murder* based upon the best-selling novel of the same title, because it found the use of words "rape" and "contraceptive" to be objectionable. . . . The Memphis censors banned *The Southerner* which dealt with poverty among tenant farmers because "it reflects on the south." *Brewster's Millions*, an innocuous comedy of fifty years ago, was recently forbidden in Memphis because the radio and film character Rochester, a Negro, was deemed "too familiar." . . . *Witchcraft*, a study of superstition through the ages, was suppressed for years because it depicted the devil as a genial rake with amorous leanings, and because it was feared that certain historical scenes, portraying the excesses of religious fanatics, might offend religion. *Scarface*, thought by some as the best of the gangster films, was held up for months; then it was so badly mutilated that retakes costing a hundred thousand dollars were required to preserve continuity. The New York censors banned *Damaged Lives*, a film dealing with venereal disease, although it treated a difficult theme with dignity and had the sponsorship of the American Social Hygiene Society. The picture of Lenin's tomb bearing the inscription "Religion is the opiate of the people" was excised from *Potemkin*. From *Joan of Arc* the Maryland board eliminated Joan's exclamation as she stood at the stake: "Oh, God, why hast thou forsaken me?" and from *Idiot's Delight*, the sentence: "We, the workers of the world, will take care of that." *Professor Mamlock* was produced in Russia and portrayed the persecution of the Jews by Nazis. The Ohio censors condemned it as "harmful" and calculated to "stir up hatred and ill will and gain nothing." It was released only after substantial deletions were made. The police refused to permit its showing in Providence, Rhode Island, on the ground that it was communistic propaganda. . . . A member of the Chicago censor board explained that she rejected a film because "it was immoral, corrupt, indecent, against my . . . religious principles." . . . A police sergeant attached to the censor board explained, "Coarse language or anything that would be derogatory to the government—propaganda" is ruled out of foreign films. "Nothing pink or red is allowed," he added. . . . The police sergeant in charge of the censor unit has said: "Children should be allowed to see any movie that plays in Chicago. If a picture is objectionable for a child, it is objectionable period." . . . And this is but a smattering produced from limited research. . . .

If the censor denies rights protected by the First and Fourteenth Amendments, the courts might be called upon to correct the abuse if the exhibitor decides to pursue judicial remedies. But, this is not a satisfactory answer as emphasized by this very case. The delays in adjudication may well result in irreparable damage, both to the litigants and to the public. Vindication by the courts of *The Miracle* was not had until five years after the Chicago censor refused to license it. And then the picture was never shown in Chicago. Brief for Petitioner, p. 17. The instant litigation has now consumed almost three years. This is the delay occasioned by the censor; this is the injury done to the free communication of ideas. This damage is not inflicted by the ordinary criminal penalties. The threat of these penalties, intelligently applied, will ordinarily be sufficient to deter the exhibition of obscenity. However, if the exhibitor believes that his film is constitutionally protected, he will show the film, and, if prosecuted under criminal statute, will have ready that defense. The perniciousness of a system of censorship is that the exhibitor's belief that his film is constitutionally protected is irrelevant. Once the censor has made his estimation that the film is "bad" and has refused to issue a permit, there is ordinarily no defense to a prosecution for showing the film without a license. Thus, the film is not shown, perhaps not for years and sometimes not ever. . . .

It seems to me that the Court's opinion comes perilously close to holding that not only may motion pictures be censored but that a licensing scheme may also be applied to newspapers, books and periodicals, radio, television, public speeches, and every other medium of expression. . . . The Court, in no way, explains why moving pictures should be treated differently than any other form of expression, why moving pictures should be denied the protection against censorship. . . . When pressed during oral argument, counsel for the city could make no meaningful distinction between the censorship of newspapers and motion pictures. . . . The Chicago ordinance makes no exception for newsreels, documentaries, instructional and educational films or the like. All must undergo the censor's inquisition. . . .

The contention may be advanced that the impact of motion pictures is such that a licensing system of prior censorship is permissible. There are several answers to this, the first of which I think is the Constitution itself. Although it is an open question whether the impact of motion pictures is greater or less than that of other media, there is not much doubt that the exposure of television far exceeds that of the motion picture. . . . But, even if the impact of the motion picture is greater than that of some other media, that fact constitutes no basis for the argument that motion pictures should be subject to greater suppression. This is the traditional argument made in the censor's behalf; this is the argument advanced against newspapers at the time of the invention of the printing press. The argument was ultimately rejected in England, and has consistently been held to be contrary to our Constitution. No compelling reason has been predicated for accepting the contention now. . . .

MR. JUSTICE DOUGLAS, with whom THE CHIEF JUSTICE and MR. JUSTICE BLACK concur, dissenting.

My view that censorship of movies is unconstitutional because it is a prior restraint and violative of the First Amendment has been expressed on prior occasions. . . .

While the problem of movie censorship is relatively new, the censorship device is an ancient one. . . . Censorship has had many champions throughout time.

Socrates: "And shall we just carelessly allow children to hear any casual tales which may be devised by casual persons, and to receive into their minds ideas for the most part the very opposite of those which we should wish them to have when they are grown up?"

Glaucon: "We cannot."

Socrates: "Then the first thing will be to establish a censorship of the writers of fiction, and let the censors receive any tale of fiction which is good, and reject the bad; and we will desire mothers and nurses to tell their children the authorised ones only. Let them fashion the mind with such tales, even more fondly than they mould the body with their hands; but most of those which are now in use must be discarded." Plato, Republic, Bk. II. . . .

Regimes of censorship are common in the world today. Every dictator has one; every Communist regime finds it indispensable. . . .

Yet as long as the First Amendment survives, the censor, no matter how respectable his cause, cannot have the support of government. It is not for government to pick and choose according to the standards of any religious, political, or philosophical group. It is not permissible, as I read the Constitution, for government to release one movie and refuse to release another because of an official's concept of the prevailing need or the public good. . . .

The First Amendment was designed to enlarge, not to limit, freedom in literature and in the arts as well as in politics, economics, law, and other fields. . . . Its aim was to unlock all ideas for argument, debate, and dissemination. No more potent force in defeat of that freedom could be designed than censorship. It is a weapon that no minority or majority group, acting through government, should be allowed to wield over any of us.

Chapter 26

THE RIGHT TO ASSOCIATE

There is no provision in the Constitution specifically protecting freedom of association, yet the right of individuals to organize into groups for political, economic, religious, and social purposes is universally recognized. The constitutional basis for this freedom must be derived from the right of assembly and the freedom of speech, press, and religion, but the fact that it is derivative does not make this freedom any the less real.

Of course associational freedom is not absolute for any group, any more than are the freedoms of speech, press, and assembly of which it is compounded. The freedom of group life is always subject to regulation in the public interest. Totalitarians carry this regulation to the point of completely subjecting all groups to the purposes of the state. Anarchists go to the other extreme in proposing that the state abdicate its functions to groups. The liberal state seeks to encourage the maximum of group freedom compatible with the general public welfare.

A systematic study of the relationships between government and groups would distinguish three general categories. First, there is the norm of freedom from governmental interference. The government simply keeps hands off. Individuals are free to associate and their organizations are free to carry on their programs without any public authorization or recognition. No constitutional problems are raised by such a laissez-faire policy.

Second, the government may undertake to assist groups in formation or in the achievement of their purposes by granting them appropriate privileges and powers. By permitting groups the privilege of incorporation, the government grants a set of legal rights which makes much more effective organizations possible. The government may grant financial or other types of aid to groups, though so far as religious groups are concerned, there are constitutional limits on such assistance growing out of the establishment of religion clause in the Constitution which will be discussed in Chapter 29. Government assistance may also take the form of forbidding private individuals to interfere with the rights of persons who are members of groups or wish to form groups, or even require individuals to enter into legal relations with groups. Here we may recall, for example, the many regulations forbidding discrimination against racial groups or interference with the formation of labor unions, or requiring employers to bargain collectively with unions.

Finally, the government's interest in groups may take the form of restricting or forbidding them and of penalizing or punishing their members. Associations have power and resources; they are formed in fact because through them individuals can do things which they lack the power or resources to do as individuals. But groups may use their powers to injure other persons, or even members of their own groups. Corporations may form combinations in restraint of trade. Labor unions may wrongfully expel members and thus cause them to lose their jobs. "Hate organizations" may be formed to harass or discriminate against certain racial or religious groups. Subversive organizations may seek to undermine the authority of the government itself. Under these circumstances public regulation or control of group abuses will inevitably be forthcoming.

It is this third regulatory relationship which develops constitutional issues concerning freedom of association. During the past several decades the most controversial associational problems have arisen out of public concern about the activities of the Communist Party and its members, and most, though not all, of the recent constitutional decisions have involved the application of antisubversive legislation or measures.

For purposes of this analysis, government programs against group threats may be divided into two classes. In one the government seeks to discourage membership in the group or to limit the harm it may do by keeping its members out of posts of public importance. In the second the government goes further and seeks to punish membership in the group by criminal prosecution, or in extreme cases to declare the organization itself illegal. The first of these approaches will be examined in this chapter.

Non-Communist Oaths. In the Labor Management Relations Act of 1947, better known as the Taft-Hartley Act, Congress sought to discourage the selection of members of the Communist Party as officers of labor unions. Section 9 (h) of this act denied the protections and services of the act to any labor organization unless each of its officers filed an affidavit with the National Labor Relations Board "that he is not a member of the Communist Party or affiliated with such party, and that he does not believe in, and is not a member of or supports any organization that believes in or teaches, the overthrow of the United States Government by force or by any illegal or unconstitutional methods."

This statutory discrimination against members of the Communist Party was held in *American Communications Association* v. *Douds,* 339 U.S. 382 (1950), not to be an unconstitutional limitation on the freedom of beliefs and affiliations. The congressional purpose was to remove "political" strikes as an obstruction to interstate commerce. Congress was held to have such power under the commerce clause unless results were achieved which were forbidden by other provisions of the Constitution. Admittedly political freedoms were limited by the statute because its effect was to exert "pressures upon labor unions to deny positions of leadership to certain persons who are identified by particular beliefs and political affiliations." Normally, beliefs and affiliations are "irrelevant to permissible subjects of government action," but that does not mean that they are never relevant. Here the Court conceived that beliefs and affiliations bore a reasonable relation to the apprehended evil. The persons identified by the statute did not cause damage by speech, and it was not their speech that the statute sought to restrain, but rather their use of force through the political strike. "Speech may be fought with speech. . . . But force may and must be met with force."

Many states have required non-Communist oaths from their public employees.

A Los Angeles city ordinance requiring the filing of an affidavit by city employees that they were not and never had been members of the Communist Party was upheld in *Garner* v. *Board of Public Works*, 341 U.S. 716 (1951), Justice Frankfurter saying: "In the context of our time, such membership is sufficiently relevant to effective and dependable government, and to the confidence of the electorate in its government."

But shortly thereafter the Court made it clear that it was not endorsing the principle of guilt by association. In *Wieman* v. *Updegraff*, 344 U.S. 183 (1952), the justices unanimously invalidated an Oklahoma oath for state employees which, as interpreted by the state supreme court, adopted the guilt by association test. Persons who had been or still were members of proscribed organizations were to be excluded from the state service, regardless of their knowledge concerning the organizations to which they had belonged. Justice Clark said:

Under the Oklahoma Act, the fact of association alone determines disloyalty and disqualification; it matters not whether association existed innocently or knowingly. To thus inhibit individual freedom of movement is to stifle the flow of democratic expression and controversy at one of its chief sources. . . . Indiscriminate classification of innocent with knowing activity must fall as an assertion of arbitrary power. The oath offends due process.

Removal of Public Employees. Going beyond the non-Communist oath, many states and cities have provided for removal of public employees belonging to organizations regarded as subversive or dangerous. The New York law to this effect was upheld by the Supreme Court in *Adler* v. *Board of Education of City of New York*, 342 U.S. 485 (1952). The law required the school authorities to make a list of organizations found to advocate, advise, teach, or embrace the doctrine that the government should be overthrown by force or violence or any unlawful means. Membership of a schoolteacher in any such listed organization was "prima facie evidence for disqualification for appointment to or retention in" any school position.

Another rather common state action has been the removal of public employees who refuse to give information about alleged subversive associations, whether by taking the Fifth Amendment before a legislative committee or by some other method. In *Slochower* v. *Board of Higher Education of New York City*, 350 U.S. 551 (1956), a Brooklyn College professor had taken the Fifth Amendment before a Senate committee on all questions covering his political associations before 1941. His discharge was voided by the Supreme Court because the New York charter treated the claim of privilege as "a conclusive presumption of guilt." However, the Court indicated it would see no objection to discharge if the city authorities made their own independent investigation of an employee's "fitness."

This was precisely what happened in *Lerner* v. *Casey*, 357 U.S. 468 (1958), and *Beilan* v. *Board of Public Education*, 357 U.S. 399 (1958). Lerner refused to tell New York City authorities whether he was a member of the Communist Party, and was dismissed from his post as subway conductor as a person of "doubtful trust and reliability" because of his "lack of candor." Beilan, a public school teacher, refused to tell his superintendent whether he had held a certain position in the Communist Party in 1944, and later took the Fifth Amendment before a House committee; he was dismissed for "incompetency."

The Court majority upheld the official action in both cases, contending that the employees were not removed because of a Fifth Amendment plea (as in Slochower's case), or because of their beliefs or associations, or because they were security risks, but only because their refusal to answer questions put by their employers constituted evidence of their unreliability and incompetency.

The Court took an even stronger line in *Nelson and Globe* v. *County of Los Angeles*, 362 U.S. 1 (1960), upholding the dismissal of local California employees who had refused to answer a congressional committee's questions about alleged subversive activities. While the majority distinguished *Slochower* here, it seemed obvious that the *Slochower* principle had been abandoned. However, an Arkansas statute compelling teachers, as a condition of employment, to list every organization to which they had belonged or regularly contributed within the preceding five years was held in *Shelton* v. *Tucker*, 364 U.S. 479 (1960), to go far beyond any justifiable grounds in interference with "associational freedom."

Admission to the Bar. Several Supreme Court decisions have considered state refusal to admit to the bar candidates suspected of some kind of subversive association. In *Schware* v. *New Mexico Board of Bar Examiners*, 353 U.S. 232 (1957), a man who admitted membership in the Communist Party between 1932 and 1940 had been denied admission to the bar, but the Court unanimously reversed the state action. During that period the party was a lawful political organization on the ballot in many states, and the fact that some members might have had illegal aims did not permit an automatic inference "that all members shared their evil purposes or participated in their illegal conduct."

Konigsberg v. *State Bar of California*, 353 U.S. 252 (1957), involved a bar candidate who declined on constitutional grounds to discuss his political beliefs with the examining committee. There was some disagreement on the Supreme Court as to whether the examiners had barred him because of his non-co-operation, or because of negative findings as to character and loyalty. A five-judge majority adopted the latter explanation, and reversed the board's conclusion as contrary to the evidence.

Following this decision, the state bar committee again held hearings at which Konigsberg again refused to answer any questions relating to his alleged membership in the Communist Party. The committee refused to certify him, this time clearly on the ground that his refusals to answer had obstructed a full investigation into his qualifications. In the second *Konigsberg* case, 366 U.S. 36 (1961), the Supreme Court upheld the state action by a vote of five to four, on the ground that a state can require a bar applicant "to provide unprivileged answers to questions having a substantial relevance to his qualifications." In another case decided the same day, *In re Anastaplo*, 366 U.S. 82 (1961), the Court by the same division upheld the action of an Illinois bar committee in denying George Anastaplo admission to the bar. In Anastaplo's case there was never any suggestion from any source of Communist Party membership. He had simply taken a stand on principle against discussing his political beliefs with the examiners.

Disclosure of Membership Lists. One of the most significant decisions in the associational field, *National Association for the Advancement of Colored People* v. *Alabama*, 357 U.S. 449 (1958), grew out of the desegregation controversy in the South. Alabama, like other states, has a statute requiring out-of-state corporations to register and meet certain requirements before doing business in the state. The NAACP, organized under the laws of New York, had a regional office in Alabama, but considered itself exempt from the statute. Alabama officials brought court action in 1956 to enjoin the association from conducting business in the state, in the course of which the organization was ordered to produce its records, including names and addresses of all members in Alabama. The association filed the qualifying forms and produced all records except the membership lists, the disclosure of which it resisted on constitutional grounds. For this failure the organization was held in contempt and fined $100,000.

The Supreme Court unanimously ruled that compelled disclosure of the membership lists would abridge the rights of members to engage in lawful association in support of their common beliefs. For the association was able to make "an uncontroverted showing that on past occasions revelation of the identity of its rank-and-file members has exposed these members to economic reprisal, loss of employment, threat of physical coercion, and other manifestations of public hostility." The fact that it was "private community pressures" rather than state action which would penalize disclosure of membership was irrelevant. "The crucial factor is the interplay of governmental and private action. . . ." Alabama's announced purpose of determining whether the association was doing business in the state in violation of the foreign corporation registration act was not "a controlling justification for the deterrent effect on the free enjoyment of the right to associate which disclosure of membership lists is likely to have."

In *Bates v. City of Little Rock*, 361 U.S. 516 (1960), the Court unanimously invalidated a demand that city officials be furnished with a list of the members of a local branch of the NAACP. This information was called for under amendments to the occupation license tax ordinance, adopted in 1957, on the ground that it was necessary to determine whether the organization was subject to tax, but the Court ruled that there was no showing that production of the membership list bore any "reasonable relationship" to achievement of the governmental purpose of taxation.

ADLER v. BOARD OF EDUCATION OF CITY OF NEW YORK
342 U.S. 485, 72 S. Ct. 380, 96 L. Ed. 517 (1952)

Mr. Justice Minton delivered the opinion of the Court. . . .

Section 3022 of the Education Law, added by the Feinberg Law, provides that the Board of Regents, which has charge of the public school system in the State of New York, shall, after full notice and hearing, make a listing of organizations which it finds advocate, advise, teach, or embrace the doctrine that the government should be overthrown by force or violence or any other unlawful means, and that such listing may be amended and revised from time to time. . . .

The Board of Regents is further authorized to provide in rules and regulations, and has so provided, that membership in any listed organization, after notice and hearing, "shall constitute prima facie evidence for disqualification for appointment to or retention in any office or position in the school system"; but before one who is an employee or seeks employment is severed from or denied employment, he likewise must be given a full hearing with the privilege of being represented by counsel and the right to judicial review. It is § 12-a of the Civil Service Law, as implemented by the Feinberg Law as above indicated, that is under attack here.

It is first argued that the Feinberg Law and the rules promulgated thereunder constitute an abridgment of the freedom of speech and assembly of persons employed or seeking employment in the public schools of the State of New York.

It is clear that such persons have the right under our law to assemble, speak, think and believe as they will. *Communications Assn.* v. *Douds,* 339 U.S. 382. It is equally clear that they have no right to work for the State in the school system on their own terms. *United Public Workers* v. *Mitchell,* 330 U.S. 75. They may work for the school system upon the reasonable terms laid down by the proper authorities of New York. If they do not choose to work on such terms, they are at liberty to retain their beliefs and associations and go elsewhere. Has the State thus deprived them of any right to free speech or assembly? We think not. . . .

. . . It is rather subtly suggested that we should not follow our recent decision in *Garner* v. *Los Angeles Board,* 341 U.S. 716. We there said:

"We think that a municipal employer is not disabled because it is an agency of the State from inquiring of its employees as to matters that may prove relevant to their fitness and suitability for the public service. Past conduct may well relate to present fitness; past loyalty may have a reasonable relationship to present and future trust. Both are commonly inquired into in determining fitness for both high and low positions in private industry and are not less relevant in public employment." 341 U.S., at p. 720.

We adhere to that case. A teacher works in a sensitive area in a schoolroom. There he shapes the attitude of young minds towards the society in which they live. In this, the state has a vital concern. It must preserve the integrity of the schools. That the school authorities have the right and the duty to screen the officials, teachers, and employees as to their fitness to maintain the integrity of the schools as a part of ordered society, cannot be doubted. One's associates, past and present, as well as one's conduct, may properly be considered in determining fitness and loyalty. From time immemorial, one's reputation has been determined in part by the company he keeps. In the employment of officials and teachers of the school system, the state may very properly inquire into the company they keep, and we know of no rule, constitutional or otherwise, that prevents the state, when determining the fitness and loyalty of such persons, from considering the organizations and persons with whom they associate. . . .

It is next argued by appellants that the provision in § 3022 directing the Board of Regents to provide in rules and regulations that membership in any organization listed by the Board after notice and hearing, with provision for review in accordance with the statute, shall constitute prima facie evidence of disqualification, denies due process, because the fact found bears no relation to the fact presumed. In other words, from the fact found that the organization was one that advocated the overthrow of government by unlawful means and that the person employed or to be employed was a member of the organization and knew of its purpose, to presume that such member is disqualified for employment is so unreasonable as to be a denial of due process of law. We do not agree. . . .

Membership in a listed organization found to be within the statute and known by the member to be within the statute is a legislative finding that the member by his membership supports the thing the organization stands for, namely, the overthrow of government by unlawful means. We cannot say that such a finding is contrary to fact or that "generality of experience" points to a different conclusion. Disqualification follows therefore as a reasonable presumption from such membership and support. Nor is there here a problem of procedural due process. The presumption is not conclusive but arises only in a hearing where the person against whom it may arise has full opportunity to rebut it. . . .

We find no constitutional infirmity in § 12-a of the Civil Service Law of New York or in the Feinberg Law which implemented it, and the judgment is

Affirmed.

Mr. Justice Black, dissenting.

While I fully agree with the dissent of Mr. Justice Douglas, the importance of this holding prompts me to add these thoughts.

This is another of those rapidly multiplying legislative enactments which make it dangerous—this time for school teachers—to think or say anything except what a transient majority happen to approve at the moment. Basically these laws rest on the belief that government should supervise and limit the flow of ideas into the minds of men. The tendency of such governmental policy is to mould people into a common intellectual pattern. Quite a different governmental policy rests on the belief that government should leave the mind and spirit of man absolutely free. Such a governmental policy encourages varied intellectual outlooks in the belief that the best views will prevail. This policy of freedom is in my judgment embodied in the First Amendment and made applicable to the states by the Fourteenth. Because of this policy public officials cannot be constitutionally vested with powers to select the ideas people can think about, censor the public views they can express, or choose the persons or groups people can associate with. Public officials with such powers are not public servants; they are public masters.

I dissent from the Court's judgment sustaining this law which effectively penalizes school teachers for their thoughts and their associates.

Mr. Justice Frankfurter, dissenting.

We are asked to pass on a scheme to counteract what are currently called "subversive" influences in the public school system of New York. The scheme is formulated partly in statutes and partly in administrative regulations, but all of it is still an unfinished blueprint. We are asked to adjudicate claims against its constitutionality before the scheme has been put into operation, before the limits that it imposes upon free inquiry and association, the scope of scrutiny that it sanctions, and the procedural safeguards that will be found to be implied for its enforcement have been authoritatively defined. I think we should adhere to the teaching of this Court's history to avoid constitutional adjudications on merely abstract or speculative issues and to base them on the concreteness afforded by an actual, present, defined controversy, appropriate for judicial judgment, between adversaries immediately affected by it. In accordance with the settled limits upon our jurisdiction I would dismiss this appeal. . . .

Mr. Justice Douglas, with whom Mr. Justice Black concurs, dissenting.

I have not been able to accept the recent doctrine that a citizen who enters the public service can be forced to sacrifice his civil rights. I cannot for example find in our constitutional scheme the power of a state to place its employees in the category of second-class citizens by denying them freedom of thought and expression. The Constitution guarantees freedom of thought and expression to everyone in our society. All are entitled to it; and none needs it more than the teacher.

The public school is in most respects the cradle of our democracy. The increasing role of the public school is seized upon by proponents of the type of legislation represented by New York's Feinberg law as proof of the importance and need for keeping the school free of "subversive influences." But that is to misconceive the effect of this type of legislation. Indeed the impact of this kind of censorship on the public school system illustrates the high purpose of the First Amendment in freeing speech and thought from censorship.

The present law proceeds on a principle repugnant to our society—guilt by association. A teacher is disqualified because of her membership in an organization found to be "subversive." The finding as to the "subversive" character of the organization is made in a proceeding to which the teacher is not a party and in which it is not clear that she may even be heard. To be sure, she may have a hearing when charges of disloyalty are leveled against her. But in that hearing the finding as to the "subversive" character of the organization apparently may not be reopened in order to allow her to show the truth of the matter. The irrebuttable charge that the organization is "subversive" therefore hangs as an ominous cloud over her own hearing. The mere fact of membership in the organization raises a prima facie case of her own guilt. She may, it is said, show her innocence. But innocence in this case turns on knowledge; and when the witch hunt is on, one who must rely on ignorance leans on a feeble reed.

The very threat of such a procedure is certain to raise havoc with academic freedom. Youthful indiscretions, mistaken causes, misguided enthusiasms—all long forgotten— become the ghosts of a harrowing present. Any organization committed to a liberal cause, any group organized to revolt against an hysterical trend, any committee launched to sponsor an unpopular program becomes suspect. These are the organizations into which Communists often infiltrate. Their presence infects the whole, even though the project was not conceived in sin. A teacher caught in that mesh is almost certain to stand condemned. Fearing condemnation, she will tend to shrink from any association that stirs controversy. In that manner freedom of expression will be stifled.

But that is only part of it. Once a teacher's connection with a listed organization is shown, her views become subject to scrutiny to determine whether her membership in the organization is innocent or, if she was formerly a member, whether she has *bona fide* abandoned her membership.

The law inevitably turns the school system into a spying project. Regular loyalty reports on the teachers must be made out. The principals become detectives; the students, the parents, the community become informers. Ears are cocked for tell-tale signs of disloyalty. The prejudices of the community come into play in searching out the disloyal. This is not the usual type of supervision which checks a teacher's competency; it is a system which searches for hidden meanings in a teacher's utterances.

What was the significance of the reference of the art teacher to socialism? Why was the history teacher so openly hostile to Franco Spain? Who heard overtones of revolution in the English teacher's discussion of the Grapes of Wrath? What was behind the praise of Soviet progress in metallurgy in the chemistry class? Was it not "subversive" for the teacher to cast doubt on the wisdom of the venture in Korea?

What happens under this law is typical of what happens in a police state. Teachers are under constant surveillance; their pasts are combed for signs of disloyalty; their utterances are watched for clues to dangerous thoughts. A pall is cast over the classrooms. There can be no real academic freedom in that environment. Where suspicion fills the air and holds scholars in line for fear of their jobs, there can be no exercise of the free intellect. Supineness and dogmatism take the place of inquiry. A "party line"—as dangerous as the "party line" of the Communists—lays hold. It is the "party line" of the orthodox view, of the conventional thought, of the accepted approach. A problem can no longer be pursued with impunity to its edges. Fear stalks the classroom. The teacher is no longer a stimulant to adventurous thinking; she becomes instead a pipe line for safe and sound information. A deadening dogma takes the place of free inquiry. Instruction tends to become sterile; pursuit of knowledge is discouraged; discussion often leaves off where it should begin.

This, I think, is what happens when a censor looks over a teacher's shoulder. This system of spying and surveillance with its accompanying reports and trials cannot go hand in hand with academic freedom. It produces standardized thought, not the pursuit of truth. Yet it was the pursuit of truth which the First Amendment was designed to protect. A system which directly or inevitably has that effect is alien to our system and should be struck down. Its survival is a real threat to our way of life. We need be bold and adventuresome in our thinking to survive. A school system producing students trained as robots threatens to rob a generation of the versatility that has been perhaps our greatest distinction. The Framers knew the danger of dogmatism; they also knew the strength that comes when the mind is free, when ideas may be pursued wherever they lead. We forget these teachings of the First Amendment when we sustain this law.

Of course the school systems of the country need not become cells for Communist activities; and the classrooms need not become forums for propagandizing the Marxist creed. But the guilt of the teacher should turn on overt acts. So long as she is a law-abiding citizen, so long as her performance within the public school system meets professional standards, her private life, her political philosophy, her social creed should not be the cause of reprisals against her.

SHELTON v. TUCKER
364 U.S. 479, 81 S. Ct. 247, 5 L. Ed. 2d 231 (1960)

Mr. Justice Stewart delivered the opinion of the Court.

An Arkansas statute compels every teacher, as a condition of employment in a State supported school or college, to file annually an affidavit listing without limitation every organization to which he has belonged or regularly contributed within the preceding five years. At issue in these two cases is the validity of that statute under the Fourteenth Amendment to the Constitution. . . . The statute in question is Act 10 of the Second Extraordinary Session of the Arkansas General Assembly of 1958. . . .

These provisions must be considered against the existing system of teacher employment required by Arkansas law. Teachers there are hired on a year-to-year basis. They are not covered by a civil service system, and they have no job security beyond the end of each school year. The closest approach to tenure is a statutory provision for the automatic renewal of a teacher's contract if he is not notified within ten days after the end of a school year that the contract has not been renewed. . . .

I.

It is urged here, as it was unsuccessfully urged throughout the proceedings in both the Federal and State courts, that Act 10 deprives teachers in Arkansas of their rights to personal, associational, and academic liberty, protected by the Due Process Clause of the Fourteenth Amendment from invasion by state action. In considering this contention, we deal with two basic postulates.

First. There can be no doubt of the right of a state to investigate the competence and fitness of those whom it hires to teach in its schools, as this Court before now has had occasion to recognize. "A teacher works in a sensitive area in a schoolroom. There he shapes the attitude of young minds towards the society in which they live. In this, the state has a vital concern." *Adler v. Board of Education,* 342 U.S. 485, 493. There is "no requirement in the Federal Constitution that a teacher's classroom conduct be the sole basis for determining his fitness. Fitness for teaching depends on a broad range of factors." *Beilan* v. *Board of Education,* 357 U.S. 399, 406.

This controversy is thus not of a pattern with such cases as *N.A.A.C.P.* v. *Alabama,* 357 U.S. 449, and *Bates* v. *Little Rock,* 361 U.S. 516. In those cases the Court held that there was no substantially relevant correlation between the governmental interest asserted and the state's effort to compel disclosure of the membership lists involved. Here, by contrast, there can be no question of the relevance of a state's inquiry into the fitness and competence of its teachers.

Second. It is not disputed that to compel a teacher to disclose his every associational tie is to impair that teacher's right of free association, a right closely allied to freedom of speech and a right which, like free speech, lies at the foundation of a free society. . . . Such interference with personal freedom is conspicuously accented when the teacher serves at the absolute will of those to whom the disclosure must be made—those who any year can terminate the teacher's employment without bringing charges, without notice, without a hearing, without affording an opportunity to explain.

The statute does not provide that the information it requires be kept confidential. Each school board is left free to deal with the information as it wishes. The record contains evidence to indicate that fear of public disclosure is neither theoretical nor groundless. Even if there were no disclosure to the general public, the pressure upon a teacher to avoid any ties which might displease those who control his professional destiny would be constant and heavy. Public exposure, bringing with it the possibility of public pressures upon school boards to discharge teachers who belong to unpopular or minority organizations, would simply operate to widen and aggravate the impairment of constitutional liberty.

The vigilant protection of constitutional freedoms is nowhere more vital than in the community of American schools. "By limiting the power of the States to interfere with freedom of speech and freedom of inquiry and freedom of association, the Fourteenth Amendment protects all persons, no matter what their calling. But, in view of the nature of the teacher's relation to the effective exercise of the rights which are safeguarded by the Bill of Rights and by the Fourteenth Amendment, inhibition of freedom of thought, and of action upon thought, in the case of teachers brings the safeguards of those amendments vividly into operation. Such unwarranted inhibition upon the free spirit of teachers . . . has an unmistakable tendency to chill that free play of the spirit which all teachers ought especially to cultivate and practice; it makes for caution and timidity in their associations by potential teachers." *Wieman* v. *Updegraff,* 344 U.S. 183, 195 (concurring opinion). "Scholarship cannot flourish in an atmosphere of suspicion and distrust. Teachers and students must always remain free to inquire, to study and to evaluate. . . ." *Sweezy* v. *New Hampshire,* 354 U.S. 234, 250.

II.

The question to be decided here is not whether the State of Arkansas can ask certain of its teachers about all their organizational relationships. It is not whether the State can ask all of its teachers about certain of their associational ties. It is not whether teachers can be asked how many organizations they belong to, or how much time they spend in organizational activity. The question is whether the State can ask every one of its teachers to disclose every single organization with which he has been associated over a five-year period. The scope of the inquiry required by Act 10 is completely unlimited. The statute requires a teacher to reveal the church to which he belongs, or to which he has given financial support. It requires him to disclose his political party, and every political organization to which he may have contributed over a five-year period. It requires him to list, without number, every conceivable kind of associational tie—social, professional, political, avocational, or religious. Many such relationships could have no possible bearing upon the teacher's occupational competence or fitness.

In a series of decisions this Court has held that, even though the governmental purpose be legitimate and substantial, that purpose cannot be pursued by means that broadly stifle fundamental personal liberties when the end can be more narrowly achieved. The breadth of legislative abridgement must be viewed in the light of less drastic means for achieving the same basic purpose.

In *Lovell* v. *Griffin*, 303 U.S. 444, the Court invalidated an ordinance prohibiting all distribution of literature at any time or place in Griffin, Georgia, without a license, pointing out that so broad an interference was unnecessary to accomplish legitimate municipal aims. In *Schneider* v. *State*, 308 U.S. 147, the Court dealt with ordinances of four different municipalities which either banned or imposed prior restraints upon the distribution of handbills. In holding the ordinances invalid, the Court noted that where legislative abridgment of "fundamental personal rights and liberties" is asserted, "the courts should be astute to examine the effect of the challenged legislation. Mere legislative preferences or beliefs respecting matters of public convenience may well support regulation directed at other personal activities, but be insufficient to justify such as diminishes the exercise of rights so vital to the maintenance of democratic institutions." 308 U.S., at 161. In *Cantwell* v. *Connecticut*, 310 U.S. 296, the Court said that "conduct remains subject to regulation for the protection of society," but pointed out that in each case "the power to regulate must be so exercised as not, in attaining a permissible end, unduly to infringe the protected freedom." . . .

As recently as last Term we held invalid an ordinance prohibiting the distribution of handbills because the breadth of its application went far beyond what was necessary to achieve a legitimate governmental purpose. *Talley* v. *California*, 362 U.S. 60. In that case the Court noted that it had been "urged that this ordinance is aimed at providing a way to identify those responsible for fraud, false advertising and libel. Yet the ordinance is in no manner so limited. . . . Therefore we do not pass on the validity of an ordinance limited to prevent these or any other supposed evils. This ordinance simply bars all handbills under all circumstances anywhere that do not have the names and addresses printed on them in the place the ordinance requires." 362 U.S., at 64.

The unlimited and indiscriminate sweep of the statute now before us brings it within the ban of our prior cases. The statute's comprehensive interference with associational freedom goes far beyond what might be justified in the exercise of the State's legitimate inquiry into the fitness and competency of its teachers. The judgments in both cases must be reversed.

It is so ordered.

Mr. Justice Frankfurter, dissenting.

As one who has strong views against crude intrusions by the state into the atmosphere of creative freedom in which alone the spirit and mind of a teacher can fruitfully function, I may find displeasure with the Arkansas legislation now under review. But in maintaining the distinction between private views and constitutional restrictions, I am constrained to find that it does not exceed the permissible range of state action limited by the Fourteenth Amendment. By way of emphasis I therefore add a few words to the dissent of Mr. Justice Harlan, in which I concur.

It is essential, at the outset, to establish what is not involved in this litigation:

(1) As the Court recognizes, this is not a case where, as in *N.A.A.C.P.* v. *Alabama*,

357 U.S. 449, and *Bates* v. *Little Rock,* 361 U.S. 516, a State, asserting the power to compel disclosure of organizational affiliations, can show no rational relation between disclosure and a governmental interest justifying it. Those cases are relevant here only because of their recognition that an interest in privacy, in non-disclosure, may under appropriate circumstances claim constitutional protection. The question here is whether that interest is overborne by a countervailing public interest. To this concrete, limited question—whether the State's interest in knowing the nature of the organizational activities of teachers employed by it or by institutions which it supports, as a basis for appraising the fitness of those teachers for the positions which they hold, outweighs the interest recognized in *N.A.A.C.P.* and *Bates*—those earlier decisions themselves give no answer.

(2) The Court's holding that the Arkansas statute is unconstitutional does not, apparently, rest upon the threat that the information which it requires of teachers will be revealed to the public. In view of the opinion of the Supreme Court of Arkansas, decision here could not, I believe, turn on a claim that the teachers' affidavits will not remain confidential. . . .

(3) This is not a case in which *Lovell* v. *Griffin,* 303 U.S. 444; *Cantwell* v. *Connecticut,* 310 U.S. 296; *Saia* v. *New York,* 334 U.S. 558; and *Kunz* v. *New York,* 340 U.S. 290, call for condemnation of the "breadth" of the statute. Those decisions struck down licensing laws which vested in administrative officials a power of censorship over communications not confined within standards designed to curb the dangers of arbitrary or discriminatory official action. The "breadth" with which the cases were concerned was the breadth of unrestricted discretion left to a censor, which permitted him to make his own subjective opinions the practically unreviewable measure of permissible speech. Nor is this a case of the nature of *Thornhill* v. *Alabama,* 310 U.S. 88, and *Herndon* v. *Lowry,* 301 U.S. 242, involving penal statutes which the Court found impermissibly "broad" in quite another sense. Prohibiting, indiscriminately, activity within and without the sphere of the Fourteenth Amendment's protection of free expression, those statutes had the double vice of deterring the exercise of constitutional freedoms by making the uncertain line of the Amendment's application determinative of criminality and of prescribing indefinite standards of guilt, thereby allowing the potential vagaries and prejudices of juries, effectively insulated against control by reviewing courts, the power to intrude upon the protected sphere. The statute challenged in the present cases involves neither administrative discretion to censor nor vague, overreaching tests of criminal responsibility. . . .

In the present case the Court strikes down an Arkansas statute requiring that teachers disclose to school officials all of their organizational relationships, on the ground that "many such relationships could have no possible bearing upon the teacher's occupational competence or fitness." Granted that a given teacher's membership in the First Street Congregation is, standing alone, of little relevance to what may rightly be expected of a teacher, is that membership equally irrelevant when it is discovered that the teacher is in fact a member of the First Street Congregation *and* the Second Street Congregation *and* the Third Street Congregation *and* the 4-H Club *and* the 3-H Club *and* half a dozen other groups? Presumably, a teacher may have so many divers associations, so many divers commitments, that they consume his time and energy and interest at the expense of his work or even of his professional dedication. Unlike wholly individual interests, organizational connections—because they involve obligations undertaken with relation to other persons—may become inescapably demanding and distracting. Surely, a school board is entitled to inquire whether any of its teachers has placed himself, or is placing himself, in a condition where his work may suffer. Of course, the State might ask: "To how many organizations do you belong?" or "How much time do you expend at organizational activity?" But the answer to such questions could reasonably be regarded by a state legislature as insufficient, both because the veracity of the answer is more difficult to test, in cases where doubts as to veracity may arise, than in the case of the answers required by the Arkansas statute, and because an estimate of time presently spent in organizational activity reveals nothing as to the quality and nature of that activity, upon the basis of which, necessarily, judgment or prophesy of the extent of future involvement must be based. A teacher's answers to the questions which Arkansas asks, moreover, may serve the purpose of making known to school authorities persons who come into contact with the teacher in all of the phases of his activity in the community, and who can be questioned, if need be, concerning the teacher's conduct in matters which this Court can certainly not now say are lacking in any pertinence to professional fitness. It is difficult to understand how these particular ends could be achieved by asking "certain of [the State's] teachers about all their organizational relationships," or "all of its teachers about certain of their associational ties," or all of its teachers how many associations currently involve them, or during how many hours; and difficult, therefore, to appreciate why the Court deems unreasonable and forbids what Arkansas does ask.

If I dissent from the Court's disposition in these cases, it is not that I put a low value on academic freedom. . . . It is because that very freedom, in its most creative reaches, is dependent in no small part upon the careful and discriminating selection of teachers. This process of selection is an intricate affair, a matter of fine judgment, and if it is to be informed, it must be based upon a comprehensive range of information. I am unable to say, on the face of this statute, that Arkansas could not reasonably find that the information which the statute requires—and which may not be otherwise acquired than by asking the question which it asks—is germane to that selection. Nor, on this record, can I attribute to the State a purpose to employ the enactment as a device for the accomplishment of what is constitutionally forbidden. Of course, if the information gathered by the required affidavits is used to further a scheme of terminating the employment of teachers solely because of their membership in unpopular organizations, that use will run afoul of the Fourteenth Amendment. It will be time enough, if such use is made, to hold the application of the statute unconstitutional. See *Yick Wo* v. *Hopkins,* 118 U.S. 356. Because I do not find that the disclosure of teachers' associations to their school boards is, without more, such a restriction upon their liberty, or upon that of the community, as to overbalance the State's interest in asking the question, I would affirm the judgments below.

I am authorized to say that Mr. Justice Clark, Mr. Justice Harlan and Mr. Justice Whittaker agree with this opinion.

Mr. Justice Harlan, whom Mr. Justice Frankfurter, Mr. Justice Clark and Mr. Justice Whittaker join, dissenting.

Of course this decision has a natural tendency to enlist support, involving as it does an unusual statute that touches constitutional rights whose protection in the context of the racial situation in various parts of the country demands the unremitting vigilance of the courts. Yet that very circumstance also serves to remind of the restraints that attend constitutional adjudication. It must be emphasized that neither of these cases actually presents an issue of racial discrimination. The statute on its face applies to *all* Arkansas teachers irrespective of race, and there is no showing that it has been discriminatorily administered.

The issue is whether, consistently with the Fourteenth Amendment, a State may require teachers in its public schools or colleges to disclose, as a condition precedent to their initial or continued employment, all organizations to which they have belonged, paid dues, or contributed within the past five years. Since I believe that such a requirement cannot be said to transgress the constitutional limits of a State's conceded authority to determine the qualifications of those serving it as teachers, I am bound to consider that Arkansas had the right to pass the statute in question, and therefore conceive it my duty to dissent. . . .

Chapter 27

SUBVERSIVE ASSOCIATIONS

The most serious test of the American doctrine of freedom of association has been that presented by the Communist Party since the Russian Revolution established a basis for its world-wide operations. The Supreme Court's introduction to the interpretation of statutes imposing criminal punishment on radicals came during and immediately after World War I, involving the Espionage Act of 1917 and the Sedition Act of 1918. The most significant of these wartime decisions, the *Abrams* and *Schenck* cases, have already been commented on, and the ineffectiveness of the clear and present danger test, first developed in these cases, has been noted.

The passing of the wartime hysteria and the repeal of the Sedition Act in 1921 largely terminated federal prosecutions. But many of the states had legislation on the books aimed at radicals of various sorts. Some of these laws had been passed after the assassination of President McKinley in 1901 by an anarchist, and were directed at "criminal anarchy" or "criminal syndicalism." It was a New York statute of this sort which was involved in *Gitlow* v. *New York,* 268 U.S. 652 (1925). Gitlow, a Communist, was business manager of the Party paper in which a "manifesto" was published containing typical Communist language about the necessity of accomplishing the Communist revolution through class struggle, general strikes, and the power of the proletariat. Gitlow was convicted of criminal anarchy on the basis of this publication, and the Supreme Court upheld the conviction, though in the process it made the startling and unexpected concession that First Amendment freedoms were effective against the states.

Thus the *Gitlow* case opened the way for Supreme Court review of all state laws under which political radicals were convicted, and the 1930s found the Court using this power to formulate some significant new standards to control state action. In three important decisions—*Stromberg* v. *California,* 283 U.S. 359 (1931), *DeJonge* v. *Oregon,* 299 U.S. 353 (1937), and *Herndon* v. *Lowry,* 301 U.S. 242 (1937)—the convictions of admitted Communists were reversed. Miss Stromberg had raised a red flag every morning at a children's summer camp. DeJonge had addressed a public meeting called by the Communist Party to protest police violence against strikers. Herndon was a Communist organizer in Georgia who possessed inflammatory literature addressed to Negroes.

The most significant feature of these decisions was the insistence of the Court that conviction must be for personal guilt and not on the basis of guilt by association. Miss Stromberg's Communist affiliations were ignored. In the DeJonge affair, the objectives of the Communist Party, to which the state courts had devoted a great deal of attention, were set aside as irrelevant, Chief Justice Hughes saying: "Notwithstanding those objectives, the defendant still enjoyed his personal right of free speech and to take part in a peaceable assembly having a lawful purpose, although called by that Party." As for Herndon, convicted for holding recruiting meetings for the Communist Party and possessing Party literature, Justice Roberts ruled there was no evidence that he used inciting language in his meetings. As for the incendiary literature, the proof wholly failed to show that he had read these documents, approved of them, or distributed them.

Thus this series of cases gave considerable support for associative freedom as applied to members of the Communist Party. Gitlow was held guilty of issuing a publication with a forbidden and illegal purpose, but Stromberg, DeJonge, and Herndon, judged on their own actions, and not on the basis of motives which might be imputed to them because of their membership in the Communist Party, were within the protection of the Constitution.

The one exception to the rule of no guilt by association was the case of *Whitney* v. *California*, 274 U.S. 357 (1927). Miss Whitney's crime, under the California Syndicalism Act, was that she participated, without protest, in the convention which set up the Communist Labor party of California, and was elected a member of its state executive committee. She testified that it was not her purpose that this party should be an instrument of terrorism or violence, but the party was found to have been formed to teach criminal syndicalism, and as a member of the party she participated in the crime. Justices Brandeis and Holmes protested that Miss Whitney was being convicted for "association with those who propose to preach" criminal syndicalism, but because of certain errors made by the defense concurred in the Court's judgment.

In more recent times, the most famous of the anti-Communist measures has been the Alien Registration Act of 1940, better known as the Smith Act. Actually alien registration was only one of the five purposes of the act. Its major importance was as a peacetime sedition act, the first federal peacetime restrictions on speaking and writing by American citizens since the ill-fated Sedition Act of 1798. Section 2 of the statute made it unlawful knowingly to advocate or teach the overthrow of any government in the United States by force or violence, to print or distribute written matter so advocating, or to organize or knowingly become a member of any group which so advocates. Section 3 made punishable conspiracy to accomplish any of these ends.

The act did not mention the Communist Party by name, but there can be no doubt that the framers of the statute believed the party advocated force and violence and intended the act to apply to it and its members. The Supreme Court, however, was initially less clear on this point. On two noteworthy occasions shortly after the Smith Act was passed, the Court refused to proceed on such an assumption. In *Schneiderman* v. *United States*, 320 U.S. 118 (1943), the Court voided the government's effort to cancel the naturalization of an admitted Communist, on the ground that it had not been proved that a Communist necessarily believed in force and violence. In *Bridges* v. *Wixon*, 326 U.S. 135 (1945), deportation proceedings against Harry Bridges, a labor leader, were nullified on the ground that his cooperation with the Communist Party had been in the attainment of legitimate trade union goals.

The first important use of the Smith Act came in 1948 when eleven leaders of the American Communist Party were indicted in New York. The indictment made two charges against them: (1) willfully and knowingly conspiring to organize as the United States Communist Party a society, group, and assembly of persons who teach and advocate the overthrow and destruction of the government of the United States by force and violence, and (2) knowingly and willfully advocating and teaching the duty and necessity of overthrowing and destroying the government by force and violence. No overt revolutionary acts other than teaching and advocating were alleged.

The trial of the case was full of sensations and lasted for nine months. The ultimate conviction was upheld by the court of appeals, Chief Judge Learned Hand writing the opinion. The Supreme Court then granted certiorari limited to questions of the constitutionality of the Smith Act, "inherently or as construed and applied in the instant case." By a vote of six to two, with Chief Justice Vinson writing the opinion, the Court confirmed the convictions in *Dennis* v. *United States*, 341 U.S. 494 (1951).

By limiting the grant of certiorari, the Court had cut itself off from consideration of the evidence relied on to prove the alleged conspiracy. Actually the government's case was a most peculiar one. The evidence presented at the trial was primarily concerned with what was in the basic texts of Marxism-Leninism extending all the way back to 1848, as distributed by the Communist Party and discussed at their meetings. The guilt of the Communist leaders was established by connecting them with the organization of the Party and the teaching of these texts. By allowing the validity of convictions based on such textual analysis to be established by default, the Supreme Court permitted the assumption that it had accepted the principle of guilt by association. Illegal conspiracy could be established by demonstrating activities—any kind of activities—in furtherance of the organizational work of the Communist Party.

The *Dennis* decision encouraged the government to bring similar prosecutions, based on similar evidence, against the lesser Party leaders throughout the country. The government was almost uniformly successful in these subsidiary suits, in none of which did the Supreme Court grant certiorari until October, 1955, when it agreed to review the conviction of fourteen California Communists. This time no limitation was imposed on the grant of certiorari, and the result was the shattering decision in *Yates* v. *United States*, 354 U.S. 298 (1957). By a vote of six to one the Court, while not challenging the constitutionality of the Smith Act as established by the *Dennis* decision, reversed the convictions of five of the fourteen defendants and laid down conditions for Smith Act trials which made it much more difficult to secure any future convictions.

Justice Harlan, writing the majority decision, concerned himself with three main issues. First, he held that when the Smith Act made it unlawful to "organize" a group advocating overthrow of the government by force and violence, it referred to the initial formation of the group, not to continuing organizational activities. On this basis the Communist Party had been "organized" in 1945, and consequently the three-year statute of limitations would outlaw a prosecution begun in 1951.

Harlan's second point was that the trial judge's instructions to the jury did not adequately distinguish between "advocacy of abstract doctrine and advocacy directed at promoting unlawful action." He restated the Court's holding in the *Dennis* case, completely abandoning any reliance on the clear and present danger test. The problem of the prosecution in both cases was to prove advocacy directed at promoting unlawful action. The *Dennis* ruling, said Harlan, was not based on any contention that "the defendants' advocacy was directed at, or created any danger of, immediate overthrow." Rather, "it did establish that the advocacy was aimed at building up a seditious group and maintaining it in readiness for action at a propitious time." Harlan continued:

The essence of the *Dennis* holding was that indoctrination of a group in preparation for future violent action, as well as exhortation to immediate action, by advocacy found to be directed to "action for the accomplishment" of forcible overthrow, to violence "as a rule or principle of action," and employing "language of incitement" . . . is not constitutionally protected when the group is of sufficient size and cohesiveness, is sufficiently oriented towards action, and other circumstances are such as reasonably to justify apprehension that action will occur.

As so interpreted, *Dennis* provided a clear contrast to the view of the *Yates* trial judge that "mere doctrinal justification of forcible overthrow, if engaged in with the intent to accomplish overthrow, is punishable *per se* under the Smith Act." That sort of advocacy, Harlan concluded, "even though uttered with the hope that it may ultimately lead to violent revolution, is too remote from concrete action to be regarded as the kind of indoctrination preparatory to action which was condemned in *Dennis*." Consequently, the trial judge's charge to the jury furnished it "wholly inadequate guidance" on the central point in the case and supplied a second reason why the convictions could not be allowed to stand.

Third, Harlan looked at the evidence on which the convictions had been secured. There had to be in the record some evidence of "Party advocacy or teaching in the sense of a call to forcible action at some future time." The government's theory was that the Marxist-Leninist texts which it offered in evidence demonstrated the conspiratorial character of the Communist Party, and that conspiracy on the part of the defendants was proved by then connecting them with the Party. But Harlan insisted that the Party's advocacy of forcible action had to be shown by acts, not by texts. On this basis five of the defendants were completely cleared, since there was no evidence in the record to connect them with the conspiracy except their membership in the Communist Party of California.

As for the other nine defendants, the Court was not prepared to go so far. There was evidence involving them—Party classes, an "underground apparatus," board meetings held in a devious and conspiratorial manner—which might meet the Court's tests. Consequently new trials were ordered for these defendants.

The Black-Douglas dissents in the *Dennis* case were partially vindicated by the *Yates* decision, though again in *Yates* Black and Douglas found themselves in disagreement with the majority decision. While concurring in the result, they would have held the Smith Act completely unconstitutional and directed the acquittal of all defendants. In fact, this latter result was achieved six months later when the Department of Justice "reluctantly" requested the trial court to dismiss the indictments against the remaining nine defendants on the ground that "the evidentiary requirements laid down by the Supreme Court" could not be satisfied. Also on the basis of the *Yates* ruling, all pending indictments under section 3 were dismissed and all convictions under appeal were reversed.

Efforts to secure a Supreme Court ruling on section 2 of the Smith Act, which makes unlawful mere membership in a group advocating forcible overthrow of the government, did not succeed until 1961. The government had apparently regarded the constitutionality of section 2 as more doubtful than section 3, and did not bring any prosecutions under section 2 until after the *Dennis* decision had cleared section 3. Initial convictions in two section 2 cases were reversed by the Supreme Court in 1957 after a government confession of procedural error (*Scales* v. *United States*, 355 U.S. 1; *Lightfoot* v. *United States*, 355 U.S. 2). However, in *Scales* v. *United States*, 367 U.S. 203 (1961), the Court by a five to four vote held that a person who was a "knowing," "active" member of a subversive group, and who personally had a "specific intent to bring about violent overthrow," could be convicted under section 2 without raising any First Amendment questions. In a second case decided the same day, *Noto* v. *United States*, 367 U.S. 290 (1961), the Court ruled that the government had not proved the kind of advocacy necessary to meet the tests laid down in the *Scales* case.

The registration provisions of the Internal Security Act of 1950, as applied to the Communist Party, were upheld after a long delay in 1961. Under this act Communist organizations were ordered to register with the Attorney General, and a Subversive Activities Control Board was established to determine which organizations should be required to register. On registration, organizations must disclose names and addresses of officers and give an accounting of sources of funds and expenditures. Among the sanctions incurred by a registered organization are the following: Its mail and radio broadcasts must be identified as Communist propaganda; members may not hold nonelective federal positions; they commit a crime if they apply for or use a United States passport; and their right to work in defense plants is limited.

The initial order requiring the Communist Party to register was reversed by the Supreme Court in 1956 because the "professional informers" used by the government had been charged with perjury (*Communist Party* v. *Subversive Activities Control Board*, 351 U.S. 115). In the 1961 decision, 367 U.S. 1, the Court held only that the registration requirement did not violate the First Amendment by forced disclosure of members' names. The Court did not rule on the claim that registration would constitute forced self-incrimination in violation of the Fifth Amendment. Nor did it rule on the validity of any of the sanctions provided by the act for members of registered organizations, holding that it would be premature to consider these matters until the sanctions were actually applied to the Party or its members.

DENNIS v. UNITED STATES
341 U.S. 494, 71 S. Ct. 857, 95 L. Ed. 1137 (1951)

Mr. Chief Justice Vinson announced the judgment of the Court and an opinion in which Mr. Justice Reed, Mr. Justice Burton and Mr. Justice Minton join. . . .

The indictment charged the petitioners with wilfully and knowingly conspiring (1) to organize as the Communist Party of the United States of America a society, group and assembly of persons who teach and advocate the overthrow and destruction of the Government of the United States by force and violence, and (2) knowingly and wilfully to advocate and teach the duty and necessity of overthrowing and destroying the Government of the United States by force and violence. The indictment further alleged that § 2 of the Smith Act proscribes these acts and that any conspiracy to take such action is a violation of § 3 of the Act.

The trial of the case extended over nine months, six of which were devoted to the taking of evidence, resulting in a record of 16,000 pages. Our limited grant of the writ of certiorari has removed from our consideration any question as to the sufficiency of the evidence to support the jury's determination that petitioners are guilty of the offense charged. Whether on this record petitioners did in fact advocate the overthrow of the Government by force and violence is not before us, and we must base any discussion of this point upon the conclusions stated in the opinion of the Court of Appeals, which treated the issue in great detail. That court held that the record in this case amply supports the necessary finding of the jury that petitioners, the leaders of the Communist Party in this country, were unwilling to work within our framework of democracy, but intended to initiate a violent revolution whenever the propitious occasion appeared. . . .

The obvious purpose of the statute is to protect existing Government, not from change by peaceable, lawful and constitutional means, but from change by violence, revolution and terrorism. That it is within the *power* of the Congress to protect the Government of the United States from armed rebellion is a proposition which requires little discussion. Whatever theoretical merit there may be to the argument that there is a "right" to rebellion against dictatorial governments is without force where the existing structure of the government provides for peaceful and orderly change. We reject any principle of governmental helplessness in the face of preparation for revolution, which principle, carried to its logical conclusion, must lead to anarchy. No one could conceive that it is not within the power of Congress to prohibit acts intended to overthrow the Government by force and violence. The question with which we are concerned here is not whether Congress has such *power,* but whether the *means* which it has employed conflict with the First and Fifth Amendments to the Constitution.

One of the bases for the contention that the means which Congress has employed are invalid takes the form of an attack on the face of the statute on the grounds that by its terms it prohibits academic discussion of the merits of Marxism-Leninism, that it stifles ideas and is contrary to all concepts of a free speech and a free press. Although we do not agree that the language itself has that significance, we must bear in mind that it is the duty of the federal courts to interpret federal legislation in a manner not inconsistent with the demands of the Constitution. *American Communications Assn.* v. *Douds,* 339 U.S. 382, 407 (1950). . . .

The very language of the Smith Act negates the interpretation which petitioners would have us impose on that Act. It is directed at advocacy, not discussion. Thus, the trial judge properly charged the jury that they could not convict if they found that petitioners did "no more than pursue peaceful studies and discussions or teaching and advocacy in the realm of ideas." He further charged that it was not unlawful "to conduct in an American college or university a course explaining the philosophical theories set forth in the books which have been placed in evidence." Such a charge is in strict accord with the statutory language, and illustrates the meaning to be placed on those words. Congress did not intend to eradicate the free discussion of political theories, to destroy the traditional rights of Americans to discuss and evaluate ideas without fear of governmental sanction. Rather Congress was concerned with the very kind of activity in which the evidence showed these petitioners engaged.

But although the statute is not directed at the hypothetical cases which petitioners have conjured, its application in this case has resulted in convictions for the teaching and advocacy of the overthrow of the Government by force and violence, which, even though coupled with the intent to accomplish that overthrow, contains an element of speech. For this reason, we must pay special heed to the demands of the First Amendment marking out the boundaries of speech.

We pointed out in *Douds, supra,* that the basis of the First Amendment is the hypothesis that speech can rebut speech, propaganda will answer propaganda, free debate of ideas will result in the wisest governmental policies. It is for this reason that this Court has recognized the inherent value of free discourse. An analysis of the leading cases in this Court which have involved direct limitations on speech, however, will demonstrate that both the majority of the Court and the dissenters in particular cases have recognized that this is not an unlimited, unqualified right, but that the societal value of speech must, on occasion, be subordinated to other values and considerations.

No important case involving free speech was decided by this Court prior to *Schenck v. United States,* 249 U.S. 47 (1919). . . . That case involved a conviction under the Criminal Espionage Act, 40 Stat. 217. The question the Court faced was whether the evidence was sufficient to sustain the conviction. Writing for a unanimous Court Justice Holmes stated that the "question in every case is whether the words used are used in such circumstances and are of such a nature as to create a clear and present danger that they will bring about the substantive evils that Congress has a right to prevent." . . .

The next important case before the Court in which free speech was the crux of the conflict was *Gitlow v. New York,* 268 U.S. 652 (1925). There New York had made it a crime to advocate "the necessity or propriety of overthrowing . . . organized government by force. . . ." The evidence of violation of the statute was that the defendant had published a Manifesto attacking the Government and capitalism. The convictions were sustained, Justices Holmes and Brandeis dissenting. The majority refused to apply the "clear and present danger" test to the specific utterance. Its reasoning was as follows: The "clear and present danger" test was applied to the utterance itself in *Schenck* because the question was merely one of sufficiency of evidence under an admittedly constitutional statute. *Gitlow,* however, presented a different question. There a legislature had found that a certain kind of speech was, itself, harmful and unlawful. The constitutionality of such a state statute had to be adjudged by this Court just as it determined the constitutionality of any state statute, namely, whether the statute was "reasonable." Since it was entirely reasonable for a state to attempt to protect itself from violent overthrow, the statute was perforce reasonable. The only question remaining in the case became whether there was evidence to support the conviction, a question which gave the majority no difficulty. Justices Holmes and Brandeis refused to accept this approach, but insisted that wherever speech was the evidence of the violation, it was necessary to show that the speech created the "clear and present danger" of the substantive evil which the legislature had the right to prevent. Justices Holmes and Brandeis, then, made no distinction between a federal statute which made certain acts unlawful, the evidence to support the conviction being speech, and a statute which made speech itself the crime. This approach was emphasized in *Whitney v. California,* 274 U.S. 357 (1927), where the Court was confronted with a conviction under the California Criminal Syndicalist statute. The Court sustained the conviction, Justices Brandeis and Holmes concurring in the result. In their concurrence they repeated that even though the legislature had designated certain speech as criminal, this could not prevent the defendant from showing that there was no danger that the substantive evil would be brought about.

Although no case subsequent to *Whitney* and *Gitlow* has expressly overruled the majority opinions in those cases, there is little doubt that subsequent opinions have inclined toward the Holmes-Brandeis rationale. And in *American Communications Assn.* v. *Douds, supra,* we . . . suggested that the Holmes-Brandeis philosophy insisted that where there was a direct restriction upon speech, a "clear and present danger" that the substantive evil would be caused was necessary before the statute in question could be constitutionally applied. . . . But we further suggested that neither Justice Holmes nor Justice Brandeis ever envisioned that a shorthand phrase should be crystallized into a rigid rule to be applied inflexibly without regard to the circumstances of each case. Speech is not an absolute, above and beyond control by the legislature when its judgment, subject to review here, is that certain kinds of speech are so undesirable as to warrant criminal sanction. Nothing is more certain in modern society than the principle that there are no absolutes, that a name, a phrase, a standard has meaning only when associated with the considerations which gave birth to the nomenclature. See *American Communications Assn.* v. *Douds,* 339 U.S. at 397. To those who would paralyze our Government in the face of impending threat by encasing it in a semantic straitjacket we must reply that all concepts are relative.

In this case we are squarely presented with the application of the "clear and present danger" test, and must decide what that phrase imports. We first note that many of the cases in which this Court has reversed convictions by use of this or similar tests have been based on the fact that the interest which the State was attempting to protect was itself too insubstantial to warrant restriction of speech. . . . Overthrow of the Government by force and violence is certainly a substantial enough interest for the Government to limit speech. Indeed, this is the ultimate value of any society, for if a society cannot protect its very structure from armed internal attack, it must follow that no subordinate value can be protected. If, then, this interest may be protected, the literal problem which is presented is what has been meant by the use of the phrase "clear and present danger" of the utterances bringing about the evil within the power of Congress to punish.

Obviously, the words cannot mean that before the Government may act, it must wait until the *putsch* is about to be executed, the plans have been laid and the signal is awaited. If Government is aware that a group aiming at its overthrow is attempting to indoctrinate its members and to commit them to a course whereby they will strike when the leaders feel the circumstances permit, action by the Government is required. The argument that there is no need for Government to concern itself, for Government is strong, it possesses ample powers to put down a rebellion, it may defeat the revolution with ease needs no answer. For that is not the question. Certainly an attempt to overthrow the Government by force, even though doomed from the outset because of inadequate numbers or power of the revolutionists, is a sufficient evil for Congress to prevent. The damage which such attempts create both physically and politically to a nation makes it impossible to measure the validity in terms of the probability of success, or the immediacy of a successful attempt. In the instant case the trial judge charged the jury that they could not convict unless they found that petitioners intended to overthrow the Government "as speedily as circumstances would permit." This does not mean, and could not properly mean, that they would not strike until there was certainty of success. What was meant was that the revolutionists would strike when they thought the time was ripe. We must therefore reject the contention that success or probability of success is the criterion.

The situation with which Justices Holmes and Brandeis were concerned in *Gitlow* was a comparatively isolated event, bearing little relation in their minds to any substantial threat to the safety of the community. . . . They were not confronted with any situation comparable to the instant one—the development of an apparatus designed and dedicated to the overthrow of the Government, in the context of world crisis after crisis.

Chief Judge Learned Hand, writing for the majority below, interpreted the phrase as follows: "In each case [courts] must ask whether the gravity of the 'evil,' discounted by its improbability, justifies such invasion of free speech as is necessary to avoid the danger." 183 F. 2d at 212. We adopt this statement of the rule. As articulated by Chief Judge Hand, it is as succinct and inclusive as any other we might devise at this time. It takes into consideration those factors which we deem relevant, and relates their significances. More we cannot expect from words.

Likewise, we are in accord with the court below, which affirmed the trial court's finding that the requisite danger existed. The mere fact that from the period 1945 to 1948 petitioners' activities did not result in an attempt to overthrow the Government by force and violence is of course no answer to the fact that there was a group that was ready to make the attempt. The formation by petitioners of such a highly organized conspiracy, with rigidly disciplined members subject to call when the leaders, these petitioners, felt that the time had come for action, coupled with the inflammable nature of world conditions, similar uprisings in other countries, and the touch-and-go nature of our relations with countries with whom petitioners were in the very least ideologically attuned, convince us that their convictions were justified on this score. And this analysis disposes of the contention that a conspiracy to advocate, as distinguished from the advocacy itself, cannot be constitutionally restrained, because it comprises only the preparation. It is the existence of the conspiracy which creates the danger. . . . If the ingredients of the reaction are present, we cannot bind the Government to wait until the catalyst is added. . . .

Affirmed.

MR. JUSTICE CLARK took no part in the consideration or decision of this case.

MR. JUSTICE FRANKFURTER, concurring in affirmance of the judgment. . . .

. . . the controversy in this Court turns essentially on the instructions given to the jury for determining guilt or innocence. . . . The first question is whether—wholly apart from constitutional matters—the judge's charge properly explained to the jury what it is that the Smith Act condemns. The conclusion that he did so requires no labored argument. On the basis of the instructions, the jury found, for the purpose of our review, that the advocacy which the defendants conspired to promote was to be a rule of action, by language reasonably calculated to incite persons to such action, and was intended to cause the overthrow of the Government by force and violence as soon as circumstances permit. This brings us to the ultimate issue. In enacting a statute which makes it a crime for the defendants to conspire to do what they have been found to have conspired to do, did Congress exceed its constitutional power? . . .

The language of the First Amendment is to be read not as barren words found in a dictionary but as symbols of historic experience illumined by the presuppositions of those who employed them. Not what words did Madison and Hamilton use, but what was it in their minds which they conveyed? Free speech is subject to prohibition of those abuses of expression which a civilized society may forbid. . . . Absolute rules would inevitably lead to absolute exceptions, and such exceptions would eventually corrode the rules. The demands of free speech in a democratic society as well as the interest in national security are better served by candid and informed weighing of the competing interests, within the confines of the judicial process, than by announcing dogmas too inflexible for the non-Euclidian problems to be solved.

But how are competing interests to be assessed? Since they are not subject to quantitative ascertainment, the issue necessarily resolves itself into asking, who is to make the adjustment?—who is to balance the relevant factors and ascertain which interest is in the circumstances to prevail? Full responsibility for the choice cannot be given to the courts. Courts are not representative bodies. They are not designed to be a good reflex of a democratic society. Their judgment is best informed, and therefore most dependable, within narrow limits. Their essential quality is detachment, founded on independence. History teaches that the independence of the judiciary is jeopardized when courts become embroiled in the passions of the day and assume primary responsibility in choosing between competing political, economic and social pressures.

Primary responsibility for adjusting the interests which compete in the situation before us of necessity belongs to the Congress. . . .

A generation ago this distribution of responsibility would not have been questioned. . . . But in recent decisions we have made explicit what has long been implicitly recognized. In reviewing statutes which restrict freedoms protected by the First Amendment, we have emphasized the close relation which those freedoms bear to maintenance of a free society. See *Kovacs* v. *Cooper,* 336 U.S. 77, 89, 95 (concurring). Some members of the Court—and at times a majority—have done more. They have suggested that our function in reviewing statutes restricting freedom of expression differs sharply from our normal duty in sitting in judgment on legislation. It has been said that such statutes "must be justified by clear public interest, threatened not doubtfully or remotely, but by clear and present danger. The rational connection between the remedy provided and the evil to be curbed, which in other contexts might support legislation against attack on due process grounds, will not suffice." *Thomas* v. *Collins,* 323 U.S. 516, 530. It has been suggested, with the casualness of a footnote, that such legislation is not presumptively valid, see *United States* v. *Carolene Products Co.,* 304 U.S. 144, 152, n. 4, and it has been weightily reiterated that freedom of speech has a "preferred position" among constitutional safeguards. *Kovacs* v. *Cooper,* 336 U.S. 77, 88.

The precise meaning intended to be conveyed by these phrases need not now be pursued. It is enough to note that they have recurred in the Court's opinions, and their cumulative force has, not without justification, engendered belief that there is a constitutional principle, expressed by those attractive but imprecise words, prohibiting restriction upon utterance unless it creates a situation of "imminent" peril against which legislation may guard. It is on this body of the Court's pronouncements that the defendants' argument here is based. . . .

. . . Unless we are to compromise judicial impartiality and subject these defendants to the risk of an *ad hoc* judgment influenced by the impregnating atmosphere of the times, the constitutionality of their conviction must be determined by principles established in cases decided in more tranquil periods. If those decisions are to be used as a guide and not as an argument, it is important to view them as a whole and to distrust the easy generalizations to which some of them lend themselves. Viewed as a whole . . . the decisions express an attitude toward the judicial function and a standard of values which for me are decisive of the case before us.

First.—Free-speech cases are not an exception to the principle that we are not legislators, that direct policy-making is not our province. How best to reconcile competing interests is the business of legislatures, and the balance they strike is a judgment not to be displaced by ours, but to be respected unless outside the pale of fair judgment. . . .

In *Gitlow* v. *New York,* we put our respect for the legislative judgment in terms which, if they were accepted here, would make decision easy. For that case held that, when the legislature has determined that advocacy of forceful overthrow should be forbidden, a conviction may be sustained without a finding that in the particular case the advocacy had a close relation to a serious attempt at overthrow. We held that it was enough that the statute be a reasonable exercise of the legislative judgment, and that the defendant's conduct fall within the statute.

One of the judges below rested his affirmance on the *Gitlow* decision, and the defendants do not attempt to distinguish the case. They place their argument squarely on the ground that the case has been overruled by subsequent decisions. It has not been explicitly overruled. But it would be disingenuous to deny that the dissent in *Gitlow* has been treated with the respect usually accorded to a decision.

The result of the *Gitlow* decision was to send a left-wing Socialist to jail for publishing a Manifesto expressing Marxist exhortations. It requires excessive tolerance of the legislative judgment to suppose that the *Gitlow* publication in the circumstances could justify serious concern.

In contrast, there is ample justification for a legislative judgment that the conspiracy now before us is a substantial threat to national order and security. If the Smith Act is justified at all, it is justified precisely because it may serve to prohibit the type of conspiracy for which these defendants were convicted. . . .

Second.—A survey of the relevant decisions indicates that the results which we have reached are on the whole those that would ensue from careful weighing of conflicting interests. The complex issues presented by regulation of speech in public places, by picketing, and by legislation prohibiting advocacy of crime have been resolved by scrutiny of many factors besides the imminence and gravity of the evil threatened. . . .

It is a familiar experience in the law that new situations do not fit neatly into legal conceptions that arose under different circumstances to satisfy different needs. . . . So it is with the attempt to use the direction of thought lying behind the criterion of "clear and present danger" wholly out of the context in which it originated, and to make of it an absolute dogma and definitive measuring rod for the power of Congress to deal with assaults against security through devices other than overt physical attempts. . . .

. . . The phrase "clear and present danger," in its origin, "served to indicate the importance of freedom of speech to a free society but also to emphasize that its exercise must be compatible with the preservation of other freedoms essential to a democracy and guaranteed by our Constitution." *Pennekamp* v. *Florida,* 328 U.S. 331, 350, 352-353 (concurring). It were far better that the phrase be abandoned than that it be sounded once more to hide from the believers in an absolute right of free speech the plain fact that the interest in speech, profoundly important as it is, is no more conclusive in judicial review than other attributes of democracy or than a determination of the people's representatives that a measure is necessary to assure the safety of government itself.

Third.—Not every type of speech occupies the same position on the scale of values. There is no substantial public interest in permitting certain kinds of utterances: "the lewd and obscene, the profane, the libelous, and the insulting or 'fighting' words— those which by their very utterance inflict injury or tend to incite an immediate breach of the peace." *Chaplinsky* v. *New Hampshire,* 315 U.S. 568, 572. We have frequently indicated that the interest in protecting speech depends on the circum-

stances of the occasion. See cases collected in *Niemotko v. Maryland,* 340 U.S. at
275–283. It is pertinent to the decision before us to consider where on the scale of
values we have in the past placed the type of speech now claiming constitutional
immunity.

The defendants have been convicted of conspiring to organize a party of persons
who advocate the overthrow of the Government by force and violence. The jury has
found that the object of the conspiracy is advocacy as "a rule or principle of action,"
"by language reasonably and ordinarily calculated to incite persons to such action,"
and with the intent to cause the overthrow "as speedily as circumstances would
permit."

On any scale of values which we have hitherto recognized, speech of this sort
ranks low. . . .

These general considerations underlie decision of the case before us.

On the one hand is the interest in security. The Communist Party was not designed by these defendants as an ordinary political party. For the circumstances of its
organization, its aims and methods, and the relation of the defendants to its organization and aims we are concluded by the jury's verdict. The jury found that the Party
rejects the basic premise of our political system—that change is to be brought about
by nonviolent constitutional process. The jury found that the Party advocates the
theory that there is a duty and necessity to overthrow the Government by force and
violence. It found that the Party entertains and promotes this view, not as a prophetic
insight or as a bit of unworldly speculation, but as a program for winning adherents
and as a policy to be translated into action.

In finding that the defendants violated the statute, we may not treat as established
fact that the Communist Party in this country is of significant size, well-organized,
well-disciplined, conditioned to embark on unlawful activity when given the command. But in determining whether application of the statute to the defendants is
within the constitutional powers of Congress, we are not limited to the facts found
by the jury. We must view such a question in the light of whatever is relevant to a
legislative judgment. We may take judicial notice that the Communist doctrines
which these defendants have conspired to advocate are in the ascendancy in powerful nations who cannot be acquitted of unfriendliness to the institutions of this country. We may take account of evidence brought forward at this trial and elsewhere,
much of which has long been common knowledge. In sum, it would amply justify
a legislature in concluding that recruitment of additional members for the Party
would create a substantial danger to national security. . . .

On the other hand is the interest in free speech. The right to exert all governmental powers in aid of maintaining our institutions and resisting their physical
overthrow does not include intolerance of opinions and speech that cannot do harm
although opposed and perhaps alien to dominant, traditional opinion. The treatment
of its minorities, especially their legal position, is among the most searching tests of
the level of civilization attained by a society. It is better for those who have almost
unlimited power of government in their hands to err on the side of freedom. We
have enjoyed so much freedom for so long that we are perhaps in danger of forget-
ting how much blood it cost to establish the Bill of Rights. . . .

It is not for us to decide how we would adjust the clash of interests which this case
presents were the primary responsibility for reconciling it ours. Congress has determined that the danger created by advocacy of overthrow justifies the ensuing restriction on freedom of speech. The determination was made after due deliberation, and
the seriousness of the congressional purpose is attested by the volume of legislation
passed to effectuate the same ends.

Can we then say that the judgment Congress exercised was denied it by the

Constitution? Can we establish a constitutional doctrine which forbids the elected representatives of the people to make this choice? Can we hold that the First Amendment deprives Congress of what it deemed necessary for the Government's protection? . . .

Even when moving strictly within the limits of constitutional adjudication, judges are concerned with issues that may be said to involve vital finalities. The too easy transition from disapproval of what is undesirable to condemnation as unconstitutional, has led some of the wisest judges to question the wisdom of our scheme in lodging such authority in courts. But it is relevant to remind that in sustaining the power of Congress in a case like this nothing irrevocable is done. The democratic process at all events is not impaired or restricted. Power and responsibility remain with the people and immediately with their representatives. All the Court says is that Congress was not forbidden by the Constitution to pass this enactment and that a prosecution under it may be brought against a conspiracy such as the one before us. . . .

MR. JUSTICE JACKSON, concurring.

This prosecution is the latest of never-ending, because never successful, quests for some legal formula that will secure an existing order against revolutionary radicalism. It requires us to reappraise, in the light of our own times and conditions, constitutional doctrines devised under other circumstances to strike a balance between authority and liberty.

Activity here charged to be criminal is conspiracy—that defendants conspired to teach and advocate, and to organize the Communist Party to teach and advocate, overthrow and destruction of the Government by force and violence. There is no charge of actual violence or attempt at overthrow.

The principal reliance of the defense in this Court is that the conviction cannot stand under the Constitution because the conspiracy of these defendants presents no "clear and present danger" of imminent or foreseeable overthrow. . . .

The "clear and present danger" test was an innovation by Mr. Justice Holmes in the *Schenck* case, reiterated and refined by him and Mr. Justice Brandeis in later cases, all arising before the era of World War II revealed the subtlety and efficacy of modernized revolutionary techniques used by totalitarian parties. In those cases, they were faced with convictions under so-called criminal syndicalism statutes aimed at anarchists but which, loosely construed, had been applied to punish socialism, pacifism, and left-wing ideologies, the charges often resting on far-fetched inferences which, if true, would establish only technical or trivial violations. They proposed "clear and present danger" as a test for the sufficiency of evidence in particular cases.

I would save it, unmodified, for application as a "rule of reason" in the kind of case for which it was devised. When the issue is criminality of a hot-headed speech on a street corner, or circulation of a few incendiary pamphlets, or parading by some zealots behind a red flag, or refusal of a handful of school children to salute our flag, it is not beyond the capacity of the judicial process to gather, comprehend, and weigh the necessary materials for decision whether it is a clear and present danger of substantive evil or a harmless letting off of steam. It is not a prophecy, for the danger in such cases has matured by the time of trial or it was never present. The test applies and has meaning where a conviction is sought to be based on a speech or writing which does not directly or explicitly advocate a crime but to which such tendency is sought to be attributed by construction or by implication from external circumstances. The formula in such cases favors freedoms that are vital to our society, and, even if sometimes applied too generously, the consequences cannot be grave. But its recent expansion has extended, in particular to Communists, unprecedented immunities. Unless we are to hold our Government captive in a judge-made verbal trap, we must approach the problem of a well-organized, nation-wide conspiracy . . . as realistically as our predecessors faced the trivialities that were being prosecuted until they were checked with a rule of reason.

I think reason is lacking for applying that test to this case.

If we must decide that this Act and its application are constitutional only if we are convinced that petitioner's conduct creates a "clear and present danger" of violent overthrow, we must appraise imponderables, including international and national phenomena which baffle the best informed foreign offices and our most experienced politicians. We would have to foresee and predict the effectiveness of Communist propaganda, opportunities for infiltration, whether, and when, a time will come that they consider propitious for action, and whether and how fast our existing government will deteriorate. And we would have to speculate as to whether an approaching Communist *coup* would not be anticipated by a nationalistic fascist movement. No doctrine can be sound whose application requires us to make a prophecy of that sort in the guise of a legal decision. The judicial process simply is not adequate to a trial of such far-flung issues. The answers given would reflect our own political predilections and nothing more.

The authors of the clear and present danger test never applied it to a case like this, nor would I. If applied as it is proposed here, it means that the Communist plotting is protected during its period of incubation; its preliminary stages of organization and preparation are immune from the law; the Government can move only after imminent action is manifest, when it would, of course, be too late. . . .

Also, it is urged that since the conviction is for conspiracy to teach and advocate, and to organize the Communist Party to teach and advocate, the First Amendment is violated, because freedoms of speech and press protect teaching and advocacy regardless of what is taught or advocated. I have never thought that to be the law.

I do not suggest that Congress could punish conspiracy to advocate something, the doing of which it may not punish. Advocacy or exposition of the doctrine of communal property ownership, or any political philosophy unassociated with advocacy of its imposition by force or seizure of government by unlawful means could not be reached through conspiracy prosecution. But it is not forbidden to put down force or violence, it is not forbidden to punish its teaching or advocacy, and the end being punishable, there is no doubt of the power to punish conspiracy for the purpose. . . .

When our constitutional provisions were written, the chief forces recognized as antagonists in the struggle between authority and liberty were the Government on the one hand and the individual citizen on the other. It was thought that if the state could be kept in its place the individual could take care of himself.

In more recent times these problems have been complicated by the intervention between the state and the citizen of permanently organized, well-financed, semisecret and highly disciplined political organizations. Totalitarian groups here and abroad perfected the technique of creating private paramilitary organizations to coerce both the public government and its citizens. These organizations assert as against our Government all of the constitutional rights and immunities of individuals and at the same time exercise over their followers much of the authority which they deny to the Government. The Communist Party realistically is a state within a state, an authoritarian dictatorship within a republic. It demands these freedoms, not for its members, but for the organized party. It denies to its own members at the same time the freedom to dissent, to debate, to deviate from the party line, and enforces its authoritarian rule by crude purges, if nothing more violent.

The law of conspiracy has been the chief means at the Government's disposal to deal with the growing problems created by such organizations. I happen to think it is an awkward and inept remedy, but I find no constitutional authority for taking this weapon from the Government. There is no constitutional right to "gang up" on the Government. . . .

Mr. Justice Black, dissenting.

Here again, as in *Breard* v. *Alexandria, post,* p. 622, decided this day, my basic disagreement with the Court is not as to how we should explain or reconcile what was said in prior decisions but springs from a fundamental difference in constitutional approach. Consequently, it would serve no useful purpose to state my position at length.

At the outset I want to emphasize what the crime involved in this case is, and what it is not. These petitioners were not charged with an attempt to overthrow the Government. They were not charged with overt acts of any kind designed to overthrow the Government. They were not even charged with saying anything or writing anything designed to overthrow the Government. The charge was that they agreed to assemble and to talk and publish certain ideas at a later date: The indictment is that they conspired to organize the Communist Party and to use speech or newspapers and other publications in the future to teach and advocate the forcible overthrow of the Government. No matter how it is worded, this is a virulent form of prior censorship of speech and press, which I believe the First Amendment forbids. I would hold § 3 of the Smith Act authorizing this prior restraint unconstitutional on its face and as applied.

But let us assume, contrary to all constitutional ideas of fair criminal procedure, that petitioners although not indicted for the crime of actual advocacy, may be punished for it. Even on this radical assumption, the other opinions in this case show that the only way to affirm these convictions is to repudiate directly or indirectly the established "clear and present danger" rule. This the Court does in a way which greatly restricts the protections afforded by the First Amendment. The opinions for affirmance indicate that the chief reason for jettisoning the rule is the expressed fear that advocacy of Communist doctrine endangers the safety of the Republic. Undoubtedly, a governmental policy of unfettered communication of ideas does entail dangers. To the Founders of this Nation, however, the benefits derived from free expression were worth the risk. They embodied this philosophy in the First Amendment's command that "Congress shall make no law . . . abridging the freedom of speech, or of the press. . . ." I have always believed that the First Amendment is the keystone of our Government, that the freedoms it guarantees provide the best insurance against destruction of all freedom. At least as to speech in the realm of public matters, I believe that the "clear and present danger" test does not "mark the furthermost constitutional boundaries of protected expression" but does "no more than recognize a minimum compulsion of the Bill of Rights." *Bridges* v. *California*, 314 U.S. 252, 263.

So long as this Court exercises the power of judicial review of legislation, I cannot agree that the First Amendment permits us to sustain laws suppressing freedom of speech and press on the basis of Congress' or our own notions of mere "reasonableness." Such a doctrine waters down the First Amendment so that it amounts to little more than an admonition to Congress. The Amendment as so construed is not likely to protect any but those "safe" or orthodox views which rarely need its protection.

Public opinion being what it now is, few will protest the conviction of these Communist petitioners. There is hope, however, that in calmer times, when present pressures, passions and fears subside, this or some later Court will restore the First Amendment liberties to the high preferred place where they belong in a free society.

MR. JUSTICE DOUGLAS, dissenting.

If this were a case where those who claimed protection under the First Amendment were teaching the techniques of sabotage, the assassination of the President, the filching of documents from public files, the planting of bombs, the art of street warfare, and the like, I would have no doubts. The freedom to speak is not absolute; the teaching of methods of terror and other seditious conduct should be beyond the pale along with obscenity and immorality. This case was argued as if those were the facts. The argument imported much seditious conduct into the record. That is easy and it has popular appeal, for the activities of Communists in plotting and scheming against the free world are common knowledge. But the fact is that no such evidence was introduced at the trial. . . .

So far as the present record is concerned, what petitioners did was to organize people to teach and themselves teach the Marxist-Leninist doctrine contained chiefly in four books: Stalin, Foundations of Leninism (1924); Marx and Engels, Manifesto of the Communist Party (1848); Lenin, The State and Revolution (1917); History of the Communist Party of the Soviet Union (B.) (1939).

Those books are to Soviet Communism what Mein Kampf was to Nazism. If they are understood, the ugliness of Communism is revealed, its deceit and cunning are exposed, the nature of its activities becomes apparent, and the chances of its success less likely. That is not, of course, the reason why petitioners chose these books for their classrooms. They are fervent Communists to whom these volumes are gospel. They preached the creed with the hope that some day it would be acted upon.

The opinion of the Court does not outlaw these texts nor condemn them to the fire, as the Communists do literature offensive to their creed. But if the books themselves are not outlawed, if they can lawfully remain on library shelves, by what reasoning does their use in a classroom become a crime? It would not be a crime under the Act to introduce these books to a class, though that would be teaching what the creed of violent overthrow of the Government is. The Act, as construed, requires the element of intent—that those who teach the creed believe in it. The crime then depends not on what is taught but on who the teacher is. That is to make freedom of speech turn not on *what is said,* but on the *intent* with which it is said. Once we start down that road we enter territory dangerous to the liberties of every citizen. . . .

Intent, of course, often makes the difference in the law. An act otherwise excusable or carrying minor penalties may grow to an abhorrent thing if the evil intent is present. We deal here, however, not with ordinary acts but with speech, to which the Constitution has given a special sanction.

The vice of treating speech as the equivalent of overt acts of a treasonable or seditious character is emphasized by a concurring opinion, which by invoking the law of conspiracy makes speech do service for deeds which are dangerous to society. The doctrine of conspiracy has served divers and oppressive purposes and in its broad reach can be made to do great evil. But never until today has anyone seriously thought that the ancient law of conspiracy could constitutionally be used to turn speech into seditious conduct. Yet that is precisely what is suggested. I repeat that we deal here with speech alone, not with speech *plus* acts of sabotage or unlawful conduct. Not a single seditious act is charged in the indictment. To make a lawful speech unlawful because two men conceive it is to raise the law of conspiracy to appalling proportions. That course is to make a radical break with the past and to violate one of the cardinal principles of our constitutional scheme. . . .

There comes a time when even speech loses its constitutional immunity. Speech innocuous one year may at another time fan such destructive flames that it must be halted in the interests of the safety of the Republic. That is the meaning of the clear and present danger test. When conditions are so critical that there will be no time to avoid the evil that the speech threatens, it is time to call a halt. Otherwise, free speech which is the strength of the Nation will be the cause of its destruction.

Yet free speech is the rule, not the exception. The restraint to be constitutional must be based on more than fear, on more than passionate opposition against the speech, on more than a revolted dislike for its contents. There must be some immediate injury to society that is likely if speech is allowed. . . .

I had assumed that the question of the clear and present danger, being so critical an issue in the case, would be a matter for submission to the jury. . . .

Yet, whether the question is one for the Court or the jury, there should be evidence of record on the issue. This record, however, contains no evidence whatsoever showing that the acts charged, *viz.*, the teaching of the Soviet theory of revolution with the hope that it will be realized, have created any clear and present danger to the Nation. The Court, however, rules to the contrary. It says, "The formation by petitioners of such a highly organized conspiracy, with rigidly disciplined members subject to call when the leaders, these petitioners, felt that the time had come for action, coupled with the inflammable nature of world conditions, similar uprisings in other countries, and the touch-and-go nature of our relations with countries with whom petitioners were in the very least ideologically attuned, convince us that their convictions were justified on this score."

That ruling is in my view not responsive to the issue in the case. We might as well say that the speech of petitioners is outlawed because Soviet Russia and her Red Army are a threat to world peace.

The nature of Communism as a force on the world scene would, of course, be relevant to the issue of clear and present danger of petitioners' advocacy within the United States. But the primary consideration is the strength and tactical position of petitioners and their converts in this country. On that there is no evidence in the record. If we are to take judicial notice of the threat of Communists within the nation, it should not be difficult to conclude that *as a political party* they are of little consequence. . . .

How it can be said that there is a clear and present danger that this advocacy will succeed is, therefore, a mystery. Some nations less resilient than the United States, where illiteracy is high and where democratic traditions are only budding, might have to take drastic steps and jail these men for merely speaking their creed. But in America they are miserable merchants of unwanted ideas; their wares remain unsold. The fact that their ideas are abhorrent does not make them powerful.

The political impotence of the Communists in this country does not, of course, dispose of the problem. Their numbers; their positions in industry and government; the extent to which they have in fact infiltrated the police, the armed services, transportation, stevedoring, power plants, munitions works, and other critical places—these facts all bear on the likelihood that their advocacy of the Soviet theory of revolution will endanger the Republic. But the record is silent on these facts.

. . . Free speech—the glory of our system of government—should not be sacrificed on anything less than plain and objective proof of danger that the evil advocated is imminent. On this record no one can say that petitioners and their converts are in such a strategic position as to have even the slightest chance of achieving their aims.

The First Amendment provides that "Congress shall make no law . . . abridging the freedom of speech." The Constitution provides no exception. This does not mean, however, that the Nation need hold its hand until it is in such weakened condition that there is no time to protect itself from incitement to revolution. Seditious conduct can always be punished. But the command of the First Amendment is so clear that we should not allow Congress to call a halt to free speech except in the extreme case of peril from the speech itself. The First Amendment makes confidence in the common sense of our people and in their maturity of judgment the great postulate of our democracy. . . . Unless and until extreme and necessitous circumstances are shown, our aim should be to keep speech unfettered and to allow the processes of law to be invoked only when the provocateurs among us move from speech to action. . . .

SCALES v. UNITED STATES
367 U.S. 203, 81 S. Ct. 1469, 6 L. Ed. 2d 782 (1961)

MR. JUSTICE HARLAN delivered the opinion of the Court. . . .

The Smith Act . . . among other things, makes a felony the acquisition or holding of knowing membership in any organization which advocates the overthrow of the Government of the United States by force or violence. The indictment charged that from January 1946 to the date of its filing (November 18, 1954) the Communist Party of the United States was such an organization, and that petitioner throughout that period was a member thereof, with knowledge of the Party's illegal purpose and a specific intent to accomplish overthrow "as speedily as circumstances would permit." . . .

It will bring the constitutional issues into clear focus to notice first the premises on which the case was submitted to the jury. The jury was instructed that in order to convict it must find that within the three-year limitations period (1) the Communist Party advocated the violent overthrow of the Government, in the sense of present "advocacy of action" to accomplish that end as soon as circumstances were propitious; and (2) petitioner was an "active" member of the Party, and not merely "a nominal, passive, inactive or purely technical" member, with knowledge of the Party's illegal advocacy and a specific intent to bring about violent overthrow "as speedily as circumstances would permit."

The constitutional attack upon the membership clause, as thus construed, is that the statute offends (1) the Fifth Amendment, in that it impermissibly imputes guilt to an individual merely on the basis of his associations and sympathies, rather than because of some concrete personal involvement in criminal conduct; and (2) the First Amendment, in that it infringes free political expression and association. . . .

Fifth Amendment.

In our jurisprudence guilt is personal, and when the imposition of punishment on a status or on conduct can only be justified by reference to the relationship of that status or conduct to other concededly criminal activity (here advocacy of violent overthrow), that relationship must be sufficiently substantial to satisfy the concept of personal guilt in order to withstand attack under the Due Process Clause of the Fifth Amendment. Membership, without more, in an organization engaged in illegal advocacy, it is now said, has not heretofore been recognized by this Court to be such a relationship. This claim stands, and we shall examine it, independently of that made under the First Amendment.

Any thought that due process puts beyond the reach of the criminal law all individual associational relationships, unless accompanied by the commission of specific acts of criminality, is dispelled by familiar concepts of the law of conspiracy and complicity. While both are commonplace in the landscape of the criminal law, they are not natural features. Rather they are particular legal concepts manifesting the more general principle that society, having the power to punish dangerous behavior, cannot be powerless against those who work to bring about that behavior. The fact that Congress has not resorted to either of these familiar concepts means only that the enquiry here must direct itself to an analysis of the relationship between the fact of membership and the underlying substantive illegal conduct, in order to determine whether that relationship is indeed too tenuous to permit its use as the basis of criminal liability. In this instance it is an organization which engages in criminal activity, and we can perceive no reason why one who actively and knowingly works in the ranks of that organization, intending to contribute to the success of those specifically illegal activities, should be any more immune from prosecution than he to whom the organization has assigned the task of carrying out the substantive criminal act. Nor should the fact that Congress has focussed here on "membership," the characteristic relationship between an individual and the type of conspiratorial quasi-political associations with the criminal aspect of whose activities Congress was concerned, of itself require the conclusion that the legislature has traveled outside the familiar and permissible bounds of criminal imputability. In truth, the specificity of the proscribed relationship is not necessarily a vice; it provides instruction and warning.

What must be met, then, is the argument that membership, even when accompanied by the elements of knowledge and specific intent, affords an insufficient quantum of participation in the organization's alleged criminal activity, that is, an insufficiently significant form of aid and encouragement to permit the imposition of criminal sanctions on that basis. It must indeed be recognized that a person who merely becomes a member of an illegal organization, by that "act" alone need be doing nothing more than signifying his assent to its purposes and activities on one hand, and providing, on the other, only the sort of moral encouragement which comes from the knowledge that others believe in what the organization is doing. It may indeed be argued that such assent and encouragement do fall short of the concrete, practical impetus given to a criminal enterprise which is lent for instance by a commitment on the part of a conspirator to act in furtherance of that enterprise. A member, as distinguished from a conspirator, may indicate his approval of a criminal enterprise by the very fact of his membership without thereby necessarily committing himself to further it by any act or course of conduct whatever.

In an area of the criminal law which this Court has indicated more than once demands its watchful scrutiny . . . these factors have weight and must be found to be overborne in a total constitutional assessment of the statute. We think, however, they are duly met when the statute is found to reach only "active" members having also a guilty knowledge and intent, and which therefore prevents a conviction on what otherwise might be regarded as merely an expression of sympathy with the alleged criminal enterprise, unaccompanied by any significant action in its support or any commitment to undertake such action.

Thus, given the construction of the membership clause already discussed, we think the factors called for in rendering members criminally responsible for the illegal advocacy of the organization fall within established, and therefore presumably constitutional standards of criminal imputability.

First Amendment.

Little remains to be said concerning the claim that the statute infringes First Amendment freedoms. It was settled in *Dennis* that the advocacy with which we are here concerned is not constitutionally protected speech, and it was further established that a combination to promote such advocacy, albeit under the aegis of what purports to be a political party, is not such association as is protected by the First Amendment. We can discern no reason why membership, when it constitutes a purposeful form of complicity in a group engaging in this same forbidden advocacy, should receive any greater degree of protection from the guarantees of that Amendment.

If it is said that the mere existence of such an enactment tends to inhibit the exercise of constitutionally protected rights, in that it engenders an unhealthy fear that one may find himself unwittingly embroiled in criminal liability, the answer surely is that the statute provides that a defendant must be proven to have knowledge of the proscribed advocacy before he may be convicted. It is, of course, true that quasi-political parties or other groups that may embrace both legal and illegal aims differ from a technical conspiracy, which is defined by its criminal purpose, so that *all* knowing association with the conspiracy is a proper subject for criminal proscription as far as First Amendment liberties are concerned. If there were a similar blanket prohibition of association with a group having both legal and illegal aims, there would indeed be a real danger that legitimate political expression or association would be impaired, but the membership clause, as here construed, does not cut deeper into the freedom of association than is necessary to deal with "the substantive evils that Congress has a right to prevent." *Schenck* v. *United States,* 249 U.S. 47, 52. The clause does not make criminal all association with an organization, which has been shown to engage in illegal advocacy. There must be clear proof that a defendant "specifically intend[s] to accomplish [the aims of the organization] by resort to violence." *Noto* v. *United States.* . . . Thus the member for whom the organization is a vehicle for the advancement of legitimate aims and policies does not fall within the ban of the statute: he lacks the requisite specific intent "to bring about the overthrow of the government as speedily as circumstances would permit." Such a person may be foolish, deluded, or perhaps merely optimistic, but he is not by this statute made a criminal.

We conclude that petitioner's constitutional challenge must be overruled. . . .

The judgment of the Court of Appeals must be

Affirmed.

MR. JUSTICE BLACK, dissenting. . . .

I think it is important to point out the manner in which this case re-emphasizes the freedom-destroying nature of the "balancing test" presently in use by the Court to justify its refusal to apply specific constitutional protections of the Bill of Rights. In some of the recent cases in which it has "balanced" away the protections of the First Amendment, the Court has suggested that it was justified in the application of this "test" because no direct abridgment of First Amendment freedoms was involved, the abridgment in each of these cases being, in the Court's opinion, nothing more than "an incident of the informed exercise of a valid governmental function." A possible implication of that suggestion was that if the Court were confronted with what it would call a direct abridgment of speech, it would not apply the "balancing test" but would enforce the protections of the First Amendment according to its own terms. This case causes me to doubt that such an implication is justified. Petitioner is being sent to jail for the express reason that he has associated with people who have entertained unlawful ideas and said unlawful things, and that of course is a *direct* abridgment of his freedoms of speech and assembly—under any definition that has ever been used for that term. Nevertheless, even as to this admittedly direct abridgment, the Court relies upon its prior decisions to the effect that the Government has power to abridge speech and assembly if its interest in doing so is sufficient to outweigh the interest in protecting these First Amendment freedoms.

This, I think, demonstrates the unlimited breadth and danger of the "balancing test" as it is currently being applied by a majority of this Court. Under that "test," the question in every case in which a First Amendment right is asserted is not whether there has been an abridgment of that right, not whether the abridgment of that right was intentional on the part of the Government, and not whether there is any other way in which the Government could accomplish a lawful aim without an invasion of the constitutionally guaranteed rights of the people. It is, rather, simply whether the Government has an interest in abridging the right involved and, if so, whether that interest is of sufficient importance, in the opinion of a majority of this Court, to justify the Government's action in doing so. This doctrine, to say the very least, is capable of being used to justify almost any action Government may wish to take to suppress First Amendment freedoms.

Mr. Justice Douglas, dissenting.

When we allow petitioner to be sentenced to prison for six years for being a "member" of the Communist Party, we make a sharp break with traditional concepts of First Amendment rights and make serious Mark Twain's lighthearted comment that "It is by the goodness of God that in our country we have those three unspeakably precious things: freedom of speech, freedom of conscience, and the prudence never to practice either of them." . . .

There is here no charge of conspiracy, no charge of any overt act to overthrow the Government by force and violence, no charge of any other criminal act. The charge is being a "member" of the Communist Party, "well-knowing" that it advocated the overthrow of the Government by force and violence, "said defendant intending to bring about such overthrow by force and violence as speedily as circumstances would permit." That falls far short of a charge of conspiracy. Conspiracy rests not in intention alone but in an agreement with one or more others to promote an unlawful project. . . . No charge of any kind or sort of agreement hitherto embraced in the concept of a conspiracy is made here.

We legalize today guilt by association, sending a man to prison when he committed no unlawful act. . . .

The case is not saved by showing that petitioner was an active member. None of the activity constitutes a crime. The record contains evidence that Scales was the Chairman of the North and South Carolina Districts of the Communist Party. He recruited new members into the Party, and promoted the advanced education of selected young Party members in the theory of communism to be undertaken at secret schools. He was a director of one such school. He explained the principles of the Party to an FBI agent who posed as someone interested in joining the Party, and furnished him literature, including articles which criticized in vivid language the American "aggression" in Korea and described American "atrocities" committed on Korean citizens. He once remarked that the Party was setting up underground means of communication, and in 1951 he himself "went underground." At the school of which Scales was director, students were told (by someone else) that one of the Party's weaknesses was in failing to place people in key industrial positions. One witness told of a meeting arranged by Scales at which the staff of the school urged him to remain in his position in an industrial plant rather than return to college. In Scales' presence, students at the school were once shown how to kill a person with a pencil, a device which, it was said, might come in handy on a picket line. Other evidence showed Scales to have made several statements or distributed literature containing implicating passages. Among them were comments to the effect that the Party line was that the Negroes in the South and the working classes should be used to foment a violent revolution; that a Communist government could not be voted into power in this country because the Government controlled communication media, newspapers, the military, and the educational systems, and that force was the only way to achieve the revolution; that if a depression were to come the Communist America would be closer at hand than predicted by William Z. Foster; that the revolution would come within a generation; that it would be easier in the United States than in Russia to effectuate the revolution because of assistance and advice from Russian Communists. Petitioner at different times said or distributed literature which said that the goals of communism could only be achieved by violent revolution that would have to start internally with the working classes.

Not one single illegal act is charged to petitioner. That is why the essence of the crime covered by the indictment is merely belief—belief in the proletarian revolution, belief in Communist creed. . . .

Nothing but beliefs are on trial in this case. They are unpopular and to most of us revolting. But they are nonetheless ideas or dogma or faith within the broad framework of the First Amendment. . . .

Belief in the principle of revolution is deep in our traditions. The Declaration of Independence proclaims it:

"whenever any Form of Government becomes destructive of these ends, it is the Right of the People to alter or abolish it, and to institute new Government, laying its foundation on such principles and organizing its powers in such form, as to them shall seem most likely to effect their Safety and Happiness."

This right of revolution has been and is a part of the fabric of our institutions. . . .

Of course, government can move against those who take up arms against it. Of course, the constituted authority has the right of self-preservation. But we deal in this prosecution of Scales only with the legality of ideas and beliefs, not with overt acts. The Court speaks of the prevention of "dangerous behavior" by punishing those "who work to bring about that behavior." That formula returns man to the dark days when government determined what behavior was "dangerous" and then policed the dissidents for tell-tale signs of advocacy. . . .

MR. JUSTICE BRENNAN with whom THE CHIEF JUSTICE and MR. JUSTICE DOUGLAS join, dissenting.

I think that in § 4 (f) of the Internal Security Act Congress legislated immunity from prosecution under the membership clause of the Smith Act. The first sentence of § 4 (f) is: "Neither the holding of office nor membership in any Communist organization by any person shall constitute per se a violation of subsection (a) or subsection (c) of this section or of any other criminal statute." The immunity granted by that sentence is not in my view restricted, as the Court holds, to *mere* membership, that is to membership which is nominal, passive or theoretical. The immunity also extends to "active and purposive membership, purposive that is as to the organization's criminal ends," which is the character of membership to which the Court today restricts the application of the membership clause of the Smith Act. . . .

Chapter 28

FREEDOM OF RELIGION

> Congress shall make no law respecting an establishment of religion, or prohibiting the free exercise thereof. . . .   FIRST AMENDMENT

Freedom to worship God according to the dictates of individual conscience was one of the dominant motives in the founding of the American Colonies, and it might have been expected that provisions guaranteeing that right would have an important place in the Constitution. In fact, the Founders left the original Constitution almost devoid of language on the relationships of government and religion, thus conforming with their general practice in the civil liberties field. The sole exception was the provision of Article VI that "no religious test shall ever be required as a qualification to any office or public trust under the United States."

The adoption of the First Amendment repaired the omissions of the original Constitution. The language of the amendment specifically excluded the states from its coverage, though many states had similar provisions in their own constitutions. In 1940, however, the Supreme Court held that the freedom of religion clause in the First Amendment had been made applicable to the states by the Fourteenth Amendment's guarantee of "liberty." This step was a logical sequence to the Court's ruling in the 1925 *Gitlow* decision applying the free speech and press provisions of the First Amendment to the states. Clearly, freedom to propagate religious convictions is hardly distinguishable from free speech generally, and the Supreme Court so held in *Cantwell* v. *Connecticut,* 310 U.S. 296 (1940).

Previous Restraint. A fundamental element in freedom of religion, as in freedom of speech, is that religious activity shall not be subjected to previous restraint. *Cantwell* v. *Connecticut* was such a case. A state statute made it a crime for any person to solicit or canvass from house to house for any religious or philanthropic cause without securing the prior approval of the secretary of the county welfare council, who was authorized to determine whether the cause was a bona fide religious one, conforming to reasonable standards of efficiency and integrity. The Court unanimously held this statute to abridge freedom of religion; a requirement of prior approval by a public official, which may be refused in his discretion, constitutes "a censorship of religion as the means of determining its right to survive," said Justice Roberts.

Prior restraint may take the form of a permit for speaking, as has already been illustrated by the case of *Kunz* v. *New York* in Chapter 21. Taxes may also be a restraint. Two decisions on the tax issue resulted from the unorthodox methods of Jehovah's Witnesses in financing their cause. In *Jones* v. *Opelika,* 316 U.S.

584 (1942), the Court upheld the validity of municipal license fees on transient merchants or book agents as applied in three different cities to Witnesses engaged in door-to-door peddling of religious tracts. None of these ordinances discriminated against the sale of religious literature, nor were they drafted with the Witnesses in mind. They were ordinary taxes on the privilege of peddling. When religious advocates resort to commercial methods to raise funds, the Court held, it is natural and proper to subject them to the payment of a fee. "The First Amendment does not require a subsidy in the form of fiscal exemption."

Four dissenting justices, however, thought these taxes were "in reality taxes upon the dissemination of religious ideas, a dissemination carried on by the distribution of religious literature for religious reasons alone and not for personal profit." With the appointment of Justice Rutledge to the Court a few months after this case was decided, the issue was reconsidered and in *Murdock* v. *Pennsylvania*, 319 U.S. 105 (1943), the decision of the previous year was overruled. The incidental collection of small sums for books or tracts to help finance the spread of religion was not regarded by the new Court majority as making this evangelism commercial, any more than passing the collection plate makes a church service commercial.

Antisocial Conduct. One of the clear limitations on religious freedom is its subjection to the criminal laws of the land. Thought and belief are protected, but actions or practices which are made criminal by law or are outrageously offensive to public morals are not rendered immune from punishment because of alleged religious motivation. Obviously, to permit individuals to excuse criminal activity on the ground of religion "would be to make the professed doctrines of religious belief superior to the law of the land, and in effect to permit every citizen to become a law unto himself," the Supreme Court said in *Reynolds* v. *United States*, 98 U.S. 145 (1879).

In the *Reynolds* case federal statutes making criminal the practice or advocacy of polygamy in territories of the United States were applied to Mormon sects in Utah. The Mormon Church renounced the doctrine of plural marriage in 1890, but a fundamentalist group which broke off from the main church persisted in polygamy. In *Cleveland* v. *United States*, 329 U.S. 14 (1946), the Mann Act, which forbids transportation of women in interstate commerce for prostitution "or for any other immoral purpose," was held to apply to this polygamous sect.

Prince v. *Massachusetts*, 321 U.S. 158 (1944), also illustrates the successful application of state criminal law against a religious defense. A nine-year-old girl, accompanied by her aunt, who was a Jehovah's Witness, sold literature of the Witnesses on downtown street corners at night. A Massachusetts law forbids boys under twelve and girls under eighteen to sell newspapers or other merchandise on the streets, and punishes parents or guardians who permit children to do so. By a five to four vote the Court held this statute to be a reasonable police regulation designed to protect the welfare of children, taking precedence over the competing claims of religious freedom.

Conscientious Objectors. Compulsory military service creates a problem of constitutional significance for persons who object to war or armed service on grounds of religion or conscience. Actually, the direct constitutional issue here has never been raised before the Supreme Court, because every American conscription law since the first one was passed in 1917 has granted exemption from military service to conscientious objectors who meet the statutory definition. There were numerous cases during World War II involving denial of claims of conscientious objectors by draft boards, but the issues were usually those of administrative procedure rather than religious freedom. Examples are *Falbo* v. *United States,* 320 U.S. 549 (1944), and *Estep* v. *United States,* 327 U.S. 114 (1946).

Hamilton v. *Regents of University of California,* 293 U.S. 245 (1934), resulted from a refusal of two Methodist students to take a required course in military science at a state university. The Court ruled against them on the ground that they were not compelled to go to the university, and also that instruction in military science was too indirectly related to the bearing of arms for hostile purposes to claim religious exemption.

The Supreme Court initially held in *United States* v. *Schwimmer,* 279 U.S. 644 (1929), that an alien who expressed unwillingness to defend the United States by force of arms should be refused naturalization. However, this view was reversed in *Girouard* v. *United States,* 328 U.S. 61 (1946). Girouard was a Seventh Day Adventist who was willing to serve in the army as a noncombatant, but refused to bear arms. The Court noted that his religious scruples would not disqualify him from becoming a member of Congress or holding other public offices, and refused to believe that Congress had "set a stricter standard for aliens seeking admission to citizenship than it did for officials who make and enforce the laws of the nation."

Liberty of Churches. Freedom of religion requires the secular authority to refrain from imposing its will in the settlement of internal church disputes. In *Kedroff* v. *St. Nicholas Cathedral of Russian Orthodox Church,* 344 U.S. 94 (1952), the New York Legislature had sought to free the Russian Orthodox churches in America from control by the Moscow church authorities by making them subject to an autonomous Russian church in America. The Court held that a law transferring control over churches from one group of persons to another was an inadmissible use of state power. Justice Frankfurter said: "What is at stake here is the power to exercise religious authority." The church, not the state, must make the decisions on the location of such power.

Public Education. In two important areas of educational policy, state educational requirements have been challenged as infringements on religious freedom. Oregon raised a fundamental issue in 1922 when the state adopted by the initiative process a compulsory education act requiring all children to attend public schools for the first eight grades. In *Pierce* v. *Society of Sisters,* 268 U.S. 510 (1925), the Supreme Court unanimously held the law invalid. This decision was handed down one week before the *Gitlow* ruling made the First Amendment applicable to the states, and consequently there was no clear-cut statement that the *Pierce* case, though brought by a religious order, was being handled as an issue of religious freedom. Rather, the "liberty" which was being protected by the Court, in Justice McReynolds's words, was that of the "business and property" of private and parochial schools, which were being "threatened with destruction through the unwarranted compulsion which appellants are exercising over present and prospective patrons of their schools." This was. moreover, the "liberty of parents and guardians to direct the upbringing and education of children under their control."

The second issue concerns the salute to the flag which is a part of the daily routine in many American public schools. The children of Jehovah's Witnesses are instructed that saluting the flag constitutes worship of a "graven image," contrary to Bible teaching. The conflict in conscience thus set up in schools requiring the salute was brought to the Supreme Court in *Minersville School District* v. *Gobitis,* 310 U.S. 586 (1940), where the Court decided, with only Justice Stone dissenting, that the compulsory flag salute did not infringe constitutional rights of the protesting children. Justice Frankfurter, who wrote the majority opinion, stressed that "national unity is the basis of national security," and such unity

. . . is fostered by all those agencies of the mind and spirit which may serve to gather up the traditions of a people, transmit them from generation to generation, and thereby create that continuity of a treasured common life which constitutes a civilization. "We live by symbols." The flag is the symbol of our national unity, transcending all internal differences, however large, within the framework of the Constitution.

Frankfurter's second principal contention was that the rule of the local school board must be viewed as though it were the action of the state legislature, and that a legislative judgment on the means most likely to promote an attachment to the institutions of the country was entitled to great respect. For the Court to hold the flag salute requirement void "would amount to no less than the pronouncement of pedagogical and psychological dogma in a field where courts possess no marked and certainly no controlling competence." Justice Stone, dissenting, thought that the flag salute requirement not only suppressed freedom of speech and the free exercise of religion, but actually sought to coerce children to express a sentiment violative of their deepest religious convictions.

The *Gobitis* decision was not the Court's last word on this problem, however. Justices Black, Douglas, and Murphy had second thoughts, and in *Jones* v. *Opelika,* which had nothing to do with the flag salute, they volunteered their conclusion that the *Gobitis* case had been wrongly decided. That made four votes against the flag salute, and when another case raising the same issue came up the next year, Justices Jackson and Rutledge, who had joined the Court since 1940, voted with them to reverse the *Gobitis* ruling in *West Virginia State Board of Education* v. *Barnette,* 319 U.S. 624 (1943).

Religious Oaths for Public Officials. In *Torcaso* v. *Watkins,* 367 U.S. 488 (1961), a Maryland requirement of a "declaration of belief in the existence of God" as a qualification for public office in the state was declared unconstitutional by a unanimous vote of the Supreme Court, as an invasion of "freedom of belief and religion."

WEST VIRGINIA STATE BOARD OF EDUCATION v. BARNETTE
319 U.S. 624, 63 S. Ct. 1178, 87 L. Ed. 1628 (1943)

MR. JUSTICE JACKSON delivered the opinion of the Court.

Following the decision by this Court on June 3, 1940, in *Minersville School District* v. *Gobitis,* 310 U.S. 586. the West Virginia legislature amended its statutes to require all schools therein to conduct courses of instruction in history, civics, and in the Constitutions of the United States and of the State "for the purpose of teaching, fostering and perpetuating the ideals, principles and spirit of Americanism, and increasing the knowledge of the organization and machinery of the government." Appellant Board of Education was directed, with advice of the State Superintendent of Schools, to "prescribe the courses of study covering these subjects" for public schools. The Act made it the duty of private, parochial and denominational schools to prescribe courses of study "similar to those required for the public schools."

The Board of Education on January 9, 1942, adopted a resolution containing recitals taken largely from the Court's *Gobitis* opinion and ordering that the salute to the flag become "a regular part of the program of activities in the public schools," that all teachers and pupils "shall be required to participate in the salute honoring the Nation represented by the Flag; provided, however, that refusal to salute the Flag be regarded as an act of insubordination, and shall be dealt with accordingly." . . .

Appellees, citizens of the United States and of West Virginia, brought suit in the United States District Court for themselves and others similarly situated asking its injunction to restrain enforcement of these laws and regulations against Jehovah's Witnesses. The Witnesses are an unincorporated body teaching that the obligation imposed by law of God is superior to that of laws enacted by temporal government. Their religious beliefs include a literal version of Exodus, Chapter 20, verses 4 and 5, which says: "Thou shalt not make unto thee any graven image, or any likeness of anything that is in heaven above, or that is in the earth beneath, or that is in the water under the earth; thou shalt not bow down thyself to them nor serve them." They consider that the flag is an "image" within this command. For this reason they refuse to salute it.

Children of this faith have been expelled from school and are threatened with exclusion for no other cause. Officials threaten to send them to reformatories maintained for criminally inclined juveniles. Parents of such children have been prosecuted and are threatened with prosecutions for causing delinquency. . . .

The freedom asserted by these appellees does not bring them into collision with rights asserted by any other individual. It is such conflicts which most frequently require intervention of the State to determine where the rights of one end and those of another begin. But the refusal of these persons to participate in the ceremony does not interfere with or deny rights of others to do so. Nor is there any question in this case that their behavior is peaceable and orderly. The sole conflict is between authority and rights of the individual. The State asserts power to condition access to public education on making a prescribed sign and profession and at the same time to coerce attendance by punishing both parent and child. The latter stand on a right of self-determination in matters that touch individual opinion and personal attitude. . . .

. . . The compulsory flag salute and pledge requires affirmation of a belief and an attitude of mind. It is not clear whether the regulation contemplates that pupils forego any contrary convictions of their own and become unwilling converts to the prescribed ceremony or whether it will be acceptable if they simulate assent by words without belief and by a gesture barren of meaning. It is now a commonplace that censorship or suppression of expression of opinion is tolerated by our Constitution only when the expression presents a clear and present danger of action of a kind the State is empowered to prevent and punish. It would seem that involuntary affirmation could be commanded only on even more immediate and urgent grounds than silence. But here the power of compulsion is invoked without any allegation that remaining passive during a flag salute ritual creates a clear and present danger that would justify an effort even to muffle expression. To sustain the compulsory flag salute we are required to say that a Bill of Rights which guards the individual's right to speak his own mind, left it open to public authorities to compel him to utter what is not in his mind.

Whether the First Amendment to the Constitution will permit officials to order observance of ritual of this nature does not depend upon whether as a voluntary exercise we would think it to be good, bad or merely innocuous. Any credo of nationalism is likely to include what some disapprove or to omit what others think essential, and to give off different overtones as it takes on different accents or interpretations. If official power exists to coerce acceptance of any patriotic creed, what it shall contain cannot be decided by courts, but must be largely discretionary with the ordaining authority, whose power to prescribe would no doubt include power to amend. Hence validity of the asserted power to force an American citizen publicly to profess any statement of belief or to engage in any ceremony of assent to one, presents questions of power that must be considered independently of any idea we may have as to the utility of the ceremony in question.

Nor does the issue as we see it turn on one's possession of particular religious views or the sincerity with which they are held. While religion supplies appellees' motive for enduring the discomforts of making the issue in this case, many citizens who do not share these religious views hold such a compulsory rite to infringe constitutional liberty of the individual. It is not necessary to inquire whether non-conformist beliefs will exempt from the duty to salute unless we first find power to make the salute a legal duty.

The *Gobitis* decision, however, *assumed,* as did the argument in that case and in this, that power exists in the State to impose the flag salute discipline upon school children in general. The Court only examined and rejected a claim based on religious beliefs of immunity from an unquestioned general rule. The question which underlies the flag salute controversy is whether such a ceremony so touching matters of opinion and political attitude may be imposed upon the individual by official authority under powers committed to any political organization under our Constitution. We examine rather than assume existence of this power and, against this broader definition of issues in this case, reëxamine specific grounds assigned for the *Gobitis* decision.

1. It was said that the flag-salute controversy confronted the Court with "the problem which Lincoln cast in memorable dilemma: 'Must a government of necessity be too *strong* for the liberties of its people, or too *weak* to maintain its own existence?' " and that the answer must be in favor of strength. . . .

Government of limited power need not be anemic government. Assurance that rights are secure tends to diminish fear and jealousy of strong government, and by making us feel safe to live under it makes for its better support. Without promise of a limiting Bill of Rights it is doubtful if our Constitution could have mustered enough strength to enable its ratification. To enforce those rights today is not to choose weak government over strong government. It is only to adhere as a means of strength to individual freedom of mind in preference to officially disciplined uniformity for which history indicates a disappointing and disastrous end. . . .

2. It was also considered in the *Gobitis* case that functions of educational officers in States, counties and school districts were such that to interfere with their authority "would in effect make us the school board for the country." . . .

The Fourteenth Amendment, as now applied to the States, protects the citizen against the State itself and all of its creatures—Boards of Education not excepted. These have, of course, important, delicate, and highly discretionary functions, but none that they may not perform within the limits of the Bill of Rights. That they are educating the young for citizenship is reason for scrupulous protection of Constitutional freedoms of the individual, if we are not to strangle the free mind at its source

and teach youth to discount important principles of our government as mere plati-
tudes. . . .

3. The *Gobitis* opinion reasoned that this is a field "where courts possess no marked
and certainly no controlling competence," that it is committed to the legislatures as
well as the courts to guard cherished liberties and that it is constitutionally appropriate to "fight out the wise use of legislative authority in the forum of public opinion
and before legislative assemblies rather than to transfer such a contest to the judicial
arena," since all the "effective means of inducing political changes are left free." . . .

The very purpose of a Bill of Rights was to withdraw certain subjects from the
vicissitudes of political controversy, to place them beyond the reach of majorities and
officials and to establish them as legal principles to be applied by the courts. One's
right to life, liberty, and property, to free speech, a free press, freedom of worship
and assembly, and other fundamental rights may not be submitted to vote; they
depend on the outcome of no elections. . . .

In weighing arguments of the parties it is important to distinguish between the due
process clause of the Fourteenth Amendment as an instrument for transmitting the
principles of the First Amendment and those cases in which it is applied for its own
sake. The test of legislation which collides with the Fourteenth Amendment, because
it also collides with the principles of the First, is much more definite than the test
when only the Fourteenth is involved. Much of the vagueness of the due process
clause disappears when the specific prohibitions of the First become its standard. The
right of a State to regulate, for example, a public utility may well include, so far as
the due process test is concerned, power to impose all of the restrictions which a legislature may have a "rational basis" for adopting. But freedoms of speech and of press,
of assembly, and of worship may not be infringed on such slender grounds. They are
susceptible of restriction only to prevent grave and immediate danger to interests which
the State may lawfully protect. It is important to note that while it is the Fourteenth
Amendment which bears directly upon the State it is the more specific limiting principles of the First Amendment that finally govern this case.

Nor does our duty to apply the Bill of Rights to assertions of official authority depend
upon our possession of marked competence in the field where the invasion of rights
occurs. True, the task of translating the majestic generalities of the Bill of Rights,
conceived as part of the pattern of liberal government in the eighteenth century, into
concrete restraints on officials dealing with the problems of the twentieth century, is
one to disturb self-confidence. These principles grew in soil which also produced a
philosophy that the individual was the center of society, that his liberty was attainable through mere absence of governmental restraints, and that government should be
entrusted with few controls and only the mildest supervision over men's affairs. We
must transplant these rights to a soil in which the *laissez-faire* concept or principle of
non-interference has withered at least as to economic affairs, and social advancements
are increasingly sought through closer integration of society and through expanded
and strengthened governmental controls. These changed conditions often deprive
precedents of reliability and cast us more than we would choose upon our own judgment. But we act in these matters not by authority of our competence but by force
of our commissions. We cannot, because of modest estimates of our competence in
such specialties as public education, withhold the judgment that history authenticates
as the function of this Court when liberty is infringed.

4. Lastly, and this is the very heart of the *Gobitis* opinion, it reasons that "National unity is the basis of national security," that the authorities have "the right to
select appropriate means for its attainment," and hence reaches the conclusion that
such compulsory measures toward "national unity" are constitutional. . . . Upon the
verity of this assumption depends our answer in this case.

National unity as an end which officials may foster by persuasion and example is not in question. The problem is whether under our Constitution compulsion as here employed is a permissible means for its achievement.

Struggles to coerce uniformity of sentiment in support of some end thought essential to their time and country have been waged by many good as well as by evil men. Nationalism is a relatively recent phenomenon but at other times and places the ends have been racial or territorial security, support of a dynasty or regime, and particular plans for saving souls. As first and moderate methods to attain unity have failed, those bent on its accomplishment must resort to an ever-increasing severity. . . . Ultimate futility of such attempts to compel coherence is the lesson of every such effort from the Roman drive to stamp out Christianity as a disturber of its pagan unity, the Inquisition, as a means of religious and dynastic unity, the Siberian exiles as a means to Russian unity, down to the fast failing efforts of our present totalitarian enemies. Those who begin coercive elimination of dissent soon find themselves exterminating dissenters. Compulsory unification of opinion achieves only the unanimity of the graveyard.

It seems trite but necessary to say that the First Amendment to our Constitution was designed to avoid these ends by avoiding these beginnings. There is no mysticism in the American concept of the State or of the nature or origin of its authority. We set up government by consent of the governed, and the Bill of Rights denies those in power any legal opportunity to coerce that consent. Authority here is to be controlled by public opinion, not public opinion by authority.

The case is made difficult not because the principles of its decision are obscure but because the flag involved is our own. Nevertheless, we apply the limitations of the Constitution with no fear that freedom to be intellectually and spiritually diverse or even contrary will disintegrate the social organization. To believe that patriotism will not flourish if patriotic ceremonies are voluntary and spontaneous instead of a compulsory routine is to make an unflattering estimate of the appeal of our institutions to free minds. We can have intellectual individualism and the rich cultural diversities that we owe to exceptional minds only at the price of occasional eccentricity and abnormal attitudes. When they are so harmless to others or to the State as those we deal with here, the price is not too great. But freedom to differ is not limited to things that do not matter much. That would be a mere shadow of freedom. The test of its substance is the right to differ as to things that touch the heart of the existing order.

If there is any fixed star in our constitutional constellation, it is that no official, high or petty, can prescribe what shall be orthodox in politics, nationalism, religion, or other matters of opinion or force citizens to confess by word or act their faith therein. If there are any circumstances which permit an exception, they do not now occur to us. . . .

Affirmed.

Mr. Justice Roberts and Mr. Justice Reed adhere to the views expressed by the Court in *Minersville School District* v. *Gobitis,* 310 U.S. 586, and are of the opinion that the judgment below should be reversed.

Mr. Justice Black and Mr. Justice Douglas, concurring:

We are substantially in agreement with the opinion just read, but since we originally joined with the Court in the *Gobitis* case, it is appropriate that we make a brief statement of reasons for our change of view.

Reluctance to make the Federal Constitution a rigid bar against state regulation of conduct thought inimical to the public welfare was the controlling influence which moved us to consent to the *Gobitis* decision. Long reflection convinced us that although the principle is sound, its application in the particular case was wrong. *Jones v. Opelika,* 316 U.S. 584, 623. We believe that the statute before us fails to accord full scope to the freedom of religion secured to the appellees by the First and Fourteenth Amendments. . . .

No well-ordered society can leave to the individuals an absolute right to make final decisions, unassailable by the State, as to everything they will or will not do. The First Amendment does not go so far. Religious faiths, honestly held, do not free individuals from responsibility to conduct themselves obediently to laws which are either imperatively necessary to protect society as a whole from grave and pressingly imminent dangers or which, without any general prohibition, merely regulate time, place or manner of religious activity. Decision as to the constitutionality of particular laws which strike at the substance of religious tenets and practices must be made by this Court. The duty is a solemn one, and in meeting it we cannot say that a failure, because of religious scruples, to assume a particular physical position and to repeat the words of a patriotic formula creates a grave danger to the nation. Such a statutory exaction is a form of test oath, and the test oath has always been abhorrent in the United States. . . .

Neither our domestic tranquillity in peace nor our martial effort in war depend on compelling little children to participate in a ceremony which ends in nothing for them but a fear of spiritual condemnation. If, as we think, their fears are groundless, time and reason are the proper antidotes for their errors. The ceremonial, when enforced against conscientious objectors, more likely to defeat than to serve its high purpose, is a handy implement for disguised religious persecution. As such, it is inconsistent with our Constitution's plan and purpose.

Mr. Justice Murphy, concurring:

I agree with the opinion of the Court and join in it. . . .

Mr. Justice Frankfurter, dissenting:

One who belongs to the most vilified and persecuted minority in history is not likely to be insensible to the freedoms guaranteed by our Constitution. Were my purely personal attitude relevant I should wholeheartedly associate myself with the general libertarian views in the Court's opinion, representing as they do the thought and action of a lifetime. But as judges we are neither Jew nor Gentile, neither Catholic nor agnostic. We owe equal attachment to the Constitution and are equally bound by our judicial obligations whether we derive our citizenship from the earliest or the latest immigrants to these shores. As a member of this Court I am not justified in writing my private notions of policy into the Constitution, no matter how deeply I may cherish them or how mischievous I may deem their disregard. The duty of a judge who must decide which of two claims before the Court shall prevail, that of a State to enact and enforce laws within its general competence or that of an individual to refuse obedience because of the demands of his conscience, is not that of the ordinary person. It can never be emphasized too much that one's own opinion about the wisdom or evil of a law should be excluded altogether when one is doing one's duty on the bench. The only opinion of our own even looking in that direction that is material is our opinion whether legislators could in reason have enacted such a law. In the light of all the circumstances, including the history of this question in this Court, it would require more daring than I possess to deny that reasonable legislators could have taken the action which is before us for review. Most unwillingly, therefore, I must differ from my brethren with regard to legislation like this. I cannot bring my mind to believe that the "liberty" secured by the Due Process Clause gives this Court authority to deny to the State of West Virginia the attainment of that which we all recognize as a legitimate legislative end, namely, the promotion of good citizenship, by employment of the means here chosen.

Not so long ago we were admonished that "the only check upon our own exercise of power is our own sense of self-restraint. For the removal of unwise laws from the statute books appeal lies not to the courts but to the ballot and to the processes of democratic government." *United States* v. *Butler*, 297 U.S. 1, 79 (dissent). We have been told that generalities do not decide concrete cases. But the intensity with which a general principle is held may determine a particular issue, and whether we put first things first may decide a specific controversy. . . .

Under our constitutional system the legislature is charged solely with civil concerns of society. If the avowed or intrinsic legislative purpose is either to promote or to discourage some religious community or creed, it is clearly within the constitutional restrictions imposed on legislatures and cannot stand. But it by no means follows that legislative power is wanting whenever a general non-discriminatory civil regulation in fact touches conscientious scruples or religious beliefs of an individual or a group. Regard for such scruples or beliefs undoubtedly presents one of the most reasonable claims for the exertion of legislative accommodation. It is, of course, beyond our power to rewrite the State's requirement, by providing exemptions for those who do not wish to participate in the flag salute or by making some other accommodations to meet their scruples. That wisdom might suggest the making of such accommodations and that school administration would not find it too difficult to make them and yet maintain the ceremony for those not refusing to conform, is outside our province to suggest. Tact, respect, and generosity toward variant views will always commend themselves to those charged with the duties of legislation so as to achieve a maximum of good will and to require a minimum of unwilling submission to a general law. But the real question is, who is to make such accommodations, the courts or the legislature? . . .

Law is concerned with external behavior and not with the inner life of man. It rests in large measure upon compulsion. Socrates lives in history partly because he gave his life for the conviction that duty of obedience to secular law does not presuppose consent to its enactment or belief in its virtue. The consent upon which free government rests is the consent that comes from sharing in the process of making and unmaking laws. The state is not shut out from a domain because the individual conscience may deny the state's claim. The individual conscience may profess what faith it chooses. It may affirm and promote that faith—in the language of the Constitution, it may "exercise" it freely—but it cannot thereby restrict community action through political organs in matters of community concern, so long as the action is not asserted in a discriminatory way either openly or by stealth. One may have the right to practice one's religion and at the same time owe the duty of formal obedience to laws that run counter to one's beliefs. Compelling belief implies denial of opportunity to combat it and to assert dissident views. Such compulsion is one thing. Quite another matter is submission to conformity of action while denying its wisdom or virtue and with ample opportunity for seeking its change or abrogation. . . .

We are told that a flag salute is a doubtful substitute for adequate understanding of our institutions. The states that require such a school exercise do not have to justify it as the only means for promoting good citizenship in children, but merely as one of diverse means for accomplishing a worthy end. We may deem it a foolish measure, but the point is that this Court is not the organ of government to resolve doubts as to whether it will fulfill its purpose. Only if there be no doubt that any reasonable mind could entertain can we deny to the states the right to resolve doubts their way and not ours.

That which to the majority may seem essential for the welfare of the state may offend the consciences of a minority. But, so long as no inroads are made upon the actual exercise of religion by the minority, to deny the political power of the majority to enact laws concerned with civil matters, simply because they may offend the consciences of a minority, really means that the consciences of a minority are more sacred and more enshrined in the Constitution than the consciences of a majority. . . .

The right of West Virginia to utilize the flag salute as part of its educational process is denied because, so it is argued, it cannot be justified as a means of meeting a "clear and present danger" to national unity. . . . To talk about "clear and present danger" as the touchstone of allowable educational policy by the states whenever school curricula may impinge upon the boundaries of individual conscience, is to take a felicitous phrase out of the context of the particular situation where it arose and for which it was adapted. Mr. Justice Holmes . . . was not enunciating a formal rule that there can be no restriction upon speech and, still less, no compulsion where conscience balks, unless imminent danger would thereby be wrought "to our institutions or our government."

The flag salute exercise has no kinship whatever to the oath tests so odious in history. For the oath test was one of the instruments for suppressing heretical beliefs. Saluting the flag suppresses no belief nor curbs it. Children and their parents may believe what they please, avow their belief and practice it. It is not even remotely suggested that the requirement for saluting the flag involves the slightest restriction against the fullest opportunity on the part both of the children and of their parents to disavow as publicly as they choose to do so the meaning that others attach to the gesture of salute. . . .

The uncontrollable power wielded by this Court brings it very close to the most sensitive areas of public affairs. As appeal from legislation to adjudication becomes more frequent, and its consequences more far-reaching, judicial self-restraint becomes more and not less important, lest we unwarrantably enter social and political domains wholly outside our concern. I think I appreciate fully the objections to the law before us. But to deny that it presents a question upon which men might reasonably differ appears to me to be intolerance. And since men may so reasonably differ, I deem it beyond my constitutional power to assert my view of the wisdom of this law against the view of the State of West Virginia. . . .

Of course patriotism can not be enforced by the flag salute. But neither can the liberal spirit be enforced by judicial invalidation of illiberal legislation. Our constant preoccupation with the constitutionality of legislation rather than with its wisdom tends to preoccupation of the American mind with a false value. The tendency of focussing attention on constitutionality is to make constitutionality synonymous with wisdom, to regard a law as all right if it is constitutional. Such an attitude is a great enemy of liberalism. Particularly in legislation affecting freedom of thought and freedom of speech much which should offend a free-spirited society is constitutional. Reliance for the most precious interests of civilization, therefore, must be found outside of their vindication in courts of law. Only a persistent positive translation of the faith of a free society into the convictions and habits and actions of a community is the ultimate reliance against unabated temptations to fetter the human spirit.

Chapter 29

ESTABLISHMENT OF RELIGION

It is significant that the First Amendment, in forbidding Congress to pass any law "respecting an establishment of religion," uses the broadest possible term, "religion," rather than a narrower word such as "church." If the intention was simply to prevent the setting up of an official church, as in England, the narrower term would have seemed more appropriate. The contemporary state constitutions dealing with the subject of establishment employed more limited terms such as "religious sect" or "denomination." Moreover, the language adopted was clearly broader than Madison's first version of the amendment—"nor shall any national religion be established."

As for the original meaning of the word "establishment," it covered of course the full-fledged system of church-state relation in England, where there was one official church entitled to public financial support. But the essential features of this system had already been eliminated in America by 1790, and "establishment" had come to connote the somewhat different local practices. These included a tendency to accept Protestantism as the official religion, but in most states without preference for any one Protestant sect. There was also in some states the practice of collecting from all people tithes in the form of taxes, the funds so collected being turned over to the church designated by the taxpayer. If the taxpayer did not specify a church, the funds were sometimes used for support of the local almshouse. This system was referred to as "multiple establishment," with the power of government being used to assist several or all sects equally.

It was this system, embodied in a "Bill Establishing a Provision for Teachers of the Christian Religion," presented to the Virginia Legislature in 1784, which James Madison attacked in his famous and influential "Memorial and Remonstrance." The bill provided for tax support of religion, though those who professed no religion were permitted to direct that their tax be used for general educational purposes. Madison and Jefferson joined in defeating the bill, and then secured the adoption of Jefferson's Act for Establishing Religious Freedom.

During the nation's early history, interpretation of the establishment clause tended, by present standards, to be rather extreme. Thus, both Jefferson and Madison believed that presidential proclamations of national days of prayer and religious observance were contrary to the Constitution. Doubts were widely felt about the constitutionality of the office of chaplain in the legislature and the armed forces. But long practice has overruled such strict concepts of separation of church and state.

Perhaps the most authoritative indication of what cannot be done by Congress under the establishment clause was given by a Senate committee which in 1853 investigated the constitutionality of chaplains. Its conclusion was that laws "in favor of any church, or ecclesiastical association, or system of religious faith" would be invalid if they provided "endowment at the public expense, peculiar privileges to its members, or disadvantages or penalties upon those who should reject its doctrines or belong to other communions."

The principal present-day controversy over establishment problems concerns public assistance to sectarian education. Since education has traditionally been a local function, the First Amendment did not initially provide any limitation on educational policy or the expenditure of educational funds. In 1925 the Supreme Court made the First Amendment applicable to the states by way of the "liberty" language in the Fourteenth, but even so there was no immediate application of this principle in the establishment field. The issue was ignored in a 1930 case, *Cochran* v. *Louisiana State Board of Education*, 281 U.S. 370, where free textbooks were supplied to parochial as well as public schools. The issue the Court considered was whether this was a taking of property for private use, and they held it was not.

Everson v. *Board of Education of Ewing Township*, 330 U.S. 1 (1947), was the first case in which the Supreme Court did discuss state educational practices in an establishment context. Under authorization by the state, a New Jersey township had reimbursed parents of public and Catholic school pupils for the transportation of their children to school on regular public transportation. The Supreme Court upheld these payments to parents of parochial school students by a five to four vote. To assist in applying the establishment clause to the New Jersey bus problem, Justice Black stated the following formulation of principles:

Neither a state nor the Federal Government can set up a church. Neither can pass laws which aid one religion, aid all religions, or prefer one religion over another. Neither can force nor influence a person to go to or to remain away from church against his will or force him to profess a belief or disbelief in any religion. No person can be punished for entertaining or professing religious beliefs or disbeliefs, for church attendance or non-attendance. No tax in any amount, large or small, can be levied to support any religious activities or institutions, whatever they may be called, or whatever form they may adopt to teach or practice religion.

On the basis of these principles Black acknowledged that the New Jersey statute approached the "verge" of constitutional power. But he was able to uphold transportation payment by regarding the law as "welfare legislation," the benefits of which should not be denied to any individuals "because of their faith, or lack of it. . . ." But Justice Rutledge, one of the dissenters, thought that transportation "is as essential to education as any other element," and added that if providing transportation is merely "public welfare legislation," then there can be "no possible objection to more extensive support of religious education by New Jersey."

The following year the Court ruled unconstitutional a "released time" program of religious education in the public schools of Champaign, Illinois, in *McCollum* v. *Board of Education*, 333 U.S. 203 (1948). Under this program public school children, on consent of their parents, attended classes in Protestant, Catholic, or Jewish religious instruction during school hours and in the school building. The religious teachers were not paid by the schools, but were under the supervision of the school superintendents, and attendance was compulsory for participants in the program.

Justice Black, speaking for six justices, held that under this plan tax-supported school buildings were being used in disseminating religious doctrines, and the state's public school machinery was being employed to provide pupils for religious classes. Justice Jackson, concurring, agreed that the Champaign religious classes went beyond permissible limits, but he was worried over the prospect of the Supreme Court becoming a "super board of education for every school district in the nation." Only Justice Reed would have held the Champaign plan constitutional.

The *McCollum* decision created a furore in church circles, for similar released time programs were widely in effect throughout the country. It was against this background that the Court was offered a second opportunity to consider the issue, in ruling on the New York program of released time religious education in *Zorach* v. *Clauson*, 343 U.S. 306 (1952). The New York plan called for religious instruction outside the schools. Students were released from classes during the school day, on written request of their parents, in order to attend religious exercises or classes in religious centers off the school grounds. Those not released stayed in the school classrooms. The churches made weekly reports to the schools on children who had not reported for religious instruction. This plan differed sufficiently from the Champaign arrangement to win the approval of six members of the Court, including three (Douglas, Vinson, and Burton) who had voted against the Champaign plan.

Bible reading in the public schools was declared contrary to the constitutions of several states as early as the 1870s. The problem reached the Supreme Court in *Doremus* v. *Board of Education*, 342 U.S. 429 (1952), but the Court refused to decide the issue on the technical ground that the plaintiffs lacked standing to maintain the suit.

The Supreme Court in 1961 considered the constitutionality of state statutes banning certain activities and the operation of some businesses on Sunday. In four separate decisions, known as the *Sunday Closing Cases*, 366 U.S. 420, the Court denied that such statutes were an infringement of either the establishment or the free exercise of religion provisions.

ZORACH v. CLAUSON
343 U.S. 306, 72 S. Ct. 679, 96 L. Ed. 954 (1952)

MR. JUSTICE DOUGLAS delivered the opinion of the Court.

New York City has a program which permits its public schools to release students during the school day so that they may leave the school buildings and school grounds and go to religious centers for religious instruction or devotional exercises. A student is released on written request of his parents. Those not released stay in the classrooms. The churches make weekly reports to the schools, sending a list of children who have been released from public school but who have not reported for religious instruction.

This "released time" program involves neither religious instruction in public school classrooms nor the expenditure of public funds. All costs, including the application blanks, are paid by the religious organizations. The case is therefore unlike *McCollum*

v. *Board of Education,* 333 U.S. 203, which involved a "released time" program from Illinois. In that case the classrooms were turned over to religious instructors. We accordingly held that the program violated the First Amendment which (by reason of the Fourteenth Amendment) prohibits the states from establishing religion or prohibiting its free exercise.

Appellants, who are taxpayers and residents of New York City and whose children attend its public schools, challenge the present law, contending it is in essence not different from the one involved in the *McCollum* case. Their argument, stated elaborately in various ways, reduces itself to this: the weight and influence of the school is put behind a program for religious instruction; public school teachers police it, keeping tab on students who are released; the classroom activities come to a halt while the students who are released for religious instruction are on leave; the school is a crutch on which the churches are leaning for support in their religious training; without the cooperation of the schools this "released time" program, like the one in the *McCollum* case, would be futile and ineffective. The New York Court of Appeals sustained the law against this claim of unconstitutionality. . . .

The briefs and arguments are replete with data bearing on the merits of this type of "released time" program. Views *pro* and *con* are expressed, based on practical experience with these programs and with their implications. We do not stop to summarize these materials nor to burden the opinion with an analysis of them. For they involve considerations not germane to the narrow constitutional issue presented. They largely concern the wisdom of the system, its efficiency from an educational point of view, and the political considerations which have motivated its adoption or rejection in some communities. Those matters are of no concern here, since our problem reduces itself to whether New York by this system has either prohibited the "free exercise" of religion or has made a law "respecting an establishment of religion" within the meaning of the First Amendment.

It takes obtuse reasoning to inject any issue of the "free exercise" of religion into the present case. No one is forced to go to the religious classroom and no religious exercise or instruction is brought to the classrooms of the public schools. A student need not take religious instruction. He is left to his own desires as to the manner or time of his religious devotions, if any.

There is a suggestion that the system involves the use of coercion to get public school students into religious classrooms. There is no evidence in the record before us that supports that conclusion. The present record indeed tells us that the school authorities are neutral in this regard and do no more than release students whose parents so request. If in fact coercion were used, if it were established that any one or more teachers were using their office to persuade or force students to take the religious instruction, a wholly different case would be presented. Hence we put aside that claim of coercion both as respects the "free exercise" of religion and "an establishment of religion" within the meaning of the First Amendment.

Moreover, apart from that claim of coercion, we do not see how New York by this type of "released time" program has made a law respecting an establishment of religion within the meaning of the First Amendment. There is much talk of the separation of Church and State in the history of the Bill of Rights and in the decisions clustering around the First Amendment. . . . There cannot be the slightest doubt that the First Amendment reflects the philosophy that Church and State should be separated. And so far as interference with the "free exercise" of religion and an "establishment" of religion are concerned, the separation must be complete and unequivocal. The First Amendment within the scope of its coverage permits no exception; the prohibition is absolute. The First Amendment, however, does not say that in every and all respects there shall be a separation of Church and State. Rather, it studiously defines the manner, the specific ways, in which there shall be no concert or union or dependency one on the other. That is the common sense of the matter. Otherwise the state and religion would be aliens to each other—hostile, suspicious, and even unfriendly. Churches could not be required to pay even property taxes. Municipalities would not be permitted to render police or fire protection to religious groups. Policemen who helped parishioners into their places of worship would violate the Constitution. Prayers in our legislative halls; the appeals to the Almighty in the messages of the Chief Executive; the proclamations making Thanksgiving Day a holiday; "so help me God" in our courtroom oaths—these and all other references to the Almighty that run through our laws, our public rituals, our ceremonies would be flouting the First Amendment. A fastidious atheist or agnostic could even object to the supplication with which the Court opens each session: "God save the United States and this Honorable Court."

We would have to press the concept of separation of Church and State to these extremes to condemn the present law on constitutional grounds. The nullification of this law would have wide and profound effects. A Catholic student applies to his teacher for permission to leave the school during hours on a Holy Day of Obligation to attend a mass. A Jewish student asks his teacher for permission to be excused for Yom Kippur. A Protestant wants the afternoon off for a family baptismal ceremony. In each case the teacher requires parental consent in writing. In each case the teacher, in order to make sure the student is not a truant, goes further and requires a report from the priest, the rabbi, or the minister. The teacher in other words cooperates in a religious program to the extent of making it possible for her students to participate in it. Whether she does it occasionally for a few students, regularly for one, or pursuant to a systematized program designed to further the religious needs of all the students does not alter the character of the act.

We are a religious people whose institutions presuppose a Supreme Being. We guarantee the freedom to worship as one chooses. We make room for as wide a variety of beliefs and creeds as the spiritual needs of man deem necessary. We sponsor an attitude on the part of government that shows no partiality to any one group and that lets each flourish according to the zeal of its adherents and the appeal of its dogma. When the state encourages religious instruction or cooperates with religious authorities by adjusting the schedule of public events to sectarian needs, it follows the best of our traditions. For it then respects the religious nature of our people and accommodates the public service to their spiritual needs. To hold that it may not would be to find in the Constitution a requirement that the government show a callous indifference to religious groups. That would be preferring those who believe in no religion over those who do believe. Government may not finance religious groups nor undertake religious instruction nor blend secular and sectarian education nor use secular institutions to force one or some religion on any person. But we find no constitutional requirement which makes it necessary for government to be hostile to religion and to throw its weight against efforts to widen the effective scope of religious influence. The government must be neutral when it comes to competition between sects. It may not thrust any sect on any person. It may not make a religious observance compulsory. It may not coerce anyone to attend church, to observe a religious holiday, or to take religious instruction. But it can close its doors or suspend its operations as to those who want to repair to their religious sanctuary for worship or instruction. No more than that is undertaken here. . . .

In the *McCollum* case the classrooms were used for religious instruction and the force of the public school was used to promote that instruction. Here, as we have said, the public schools do no more than accommodate their schedules to a program of outside religious instruction. We follow the *McCollum* case. But we cannot expand it to cover the present released time program unless separation of Church and State means that public institutions can make no adjustments of their schedules to accommodate the religious needs of the people. We cannot read into the Bill of Rights such a philosophy of hostility to religion.

Affirmed.

Mr. Justice Black, dissenting.

Illinois ex. rel. McCollum v. *Board of Education,* 333 U.S. 203, held invalid as an "establishment of religion" an Illinois system under which school children, compelled by law to go to public schools, were freed from some hours of required school work on condition that they attend special religious classes held in the school buildings. Although the classes were taught by sectarian teachers neither employed nor paid by the state, the state did use its power to further the program by releasing some of the children from regular class work, insisting that those released attend the religious classes, and requiring that those who remained behind do some kind of academic work while the others received their religious training. . . .

I see no significant difference between the invalid Illinois system and that of New York here sustained. Except for the use of the school buildings in Illinois, there is no difference between the systems which I consider even worthy of mention. In the New York program, as in that of Illinois, the school authorities release some of the children on the condition that they attend the religious classes, get reports on whether they attend, and hold the other children in the school building until the religious hour is over. . . . *McCollum* . . . held that Illinois could not constitutionally manipulate the compelled classroom hours of its compulsory school machinery so as to channel children into sectarian classes. Yet that is exactly what the Court holds New York can do.

I am aware that our *McCollum* decision on separation of Church and State has been subjected to a most searching examination throughout the country. Probably few opinions from this Court in recent years have attracted more attention or stirred wider debate. Our insistence on "a wall between Church and State which must be kept high and impregnable" has seemed to some a correct exposition of the philosophy and a true interpretation of the language of the First Amendment to which we should strictly adhere. With equal conviction and sincerity, others have thought the *McCollum* decision fundamentally wrong and have pledged continuous warfare against it. The opinions in the court below and the briefs here reflect these diverse viewpoints. In dissenting today, I mean to do more than give routine approval to our *McCollum* decision. I mean also to reaffirm my faith in the fundamental philosophy expressed in *McCollum* and *Everson* v. *Board of Education,* 330 U.S. 1. That reaffirmance can be brief because of the exhaustive opinions in those recent cases.

Difficulty of decision in the hypothetical situations mentioned by the Court, but not now before us, should not confuse the issues in this case. Here the sole question is whether New York can use its compulsory education laws to help religious sects get attendants presumably too unenthusiastic to go unless moved to do so by the pressure of this state machinery. That this is the plan, purpose, design and consequence of the New York program cannot be denied. The state thus makes religious sects beneficiaries of its power to compel children to attend secular schools. Any use of such coercive power by the state to help or hinder some religious sects or to prefer all religious sects over nonbelievers or vice versa is just what I think the First Amendment forbids. In considering whether a state has entered this forbidden field the question is not whether it has entered too far but whether it has entered at all. New York is manipulating its compulsory education laws to help religious sects get pupils. This is not separation but combination of Church and State.

The Court's validation of the New York system rests in part on its statement that Americans are "a religious people whose institutions presuppose a Supreme Being." This was at least as true when the First Amendment was adopted; and it was just as true when eight Justices of this Court invalidated the released time system in *McCollum* on the premise that a state can no more "aid all religions" than it can aid one. It was precisely because Eighteenth Century Americans were a religious people divided into many fighting sects that we were given the constitutional mandate to keep Church and State completely separate. Colonial history had already shown that, here as elsewhere zealous sectarians entrusted with governmental power to further their causes would sometimes torture, maim and kill those they branded "heretics," "atheists" or "agnostics." The First Amendment was therefore to insure that no one powerful sect or combination of sects could use political or governmental power to punish dissenters whom they could not convert to their faith. Now as then, it is only by wholly isolating the state from the religious sphere and compelling it to be completely neutral, that the freedom of each and every denomination and of all nonbelievers can be maintained. It is this neutrality the Court abandons today when it treats New York's coercive system as a program which *merely* "encourages religious instruction or cooperates with religious authorities." The abandonment is all the more dangerous to liberty because of the Court's legal exaltation of the orthodox and its derogation of unbelievers.

Under our system of religious freedom, people have gone to their religious sanctuaries not because they feared the law but because they loved their God. The choice of all has been as free as the choice of those who answered the call to worship moved only by the music of the old Sunday morning church bells. The spiritual mind of man has thus been free to believe, disbelieve, or doubt, without repression, great or small, by the heavy hand of government. Statutes authorizing such repression have been stricken. Before today, our judicial opinions have refrained from drawing invidious distinctions between those who believe in no religion and those who do believe. The First Amendment has lost much if the religious follower and the atheist are no longer to be judicially regarded as entitled to equal justice under law.

State help to religion injects political and party prejudices into a holy field. It too often substitutes force for prayer, hate for love, and persecution for persuasion. Government should not be allowed, under cover of the soft euphemism of "co-operation," to steal into the sacred area of religious choice.

Mr. Justice Frankfurter, dissenting. . . .

Mr. Justice Jackson, dissenting.

This released time program is founded upon a use of the State's power of coercion, which, for me, determines its unconstitutionality. Stripped to its essentials, the plan has two stages: first, that the State compel each student to yield a large part of his time for public secular education; and, second, that some of it be "released" to him on condition that he devote it to sectarian religious purposes.

No one suggests that the Constitution would permit the State directly to require this "released" time to be spent "under the control of a duly constituted religious body." This program accomplishes that forbidden result by indirection. If public education were taking so much of the pupils' time as to injure the public or the students' welfare by encroaching upon their religious opportunity, simply shortening everyone's school day would facilitate voluntary and optional attendance at Church classes. But that suggestion is rejected upon the ground that if they are made free many students will not go to the Church. Hence, they must be deprived of freedom for this period, with Church attendance put to them as one of the two permissible ways of using it.

The greater effectiveness of this system over voluntary attendance after school hours is due to the truant officer who, if the youngster fails to go to the Church school, dogs him back to the public schoolroom. Here schooling is more or less suspended during the "released time" so the nonreligious attendants will not forge ahead of the churchgoing absentees. But it serves as a temporary jail for a pupil who will not go to Church. It takes more subtlety of mind than I possess to deny that this is governmental constraint in support of religion. It is as unconstitutional, in my view, when exerted by indirection as when exercised forthrightly.

As one whose children, as a matter of free choice, have been sent to privately supported Church schools, I may challenge the Court's suggestion that opposition to this plan can only be antireligious, atheistic, or agnostic. My evangelistic brethren confuse an objection to compulsion with an objection to religion. It is possible to hold a faith with enough confidence to believe that what should be rendered to God does not need to be decided and collected by Caesar.

The day that this country ceases to be free for irreligion it will cease to be free for religion except for the sect that can win political power. The same epithetical jurisprudence used by the Court today to beat down those who oppose pressuring children into some religion can devise as good epithets tomorrow against those who object to pressuring them into a favored religion. And, after all, if we concede to the State power and wisdom to single out "duly constituted religious" bodies as exclusive alternatives for compulsory secular instruction, it would be logical to also uphold the power and wisdom to choose the true faith among those "duly constituted." We start down a rough road when we begin to mix compulsory public education with compulsory godliness.

A number of Justices just short of a majority of the majority that promulgates today's passionate dialectics joined in answering them in *Illinois ex rel. McCollum v. Board of Education,* 333 U.S. 203. The distinction attempted between that case and this is trivial, almost to the point of cynicism, magnifying its nonessential details and disparaging compulsion which was the underlying reason for invalidity. A reading of the Court's opinion in that case along with its opinion in this case will show such difference of overtones and undertones as to make clear that the *McCollum* case has passed like a storm in a teacup. The wall which the Court was professing to erect between Church and State has become even more warped and twisted than I expected. Today's judgment will be more interesting to students of psychology and of the judicial processes than to students of constitutional law.

SUNDAY CLOSING CASES

McGOWAN v. MARYLAND
GALLAGHER v. CROWN KOSHER SUPER MARKET
TWO GUYS FROM HARRISON-ALLENTOWN v. McGINLEY
BRAUNFELD v. BROWN
366 U.S. 420, 81 S. Ct. 1101, 6 L. Ed. 2d 393 (1961)

Two of these four cases, *McGowan* and *Two Guys,* were challenges by regular commercial establishments of the Sunday closing laws of Maryland and Pennsylvania, respectively. The other two cases, *Crown Kosher* and *Braunfeld,* arising in Massachusetts and Pennsylvania, involved businesses operated by Orthodox Jews who had a special grievance in that, since their religion required that they close their shops on Saturday, a Sunday closing law limited them to a five-day week. The establishment of religion issue was considered by the Court in all four cases, but the free exercise of religion was an issue in only the two cases brought by Jewish merchants.

The Sunday closing laws in all three of the states had been repeatedly amended over the years and were filled with exceptions for certain kinds of activities or commercial activities. Often there seemed no rational explanation why the statutes permitted certain goods to be sold on Sundays and not others. Consequently, in all the cases the statutes were attacked as denying equal protection of the laws contrary to the Fourteenth Amendment. The Court uniformly denied these claims, and the argument on this issue is not reproduced below.

In all of the cases except *Crown Kosher,* the state law had been upheld in the lower court. The *Crown Kosher, Two Guys,* and *Braunfeld* cases had originated as suits to enjoin enforcement of the state laws, and had been tried before three-judge federal district courts. *McGowan* was a prosecution by the state for violation of the Maryland Sunday closing law, and the appeal was from the judgment of the Maryland supreme court.

Chief Justice Warren and Justices Black, Frankfurter, Harlan, Clark, and Whittaker upheld the state laws on all issues in all four cases. Justices Brennan and Stewart dissented in *Crown Kosher* and *Braunfeld* on the issue of free exercise of religion. Justice Douglas dissented in all four cases on both the establishment and free exercise of religion grounds. Justice Frankfurter, joined by Justice Harlan, stated his views in an extended separate opinion, which with appendices and tables ran to over one hundred pages in the Reports.

MR. CHIEF JUSTICE WARREN [from *McGowan v. Maryland*]. . . .

Appellants contend that the statutes violate the guarantee of separation of church and state in that the statutes are laws respecting an establishment of religion contrary to the First Amendment, made applicable to the states by the Fourteenth Amendment. . . .

The essence of appellants' "establishment" argument is that Sunday is the Sabbath day of the predominant Christian sects; that the purpose of the enforced stoppage of labor on that day is to facilitate and encourage church attendance; that the purpose of setting Sunday as a day of universal rest is to induce people with no religion or people with marginal religious beliefs to join the predominant Christian sects; that the purpose of the atmosphere of tranquility created by Sunday closing is to aid the conduct of church services and religious observance of the sacred day. . . . There is no dispute that the original laws which dealt with Sunday labor were motivated by religious forces. But what we must decide is whether present Sunday legislation, having undergone extensive changes from the earliest forms, still retains its religious character.

Sunday Closing Laws go far back into American history having been brought to the colonies with a background of English legislation dating to the thirteenth century. . . . Clearly . . . the English Sunday legislation was in aid of the established church.

The American colonial Sunday restrictions arose soon after settlement. Starting in 1650, the Plymouth Colony proscribed servile work, unnecessary traveling, sports, and the sale of alcoholic beverages on the Lord's day and enacted laws concerning church attendance. The Massachusetts Bay Colony and the Connecticut and New

Haven Colonies enacted similar prohibitions. . . . The religious orientation of the colonial statutes was equally apparent. . . .

But, despite the strongly religious origin of these laws, beginning before the eighteenth century, nonreligious arguments for Sunday closing began to be heard more distinctly and the statutes began to lose some of their totally religious flavor. In the middle 1700's, Blackstone wrote, "[T]he keeping one day in the seven holy, as a time of relaxation and refreshment as well as for public worship, is of admirable service to a state considered merely as a civil institution. It humanizes, by the help of conversation and society, the manners of the lower classes; which would otherwise degenerate into a sordid ferocity and savage selfishness of spirit; it enables the industrious workman to pursue his occupation in the ensuing week with health and cheerfulness." 4 Bl. Comm. 63. . . . The preamble to a 1679 Rhode Island enactment stated that the reason for the ban on Sunday employment was that "persons being evill minded, have presumed to employ in servile labor, more than necessity requireth, their servants. . . ." . . . With the advent of the First Amendment, the colonial provisions requiring church attendance were soon repealed. . . .

More recently, further secular justifications have been advanced for making Sunday a day of rest, a day when people may recover from the labors of the week just passed and may physically and mentally prepare for the week's work to come. . . . The proponents of Sunday closing legislation are no longer exclusively representatives of religious interests. Recent New Jersey Sunday legislation was supported by labor groups and trade associations. . . . Almost every State in our country presently has some type of Sunday regulation and over forty possess a relatively comprehensive system. . . . Some of our States now enforce their Sunday legislation through Departments of Labor. . . . Thus have Sunday laws evolved from the wholly religious sanctions that originally were enacted. . . .

In order to dispose of the case before us, we must consider the standards by which the Maryland statutes are to be measured. . . . The First Amendment, in its final form, did not simply bar a congressional enactment *establishing a church;* it forbade all laws *respecting an establishment of religion.* Thus, this Court has given the Amendment a "broad interpretation . . . in the light of its history and the evils it was designed forever to suppress. . . ." *Everson v. Board of Education.* . . . It has found that the First and Fourteenth Amendments afford protection against religious establishment far more extensive than merely to forbid a national or state church. . . .

However, it is equally true that the "Establishment" Clause does not ban federal or state regulation of conduct whose reason or effect merely happens to coincide or harmonize with the tenets of some or all religions. In many instances, the Congress or state legislatures conclude that the general welfare of society, wholly apart from any religious considerations, demands such regulation. Thus, for temporal purposes, murder is illegal. And the fact that this agrees with the dictates of the Judaeo-Christian religions while it may disagree with others does not invalidate the regulation. So too with the questions of adultery and polygamy. . . . The same could be said of theft, fraud, etc., because those offenses were also proscribed in the Decalogue. . . .

Throughout this century and longer, both the federal and state governments have oriented their activities very largely toward improvement of the health, safety, recreation and general well-being of our citizens. Numerous laws affecting public health, safety factors in industry, laws affecting hours and conditions of labor of women and children, week-end diversion at parks and beaches, and cultural activities of various kinds, now point the way toward the good life for all. Sunday Closing Laws, like those before us, have become part and parcel of this great governmental concern wholly apart from their original purposes or connotations. The present purpose and effect of most of them is to provide a uniform day of rest for all citizens; the fact that

350 First Amendment Freedoms

this day is Sunday, a day of particular significance for the dominant Christian sects, does not bar the State from achieving its secular goals. To say that the States cannot prescribe Sunday as a day of rest for these purposes solely because centuries ago such laws had their genesis in religion would give a constitutional interpretation of hostility to the public welfare rather than one of mere separation of church and State. . . .

But, this does not answer all of appellants' contentions. We are told that the State has other means at its disposal to accomplish its secular purpose, other courses that would not even remotely or incidentally give state aid to religion. . . . It is true that if the State's interest were simply to provide for its citizens a periodic respite from work, a regulation demanding that everyone rest one day in seven, leaving the choice of the day to the individual, would suffice.

However, the State's purpose is not merely to provide a one-day-in-seven work stoppage. In addition to this, the State seeks to set one day apart from all others as a day of rest, repose, recreation and tranquility—a day which all members of the family and community have the opportunity to spend and enjoy together, a day in which there exists relative quiet and disassociation from the everyday intensity of commercial activities, a day in which people may visit friends and relatives who are not available during working days.

Obviously, a state is empowered to determine that a rest-one-day-in-seven statute would not accomplish this purpose; that it would not provide for a general cessation of activity, a special atmosphere of tranquility, a day which all members of the family or friends and relatives might spend together. Furthermore, it seems plain that the problems involved in enforcing such a provision would be exceedingly more difficult than those in enforcing a common-day-of-rest provision.

Moreover, it is common knowledge that the first day of the week has come to have special significance as a rest day in this country. People of all religions and people with no religion regard Sunday as a time for family activity, for visiting friends and relatives, for late-sleeping, for passive and active entertainments, for dining out and the like. . . . Sunday is a day apart from all others. The cause is irrelevant; the fact exists. It would seem unrealistic for enforcement purposes and perhaps detrimental to the general welfare to require a state to choose a common-day-of-rest other than that which most persons would select of their own accord. For these reasons, we hold that the Maryland statutes are not laws respecting an establishment of religion. . . .

MR. CHIEF JUSTICE WARREN [from *Braunfeld* v. *Brown*]. . . .

Concededly, appellants and all other persons who wish to work on Sunday will be burdened economically by the State's day of rest mandate; and appellants point out that their religion requires them to refrain from work on Saturday as well. Our inquiry then is whether, in these circumstances, the First and Fourteenth Amendments forbid application of the Sunday Closing Law to appellants.

Certain aspects of religious exercise cannot, in any way, be restricted or burdened by either federal or state legislation. Compulsion by law of the acceptance of any creed or the practice of any form of worship is strictly forbidden. The freedom to hold religious beliefs and opinions is absolute. . . .

However, the freedom to act, even when the action is in accord with one's religious convictions, is not totally free from legislative restrictions. . . . The statute at bar does not make unlawful any religious practices of appellants; the Sunday law simply regulates a secular activity and, as applied to appellants, operates so as to make the practice of their religious beliefs more expensive. Furthermore, the law's effect does not inconvenience all members of the Orthodox Jewish faith but only those who believe it necessary to work on Sunday. And even these are not faced with as serious a choice as forsaking their religious practices or subjecting themselves to criminal prosecution. Fully recognizing that the alternatives open to appellants and others similarly situated—retaining their present occupations and incurring economic disadvantage or engaging in some other commercial activity which does not call for either Saturday or Sunday labor—may well result in some financial sacrifice in order to observe their religious beliefs, still the option is wholly different than when the legislation attempts to make a religious practice itself unlawful.

To strike down, without the most critical scrutiny, legislation which imposes only an indirect burden on the exercise of religion, i.e., legislation whch does not make unlawful the religious practice itself, would radically restrict the operating latitude of the legislature. Statutes which tax income and limit the amount which may be deducted for religious contributions impose an indirect economic burden on the observance of the religion of the citizen whose religion requires him to donate a greater amount to his church; statutes which require the courts to be closed on Saturday and Sunday impose a similar indirect burden on the observance of the religion of the trial lawyer whose religion requires him to rest on a weekday. The list of legislation of this nature is nearly limitless.

Needless to say, when entering the area of religious freedom, we must be fully cognizant of the particular protection that the Constitution has accorded it. Abhorrence of religious persecution and intolerance is a basic part of our heritage. But we are a cosmopolitan nation made up of people of almost every conceivable religious preference. These denominations number almost three hundred. . . . Consequently, it cannot be expected, much less required, that legislators enact no law regulating conduct that may in some way result in an economic disadvantage to some religious sects and not to others because of the special practices of the various religions. We do not believe that such an effect is an absolute test for determining whether the legislation violates the freedom of religion protected by the First Amendment. . . .

. . . If the purpose or effect of a law is to impede the observance of one or all religions or is to discriminate invidiously between religions, that law is constitutionally invalid even though the burden may be characterized as being only indirect. But if the State regulates conduct by enacting a general law within its power, the purpose and effect of which is to advance the State's secular goals, the statute is valid despite its indirect burden on religious observance unless the State may accomplish its purpose by means which do not impose such a burden. . . .

Appellants . . . contend that the State should cut an exception from the Sunday labor proscription for those people who, because of religious conviction, observe a day of rest other than Sunday. By such regulation, appellants contend, the economic disadvantages imposed by the present system would be removed and the State's interest in having all people rest one day would be satisfied.

A number of States provide such an exemption, and this may well be the wiser solution to the problem. But our concern is not with the wisdom of legislation but its constitutional limitation. Thus, reason and experience teach that to permit the exemption might well undermine the State's goal of providing a day that, as best possible, eliminates the atmosphere of commercial noise and activity. Although not dispositive of the issue, enforcement problems would be more difficult since there would be two or more days to police rather than one and it would be more difficult to observe whether violations were occurring.

Additional problems might also be presented by a regulation of this sort. To allow only people who rest on a day other than Sunday to keep their businesses open on that day might well provide these people with an economic advantage over their competitors who must remain closed on that day; this might cause the Sundayobservers to complain that their religions were being discriminated against. With this competitive advantage existing, there could well be the temptation for some, in order to keep their businesses open on Sunday, to assert that they have religious convictions which compel them to close their businesses on what had formerly been their least profitable day. This might make necessary a state-conducted inquiry into the sincerity of the individual's religious beliefs, a practice which a State might believe would itself run afoul of the spirit of constitutionally protected religious guarantees. Finally, in order to keep the disruption of the day at a minimum, exempted employers would probably have to hire employees who themselves qualified for the exemption because of their own religious beliefs, a practice which a State might feel to be opposed to its general policy prohibiting religious discrimination in hiring. For all of these reasons, we cannot say that the Pennsylvania statute before us is invalid, either on its face or as applied. . . .

MR. JUSTICE BRENNAN, concurring and dissenting [from *Braunfeld* v. *Brown*].

I agree with the Chief Justice that there is no merit in appellants' establishment and equal-protection claims. I dissent, however, as to the claim that Pennsylvania has prohibited the free exercise of appellants' religion. . . .

. . . The issue in this case . . . is whether a State may put an individual to a choice between his business and his religion. The Court today holds that it may. But I dissent, believing that such a law prohibits the free exercise of religion. . . .

Admittedly, these laws . . . do not say that appellants must work on Saturday. But their effect is that appellants may not simultaneously practice their religion and their trade, without being hampered by a substantial competitive disadvantage. Their effect is that no one may at one and the same time be an Orthodox Jew and compete effectively with his Sunday-observing fellow tradesmen. This clog upon the exercise of religion, this state-imposed burden on Orthodox Judaism, has exactly the same economic effect as a tax levied upon the sale of religious literature. . . .

What . . . is the compelling state interest which impels the Commonwealth of Pennsylvania to impede appellants' freedom of worship? What overbalancing need is so weighty in the constitutional scale that it justifies this substantial, though indirect, limitation of appellants' freedom? . . . It is the mere convenience of having everyone rest on the same day. It is to defend this interest that the Court holds that a State need not follow the alternative route of granting an exemption for those who in good faith observe a day of rest other than Sunday.

It is true, I suppose, that the granting of such an exemption would make Sundays a little noisier, and the task of police and prosecutor a little more difficult. It is also true that a majority—21—of the 34 States which have general Sunday regulations have exemptions of this kind. We are not told that those States are significantly noisier, or that their police are significantly more burdened, than Pennsylvania's. . . . The Court conjures up several difficulties with such a system which seem to me more fanciful than real. . . .

In fine, the Court, in my view, has exalted administrative convenience to a constitutional level high enough to justify making one religion economically disadvantageous. . . .

MR. JUSTICE STEWART, dissenting [from *Braunfeld* v. *Brown*]. . . .

Pennsylvania has passed a law which compels an Orthodox Jew to choose between his religious faith and his economic survival. That is a cruel choice. It is a choice which I think no State can constitutionally demand. For me this is not something that can be swept under the rug and forgotten in the interest of enforced Sunday togetherness. I think the impact of this law upon these appellants grossly violates their constitutional right to the free exercise of religion.

Mr. Justice Douglas, dissenting [in all four cases]. . . .

I do not see how a State can make protesting citizens refrain from doing innocent acts on Sunday because the doing of those acts offends sentiments of their Christian neighbors.

The institutions of our society are founded on the belief that there is an authority higher than the authority of the State; that there is a moral law which the state is powerless to alter; that the individual possesses rights, conferred by the Creator, which government must respect. . . .

Those who fashioned the Constitution decided that if and when God is to be served, His service will not be motivated by coercive measures of government. . . . The First Amendment . . . means, as I understand it, that if a religious leaven is to be worked into the affairs of our people, it is to be done by individuals and groups, not by the government. This necessarily means, *first,* that the dogma, creed, scruples, or practices of no religious group or sect are to be preferred over those of any others; *second,* that no one shall be interfered with by government for practicing the religion of his choice; *third,* that the state may not require anyone to practice a religion or even any religion; and *fourth,* that the state cannot compel one so to conduct himself as not to offend the religious scruples of another. The idea, as I understand it, was to limit the power of government to act in religious matters . . . not to limit the freedom of religious men to act religiously nor to restrict the freedom of atheists or agnostics.

The First Amendment commands government to have no interest in theology or ritual; it admonishes government to be interested in allowing religious freedom to flourish—whether the result is to produce Catholics, Jews, or Protestants, or to turn the people toward the path of Buddha, or to end in a predominantly Moslem nation, or to produce in the long run atheists or agnostics. On matters of this kind government must be neutral. This freedom plainly includes freedom *from* religion with the right to believe, speak, write, publish and advocate antireligious programs. . . . Certainly the "free exercise" clause does not require that everyone embrace the theology of some church or of some faith, or observe the religious practices of any majority or minority sect. . . . The "establishment" clause protects citizens also against any law which selects any religious custom, practice, or ritual, puts the force of government behind it, and fines, imprisons or otherwise penalizes a person for not observing it. The Government plainly could not join forces with one religious group and decree a universal and symbolic circumcision. Nor could it require all children to be baptized or give tax exemptions only to those whose children were baptized.

Could it require a fast from sunrise to sunset throughout the Moslem month of Ramadan? I should think not. Yet why then can it make criminal the doing of other acts, as innocent as eating, during the day that Christians revere? . . .

The issue of these cases would . . . be in better focus if we imagined that a state legislature, controlled by orthodox Jews and Seventh Day Adventists, passed a law making it a crime to keep a shop open on Saturdays. Would a Baptist, Catholic, Methodist, or Presbyterian be compelled to obey that law or go to jail or pay a fine? Or suppose Moslems grew in political strength here and got a law through a state legislature making it a crime to keep a shop open on Fridays? Would the rest of us have to submit under the fear of criminal sanctions? . . .

The Court picks and chooses language from various decisions to bolster its conclusion that these Sunday Laws in the modern setting are "civil regulations." No matter how much is written, no matter what is said, the parentage of these laws is the Fourth Commandment; and they serve and satisfy the religious predispositions of our Christian communities. . . .

It seems to me plain that by these laws the States compel one, under sanction of law, to refrain from work or recreation on Sunday because of the majority's religious views about that day. The State by law makes Sunday a symbol of respect or adherence. Refraining from work or recreation in deference to the majority's religious feelings about Sunday is within every person's choice. By what authority can government compel it? . . .

These laws are sustained because, it is said, the First Amendment is concerned with religious convictions or opinion, not with conduct. But it is a strange Bill of Rights that makes it possible for the dominant religious group to bring the minority to heel because the minority, in the doing of acts which intrinsically are wholesome and not antisocial, does not defer to the majority's religious beliefs. Some have religious scruples against eating pork. Those scruples, no matter how bizarre they might seem to some, are within the ambit of the First Amendment. . . . Is it possible that a majority of a state legislature having those religious scruples could make it criminal for the nonbeliever to sell pork? Some have religious scruples against slaughtering cattle. Could a state legislature, dominated by that group, make it criminal to run an abattoir?

The Court balances the need of the people for rest, recreation, late-sleeping, family visiting and the like against the command of the First Amendment that no one need bow to the religious beliefs of another. There is in this realm no room for balancing. I see no place for it in the constitutional scheme. A legislature of Christians can no more make minorities conform to their weekly regime than a legislature of Moslems, or a legislature of Hindus. The religious regime of every group must be respected—unless it crosses the line of criminal conduct. But no one can be forced to come to a halt before it, or refrain from doing things that would offend it. That is my reading of the Establishment Clause and the Free Exercise Clause. . . .

The State can of course require one day of rest a week: one day when every shop or factory is closed. Quite a few States make that requirement. Then the "day of rest" becomes purely and simply a health measure. But the Sunday laws operate differently. They force minorities to obey the majority's religious feelings of what is due and proper for a Christian community; they provide a coercive spur to the "weaker brethren," to those who are indifferent to the claims of a Sabbath through apathy or scruple. . . .

There is an "establishment" of religion in the constitutional sense if any practice of any religious group has the sanction of law behind it. There is an interference with the "free exercise" of religion if what in conscience one can do or omit doing is required because of the religious scruples of the community. Hence I would declare each of those laws unconstitutional as applied to the complaining parties, whether or not they are members of a sect which observes as their Sabbath a day other than Sunday.

When these laws are applied to Orthodox Jews . . . or to Sabbatarians their vice is accentuated. If the Sunday laws are constitutional, Kosher markets are on a five-day week. Thus those laws put an economic penalty on those who observe Saturday rather than Sunday as the Sabbath. For the economic pressures on these minorities, created by the fact that our communities are predominantly Sunday-minded, there is no recourse. When, however, the State uses its coercive powers—here the criminal law—to compel minorities to observe a second Sabbath, not their own, the

State undertakes to aid and "prefer one religion over another"—contrary to the command of the Constitution. . . .

SELECTED REFERENCES

Abernathy, Glenn, *The Right of Assembly and Association.* Columbia, S.C.: University of South Carolina Press, 1961.

Berns, Walter, *Freedom, Virtue and the First Amendment.* Baton Rouge, La.: Louisiana State University Press, 1957.

Chafee, Zechariah, Jr., *Free Speech in the United States.* Cambridge, Mass.: Harvard University Press, 1941.

Corwin, Edward S. (ed.), *The Constitution of the United States of America: Analysis and Interpretation,* pp. 745–810. Washington: Government Printing Office, 1953.

Cushman, Robert E., *Civil Liberties in the United States: A Guide to Current Problems and Experience.* Ithaca, N.Y.: Cornell University Press, 1956.

Fellman, David, *The Limits of Freedom.* New Brunswick, N.J.: Rutgers University Press, 1959.

Gellhorn, Walter, *American Rights.* New York: The Macmillan Company, 1960.

——— (ed.), *The States and Subversion.* Ithaca, N.Y.: Cornell University Press, 1952.

Hand, Learned, *The Bill of Rights.* Cambridge, Mass.: Harvard University Press, 1958.

Horn, Robert A., *Groups and the Constitution.* Stanford, Calif.: Stanford University Press, 1956.

Kerwin, Jerome G., *Catholic Viewpoint on Church and State.* New York: Doubleday & Company, Inc., 1960.

Konefsky, Samuel J., *The Legacy of Holmes and Brandeis.* New York: The Macmillan Company, 1956.

Konvitz, Milton R., *Fundamental Liberties of a Free People: Religion, Speech, Press, Assembly.* Ithaca, N.Y.: Cornell University Press, 1957.

——— and Clinton Rossiter, *Aspects of Liberty.* Ithaca, N.Y.: Cornell University Press, 1958.

Levy, Leonard W., *Legacy of Suppression: Freedom of Speech and Press in Early American History.* Cambridge, Mass.: Harvard University Press, 1960.

Meiklejohn, Alexander, *Political Freedom.* New York: Harper & Brothers, 1960.

Pritchett, C. Herman, *The American Constitution,* part 6. New York: McGraw-Hill Book Company, Inc., 1959.

——— *The Political Offender and the Warren Court.* Boston: Boston University Press, 1958.

Rutland, Robert A., *The Birth of the Bill of Rights, 1776–1791.* Chapel Hill, N.C.: The University of North Carolina Press, 1955.

Stokes, Anson Phelps, *Church and State in the United States.* 3 vols. New York: Harper & Brothers, 1950.

PART SIX

Due Process Rights

INTRODUCTION

> . . . nor shall any person . . . be deprived of life, liberty, or property, without due process of law. . . . FIFTH AMENDMENT

> . . . nor shall any State deprive any person of life, liberty, or property, without due process of law. . . . FOURTEENTH AMENDMENT

Due process in its widest sense can be said to encompass all individual rights under the Constitution other than those stated in the First Amendment. The breadth and the far-reaching character of the due process concept have been well stated by Justice Frankfurter:

. . . "due process," unlike some legal rules, is not a technical conception with a fixed content unrelated to time, place and circumstances. Expressing as it does in its ultimate analysis respect enforced by law for that feeling of just treatment which has been evolved through centuries of Anglo-American constitutional history and civilization, "due process" cannot be imprisoned within the treacherous limits of any formula. Representing a profound attitude of fairness between man and man, and more particularly between the individual and government, "due process" is compounded of history, reason, the past course of decisions, and stout confidence in the strength of the democratic faith which we profess. Due process is not a mechanical instrument. It is not a yardstick. It is a process.[1]

The due process concept does not depend for its constitutional foundation solely on the two clauses of the Fifth and Fourteenth Amendments quoted above. All of the amendments from the Fourth through the Eighth state important due process rights, mostly concerned with protection against malpractices or abuses in the process of criminal prosecutions. Moreover, the Fourteenth Amendment contains the related, and somewhat more specific, guarantee of equal protection of the laws, as well as the looser and less significant standard of privileges and immunities of citizens of the United States. All these provisions add up to a set of vital guarantees of the status of free individuals in an open society.

Legislative Due Process. The concept of due process is generally traced to the

[1] *Joint Anti-Fascist Refugee Committee* v. *McGrath*, 341 U.S. 123 (1951).

Magna Carta of 1215, in one chapter of which the king promised: "No freeman shall be arrested, or imprisoned, or disseized, or outlawed, or exiled, or in any way molested; nor will we proceed against him, unless by the lawful judgment of his peers or by the law of the land." In England it was thus the king who was limited by due process. By contrast, anything Parliament enacted was the "law of the land," and not subject to judicial review. But in one of its first decisions interpreting the due process clause, *Murray's Lessee* v. *Hoboken Land & Improvement Co.*, 18 How. 272 (1856), the Supreme Court held that in America due process was a limitation on the legislature as well as the executive and judicial powers. The Fifth Amendment, the Court said, "cannot be so construed as to leave congress free to make any process 'due process of law' by its mere will."

The adoption of the Fourteenth Amendment meant that state legislation could also be subjected to tests for conformity with due process standards. In fact, it was under the Fourteenth Amendment that the principal judicial concern with due process occurred. It was in the interpretation and application of the Fourteenth Amendment that the Supreme Court developed the due process clause from a control over legislative procedure into a device for reviewing and nullifying the substance of legislative programs, thereby substantially expanding the power of the courts over legislative policy. Substantive due process will be considered in Chapters 36 and 37.

Judicial Due Process. Due process in judicial proceedings requires that litigants have the benefit of a full and fair trial in the courts, and that their rights be measured, not by laws made to affect them individually, but by general provisions of law applicable to all those in like condition. Due process of law, it has been well said, means the process which is due, that is, just or appropriate. Judicial procedures may vary according to circumstances, but they will be *due* procedures if they follow the established forms of law or if, adapting old forms to new problems, they preserve the principles of liberty and justice.

The basic elements in a valid judicial proceeding are jurisdiction, notice, and hearing. Beyond these basic requirements, federal judicial proceedings are controlled by provisions of the Fourth through the Eighth Amendments, while state courts come under the somewhat more flexible purview of the Fourteenth Amendment. As the Supreme Court said in *Snyder* v. *Massachusetts*, 291 U.S. 97 (1934), a state "is free to regulate the procedure of its courts in accordance with its own conception of policy and fairness unless in so doing it offends some principle of justice so rooted in the traditions and conscience of our people as to be ranked as fundamental." Chapters 30 to 35 deal with due process standards for the courts.

Administrative Due Process. Due process is not necessarily judicial process. Administrative agencies and officers often have considerable authority to take action affecting the rights of property and of person. When they are given such power, however, the obligations of due process become applicable to them. This means that the requirements of jurisdiction, notice, hearing, and general fairness of procedure must be observed in administrative action. An enormous body of what is called "administrative law" has grown up as a consequence, which is for the most part outside the scope of this volume. However, in Chapter 39, which deals with the rights of citizenship, there will be some opportunity to consider the application of due process concepts in the work of such administrative agencies as the Department of State and the Immigration and Naturalization Service.

Equal Protection. Unlike due process, equal protection is not concerned with the minimum standards which must be observed in order to meet constitutional requirements. Equal protection merely insists that, whatever the standards applied, they must be enforced uniformly, without discrimination. The equal protection clause was placed in the Fourteenth Amendment primarily to protect the rights of the newly freed Negroes. In fact, Justice Miller said in the *Slaughter-House Cases,* 16 Wall. 36 (1873), that he doubted "very much whether any action of a State not directed by way of discrimination against the negroes as a class, or on account of their race, will ever be held to come within the purview" of the clause.

This was a very bad piece of prophecy, which Miller himself soon recanted. It is true that equal protection has been the constitutional concept most often utilized in dealing with racial discrimination problems, as illustrated in Chapter 38. But equal protection has also been widely employed in testing all kinds of legislative or administrative classifications, and the concept has now been assimilated into the more general notion of due process. Though the Fifth Amendment has no equal protection provision, the Supreme Court has seen to it that there is no difference between federal and state obligations on such problems as racial discrimination in access to housing or to the public schools.

Chapter 30
DUE PROCESS STANDARDS

The concept of due process is very broad and imprecise, and in application to particular problems requires substantial judicial refinement and rationalization. One obvious problem which the Supreme Court faced in interpreting the due process clause of the Fifth Amendment was to determine its relationship to the other more specific due process types of limitations found in the Bill of Rights.

The Court first dealt with this issue in *Murray's Lessee* v. *Hoboken Land & Improvement Co.*, 18 How. 272 (1856). In that decision the problem was whether legislation providing for distress warrant levies on the property of federal tax collectors indebted to the United States violated the due process provision. In holding that it did not, the Court suggested two tests for determining what was due process. First, "we must examine the constitution itself, to see whether this process be in conflict with any of its provisions." If this search turned up a conflict, then of course the process could not be "due process."

In the *Murray* situation, however, no such conflict was found, and so the Court went on to announce a second test—"those settled usages and modes of proceeding existing in the common and statute law of England, before the emigration of our ancestors, and which are shown not to have been unsuited to their civil and political condition by having been acted on by them after the settlement of this country." Applying this test, the Court conducted a search of the records which showed that a summary method for the recovery of debts due the government had been provided for "by the common and statute law of England prior to the emigration of our ancestors, and by the laws of many of the States at the time of the adoption of this amendment," and consequently the statute could not "be denied to be due process of law."

After adoption of the Fourteenth Amendment, the Court had the same problem of applying the due process test to state legislation. There was some delay in this process, for at first litigation under the Fourteenth Amendment centered on the privileges and immunities clause, which was thought to be more promising in its protective potentialities than the due process clause. But in the *Slaughter-House Cases,* 16 Wall. 36 (1873), the Court very narrowly confined the privileges and immunities clause to the protection of those rights peculiar to national citizenship, making it inapplicable to property rights and trials in state courts.

Consequently attention turned to the due process concept, which as embodied in the Fifth Amendment had attracted very little attention. The first significant decision was *Hurtado* v. *California,* 110 U.S. 516 (1884). California, instead of indicting Hurtado for murder by a grand jury, had brought him to trial on infor-

mation after examination and commitment by a magistrate, as permitted by the
state constitution. The question before the Court was whether such departure
from the practice of grand jury indictment violated due process of law.

On the basis of the first *Murray* test, this was clearly not due process, for the
Fifth Amendment makes indictment by grand jury mandatory for all capital or
otherwise infamous crimes. However, the Court had held in *Barron* v. *Baltimore*,
7 Pet. 243 (1833), that the provisions of the Bill of Rights are applicable only
to the federal government. Consequently the *Hurtado* decision went on to the
second *Murray* test of historical practice, and was able to show that grand jury
indictment was not even known at the time of Magna Carta, or for centuries
thereafter. In any case, the Court thought it would not be wise for the states to
be bound to any fixed set of procedures in criminal cases. "It is more consonant
to the true philosophy of our historical legal institutions to say that the spirit of
personal liberty and individual right, which they embodied, was preserved and
developed by a progressive growth and wise adaptation to new circumstances
and situations of the forms and processes found fit to give, from time to time,
new expression and greater effect to modern ideas of self-government."

Justice Harlan was the only dissenter in the *Hurtado* case. To him the Fourteenth Amendment evinced "a purpose to impose upon the States the same
restrictions, in respect of proceedings involving life, liberty and property, which
had been imposed upon the general government" by the Bill of Rights. But the
Supreme Court majority has never agreed that the Fourteenth Amendment was
intended to incorporate all the provisions of the first eight amendments and to
make them effective on the states, in spite of the severest attacks on the *Hurtado*
doctrine.

The arguments on this matter were repeated in *Twining* v. *New Jersey*, 211
U.S. 78 (1908). Here the state practice upheld by the Court was compulsory
self-incrimination, which would be forbidden in a federal court by the Fifth
Amendment. The jury, under state law, had been instructed that they might
draw an unfavorable inference from the defendant's failure to testify in denial
of evidence offered against him. The important thing for the Court was whether
exemption from self-incrimination was "a fundamental principle of liberty and
justice which inheres in the very idea of free government and is the inalienable
right of a citizen of such a government."

The Court sought to answer the question by inquiring how the right against
self-incrimination "was rated during the time when the meaning of due process
was in a formative state and before it was incorporated in American constitutional law." They found that it was omitted from the great declarations of English
liberty, and that in fact English courts and Parliaments dealt with the exemption
"as they would have dealt with any other rule of evidence." Moreover, only four
of the thirteen original states insisted that this rule should be included in the
Constitution, and two of those states did not have it in their own constitutions
at the time. Thus the historical evidence demonstrated that "the privilege was
not conceived to be inherent in due process of law, but on the other hand a
right separate, independent, and outside of due process." Moreover, the exemption was unknown outside the common-law countries, and was not observed
"among our own people in the search for truth outside the administration of the

law." So, "salutary as the principle may seem to the great majority, it cannot be ranked with the right to hearing before condemnation, the immunity from arbitrary power not acting by general laws, and the inviolability of private property."

After the *Twining* decision the incorporation controversy was relatively quiescent at the Supreme Court level for three decades. Then in 1937 *Palko* v. *Connecticut,* 302 U.S. 319, offered an opportunity for reexamining the issue. In the interim the incorporation theory had achieved a very great success in another area. As already noted, *Gitlow* v. *New York,* 268 U.S. 652 (1925), had admitted that the "liberty" protected by the Fourteenth Amendment against deprivation without due process included the freedoms of speech and press guaranteed by the First Amendment. If the First Amendment was incorporated into the Fourteenth, why were not the other guarantees in the Bill of Rights similarly situated?

It fell to Justice Cardozo to answer this question in the *Palko* case. The defendant had been convicted of second-degree murder and given a life sentence, but the state appealed the conviction, as was authorized by state law, and the state supreme court, finding that there had been error in the trial to the prejudice of the state, ordered a new trial. The second time the defendant was convicted of murder in the first degree and sentenced to death. The question was whether the effect of the second trial was to place the defendant twice in jeopardy for the same offense.

Cardozo began by once more flatly rejecting the incorporation thesis. To the extent that some of the first eight amendments had been made effective against the states, that was not because they were incorporated in the Fourteenth Amendment when it was adopted, but because they had been found by the Supreme Court "to be implicit in the concept of ordered liberty." He summed up:

> The right to trial by jury and the immunity from prosecution except as the result of an indictment may have value and importance. Even so, they are not of the very essence of a scheme of ordered liberty. To abolish them is not to violate a "principle of justice so rooted in the traditions and conscience of our people as to be ranked as fundamental." . . . Few would be so narrow or provincial as to maintain that a fair and enlightened system of justice would be impossible without them. What is true of jury trials and indictments is true also . . . of the immunity from compulsory self-incrimination. . . . This too might be lost, and justice still be done.

> On the other hand, freedom of thought and speech, as guaranteed by the First Amendment, is on "a different plane of social and moral values. . . . Of that freedom one may say that it is the matrix, the indispensable condition, of nearly every other form of freedom." So these freedoms have been "absorbed" into the Fourteenth Amendment, for "neither liberty nor justice would exist if they were sacrificed."

With this groundwork, it remained only for Cardozo to conclude that double jeopardy of the type presented in this case was not a value on the high plane represented by the First Amendment. All the state was asking was that the case against the defendant go on "until there shall be a trial free from the corrosion of substantial legal error." If there had been an error adverse to the accused, admittedly he could get another trial. To give the state a reciprocal privilege was "no seismic innovation. The edifice of justice stands, its symmetry, to many, greater than before."

Justice Black was in his first term on the Court when the *Palko* decision was made, and he did not dissent, though Butler did. This is interesting, for ten years later, in *Adamson* v. *California,* 332 U.S. 46 (1947), Black led an assault on this entire line of cases which lacked only one vote of achieving success. The issue was again self-incrimination, this time presented by a state statute permitting the failure of a defendant to explain or to deny evidence against him to be commented on by the court and by counsel and to be considered by the judge and the jury. For the defendant with a previous criminal record, the problem posed by this rule is that if he chooses to go on the witness stand to explain or deny evidence, he is then subject to cross-examination which can bring out his prior convictions. If he fails to take the stand, the assumption is that he cannot refute the evidence or has something to hide. By a five to four vote, the Court held this statutory provision not contrary to due process, and so once again rejected the argument that the Fourteenth Amendment incorporated the entire Bill of Rights. The meaning of due process was to be determined by the "ordered liberty" test.

ADAMSON v. CALIFORNIA
332 U.S. 46, 67 S. Ct. 1672, 91 L. Ed. 1903 (1947)

MR. JUSTICE REED delivered the opinion of the Court.

The appellant, Adamson, a citizen of the United States, was convicted, without recommendation for mercy, by a jury in a Superior Court of the State of California of murder in the first degree. After considering the same objections to the conviction that are pressed here, the sentence of death was affirmed by the Supreme Court of the state. . . . The provisions of California law which were challenged in the state proceedings as invalid under the Fourteenth Amendment to the Federal Constitution are those of the state constitution and penal code. . . . They permit the failure of a defendant to explain or to deny evidence against him to be commented upon by court and by counsel and to be considered by court and jury. The defendant did not testify. As the trial court gave its instructions and the District Attorney argued the case in accordance with the constitutional and statutory provisions just referred to, we have for decision the question of their constitutionality in these circumstances under the limitations of § 1 of the Fourteenth Amendment.

The appellant was charged in the information with former convictions for burglary, larceny and robbery and pursuant to § 1025, California Penal Code, answered that he had suffered the previous convictions. This answer barred allusion to these charges of convictions on the trial. Under California's interpretation of § 1025 of the Penal Code and § 2051 of the Code of Civil Procedure, however, if the defendant, after answering affirmatively charges alleging prior convictions, takes the witness stand to deny or explain away other evidence that has been introduced "the commission of these crimes could have been revealed to the jury on cross-examination to impeach his testimony." . . . This forces an accused who is a repeated offender to choose between the risk of having his prior offenses disclosed to the jury or of having it draw harmful inferences from uncontradicted evidence that can only be denied or explained by the defendant. . . .

We shall assume, but without any intention thereby of ruling upon the issue, that permission by law to the court, counsel and jury to comment upon and consider the failure of defendant "to explain or to deny by his testimony any evidence or facts in the case against him" would infringe defendant's privilege against self-incrimination under the Fifth Amendment if this were a trial in a court of the United States under a similar law. Such an assumption does not determine appellant's rights under the Fourteenth Amendment. It is settled law that the clause of the Fifth Amendment, protecting a person against being compelled to be a witness against himself, is not made effective by the Fourteenth Amendment as a protection against state action on the ground that freedom from testimonial compulsion is a right of national citizenship, or because it is a personal privilege or immunity secured by the Federal Constitution as one of the rights of man that are listed in the Bill of Rights.

The reasoning that leads to those conclusions starts with the unquestioned premise that the Bill of Rights, when adopted, was for the protection of the individual against the federal government and its provisions were inapplicable to similar actions done by the states. *Barron* v. *Baltimore*, 7 Pet. 243. . . . With the adoption of the Fourteenth Amendment, it was suggested that the dual citizenship recognized by its first sentence secured for citizens federal protection for their elemental privileges and immunities of state citizenship. The *Slaughter-House Cases* decided, contrary to the suggestion, that these rights, as privileges and immunities of state citizenship, remained under the sole protection of the state governments. This Court . . . has approved this determination. . . . The power to free defendants in state trials from self-incrimination was specifically determined to be beyond the scope of the privileges and immunities clause of the Fourteenth Amendment in *Twining* v. *New Jersey*, 211 U.S. 78. . . . "The privilege against self-incrimination may be withdrawn and the accused put upon the stand as a witness for the state." The *Twining* case likewise disposed of the contention that freedom from testimonial compulsion, being specifically granted by the Bill of Rights, is a federal privilege or immunity that is protected by the Fourteenth Amendment against state invasion. This Court held that the inclusion in the Bill of Rights of this protection against the power of the national government did not make the privilege a federal privilege or immunity secured to citizens by the Constitution against state action. . . . After declaring that state and national citizenship coexist in the same person, the Fourteenth Amendment forbids a state from abridging the privileges and immunities of citizens of the United States. As a matter of words, this leaves a state free to abridge, within the limits of the due process clause, the privileges and immunities flowing from state citizenship. This reading of the Federal Constitution has heretofore found favor with the majority of this Court as a natural and logical interpretation. It accords with the constitutional doctrine of federalism by leaving to the states the responsibility of dealing with the privileges and immunities of their citizens except those inherent in national citizenship. It is the construction placed upon the amendment by justices whose own experience had given them contemporaneous knowledge of the purposes that led to the adoption of the Fourteenth Amendment. This construction has become embedded in our federal system as a functioning element in preserving the balance between national and state power. We reaffirm the conclusion of the *Twining* and *Palko* cases that protection against self-incrimination is not a privilege or immunity of national citizenship.

Appellant secondly contends that if the privilege against self-incrimination is not a right protected by the privileges and immunities clause of the Fourteenth Amendment against state action, this privilege, to its full scope under the Fifth Amendment, inheres in the right to a fair trial. A right to a fair trial is a right admittedly protected by the due process clause of the Fourteenth Amendment. Therefore, appellant argues, the due process clause of the Fourteenth Amendment protects his privilege against self-incrimination. The due process clause of the Fourteenth Amendment, however, does not draw all the rights of the federal Bill of Rights under its protection. That contention was made and rejected in *Palko* v. *Connecticut*. . . .

Nothing has been called to our attention that either the framers of the Fourteenth Amendment or the states that adopted intended its due process clause to draw within its scope the earlier amendments to the Constitution. *Palko* held that such provisions of the Bill of Rights as were "implicit in the concept of ordered liberty," . . . became secure from state interference by the clause. But it held nothing more.

Specifically, the due process clause does not protect, by virtue of its mere existence, the accused's freedom from giving testimony by compulsion in state trials that is secured to him against federal interference by the Fifth Amendment. . . . For a state to require testimony from an accused is not necessarily a breach of a state's obligation to give a fair trial. Therefore, we must examine the effect of the California law applied in this trial to see whether the comment on failure to testify violates the protection against state action that the due process clause does grant to an accused. The due process clause forbids compulsion to testify by fear of hurt, torture or exhaustion. It forbids any other type of coercion that falls within the scope of due process. California follows Anglo-American legal tradition in excusing defendants in criminal prosecutions from compulsory testimony. . . . That is a matter of legal policy and not because of the requirements of due process under the Fourteenth Amendment. So our inquiry is directed, not at the broad question of the constitutionality of compulsory testimony from the accused under the due process clause, but to the constitutionality of the provision of the California law that permits comment upon his failure to testify. It is, of course, logically possible that while an accused might be required, under appropriate penalties, to submit himself as a witness without a violation of due process, comment by judge or jury on inferences to be drawn from his failure to testify, in jurisdictions where an accused's privilege against self-incrimination is protected, might deny due process. For example, a statute might declare that a permitted refusal to testify would compel an acceptance of the truth of the prosecution's evidence.

Generally, comment on the failure of an accused to testify is forbidden in American jurisdictions. This arises from state constitutional or statutory provisions similar in character to the federal provisions. . . . California, however, is one of a few states that permit limited comment upon a defendant's failure to testify. That permission is narrow. The California law . . . authorizes comment by court and counsel upon the "failure of the defendant to explain or to deny by his testimony any evidence or facts in the case against him." This does not involve any presumption, rebuttable or irrebuttable, either of guilt or of the truth of any fact, that is offered in evidence. . . . It allows inferences to be drawn from proven facts. Because of this clause, the court can direct the jury's attention to whatever evidence there may be that a defendant could deny and the prosecution can argue as to inferences that may be drawn from the accused's failure to testify. . . . There is here no lack of power in the trial court to adjudge and no denial of a hearing. California has prescribed a method for advising the jury in the search for truth. However sound may be the legislative conclusion that an accused should not be compelled in any criminal case to be a witness against himself, we see no reason why comment should not be made upon his silence. It seems quite natural that when a defendant has opportunity to deny or explain facts and determines not to do so, the prosecution should bring out the strength of the evidence by commenting upon defendant's failure to explain or deny it. The prosecution evidence may be of facts that may be beyond the knowledge of the accused. If so, his failure to testify would have little if any weight. But the facts may be such as are necessarily in the knowledge of the accused. In that case a failure to explain would point to an inability to explain.

Appellant sets out the circumstances of this case, however, to show coercion and unfairness in permitting comment. The guilty person was not seen at the place and time of the crime. There was evidence, however, that entrance to the place or room where the crime was committed might have been obtained through a small door. It was freshly broken. Evidence showed that six fingerprints on the door were petitioner's. Certain diamond rings were missing from the deceased's possession. There was evidence that appellant, sometime after the crime, asked an unidentified person whether the latter would be interested in purchasing a diamond ring. As has been stated, the information charged other crimes to appellant and he admitted them. His argument here is that he could not take the stand to deny the evidence against him because he would be subjected to a cross-examination as to former crimes to impeach his veracity and the evidence so produced might well bring about his conviction. Such cross-examination is allowable in California. . . . Therefore, appellant contends the California statute permitting comment denies him due process.

It is true that if comment were forbidden, an accused in this situation could remain silent and avoid evidence of former crimes and comment upon his failure to testify. We are of the view, however, that a state may control such a situation in accordance with its own ideas of the most efficient administration of criminal justice. The purpose of due process is not to protect an accused against a proper conviction but against an unfair conviction. When evidence is before a jury that threatens conviction, it does not seem unfair to require him to choose between leaving the adverse evidence unexplained and subjecting himself to impeachment through disclosure of former crimes. Indeed, this is a dilemma with which any defendant may be faced. If facts, adverse to the defendant, are proven by the prosecution, there may be no way to explain them favorably to the accused except by a witness who may be vulnerable to impeachment on cross-examination. The defendant must then decide whether or not to use such a witness. The fact that the witness may also be the defendant makes the choice more difficult but a denial of due process does not emerge from the circumstances.

There is no basis in the California law for appellant's objection on due process or other grounds that the statutory authorization to comment on the failure to explain or deny adverse testimony shifts the burden of proof or the duty to go forward with the evidence. Failure of the accused to testify is not an admission of the truth of the adverse evidence. Instructions told the jury that the burden of proof remained upon the state and the presumption of innocence with the accused. Comment on failure to deny proven facts does not in California tend to supply any missing element of proof of guilt. . . . It only directs attention to the strength of the evidence for the prosecution or to the weakness of that for the defense. The Supreme Court of California called attention to the fact that the prosecutor's argument approached the borderline in a statement that might have been construed as asserting "that the jury should infer guilt solely from defendant's silence." That court felt that it was improbable the jury was misled into such an understanding of their power. We shall not interfere with such a conclusion. . . .

We find no other error that gives ground for our intervention in California's administration of criminal justice.

Affirmed.

MR. JUSTICE FRANKFURTER, concurring.

Less than ten years ago, Mr. Justice Cardozo announced as settled constitutional law that while the Fifth Amendment, "which is not directed to the states, but solely to the federal government," provides that no person shall be compelled in any criminal case to be a witness against himself, the process of law assured by the

Fourteenth Amendment does not require such immunity from self-crimination: "in prosecutions by a state, the exemption will fail if the state elects to end it." *Palko* v. *Connecticut*, 302 U.S. 319. . . . Mr. Justice Cardozo spoke for the Court, consisting of Mr. Chief Justice Hughes, and McReynolds, Brandeis, Sutherland, Stone, Roberts, Black, JJ. (Mr. Justice Butler dissented.) The matter no longer called for discussion; a reference to *Twining* v. *New Jersey*, 211 U.S. 78, decided thirty years before the *Palko* case, sufficed.

. . . After enjoying unquestioned prestige for forty years, the *Twining* case should not now be diluted, even unwittingly, either in its judicial philosophy or in its particulars. As the surest way of keeping the *Twining* case intact, I would affirm this case on its authority. . . .

The short answer to the suggestion that the provision of the Fourteenth Amendment, which ordains "nor shall any State deprive any person of life, liberty, or property, without due process of law," was a way of saying that every State must thereafter initiate prosecutions through indictment by a grand jury, must have a trial by a jury of twelve in criminal cases, and must have trial by such a jury in common law suits where the amount in controversy exceeds twenty dollars, is that it is a strange way of saying it. It would be extraordinarily strange for a Constitution to convey such specific commands in such a roundabout and inexplicit way. . . . The notion that the Fourteenth Amendment was a covert way of imposing upon the States all the rules which it seemed important to Eighteenth Century statesmen to write into the Federal Amendments, was rejected by judges who were themselves witnesses of the process by which the Fourteenth Amendment became part of the Constitution. Arguments that may now be adduced to prove that the first eight Amendments were concealed within the historic phrasing of the Fourteenth Amendment were not unknown at the time of its adoption. A surer estimate of their bearing was possible for judges at the time than distorting distance is likely to vouchsafe. Any evidence of design or purpose not contemporaneously known could hardly have influenced those who ratified the Amendment. Remarks of a particular proponent of the Amendment, no matter how influential, are not to be deemed part of the Amendment. What was submitted for ratification was his proposal, not his speech. Thus, at the time of the ratification of the Fourteenth Amendment the constitutions of nearly half of the ratifying States did not have the rigorous requirements of the Fifth Amendment for instituting criminal proceedings through a grand jury. It could hardly have occurred to these States that by ratifying the Amendment they uprooted their established methods for prosecuting crime and fastened upon themselves a new prosecutorial system.

Indeed, the suggestion that the Fourteenth Amendment incorporates the first eight Amendments as such is not unambiguously urged. Even the boldest innovator would shrink from suggesting to more than half the States that they may no longer initiate prosecutions without indictment by grand jury, or that thereafter all the States of the Union must furnish a jury of twelve for every case involving a claim above twenty dollars. There is suggested merely a selective incorporation of the first eight Amendments into the Fourteenth Amendment. Some are in and some are out, but we are left in the dark as to which are in and which are out. Nor are we given the calculus for determining which go in and which stay out. If the basis of selection is merely that those provisions of the first eight Amendments are incorporated which commend themselves to individual justices as indispensable to the dignity and happiness of a free man, we are thrown back to a merely subjective test. The protection against unreasonable search and seizure might have primacy for one judge, while trial by a jury of twelve for every claim above twenty dollars might appear to another as an ultimate need in a free society. In the history of thought "natural law" has a much longer and much better founded meaning and justification than such subjective selection of the first eight Amendments for incorporation into the Fourteenth. . . .

And so, when, as in a case like the present, a conviction in a State court is here for review under a claim that a right protected by the Due Process Clause of the Fourteenth Amendment has been denied, the issue is not whether an infraction of one of the specific provisions of the first eight Amendments is disclosed by the record. The relevant question is whether the criminal proceedings which resulted in conviction deprived the accused of the due process of law to which the United States Constitution entitled him. Judicial review of that guaranty of the Fourteenth Amendment inescapably imposes upon this Court an exercise of judgment upon the whole course of the proceedings in order to ascertain whether they offend those canons of decency and fairness which express the notions of justice of English-speaking peoples even toward those charged with the most heinous offenses. These standards of justice are not authoritatively formulated anywhere as though they were prescriptions in a pharmacopoeia. But neither does the application of the Due Process Clause imply that judges are wholly at large. The judicial judgment in applying the Due Process Clause must move within the limits of accepted notions of justice and is not to be based upon the idiosyncrasies of a merely personal judgment. The fact that judges among themselves may differ whether in a particular case a trial offends accepted notions of justice is not disproof that general rather than idiosyncratic standards are applied. An important safeguard against such merely individual judgment is an alert deference to the judgment of the State court under review.

MR. JUSTICE BLACK, dissenting. . . .

This decision reasserts a constitutional theory spelled out in *Twining* v. *New Jersey*, 211 U.S. 78, that this Court is endowed by the Constitution with boundless power under "natural law" periodically to expand and contract constitutional standards to conform to the Court's conception of what at a particular time constitutes "civilized decency" and "fundamental liberty and justice." Invoking this *Twining* rule, the Court concludes that although comment upon testimony in a federal court would violate the Fifth Amendment, identical comment in a state court does not violate today's fashion in civilized decency and fundamentals and is therefore not prohibited by the Federal Constitution as amended.

The *Twining* case was the first, as it is the only, decision of this Court which has squarely held that states were free, notwithstanding the Fifth and Fourteenth Amendments, to extort evidence from one accused of crime. I agree that if *Twining* be reaffirmed, the result reached might appropriately follow. But I would not reaffirm the *Twining* decision. I think that decision and the "natural law" theory of the Constitution upon which it relies degrade the constitutional safeguards of the Bill of Rights and simultaneously appropriate for this Court a broad power which we are not authorized by the Constitution to exercise. . . . My reasons for believing that the *Twining* decision should not be revitalized can best be understood by reference to the constitutional, judicial, and general history that preceded and followed the case. That reference must be abbreviated far more than is justified but for the necessary limitations of opinion-writing. . . .

My study of the historical events that culminated in the Fourteenth Amendment, and the expressions of those who sponsored and favored, as well as those who opposed its submission and passage, persuades me that one of the chief objects that the provisions of the Amendment's first section, separately, and as a whole, were intended to accomplish was to make the Bill of Rights, applicable to the states. With full knowledge of the import of the *Barron* decision, the framers and backers of the Fourteenth Amendment proclaimed its purpose to be to overturn the constitutional rule that case had announced. This historical purpose has never received full consideration or exposition in any opinion of this Court interpreting the Amendment. . . .

. . . I am attaching to this dissent an appendix which contains a résumé, by no means complete, of the Amendment's history. In my judgment that history conclusively demonstrates that the language of the first section of the Fourteenth Amendment, taken as a whole, was thought by those responsible for its submission to the people, and by those who opposed its submission, sufficiently explicit to guarantee that thereafter no state could deprive its citizens of the privileges and protections of the Bill of Rights. . . . And I further contend that the "natural law" formula which the Court uses to reach its conclusion in this case should be abandoned as an incongruous excrescence on our Constitution. I believe that formula to be itself a violation of our Constitution, in that it subtly conveys to courts, at the expense of legislatures, ultimate power over public policies in fields where no specific provision of the Constitution limits legislative power. . . .

I cannot consider the Bill of Rights to be an outworn 18th Century "strait jacket" as the *Twining* opinion did. Its provisions may be thought outdated abstractions by some. And it is true that they were designed to meet ancient evils. But they are the same kind of human evils that have emerged from century to century wherever excessive power is sought by the few at the expense of the many. In my judgment the people of no nation can lose their liberty so long as a Bill of Rights like ours survives and its basic purposes are conscientiously interpreted, enforced and respected so as to afford continuous protection against old, as well as new, devices and practices which might thwart those purposes. I fear to see the consequences of the Court's practice of substituting its own concepts of decency and fundamental justice for the language of the Bill of Rights as its point of departure in interpreting and enforcing that Bill of Rights. If the choice must be between the selective process of the *Palko* decision applying some of the Bill of Rights to the States, or the *Twining* rule applying none of them, I would choose the *Palko* selective process. But rather than accept either of these choices, I would follow what I believe was the original purpose of the Fourteenth Amendment—to extend to all the people of the nation the complete protection of the Bill of Rights. To hold that this Court can determine what, if any, provisions of the Bill of Rights will be enforced, and if so to what degree, is to frustrate the great design of a written Constitution.

Conceding the possibility that this Court is now wise enough to improve on the Bill of Rights by substituting natural law concepts for the Bill of Rights, I think the possibility is entirely too speculative to agree to take that course. I would therefore hold in this case that the full protection of the Fifth Amendment's proscription against compelled testimony must be afforded by California. This I would do because of reliance upon the original purpose of the Fourteenth Amendment. . . .

Since *Marbury* v. *Madison*, 1 Cranch 137, was decided, the practice has been firmly established, for better or worse, that courts can strike down legislative enactments which violate the Constitution. This process, of course, involves interpretation, and since words can have many meanings, interpretation obviously may result in contraction or extension of the original purpose of a constitutional provision, thereby affecting policy. But to pass upon the constitutionality of statutes by looking to the particular standards enumerated in the Bill of Rights and other parts of the Constitution is one thing; to invalidate statutes because of application of "natural law" deemed to be above and undefined by the Constitution is another. "In the one instance, courts proceeding within clearly marked constitutional boundaries seek to execute policies written into the Constitution; in the other, they roam at will in the limitless area of their own beliefs as to reasonableness and actually select policies, a responsibility which the Constitution entrusts to the legislative representatives of the people." *Federal Power Commission* v. *Pipeline Co.,* 315 U.S. 575, 599, 601, n. 4.

MR. JUSTICE DOUGLAS joins in this opinion.

MR. JUSTICE MURPHY, with whom MR. JUSTICE RUTLEDGE concurs, dissenting.

While in substantial agreement with the views of MR. JUSTICE BLACK, I have one reservation and one addition to make.

I agree that the specific guarantees of the Bill of Rights should be carried over intact into the first section of the Fourteenth Amendment. But I am not prepared to say that the latter is entirely and necessarily limited by the Bill of Rights. Occasions may arise where a proceeding falls so far short of conforming to fundamental standards of procedure as to warrant constitutional condemnation in terms of a lack of due process despite the absence of a specific provision in the Bill of Rights. . . .

Chapter 31

SEARCHES AND SEIZURES

The right of the people to be secure in their persons, houses, papers, and effects, against unreasonable searches and seizures, shall not be violated, and no warrants shall issue, but upon probable cause, supported by oath or affirmation, and particularly describing the place to be searched, and the persons or things to be seized. FOURTH AMENDMENT

The Fourth Amendment was drafted by men who had had experience with the hated "writs of assistance," general warrants of the colonial period under which British officers burst into private homes and conducted searches for smuggled goods. The amendment did not deny the right of search, but it did forbid "unreasonable" searches and seizures, and a warrant issued by a judicial officer, and meeting the test of particularity, was one of the necessary conditions. The purpose of the warrant was to require federal law-enforcement officers to make some kind of prima facie showing of law violation before an impartial judicial officer prior to use of the search and seizure power.

The particularity requirement of the Fourth Amendment may be illustrated by *Federal Trade Commission v. American Tobacco Co.*, 264 U.S. 298 (1924), where the federal agency had sought to compel the company to turn over all the letters and telegrams received by it from its jobber customers for an entire year. Justice Holmes condemned this venture as a "fishing expedition" into private papers "on the possibility that they may disclose evidence of crime," and said this was contrary to the spirit of the Fourth Amendment.

Most constitutional issues under the search and seizure clause, however, arise not out of failure to observe the particularity requirement, but out of failure to secure any search warrant at all. Such failure does not automatically void a search or seizure. It depends upon the circumstances.

First, search without a warrant may be made in connection with a valid arrest. For example, an officer making an arrest, either with a warrant of arrest, or for a crime committed in the officer's presence, may search the person of the suspect and seize any instruments of the crime which are in plain sight. However, the officer must have a justification for the arrest if any accompanying search is to be upheld. In *Henry v. United States*, 361 U.S. 98 (1959), two FBI agents investigating interstate whiskey thefts had received a tip that a certain person might be implicated in interstate shipments. After observing the loading of cartons into his auto on two occasions, they stopped the car, took the cartons to their office, and discovered that they were stolen radios. The Supreme Court held that the arrest had occurred when the car was stopped, and that the agents had inadequate grounds for an arrest at that time. Consequently the seizure was illegal. However, in *Draper* v. *United States,* 358 U.S. 307 (1959), an arrest and seizure by federal narcotics agents was ruled valid where the agents had only a tip that a man arriving on a certain train, dressed in a certain way, walking fast, and carrying a tan bag, would be carrying narcotics.

The "plain sight" rule has been somewhat expanded in recent years. In *United States* v. *Rabinowitz,* 339 U.S. 56 (1950), a stamp dealer was arrested on a warrant in his one-room office for selling counterfeit stamps. A search, made without a warrant, revealed over five hundred additional fraudulent stamps in the office. By a five to three vote the Court held that the search was reasonable, since the office was open to the public, small, and under the immediate control of the occupant.

The Russian spy case, *Abel* v. *United States,* 362 U.S. 217 (1960), upheld the use of an administrative warrant of arrest rather than one issued by a judicial officer. Abel, an alien, was arrested in his hotel room by agents of the Immigration and Naturalization Service as a preliminary to deportation proceedings. They acted under authority of a warrant issued by their own agency, since deportation is a civil proceeding, not punishment for crime. FBI agents were present at the time of the arrest but did not participate in it or in the search of Abel's person and his room. After the prisoner had been taken away by the INS men, the FBI agents did search the room, with the consent of the hotel management. Abel was subsequently convicted of espionage with the assistance of evidence secured by these searches.

The Supreme Court by a five to four vote upheld the validity of this arrest on an administrative warrant. The dissenters charged that the FBI, suspecting espionage but unable to prove it, wanted to avoid having to secure a regular judicial warrant of arrest which would require a description of the things to be seized. So the FBI called in the immigration people to make the arrest with an administrative warrant on a charge of illegal residence in the United States, under cover of which they could pursue their own investigation. But the Court majority concluded that the decision to proceed administratively was made in good faith and not for the purpose of securing evidence for a criminal prosecution. Since the arrest was valid, the search was valid as incident to a lawful arrest.

Normally the search and seizure clause protects against the seizure of physical objects useful in effecting criminal convictions, but it may also be invoked against unreasonable "search" of a person's spoken words. This possibility was illustrated by the famous wire-tapping case, *Olmstead* v. *United States,* 277 U.S. 438 (1928). Federal prohibition agents had secured evidence against a gang of rumrunners by tapping their telephones and recording the conversations, and convictions were secured on the basis of this evidence. If such wire tapping amounted to unreasonable search and seizure, not only would the Fourth Amendment have been violated, but also the Fifth Amendment's ban on self-incrimination would be involved.

The Court majority, however, determined that there had been no actual search and seizure in this case. The agents had never entered the quarters of the suspects, but had done the tapping in the basements of apartment buildings. "The evidence was secured by the use of the sense of hearing and that only." Justice

Holmes, dissenting, noted that wire tapping was a crime in the state of Washington, where these acts occurred, and said that the United States should have no part in such a "dirty business."

In 1934 Congress adopted a statute which the Supreme Court construed in *Nardone* v. *United States,* 302 U.S. 379 (1937), as forbidding the introduction in federal trials of evidence secured by wire tapping. Government law-enforcement agencies have persistently attempted to persuade Congress to modify this wire-tapping ban, particularly in national security cases, but thus far without success.

The use of electronic eavesdropping devices for picking up conversations without wire tapping has been upheld on the same reasoning as in the *Olmstead* case, so long as there is no physical invasion of privacy. *Goldman* v. *United States,* 316 U.S. 129 (1942); *On Lee* v. *United States,* 343 U.S. 747 (1952). But in *Silverman* v. *United States,* 365 U.S. 505 (1961), police officers in the District of Columbia had occupied a vacant house and driven a "spike mike" through the party wall of an adjoining row house. The spike made contact with the heating duct of the house next door and all the conversations in the house were audible to the officers. The Supreme Court held that the projection of the spike into the adjoining house amounted to an "unauthorized physical penetration" of a constitutionally protected area, and consequently the evidence had been illegally obtained.

In general, evidence secured by unreasonable search and seizure cannot be employed in a federal criminal trial. This exclusion of illegally procured evidence was established by the Supreme Court in *Weeks* v. *United States,* 232 U.S. 383 (1914). Originally this exclusionary rule applied only if federal agents were the guilty parties in procuring the evidence. If the evidence was illegally secured by state police agents or stolen by private parties and then turned over to federal officers on a "silver platter," it could be employed in a federal trial. But in *Elkins* v. *United States,* 364 U.S. 206 (1960), the Supreme Court by a five to four vote abandoned the "silver platter" doctrine.

The "silver platter" rule never did apply to evidence secured by wire tapping, because wire-tap evidence was banned in federal courts by the Communications Act of 1934. In *Benanti* v. *United States,* 355 U.S. 96 (1957), the Court held that this statute forbids the use in federal courts of evidence secured by state officers under a state-approved wire-tap system, even though no federal officers participated in the tapping.

State Searches and Seizures. The Supreme Court had no occasion to make a definitive ruling on the application of the unreasonable search and seizure requirements of the Fourth Amendment to the states until *Wolf* v. *Colorado,* 338 U.S. 25 (1949). This case involved an abortionist who had been convicted on the basis of records seized in an unauthorized search of his office. Justice Frankfurter, writing the Court's opinion, concluded that freedom from unreasonable search and seizure was an essential element in the concept of "ordered liberty," and so entitled to Fourteenth Amendment protection against state action.

The security of one's privacy against arbitrary intrusion by the police—which is at the core of the Fourth Amendment—is basic to a free society. . . . The knock at the door, whether by day or by night, as a prelude to a search, without authority of law but solely on the authority of the police, did not need the commentary of recent history to be condemned as inconsistent with the conception of human rights enshrined in the history and the basic constitutional documents of English-speaking peoples.

The next question was whether the state was forbidden to use the illegally secured evidence in the trial. It would not be admissible in a federal court, under the *Weeks* rule. But in *Wolf* six justices voted not to embody this rule of evidence in the Fourteenth Amendment. Justice Frankfurter, after a survey of practice on this point, concluded that "most of the English-speaking world does not regard as vital . . . the exclusion of evidence thus obtained." Accordingly the Court "must hesitate to treat this remedy as an essential ingredient of the right." The sanctions suggested by Frankfurter, if evidence secured by illegal invasion of privacy was nonetheless used in court, were "the remedies of private action and such protection as the internal discipline of the police, under the eyes of an alert public opinion, may afford."

The Court's subsequent dilemmas in applying the *Wolf* rule may be illustrated by three decisions. The first, *Rochin v. California,* 342 U.S. 165 (1952), was a prosecution for illegal possession of narcotics. Having information that Rochin was selling dope, three deputy sheriffs entered his house and forced open his bedroom door. There were two capsules on the nightstand, which Rochin seized and put in his mouth. The deputies jumped on him and tried to extricate the capsules. This failing, they handcuffed him and took him to a hospital, where at the direction of the officers a doctor pumped his stomach and produced the capsules, which contained morphine. The capsules were the chief evidence on which he was convicted.

Justice Frankfurter for a unanimous Court invalidated the conviction. The *Wolf* rule would have admitted evidence secured illegally, but the conduct here went beyond any acceptable bounds.

It is conduct that shocks the conscience. Illegally breaking into the privacy of the petitioner, the struggle to open his mouth and remove what was there, the forcible extraction of his stomach's contents—this course of proceeding by agents of government to obtain evidence is bound to offend even hardened sensibilities. They are methods too close to the rack and the screw to permit of constitutional differentiation.

Next came *Irvine v. California,* 347 U.S. 128 (1954), where official conduct was also shocking, but not too shocking to permit application of the *Wolf* rule. The police suspected Irvine of illegal bookmaking. In his absence from home, they had a locksmith go there and make a door key. Then they entered the house with this key and installed a concealed microphone, boring a hole in the roof through which wires were strung to a neighboring garage, where officers were posted with listening devices. They twice reentered the house to move the microphone to better positions. At the trial, the officers were allowed to testify to conversations heard by this method.

The Court majority, through Justice Jackson, said that this was "trespass, and probably a burglary," but according to *Wolf* there was no basis for denying the state's right to get a conviction by use of such methods. "We adhere to *Wolf* as stating the law of search-and-seizure cases." Four justices dissented, including

Frankfurter, author of *Wolf*. He contended that the *Wolf* ruling did not affect the decision on exclusion of the evidence in this case, because here there was "additional aggravating conduct which the Court finds repulsive," as there had also been in the *Rochin* case. There had been no direct physical violence in *Irvine*, as there had been in *Rochin*, but there had been "a more powerful and offensive control over the Irvines' life," a control which enabled police to hear every word said in a private home for an entire month.

The third case was *Breithaupt v. Abram*, 352 U.S. 432 (1957). A truck driven by Breithaupt in New Mexico collided with a car, and three persons were killed. An almost empty whiskey bottle was found in the truck. Breithaupt, seriously injured, was taken to a hospital unconscious. When liquor was detected on his breath, the police directed a doctor to secure a sample of his blood by use of a hypodermic needle. Testimony regarding the blood test was admitted in evidence at the trial, and an expert gave his opinion that the amount of alcohol found in the blood was sufficient to induce intoxication.

By a six to three vote the Court distinguished these circumstances from those in the *Rochin* case and upheld the conviction. Justice Clark pointed out that blood tests are "routine"; they do not shock the conscience or offend the sense of justice; there is nothing offensive or brutal about them. Intoxication is one of the reasons for the "increasing slaughter on our highways," and the interests of society in reducing these hazards outweigh "so slight an intrusion" on the person.

But three justices found these efforts to distinguish the *Rochin* case unconvincing. In both instances the operation was performed by a doctor in a hospital. In each case body fluids were extracted. Both operations are common, "scientific," and cause no lasting ill effects. The only possible distinction was that force had to be used on Rochin, but not on Breithaupt because he was unconscious. If this is the justification, then it follows that one has constitutional rights only when he is physically able to assert them.

The *Wolf* rule on evidence had apparently emerged unscathed from this series of encounters, but actually its days were numbered. In the 1960 *Elkins* decision, where the Court abandoned the "silver platter" rule for federal prosecutions, the Court majority through Justice Stewart took note of the fact that the states were definitely moving away from the freedom the *Wolf* decision gave them and toward adoption of the federal exclusionary rule.

Then in *Mapp v. Ohio*, 367 U.S. 643 (1961), the Court by a five to three vote overruled the *Wolf* decision. Cleveland police officers, suspecting that a law violator was hiding in a certain house, broke in the door, manhandled a woman resident, searched the entire premises, and discovered some obscene materials in a trunk. The woman was convicted of possession of these materials. The state court, pointing out that the objects had not been taken from the defendant's person by brutal or offensive physical force (as in *Rochin*), permitted their use in evidence on the basis of the *Wolf* rule. But the Supreme Court disposed of *Wolf*, Justice Clark saying:

The ignoble shortcut to conviction left open to the State [by *Wolf*] tends to destroy the entire system of constitutional restraints on which the liberties of the people rest. Having once recognized that the right to privacy embodied in the Fourth

Amendment is enforceable against the States, and that the right to be secure against rude invasions of privacy by state officers is, therefore, constitutional in origin, we can no longer permit that right to remain an empty promise.

An interesting limitation on individual power to resist official searches was imposed by the Supreme Court in *Frank* v. *Maryland,* 359 U.S. 360 (1959). A Baltimore city ordinance obliged householders to admit city health inspectors who suspected that a nuisance existed in a house, and provided for a fine of $20 for each refusal to admit. The Court by a vote of five to four held that a search warrant was not required for inspections of this kind.

FRANK v. MARYLAND
359 U.S. 360, 79 S. Ct. 804, 3 L. Ed. 2d 877 (1959)

Mr. Justice Frankfurter delivered the opinion of the Court.

Acting on a complaint from a resident of the 4300 block of Reisterstown Road, Baltimore, Maryland, that there were rats in her basement, Gentry, an inspector of the Baltimore City Health Department, began an inspection of the houses in the vicinity looking for the source of the rats. In the middle of the afternoon of February 27 Gentry knocked on the door of the appellant's detached frame home at 4335 Reisterstown Road. After receiving no response he proceeded to inspect the area outside the house. This inspection revealed that the house was in an "extreme state of decay," and that in the rear of the house there was a pile later identified as "rodent feces mixed with straw and trash and debris to approximately half a ton." During this inspection appellant came around the side of the house and asked Gentry to explain his presence. Gentry responded that he had evidence of rodent infestation and asked appellant for permission to inspect the basement area. Appellant refused. At no time did Gentry have a warrant authorizing him to enter. The next forenoon Gentry, in the company of two police officers, returned to appellant's house. After receiving no response to his knock, he reinspected the exterior of the premises. He then swore out a warrant for appellant's arrest alleging a violation of § 120 of Art. 12 of the Baltimore City Code. That section provides:

"Whenever the Commissioner of Health shall have cause to suspect that a nuisance exists in any house, cellar or enclosure, he may demand entry therein in the day time, and if the owner or occupier shall refuse or delay to open the same and admit a free examination, he shall forfeit and pay for every such refusal the sum of Twenty Dollars."

Appellant was arrested on March 5, and the next day was found guilty of the offense alleged in the warrant by a Police Justice for the Northern District of Baltimore and fined twenty dollars. On appeal, the Criminal Court of Baltimore, in a *de novo* proceeding, also found appellant guilty. The Maryland Court of Appeals denied certiorari. The case came here under a challenge to the validity of § 120 . . . to determine whether appellant's conviction for resisting an inspection of his house without a warrant was obtained in violation of the Fourteenth Amendment. . . .

We have said that "[t]he security of one's privacy against arbitrary intrusion by the police" is fundamental to a free society and as such protected by the Fourteenth Amendment. *Wolf* v. *Colorado,* 338 U.S. 25, 27. Application of the broad restraints of due process compels inquiry into the nature of the demand being made upon individual freedom in a particular context and the justification of social need on which the demand rests.

The history of the constitutional protection against official invasion of the citizen's home makes explicit the human concerns which it was meant to respect. In years prior to the Revolution leading voices in England and the Colonies protested against the ransacking by Crown officers of the homes of citizens in search of evidence of crime or of illegally imported goods. The vivid memory by the newly independent Americans of these abuses produced the Fourth Amendment as a safeguard against such arbitrary official action by officers of the new Union, as like provisions had already found their way into State Constitutions.

In 1765, in England, what is properly called the great case of *Entick* v. *Carrington*, 19 Howell's State Trials, col. 1029, announced the principle of English law which became part of the Bill of Rights and whose basic protection has become imbedded in the concept of due process of law. It was there decided that English law did not allow officers of the Crown to break into a citizen's home, under cover of a general executive warrant, to search for evidence of the utterance of libel. Among the reasons given for that decision were these:

"It is very certain, that the law obligeth no man to accuse himself; because the necessary means of compelling self-accusation, falling upon the innocent as well as the guilty, would be both cruel and unjust; and it should seem, that search for evidence is disallowed upon the same principle. There too the innocent would be confounded with the guilty." *Id.*, at col. 1073.

These were not novel pronouncements to the colonists. A few years earlier, in Boston, revenue officers had been authorized to use Writs of Assistance, empowering them to search suspected places, including private houses, for smuggled goods. In 1761 the validity of the use of the Writs was contested in the historic proceedings in Boston. James Otis attacked the Writ of Assistance because its use placed "the liberty to every man in the hands of every petty officer." His powerful argument so impressed itself first on his audience and later on the people of all the Colonies that President Adams was moved to say that "American Independence was then and there born." . . .

Against this background two protections emerge from the broad constitutional proscription of official invasion. The first of these is the right to be secure from intrusion into personal privacy, the right to shut the door on officials of the state unless their entry is under proper authority of law. The second, and intimately related protection, is self-protection: the right to resist unauthorized entry which has as its design the securing of information to fortify the coercive power of the state against the individual, information which may be used to effect a further deprivation of life or liberty or property. Thus, evidence of criminal action may not, save in very limited and closely confined situations, be seized without a judicially issued search warrant. . . .

But giving the fullest scope to this constitutional right to privacy, its protection cannot be here invoked. The attempted inspection of appellant's home is merely to determine whether conditions exist which the Baltimore Health Code proscribes. If they do appellant is notified to remedy the infringing conditions. No evidence for criminal prosecution is sought to be seized. Appellant is simply directed to do what he could have been ordered to do without any inspection, and what he cannot properly resist, namely, act in a manner consistent with the maintenance of minimum community standards of health and well-being, including his own. Appellant's resistance can only be based, not on admissible self-protection, but on a rarely voiced denial of any official justification for seeking to enter his home. The constitutional "liberty" that is asserted is the absolute right to refuse consent for an inspection designed and pursued solely for the protection of the community's health, even when the inspection is conducted with due regard for every convenience of time and place.

The power of inspection granted by the Baltimore City Code is strictly limited, more exacting than the analogous provisions of many other municipal codes. Valid grounds for suspicion of the existence of a nuisance must exist. Certainly the presence of a pile of filth in the back yard combined with the run-down condition of the house gave adequate grounds for such suspicion. The inspection must be made in the day time. Here was no midnight knock on the door, but an orderly visit in the middle of the afternoon with no suggestion that the hour was inconvenient. Moreover, the inspector has no power to force entry and did not attempt it. A fine is imposed for resistance, but officials are not authorized to break past the unwilling occupant.

Thus, not only does the inspection touch at most upon the periphery of the important interests safeguarded by the Fourteenth Amendment's protection against official intrusion, but it is hedged about with safeguards designed to make the least possible demand on the individual occupant, and to cause only the slightest restriction on his claims of privacy. Such a demand must be assessed in the light of the needs which have produced it.

Inspection without a warrant, as an adjunct to a regulatory scheme for the general welfare of the community and not as a means of enforcing the criminal law, has antecedents deep in our history. For more than 200 years Maryland has empowered its officers to enter upon ships, carriages, shops, and homes in the service of the common welfare. . . .

. . . the system of inspection here under attack, having its beginning in Maryland's colonial history, has been an integral part of the enforcement of Baltimore's health laws for more than a century and a half. The legal significance of such a long and consistent history of state practice has been illuminated for us by Mr. Justice Holmes:

"The Fourteenth Amendment, itself a historical product, did not destroy history for the States and substitute mechanical compartments of law all exactly alike. If a thing has been practised for two hundred years by common consent, it will need a strong case for the Fourteenth Amendment to affect it, . . ." *Jackman v. Rosenbaum Co.*, 260 U.S. 22, 31. . . .

The power here challenged rests not only on a long history of its exercise. It is a power which was continually strengthened and applied to wider concerns through those very years when the right of individuals to be free from peremptory official invasion received increasing legislative and judicial protection. Nor is this a situation where a new body of knowledge displaces previous premises of action. There is a total want of important modification in the circumstances or the structure of society which calls for a disregard of so much history. On the contrary, the problems which gave rise to these ordinances have multiplied manifold, as have the difficulties of enforcement. The need to maintain basic, minimal standards of housing, to prevent the spread of disease and of that pervasive breakdown in the fiber of a people which is produced by slums and the absence of the barest essentials of civilized living, has mounted to a major concern of American government. The growth of cities, the crowding of populations, the increased awareness of the responsibility of the state for the living conditions of its citizens, all have combined to create problems of the enforcement of minimum standards of far greater magnitude than the writers of these ancient inspection laws ever dreamed. Time and experience have forcefully taught that the power to inspect dwelling places, either as a matter of systematic area-by-area search or, as here, to treat a specific problem, is of indispensable importance to the maintenance of community health; a power that would be greatly hobbled by the blanket requirement of the safeguards necessary for a search of evidence of criminal acts. The need for preventive action is great, and city after city has seen this need and granted the power of inspection to its health officials; and these inspections are apparently welcomed by all but an insignificant few. Certainly, the nature of our society has not vitiated the need for inspections first thought necessary 158 years ago, nor has experience revealed any abuse or inroad on freedom in meeting this need by means that history and dominant public opinion have sanctioned. . . .

In light of the long history of this kind of inspection and of modern needs, we cannot say that the carefully circumscribed demand which Maryland here makes on appellant's freedom has deprived him of due process of law.

Affirmed.

Mr. Justice Whittaker, concurring. . . .

Mr. Justice Douglas, with whom The Chief Justice, Mr. Justice Black and Mr. Justice Brennan concur, dissenting.

The decision today greatly dilutes the right of privacy which every homeowner had the right to believe was part of our American heritage. We witness indeed an inquest over a substantial part of the Fourth Amendment.

The question in this case is whether a search warrant is needed to enter a citizen's home to investigate sanitary conditions. The Court holds that no search warrant is needed, that a knock on the door is all that is required, that for failure of the citizen to open the door he can be punished. From these conclusions I am forced to dissent.

The Due Process Clause of the Fourteenth Amendment enjoins upon the States the guarantee of privacy embodied in the Fourth Amendment (*Wolf v. Colorado,* 338 U.S. 25)—whatever may be the means established under the Fourth Amendment to enforce that guarantee. The Court now casts a shadow over that guarantee as respects searches and seizures in civil cases. Any such conclusion would require considerable editing and revision of the Fourth Amendment. For by its terms it protects the citizen against unreasonable searches and seizures by government, whatever may be the complaint. . . .

The Court said in *Wolf v. Colorado, supra,* at 27, that "The security of one's privacy against arbitrary intrusion by the police—which is at the core of the Fourth Amendment—is basic to a free society." Now that resounding phrase is watered down to embrace only certain invasions of one's privacy. If officials come to inspect sanitary conditions, they may come without a warrant and demand entry as of right. This is a strange deletion to make from the Fourth Amendment. In some States the health inspectors are none other than the police themselves. In some States the presence of unsanitary conditions gives rise to criminal prosecutions. Baltimore City Code, Art. 12, §§ 112 and 119—the one involved in the present case—makes the failure to abate a nuisance a misdemeanor. The knock on the door in any health inspection case may thus lay the groundwork for a criminal prosecution. The resistance of the citizen in the present case led to the imposition of a fine. If a fine may be imposed, why not a prison term?

It is said, however, that this fine is so small as to amount only to an assessment to cover the costs of the inspection. Yet if this fine can be imposed, the premises can be revisited without a warrant and repeated fines imposed. The truth is that the amount of the fine is not the measure of the right. The right is the guarantee against invasion of the home by officers without a warrant. No officer of government is authorized to penalize the citizen because he invokes his constitutional protection.

Moreover, the protection of the Fourth Amendment has heretofore been thought to protect privacy when civil litigation, as well as criminal prosecutions, were in the offing. . . .

The Court misreads history when it relates the Fourth Amendment primarily to searches for evidence to be used in criminal prosecutions. That certainly is not the teaching of *Entick v. Carrington,* 19 Howell's St. Tr. col. 1029. At that time—1765

—it was the search for the nonconformist that led British officials to ransack private homes. The commands of our First Amendment (as well as the prohibitions of the Fourth and the Fifth) reflect the teachings of *Entick* v. *Carrington, supra.* These three amendments are indeed closely related, safeguarding not only privacy and protection against self-incrimination but "conscience and human dignity and freedom of expression as well." . . .

The well-known protest of the elder Pitt against invasion of the home by the police, had nothing to do with criminal proceedings.

"The poorest man may in his cottage bid defiance to all the force of the Crown. It may be frail; its roof may shake; the wind may blow through it; the storm may enter, the rain may enter,—but the King of England cannot enter; all his force dares not cross the threshold of the ruined tenement!"

While this statement did not specifically refer to the general warrant, it was said in reference to the danger of excise officers entering private homes to levy the "Cyder Tax." . . .

Some of the statutes which James Otis denounced did not involve criminal proceedings. They in the main regulated customs and allowed forfeitures of goods shipped into the Colonies in violation of English shipping regulations. The twenty-dollar forfeiture involved here is no different in substance from the ones that Otis and the colonists found so objectionable. For their objection went not to the amount or size of the forfeiture but to the lawless manner in which it was collected. . . .

The philosophy of the Fourth Amendment was well expressed by Mr. Justice Butler speaking for the Court in *Agnello* v. *United States,* 269 U.S. 20, 32. "The search of a private dwelling without a warrant is in itself unreasonable and abhorrent to our laws." We have emphasized over and again that a search without a warrant can be made only in exceptional circumstances. If a house is on fire or if the police see a fugitive enter a building, entry without a search warrant can of course be made. Yet absent such extraordinary situations, the right of privacy must yield only when a judicial officer issues a warrant for a search on a showing of probable cause. . . . As we said in *McDonald* v. *United States,* [335 U.S. 451] 455–456:

"The presence of a search warrant serves a high function. Absent some grave emergency, the Fourth Amendment has interposed a magistrate between the citizen and the police. This was done not to shield criminals nor to make the home a safe haven for illegal activities. It was done so that an objective mind might weigh the need to invade that privacy in order to enforce the law. The right of privacy was deemed too precious to entrust to the discretion of those whose job is the detection of crime and the arrest of criminals. Power is a heady thing; and history shows that the police acting on their own cannot be trusted. And so the Constitution requires a magistrate to pass on the desires of the police before they violate the privacy of the home. We cannot be true to that constitutional requirement and excuse the absence of a search warrant without a showing by those who seek exemption from the constitutional mandate that the exigencies of the situation made that course imperative."

In the present case, the homeowner agreed to let the inspector in, if he got a search warrant. But none was ever sought. No excuse exists here for not getting a search warrant. A whole day elapsed between the first inspection and the arrest. The only reasons given for not getting a warrant was the officer's convenience:

"Q. Could you not just as well have made your inspection one hour or two hours later than at the time you demanded entry?"

"A. I could not. I had two students I had to release at three o'clock. I have to be in the office at three-thirty every day to take care of my reports."

That is indeed flimsy ground for denying this homeowner the constitutional protection afforded by a search warrant. . . .

[The Fourth Amendment] was designed to protect the citizen against uncontrolled invasion of his privacy. It does not make the home a place of refuge from the law. It only requires the sanction of the judiciary rather than the executive before that privacy may be invaded. History shows that all officers tend to be officious; and health inspectors, making out a case for criminal prosecution of the citizen, are no exception. . . .

One invasion of privacy by an official of government can be as oppressive as another. Health inspections are important. But they are hardly more important than the search for narcotic peddlers, rapists, kidnappers, murderers, and other criminal elements. As we have seen, searches were once in their heyday when the government was out to suppress the nonconformists. That is the true explanation of *Entick v. Carrington, supra.* Many today would think that the search for subversives was even more important than the search for unsanitary conditions. It would seem that the public interest in protecting privacy is equally as great in one case as in another. The fear that health inspections will suffer if constitutional safeguards are applied is strongly held by some. Like notions obtain by some law enforcement officials who take shortcuts in pursuit of criminals. The same pattern appears over and again whenever government seeks to use its compulsive force against the citizen. . . . The official's measure of his own need often does not square with the Bill of Rights.

Certainly this is a poor case for dispensing with the need for a search warrant. Evidence to obtain one was abundant. The house was in a state of extreme decay; and in the rear of the house was a pile of "rodent feces mixed with straw and debris to approximately half a ton." This is not to suggest that a health official need show the same kind of proof to a magistrate to obtain a warrant as one must who would search for the fruits or instrumentalities of crime. Where considerations of health and safety are involved, the facts that would justify an inference of "probable cause" to make an inspection are clearly different from those that would justify such an inference where a criminal investigation has been undertaken. Experience may show the need for periodic inspections of certain facilities without a further showing of cause to believe that substandard conditions dangerous to the public are being maintained. The passage of a certain period without inspection might of itself be sufficient in a given situation to justify the issuance of a warrant. The test of "probable cause" required by the Fourth Amendment can take into account the nature of the search that is being sought. This is not to sanction synthetic search warrants but to recognize that the showing of probable cause in a health case may have quite different requirements than the one required in graver situations. It can hardly be denied, unless history is ignored, that the policeman's or the inspector's knock on the door is one of these "official acts and proceedings" which *Boyd v. United States, supra,* 624, brought squarely within the Fourth Amendment. That being true, it seems to us plain that there is nothing in the Fourth Amendment that relieves the health inspector altogether from making an appropriate showing to a magistrate if he would enter a private dwelling without the owner's consent.

That problem, while important overall, is not important to the situation with which we deal. Figures submitted by the Baltimore Health Department show that citizens are mostly cooperative in granting entrance to inspectors. There were 28,081 inspections in 1954; 25,021 in 1955; 35,120 in 1956; 33,573 in 1957; and 36,119 in 1958. *And in all these instances the number of prosecutions was estimated to average one a year.* Submission by the overwhelming majority of the populace indicates there is no peril to the health program. One rebel a year (cf. Whyte, *The Organization Man*) is not too great a price to pay for maintaining our guarantee of civil rights in full vigor.

England—a nation no less mindful of public health than we and keenly conscious of civil liberties—has long proceeded on the basis that where the citizen denies entrance to a health inspector, a search warrant is needed. . . .

We cannot do less and still be true to the command of the Fourth Amendment which protects even the lowliest home in the land from intrusion on the mere say-so of an official.

Chapter 32

SELF-INCRIMINATION AND
COERCED CONFESSIONS

> . . . nor shall any person . . . be compelled in any criminal case to be a
> witness against himself. . . .   FIFTH AMENDMENT

The privilege against self-incrimination was well established in England by the last half of the seventeenth century, its adoption marking a great advance over earlier practices when suspects not only were required to give such testimony but were tortured to force them to do so. The privilege came to this country as part of the English common law, and was included in the Virginia Bill of Rights of 1776.

The Fifth Amendment by its terms protects persons only from compulsion to testify against themselves in criminal prosecutions, but it has long been interpreted as applicable to grand jury proceedings and legislative inquires as well. There has been considerable diversity of opinion concerning the privilege. On the one hand, Dean Erwin N. Griswold says it is "one of the great landmarks in man's struggle to make himself civilized," and the epitome of the Anglo-Saxon assumption that a man is innocent until proved guilty. Justice Stephen J. Field said: "The essential and inherent cruelty of compelling a man to expose his own guilt is obvious to every one." On the other hand, it was subjected to a classic attack by Jeremy Bentham, in 1925 Charles Evans Hughes recommended serious consideration of its abolition, and in the early 1950s Senator Joseph McCarthy made "Fifth Amendment Communists" objects of derision and scorn.

The first, and most obvious, effect of the Fifth Amendment is that the defendant in a criminal trial cannot be required to take the witness stand. It is improper for opposing counsel to call attention to failure of a defendant to take the stand in his own defense, and by federal statute a jury must be instructed that the defendant's failure to testify creates no presumption against him.

Before a grand jury, congressional committee, or administrative tribunal, the situation is different. Since there has been no indictment for crime, a person from whom evidence is sought cannot refuse to be a witness, but once he has gone on the witness stand, he can decline to answer particular questions on the ground of self-incrimination. It is normally very difficult to challenge a witness who refuses to testify on Fifth Amendment grounds, without forcing him to reveal the conduct which the Constitution entitles him to conceal. It is agreed that a witness may refuse to give not only answers which constitute an admission of guilt, but

383

also those which merely furnish evidence of guilt or supply a lead to obtaining such evidence. However, he may not refuse to talk when the danger of incrimination is "of an imaginary and unsubstantial character, having reference to some extraordinary and barely possible contingency, so improbable that no reasonable man would suffer it to influence his conduct. . . ."

This is the "real danger versus imaginary possibility" test, but in 1955 Justice Harlan in *Emspak* v. *United States*, 349 U.S. 190, charged that the Supreme Court had practically given up this standard, and was approving the refusal of witnesses to answer questions on Fifth Amendment grounds which could not conceivably be incriminatory. In the *Emspak* case the fifty-eight questions the witness had refused to answer all had to do with persons under suspicion of communism. The Court majority held that this circumstance justified Emspak in refusing to answer, but Harlan thought this was "painting with too broad a brush." The inference he drew from the record was that Emspak's real motive was to avoid being a "stool pigeon" against his associates, and this was not a "legal excuse for refusing to answer nonincriminatory questions."

The Fifth Amendment does not justify a person in refusing to testify about matters which would merely impair his reputation or tend to disgrace him. Moreover, even if criminal conduct would be disclosed by the answers, a person may not refuse if the conduct is no longer punishable because the statute of limitations has run, or because he has been granted immunity from prosecution by statute.

The granting of immunity to witnesses whose testimony is particularly wanted has been authorized by Congress in several statutes. The constitutionality of its use by the Interstate Commerce Commission under an act of 1893 was upheld by a five to four vote in *Brown* v. *Walker*, 161 U.S. 591 (1896). The majority opinion admitted that, interpreted literally, the self-incrimination clause authorizes a witness "to refuse to disclose any fact which might tend to incriminate, disgrace or expose him to unfavorable comments," and as so interpreted would render the immunity act unconstitutional. But the Fifth Amendment could also be read as having for its object only "to secure the witness against a criminal prosecution, which might be aided directly or indirectly by his disclosure." The Court regarded this second interpretation as yielding a better balance between private right and public welfare. If a witness secures legal immunity from prosecution, "the possible impairment of his good name is a penalty which it is reasonable he should be compelled to pay for the common good."

The Supreme Court maintained this position when it faced the same issue sixty years later in *Ullmann* v. *United States*, 350 U.S. 422 (1956). In 1954 Congress had adopted an immunity act under which witnesses could be compelled to testify before courts, grand juries, and congressional committees in national security cases by granting them immunity from prosecution for any criminal acts they might confess. Ullmann, who had earlier pleaded the Fifth Amendment before a congressional committee and a grand jury when questioned about a wartime espionage ring in Washington, was granted immunity under the 1954 act so that a grand jury could secure his testimony.

Coerced Confessions in Federal Courts. The Fifth Amendment forbids the use in federal courts of confessions secured under conditions of physical or mental coercion, for in such cases the defendant would obviously have been under compulsion to testify against himself. But the Amendment does not forbid the admission in evidence of a confession made while the accused was in custody of the law, if the confession was made voluntarily and without compulsion of any kind.

Federal statutes require suspects on apprehension to be taken before the nearest judicial officer "without unnecessary delay" for hearing, commitment, or release on bail. When suspects are taken before a committing magistrate, the law officers must show probable cause for the arrests, and the suspects must be informed of their right to remain silent and to have counsel. The motive of the police in delaying this process is usually to attempt to secure a confession before the suspect learns of his rights.

In *McNabb* v. *United States*, 318 U.S. 332 (1943), two men suspected of shooting a revenue officer were taken into custody by federal officials and questioned over a period of two days, without the presence of friends or counsel, until a confession was secured. The Supreme Court voided the conviction, not on the ground that the confession was coerced, but because of violation of the "without unnecessary delay" provision. There was considerable criticism of the *McNabb* rule as placing a substantial impediment in the path of law enforcement, but the Supreme Court reaffirmed it in *Mallory* v. *United States*, 354 U.S. 449 (1957). This decision, which voided a death sentence for rape in the District of Columbia, set off a concerted effort in Congress to revise the *McNabb* rule by new legislation providing that a confession or other evidence otherwise admissible should not be excluded solely because of delay in the arraignment, but the measure failed of adoption.

Self-incrimination in State Courts. The Fifth Amendment ban on self-incrimination does not carry through to the state level to prevent the drawing of unfavorable inferences from a defendant's failure to take the witness stand in a criminal prosecution. The reason, as already noted in the *Twining* and *Adamson* cases, is that the privilege against self-incrimination is not regarded by the Supreme Court as necessary to a system of "ordered liberty." Nor, according to two divided Supreme Court decisions, does the Fifth Amendment protect a person in refusing to give testimony before a state body which might lead to a federal prosecution. In *Feldman* v. *United States*, 322 U.S. 487 (1944), a man was compelled to testify in a state court proceeding, with a guarantee of immunity from state prosecution for any state crime he might confess. The transcript of his compelled testimony was then used by federal authorities to convict him of a federal crime in a federal court.

In a four to three decision Justice Frankfurter upheld this result as required by our system of dual sovereignties, and the only limitation he admitted on the practice was that there must be no "complicity" of federal officers in the state proceeding. Justice Black, dissenting, bitterly attacked this ruling as cutting into the "very substance" of the Fifth Amendment on the basis of "dialectics" and "syllogistic reasoning" about the necessities of the federal system. The argument was repeated in *Knapp* v. *Schweitzer*, 357 U.S. 371 (1958), with the same result, but with four justices favoring reconsideration of the *Feldman* rule.

In *Cohen* v. *Hurley*, 366 U.S. 117 (1961), the Court by another five to four vote ruled that New York could disbar an attorney who invoked his privilege against self-incrimination and refused to testify before a judicially established committee of inquiry looking into "ambulance chasing." The majority held that disbarment was based, not on his exercise of the self-incrimination privilege, but on his refusal to discharge obligations which as a lawyer he owed the court.

Coerced Confessions in State Courts. Confessions extorted by force and violence will be regarded by the Supreme Court as voiding any convictions in state courts based on them. In *Brown* v. *Mississippi,* 297 U.S. 278 (1936), the facts of brutality and torture by state officers were uncontroverted, and no evidence other than the coerced confessions of murder was presented at the trial. The state's defense was the *Twining* argument that immunity from self-incrimination was not an essential element in due process of law. Chief Justice Hughes replied for a unanimous Court that the *Twining* principle simply gave a state some freedom to experiment with the procedures of criminal prosecution. But that freedom is "the freedom of constitutional government and is limited by the requirement of due process of law. Because a State may dispense with a jury trial, it does not follow that it may substitute trial by ordeal. The rack and torture chamber may not be substituted for the witness stand."

More difficult problems arise where confessions are secured by coercion which is mental rather than physical. In *Ashcraft* v. *Tennessee,* 322 U.S. 143 (1944), a man was convicted of murder on a confession elicited by thirty-six hours of continuous questioning under powerful electric lights by relays of officers, investigators, and lawyers. The Court held such a situation to be "so inherently coercive that its very existence is irreconcilable with the possession of mental freedom by a lone suspect against whom the full coercive force is brought to bear." Justice Jackson disagreed on the ground that a confession obtained by questioning, "even if persistent and prolonged," is different from one obtained by the use of violence. "Interrogation *per se* is not, while violence *per se* is, an outlaw."

This division of opinion on the validity of confessions obtained by mental coercion has continued, though generally such confessions have been voided. For example, in *Leyra* v. *Denno,* 347 U.S. 556 (1954), a man suspected of having murdered his parents was questioned intensively for three days. Then, because he had a sinus condition, a doctor was brought in who was a state-employed psychiatrist with experience in hypnosis. After a short time, the completely exhausted suspect was at the stage of accepting suggestions of his guilt from the psychiatrist, who then called in the police to take the confession, which the suspect subsequently repeated to his business partner. The trial court accepted the latter confession, but the Supreme Court majority rejected all the confessions as parts of one continuous process, during which "an already physically and emotionally exhausted suspect's ability to resist interrogation was broken to almost trance-like submission by use of the arts of a highly skilled psychiatrist."

Fikes v. *Alabama,* 352 U.S. 191 (1957), another split decision, concerned a Negro of low mentality who had been kept incommunicado for a week, had not been arraigned, and had been questioned intermittently. Justice Frankfurter's conclusion for the Court was that none of these circumstances standing alone would justify a reversal, but that "in combination they bring the result below the Plimsoll line of 'due process.'"

ULLMANN *v.* UNITED STATES
350 U.S. 422, 76 S. Ct. 497, 100 L. Ed. 511 (1956)

The Immunity Act of 1954 was adopted by Congress to provide a means of securing information on national security matters by granting immunity from prosecution to unwilling witnesses whose testimony was desired. Immunity orders were to be granted by a federal judge on requests initiated by a United States attorney with the approval of the Attorney General. Ullmann, having been ordered to testify before a federal grand jury under the act and having refused to do so, was convicted of contempt of court and sentenced to six months' imprisonment unless he should purge himself of the contempt.

Mr. Justice Frankfurter delivered the opinion of the Court. . . .

Is the immunity provided by the Act sufficiently broad to displace the protection afforded by the privilege against self-incrimination? . . . Does the Fifth Amendment prohibit compulsion of what would otherwise be self-incriminating testimony no matter what the scope of the immunity statute?

It is relevant to define explicitly the spirit in which the Fifth Amendment's privilege against self-incrimination should be approached. This command of the Fifth Amendment . . . registers an important advance in the development of our liberty. . . . Time has not shown that protection from the evils against which this safeguard was directed is needless or unwarranted. This constitutional protection must not be interpreted in a hostile or niggardly spirit. Too many, even those who should be better advised, view this privilege as a shelter for wrongdoers. They too readily assume that those who invoke it are either guilty of crime or commit perjury in claiming the privilege. Such a view does scant honor to the patriots who sponsored the Bill of Rights as a condition to acceptance of the Constitution by the ratifying States. . . .

Nothing new can be put into the Constitution except through the amendatory process. Nothing old can be taken out without the same process.

No doubt the constitutional privilege may, on occasion, save a guilty man from his just deserts. It was aimed at a more far-reaching evil—a recurrence of the Inquisition and the Star Chamber, even if not in their stark brutality. Prevention of the greater evil was deemed of more importance than occurrence of the lesser evil. Having had much experience with a tendency in human nature to abuse power, the Founders sought to close the doors against like future abuses by law-enforcing agencies.

As no constitutional guarantee enjoys preference, so none should suffer subordination or deletion. . . . It is in this spirit of strict, not lax, observance of the constitutional protection of the individual that we approach the claims made by petitioner in this case. The attack on the Immunity Act as violating the Fifth Amendment is not a new one. Sixty years ago this Court considered, in *Brown* v. *Walker,* 161 U.S. 591, the constitutionality of a similar Act. . . . In that case, Brown, auditor for a railroad company, had been subpoenaed to testify before a grand jury which was investigating charges that officers and agents of the company had violated the Interstate Commerce Act. Invoking the privilege against self-incrimination, he refused to answer certain questions concerning the operations and the rebate policy of the railroad. . . .

The Court [held] that a statute which compelled testimony but secured the witness against a criminal prosecution which might be aided directly or indirectly by his disclosures did not violate the Fifth Amendment's privilege against self-incrimination and that the 1893 statute did provide such immunity. "While the constitutional provision in question is justly regarded as one of the most valuable prerogatives of the citizen, its object is fully accomplished by the statutory immunity, and we are therefore of opinion that the witness was compellable to answer. . . ."

Petitioner, however, attempts to distinguish *Brown* v. *Walker*. He argues that this case is different from *Brown* v. *Walker* because the impact of the disabilities imposed by federal and state authorities and the public in general—such as loss of job, expulsion from labor unions, state registration and investigation statutes, passport eligibility, and general public opprobrium—is so oppressive that the statute does not give him true immunity. This, he alleges, is significantly different from the impact of testifying on the auditor in *Brown* v. *Walker,* who could the next day resume his job with reputation unaffected. But, as this Court has often held, the immunity granted need only remove those sanctions which generate the fear justifying invocation of the privilege: "The interdiction of the 5th Amendment operates only where a witness is asked to incriminate himself,—in other words, to give testimony which may possibly expose him to a criminal charge. But if the criminality has already been taken away, the amendment ceases to apply." *Hale* v. *Henkel,* 201 U.S. 43, 67. . . .

Petitioner also urges that if *Brown* v. *Walker* is found nondistinguishable and controlling, then that case should be reconsidered and overruled. He also urges upon us a "return" to a literal reading of the Fifth Amendment. *Brown* v. *Walker* was the second case to deal with an immunity statute. Four years previously, in *Counselman* v. *Hitchcock,* 142 U.S. 547, a unanimous Court had found constitutionally inadequate the predecessor to the 1893 statute because the immunity granted was incomplete, in that it merely forbade the use of the testimony given and failed to protect a witness from future prosecution based on knowledge and sources of information obtained from the compelled testimony. It was with this background that the 1893 statute, providing complete immunity from prosecution, was passed and that *Brown* v. *Walker* was argued and decided. . . . The Court was closely divided in upholding the statute, and the opinions reflect the thoroughness with which the issues were considered. Since that time the Court's holding in *Brown* v. *Walker* has never been challenged; the case and the doctrine it announced have consistently and without question been treated as definitive by this Court. . . . The 1893 statute has become part of our constitutional fabric and has been included "in substantially the same terms, in virtually all of the major regulatory enactments of the Federal Government." . . .

We are not dealing here with one of the vague, undefinable, admonitory provisions of the Constitution whose scope is inevitably addressed to changing circumstances. The privilege against self-incrimination is a specific provision of which it is peculiarly true that "a page of history is worth a volume of logic." . . . For the history of the privilege establishes not only that it is not to be interpreted literally, but also that its sole concern is, as its name indicates, with the danger to a witness forced to give testimony leading to the infliction of "penalties affixed to the criminal acts. . . ." *Boyd* v. *United States,* 116 U.S. 616. . . . Immunity displaces the danger. Once the reason for the privilege ceases, the privilege ceases. We reaffirm *Brown* v. *Walker.* . . .

The judgment of the Court of Appeals is affirmed.

Affirmed.

MR. JUSTICE REED concurs in the opinion and judgment of the Court except as to the statement that no constitutional guarantee enjoys preference. . . .

MR. JUSTICE DOUGLAS, with whom MR. JUSTICE BLACK concurs, dissenting.

I would reverse the judgment of conviction. I would base the reversal on *Boyd* v. *United States,* 116 U.S. 616, or, in the alternative, I would overrule the five-to-four decision of *Brown* v. *Walker* . . . and adopt the view of the minority in that case that the right of silence created by the Fifth Amendment is beyond the reach of Congress.

First, as to the *Boyd* case. There are numerous disabilities created by federal law that attach to a person who is a Communist. These disabilities include ineligibility for employment in the Federal Government and in defense facilities, disqualification for a passport, the risk of internment, the risk of loss of employment as a longshoreman —to mention only a few. These disabilities imposed by federal law are forfeitures within the meaning of our cases and as much protected by the Fifth Amendment as criminal prosecution itself. But there is no indication that the Immunity Act . . . grants protection against those disabilities. The majority will not say that it does. I think, indeed, that it must be read as granting only partial, not complete, immunity for the matter disclosed under compulsion. . . .

Boyd v. *United States, supra,* involved a proceeding to establish a forfeiture of goods alleged to have been fraudulently imported without payment of duties. The claimants resisted an order requiring the production of an invoice to be used against them in the forfeiture proceedings. The Court in an opinion by Mr. Justice Bradley sustained the defense of the Fifth Amendment. The Court said, "A witness, as well as a party, is protected by the law from being compelled to give evidence that tends to criminate him, or to subject his property to forfeiture." . . .

The forfeiture of property on compelled testimony is no more abhorrent than the forfeiture of rights of citizenship. Any forfeiture of rights as a result of compelled testimony is at war with the Fifth Amendment.

The Court apparently distinguishes the *Boyd* case on the ground that the forfeiture of property was a penalty affixed to a criminal act. The loss of a job and the ineligibility for a passport are also penalties affixed to a criminal act. For the case of *Dennis* v. *United States,* 341 U.S. 494, makes plain that membership in the Communist Party is a crucial link of evidence for conviction under the Smith Act. . . . When a man loses his job because he is a Communist, there is as much a penalty suffered as when an importer loses property because he is a tax evader. When a man loses his right to a passport because he is a Communist, there is as much a penalty suffered as when property is lost for violation of the revenue laws. If there was a penalty suffered in the *Boyd* case, there are penalties suffered here. Both are hitched to criminal acts. . . .

Second, as to *Brown* v. *Walker.* The difficulty I have with that decision and with the majority of the Court in the present case is that they add an important qualification to the Fifth Amendment. The guarantee is that no person "shall be compelled in any criminal case to be a witness against himself." The majority does not enforce that guarantee as written but qualifies it; and the qualification apparently reads, "but only if criminal conviction might result." Wisely or not, the Fifth Amendment protects against the compulsory self-accusation of crime without exception or qualification. In *Counselman* v. *Hitchcock, supra,* Mr. Justice Blatchford said, "The privilege is limited to criminal matters, but it is as broad as the mischief against which it seeks to guard."

The "mischief" to be prevented falls under at least three heads.

(1) One "mischief" is not only the risk of conviction but the risk of prosecution. . . . The risk of prosecution is not a risk which the wise take lightly. As experienced a judge as Learned Hand once said, "I must say that, as a litigant, I should dread a lawsuit beyond almost anything else short of sickness and of death." . . . A part of the dread in a case such as this is the chain of events that may be put in motion once disclosure is made. The truth is, I think, that there is no control left, once the right of secrecy is broken. For the statute protects the accused only on account of the

"transaction, matter, or thing" concerning which he is compelled to testify and bars the use as evidence of the "testimony so compelled." The forced disclosure may open up vast new vistas for the prosecutor with leads to numerous accusations not within the purview of the question and answer. . . .

(2) The guarantee against self-incrimination contained in the Fifth Amendment is not only a protection against conviction and prosecution but a safeguard of conscience and human dignity and freedom of expression as well. My view is that the Framers put it beyond a power of Congress to *compel* anyone to confess his crimes. The evil to be guarded against was partly self-accusation under legal compulsion. But that was only a part of the evil. The conscience and dignity of man were also involved. So too was his right to freedom of expression guaranteed by the First Amendment. The Framers, therefore, created the federally protected right of silence and decreed that the law could not be used to pry open one's lips and make him a witness against himself. . . .

(3) This right of silence, this right of the accused to stand mute serves another high purpose. Mr. Justice Field, one of the four dissenters in *Brown* v. *Walker,* stated that it is the aim of the Fifth Amendment to protect the accused from all compulsory testimony "which would expose him to infamy and disgrace," as well as that which might lead to a criminal conviction. . . .

The history of infamy as a punishment was notorious. Luther had inveighed against excommunication. The Massachusetts Body of Liberties of 1641 had provided in Article 60 "No church censure shall degrade or depose any man from any Civill dignitie, office, or Authoritie he shall have in the Commonwealth." Loss of office, loss of dignity, loss of face were feudal forms of punishment. Infamy was historically considered to be punishment as effective as fine and imprisonment. . . .

There is great infamy involved in the present case apart from the loss of rights of citizenship under federal law which I have already mentioned. The disclosure that a person is a Communist practically excommunicates him from society. School boards will not hire him. . . . A lawyer risks exclusion from the bar . . . ; a doctor, the revocation of his license to practice. . . . If an actor, he is on a black list. . . . And he will be able to find no employment in our society except at the lowest level, if at all. . . .

It is no answer to say that a witness who exercises his Fifth Amendment right of silence and stands mute may bring himself into disrepute. If so, that is the price he pays for exercising the right of silence granted by the Fifth Amendment. The critical point is that the Constitution places the right of silence *beyond the reach of government.* The Fifth Amendment stands between the citizen and his government. When public opinion casts a person into the outer darkness, as happens today when a person is exposed as a Communist, the government brings infamy on the head of the witness when it compels disclosure. That is precisely what the Fifth Amendment prohibits.

Finally, it is said that we should not disturb *Brown* v. *Walker* because it is an old and established decision. But this Court has always been willing to re-examine and overrule constitutional precedents, even those old and established. . . . *Brown* v. *Walker,* decided by a bare majority of the Court and now 60 years old, has no greater claim to sanctity than the other venerable decisions which history showed had outlived their usefulness or were conceived in error. . . .

Chapter 33

DOUBLE JEOPARDY

> . . . nor shall any person be subject for the same offence to be twice put in jeopardy of life or limb. . . .
>
> FIFTH AMENDMENT

The Fifth Amendment in archaic language forbids the government to place any person twice "in jeopardy of life or limb" for the same offense. The underlying idea, as Justice Black said in *Green v. United States,* 355 U.S. 184 (1957), "is that the State with all its resources and power should not be allowed to make repeated attempts to convict an individual for an alleged offense, thereby subjecting him to embarrassment, expense and ordeal and compelling him to live in a continuing state of anxiety and insecurity, as well as enhancing the possibility that even though innocent he may be found guilty." Enforcement of this provision depends upon the views taken as to what constitutes "jeopardy" in a legal proceeding, and what constitutes "sameness" in an offense.

On the first question, an accused person has of course been placed in jeopardy when he has been tried by a court of competent jurisdiction and either acquitted or convicted. The government may not appeal such a verdict or institute a second prosecution for the same offense. It is not even necessary for a trial to have reached the stage of a verdict to bring the jeopardy rule into operation; otherwise a prosecutor or judge would be able to stop a trial when it began to appear that the jury might not convict, in order to leave the way open for a second trial. On the other hand, when a jury fails to agree on a verdict and is discharged by the judge, a second trial is permissible, the theory being that it is merely a continuation of the first. Trial by a court which is subsequently found to lack jurisdiction cannot place the defendant in jeopardy, no matter how far the proceedings are carried.

The accused may waive his constitutional immunity against double jeopardy. He does this when he requests a new trial, or appeals from a verdict of guilty. If a conviction is set aside on appeal, the defendant may be tried a second time for the same offense, and the accused assumes the risk of receiving a heavier penalty than in the first trial. But according to *Green v. United States* (1957), he cannot be subjected to the risk of being convicted on a more serious charge than in the first trial.

The "same offense" provision means the same identical offense as defined by the same governmental jurisdiction. The test of identity of offenses is whether the same evidence is required to prove them. If not, the fact that two charges grow out of one transaction does not make a single offense where two or more are defined by the statutes. Thus Congress may provide for both civil and criminal prosecution for the same act or failure to act, or it may separate a conspiracy to commit a substantive offense from the actual commission of the offense, and attach a different penalty to each. A person who refused to testify before a Senate committee was not subjected to double jeopardy by being punished for contempt of the Senate and also indicted for a misdemeanor for such refusal, according to *In re Chapman*, 166 U.S. 661 (1897).

Double Jeopardy in State Courts. As already noted in Chapter 30, *Palko* v. *Connecticut*, 302 U.S. 319 (1937), held that the federal double jeopardy rule was not binding on the states, and that a statute permitting the state to appeal a criminal conviction was not inconsistent with the standard of "ordered liberty."

A bizarre form of double jeopardy problem came before the Court in *Louisiana ex rel. Francis* v. *Resweber*, 329 U.S. 459 (1947). Francis had been convicted of murder and sentenced to death. He was placed in the electric chair, but because of some mechanical difficulty it did not operate, and the prisoner was returned to his cell. Redress was then sought in the courts on the ground that a second trip to the chair would constitute double jeopardy contrary to the Fifth Amendment as well as cruel and unusual punishment in violation of the Eighth Amendment. The Supreme Court said: "We shall examine the circumstances under the assumption, but without so deciding, that violation of the principles of the Fifth and Eighth Amendments, as to double jeopardy and cruel and unusual punishment, would be violative of the due process clause of the Fourteenth Amendment." The Court was able to leave the constitutional problem in this equivocal state, since it found that even if the two standards were applicable, they had not been violated.

In two 1958 decisions a double jeopardy problem was raised by the prosecution of different offenses at consecutive trials even though arising out of the same occurrence. In *Hoag* v. *New Jersey*, 356 U.S. 464, a man who was alleged to have robbed five tavern patrons was tried for the robbery of three of them, and was acquitted because of the unexpected failure of four of the state's witnesses to identify the defendant. The state then tried Hoag for robbery of a fourth patron, who was the only witness at the first trial to identify the defendant, and this time the jury convicted. By a five to three vote the Supreme Court upheld the state's action on the ground that, while a single trial would have been "preferable practice," the Fourteenth Amendment did not lay down an inflexible rule making multiple trials unconstitutional, and the circumstances of this case did not result in "fundamental unfairness."

Ciucci v. *Illinois*, 356 U.S. 571, involved a man accused of killing his wife and three children. The initial prosecution for one of the murders brought conviction and a twenty-year sentence. Dissatisfied with this outcome, the prosecutor instituted a second trial for another of the murders, which yielded a forty-five year sentence. The state then made a third effort, and was finally rewarded by a death sentence. The Court upheld these tactics by a five to four vote.

Double Jeopardy in a Federal System. Where both federal and state governments make the same act an offense, the Supreme Court has held that it is not double jeopardy for each government to prosecute and punish. This rule provoked considerable dissatisfaction during the period of national prohibition, but the Court justified dual prosecution in *United States* v. *Lanza,* 260 U.S. 377 (1922), as resulting from our system of "two sovereignties, deriving power from different sources, capable of dealing with the same subject-matter within the same territory. . . . It follows that an act denounced as a crime by both national and state sovereignties is an offense against the peace and dignity of both. . . ."

This principle was further developed in two 1959 decisions. In *Abbate* v. *United States,* 359 U.S. 187, several individuals who conspired in Illinois to blow up telephone properties in Mississippi were convicted on a conspiracy charge in Illinois, and were subsequently found guilty of the same acts by a federal court in Mississippi. In *Bartkus* v. *Illinois,* 359 U.S. 121, a man was tried by a federal court for robbery of an Illinois bank and acquitted. He was then indicted for the same crime by an Illinois grand jury, convicted, and sentenced to life imprisonment. The Supreme Court, by a divided vote, denied that the double jeopardy standard had been violated in either case.

BARTKUS v. ILLINOIS
359 U.S. 121, 79 S. Ct. 676, 3 L. Ed. 2d 684 (1959)

MR. JUSTICE FRANKFURTER delivered the opinion of the Court.

Petitioner was tried in the Federal District Court for the Northern District of Illinois on December 18, 1953, for robbery of a federally insured savings and loan association. . . . The case was tried to a jury and resulted in an acquittal. On January 8, 1954, an Illinois grand jury indicted Bartkus. The facts recited in the Illinois indictment were substantially identical to those contained in the prior federal indictment. . . . Bartkus was tried and convicted in the Criminal Court of Cook County and was sentenced to life imprisonment under the Illinois Habitual Criminal Statute. . . .

The state and federal prosecutions were separately conducted. It is true that the agent of the Federal Bureau of Investigation who had conducted the investigation on behalf of the Federal Government turned over to the Illinois prosecuting officials all the evidence he had gathered against the petitioner. Concededly, some of that evidence had been gathered after acquittal in the federal court. The only other connection between the two trials is to be found in a suggestion that the federal sentencing of the accomplices who testified against petitioner in both trials was purposely continued by the federal court until after they testified in the state trial. The record establishes that the prosecution was undertaken by state prosecuting officials within their discretionary responsibility and on the basis of evidence that conduct contrary to the penal code of Illinois had occurred within their jurisdiction. It establishes also that federal officials acted in cooperation with state authorities, as is the conventional practice between the two sets of prosecutors throughout the country. It does not support the claim that the State of Illinois in bringing its prosecution was merely a tool of the federal authorities, who thereby avoided the prohibition of the Fifth Amendment against a retrial of a federal prosecution after an acquittal. It does not sustain a conclusion that the state prosecution was a sham and a cover for a federal prosecution, and thereby in essential fact another federal prosecution.

Since the new prosecution was by Illinois, and not by the Federal Government, the claim of unconstitutionality must rest upon the Due Process Clause of the Fourteenth Amendment. Prior cases in this Court relating to successive state and federal prosecutions have been concerned with the Fifth Amendment, and the scope of its proscription of second prosecutions by the Federal Government, not with the Fourteenth Amendment's effect on state action. We are now called upon to draw on the considerations which have guided the Court in applying the limitations of the Fourteenth Amendment on state powers. We have held from the beginning and uniformly that the Due Process Clause of the Fourteenth Amendment does not apply to the States any of the provisions of the first eight amendments as such. The relevant historical materials have been canvassed by this Court and by legal scholars. These materials demonstrate conclusively that Congress and the members of the legislatures of the ratifying States did not contemplate that the Fourteenth Amendment was a shorthand incorporation of the first eight amendments making them applicable as explicit restrictions upon the States. . . .

Decisions of this Court concerning the application of the Due Process Clause reveal the necessary process of balancing relevant and conflicting factors in the judicial application of that Clause. In *Chambers* v. *Florida,* 309 U.S. 227, we held that a state conviction of murder was void because it was based upon a confession elicited by applying third-degree methods to the defendant. But we have also held that a second execution necessitated by a mechanical failure in the first attempt was not in violation of due process. *Louisiana ex rel. Francis* v. *Resweber,* 329 U.S. 459. Decisions under the Due Process Clause require close and perceptive inquiry into fundamental principles of our society. The Anglo-American system of law is based not upon transcendental revelation but upon the conscience of society ascertained as best it may be by a tribunal disciplined for the task and environed by the best safeguards for disinterestedness and detachment.

Constitutional challenge to successive state and federal prosecutions based upon the same transaction or conduct is not a new question before the Court though it has now been presented with conspicuous ability. The Fifth Amendment's proscription of double jeopardy has been invoked and rejected in over twenty cases of real or hypothetical successive state and federal prosecution cases before this Court. While *United States* v. *Lanza,* 260 U.S. 377, was the first case in which we squarely held valid a federal prosecution arising out of the same facts which had been the basis of a state conviction, the validity of such a prosecution by the Federal Government has not been questioned by this Court since the opinion in *Fox* v. *Ohio,* 5 How. 410, more than one hundred years ago. . . .

Since *Lanza* the Court has five times repeated the rule that successive state and federal prosecutions are not in violation of the Fifth Amendment. Indeed Mr. Justice Holmes once wrote of this rule that it "is too plain to need more than statement." One of the post-*Lanza* cases, *Jerome* v. *United States,* 318 U.S. 101, involved the same federal statute under which Bartkus was indicted and in *Jerome* this Court recognized that successive state and federal prosecutions were thereby made possible because all States had general robbery statutes. Nonetheless, a unanimous Court, as recently as 1943, accepted as unquestioned constitutional law that such successive prosecutions would not violate the proscription of double jeopardy included in the Fifth Amendment. . . .

The experience of state courts in dealing with successive prosecutions by different governments is obviously also relevant in considering whether or not the Illinois prosecution of Bartkus violated due process of law. Of the twenty-eight States which have considered the validity of successive state and federal prosecutions as against a challenge of violation of either a state constitutional double-jeopardy provision or a common-law evidentiary rule of *autrefois acquit* and *autrefois convict,* twenty-seven have refused to rule that the second prosecution was or would be barred. These States were not bound to follow this Court and its interpretation of the Fifth Amendment. The rules, constitutional, statutory, or common law which bound them, drew upon the same experience as did the Fifth Amendment, but were and are of separate and independent authority. . . .

With this body of precedent as irrefutable evidence that state and federal courts have for years refused to bar a second trial even though there had been a prior trial by another government for a similar offense, it would be disregard of a long, unbroken, unquestioned course of impressive adjudication for the Court now to rule that due process compels such a bar. A practical justification for rejecting such a reading of due process also commends itself in aid of this interpretation of the Fourteenth Amendment. In *Screws v. United States*, 325 U.S. 91, defendants were tried and convicted in a federal court under federal statutes with maximum sentences of a year and two years respectively. But the state crime there involved was a capital offense. Were the federal prosecution of a comparatively minor offense to prevent state prosecution of so grave an infraction of state law, the result would be a shocking and untoward deprivation of the historic right and obligation of the States to maintain peace and order within their confines. It would be in derogation of our federal system to displace the reserved power of States over state offenses by reason of prosecution of minor federal offenses by federal authorities beyond the control of the States.[1]

Some recent suggestions that the Constitution was in reality a deft device for establishing a centralized government are not only without factual justification but fly in the face of history. It has more accurately been shown that the men who wrote the Constitution as well as the citizens of the member States of the Confederation were fearful of the power of centralized government and sought to limit its power. Mr. Justice Brandeis has written that separation of powers was adopted in the Constitution "not to promote efficiency but to preclude the exercise of arbitrary power." Time has not lessened the concern of the Founders in devising a federal system which would likewise be a safeguard against arbitrary government. The greatest self-restraint is necessary when that federal system yields results with which a court is in little sympathy. . . .

Precedent, experience, and reason alike supoprt the conclusion that Alfonse Bartkus has not been deprived of due process of law by the State of Illinois.

Affirmed.

MR. JUSTICE BLACK, with whom THE CHIEF JUSTICE and MR. JUSTICE DOUGLAS concur, dissenting.

Petitioner, Bartkus, was indicted in a United States District Court for bank robbery. He was tried by a jury and acquitted. So far as appears the trial was conducted fairly by an able and conscientious judge. Later, Bartkus was indicted in an Illinois state court for the same bank robbery. This time he was convicted and sentenced to life imprisonment. His acquittal in the federal court would have barred a second trial in any court of the United States because of the provision in the Fifth Amendment that no person shall "be subject for the same offence to be twice put in jeopardy of life or limb." The Court today rejects Bartkus' contention that his state conviction after a federal acquittal violates the Fourteenth Amendment to our Constitution. I cannot agree.

The Court's holding further limits our already weakened constitutional guarantees

---

[1] Illinois had an additional and unique interest in Bartkus beyond the commission of this particular crime. If Bartkus was guilty of the crime charged he would be an habitual offender in Illinois and subject to life imprisonment. The Illinois court sentenced Bartkus to life imprisonment on this ground.

against double prosecutions. *United States* v. *Lanza,* 260 U.S. 377, decided in 1922, allowed federal conviction and punishment of a man who had been previously convicted and punished for the identical acts by one of our States. Today, for the first time in its history, this Court upholds the state conviction of a defendant who had been *acquitted* of the same offense in the federal courts. I would hold that a federal trial following either state acquittal or conviction is barred by the Double Jeopardy Clause of the Fifth Amendment. . . . And, quite apart from whether that clause is as fully binding on the States as it is on the Federal Government, see *Adamson* v. *California,* 332 U.S. 46, 68 (dissenting opinion), I would hold that Bartkus' conviction cannot stand. For I think double prosecutions for the same offense are so contrary to the spirit of our free country that they violate even the prevailing view of the Fourteenth Amendment, expressed in *Palko* v. *Connecticut,* 302 U.S. 319. . . .

Fear and abhorrence of governmental power to try people twice for the same conduct is one of the oldest ideas found in western civilization. Its roots run deep into Greek and Roman times. Even in the Dark Ages, when so many other principles of justice were lost, the idea that one trial and one punishment were enough remained alive through the canon law and the teachings of the early Christian writers. By the thirteenth century it seems to have been firmly established in England, where it came to be considered as a "universal maxim of the common law." It is not surprising, therefore, that the principle was brought to this country by the earliest settlers as part of their heritage of freedom, and that it has been recognized here as fundamental again and again. Today it is found, in varying forms, not only in the Federal Constitution, but in the jurisprudence or constitutions of every State, as well as most foreign nations. It has, in fact, been described as a part of all advanced systems of law and as one of those universal principles "of reason, justice, and conscience, of which Cicero said: 'Nor is it one thing at Rome and another at Athens, one now and another in the future, but among all nations it is the same.'" While some writers have explained the opposition to double prosecutions by emphasizing the injustice inherent in two punishments for the same act, and others have stressed the dangers to the innocent from allowing the full power of the state to be brought against them in two trials, the basic and recurring theme has always simply been that it is wrong for a man to "be brought into Danger for the same Offence more than once." Few principles have been more deeply "rooted in the traditions and conscience of our people."

The Court apparently takes the position that a second trial for the same act is somehow less offensive if one of the trials is conducted by the Federal Government and the other by a State. Looked at from the standpoint of the individual who is being prosecuted, this notion is too subtle for me to grasp. If double punishment is what is feared, it hurts no less for two "Sovereigns" to inflict it than for one. If danger to the innocent is emphasized, that danger is surely no less when the power of State and Federal Governments is brought to bear on one man in two trials, than when one of these "Sovereigns" proceeds alone. In each case, inescapably, a man is forced to face danger twice for the same conduct.

The Court, without denying the almost universal abhorrence of such double prosecutions, nevertheless justifies the practice here in the name of "federalism." This, it seems to me, is a misuse and desecration of the concept. Our Federal Union was conceived and created "to establish Justice" and to "secure the Blessings of Liberty," not to destroy any of the bulwarks on which both freedom and justice depend. We should, therefore, be suspicious of any supposed "requirements" of "federalism" which result in obliterating ancient safeguards. I have been shown nothing in the history of our Union, in the writings of its Founders, or elsewhere, to indicate that individual rights deemed essential by both State and Nation were to be lost through the combined operations of the two governments. Nor has the Court given any sound reason for thinking that the successful operation of our dual system of government depends in the slightest on the power to try people twice for the same act.

Implicit in the Court's reliance on "federalism" is the premise that failure to allow double prosecutions would seriously impair law enforcement in both State and Nation. For one jurisdiction might provide minor penalties for acts severely punished by the other and by accepting pleas of guilty shield wrongdoers from justice. I believe this argument fails on several grounds. In the first place it relies on the unwarranted assumption that State and Nation will seek to subvert each other's laws. . . .

The Court's argument also ignores the fact that our Constitution allocates power between local and federal governments in such a way that the basic rights of each can be protected without double trials. The Federal Government is given power to act in limited areas only, but in matters properly within its scope it is supreme. It can retain exclusive control of such matters, or grant the States concurrent power on its own terms. If the States were to subvert federal laws in these areas by imposing inadequate penalties, Congress would have full power to protect the national interest, either by defining the crime to be punished and establishing minimum penalties applicable in both state and federal courts, or by excluding the States altogether. Conversely, in purely local matters the power of the States is supreme and exclusive. State courts can and should, therefore, protect all essentially local interests in one trial without federal interference. . . . In areas, however, where the Constitution has vested power in the Federal Government the States necessarily act only to the extent Congress permits, and it is no infringement on their basic rights if Congress chooses to fix penalties smaller than some of them might wish. In fact, this will rarely occur, for Congress is not likely to use indirect means to limit state power when it could accomplish the same result directly by pre-empting the field.

Ultimately the Court's reliance on federalism amounts to no more than the notion that, somehow, one act becomes two because two jurisdictions are involved. . . .

To bolster its argument that successive state and federal prosecutions do not violate basic principles of justice, the Court cites many cases. . . . Despite its exhaustive research, the Court has cited only three cases before *Lanza* where a new trial after an *acquittal* was upheld. . . .

One may, I think, infer from the fewness of the cases that retrials after acquittal have been considered particularly obnoxious, worse even, in the eyes of many, than retrials after conviction. I doubt, in fact, if many practices which have been found to violate due process can boast of so little actual support. Yet it is on this meager basis that the Court must ultimately rest its finding that Bartkus' retrial does not violate fundamental principles "rooted in the traditions and conscience of our peoples." . . .

Since *Lanza* people have apparently become more accustomed to double trials, once deemed so shocking, just as they might, in time, adjust themselves to all other violations of the Bill of Rights should they be sanctioned by this Court. The Court is therefore able to find a 1943 state case, as well as four federal cases in the last five years, in which a conviction following acquittal was sustained. Thus this practice, which for some 150 years was considered so undesirable that the Court must strain to find examples, is now likely to become a commonplace. For, after today, who will be able to blame a conscientious prosecutor for failing to accept a jury verdict of acquittal when he believes a defendant guilty and knows that a second try is available in another jurisdiction and that such a second try is approved by the Highest Court in the Land? Inevitably, the victims of such double prosecutions will most often be the poor and the weak in our society, individuals without friends in high places who can influence prosecutors not to try them again. The power to try a second time will be used, as have all similar procedures, to make scapegoats of helpless, political, religious, or racial minorities and those who differ, who do not conform and who resist tyranny. . . .

There are some countries that allow the dangerous practice of trying people twice. I am inserting below a recent news item about a man who was tried, convicted, sentenced to prison and then was tried again, convicted and sentenced to death [in Moscow]. Similar examples are not hard to find in lands torn by revolution or crushed by dictatorship. I had thought that our constitutional protections embodied in the Double Jeopardy and Due Process Clauses would have barred any such things happening here. Unfortunately, last year's holdings by this Court in *Ciucci* v. *Illinois,* 356 U.S. 571, and *Hoag* v. *New Jersey,* 356 U.S. 464, and today's affirmance of the convictions of Bartkus and Abbate cause me to fear that in an important number of cases it can happen here.

I would reverse.

MR. JUSTICE BRENNAN, whom THE CHIEF JUSTICE and MR. JUSTICE DOUGLAS join, dissenting. . . .

The Government's case against Bartkus on the federal trial rested primarily upon the testimony of two of the robbers, Joseph Cosentino and James Brindis, who confessed their part in the crime and testified that Bartkus was their confederate. The defense was that Bartkus was getting a haircut in a barber shop several miles away at the time the robbery was committed. The owner of the barber shop, his son and other witnesses placed Bartkus in the shop at the time. The federal jury in acquitting Bartkus apparently believed the alibi witnesses and not Cosentino and Brindis.

The federal authorities were highly displeased with the jury's resolution of the conflicting testimony, and the trial judge sharply upbraided the jury for its verdict. . . . The federal authorities obviously decided immediately after the trial to make a second try at convicting Bartkus, and since the federal courthouse was barred to them by the Fifth Amendment, they turned to a state prosecution for that purpose. It is clear that federal officers solicited the state indictment, arranged to assure the attendance of key witnesses, unearthed additional evidence to discredit Bartkus and one of his alibi witnesses, and in general prepared and guided the state prosecution. Thus the State's Attorney stated at the state trial: "I am particularly glad to see a case where the federal authorities came to see the state's attorney." And Illinois conceded with commendable candor on the oral argument in this Court "that the federal officers did instigate and guide this state prosecution" and "actually prepared this case." Indeed, the State argued the case on the basis that the record showed as a matter of "fair inference" that the case was one in which "federal officers bring to the attention of the state prosecuting authority the commission of an act and furnish and provide him with evidence of defendant's guilt."

I think that the record before us shows that the extent of participation of the federal authorities here constituted this state prosecution actually a second federal prosecution of Bartkus. . . . In allowing the use of federal resources to bring about this second try at Bartkus, the Court denies Bartkus the protection which the Fifth Amendment assures him. Given the fact that there must always be state officials involved in a state prosecution, I cannot see how there can be more complete federal participation in a state prosecution than there was in this case. I see no escape from the conclusion that this particular state trial was in actuality a second federal prosecution—a second federal try at Bartkus in the guise of a state prosecution. If this state conviction is not overturned, then, as a practical matter, there will be no restraints on the use of state machinery by federal officers to bring what is in effect a second federal prosecution.

To set aside this state conviction because infected with constitutional violations by federal officers implies no condemnation of the state processes as such. The conviction is set aside not because of any infirmities resulting from fault of the State but because it is the product of unconstitutional federal action. I cannot grasp the merit of an argument that protection against federal oppression in the circumstances shown by this record would do violence to the principles of federalism. Of course, cooperation between federal and state authorities in criminal law enforcement is to be desired and encouraged, for cooperative federalism in this field can indeed profit the Nation and the States in improving methods for carrying out the endless fight against crime. But the normal and healthy situation consists of state and federal officers cooperating to apprehend lawbreakers and present the strongest case against them at a single trial, be it state or federal. Cooperation in order to permit the Federal Government to harass the accused so as to deny him his protection under the Fifth Amendment is not to be tolerated as a legitimate requirement of federalism. . . .

Chapter 34

RIGHT TO COUNSEL

> In all criminal prosecutions the accused shall enjoy the right . . . to have
> the assistance of counsel for his defence.   SIXTH AMENDMENT

In establishing an accused person's right to have the assistance of counsel, the Sixth Amendment represented an important advance over common-law practices. The actual wording of the amendment implies that the assistance of counsel is a privilege of which the accused has a right to avail himself, but not a mandatory feature of all criminal trials. In the Federal Crimes Act of 1790, Congress imposed a statutory duty on the courts to assign counsel to represent the defendant in capital cases, from which it could be implied that there was no such obligation in other types of cases. Up until 1938 it was the general understanding that where a person desired counsel, but for lack of funds or any other reason was not able to obtain counsel, the court was under no obligation in a noncapital case to secure counsel for him.

The Supreme Court abruptly changed this rule in *Johnson* v. *Zerbst*, 304 U.S. 458 (1938), a counterfeiting prosecution in which it held that "the Sixth Amendment withholds from federal courts, in all criminal proceedings, the power and authority to deprive an accused of his life or liberty unless he has or waives the assistance of counsel." The Court justified this new interpretation of the amendment by adding that the "right to be heard would be, in many cases, of little avail if it did not comprehend the right to be heard by counsel."

The right to counsel can be waived, but the waiver must be intelligent and understanding. It is conceivable that the requirement of representation by counsel may be met in form but not in substance. A conviction may be attacked on the ground that counsel assigned by the court was incompetent, but in any such claim a heavy burden of proof rests on the defendant. Of course, counsel to be effective should have adequate opportunity to prepare and present his case, and should be present at all stages of the trial.

Right to Counsel in State Courts. In state courts there is no such clear-cut rule on right to counsel as that laid down in *Johnson* v. *Zerbst*. The Supreme Court first dealt with the state problem in the famous First Scottsboro case, *Powell* v. *Alabama*, 287 U.S. 45 (1932). The case involved seven Negro boys, ignorant and illiterate, who were charged with the rape of two white girls in an open gondola car of a freight train passing through Alabama. They were taken from the train near Scottsboro and jailed there. Public excitement was high, and the defendants were guarded by state militia at all stages of the proceedings. At the arraignment they pleaded not guilty. They were not asked whether they had, or were able to employ, counsel, or wished to have counsel appointed. The presiding judge did appoint "all the members of the bar" as counsel for the purpose of arraigning the defendants, but this "expansive gesture" produced no results.

The first case came to trial with no counsel for the defense. As the trial began an out-of-state lawyer said some people had asked him to come down, and that he would be willing to appear along with local counsel that the court might appoint. A member of the local bar then agreed that he would help the out-of-state lawyer. As the Supreme Court subsequently noted:

> With this dubious understanding, the trials immediately proceeded. The defendants, young, ignorant, illiterate, surrounded by hostile sentiment, haled back and forth under guard of soldiers, charged with an atrocious crime regarded with especial horror in the community where they were to be tried, were thus put in peril of their lives within a few moments after counsel for the first time charged with any degree of responsibility began to represent them.

The state supreme court ruled that this arrangement met the requirements of the state constitution. The Supreme Court, however, said that did not decide the matter under the Fourteenth Amendment. "The right to the aid of counsel," said Justice Sutherland, is of a "fundamental character." In this country, "historically and in practice," a hearing has always included "the right to the aid of counsel when desired and provided by the party asserting the right." The Court went on to indicate why this should be so:

> The right to be heard would be, in many cases, of little avail if it did not comprehend the right to be heard by counsel. Even the intelligent and educated layman has small and sometimes no skill in the science of law. If charged with crime, he is incapable, generally, of determining for himself whether the indictment is good or bad. He is unfamiliar with the rules of evidence. Left without the aid of counsel he may be put on trial without a proper charge, and convicted upon incompetent evidence, or evidence irrelevant to the issue or otherwise inadmissible. He lacks both the skill and knowledge adequately to prepare his defense, even though he have a perfect one. He requires the guiding hand of counsel at every step in the proceedings against him. Without it, though he be not guilty, he faces the danger of conviction because he does not know how to establish his innocence.

All these factors would operate even with intelligent defendants. Considering all the additional prejudicial circumstances in this case, the Court was clear that "the failure of the trial court to give . . . reasonable time and opportunity to secure counsel was a clear denial of due process." But the Court went on to hold that if these defendants were unable to get counsel, even though opportunity were offered, then the due process clause required the trial court "to make an effective appointment of counsel." This was new law, and so it was natural that the Court should state careful limits for the new principle:

> Whether this would be so in other criminal prosecutions, or under other circumstances, we need not determine. All that it is necessary now to decide, as we do decide, is that in a capital case, where the defendant is unable to employ counsel, and is incapable adequately of making his own defense because of ignorance, feeble-mindedness, illiteracy, or the like, it is the duty of the court, whether requested or not, to assign counsel for him as a necessary requisite of due process of law; and that

duty is not discharged by an assignment at such time or under such circumstances as to preclude the giving of effective aid in the preparation and trial of the case.

To an unusual degree the principle of the *Powell* case was tied to the individual circumstances of that case. In *Betts* v. *Brady,* 316 U.S. 455 (1942), the circumstances were different and the Court's holding was different. Betts, under indictment for robbery in Maryland, requested the court to appoint counsel for him, since he was financially unable to secure legal aid. The judge refused, on the ground that it was not the practice in that county to appoint counsel for indigent defendants except in murder and rape prosecutions. The trial proceeded before the judge, acting without a jury. The Supreme Court upheld the conviction.

A great many cases involving state refusal to assign counsel have come to the Supreme Court since *Betts* v. *Brady.* In a very considerable number of these cases the Court has held that due process does require the furnishing of counsel. This is very likely to be the holding, for example, when the offense is a capital one; where the conduct of the trial judge appears to be questionable; where the defendant is young or ignorant or otherwise handicapped; or where the points of law involved are too technical for a layman to grasp.

On the other hand, in several instances absence of counsel has been regarded as constitutionally unobjectionable even though the possibility of serious unfairness might have seemed to exist. In *Canizio* v. *New York,* 327 U.S. 82 (1946), a nineteen-year-old boy, charged with first-degree robbery, was not informed of his right to counsel, and in fact had none until two days before he was sentenced. When he raised the issue of failure to assign counsel fourteen years later, the Supreme Court ruled he had enjoyed the assistance of counsel.

The issue of right to counsel is, then, simply a special case of the general problem of interrelationship between the Bill of Rights and the Fourteenth Amendment. Instead of the Sixth Amendment, the Supreme Court applies to the states the more flexible doctrine that due process may be denied if absence of counsel deprives a trial of the essential element of fairness. By the same token a trial may be adjudged fair even though the defendant is not represented by counsel. The due process clause, Justice Frankfurter summed up in *Foster* v. *Illinois,* 332 U.S. 134 (1947), "does require that a State give a defendant ample opportunity to meet an accusation," but this does not mean that counsel must be assigned in all cases. Such a rigid rule would turn the Fourteenth Amendment "into a destructive dogma in the administration of systems of criminal justice." The adverse position was stated by Justice Douglas in *Bute* v. *Illinois,* 333 U.S. 640 (1948): "I fail to see why it is due process to deny an accused the benefit of counsel in a state court when by constitutional standards that benefit could not be withheld from him in a federal court."

BETTS v. BRADY
316 U.S. 455, 62 S. Ct. 1252, 86 L. Ed. 1595 (1942)

Mr. Justice Roberts delivered the opinion of the Court.

The petitioner was indicted for robbery in the Circuit Court of Carroll County, Maryland. Due to lack of funds, he was unable to employ counsel, and so informed the judge at his arraignment. He requested that counsel be appointed for him. The judge advised him that this would not be done, as it was not the practice in Carroll County to appoint counsel for indigent defendants, save in prosecutions for murder and rape.

Without waiving his asserted right to counsel, the petitioner pleaded not guilty and elected to be tried without a jury. At his request witnesses were summoned in his behalf. He cross-examined the State's witnesses and examined his own. The latter gave testimony tending to establish an alibi. Although afforded the opportunity, he did not take the witness stand. The judge found him guilty and imposed a sentence of eight years. . . .

Was the petitioner's conviction and sentence a deprivation of his liberty without due process of law, in violation of the Fourteenth Amendment, because of the court's refusal to appoint counsel at his request?

The Sixth Amendment of the national Constitution applies only to trials in federal courts. The due process clause of the Fourteenth Amendment does not incorporate, as such, the specific guarantees found in the Sixth Amendment, although a denial by a State of rights or privileges specifically embodied in that and others of the first eight amendments may, in certain circumstances, or in connection with other elements, operate, in a given case, to deprive a litigant of due process of law in violation of the Fourteenth. Due process of law is secured against invasion by the federal Government by the Fifth Amendment, and is safeguarded against state action in identical words by the Fourteenth. The phrase formulates a concept less rigid and more fluid than those envisaged in other specific and particular provisions of the Bill of Rights. Its application is less a matter of rule. Asserted denial is to be tested by an appraisal of the totality of facts in a given case. That which may, in one setting, constitute a denial of fundamental fairness, shocking to the universal sense of justice, may, in other circumstances, and in the light of other considerations, fall short of such denial. In the application of such a concept, there is always the danger of falling into the habit of formulating the guarantee into a set of hard and fast rules, the application of which in a given case may be to ignore the qualifying factors therein disclosed.

The petitioner, in this instance, asks us, in effect, to apply a rule in the enforcement of the due process clause. He says the rule to be deduced from our former decisions is that, in every case, whatever the circumstances, one charged with crime, who is unable to obtain counsel, must be furnished counsel by the State. Expressions in the opinions of this court lend color to the argument, but, as the petitioner admits, none of our decisions squarely adjudicates the question now presented.

In *Powell* v. *Alabama*, 287 U.S. 45, ignorant and friendless negro youths, strangers in the community, without friends or means to obtain counsel, were hurried to trial for a capital offense without effective appointment of counsel on whom the burden of preparation and trial would rest, and without adequate opportunity to consult even the counsel casually appointed to represent them. This occurred in a State whose statute law required the appointment of counsel for indigent defendants prosecuted for the offense charged. Thus the trial was conducted in disregard of every principle of fairness and in disregard of that which was declared by the law of the State a requisite of a fair trial. This court held the resulting convictions were without due process of law. It said that, in the light of all the facts, the failure of the trial court to afford the defendants reasonable time and opportunity to secure counsel was a clear denial of due process. The court stated further that "under the circumstances . . . the necessity of counsel was so vital and imperative that the failure of the trial court to make an effective appointment of counsel was likewise a denial of due process," but added: "Whether this would be so in other criminal prosecutions, or under other circumstances, we need not determine. All that it is necessary now to decide, as we do decide, is that, in a capital case, where the defendant is unable to employ counsel, and is incapable adequately of making his own defense because of ignorance, feeble-mindedness, illiteracy, or the like, it is the duty of the court, whether requested or not, to assign counsel for him as a necessary requisite of due process of law, . . ."

. . . The question we are now to decide is whether due process of law demands that in every criminal case, whatever the circumstances, a State must furnish counsel to an indigent defendant. Is the furnishing of counsel in all cases whatever dictated by natural, inherent, and fundamental principles of fairness? The answer to the question may be found in the common understanding of those who have lived under the Anglo-American system of law. By the Sixth Amendment the people ordained that, in all criminal prosecutions, the accused should "enjoy the right . . . to have the assistance of counsel for his defence." We have construed the provision to require appointment of counsel in all cases where a defendant is unable to procure the services of an attorney, and where the right has not been intentionally and competently waived. Though, as we have noted, the Amendment lays down no rule for the conduct of the States, the question recurs whether the constraint laid by the Amendment upon the national courts expresses a rule so fundamental and essential to a fair trial, and so, to due process of law, that it is made obligatory upon the States by the Fourteenth Amendment. Relevant data on the subject are afforded by constitutional and statutory provisions subsisting in the colonies and the States prior to the inclusion of the Bill of Rights in the national Constitution, and in the constitutional, legislative, and judicial history of the States to the present date. These constitute the most authoritative sources for ascertaining the considered judgment of the citizens of the States upon the question.

The Constitutions of the thirteen original States, as they were at the time of federal union, exhibit great diversity in respect of the right to have counsel in criminal cases. Rhode Island had no constitutional provision on the subject until 1843, North Carolina and South Carolina had none until 1868. Virginia has never had any. Maryland, in 1776, and New York, in 1777, adopted provisions to the effect that a defendant accused of crime should be "allowed" counsel. A constitutional mandate that the accused should have a right to be heard by himself and by his counsel was adopted by Pennsylvania in 1776, New Hampshire in 1774, by Delaware in 1782, and by Connecticut in 1818. In 1780 Massachusetts ordained that the defendant should have the right to be heard by himself or his counsel at his election. In 1798 Georgia provided that the accused might be heard by himself or counsel, or both. In 1776 New Jersey guaranteed the accused the same privileges of witnesses and counsel as their prosecutors "are or shall be entitled to."

The substance of these provisions of colonial and early state constitutions is explained by the contemporary common law. Originally, in England, a prisoner was not permitted to be heard by counsel upon the general issue of not guilty on any indictment for treason or felony. The practice of English judges, however, was to permit counsel to advise with a defendant as to the conduct of his case and to represent him in collateral matters and as respects questions of law arising upon the trial. In 1695 the rule was relaxed by statute to the extent of permitting one accused of treason the privilege of being heard by counsel. The rule forbidding the participation of counsel stood, however, as to indictments for felony, until 1836, when a statute accorded the right to defend by counsel against summary convictions and charges of felony. In misdemeanor cases and, after 1695, in prosecutions for treason, the rule was that the defense must be conducted either by the defendant in person or by counsel, but that both might not participate in the trial.

In the light of this common law practice, it is evident that the constitutional provisions to the effect that a defendant should be "allowed" counsel or should have a right "to be heard by himself and his counsel," or that he might be heard by "either or both," at his election, were intended to do away with the rules which denied representation, in whole or in part, by counsel in criminal prosecutions, but were not aimed to compel the State to provide counsel for a defendant. At the least, such a construction by State courts and legislators can not be said to lack reasonable basis.

The statutes in force in the thirteen original States at the time of the adoption of the Bill of Rights are also illuminating. It is of interest that the matter of appointment of counsel for defendants, if dealt with at all, was dealt with by statute rather than by constitutional provision. The contemporary legislation exhibits great diversity of policy.

The constitutions of all the States, presently in force, save that of Virginia, contain provisions with respect to the assistance of counsel in criminal trials. Those of nine States may be said to embody a guarantee textually the same as that of the Sixth Amendment, or of like import. In the fundamental law of most States, however, the language used indicates only that a defendant is not to be denied the privilege of representation by counsel of his choice. . . .

This material demonstrates that, in the great majority of the States, it has been the considered judgment of the people, their representatives and their courts that appointment of counsel is not a fundamental right, essential to a fair trial. On the contrary, the matter has generally been deemed one of legislative policy. In the light of this evidence, we are unable to say that the concept of due process incorporated in the Fourteenth Amendment obligates the States, whatever may be their own views, to furnish counsel in every such case. Every court has power, if it deems proper, to appoint counsel where that course seems to be required in the interest of fairness.

The practice of the courts of Maryland gives point to the principle that the States should not be straight-jacketed in this respect, by a construction of the Fourteenth Amendment. Judge Bond's opinion states, and counsel at the bar confirmed the fact, that in Maryland the usual practice is for the defendant to waive a trial by jury. This the petitioner did in the present case. Such trials, as Judge Bond remarks, are much more informal than jury trials and it is obvious that the judge can much better control the course of the trial and is in a better position to see impartial justice done than when the formalities of a jury trial are involved.

In this case there was no question of the commission of a robbery. The State's case consisted of evidence identifying the petitioner as the perpetrator. The defense was an alibi. Petitioner called and examined witnesses to prove that he was at another place at the time of the commission of the offense. The simple issue was the veracity of the testimony for the State and that for the defendant. As Judge Bond says, the accused was not helpless, but was a man forty-three years old, of ordinary intelligence, and ability to take care of his own interests on the trial of that narrow issue. He had once before been in a criminal court, pleaded guilty to larceny and served a sentence and was not wholly unfamiliar with criminal procedure. It is quite clear that in Maryland, if the situation had been otherwise and it had appeared that the petitioner was, for any reason, at a serious disadvantage by reason of the lack of counsel, a refusal to appoint would have resulted in the reversal of a judgment of conviction. Only recently the Court of Appeals has reversed a conviction because it was convinced on the whole record that an accused, tried without counsel, had been handicapped by the lack of representation.

To deduce from the due process clause a rule binding upon the States in this matter would be to impose upon them, as Judge Bond points out, a requirement without distinction between criminal charges of different magnitude or in respect of courts of varying jurisdiction. As he says: "Charges of small crimes tried before justices of the peace and capital charges tried in the higher courts would equally require the appointment of counsel. Presumably it would be argued that trials in the Traffic Court would require it." And, indeed, it was said by petitioner's counsel both below and in this court, that as the Fourteenth Amendment extends the protection of due process to property as well as to life and liberty, if we hold with the petitioner, logic would require the furnishing of counsel in civil cases involving property.

As we have said, the Fourteenth Amendment prohibits the conviction and incarceration of one whose trial is offensive to the common and fundamental ideas of fairness and right, and while want of counsel in a particular case may result in a conviction lacking in such fundamental fairness, we cannot say that the Amendment embodies an inexorable command that no trial for any offense, or in any court, can be fairly conducted and justice accorded a defendant who is not represented by counsel.

The judgment is

Affirmed.

MR. JUSTICE BLACK, dissenting, with whom MR. JUSTICE DOUGLAS and MR. JUSTICE MURPHY concur.

To hold that the petitioner had a constitutional right to counsel in this case does not require us to say that "no trial for any offense, or in any court, can be fairly conducted and justice accorded a defendant who is not represented by counsel." This case can be determined by a resolution of a narrower question: whether in view of the nature of the offense and the circumstances of his trial and conviction, this petitioner was denied the procedural protection which is his right under the Federal Constitution. I think he was.

The petitioner, a farm hand, out of a job and on relief, was indicted in a Maryland state court on a charge of robbery. He was too poor to hire a lawyer. He so informed the court and requested that counsel be appointed to defend him. His request was denied. Put to trial without a lawyer, he conducted his own defense, was found guilty, and was sentenced to eight years' imprisonment. The court below found that the petitioner had "at least an ordinary amount of intelligence." It is clear from his examination of witnesses that he was a man of little education.

If this case had come to us from a federal court, it is clear we should have to reverse it, because the Sixth Amendment makes the right to counsel in criminal cases inviolable by the Federal Government. I believe that the Fourteenth Amendment made the Sixth applicable to the states. But this view, although often urged in dissents, has never been accepted by a majority of this Court and is not accepted today. A statement of the grounds supporting it is, therefore, unnecessary at this time. I believe, however, that, under the prevailing view of due process, as reflected in the opinion just announced, a view which gives this Court such vast supervisory powers that I am not prepared to accept it without grave doubts, the judgment below should be reversed.

This Court has just declared that due process of law is denied if a trial is conducted in such manner that it is "shocking to the universal sense of justice" or "offensive to the common and fundamental ideas of fairness and right." On another occasion, this Court has recognized that whatever is "implicit in the concept of ordered liberty" and "essential to the substance of a hearing" is within the procedural protection afforded by the constitutional guaranty of due process. *Palko* v. *Connecticut,* 302 U.S. 319, 325, 327.

The right to counsel in a criminal proceeding is "fundamental." *Powell* v. *Alabama,*

287 U.S. 45, 70; *Grosjean* v. *American Press Co.*, 297 U.S. 233, 243–244. It is guarded from invasion by the Sixth Amendment, adopted to raise an effective barrier against arbitrary or unjust deprivation of liberty by the Federal Government. *Johnson* v. *Zerbst*, 304 U.S. 458, 462.

An historical evaluation of the right to a full hearing in criminal cases, and the dangers of denying it, were set out in the *Powell* case, where this Court said: "What . . . does a hearing include? Historically and in practice, in our own country at least, it has always included the right to the aid of counsel when desired and provided by the person asserting the right . . . Even the intelligent and educated layman . . . lacks both the skill and knowledge adequately to prepare his defense, even though he have a perfect one. He requires the guiding hand of counsel in every step in the proceedings against him. Without it, though he be not guilty, he faces the danger of conviction because he does not know how to establish his innocence." *Powell* v. *Alabama, supra*, 68–69. Cf. *Johnson* v. *Zerbst, supra*, 462–463.

A practice cannot be reconciled with "common and fundamental ideas of fairness and right," which subjects innocent men to increased dangers of conviction merely because of their poverty. Whether a man is innocent cannot be determined from a trial in which, as here, denial of counsel has made it impossible to conclude, with any satisfactory degree of certainty, that the defendant's case was adequately presented. No one questions that due process requires a hearing before conviction and sentence for the serious crime of robbery. As the Supreme Court of Wisconsin said, in 1859, ". . . would it not be a little like mockery to secure to a pauper these solemn constitutional guaranties for a fair and full trial of the matters with which he was charged, and yet say to him when on trial, that he must employ his own counsel, who could alone render these guaranties of any real permanent value to him. . . . Why this great solicitude to secure him a fair trial if he cannot have the benefit of counsel?" *Carpenter* v. *Dane County*, 9 Wis. 274, 276–277.

Denial to the poor of the request for counsel in proceedings based on charges of serious crime has long been regarded as shocking to the "universal sense of justice" throughout this country. In 1854, for example, the Supreme Court of Indiana said: "It is not to be thought of, in a civilized community, for a moment, that any citizen put in jeopardy of life or liberty, should be debarred of counsel because he was too poor to employ such aid. No Court could be respected, or respect itself, to sit and hear such a trial. The defence of the poor, in such cases, is a duty resting somewhere, which will be at once conceded as essential to the accused, to the Court, and to the public." *Webb* v. *Baird*, 6 Ind. 13, 18. And most of the other States have shown their agreement by constitutional provisions, statutes, or established practice judicially approved, which assure that no man shall be deprived of counsel merely because of his poverty. Any other practice seems to me to defeat the promise of our democratic society to provide equal justice under the law.

Chapter 35

TRIAL PROCEDURE

No person shall be held to answer for a capital, or otherwise infamous crime, unless on a presentment or indictment of a grand jury. . . .
                                                                    FIFTH AMENDMENT

In all criminal prosecutions the accused shall enjoy the right to a speedy and public trial, by an impartial jury of the State and district wherein the crime shall have been committed . . . and to be informed of the nature and cause of the accusation; to be confronted with the witnesses against him; to have compulsory process for obtaining witnesses in his favor, and to have the assistance of counsel for his defence.   SIXTH AMENDMENT

The original language of the Constitution gave little attention to the procedures of criminal trials. The grand jury, which was an important common-law device for protection against harassment or arbitrary decisions by prosecuting officers, was not mentioned. Trial by jury for all crimes except impeachment was required by Article III, section 2, but the various state constitutions typically contained much fuller guarantees concerning jury trial and its incidents. Consequently the Bill of Rights remedied these faults by the provisions of the Fifth and Sixth Amendments.

The trial jury provided for by the Sixth Amendment in federal criminal prosecutions is the common-law jury. According to *Patton* v. *United States*, 281 U.S. 276 (1930), there are three essential elements in trial by jury—a panel of twelve, supervision by a judge, and unanimity of verdict. Elimination of any of these elements, the Court said, would constitute a denial of the constitutional right to jury trial.

The jury, according to the amendment, must be "impartial." This raises the whole question of jury composition and method of selection. Bias, although difficult to guard against, may be thought of as being (1) simply a matter of opinion, or (2) as growing out of or being associated with social or economic status of jurors. Bias in the first sense is protected against by the right to challenge prospective jurors for cause. Obviously the challenged bias must have some direct relation to the issues of the case; thus a person who has conscientious scruples against the death penalty is properly excluded from the jury in a capital case.

The main protection against bias alleged to flow from a juror's race or employment or class status is the cross-section principle of jury selection. Intentional exclusion of any group in the population from jury lists, or any system of weighting or preference which will render any group in the community more or less likely to be represented on juries, will create constitutional questions.

Allegations of discriminatory practices in the selection of juries in federal courts have been comparatively few. But the 1949 Smith Act prosecution of Communist Party leaders in New York was bogged down for seven weeks by defense efforts to establish that poor people, manual workers, Negroes, Jews, women, and members of the Communist and American Labor parties were deliberately excluded from federal jury panels in New York, in favor of the "rich, propertied and well-to-do." The trial judge found there had been no such deliberate or planned discrimination, and the trial then proceeded. Exclusion of women from federal juries in California, however, was the basis for Supreme Court reversal of a conviction in *Ballard* v. *United States,* 329 U.S. 187 (1946).

A special problem in impartiality concerns the service of government employees on federal juries, a matter of great importance in the District of Columbia. In criminal and other cases to which the government is a party, the question has been raised whether government employees can be free from bias. In *Dennis* v. *United States,* 339 U.S. 162 (1950), a well-known Communist was convicted in the District of Columbia courts of willful refusal to obey a subpoena served on him by the House Committee on Un-American Activities. Dennis had moved for a transfer of his trial from the District on the ground that he could not obtain a fair trial there, but the Supreme Court ruled against him.

State Jury Practices. Decisions already discussed establish that states can experiment with juries. According to *Hurtado* v. *California,* 110 U.S. 516 (1884), they can abolish the grand jury. According to *Maxwell* v. *Dow,* 176 U.S. 581 (1900), they can have fewer than twelve on a trial jury. However, both the due process and equal protection clauses involve the Supreme Court in the policing of jury-selection practices so as to eliminate possible discrimination.

The chief interference with free operation of the cross-section principle in jury selection has resulted from discrimination against Negroes. As early as 1880, a Virginia judge charged with excluding Negroes from jury lists because of their race and color was found guilty of denying equal protection in *Ex parte Virginia,* 100 U.S. 339. In the same year, a West Virginia statute requiring juries to be composed exclusively of white male citizens was likewise held unconstitutional in *Strauder* v. *West Virginia,* 100 U.S. 303. However, where a state statute made no discrimination against Negroes, the fact that no Negroes had sat on the grand and trial juries in a murder case was not a constitutional objection to conviction. Petitioners had no right to have Negroes on the jury, the Court said in *Virginia* v. *Rives,* 100 U.S. 313 (1880). Thus, so long as open discrimination was avoided, it was possible for the Southern states to follow a successful exclusion policy based on practice and custom.

This system operated undisturbed by the Supreme Court until 1935, when it was challenged in *Norris* v. *Alabama,* 294 U.S. 587, known as the Second Scottsboro case. Following the Supreme Court's reversal in the first case on grounds of denial of counsel, a second trial had been held in another county and the defendants again convicted. This second conviction was attacked on the ground that Negroes were systematically excluded from the grand jury in the county where the indictment was found, and from the trial jury in the county where the trial was held.

The Supreme Court unanimously sustained this contention, finding that in each of the two counties no Negroes had ever been called for jury service within the memory of the oldest inhabitants or any officer of the courts. This was in spite of the fact that there were Negro citizens in each county well able to render jury service, and that Negro citizens had been called on to serve on federal juries in that district. "For this long-continued, unvarying, and wholesale exclusion of Negroes from jury service," Chief Justice Hughes concluded, "we find no justification consistent with the constitutional mandate." The great advance of the *Norris* decision was that it permitted discriminatory practices to be inferred from the facts showing the actuality of unequal treatment.

In 1954 the Supreme Court for the first time extended the rule against racial discrimination in jury composition to a group other than Negroes. *Hernandez* v. *Texas*, 347 U.S. 475, presented the allegation that persons of Mexican descent were systematically excluded from jury service in Jackson County, Texas, and the Supreme Court unanimously agreed. It was admitted that for twenty-five years no person with a Mexican or Latin American name had served on a jury in that county, although 11 per cent of the males over twenty-one bore such names. This showing met "the burden of proof imposed in *Norris* v. *Alabama*," the Court concluded, and was not rebutted by testimony of five jury commissioners that their objective had been to select only those they thought best qualified.

Of course the Fourteenth Amendment does not require proportional representation of all the component ethnic groups of a community on every jury. Neither does it require that a defendant of a particular ethnic group have one or more representatives of his group on the grand and trial juries. What it does require is that members of the defendant's class must not be systematically excluded from juries.

Although discrimination in jury selection against non-ethnic classes has been alleged in several Supreme Court cases, no claim of this sort has yet been allowed. The case of *Brown* v. *Allen*, 344 U.S. 443 (1953), involved a North Carolina county where jurors were selected, apparently by an impartial process, from a list of the county's taxpayers. Negroes in the county amounted to 33 per cent of its population, but only 16 per cent of the listed taxpayers were Negroes. A Supreme Court majority upheld this arrangement as a "good faith" effort to secure competent juries. Justices Black and Douglas, dissenting, said: "What the Court apparently finds is that Negroes were excluded from this . . . jury box not because they were Negroes but because they happened to own less property than white people."

Fay v. *New York*, 332 U.S. 261 (1947), tested the constitutionality of New York's so-called "blue ribbon" juries. A conviction was attacked on the ground that laborers, operatives, craftsmen, foremen, and service employees were "intentionally and deliberately excluded" from the jury panels. However, Justice Jackson for the Court majority held that there was no proof of a deliberate purpose to discriminate, and went on:

Even in Negro cases, this Court has never undertaken to say that a want of proportionate representation of groups, which is not proved to be deliberate and intentional, is sufficient to violate the Constitution. . . . If the Court has hesitated to require proportional representation where but two groups need be considered and identification of each group is fairly clear, how much more imprudent would it be to require proportional representation of economic classes.

Fairness of Trial. There are occasions where a fundamental challenge to the fairness of a state court trial goes beyond any of the more specific protections recognized by the Constitution. It is possible to have a trial in which all the forms may be observed, but in which the substance is nonetheless lacking.

Consider the case of *Frank v. Mangum*, 237 U.S. 309 (1915). Frank, a native New Yorker, had gone to Georgia to manage a factory owned by his uncle. In 1913 he was convicted of the murder of a girl who worked in the plant. The trial was conducted in an atmosphere poisonous with anti-Semitism and hatred of "foreigners" from New York. After appeals to the state courts had failed, a writ of habeas corpus was sought from the federal district court, on grounds of mob domination of the trial. The Supreme Court upheld the lower court's refusal to intervene, saying that the findings of the state supreme court, far removed from the atmosphere of the trial, must be accepted.

Justices Holmes and Hughes did not think so. This was a habeas corpus action which "cuts through all forms and goes to the very tissue of the structure. It comes in from the outside, not in subordination to the proceedings, and although every form may have been preserved opens the inquiry whether they have been more than an empty shell." Holmes concluded: "It is our duty . . . to declare lynch law as little valid when practiced by a regularly drawn jury as when administered by one elected by a mob intent on death."

Eight years later, in *Moore v. Dempsey*, 261 U.S. 86 (1923), Holmes had a chance to repeat these views in a majority opinion which, in effect, though not in terms, overruled the *Frank* decision.

MOORE v. DEMPSEY
261 U.S. 86, 43 S. Ct. 265, 67 L. Ed. 543 (1923)

Mr. Justice Holmes delivered the opinion of the Court.

This is an appeal from an order of the District Court for the Eastern District of Arkansas dismissing a writ of *habeas corpus* upon demurrer, the presiding judge certifying that there was probable cause for allowing the appeal. There were two cases originally, but by agreement they were consolidated into one. The appellants are five negroes who were convicted of murder in the first degree and sentenced to death by the Court of the State of Arkansas. The ground of the petition for the writ is that the proceedings in the State Court, although a trial in form, were only a form, and that the appellants were hurried to conviction under the pressure of a mob without any regard for their rights and without according to them due process of law.

The case stated by the petition is as follows, and it will be understood that while we put it in narrative form, we are not affirming the facts to be as stated but only what we must take them to be, as they are admitted by the demurrer: On the night of September 30, 1919, a number of colored people assembled in their church were attacked and fired upon by a body of white men, and in the disturbance that followed a white man was killed. The report of the killing caused great excitement and was followed by the hunting down and shooting of many negroes and also by the killing on October 1 of one Clinton Lee, a white man, for whose murder the petitioners were indicted. They seem to have been arrested with many others on the same day. The petitioners say that Lee must have been killed by other whites, but that we leave on one side as what we have to deal with is not the petitioners' innocence or guilt but solely the question whether their constitutional rights have been preserved. They say that their meeting was to employ counsel for protection against extortions practiced upon them by the landowners and that the landowners tried to prevent their effort, but that again we pass by as not directly bearing upon the trial. It should be mentioned however that O. S. Bratton, a son of the counsel who is said to have been contemplated and who took part in the argument here, arriving for consultation on October 1, is said to have barely escaped being mobbed; that he was arrested and confined during the month on a charge of murder and on October 31 was indicted for barratry, but later in the day was told that he would be discharged but that he must leave secretly by a closed automobile to take the train at West Helena, four miles away, to avoid being mobbed. It is alleged that the judge of the Court in which the petitioners were tried facilitated the departure and went with Bratton to see him safely off.

A Committee of Seven was appointed by the Governor in regard to what the committee called the "insurrection" in the county. The newspapers daily published inflammatory articles. On the 7th a statement by one of the committee was made public to the effect that the present trouble was "a deliberately planned insurrection of the negroes against the whites, directed by an organization known as the 'Progressive Farmers' and Household Union of America' established for the purpose of banding negroes together for the killing of white people." According to the statement the organization was started by a swindler to get money from the blacks.

Shortly after the arrest of the petitioners a mob marched to the jail for the purpose of lynching them but were prevented by the presence of United States troops and the promise of some of the Committee of Seven and other leading officials that if the mob would refrain, as the petition puts it, they would execute those found guilty in the form of law. The Committee's own statement was that the reason that the people refrained from mob violence was "that this Committee gave our citizens their solemn promise that the law would be carried out." According to affidavits of two white men and the colored witnesses on whose testimony the petitioners were convicted, produced by the petitioners since the last decision of the Supreme Court hereafter mentioned, the Committee made good their promise by calling colored witnesses and having them whipped and tortured until they would say what was wanted, among them being the two relied on to prove the petitioners' guilt. However this may be, a grand jury of white men was organized on October 27 with one of the Committee of Seven and, it is alleged, with many of a posse organized to fight the blacks, upon it, and on the morning of the 29th the indictment was returned. On November 3 the petitioners were brought into Court, informed that a certain lawyer was appointed their counsel and were placed on trial before a white jury—blacks being systematically excluded from both grand and petit juries. The Court and neighborhood were thronged with an adverse crowd that threatened the most dangerous consequences to anyone interfering with the desired result. The counsel did not venture to demand delay or a change of venue, to challenge a juryman or to ask for separate trials. He had had no preliminary consultation with the accused, called no witnesses for the defence although they could have been produced, and did not put the defendants on the stand. The trial lasted about three-quarters of an hour and in less than five minutes the jury brought in a verdict of guilty of murder in the first degree. According to the allegations and affidavits there never was a chance for the petitioners to be acquitted; no juryman could have voted for an acquittal and continued to live in Phillips County and if any prisoner by any chance had been acquitted by a jury he could not have escaped the mob.

The averments as to the prejudice by which the trial was environed have some corroboration in appeals to the Governor, about a year later, earnestly urging him not to interfere with the execution of the petitioners. One came from five members of the Committee of Seven, and stated in addition to what has been quoted heretofore that "all our citizens are of the opinion that the law should take its course." Another from a part of the American Legion protests against a contemplated commutation of the sentence of four of the petitioners and repeats that a "solemn promise was given by the leading citizens of the community that if the guilty parties were not lynched, and let the law take its course, that justice would be done and the majesty of the law upheld." A meeting of the Helena Rotary Club attended by members representing, as it said, seventy-five of the leading industrial and commercial enterprises of Helena, passed a resolution approving and supporting the action of the American Legion post. The Lions Club of Helena at a meeting attended by members said to represent sixty of the leading industrial and commercial enterprises of the city passed a resolution to the same effect. In May of the same year, a trial of six other negroes was coming on and it was represented to the Governor by the white citizens and officials of Phillips County that in all probability those negroes would be lynched. It is alleged that in order to appease the mob spirit and in a measure secure the safety of the six the Governor fixed the date for the execution of the petitioners at June 10, 1921, but that the execution was stayed by proceedings in Court; we presume the proceedings before the Chancellor to which we shall advert.

In *Frank* v. *Mangum*, 237 U.S. 309, 335, it was recognized of course that if in fact a trial is dominated by a mob so that there is an actual interference with the course of justice, there is a departure from due process of law; and that "if the State, supplying no corrective process, carries into execution a judgment of death or imprisonment based upon a verdict thus produced by mob domination, the State deprives the accused of his life or liberty without due process of law." We assume in accordance with that case that the corrective process supplied by the State may be so adequate that interference by *habeas corpus* ought not to be allowed. It certainly is true that mere mistakes of law in the course of a trial are not to be corrected in that way. But if the case is that the whole proceeding is a mask—that counsel, jury and judge were swept to the fatal end by an irresistible wave of public passion, and that the State Courts failed to correct the wrong, neither perfection in the machinery for correction nor the possibility that the trial court and counsel saw no other way of avoiding an immediate outbreak of the mob can prevent this Court from securing to the petitioners their constitutional rights.

In this case a motion for a new trial on the ground alleged in this petition was overruled and upon exceptions and appeal to the Supreme Court the judgment was affirmed. The Supreme Court said that the complaint of discrimination against petitioners by the exclusion of colored men from the jury came too late and by way of answer to the objection that no fair trial could be had in the circumstances, stated that it could not say "that this must necessarily have been the case"; that eminent counsel was appointed to defend the petitioners, that the trial was had according to law, the jury correctly charged, and the testimony legally sufficient. On June 8, 1921, two days before the date fixed for their execution, a petition for *habeas corpus* was presented to the Chancellor and he issued the writ and an injunction against the execution of the petitioners; but the Supreme Court of the State held that the Chancellor had no jurisdiction under the state law whatever might be the law of the United States. The present petition perhaps was suggested by the language of the Court: "What the result would be of an application to a Federal Court we need not inquire." It was presented to the District Court on September 21. We shall not say more concerning the corrective process afforded to the petitioners than that it does not seem to us sufficient to allow a Judge of the United States to escape the duty of examining the facts for himself when if true as alleged they make the trial absolutely void. We have confined the statement to facts admitted by the demurrer. We will not say that they cannot be met, but it appears to us unavoidable that the District Judge should find whether the facts alleged are true and whether they can be explained so far as to leave the state proceedings undisturbed.

Order reversed. The case to stand for hearing before the District Court.

MR. JUSTICE McREYNOLDS, dissenting.

We are asked to overrule the judgment of the District Court discharging a writ of *habeas corpus* by means of which five negroes sought to escape electrocution for the murder of Clinton Lee. . . . They were convicted and sentenced in the Circuit Court of Phillips County, Arkansas, two years before the writ issued. The petition for the writ was supported by affidavits of these five ignorant men whose lives were at stake, the *ex parte* affidavits of three other negroes who had pleaded guilty and were then confined in the penitentiary under sentences for the same murder, and the affidavits of two white men—low villains according to their own admissions. It should be remembered that to narrate the allegations of the petition is but to repeat statements from these sources. Considering all the circumstances—the course of the cause in the state courts and upon application here for certiorari, etc.,—the District Court held the alleged facts insufficient *prima facie* to show nullity of the original judgment.

The matter is one of gravity. If every man convicted of crime in a state court may thereafter resort to the federal court and by swearing, as advised, that certain allegations of fact tending to impeach his trial are "true to the best of his knowledge and belief," thereby obtain as of right further review, another way has been added to a list already unfortunately long to prevent prompt punishment. The delays incident to enforcement of our criminal laws have become a national scandal and give serious alarm to those who observe. Wrongly to decide the present cause probably will produce very unfortunate consequences.

In *Frank v. Mangum,* 237 U.S. 309, 325, 326, 327, 329, 335, after great consideration a majority of this Court approved the doctrine which should be applied here. The doctrine is right and wholesome. I can not agree now to put it aside and substitute the views expressed by the minority of the Court in that cause. . . .

Chapter 36

HEALTH AND MORALS LEGISLATION

Due process was, by definition, a procedural concept, under which the procedures provided or employed by legislatures, executive officers, or courts would be subjected to some fundamental tests of fairness. However, this power to test actions by due process standards proved to be a great temptation to the courts. Once they had become accustomed to judging executive or legislative procedure, it was easy to use the same standards of fairness in passing on the substance of executive or legislative programs. Thus a test of the fairness of governmental procedure developed into a test of governmental ability to act at all, regardless of procedure.

This transformation occurred in connection with application of the Fourteenth rather than the Fifth Amendment. It is true that a substantive due process argument was made by Chief Justice Taney in the *Dred Scott* case, 19 How. 393 (1857). Holding the Missouri Compromise void, he argued: "An act of Congress which deprives a citizen of the United States of his liberty or property, merely because he came himself or brought his property into a particular Territory of the United States, and who had committed no offense against the laws, could hardly be dignified with the name of due process of law." But Taney was not speaking for the Court majority at this point. Again, the Court used a substantive due process argument in *Hepburn* v. *Griswold,* 8 Wall. 603 (1870), as one of the bases for setting aside the Legal Tender Act of 1862, but the authority of this decision was nullified when it was reversed a year later.

It was not until the Fourteenth Amendment came before the Supreme Court that the possibilities of judicial control over legislation on substantive due process grounds began to appear. In the *Slaughter-House Cases,* 16 Wall. 36 (1873), where a slaughterhouse monopoly granted by Louisiana was under attack, the argument was presented to the Court that the Fourteenth Amendment was intended to safeguard "laissez-faire individualism." The majority was unwilling to subscribe to this novel view, but Justice Bradley, dissenting, did. He wrote:

[The] right to choose one's calling is an essential part of that liberty which it is the object of government to protect; and a calling, when chosen, is a man's property and right. Liberty and property are not protected where these rights are arbitrarily assailed. . . . In my view, a law which prohibits a large class of citizens from adopting a lawful employment, or from following a lawful employment previously adopted, does deprive them of liberty as well as property, without due process of law.

In *Munn* v. *Illinois,* 94 U.S. 113 (1877), the Supreme Court refused to invalidate on due process grounds a state statute fixing the maximum charges for storage of grain in warehouses and elevators. The Court warned that "for protection against abuses by legislatures the people must resort to the polls, not to the courts."

But ten years later, in *Mugler v. Kansas,* 123 U.S. 623 (1887), the Court's resistance began to break down. A state prohibition law was at issue here, and the Court upheld it, but not by use of the legislative supremacy rationale of the *Munn* case. Rather, the Court approved the statute because it knew of its own knowledge, independently of the legislative finding, that intoxicating liquor could imperil the public welfare. While upholding this particular statute, Justice Harlan was careful to warn that a legislature might easily go too far in seeking to promote public purposes.

There are, of necessity, limits beyond which legislation cannot rightfully go. . . . If, therefore, a statute purporting to have been enacted to protect the public health, the public morals, or the public safety, has no real or substantial relation to those objects, or is a palpable invasion of rights secured by the fundamental law, it is the duty of the courts to so adjudge. . . .

So the Court announced its assumption of the right to pass on the substance of legislation under the due process clause, and in *Allgeyer v. Louisiana,* 165 U.S. 578 (1897), for the first time it actually set aside a state law on substantive due process grounds.

The subsequent history of substantive due process can be best traced by examining its impact on two kinds of legislation. In general, police power regulations aimed at protection of public health, safety, and morals have not encountered substantial opposition from the Supreme Court on due process grounds, as the present chapter will illustrate, whereas the reverse is true of economic regulation, as the following chapter will demonstrate.

Health Legislation. A state statute prohibiting the manufacture and sale of oleomargarine was upheld in *Powell v. Pennsylvania,* 127 U.S. 678 (1888), as a measure to "protect the public health and to prevent the adulteration of dairy products and fraud in the sale thereof," even though one might have had justifiable doubts that this was the main purpose of the legislation.

Reasonable regulation of professions or occupations which have a close relationship to the public health, such as doctors, dentists, druggists, nurses, beauticians, barbers, plumbers, and the like, is readily supportable as a protection of the public welfare. Such regulation, moreover, may extend beyond the basic considerations of health to cover activities only tangentially related. Thus in *Semler v. Oregon State Board of Dental Examiners,* 294 U.S. 608 (1935), the Court upheld a state statute which forbade dentists to advertise in any competitive or spectacular manner, as a means of preventing demoralization of the profession.

But there are two Supreme Court decisions which better than any others illustrate the presumption of validity which almost automatically attaches to legislation for health motives. The first is *Jacobson v. Massachusetts,* 197 U.S. 11 (1905), upholding a state requirement of vaccination against smallpox. The statute applied to adults in any area where the board of health certified that vaccination was necessary for the public health or safety. Jacobson refused to be vaccinated, contending it was injurious or dangerous. He offered to prove his contentions in court, but his evidence was excluded as incompetent and immaterial.

The Supreme Court, with two dissents, upheld the state court. Justice Harlan for the majority made a most illuminating statement in justification of refusal to listen to Jacobson's evidence. He was quite willing to believe that there were those, some of them perhaps even doctors, who attached little or no value to vaccination. But

. . . what everybody knows the court must know, and therefore the state court judicially knew, as this court knows, that an opposite theory accords with the common belief and is maintained by high medical authority. We must assume that when the statute in question was passed, the legislature of Massachusetts was not unaware of these opposing theories, and was compelled, of necessity, to choose between them. It was not compelled to commit a matter involving the public health and safety to the final decision of a court or jury. It is no part of the function of a court or a jury to determine which one of two modes was likely to be the most effective for the protection of the public against disease. That was for the legislative department to determine in the light of all the information it had or could obtain.

The second case is *Buck* v. *Bell*, 274 U.S. 200 (1927), which upheld a Virginia statute authorizing compulsory sexual sterilization of persons affected with hereditary insanity, idiocy, imbecility, feeblemindedness, or epilepsy. This operation could be performed only on the inmates of state institutions, and adequate provisions were made by the statute for notice, hearing, and judicial review before such operations were performed. In this case the law was applied to Carrie Buck, a seventeen-year-old "feeble-minded" inmate of a state institution whose mother was also an inmate of the same institution, and who had given birth to an allegedly mentally defective child just before admission to the institution. The contention was that if she were rendered incapable of childbearing, she could be released from the institution and become self-supporting. In the judicial proceedings held to authorize the operation there was presented, in addition to evidence concerning the mental and social status of Carrie Buck, testimony in support of the statute by eugenicists to the effect that feeblemindedness was hereditary and incurable.

It should be noted that a later Court came very close to overruling *Buck* v. *Bell*. *Skinner* v. *Oklahoma*, 316 U.S. 535 (1942), involved a state habitual criminal sterilization act, under which persons convicted two or more times of felonies involving moral turpitude could be rendered sexually sterile. The Court struck the law down on equal protection grounds, which made it unnecessary to reconsider *Buck* v. *Bell*. But both Stone and Jackson wrote concurring opinions cutting much of the ground out from under the *Buck* decision and its presumption of legislative validity. Justice Jackson warned:

I . . . think the present plan to sterilize the individual in pursuit of a eugenic plan to eliminate from the race characteristics that are only vaguely identified and which in our present state of knowledge are uncertain as to transmissibility presents . . . constitutional questions of gravity. . . . There are limits to the extent to which a legislatively represented majority may conduct biological experiments at the expense of the dignity and personality and natural powers of a minority.

Morals Legislation. Experience with state and national prohibition of liquor is illustrative of judicial permissiveness on morals legislation. In *Mugler* v. *Kansas,* already mentioned, the Court specifically recognized that the effect of the statute would be to render practically worthless property invested in the liquor business at a time when it was a perfectly legal occupation, but held this was not contrary to due process. The general attitude of the Court toward prohibition was well summed up in *Austin* v. *Tennessee,* 179 U.S. 343 (1900):

. . . intoxicating liquors belong to a class of commodities which, in the opinion of a great many estimable people, are deleterious in their effects, demoralizing in their tendencies, and often fatal in their excessive indulgence. . . . It may be that their evil effects have been exaggerated. . . . It is, however, within the power of each State to investigate the subject and to determine its policy in that particular.

The *Austin* decision then went on to hold that the same reasoning would support a Tennessee statute prohibiting the sale of cigarettes. As late as 1932 a Utah statute which forbade billboard or streetcar advertising of tobacco was upheld in *Packer Corp.* v. *Utah,* 285 U.S. 105, in these words: "The law deals confessedly with a subject within the scope of the police power. No facts are brought to our attention which establish either that the evil aimed at does not exist or that the statutory remedy is inappropriate."

Zoning Legislation. Euclid v. *Ambler Realty Co.,* 272 U.S. 365 (1926), upholding the constitutionality of zoning, was a landmark case in the development of a broader judicial attitude toward police power regulation. Zoning ordinances typically divide a city into various classes of residential, commercial, and manufacturing areas, and buildings and land used within each area must conform to the regulations for this district. Such restrictions of course constitute a serious limitation on freedom of the owner to employ his property as he sees fit, and the Supreme Court held two hearings in the *Euclid* case before it approved the zoning regulations by a five to four vote.

The most controversial part of the *Euclid* zoning ordinance was the exclusion of all businesses, trades, hotels, and apartment houses from residential districts. To support these restrictions the Court majority rehearsed the findings and the philosophy of the zoning experts as set forth in numerous reports:

These reports . . . concur in the view that the segregation of residential, business, and industrial buildings will make it easier to provide fire apparatus suitable for the character and intensity of the development in each section; that it will increase the safety and security of home life; greatly tend to prevent street accidents, especially to children, by reducing the traffic and resulting confusion in residential sections; decrease noise and other conditions which produce or intensify nervous disorders; [and] preserve a more favorable environment in which to rear children. . . .

Such considerations prevented the Court from holding that these zoning restrictions were "clearly arbitrary and unreasonable, having no substantial relation to the public health, safety, morals, or general welfare." In *Berman* v. *Parker,* 348 U.S. 26 (1954), the Court went further and accepted aesthetics as a proper purpose of zoning regulations in a District of Columbia slum clearance and redevelopment program.

Public safety, public health, morality, peace and quiet, law and order—these are some of the more conspicuous examples of the traditional application of the police power to municipal affairs. Yet they merely illustrate the scope of the power and do not delimit it. . . . Miserable and disreputable housing conditions may do more than spread disease and crime and immorality. They may also suffocate the spirit by reducing the people who live there to the status of cattle. They may indeed make living an almost unsufferable burden. They may also be an ugly sore, a blight on the community which robs it of charm, which makes it a place from which men turn. The misery of housing may despoil a community as an open sewer may ruin a river. . . .

The concept of the public welfare is broad and inclusive. . . . The values it represents are spiritual as well as physical, aesthetic as well as monetary. It is within the power of the legislature to determine that the community should be beautiful as well as healthy, spacious as well as clean, well-balanced as well as carefully patrolled.

BUCK v. BELL
274 U.S. 200, 47 S. Ct. 584, 71 L. Ed. 1000 (1927)

Mr. Justice Holmes delivered the opinion of the Court.

This is a writ of error to review a judgment of the Supreme Court of Appeals of the State of Virginia, affirming a judgment of the Circuit Court of Amherst County, by which the defendant in error, the superintendent of the State Colony for Epileptics and Feeble Minded, was ordered to perform the operation of salpingectomy upon Carrie Buck, the plaintiff in error, for the purpose of making her sterile. 143 Va. 310. The case comes here upon the contention that the statute authorizing the judgment is void under the Fourteenth Amendment as denying to the plaintiff in error due process of law and the equal protection of the laws.

Carrie Buck is a feeble minded white woman who was committed to the State Colony above mentioned in due form. She is the daughter of a feeble minded mother in the same institution, and the mother of an illegitimate feeble minded child. She was eighteen years old at the time of the trial of her case in the Circuit Court, in the latter part of 1924. An Act of Virginia, approved March 20, 1924, recites that the health of the patient and the welfare of society may be promoted in certain cases by the sterilization of mental defectives, under careful safeguard, &c.; that the sterilization may be effected in males by vasectomy and in females by salpingectomy, without serious pain or substantial danger to life; that the Commonwealth is supporting in various institutions many defective persons who if now discharged would become a menace but if incapable of procreating might be discharged with safety and become self-supporting with benefit to themselves and to society; and that experience has shown that heredity plays an important part in the transmission of insanity, imbecility, &c. The statute then enacts that whenever the superintendent of certain institutions including the above named State Colony shall be of opinion that it is for the best interests of the patients and of society that an inmate under his care should be sexually sterilized, he may have the operation performed upon any patient afflicted with hereditary forms of insanity, imbecility, &c., on complying with the very careful provisions by which the act protects the patients from possible abuse.

The superintendent first presents a petition to the special board of directors of his hospital or colony, stating the facts and the grounds for his opinion, verified by affidavit. Notice of the petition and of the time and place of the hearing in the institution is to be served upon the inmate, and also upon his guardian, and if there is no guardian the superintendent is to apply to the Circuit Court of the County to appoint one. If the inmate is a minor notice also is to be given to his parents if any with a copy of the petition. The board is to see to it that the inmate may attend the hearings if desired by him or his guardian. The evidence is all to be reduced to writing, and after the board has made its order for or against the operation, the superintendent, or the inmate, or his guardian, may appeal to the Circuit Court of the County. The Circuit Court may consider the record of the board and the evidence before it and such other admissible evidence as may be offered, and may affirm, revise, or reverse the order of the board and enter such order as it deems just. Finally any party may apply to the Supreme Court of Appeals, which, if it grants the appeal, is to hear the case upon the record of the trial in the Circuit Court and may enter such order as it thinks the Circuit Court should have entered. There can be no doubt that so far as procedure is concerned the rights of the patient are most carefully considered, and as every step in this case was taken in scrupulous compliance with the statute and after months of observation, there is no doubt that in that respect the plaintiff in error has had due process of law.

The attack is not upon the procedure but upon the substantive law. It seems to be contended that in no circumstances could such an order be justified. It certainly is contended that the order cannot be justified upon the existing grounds. The judgment finds the facts that have been recited and that Carrie Buck "is the probable potential parent of socially inadequate offspring, likewise afflicted, that she may be sexually sterilized without detriment to her general health and that her welfare and that of society will be promoted by her sterilization," and thereupon makes the order. In view of the general declarations of the legislature and the specific findings of the Court, obviously we cannot say as matter of law that the grounds do not exist, and if they exist they justify the result. We have seen more than once that the public welfare may call upon the best citizens for their lives. It would be strange if it could not call upon those who already sap the strength of the State for these lesser sacrifices, often not felt to be such by those concerned, in order to prevent our being swamped with incompetence. It is better for all the world, if instead of waiting to execute degenerate offspring for crime, or to let them starve for their imbecility, society can prevent those who are manifestly unfit from continuing their kind. The principle that sustains compulsory vaccination is broad enough to cover cutting the Fallopian tubes. *Jacobson* v. *Massachusetts*, 197 U.S. 11. Three generations of imbeciles are enough.

But, it is said, however it might be if this reasoning were applied generally, it fails when it is confined to the small number who are in the institutions named and is not applied to the multitudes outside. It is the usual last resort of constitutional arguments to point out shortcomings of this sort. But the answer is that the law does all that is needed when it does all that it can, indicates a policy, applies it to all within the lines, and seeks to bring within the lines all similarly situated so far and so fast as its means allow. Of course so far as the operations enable those who otherwise must be kept confined to be returned to the world, and thus open the asylum to others, the equality aimed at will be more nearly reached.

Judgment affirmed.

Mr. Justice Butler dissents.

Chapter 37

ECONOMIC REGULATION

Legislative intervention in the economic field has customarily aroused greater judicial concern than health or morals legislation, and it is here that substantive due process had its greatest successes in supplying a foundation for judicial veto of legislation. One of the commonest types of police power intervention in the economic sphere has been legislation affecting the hours, wages, or working conditions of industrial employees. Such regulation imposes drastic limitations on liberty of contract, one of the cornerstones of the laissez-faire economic system, and it is not surprising that courts initially exhibited some reluctance to believe that these controls amounted to substantive due process of law.

Hours Legislation. The Supreme Court encountered its first hours law in *Holden* v. *Hardy,* 169 U.S. 366 (1898). With only two dissents, the Court here upheld a Utah statute providing for an eight-hour day in mines and smelters. Freedom of contract was held to be subject to the state's police power to protect life and health of workers in a dangerous and unhealthful occupation. Moreover, the Court challenged the whole freedom of contract idea by pointing out that the workers and owners were not on an equal bargaining basis, and that the state was justified in taking some steps to equalize their bargaining position.

There could scarcely be a greater contrast than between *Holden* v. *Hardy* and the Court's five to four ruling in *Lochner* v. *New York,* 198 U.S. 45 (1905). This case involved a statute forbidding employees to work in bakeries more than ten hours a day or sixty hours a week. Lochner was an employer who had been convicted of violating the law in his plant. This time, freedom of contract was victorious over the police power, though Justice Holmes led four dissenting justices in charging that the case was decided "upon an economic theory which a large part of the country does not entertain."

Only three years later, the Court in *Muller* v. *Oregon,* 208 U.S. 412 (1908), unanimously upheld a ten-hour law which, however, applied only to women in industry. Taking judicial cognizance of factors which make women the weaker sex, the Court held that "she is properly placed in a class by herself, and legislation designed for her protection may be sustained, even when like legislation is not necessary for men and could not be sustained." So the *Lochner* decision was regarded as not controlling.

But in *Bunting* v. *Oregon,* 243 U.S. 426 (1917), the Court was confronted with another ten-hour law covering both men and women. Since the statute covered all industrial employment, it must have applied to bakers, yet the Supreme Court upheld the law by a vote of five to three in an opinion which never mentioned the *Lochner* decision. The Court's opinion disposed of the claim that the statute was not a health measure in one sentence: "The record contains no facts to support the contention, and against it is the judgment of the legislature and the [state] Supreme Court." One could well assume, as Chief Justice Taft later put it, that "the *Lochner* Case was thus overruled *sub silentio.*"

Wages Legislation. So health eventually proved to be a sufficiently flexible concept to provide the Court with police power justification for hours legislation. But would it also legitimize wages regulation, where the tie-in with health was even more indirect, and where the assault on freedom of contract was even more painful to employers? At first it seemed so. An Oregon minimum wage law for women came up to the Supreme Court in 1917, the same year as the *Bunting* case. The Oregon supreme court had upheld the law on the strength of the *Muller* principle, finding it a protection for women's health and also for their morals. In *Stettler* v. *O'Hara,* 243 U.S. 629 (1917), the Supreme Court split four to four, with Justice Brandeis abstaining, and thus the state court decision was left in effect.

In 1923, however, the Supreme Court mustered a five to three majority against the District of Columbia minimum wage law for women. *Adkins* v. *Children's Hospital,* 261 U.S. 525 (1923), stands with *Lochner* as one of the landmarks in the Supreme Court's losing battle against economic regulation. Here was another paean to freedom of contract in its purest form, with no nonsense about the special needs of women or inequality of bargaining position. The Court saw the statute as "simply and exclusively a price-fixing law, confined to adult women . . . who are legally as capable of contracting for themselves as men."

The statute was unconstitutional for two reasons, the Court said. First, the standards set up by the law to guide the administering board in fixing minimum wages were too vague and fatally uncertain. The sum necessary to maintain a woman worker in good health and protect her morals is not precise or unvarying. It will depend on her temperament, her habits, her moral standards, her independent resources, and so on.

Second, the law was invalid because it took account "of the necessities of only one party to the contract," compelling the employer to pay the minimum wage whether or not the employee was worth that much to him. "A statute which prescribes payment . . . solely with relation to circumstances apart from the contract of employment, the business affected by it and the work done under it, is so clearly the product of a naked, arbitrary exercise of power that it cannot be allowed to stand under the Constitution." But Chief Justice Taft, dissenting, thought that the *Adkins* case was controlled by the *Muller* decision, and he could see no difference in principle between regulating maximum hours and minimum wages.

Following the *Adkins* decision, many states assumed that a minimum wage law which did take into account the value-of-service-rendered principle would be constitutional, and passed statutes including such provisions. A New York law of this type came before the Supreme Court in *Morehead* v. *Tipaldo,* 298 U.S. 587 (1936), in the midst of the Court's furious battle with the New Deal, and was invalidated by a five to four vote. The value-of-service feature in the New York law was held insufficient to meet the *Adkins* objection, which was dogmatically restated in these words: "the State is without power by any form of legislation to prohibit, change or nullify contracts between employers and adult women workers as to the amount of wages to be paid."

This ruling earned the dissent of Hughes, Brandeis, Cardozo, and Stone. In Stone's dissent, for the first time in an economic regulation case, a Supreme Court justice went beyond the traditional health and morals boundaries on state police power and asserted—what was shortly to become axiomatic for the Court—that public power is as broad as is necessary to meet urgent economic problems.

The Supreme Court carried the millstone of *Morehead* v. *Tipaldo* around its neck for only one year. In 1937 Justice Roberts switched his position and made the *Morehead* dissenters a Court majority in *West Coast Hotel Co.* v. *Parrish*, 300 U.S. 379. This case arose under the Washington state minimum wage law which, like that of the District of Columbia, had no value-of-service standard, and so seemed more in defiance of the *Adkins* decision than the New York law had been. But Chief Justice Hughes upheld the Washington law, adopting the principles of Stone's *Morehead* dissent and directly overruling the *Adkins* decision. Nothing was said about *Lochner*, but this time we can be sure that it had been overruled *sub silentio*.

The Fair Labor Standards Act, passed by Congress in 1938, imposed minimum wage and maximum hours regulations for employees engaged in interstate commerce or in the production of goods for commerce. In *United States* v. *Darby Lumber Co.*, 312 U.S. 100 (1941), due process objections to the statute were disposed of in one short paragraph which cited *Holden*, *Muller*, and *Bunting* on hours, and *West Coast Hotel* on wages. The federal act covered men as well as women, so that *West Coast Hotel* was no precedent at all on minimum wages for men. The sexual distinction, which as late as 1937 had been vital in establishing constitutional power, was by 1941 unimportant to the Court.

Employee Organization. A third general area of employer-employee relations which legislatures began to regulate at the turn of the century was employee unionization. Congress in 1898 adopted legislation outlawing the so-called "yellow-dog" contract, an agreement not to join a labor union which many employers forced workers to sign as a condition of employment. Discharging an employee of an interstate railroad on grounds of his membership in a labor organization was made a criminal offense against the United States. This statute was declared unconstitutional by the Supreme Court in *Adair* v. *United States*, 208 U.S. 161 (1908), on familiar freedom of contract grounds.

Justice Holmes dissented in the *Adair* case, and also in *Coppage* v. *Kansas*, 236 U.S. 1 (1915), where the Court struck down a comparable state statute. He said in the latter case: "In present conditions a workman not unnaturally may believe that only by belonging to a union can he secure a contract that shall be fair to him. . . . If that belief, whether right or wrong, may be held by a reasonable man, it seems to me that it may be enforced by law in order to establish the equality of position between the parties in which liberty of contract begins." He would therefore have overruled the *Adair* decision.

The *Adair* and *Coppage* rule was gradually outflanked as state power was confirmed in other areas of labor relations. This process took some time, of course. For example, in *Truax* v. *Corrigan*, 257 U.S. 312 (1921), an Arizona statute forbidding use of the injunction to protect an employer's business from injury by labor picketing was held unconstitutional. But in 1937 a Wisconsin law not appreciably different was upheld in *Senn v. Tile Layers' Protective Union*, 301 U.S. 468. This act authorized the giving of publicity to labor disputes, declared peaceful picketing lawful, and prevented the granting of injunctions against such conduct.

It was not until 1949 that the *Adair-Coppage* doctrine was specifically repudiated, and it is significant that by this time the situation had so changed that it was the unions rather than the employers who claimed freedom of contract and protection by the due process clause. *Lincoln Federal Labor Union v. Northwestern Iron & Metal Co.*, 335 U.S. 525 (1949), involved a North Carolina statute and a Nebraska constitutional amendment outlawing the closed shop. No person was to be denied an opportunity to work in the two states because he either was or was not a member of a labor organization. The Supreme Court unanimously upheld these laws against free speech, equal protection, and due process charges. On the latter point Justice Black referred to "the *Allgeyer-Lochner-Adair-Coppage* constitutional doctrine [which] was for some years followed by this Court" and used to strike down state regulation. "Appellants now ask us to return, at least in part, to the due process philosophy that has been deliberately discarded." This the Court refused to do.

Price-fixing Regulation. "The thought seems . . . to have persisted," wrote Justice Roberts in 1934, "that there is something peculiarly sacrosanct about the price one may charge for what he makes or sells, and that, however able to regulate other elements of manufacture or trade, with incidental effect upon price, the state is incapable of directly controlling the price itself." This rule did not apply, of course, to the class of businesses designated as public utilities. Customarily rendering an essential service, enjoying monopoly status, and exercising the power of eminent domain, public utilities were required to pay for their preferred status by making their services available to all comers and by accepting public regulation of their rates and services.

But inevitably problems developed concerning services outside the normal public utility classifications which were nevertheless so important to the public that legislatures sought to bring their rates or charges under public control. Such a case was presented by *Munn v. Illinois*, 94 U.S. 113 (1877). Here the Court approved the fixing of rates for Chicago grain elevators on the ground that, though not public utilities, they fell in a category of businesses recognized by the common law as "affected with a public interest."

So from 1877 on the constitutionality of price fixing depended upon demonstrating to the reviewing courts that the businesses involved were either public utilities or affected with a public interest. Unfortunately the Supreme Court was never able to state very clearly what characteristics put a business in this second category, but it did recognize fire insurance companies, stockyards, and tobacco warehouses as well as grain elevators in this classification. Then abruptly in the 1920s a conservative Court began to deny public interest status to businesses where legislative price fixing had been attempted. In *Tyson and Brother v. Banton*, 273 U.S. 418 (1927), a New York law forbidding the resale of theater tickets at more than a 50-cent markup was declared unconstitutional by a five to four vote. The following year the Court by a six to three vote in *Ribnik* v. *Mc-Bride,* 277 U.S. 350 (1928), held invalid New Jersey's effort to regulate the fees charged by employment agencies.

In 1934, however, the Supreme Court returned to its earlier views in the landmark case of *Nebbia* v. *New York,* 291 U.S. 502. By a five to four vote the Court upheld a state statute which had established a milk control board with power to fix minimum and maximum resale prices. As applied in this case, the objective had been to prevent ruinous price cutting by fixing minimum prices. Justice Roberts for the Court majority admitted that the milk industry had never been regarded as affected with a public interest and had none of the characteristics relied on in the past in attributing such status—no public grant or franchise, no monopoly, no obligation to serve all comers, no devotion of property to a public use. But that made no difference, said Roberts:

It is clear that there is no closed class or category of businesses affected with a public interest, and the function of courts in the application of the Fifth and Fourteenth Amendments is to determine in each case whether circumstances vindicate the challenged regulation as a reasonable exertion of governmental authority or condemn it as arbitrary or discriminatory. . . . The phrase "affected with a public interest" can, in the nature of things, mean no more than that an industry, for adequate reason, is subject to control for the public good.

LOCHNER v. NEW YORK
198 U.S. 45, 25 S. Ct. 539, 49 L. Ed. 937 (1905)

MR. JUSTICE PECKHAM . . . delivered the opinion of the Court. . . .

The statute necessarily interferes with the right of contract between the employer and employees, concerning the number of hours in which the latter may labor in the bakery of the employer. The general right to make a contract in relation to his business is part of the liberty of the individual protected by the Fourteenth Amendment of the Federal Constitution. . . . Under that provision no State can deprive any person of life, liberty or property without due process of law. The right to purchase or to sell labor is part of the liberty protected by this Amendment, unless there are circumstances which exclude the right. There are, however, certain powers, existing in the sovereignty of each State in the Union, somewhat vaguely termed police powers, the exact description and limitation of which have not been attempted by the courts. Those powers, broadly stated, and without, at present, any attempt at a more specific limitation, relate to the safety, health, morals, and general welfare of the public. Both property and liberty are held on such reasonable conditions as may be imposed by the governing power of the State in the exercise of those powers, and with such conditions the Fourteenth Amendment was not designed to interfere. . . .

The State, therefore, has power to prevent the individual from making certain kinds of contracts, and in regard to them the Federal Constitution offers no protection. If the contract be one which the State, in the legitimate exercise of its police power, has the right to prohibit, it is not prevented from prohibiting it by the Fourteenth Amendment. Contracts in violation of a statute, either of the Federal or state government, or a contract to let one's property for immoral purposes, or to do any other unlawful act, could obtain no protection from the Federal Constitution, as coming under the liberty of person or of free contract. Therefore, when the State, by its legislature, in the assumed exercise of its police powers, has passed an act which seriously limits the right to labor or the right of contract in regard to their means of livelihood between persons who are *sui juris* (both employer and employee), it becomes of great importance to determine which shall prevail—the right of the individual to labor for such time as he may choose, or the right of the State to prevent the individual from laboring or from entering into any contract to labor, beyond a certain time prescribed by the State. . . .

It must, of course, be conceded that there is a limit to the valid exercise of the police power by the State. There is no dispute concerning this general proposition. Otherwise the Fourteenth Amendment would have no efficacy and the legislatures of the States would have unbounded power, and it would be enough to say that any piece of legislation was enacted to conserve the morals, the health or the safety of the people; such legislation would be valid, no matter how absolutely without foundation the claim might be. The claim of the police power would be a mere pretext—become another and delusive name for the supreme sovereignty of the State to be exercised free from constitutional restraint. This is not contended for. In every case that comes before this court, therefore, where legislation of this character is concerned and where the protection of the Federal Constitution is sought, the question necessarily arises: Is this a fair, reasonable and appropriate exercise of the police power of the State, or is it an unreasonable, unnecessary and arbitrary interference with the right of the individual to his personal liberty or to enter into those contracts in relation to labor which may seem to him appropriate or necessary for the support of himself and his family? Of course the liberty of contract relating to labor includes both parties to it. The one has as much right to purchase as the other to sell labor.

This is not a question of substituting the judgment of the court for that of the legislature. If the act be within the power of the State it is valid, although the judgment of the court might be totally opposed to the enactment of such a law. But the question would still remain: Is it within the police power of the State? and that question must be answered by the court.

The question whether this act is valid as a labor law, pure and simple, may be dismissed in a few words. There is no reasonable ground for interfering with the liberty of person or the right of free contract, by determining the hours of labor, in the occupation of a baker. There is no contention that bakers as a class are not equal in intelligence and capacity to men in other trades or manual occupations, or that they are not able to assert their rights and care for themselves without the protecting arm of the State, interfering with their independence of judgment and of action. They are in no sense wards of the State. Viewed in the light of a purely labor law, with no reference whatever to the question of health, we think that a law like the one before us involves neither the safety, the morals nor the welfare of the public, and that the interest of the public is not in the slightest degree affected by such an act. The law must be upheld, if at all, as a law pertaining to the health of the individual engaged in the occupation of a baker. It does not affect any other portion of the public than those who are engaged in that occupation. Clean and wholesome bread does not depend upon whether the baker works but ten hours per day or only sixty hour a week. The limitation of the hours of labor does not come within the police power on that ground.

It is a question of which of two powers or rights shall prevail—the power of the State to legislate or the right of the individual to liberty of person and freedom of contract. The mere assertion that the subject relates though but in a remote degree to the public health does not necessarily render the enactment valid. The act must have a more direct relation, as a means to an end, and the end itself must be appropriate and legitimate, before an act can be held to be valid which interferes with the general right of an individual to be free in his person and in his power to contract in relation to his own labor. . . .

We think the limit of the police power has been reached and passed in this case. There is, in our judgment, no reasonable foundation for holding this to be necessary or appropriate as a health law to safeguard the public health, or the health of the individuals who are following the trade of a baker. If this statute be valid, and if, therefore, a proper case is made out in which to deny the right of an individual, *sui juris,* as employer or employee, to make contracts for the labor of the latter under the protection of the provisions of the federal Constitution, there would seem to be no length to which legislation of this nature might not go. . . .

We think that there can be no fair doubt that the trade of a baker, in and of itself, is not an unhealthy one to that degree which would authorize the legislature to interfere with the right to labor, and with the right of free contract on the part of the individual, either as employer or employee. In looking through statistics regarding all trades and occupations, it may be true that the trade of a baker does not appear to be as healthy as some other trades, and is also vastly more healthy than still others. To the common understanding the trade of a baker has never been regarded as an unhealthy one. Very likely physicians would not recommend the exercise of that or of any other trade as a remedy for ill health. Some occupations are more healthy than others, but we think there are none which might not come under the power of the legislature to supervise and control the hours of working therein, if the mere fact that the occupation is not absolutely and perfectly healthy is to confer that right upon the legislative department of the government. It might be safely affirmed that almost all occupations more or less affect the health. There must be more than the mere fact of the possible existence of some small amount of unhealthiness to warrant legislative interference with liberty. It is unfortunately true that labor, even in any department, may possibly carry with it the seeds of unhealthiness. But are we all, on that account, at the mercy of legislative majorities? A printer, a tinsmith, a locksmith, a carpenter, a cabinetmaker, a dry-goods clerk, a bank's, a lawyer's, or a physician's clerk, or a clerk in almost any kind of business, would all come under the power of the legislature, on this assumption. No trade, no occupation, no mode of earning one's living, could escape this all-pervading power, and the acts of the legislature in limiting the hours of labor in all employments would be valid, although such limitation might seriously cripple the ability of the laborer to support himself and his family. . . .

It is also urged, pursuing the same line of argument, that it is to the interest of the State that its population should be strong and robust, and therefore any legislation which may be said to tend to make people healthy must be valid as health laws, enacted under the police power. If this be a valid argument and a justification for this kind of legislation, it follows that the protection of the Federal Constitution from undue interference with liberty of person and freedom of contract is visionary, wherever the law is sought to be justified as a valid exercise of the police power. Scarcely any law but might find shelter under such assumptions, and conduct, properly so called, as well as contract, would come under the restrictive sway of the legislature. Not only the hours of employees, but the hours of employers, could be regulated, and doctors, lawyers, scientists, all professional men, as well as athletes and artisans, could be forbidden to fatigue their brains and bodies by prolonged hours of exercise, lest the fighting strength of the State be impaired. We mention these extreme cases because the contention is extreme.

We do not believe in the soundness of the views which uphold this law. On the contrary, we think that such a law as this, although passed in the assumed exercise of the police power, and as relating to the public health, or the health of the employees named, is not within that power, and is invalid. The act is not, within any fair meaning of the term, a health law, but is an illegal interference with the rights of individuals, both employers and employees, to make contracts regarding labor upon such terms as they may think best, or which they may agree upon with the other parties to such contracts. Statutes of the nature of that under review, limiting the hours in which grown and intelligent men may labor to earn their living, are mere meddlesome interferences with the rights of the individual, and they are not saved from condemnation by the claim that they are passed in the exercise of the police power and upon the subject of the health of the individual whose rights are interfered with, unless there be some fair ground, reasonable in and of itself, to say that there is material danger to the public health, or to the health of the employees, if the hours of labor are not curtailed. . . .

It was further urged on the argument that restricting the hours of labor in the case of bakers was valid because it tended to cleanliness on the part of the workers, as a man was more apt to be cleanly when not overworked, and if cleanly then his "output" was also more likely to be so. . . . The connection, if any exists, is too shadowy and thin to build any argument for the interference of the legislature. If the man works ten hours a day it is all right, but if ten and a half or eleven his health is in danger and his bread may be unhealthful, and therefore, he shall not be permitted to do it. This, we think, is unreasonable and entirely arbitrary. When assertions such as we have adverted to become necessary in order to give, if possible, a plausible foundation for the contention that the law is a "health law," it gives rise to at least a suspicion that there was some other motive dominating the legislature than the purpose to subserve the public health or welfare. . . .

It is impossible for us to shut our eyes to the fact that many of the laws of this character, while passed under what is claimed to be the police power for the purpose of protecting the public health or welfare, are, in reality, passed from other motives. We are justified in saying so when, from the character of the law and the subject upon which it legislates, it is apparent that the public health or welfare bears but the most remote relation to the law. The purpose of a statute must be determined from the natural and legal effect of the language employed; and whether it is or is not repugnant to the Constitution of the United States must be determined from the natural effect of such statutes when put into operation, and not from their proclaimed purpose. . . .

It is manifest to us that the limitation of the hours of labor as provided for in this section of the statute under which the indictment was found, and the plaintiff in error convicted, has no such direct relation to and no such substantial effect upon the health of the employee, as to justify us in regarding the section as really a health law. It seems to us that the real object and purpose were simply to regulate the hours of labor between the master and his employees (all being men, *sui juris*), in a private business, not dangerous in any degree to morals or in any real and substantial degree, to the health of the employees. Under such circumstances the freedom of master and employee to contract with each other in relation to their employment, and in defining the same, cannot be prohibited or interfered with, without violating the Federal Constitution. . . .

Reversed.

MR. JUSTICE HARLAN, with whom MR. JUSTICE WHITE and MR. JUSTICE DAY concurred, dissenting. . . .

I take it to be firmly established that what is called the liberty of contract may, within certain limits, be subjected to regulations designed and calculated to promote the general welfare or to guard the public health, the public morals or the public safety. "The liberty secured by the Constitution of the United States to every person within its jurisdiction does not import," this court has recently said, "an absolute right in each person to be, at all times and in all circumstances, wholly freed from restraint. There are manifold restraints to which every person is necessarily subject for the common good." *Jacobson* v. *Massachusetts*, 197 U.S. 11.

Granting then that there is a liberty of contract which cannot be violated even under the sanction of direct legislative enactment, but assuming, as according to settled law we may assume, that such liberty of contract is subject to such regulations as the State may reasonably prescribe for the common good and the well-being of society, what are the conditions under which the judiciary may declare such regulations to be in excess of legislative authority and void? Upon this point there is no room for dispute; for, the rule is universal that a legislative enactment, Federal or state, is never to be disregarded or held invalid unless it be, beyond question, plainly and palpably in excess of legislative power. . . . If there be doubt as to the validity of the statute, that doubt must therefore be resolved in favor of its validity, and the courts must keep their hands off, leaving the legislature to meet the responsibility for unwise legislation. If the end which the legislature seeks to accomplish be one to which its power extends, and if the means employed to that end, although not the wisest or best, are yet not plainly and palpably unauthorized by law, then the court cannot interfere. In other words, when the validity of a statute is questioned, the burden of proof, so to speak, is upon those who assert it to be unconstitutional. *McCulloch* v. *Maryland*, 4 Wheat. 316, 421. . . .

It is plain that this statute was enacted in order to protect the physical well-being of those who work in bakery and confectionery establishments. It may be that the statute had its origin, in part, in the belief that employers and employees in such establishments were not upon an equal footing, and that the necessities of the latter often compelled them to submit to such exactions as unduly taxed their strength. Be this as it may, the statute must be taken as expressing the belief of the people of New York that, as a general rule, and in the case of the average man, labor in excess of sixty hours during a week in such establishments may endanger the health of those who thus labor. Whether or not this be wise legislation it is not the province of the court to inquire. Under our systems of government the courts are not concerned with the wisdom or policy of legislation. So that in determining the question of power to interfere with liberty of contract, the court may inquire whether the means devised by the State are germane to an end which may be lawfully accomplished and have a real or substantial relation to the protection of health, as involved in the daily work of the persons, male and female, engaged in bakery and confectionery establishments. But when this inquiry is entered upon I find it impossible, in view of common experience, to say that there is here no real or substantial relation between the means employed by the State and the end sought to be accomplished by its legislation. . . . Therefore I submit that this court will transcend its functions if it assumes to annul the statute of New York. . . .

We judicially know that the question of the number of hours during which a workman should continuously labor has been, for a long period, and is yet, a subject of serious consideration among civilized peoples, and by those having special knowledge of the laws of health. Suppose the statute prohibited labor in bakery and confectionery establishments in excess of eighteen hours each day. No one, I take it, could dispute the power of the State to enact such a statute. But the statute before us does not embrace extreme or exceptional cases. It may be said to occupy a middle ground in respect of the hours of labor. What is the true ground for the State to take between legitimate protection, by legislation, of the public health and liberty of contract is not a question easily solved, nor one in respect of which there is or can be absolute certainty. There are very few, if any, questions in political economy about which entire certainty may be predicated. . . .

I do not stop to consider whether any particular view of this economic question presents the sounder theory. What the precise facts are it may be difficult to say. It is enough for the determination of this case, and it is enough for this court to know, that the question is one about which there is room for debate and for an honest difference of opinion. There are many reasons of a weighty, substantial character, based upon the experience of mankind, in support of the theory that, all things considered, more than ten hours' steady work each day, from week to week, in a bakery or confectionery establishment, may endanger the health, and shorten the lives of the workmen, thereby diminishing their physical and mental capacity to serve the State, and to provide for those dependent upon them.

If such reasons exist that ought to be the end of this case, for the State is not amenable to the judiciary, in respect of its legislative enactments, unless such enactments are plainly, palpably, beyond all question, inconsistent with the Constitution of the United States. We are not to presume that the State of New York has acted in bad faith. Nor can we assume that its legislature acted without due deliberation, or that it did not determine this question upon the fullest attainable information, and for the common good. We cannot say that the State has acted without reason nor ought we to proceed upon the theory that its action is a mere sham. Our duty, I submit, is to sustain the statute as not being in conflict with the Federal Constitution, for the reason—and such is an all-sufficient reason—it is not shown to be plainly and palpably inconsistent with that instrument. Let the State alone in the management of its purely domestic affairs, so long as it does not appear beyond all question that it has violated the Federal Constitution. This view necessarily results from the principle that the health and safety of the people of a State are primarily for the State to guard and protect. . . .

The judgment in my opinion should be affirmed.

MR. JUSTICE HOLMES dissenting.

I regret sincerely that I am unable to agree with the judgment in this case, and that I think it my duty to express my dissent.

This case is decided upon an economic theory which a large part of the country does not entertain. If it were a question whether I agreed with that theory, I should desire to study it further and long before making up my mind. But I do not conceive that to be my duty, because I strongly believe that my agreement or disagreement has nothing to do with the right of a majority to embody their opinions in law. It is settled by various decisions of this court that state constitutions and state laws may regulate life in many ways which we as legislators might think as injudicious or if you like as tyrannical as this, and which equally with this interfere with the liberty to contract. Sunday laws and usury laws are ancient examples. A more modern one is the prohibition of lotteries. The liberty of the citizen to do as he likes so long as he does not interfere with the liberty of others to do the same, which has been a shibboleth for some well-known writers, is interfered with by school laws, by the Post Office, by every state or municipal institution which takes his money for purposes thought desirable, whether he likes it or not. The Fourteenth Amendment does not enact Mr. Herbert Spencer's Social Statics. The other day we sustained the Massachusetts vaccination law. *Jacobson* v. *Massachusetts*, 197 U.S. 11. United States and state statutes and decisions cutting down the liberty to contract by way of combination are familiar to this court. *Northern Securities Co.* v. *United States*, 193 U.S. 197. Two years ago we upheld the prohibition of sales of stock on margins or for future delivery in the constitution of California. *Otis* v. *Parker,* 187 U.S. 606. The decision sustaining an eight hour law for miners is still recent. *Holden* v. *Hardy,* 169 U.S. 366. Some of these laws embody convictions or prejudices which judges are likely to share. Some may not. But a constitution is not intended to embody a particular economic theory, whether of paternalism and the organic relation of the citizen to the State or of *laissez faire.* It is made for people of fundamentally differing views, and the accident of our finding certain opinions natural and familiar or novel and even shocking ought not to conclude our judgment upon the question whether statutes embodying them conflict with the Constitution of the United States.

General propositions do not decide concrete cases. The decision will depend on a judgment or intuition more subtle than any articulate major premise. But I think that the proposition just stated, if it is accepted, will carry us far toward the end. Every opinion tends to become a law. I think that the word liberty in the Fourteenth Amendment is perverted when it is held to prevent the natural outcome of a dominant opinion, unless it can be said that a rational and fair man necessarily would admit that the statute proposed would infringe fundamental principles as they have been understood by the traditions of our people and our law. It does not need research to show that no such sweeping condemnation can be passed upon the statute before us. A reasonable man might think it a proper measure on the score of health. Men whom I certainly could not pronounce unreasonable would uphold it as a first instalment of a general regulation of the hours of work. Whether in the latter aspect it would be open to the charge of inequality I think it unnecessary to discuss.

Chapter 38

RACIAL SEGREGATION AND EQUAL PROTECTION

Section 1. . . . No State shall . . . deny to any person within its jurisdiction the equal protection of the laws. . . .

Section 5. The Congress shall have power to enforce, by appropriate legislation, the provisions of this article.   FOURTEENTH AMENDMENT

Congress was thinking primarily of the newly freed Negroes when it drafted
the Fourteenth Amendment. Their problems were of two sorts. The first was
political. How could they be guaranteed the right to vote and to full political
participation in the Southern states? Congress sought to include some formula
for this purpose in the Fourteenth Amendment, but ultimately all it was able to
produce was the provision in section 2 of the amendment reducing representation
in the House for any state which denied the vote to qualified citizens. Contemporary discussion in Congress made it clear that the equal protection clause
had no bearing on political rights.

The second problem was guaranteeing the civil, as distinct from the political,
rights of the freedmen. This was the area that equal protection was meant to
cover—but what fields, and how fully? There can be no doubt that the equal
protection clause was meant to end discrimination enforced upon Negroes by the
"Black Codes" of certain states which limited their right to hold property, specified criminal offenses for Negroes only, and hampered their access to the courts
in a variety of ways. But congressional intent in other areas of discrimination is
less clear, and the impact which equal protection was intended to have on
segregation is certainly open to doubt.

The most significant post-Civil War effort to implement the equal protection
clause was the Civil Rights Act of 1875, which forbade racial separation or
discrimination in public conveyances, hotels, and theaters, and also required
equality in jury service. Two matters of major significance should be noted about
this act. First, apart from the jury provisions, it was directed at discriminatory
actions not primarily of public officials, but of private individuals operating services traditionally subject to public regulation.

Second, the Civil Rights Act was based on an unquestioned assumption that
Congress had plenary legislative power to enforce the protections of the Fourteenth Amendment, that its authority was as broad as was necessary to correct
abuses which might be found, and that it could be invoked to punish acts of
omission, or failure to enforce the law, as well as affirmative discriminatory acts.
There was this significant difference in the two situations. When a state discriminated by affirmative state action, redress simply required the negating of

that action. But where the discrimination arose out of actions by private individuals which the state failed to prevent or punish, then redress necessarily required the assertion of power to coerce state officials into a positive program of law enforcement. Thus the latter situation involved substantially greater congressional control over state and local government than the former.

Within a decade the Supreme Court decided that Congress had been wrong on both its assumptions. In the *Civil Rights Cases,* 109 U.S. 3 (1883), the Court pointed out that it is "states" which are the target of the amendment. "It is State action of a particular character that is prohibited. Individual invasion of individual rights is not the subject matter of the amendment." Thus Congress was stripped of any power to correct or to punish individual discriminatory action. Only *state* action was subject to the amendment.

As for section 5, it was also construed strictly by the Court; it was held to give Congress authority only to *correct affirmative* state action. "Until some State law has been passed, or some State action through its officers or agents has been taken, adverse to the rights of citizens sought to be protected by the Fourteenth Amendment, no legislation of the United States under said amendment, nor any proceeding under such legislation, can be called into activity." The amendment "does not authorize Congress to create a code of municipal law for the regulation of private rights. . . ." But this is what the Civil Rights Act was. It was not corrective legislation. It was a code of conduct which ignored state legislation. Since the law was thus based on a misconstruction of the Fourteenth Amendment, according to the Supreme Court, it was unconstitutional.

Geographical Segregation. The *Civil Rights* decision left the equal protection clause effective against state action, and therefore it would forbid state action which violated equal rights in property ownership. The Supreme Court so held in *Buchanan* v. *Warley,* 245 U.S. 60 (1917), where a municipal segregation ordinance was invalidated as an unconstitutional interference with the right of a property owner to dispose of his real estate.

Efforts to maintain residential segregation then turned to a second protective device—restrictive covenants entered into by property owners binding themselves not to sell or lease their property to Negroes or certain other social, national, or religious groups. Because this type of agreement results from action by private persons, not by the state, it was at first generally successful in meeting constitutional tests. But in 1948 the Supreme Court reconsidered this matter. *Shelley* v. *Kraemer,* 334 U.S. 1, admitted that because of their private character "restrictive agreements standing alone cannot be regarded as violative of any rights guaranteed . . . by the Fourteenth Amendment." However, these covenants could only be made effective by judicial enforcement, and that required "state action," which could not be provided without violating the amendment. Thus the restrictive covenants, though legal, were unenforceable.

This anomalous holding resulted in further litigation. *Barrows* v. *Jackson,* 346 U.S. 249 (1953), raised the question whether the signer of a covenant who breached its provisions could be sued for damages by other participants in the covenant. A California property owner who had failed to live up to the conditions of a covenant was sued by three neighbors on the ground that the value of their property had dropped sharply since Negroes moved in. But the Court also foreclosed this circuitous method of enforcing restrictive covenants, holding that state courts could not coerce a property owner to pay damages for failure to observe a covenant that California had no right to incorporate in a statute or enforce in equity and which federal courts could not enforce because contrary to public policy.

Segregation in Public Transportation. The basic decision in this field was the landmark case of *Plessy v. Ferguson,* 163 U.S. 537 (1896). Here a Louisiana statute requiring segregation of the races on public carriers was held by the Supreme Court not to violate the Fourteenth Amendment. The Court of course could not deny here, as it had in the *Civil Rights Cases,* that state action was present. But what it did was to hold that equal protection of the laws was not violated if the segregated facilities provided for Negroes were "equal" to those of whites. The Court said: "The object of the amendment was undoubtedly to enforce the absolute equality of the two races before the law, but in the nature of things it could not have been intended to abolish distinctions based upon color, or to enforce social, as distinguished from political equality, or a commingling of the two races upon terms unsatisfactory to either."

If separation of the races was enforced by law, the Court continued, it did not mean that Negroes were stamped with a "badge of inferiority." "If this be so, it is not by reason of anything found in the act, but solely because the colored race chooses to put that construction upon it." Thus "separate but equal" became the formula for reconciling the protection of the Fourteenth Amendment with a system of state-enforced segregation.

In actuality, of course, segregated transportation facilities for Negroes were almost never "equal," but it was almost fifty years before the Supreme Court finally recognized this fact. In *Mitchell v. United States,* 313 U.S. 80 (1941), the Court squarely upheld a charge of denial of equal treatment brought by a Negro congressman from Illinois who had been refused Pullman accommodations in Arkansas. Soon thereafter the Court also rediscovered the commerce clause as a bar to segregation. In *Morgan v. Virginia,* 328 U.S. 373 (1946), a Jim Crow law was declared invalid when applied to interstate bus traffic moving through a state. The mandatory reseating of passengers when a state line was crossed was a burden on commerce where uniformity was required, the Court ruled.

In 1955 the Interstate Commerce Commission reversed its previous interpretation of the Interstate Commerce Act of 1887 and issued an order banning racial segregation on trains and buses crossing state lines. This ruling did not touch intrastate practices, which could only be brought into line through the equal protection clause. In *Gayle v. Browder,* 352 U.S. 903 (1956), the Supreme Court took this step by affirming a lower court ruling that an Alabama statute and a Montgomery ordinance requiring segregation on intrastate buses violated the equal protection and due process clauses. This decision was a result of, and an anticlimax to, the historic Court decisions of May, 1954, invalidating segregation in public education.

Segregation in Education. The legality of the "separate but equal" formula was carried over from *Plessy v. Ferguson* into the area of public education without any reexamination by the Supreme Court. Neither was there any judicial effort to ensure the "equality" of the segregated schools. Not until 1938 was there any change in this pattern. In *Missouri ex rel. Gaines v. Canada,* 305 U.S. 337

(1938), the state had refused to admit Negroes to its law school, providing instead for the payment of tuition fees for any of its Negro citizens who wished to attend law schools in neighboring states where segregation was not enforced. The Supreme Court held that Missouri could not shift its responsibility to provide equal educational opportunities to some other state. By operating a white law school, the state was providing privileges to white students which it denied to Negroes because of their race.

The next test came in *McLaurin* v. *Oklahoma State Regents*, 339 U.S. 637 (1950), involving a Negro who sought a graduate degree in a state university. The Oklahoma Legislature, under pressure of the *Gaines* ruling, had amended the state law to permit the admission of Negroes to institutions of higher learning in cases where such institutions offered courses not available in Negro schools. However, the program of instruction for such Negro students was to be given on a "segregated basis," which meant that McLaurin could use only assigned areas in classrooms, library, and cafeteria. These restrictions were declared unconstitutional by the Supreme Court on the ground that they would "impair and inhibit his ability to study, to engage in discussions and exchange views with other students. . . ."

Sweatt v. *Painter*, 339 U.S. 629 (1950), involved the petition of a Negro student for admission to the University of Texas Law School. The University had set up a separate law school for Negroes in 1947, and the Texas courts ruled that Sweatt must attend it, since its facilities were "substantially equivalent" to those of the white law school. The Supreme Court disagreed. Its decision was based on the necessary and inescapable "inequality" of the education offered by the new school with its poor library and five professors, not on a condemnation of the principle of segregation.

However, the issue continued to knock on the Court's portals. The pressure now shifted from graduate professional and university education, where the breaking down of segregation barriers presented a lesser problem because of the comparatively few Negro students involved, to public education at the primary and secondary levels.

Brown v. *Board of Education of Topeka*, 347 U.S. 483, and the other public school segregation cases were finally decided on May 17, 1954, by a unanimous vote of the Court. In this epic decision the Court finally came to grips with the constitutionality of the "separate but equal" doctrine, and concluded that even though "the physical facilities and other 'tangible' factors may be equal," still the psychological effects of segregation would be to "deprive the children of the minority group of equal educational opportunities."

Bolling v. *Sharpe*, 347 U.S. 497 (1954), was handled in a separate decision from the other four cases, since it arose in the District of Columbia where the equal protection clause was not applicable. In a brief opinion Chief Justice Warren held that the due process clause of the Fifth Amendment required the same result.

These holdings still left the problem of putting this potentially explosive doctrine into effect. Further hearings were held in April, 1955, and on May 31 the Supreme Court announced its plan of action. The cases would be remanded to the courts where they had originated, which would fashion decrees of enforcement on equitable principles and with regard for "varied local school problems."

The local courts would require "a prompt and reasonable start toward full compliance" with the 1954 ruling. During the period of transition to full compliance, the courts where the cases originated would retain jurisdiction of them.

Many types of resistance to compliance with the Court's order were attempted, and in some states progress was very slow indeed. Up to 1958 the Supreme Court refused to become involved in the resulting litigation in the lower federal courts. But in the fall of 1958 the case of *Cooper* v. *Aaron*, 358 U.S. 1, brought up the continuing Little Rock controversy and required the Court to reinterpret and apply the principles of its 1954 decision. In June, 1958, the federal district judge in Little Rock had ordered a 2½-year delay in the modest program of integration in that city's high school which, when inaugurated in 1957, had brought on riotous conditions requiring the sending of federal troops. This order was unanimously reversed by the Supreme Court, which took advantage of the opportunity to rule that any "evasive schemes" for continuing segregation, such as turning public schools over to private organizations for operation as "private schools" with some kind of state financial assistance, would not be constitutional. Subsequently, in *Shuttlesworth* v. *Birmingham Board of Education*, 358 U.S. 101 (1958), the Court accepted as constitutional an Alabama pupil placement law which did not list race as a placement factor, but warned that if race was actually employed in administration of the statute to allocate students among schools, it would be declared unconstitutional.

Denial of Service. While slow progress was being made in school integration, legal tests of the color barrier in other areas were undertaken. The "sit-in" movement, dating from 1960, had remarkable success in desegregating restaurants and other places of public accommodation. The initial sit-ins were held in stores which welcomed Negroes as customers but refused to serve them at lunch counters maintained in the stores. The justification urged for segregated service was that private businesses are not subjected to the Fourteenth Amendment, which covers only "state action," and so are free to refuse service or to determine the conditions on which it will be granted. Persons conducting a sit-in on private property after being refused service and requested to leave, it was argued, are guilty of criminal trespass. In *Garner* v. *Louisiana*, 368 U.S. 157 (1961), the Supreme Court found that the persons sitting-in had not been requested to leave by the managers of the eating places, and their convictions for breach of the peace were reversed on the narrow ground that their actions were peaceful and did not constitute breach of the peace under the Louisiana statute. Justice Douglas, concurring, reached the constitutional issue and ruled that restaurants are public facilities, licensed by the state, and that the state cannot enforce a policy of segregation in such facilities.

BROWN v. BOARD OF EDUCATION OF TOPEKA
347 U.S. 483, 74 S. Ct. 686, 98 L. Ed. 873 (1954)

MR. CHIEF JUSTICE WARREN delivered the opinion of the Court.

These cases come to us from the States of Kansas, South Carolina, Virginia, and Delaware. They are premised on different facts and different local conditions, but a common legal question justifies their consideration together in this consolidated opinion.

In each of the cases, minors of the Negro race, through their legal representatives, seek the aid of the courts in obtaining admission to the public schools of their community on a nonsegregated basis. In each instance, they had been denied admission to schools attended by white children under laws requiring or permitting segregation according to race. This segregation was alleged to deprive the plaintiffs of the equal protection of the laws under the Fourteenth Amendment. In each of the cases other than the Delaware case, a three-judge federal district court denied relief to the plaintiffs on the so-called "separate but equal" doctrine announced by this Court in *Plessy* v. *Ferguson,* 163 U.S. 537. Under that doctrine, equality of treatment is accorded when the races are provided substantially equal facilities, even though these facilities be separate. In the Delaware case, the Supreme Court of Delaware adhered to that doctrine, but ordered that the plaintiffs be admitted to the white schools because of their superiority to the Negro schools.

The plaintiffs contend that segregated public schools are not "equal" and cannot be made "equal," and that hence they are deprived of the equal protection of the laws. Because of the obvious importance of the question presented, the Court took jurisdiction. Argument was heard in the 1952 Term, and reargument was heard this Term on certain questions propounded by the Court.

Reargument was largely devoted to the circumstances surrounding the adoption of the Fourteenth Amendment in 1868. It covered exhaustively consideration of the Amendment in Congress, ratification by the states, then existing practices in racial segregation, and the views of proponents and opponents of the Amendment. This discussion and our own investigation convince us that, although these sources cast some light, it is not enough to resolve the problem with which we are faced. At best, they are inconclusive. The most avid proponents of the post-War Amendments undoubtedly intended them to remove all legal distinctions among "all persons born or naturalized in the United States." Their opponents, just as certainly, were antagonistic to both the letter and the spirit of the Amendments and wished them to have the most limited effect. What others in Congress and the state legislatures had in mind cannot be determined with any degree of certainty.

An additional reason for the inconclusive nature of the Amendment's history, with respect to segregated schools, is the status of public education at that time. In the South, the movement toward free common schools, supported by general taxation, had not yet taken hold. Education of white children was largely in the hands of private groups. Education of Negroes was almost nonexistent, and practically all of the race were illiterate. In fact, any education of Negroes was forbidden by law in some states. Today, in contrast, many Negroes have achieved outstanding success in the arts and sciences as well as in the business and professional world. It is true that public school education at the time of the Amendment had advanced further in the North, but the effect of the Amendment on Northern States was generally ignored in the congressional debates. Even in the North, the conditions of public education did not approximate those existing today. The curriculum was usually rudimentary; ungraded schools were common in rural areas; the school term was but three months a year in many states; and compulsory school attendance was virtually unknown. As a consequence, it is not surprising that there should be so little in the history of the Fourteenth Amendment relating to its intended effect on public education.

In the first cases in this Court construing the Fourteenth Amendment, decided shortly after its adoption, the Court interpreted it as proscribing all state-imposed discriminations against the Negro race. The doctrine of "separate but equal" did not make its appearance in this Court until 1896 in the case of *Plessy* v. *Ferguson, supra,* involving not education but transportation. American courts have since labored with the doctrine for over half a century. In this Court, there have been six cases involving the "separate but equal" doctrine in the field of public education. In *Cumming* v. *County Board of Education,* 175 U.S. 528, and *Gong Lum* v. *Rice,* 275 U.S. 78, the validity of the doctrine itself was not challenged. In more recent cases, all on the graduate school level, inequality was found in that specific benefits enjoyed by white students were denied to Negro students of the same educational qualifications. *Missouri ex rel. Gaines* v. *Canada,* 305 U.S. 337; *Sipuel* v. *Oklahoma,* 332 U.S. 631; *Sweatt* v. *Painter,* 339 U.S. 629; *McLaurin* v. *Oklahoma State Regents,* 339 U.S. 637. In none of these cases was it necessary to re-examine the doctrine to grant relief to the Negro plaintiff. And in *Sweatt* v. *Painter, supra,* the Court expressly reserved decision on the question whether *Plessy* v. *Ferguson* should be held inapplicable to public education.

In the instant cases, that question is directly presented. Here, unlike *Sweatt* v. *Painter,* there are findings below that the Negro and white schools involved have been equalized, or are being equalized, with respect to buildings, curricula, qualifications and salaries of teachers, and other "tangible" factors. Our decision, therefore, cannot turn on merely a comparison of these tangible factors in the Negro and white schools involved in each of the cases. We must look instead to the effect of segregation itself on public education.

In approaching this problem, we cannot turn the clock back to 1868 when the Amendment was adopted, or even to 1896 when *Plessy* v. *Ferguson* was written. We must consider public education in the light of its full development and its present place in American life throughout the Nation. Only in this way can it be determined if segregation in public schools deprives these plaintiffs of the equal protection of the laws.

Today, education is perhaps the most important function of state and local governments. Compulsory school attendance laws and the great expenditures for education both demonstrate our recognition of the importance of education to our democratic society. It is required in the performance of our most basic public responsibilities, even service in the armed forces. It is the very foundation of good citizenship. Today it is a principal instrument in awakening the child to cultural values, in preparing him for later professional training, and in helping him to adjust normally to his environment. In these days, it is doubtful that any child may reasonably be expected to succeed in life if he is denied the opportunity of an education. Such an opportunity, where the state has undertaken to provide it, is a right which must be made available to all on equal terms.

We come then to the question presented: Does segregation of children in public schools solely on the basis of race, even though the physical facilities and other "tangible" factors may be equal, deprive the children of the minority group of equal educational opportunities? We believe that it does.

In *Sweatt* v. *Painter, supra,* in finding that a segregated law school for Negroes could not provide them equal educational opportunities, this Court relied in large part on "those qualities which are incapable of objective measurement but which make for greatness in a law school." In *McLaurin* v. *Oklahoma State Regents, supra,* the Court, in requiring that a Negro admitted to a white graduate school be treated like all other students, again resorted to intangible considerations: ". . . his ability to study, to engage in discussions and exchange views with other students, and, in general, to learn his profession." Such considerations apply with added force to children in grade and high schools. To separate them from others of similar age and qualifications solely because of their race generates a feeling of inferiority as to their status in the community that may affect their hearts and minds in a way unlikely ever to be undone. The effect of this separation on their educational opportunities was well stated by a finding in the Kansas case by a court which nevertheless felt compelled to rule against the Negro plaintiffs:

"Segregation of white and colored children in public schools has a detrimental effect upon the colored children. The impact is greater when it has the sanction of the law; for the policy of separating the races is usually interpreted as denoting the inferiority of the negro group. A sense of inferiority affects the motivation of a child to learn. Segregation with the sanction of law, therefore, has a tendency to [retard] the educational and mental development of negro children and to deprive them of some of the benefits they would receive in a racial[ly] integrated school system."

Whatever may have been the extent of psychological knowledge at the time of *Plessy* v. *Ferguson,* this finding is amply supported by modern authority.[1] Any language in *Plessy* v. *Ferguson* contrary to this finding is rejected.

We conclude that in the field of public education the doctrine of "separate but equal" has no place. Separate educational facilities are inherently unequal. Therefore, we hold that the plaintiffs and others similarly situated for whom the actions have been brought are, by reason of the segregation complained of, deprived of the equal protection of the laws guaranteed by the Fourteenth Amendment. This disposition makes unnecessary any discussion whether such segregation also violates the Due Process Clause of the Fourteenth Amendment.

Because these are class actions, because of the wide applicability of this decision, and because of the great variety of local conditions, the formulation of decrees in these cases presents problems of considerable complexity. On reargument, the consideration of appropriate relief was necessarily subordinated to the primary question —the constitutionality of segregation in public education. We have now announced that such segregation is a denial of the equal protection of the laws. In order that we may have the full assistance of the parties in formulating decrees, the cases will be restored to the docket, and the parties are requested to present further argument on Questions 4 and 5 previously propounded by the Court for the reargument this Term.[2] . . .

It is so ordered.

[1] K. B. Clark, Effect of Prejudice and Discrimination on Personality Development (Mid-century White House Conference on Children and Youth, 1950); Witmer and Kotinsky, Personality in the Making (1952), c. VI; Deutscher and Chein, The Psychological Effects of Enforced Segregation: A Survey of Social Science Opinion, 26 J. Psychol. 259 (1948); Chein, What are the Psychological Effects of Segregation Under Conditions of Equal Facilities?, 3 Int. J. Opinion and Attitude Res. 229 (1949); Brameld, Educational Costs, in Discrimination and National Welfare (MacIver, ed., 1949), 44–48; Frazier, The Negro in the United States (1949), 674–681. And see generally Myrdal, An American Dilemma (1944).

[2] "4. Assuming it is decided that segregation in public schools violates the Fourteenth Amendment

"(a) would a decree necessarily follow providing that, within the limits set by normal geographic school districting, Negro children should forthwith be admitted to schools of their choice, or

"(b) may this Court, in the exercise of its equity powers, permit an effective gradual adjustment to be brought about from existing segregated systems to a system not based on color distinctions?

"5. On the assumption on which questions 4 (a) and (b) are based, and assuming further that this Court will exercise its equity powers to the end described in question 4 (b),

"(a) should this Court formulate detailed decrees in these cases;

"(b) if so, what specific issues should the decrees reach;

"(c) should this Court appoint a special master to hear evidence with a view to recommending specific terms for such decrees;

"(d) should this Court remand to the courts of first instance with directions to frame decrees in these cases, and if so what general directions should the decrees of this Court include and what procedures should the courts of first instance follow in arriving at the specific terms of more detailed decrees?"

BOLLING v. SHARPE
347 U.S. 497, 74 S. Ct. 693, 98 L. Ed. 884 (1954)

MR. CHIEF JUSTICE WARREN delivered the opinion of the Court.

This case challenges the validity of segregation in the public schools of the District of Columbia. The petitioners, minors of the Negro race, allege that such segregation deprives them of due process of law under the Fifth Amendment. They were refused admission to a public school attended by white children solely because of their race. They sought the aid of the District Court for the District of Columbia in obtaining admission. That court dismissed their complaint. We granted a writ of certiorari before judgment in the Court of Appeals because of the importance of the constitutional question presented. . . .

We have this day held that the Equal Protection Clause of the Fourteenth Amendment prohibits the states from maintaining racially segregated public schools. The legal problem in the District of Columbia is somewhat different, however. The Fifth Amendment, which is applicable in the District of Columbia, does not contain an equal protection clause as does the Fourteenth Amendment which applies only to the states. But the concepts of equal protection and due process, both stemming from our American ideal of fairness, are not mutually exclusive. The "equal protection of the laws" is a more explicit safeguard of prohibited unfairness than "due process of law," and, therefore, we do not imply that the two are always interchangeable phrases. But, as this Court has recognized, discrimination may be so unjustifiable as to be violative of due process.

Classifications based solely upon race must be scrutinized with particular care, since they are contrary to our traditions and hence constitutionally suspect. As long ago as 1896, this Court declared the principle "that the constitution of the United States, in its present form, forbids, so far as civil and political rights are concerned, discrimination by the general government, or by the states, against any citizen because of his race." And in *Buchanan* v. *Warley,* 245 U.S. 60, the Court held that a statute which limited the right of a property owner to convey his property to a person of another race was, as an unreasonable discrimination, a denial of due process of law.

Although the Court has not assumed to define "liberty" with any great precision, that term is not confined to mere freedom from bodily restraint. Liberty under law extends to the full range of conduct which the individual is free to pursue, and it cannot be restricted except for a proper governmental objective. Segregation in public education is not reasonably related to any proper governmental objective, and thus it imposes on Negro children of the District of Columbia a burden that constitutes an arbitrary deprivation of their liberty in violation of the Due Process Clause.

In view of our decision that the Constitution prohibits the states from maintaining racially segregated public schools, it would be unthinkable that the same Constitution would impose a lesser duty on the Federal Government. We hold that racial segregation in the public schools of the District of Columbia is a denial of the due process of law guaranteed by the Fifth Amendment to the Constitution. . . .

BROWN v. BOARD OF EDUCATION OF TOPEKA
349 U.S. 294, 75 S. Ct. 753, 99 L. Ed. 1083 (1955)

MR. CHIEF JUSTICE WARREN delivered the opinion of the Court.

These cases were decided on May 17, 1954. The opinions of that date, declaring the fundamental principle that racial discrimination in public education is unconstitutional, are incorporated herein by reference. All provisions of federal, state, or local law requiring or permitting such discrimination must yield to this principle. There remains for consideration the manner in which relief is to be accorded.

Because these cases arose under different local conditions and their disposition will involve a variety of local problems, we requested further argument on the question of relief. In view of the nationwide importance of the decision, we invited the Attorney General of the United States and the Attorneys General of all states requiring or permitting racial discrimination in public education to present their views on that question. . . .

These presentations were informative and helpful to the Court in its consideration of complexities arising from the transition to a system of public education freed of racial discrimination. The presentations also demonstrated that substantial steps to eliminate racial discrimination in public schools have already been taken, not only in some of the communities in which these cases arose, but in some of the states appearing as *amici curiae,* and in other states as well. Substantial progress has been made in the District of Columbia and in the communities in Kansas and Delaware involved in this litigation. The defendants in the cases coming to us from South Carolina and Virginia are awaiting the decision of this Court concerning relief.

Full implementation of these constitutional principles may require solution of varied local school problems. School authorities have the primary responsibility for elucidating, assessing, and solving these problems; courts will have to consider whether the action of school authorities constitutes good faith implementation of the governing constitutional principles. Because of their proximity to local conditions and the possible need for further hearings, the courts which originally heard these cases can best perform this judicial appraisal. Accordingly, we believe it appropriate to remand the cases to those courts.

In fashioning and effectuating the decrees, the courts will be guided by equitable principles. Traditionally, equity has been characterized by a practical flexibility in shaping its remedies and by a facility for adjusting and reconciling public and private needs. These cases call for the exercise of these traditional attributes of equity power. At stake is the personal interest of the plaintiffs in admission to public schools as soon as practicable on a nondiscriminatory basis. To effectuate this interest may call for elimination of a variety of obstacles in making the transition to school systems operated in accordance with the constitutional principles set forth in our May 17, 1954, decision. Courts of equity may properly take into account the public interest in the elimination of such obstacles in a systematic and effective manner. But it should go without saying that the vitality of these constitutional principles cannot be allowed to yield simply because of disagreement with them.

While giving weight to these public and private considerations, the courts will require that the defendants make a prompt and reasonable start toward full compliance with our May 17, 1954, ruling. Once such a start has been made, the courts may find that additional time is necessary to carry out the ruling in an effective manner. The burden rests upon the defendants to establish that such time is necessary in the public interest and is consistent with good faith compliance at the earliest practicable date. To that end, the courts may consider problems related to administration, arising from the physical condition of the school plant, the school transportation system, personnel, revision of school districts and attendance areas into compact units to achieve a system of determining admission to the public schools on a nonracial basis, and revision of local laws and regulations which may be necessary in solving the foregoing problems. They will also consider the adequacy of any plans the defendants may propose to meet these problems and to effectuate a transition to a racially nondiscriminatory school system. During this period of transition, the courts will retain jurisdiction of these cases.

The judgments below, except that in the Delaware case, are accordingly reversed and remanded to the District Courts to take such proceedings and enter such orders and decrees consistent with this opinion as are necessary and proper to admit to public schools on a racially nondiscriminatory basis with all deliberate speed the parties to these cases. The judgment in the Delaware case—ordering the immediate admission of the plaintiffs to schools previously attended only by white children—is affirmed on the basis of the principles stated in our May 17, 1954, opinion. . . .

It is so ordered. . . .

Chapter 39

RIGHTS OF CITIZENSHIP

The Congress shall have power . . . to establish an uniform rule of naturalization. ART. I, SEC. 8, CLAUSE 4

All persons born or naturalized in the United States, and subject to the jurisdiction thereof, are citizens of the United States and of the State wherein they reside. FOURTEENTH AMENDMENT

The original Constitution mentioned both state and national citizens several times, but did not define either type of citizenship or indicate the relationship between them. Neither did the Constitution express a preference between the two principal rules which modern civilized nations have employed for determining citizenship—the *jus sanguinis,* under which one acquires the citizenship of one's parents, or the *jus soli,* under which one becomes a citizen of the country of birth.

These gaps were filled by the Fourteenth Amendment, which provided a definition of citizenship. One effect and purpose of this definition was to reverse the holding in the *Dred Scott* case that Negroes could never be citizens of the United States. The amendment also established that national citizenship was primary, and that state citizenship signified little more than residence within the state.

The Fourteenth Amendment adopted *jus soli* as its principal rule of citizenship. Birth in the United States confers citizenship on the children of alien parents, even if the parents themselves are ineligible for citizenship. *United States* v. *Wong Kim Ark,* 169 U.S. 649 (1898). Children born to United States citizens abroad are by act of Congress also citizens, provided the citizen parent had had a period of residence in the United States prior to the birth of the child. To this extent the United States follows the rule of *jus sanguinis* as well as *jus soli.*

Naturalization. No alien in the United States has any constitutional "right" to be naturalized. Congress may grant or withhold the privilege of naturalization upon any grounds or without any reason, as it sees fit. However, once Congress has defined eligibility for naturalization, then an alien who qualifies has a statutory right to submit his naturalization petition and supporting evidence to a court for a determination of his eligibility.

Post-Civil War statutes confined eligibility to white persons and those of African descent. Beginning in 1940 Congress widened eligibility in successive

443

statutes until in 1952 the Immigration and Nationality Act provided in sweeping language that "the rights of a person to become a naturalized citizen of the United States shall not be denied or abridged because of race." The act of 1952 also terminated the policy of denying the privilege of naturalization to conscientious objectors, which had been based on administrative practice rather than statutory requirement. *Girouard v. United States,* 328 U.S. 61 (1946).

Political opinion still remains as a restriction on naturalization, however. In fact, while limitations on all other grounds were disappearing, concern with political beliefs was increasing. This trend began in 1906, when Congress provided that anarchists could not become citizens, and wound up with the 1952 ban on naturalization of any person "who is a member of or affiliated with . . . the Communist Party of the United States."

Denaturalization. There are two ways by which American citizenship may be lost: denaturalization and expatriation. Denaturalization is the process of canceling a certificate of naturalization by official action for cause, and by definition can only be employed against persons who have secured their citizenship by naturalization.

The original purpose of denaturalization procedures, as authorized by statute in 1906, was to provide a method of canceling citizenship secured by the use of fraudulent documents or where entry into the United States was illegal. But the denaturalization process can also be employed against naturalized citizens who hold unpopular political views. During World War I a considerable number of "pro-Germans" were denaturalized, and World War II saw a similar drive on Nazis and Communists. Denaturalization has also been employed against criminals and racketeers.

The 1952 statute now controls the denaturalization process. It provides that any naturalized person who takes the oath with mental reservations or conceals beliefs and affiliations which by law disqualify one for naturalization, is subject to having his certificate canceled after an appropriate judicial proceeding. Furthermore, the 1952 act adds a new hazard. If a naturalized citizen within five years after his naturalization becomes a member of an organization which would have precluded him from being eligible for naturalization, this will be prima facie evidence that he was not attached to the principles of the Constitution at the time of naturalization, and the certificate can be canceled as having been obtained by "willful misrepresentation."

The constitutionality of the denaturalization power was attacked by Justices Murphy and Rutledge in *Knauer v. United States,* 328 U.S. 654 (1946), and *Klapprott v. United States,* 335 U.S. 601 (1949). Their position was that the Constitution makes only one distinction between natural-born and naturalized citizens; the latter are ineligible for the Presidency. They contended that in no other way could the status of naturalized citizens be made inferior, and that if they could be stripped of citizenship on grounds and by procedures not applicable to natural-born citizens, then naturalized citizens had only a second-class citizenship. This position failed to win any other converts on the Court.

Expatriation. Expatriation refers to the loss of citizenship as the result, intended or unintended, of voluntary action taken by a citizen, either natural-born or naturalized. When an individual wishes to give up his American citizenship, there is of course no constitutional problem. But Congress has stated twelve conditions under which individual action results in expatriation, at least six of which could cause loss of citizenship contrary to the intention of the individual.

Three involve relationships with a foreign state—serving in the armed forces of a foreign power without authorization and with consequent acquisition of a foreign nationality; assuming public office under the government of a foreign state, for which only nationals of that state are eligible; and voting in an election or plebiscite in a foreign state.

The constitutionality of this latter provision was upheld by a five to four vote in *Perez* v. *Brownell*, 356 U.S. 44 (1958). Congress might reasonably conclude, the Court thought, that voting by Americans in foreign political elections could jeopardize the successful conduct of international relations. Loss of nationality was upheld as one of the consequences which Congress could attach to such conduct as a means of discouraging this action.

The law states three other grounds for loss of citizenship which are essentially of a penal character—conviction and discharge from the armed services for desertion in time of war; conviction of treason or an attempt at forceful overthrow of the United States; and fleeing from or remaining outside the United States in time of war to evade military training. Since these conditions would normally not result in an expatriated person simultaneously gaining citizenship in another country, the usual consequence would be that the individual would become stateless. The first of these grounds for expatriation was considered in *Trop* v. *Dulles*, 356 U.S. 86 (1958), and declared unconstitutional by a five to four vote. The difference in result between this and the *Perez* case, which were decided on the same day, was that in *Trop* Justice Brennan voted with the four *Perez* dissenters.

Exclusion of Aliens. The absolute power of Congress to exclude aliens from the United States is firmly established. An alien who seeks admission to this country may not do so under any claim of right. Admission is a privilege granted only on such terms as Congress may prescribe.

Exclusion on racial grounds was first legislated by Congress in 1882, when Chinese immigration was suspended, a policy later made permanent. Exclusion of natives of India was accomplished in 1917, and of Japanese in 1924. The act of 1952 repealed all explicit racial restrictions on admission, but there is a quota law which heavily favors immigration from Northern and Western Europe and restricts immigrants from other parts of the world.

Exclusion on grounds of opinion has been in effect since 1903. The emphasis in recent statutes has of course been on the exclusion of Communists. The Subversive Activities Control Act of 1950 banned admission of aliens who were members of or affiliated with the Communist Party in any country. The act also excluded aliens if there is "reason to believe" that after entry they would be likely to engage in subversive activity.

Recognizing the breadth of congressional power and the need for administrative discretion in administering the statutes, the courts have placed exclusion procedures largely outside the scope of constitutional protection. *United States* v. *Ju Toy*, 198 U.S. 253 (1905). A hearing in exclusion cases rests upon congressional beneficence and not constitutional right. *United States ex rel. Knauff* v. *Shaughnessy*, 338 U.S. 537 (1950). Judicial review is limited to determining whether there has been a fair hearing when Congress provides for a hearing.

Deportation. Aliens who are in the United States illegally or who violate the conditions set by Congress for their residence in the country are subject to deportation. In *Fong Yue Ting* v. *United States,* 149 U.S. 698 (1893), the Supreme Court held that the power to deport was absolute and that deportation procedures need not meet the constitutional requirements for criminal trials since deportation was not a punishment for crime.

Recent litigation has centered around the validity of laws which require deportation of aliens for violation of a statutory condition attached to continued residence. Both the Alien Registration Act of 1940 and the Internal Security Act of 1950 provide for the deportation of legally resident aliens who have been members of the Communist Party at any time after entry into the United States, even though such membership had been terminated before passage of the statutes. In *Harisiades* v. *Shaughnessy,* 342 U.S. 580 (1952), and subsequent decisions the Court majority has ruled that it cannot interfere with the enforcement of such statutes.

TROP v. DULLES
356 U.S. 86, 78 S. Ct. 590, 2 L. Ed. 2d 630 (1958)

MR. CHIEF JUSTICE WARREN announced the judgment of the Court and delivered an opinion, in which MR. JUSTICE BLACK, MR. JUSTICE DOUGLAS, and MR. JUSTICE WHITTAKER join.

The petitioner in this case, a native-born American, is declared to have lost his United States citizenship and become stateless by reason of his conviction by court-martial for wartime desertion. As in *Perez* v. *Brownell,* 356 U.S. 44, the issue before us is whether this forfeiture of citizenship comports with the Constitution.

The facts are not in dispute. In 1944 petitioner was a private in the United States Army, serving in French Morocco. On May 22, he escaped from a stockade at Casablanca, where he had been confined following a previous breach of discipline. The next day petitioner and a companion were walking along a road towards Rabat, in the general direction back to Casablanca, when an Army truck approached and stopped. A witness testified that petitioner boarded the truck willingly and that no words were spoken. In Rabat petitioner was turned over to military police. Thus ended petitioner's "desertion." He had been gone less than a day and had willingly surrendered to an officer on an Army vehicle while he was walking back towards his base. He testified that at the time he and his companion were picked up by the Army truck, "we had decided to return to the stockade. The going was tough. We had no money to speak of, and at the time we were on foot and we were getting cold and hungry." A general court-martial convicted petitioner of desertion and sentenced him to three years at hard labor, forfeiture of all pay and allowances and a dishonorable discharge.

In 1952 petitioner applied for a passport. His application was denied on the ground that under the provisions of Section 401 (g) of the Nationality Act of 1940, as amended, he had lost his citizenship by reason of his conviction and dishonorable discharge for wartime desertion. In 1955 petitioner commenced this action in the District Court, seeking a declaratory judgment that he is a citizen. . . .

Section 401 (g) . . . is based directly on a Civil War statute, which provided that a deserter would lose his "rights of citizenship." The meaning of this phrase was not clear. When the 1940 codification and revision of the nationality laws was prepared, the Civil War statute was amended to make it certain that what a convicted deserter would lose was nationality itself. In 1944 the statute was further amended to provide that a convicted deserter would lose his citizenship only if he was dismissed from the service or dishonorably discharged. At the same time it was provided that citizenship could be regained if the deserter was restored to active duty in wartime with the permission of the military authorities.

Though these amendments were added to ameliorate the harshness of the statute, their combined effect produces a result that poses far graver problems than the ones that were sought to be solved. Section 401 (g) as amended now gives the military authorities complete discretion to decide who among convicted deserters shall continue to be Americans and who shall be stateless. By deciding whether to issue and execute a dishonorable discharge and whether to allow a deserter to re-enter the armed forces, the military becomes the arbiter of citizenship. And the domain given to it by Congress is not as narrow as might be supposed. Though the crime of desertion is one of the most serious in military law, it is by no means a rare event for a soldier to be convicted of this crime. The elements of desertion are simply absence from duty plus the intention not to return. Into this category falls a great range of conduct, which may be prompted by a variety of motives—fear, laziness, hysteria or any emotional imbalance. The offense may occur not only in combat but also in training camps for draftees in this country. The Solicitor General informed the Court that during World War II, according to Army estimates, approximately 21,000 soldiers and airmen were convicted of desertion and given dishonorable discharges by the sentencing courts-martial and that about 7,000 of these were actually separated from the service and thus rendered stateless when the reviewing authorities refused to remit their dishonorable discharges. . . .

In *Perez* v. *Brownell, supra,* I expressed the principles that I believe govern the constitutional status of United States citizenship. It is my conviction that citizenship is not subject to the general powers of the National Government and therefore cannot be divested in the exercise of those powers. The right may be voluntarily relinquished or abandoned either by express language or by language and conduct that show a renunciation of citizenship.

Under these principles, this petitioner has not lost his citizenship. Desertion in wartime, though it may merit the ultimate penalty, does not necessarily signify allegiance to a foreign state. Section 401 (g) is not limited to cases of desertion to the enemy, and there is no such element in this case. This soldier committed a crime for which he should be and was punished, but he did not involve himself in any way with a foreign state. There was no dilution of his allegiance to this country. The fact that the desertion occurred on foreign soil is of no consequence. The Solicitor General acknowledged that forfeiture of citizenship would have occurred if the entire incident had transpired in this country.

Citizenship is not a license that expires upon misbehavior. The duties of citizenship are numerous, and the discharge of many of these obligations is essential to the security and well-being of the Nation. The citizen who fails to pay his taxes or to abide by the laws safeguarding the integrity of elections deals a dangerous blow to his country. But could a citizen be deprived of his nationality for evading these basic responsibilities of citizenship? In time of war the citizen's duties include not only the military defense of the Nation but also full participation in the manifold activities of the civilian ranks. Failure to perform any of these obligations may cause the Nation serious injury, and, in appropriate circumstances, the punishing power is available to deal with derelictions of duty. But citizenship is not lost every time a duty of citizenship is shirked. And the deprivation of citizenship is not a weapon that the Government may use to express its displeasure at a citizen's conduct, however reprehensible that conduct may be. As long as a person does not voluntarily renounce or abandon his citizenship, and this petitioner has done neither, I believe his fundamental right of citizenship is secure. On this ground alone the judgment in this case should be reversed.

Since a majority of the Court concluded in *Perez* v. *Brownell* that citizenship may be divested in the exercise of some governmental power, I deem it appropriate to state additionally why the action taken in this case exceeds constitutional limits, even under the majority's decision in *Perez*. The Court concluded in *Perez* that citizenship could be divested in the exercise of the foreign affairs power. In this case, it is urged that the war power is adequate to support the divestment of citizenship. But there is a vital difference between the two statutes that purport to implement these powers by decreeing loss of citizenship. The statute in *Perez* decreed loss of citizenship—so the majority concluded—to eliminate those international problems that were thought to arise by reason of a citizen's having voted in a foreign election. The statute in this case, however, is entirely different. . . . Denationalization in this case is not even claimed to be a means of solving international problems, as was argued in *Perez*. Here the purpose is punishment, and therefore the statute is a penal law. . . .

Section 401 (g) is a penal law, and we must face the question whether the Constitution permits the Congress to take away citizenship as a punishment for crime. If it is assumed that the power of Congress extends to divestment of citizenship, the problem still remains as to this statute whether denationalization is a cruel and unusual punishment within the meaning of the Eighth Amendment. Since wartime desertion is punishable by death, there can be no argument that the penalty of denationalization is excessive in relation to the gravity of the crime. The question is whether this penalty subjects the individual to a fate forbidden by the principle of civilized treatment guaranteed by the Eighth Amendment.

At the outset, let us put to one side the death penalty as an index of the constitutional limit on punishment. Whatever the arguments may be against capital punishment, both on moral grounds and in terms of accomplishing the purposes of punishment—and they are forceful, the death penalty has been employed throughout our history, and in a day when it is still widely accepted, it cannot be said to violate the constitutional concept of cruelty. But it is equally plain that the existence of the death penalty is not a license to the Government to devise any punishment short of death within the limit of its imagination.

The exact scope of the constitutional phrase "cruel and unusual" has not been detailed by this Court. But the basic policy reflected in these words is firmly established in the Anglo-American tradition of criminal justice. The phrase in our Constitution was taken directly from the English Declaration of Rights of 1688, and the principle it represents can be traced back to the Magna Carta. The basic concept underlying the Eighth Amendment is nothing less than the dignity of man. While the State has the power to punish, the Amendment stands to assure that this power be exercised within the limits of civilized standards. . . .

We believe . . . that use of denationalization as a punishment is barred by the Eighth Amendment. There may be involved no physical mistreatment, no primitive torture. There is instead the total destruction of the individual's status in organized society. It is a form of punishment more primitive than torture, for it destroys for the individual the political existence that was centuries in the development. The punishment strips the citizen of his status in the national and international political community. His very existence is at the sufferance of the country in which he happens to find himself. While any one country may accord him some rights, and presumably as long as he remained in this country he would enjoy the limited rights of an alien, no country need do so because he is stateless. Furthermore, his enjoyment of even the limited rights of an alien might be subject to termination at any time by reason of deportation. In short, the expatriate has lost the right to have rights. . . .

The civilized nations of the world are in virtual unanimity that statelessness is not to be imposed as punishment for crime. . . . The United Nations' survey of the nationality laws of 84 nations of the world reveals that only two countries, the Philippines and Turkey, impose denationalization as a penalty for desertion. In this country the Eighth Amendment forbids this to be done.

In concluding as we do that the Eighth Amendment forbids Congress to punish by taking away citizenship, we are mindful of the gravity of the issue inevitably raised whenever the constitutionality of an Act of the National Legislature is challenged. No member of the Court believes that in this case the statute before us can be construed to avoid the issue of constitutionality. That issue confronts us, and the task of resolving it is inescapably ours. This task requires the exercise of judgment, not the reliance upon personal preferences. Courts must not consider the wisdom of statutes but neither can they sanction as being merely unwise that which the Constitution forbids.

We are oath-bound to defend the Constitution. This obligation requires that congressional enactments be judged by the standards of the Constitution. The Judiciary has the duty of implementing the constitutional safeguards that protect individual rights. When the Government acts to take away the fundamental right of citizenship, the safeguards of the Constitution should be examined with special diligence. . . .

Reversed and remanded.

MR. JUSTICE BLACK, whom MR. JUSTICE DOUGLAS joins, concurring.

While I concur in the opinion of THE CHIEF JUSTICE there is one additional thing that needs to be said.

Even if citizenship could be involuntarily divested, I do not believe that the power to denationalize may be placed in the hands of military authorities. If desertion or other misconduct is to be a basis for forfeiting citizenship, guilt should be determined in a civilian court of justice where all the protections of the Bill of Rights guard the fairness of the outcome. Such forfeiture should not rest on the findings of a military tribunal. . . . Nothing in the Constitution or its history lends the slightest support for such military control over the right to be an American citizen.

MR. JUSTICE BRENNAN, concurring.

In *Perez* v. *Brownell*, also decided today, I agreed with the Court that there was no constitutional infirmity in § 401 (e), which expatriates the citizen who votes in a foreign political election. I reach a different conclusion in this case, however, because I believe that § 401 (g), which expatriates the wartime deserter who is dishonorably discharged after conviction by court-martial, lies beyond Congress' power to enact. It is, concededly, paradoxical to justify as constitutional the expatriation of the citizen who has committed no crime by voting in a Mexican political election, yet find unconstitutional a statute which provides for the expatriation of a soldier guilty of the very serious crime of desertion in time of war. The loss of citizenship may have as ominous significance for the individual in the one case as in the other. Why then does not the Constitution prevent the expatriation of the voter as well as the deserter?

Here, as in *Perez* v. *Brownell*, we must inquire whether there exists a relevant connection between the particular legislative enactment and the power granted to Congress by the Constitution. The Court there held that such a relevant connection exists between the power to maintain relations with other sovereign nations and the power to expatriate the American who votes in a foreign election. . . .

In contrast to § 401 (e), the section with which we are now concerned, § 401 (g), draws upon the power of Congress to raise and maintain military forces to wage war. No pretense can here be made that expatriation of the deserter in any way relates to the conduct of foreign affairs, for this statute is not limited in its effects to those who desert in a foreign country or who flee to another land. Nor is this statute limited in its application to the deserter whose conduct imports "elements of an allegiance to another country in some measure, at least, inconsistent with American citizenship." *Perez* v. *Brownell, supra*. . . . The history of this provision, indeed, shows that the essential congressional purpose was a response to the needs of the military in maintaining discipline in the armed forces, especially during wartime. . . . But granting that Congress is authorized to deal with the evil of desertion, we must yet inquire whether expatriation is a means reasonably calculated to achieve this legitimate end and thereby designed to further the ultimate congressional objective—the successful waging of war. . . .

It is difficult, indeed, to see how expatriation of the deserter helps wage war except as it performs that function when imposed as punishment. It is obvious that expatriation cannot in any wise avoid the harm apprehended by Congress. After the act of desertion, only punishment can follow, for the harm has been done. The deserter, moreover, does not cease to be an American citizen at the moment he deserts. Indeed, even conviction does not necessarily effect his expatriation, for dishonorable discharge is the condition precedent to loss of citizenship. Therefore, if expatriation is made a consequence of desertion, it must stand together with death and imprisonment—as a form of punishment. . . .

It seems to me that nothing is solved by the uncritical reference to service in the armed forces as the "highest duty of American citizenship." Indeed, it is very difficult to imagine, on this theory of power, why Congress cannot impose expatriation as punishment for any crime at all—for tax evasion, for bank robbery, for narcotics offenses. As citizens we are also called upon to pay our taxes and to obey the laws, and these duties appear to me to be fully as related to the nature of our citizenship as our military obligations. But Congress' asserted power to expatriate the deserter bears to the war powers precisely the same relation as its power to expatriate the tax evader would bear to the taxing power. . . .

. . . I can only conclude that the requisite rational relation between this statute and the war power does not appear. . . .

MR. JUSTICE FRANKFURTER, whom MR. JUSTICE BURTON, MR. JUSTICE CLARK and MR. JUSTICE HARLAN join, dissenting. . . .

Probably the most important governmental action contemplated by the war power is the building up and maintenance of an armed force for the common defense. Just as Congress may be convinced of the necessity for conscription for the effective conduct of war, *Selective Draft Law Cases*, 245 U.S. 366, Congress may justifiably be of the view that stern measures—what to some may seem overly stern—are needed in order that control may be had over evasions of military duty when the armed forces are committed to the Nation's defense, and that the deleterious effects of those evasions may be kept to the minimum. Clearly Congress may deal severely with the problem of desertion from the armed forces in wartime; it is equally clear—from the face of the legislation and from the circumstances in which it was passed—that Congress was calling upon its war powers when it made such desertion an act of expatriation. . . .

Possession by an American citizen of the rights and privileges that constitute citizenship imposes correlative obligations, of which the most indispensable may well be "to take his place in the ranks of the army of his country and risk the chance of being shot down in its defense," *Jacobson* v. *Massachusetts*, 197 U.S. 11, 29. Harsh as this may sound, it is no more so than the actualities to which it responds. Can it be said that there is no rational nexus between refusal to perform this ultimate duty of American citizenship and legislative withdrawal of that citizenship? Congress may well have thought that making loss of citizenship a consequence of wartime desertion would affect the ability of the military authorities to control the forces with which they were expected to fight and win a major world conflict. It is not for us to deny that Congress might reasonably have believed the morale and fighting efficiency of our troops would be impaired if our soldiers knew that their fellows who had abandoned them in their time of greatest need were to remain in the communion of our citizens. . . .

Petitioner contends that loss of citizenship is an unconstitutionally disproportionate "punishment" for desertion and that it constitutes "cruel and unusual punishment" within the scope of the Eighth Amendment. Loss of citizenship entails undoubtedly severe—and in particular situations even tragic—consequences. . . . However, like denaturalization, see *Klapprott* v. *United States,* 335 U.S. 601, 612, expatriation under the Nationality Act of 1940 is not "punishment" in any valid constitutional sense. Cf. *Fong Yue Ting* v. *United States,* 149 U.S. 698, 730. Simply because denationalization was attached by Congress as a consequence of conduct that it had elsewhere made unlawful, it does not follow that denationalization is a "punishment," any more than it can be said that loss of civil rights as a result of conviction for a felony . . . is a "punishment" for any legally significant purposes. . . . Since there are legislative ends within the scope of Congress's war power that are wholly consistent with a "non-penal" purpose to regulate the military forces, and since there is nothing on the face of this legislation to indicate that Congress had a contrary purpose, there is no warrant for this Court's labeling the disability imposed by § 401 (g) as a "punishment."

Even assuming, *arguendo,* that § 401 (g) can be said to impose "punishment," to insist that denationalization is "cruel and unusual punishment" is to stretch that concept beyond the breaking point. It seems scarcely arguable that loss of citizenship is within the Eighth Amendment's prohibition because disproportionate to an offense that is capital and has been so from the first year of Independence. . . . Is constitutional dialectic so empty of reason that it can be seriously urged that loss of citizenship is a fate worse than death? The seriousness of abandoning one's country when it is in the grip of mortal conflict precludes denial to Congress of the power to terminate citizenship here, unless that power is to be denied to Congress under any circumstance. . . .

This legislation is the result of an exercise by Congress of the legislative power vested in it by the Constitution and of an exercise by the President of his constitutional power in approving a bill and thereby making it "a law." To sustain it is to respect the actions of the two branches of our Government directly responsive to the will of the people and empowered under the Constitution to determine the wisdom of legislation. The awesome power of this Court to invalidate such legislation, because in practice it is bounded only by our own prudence in discerning the limits of the Court's constitutional function, must be exercised with the utmost restraint. . . .

SELECTED REFERENCES

Blaustein, A. P., and C. C. Ferguson, Jr., *Desegregation and the Law.* New Brunswick, N.J.: Rutgers University Press, 1957.

Brown, Ralph S., Jr., *Loyalty and Security.* New Haven, Conn.: Yale University Press, 1958.

Carr, Robert K., *Federal Protection of Civil Rights*. Ithaca, N.Y.: Cornell University Press, 1947.

Commission on Civil Rights, *Report: Voting* (vol. 1) and *Education* (vol. 2). Washington: Government Printing Office, 1961.

Corwin, Edward S., *The Constitution of the United States of America: Analysis and Interpretation*, pp. 955–1186. Washington: Government Printing Office, 1953.

——— *Liberty against Government*. Baton Rouge, La.: Louisiana State University Press, 1948.

Dash, Samuel, *The Eavesdroppers*. New Brunswick, N.J.: Rutgers University Press, 1959.

Douglas, William O., *We the Judges*, chaps. 8, 10, 11. New York: Doubleday & Company, Inc., 1956.

Fellman, David, *The Defendant's Rights*. New York: Holt, Rinehart and Winston, Inc., 1958.

Gellhorn, Walter, *Individual Freedom and Governmental Restraints*. Baton Rouge, La.: Louisiana State University Press, 1956.

Greenberg, Jack, *Race Relations and American Law*. New York: Columbia University Press, 1959.

Harris, Robert J., *The Quest for Equality*. Baton Rouge, La.: Louisiana State University Press, 1960.

Heller, Francis H., *The Sixth Amendment to the Constitution of the United States*. Lawrence, Kan.: University of Kansas Press, 1951.

Konvitz, Milton R., *Civil Rights in Immigration*. Ithaca, N.Y.: Cornell University Press, 1953.

President's Commission on Immigration and Naturalization, *Whom We Shall Welcome*. Washington: Government Printing Office, 1952.

Pritchett, C. Herman, *The American Constitution*, part 7. New York: McGraw-Hill Book Company, Inc., 1959.

Race Relations Law Reporter. Nashville, Tenn.: Vanderbilt University School of Law, published quarterly since 1956.

Wood, Virginia, *Due Process of Law*. Baton Rouge, La.: Louisiana State University Press, 1951.

APPENDIX

CONSTITUTION OF THE UNITED STATES OF AMERICA

WE THE PEOPLE of the United States, in Order to form a more perfect Union, establish Justice, insure domestic Tranquility, provide for the common defence, promote the general Welfare, and secure the Blessings of Liberty to ourselves and our Posterity, do ordain and establish this CONSTITUTION for the United States of America.

Article I

SECTION 1. All legislative Powers herein granted shall be vested in a Congress of the United States, which shall consist of a Senate and House of Representatives.

SECTION 2. [1.] The House of Representatives shall be composed of Members chosen every second Year by the People of the several States, and the Electors in each State shall have the Qualifications requisite for Electors of the most numerous Branch of the State Legislature.

[2.] No Person shall be a Representative who shall not have attained to the Age of twenty five Years, and been seven Years a Citizen of the United States, and who shall not, when elected, be an Inhabitant of that State in which he shall be chosen.

[3.] Representatives and direct Taxes [1] shall be apportioned among the several States which may be included within this Union, according to their respective Numbers, which shall be determined by adding to the whole Number of free Persons, including those bound to Service for a Term of Years, and excluding Indians not taxed, three fifths of all other Persons.[2] The actual Enumeration shall be made within three Years after the first Meeting of the Congress of the United States, and within every subsequent Term of ten Years, in such Manner as they shall by Law direct. The Number of Representatives shall not exceed one for every thirty Thousand, but each State shall have at Least one Representative; and until such enumeration shall be made, the State of New Hampshire shall be entitled to chuse three, Massachusetts eight, Rhode-Island and Providence Plantations one, Connecticut five, New-York six, New Jersey four, Pennsylvania eight, Delaware one, Maryland six, Virginia ten, North Carolina five, South Carolina five, and Georgia three.

[4.] When vacancies happen in the Representation from any State, the Executive Authority thereof shall issue Writs of Election to fill such Vacancies.

[5.] The House of Representatives shall chuse their Speaker and other Officers; and shall have the sole Power of Impeachment.

SECTION 3. [1.] The Senate of the United States shall be composed of two Senators from each State, chosen by the Legislature thereof,[3] for six Years; and each Senator shall have one Vote.

---

[1] Modified as to direct taxes by the Sixteenth Amendment.
[2] Replaced by the Fourteenth Amendment.
[3] Modified by the Seventeenth Amendment.

[2.] Immediately after they shall be assembled in Consequence of the first Election, they shall be divided as equally as may be into three Classes. The Seats of the Senators of the first Class shall be vacated at the Expiration of the second Year, of the second Class at the Expiration of the fourth Year, and of the third Class at the Expiration of the sixth Year, so that one third may be chosen every second Year; and if Vacancies happen by Resignation, or otherwise, during the Recess of the Legislature of any State, the Executive thereof may make temporary Appointments until the next Meeting of the Legislature, which shall then fill such Vacancies.

[3.] No Person shall be a Senator who shall not have attained to the Age of thirty Years, and been nine Years a Citizen of the United States, and who shall not, when elected, be an Inhabitant of that State for which he shall be chosen.

[4.] The Vice President of the United States shall be President of the Senate, but shall have no Vote, unless they be equally divided.

[5.] The Senate shall chuse their other Officers, and also a President pro tempore, in the Absence of the Vice President, or when he shall exercise the Office of President of the United States.

[6.] The Senate shall have the sole Power to try all Impeachments. When sitting for that Purpose, they shall be on Oath or Affirmation. When the President of the United States is tried, the Chief Justice shall preside: And no Person shall be convicted without the Concurrence of two thirds of the Members present.

[7.] Judgment in Cases of Impeachment shall not extend further than to removal from Office, and disqualification to hold and enjoy any Office of honor, Trust or Profit under the United States: but the Party convicted shall nevertheless be liable and subject to Indictment, Trial, Judgment and Punishment, according to Law.

SECTION 4. [1.] The Times, Places and Manner of holding Elections for Senators and Representatives, shall be prescribed in each State by the Legislature thereof; but the Congress may at any time by Law make or alter such Regulations, except as to the Places of chusing Senators.

[2.] The Congress shall assemble at least once in every Year, and such Meeting shall be on the first Monday in December, unless they shall by Law appoint a different Day.[4]

SECTION 5. [1.] Each House shall be the Judge of the Elections, Returns and Qualifications of its own Members, and a Majority of each shall constitute a Quorum to do Business; but a smaller Number may adjourn from day to day, and may be authorized to compel the attendance of absent Members, in such Manner, and under such Penalties as each House may provide.

[2.] Each House may determine the Rules of its Proceedings, punish its Members for Disorderly Behaviour, and, with the Concurrence of two thirds, expel a Member.

[3.] Each House shall keep a Journal of its Proceedings, and from time to time publish the same, excepting such Parts as may in their Judgment require Secrecy; and the Yeas and Nays of the Members of either House on any question shall, at the Desire of one fifth of those Present, be entered on the Journal.

[4.] Neither House, during the Session of Congress, shall, without the Consent of the other, adjourn for more than three days, nor to any other Place than that in which the two Houses shall be sitting.

SECTION 6. [1.] The Senators and Representatives shall receive a Compensation for their Services, to be ascertained by Law, and paid out of the Treasury of the United States. They shall in all Cases, except Treason, Felony and Breach of the Peace, be privileged from Arrest during their Attendance at the Session of their respective Houses, and in going to and returning from the same; and for any Speech or Debate in either House, they shall not be questioned in any other Place.

---

[4] Modified by the Twentieth Amendment.

[2.] No Senator or Representative shall, during the Time for which he was elected, be appointed to any civil Office under the Authority of the United States, which shall have been created, or the Emoluments whereof shall have been encreased during such time; and no Person holding any Office under the United States, shall be a member of either House during his Continuance in Office.

SECTION 7. [1.] All Bills for raising Revenue shall originate in the House of Representatives; but the Senate may propose or concur with Amendments as on other Bills.

[2.] Every Bill which shall have passed the House of Representatives and the Senate, shall, before it become a Law, be presented to the President of the United States; If he approve he shall sign it, but if not he shall return it, with his Objections to that House in which it shall have originated, who shall enter the Objections at large on their Journal, and proceed to reconsider it. If after such Reconsideration two thirds of that House shall agree to pass the Bill, it shall be sent, together with the Objections, to the other House, by which it shall likewise be reconsidered, and if approved by two thirds of that House, it shall become a Law. But in all such Cases the Votes of both Houses shall be determined by yeas and Nays, and the Names of the Persons voting for and against the Bill shall be entered on the Journal of each House respectively. If any Bill shall not be returned by the President within ten Days (Sundays excepted) after it shall have been presented to him, the same shall be a Law, in like Manner as if he had signed it, unless the Congress by their Adjournment prevent its Return, in which Case it shall not be a Law.

[3.] Every Order, Resolution, or Vote to which the Concurrence of the Senate and House of Representatives may be necessary (except on a question of Adjournment) shall be presented to the President of the United States; and before the same shall take Effect, shall be approved by him, or being disapproved by him, shall be repassed by two thirds of the Senate and House of Representatives, according to the Rules and Limitations prescribed in the Case of a Bill.

SECTION 8. The Congress shall have Power [1.] To lay and collect Taxes, Duties, Imposts and Excises, to pay the Debts and provide for the common Defence and general Welfare of the United States; but all Duties, Imposts and Excises shall be uniform throughout the United States;

[2.] To borrow Money on the credit of the United States;

[3.] To regulate Commerce with foreign Nations, and among the several States, and with the Indian Tribes;

[4.] To establish an uniform Rule of Naturalization, and uniform Laws on the subject of Bankruptcies throughout the United States;

[5.] To coin Money, regulate the Value thereof, and of foreign Coin, and fix the Standard of Weights and Measures;

[6.] To provide for the Punishment of counterfeiting the Securities and current Coin of the United States;

[7.] To establish Post Offices and post Roads;

[8.] To promote the Progress of Science and useful Arts, by securing for limited Times to Authors and Inventors the exclusive Right to their respective Writings and Discoveries;

[9.] To constitute Tribunals inferior to the supreme Court;

[10.] To define and punish Piracies and Felonies committed on the high Seas, and Offences against the Law of Nations;

[11.] To declare War, grant Letters of Marque and Reprisal, and make Rules concerning Captures on Land and Water;

[12.] To raise and support Armies, but no Appropriation of Money to that Use shall be for a longer Term than two Years;

[13.] To provide and maintain a Navy;

]14.[To make Rules for the Government and Regulation of the land and naval Forces;

[15.] To provide for calling forth the Militia to execute the Laws of the Union, suppress Insurrections and repel Invasions;

[16.] To provide for organizing, arming, and disciplining, the Militia, and for governing such Part of them as may be employed in the Service of the United States, reserving to the States respectively, the Appointment of the Officers, and the Authority of training the Militia according to the discipline prescribed by Congress;

[17.] To exercise exclusive Legislation in all Cases whatsoever, over such District (not exceeding ten Miles square) as may, by Cession of particular States, and the Acceptance of Congress, become the Seat of the Government of the United States, and to exercise like Authority over all Places purchased by the Consent of the Legislature of the State in which the same shall be, for the Erection of Forts, Magazines, Arsenals, dock-Yards, and other needful Buildings;—And

[18.] To make all Laws which shall be necessary and proper for carrying into Execution the foregoing Powers, and all other Powers vested by this Constitution in the Government of the United States, or in any Department or Officer thereof.

SECTION 9. [1.] The Migration or Importation of such Persons as any of the States now existing shall think proper to admit, shall not be prohibited by the Congress prior to the Year one thousand eight hundred and eight, but a Tax or duty may be imposed on such Importation, not exceeding ten dollars for each Person.

[2.] The Privilege of the Writ of Habeas Corpus shall not be suspended, unless when in Cases of Rebellion or Invasion the public Safety may require it.

[3.] No Bill of Attainder or ex post facto Law shall be passed.

[4.] No Capitation, or other direct, Tax shall be laid, unless in Proportion to the Census or Enumeration herein before directed to be taken.[5]

[5.] No Tax or Duty shall be laid on Articles exported from any State.

[6.] No Preference shall be given by any Regulation of Commerce or Revenue to the Ports of one State over those of another: nor shall Vessels bound to, or from, one State, be obliged to enter, clear, or pay Duties in another.

[7.] No Money shall be drawn from the Treasury, but in Consequence of Appropriations made by Law; and a regular Statement and Account of the Receipts and Expenditures of all public Money shall be published from time to time.

[8.] No Title of Nobility shall be granted by the United States: And no Person holding any Office of Profit or Trust under them, shall, without the Consent of the Congress, accept of any present, Emolument, Office, or Title, of any kind whatever, from any King, Prince, or foreign State.

SECTION 10. [1.] No State shall enter into any Treaty, Alliance, or Confederation; grant Letters of Marque and Reprisal; coin Money; emit Bills of Credit; make any Thing but gold and silver Coin a Tender in Payment of Debts; pass any Bill of Attainder, ex post facto Law, or Law impairing the Obligation of Contracts, or grant any Title of Nobility.

[2.] No State shall, without the Consent of the Congress, lay any Imposts or Duties on Imports or Exports, except what may be absolutely necessary for executing its inspection Laws: and the net Produce of all Duties and Imposts, laid by any State on Imports or Exports, shall be for the Use of the Treasury of the United States; and all such Laws shall be subject to the Revision and Controul of the Congress.

[3.] No State shall, without the Consent of Congress, lay any Duty of Tonnage, keep Troops, or Ships of War in time of Peace, enter into any Agreement or Compact

[5] Modified by the Sixteenth Amendment.

with another State, or with a foreign Power, or engage in War, unless actually invaded, or in such imminent Danger as will not admit of delay.

Article II

SECTION 1. [1.] The executive Power shall be vested in a President of the United States of America. He shall hold his Office during the Term of four Years, and, together with the Vice President, chosen for the same Term, be elected, as follows.

[2.] Each State shall appoint, in such Manner as the Legislature thereof may direct, a Number of Electors, equal to the whole Number of Senators and Representatives to which the State may be entitled in the Congress: but no Senator or Representative, or Person holding an Office of Trust or Profit under the United States, shall be appointed an Elector.

[3.] The Electors shall meet in their respective States, and vote by Ballot for two Persons, of whom one at least shall not be an Inhabitant of the same State with themselves. And they shall make a List of all the Persons voted for, and of the Number of Votes for each; which List they shall sign and certify, and transmit sealed to the Seat of Government of the United States, directed to the President of the Senate. The President of the Senate shall, in the Presence of the Senate and House of Representatives, open all the Certificates, and the Votes shall then be counted. The Person having the greatest Number of Votes shall be the President, if such Number be a Majority of the whole Number of Electors appointed; and if there be more than one who have such Majority, and have an equal Number of Votes, then the House of Representatives shall immediately chuse by Ballot one of them for President; and if no Person have a Majority, then from the five highest on the List the said House shall in like Manner chuse the President. But in chusing the President, the Votes shall be taken by States, the Representation from each State having one Vote; A quorum for this Purpose shall consist of a Member or Members from two thirds of the States, and a Majority of all the States shall be necessary to a Choice. In every Case, after the Choice of the President, the Person having the greatest Number of Votes of the Electors shall be the Vice President. But if there should remain two or more who have equal Votes, the Senate shall chuse from them by Ballot the Vice President.[6]

[4.] The Congress may determine the Time of chusing the Electors, and the Day on which they shall give their Votes; which Day shall be the same throughout the United States.

[5.] No Person except a natural born Citizen, or a Citizen of the United States, at the time of the Adoption of this Constitution, shall be eligible to the Office of President; neither shall any Person be eligible to that Office who shall not have attained to the Age of thirty five Years, and been fourteen Years a Resident within the United States.

[6.] In Case of the Removal of the President from Office, or of his Death, Resignation, or Inability to discharge the Powers and Duties of the said Office, the Same shall devolve on the Vice President, and the Congress may by Law provide for the Case of Removal, Death, Resignation, or Inability, both of the President and Vice President, declaring what Officer shall then act as President, and such Officer shall act accordingly, until the Disability be removed, or a President shall be elected.

[7.] The President shall, at stated Times, receive for his Services, a Compensation, which shall neither be encreased nor diminished during the Period for which he shall have been elected, and he shall not receive within that Period any other Emolument from the United States, or any of them.

[8.] Before he enter on the Execution of his Office, he shall take the following

[6] This paragraph was replaced in 1804 by the Twelfth Amendment.

Oath or Affirmation:—"I do solemnly swear (or affirm) that I will faithfully execute the Office of President of the United States, and will to the best of my Ability, preserve, protect and defend the Constitution of the United States."

SECTION 2. [1.] The President shall be Commander in Chief of the Army and Navy of the United States, and of the Militia of the several States, when called into the actual Service of the United States; he may require the Opinion, in writing, of the principal Officer in each of the executive Departments, upon any Subject relating to the Duties of their respective Offices, and he shall have Power to grant Reprieves and Pardons for Offences against the United States, except in Cases of Impeachment.

[2.] He shall have Power, by and with the Advice and Consent of the Senate, to make Treaties, provided two thirds of the Senators present concur; and he shall nominate, and by and with the Advice and Consent of the Senate, shall appoint Ambassadors, other public Ministers and Consuls, Judges of the supreme Court, and all other Officers of the United States, whose Appointments are not herein otherwise provided for, and which shall be established by Law: but the Congress may by Law vest the Appointment of such inferior Officers, as they think proper, in the President alone, in the Courts of Law, or in the Heads of Departments.

[3.] The President shall have Power to fill up all Vacancies that may happen during the Recess of the Senate, by granting Commissions which shall expire at the End of their next Session.

SECTION 3. He shall from time to time give to the Congress Information of the State of the Union, and recommend to their Consideration such Measures as he shall judge necessary and expedient; he may, on extraordinary Occasions, convene both Houses, or either of them, and in Case of Disagreement between them, with Respect to the Time of Adjournment, he may adjourn them to such Time as he shall think proper; he shall receive Ambassadors and other public Ministers; he shall take Care that the Laws be faithfully executed, and shall Commission all the Officers of the United States.

SECTION 4. The President, Vice President and all civil Officers of the United States, shall be removed from Office on Impeachment for, and Conviction of, Treason, Bribery, or other high Crimes and Misdemeanors.

Article III

SECTION 1. The Judicial Power of the United States, shall be vested in one supreme Court, and in such inferior Courts as the Congress may from time to time ordain and establish. The Judges, both of the supreme and inferior Courts, shall hold their Offices during good Behaviour, and shall, at stated Times, receive for their Services, a Compensation, which shall not be diminished during their Continuance in Office.

SECTION 2. [1.] The judicial Power shall extend to all Cases, in Law and Equity, arising under this Constitution, the Laws of the United States, and Treaties made, or which shall be made, under their Authority;—to all Cases affecting Ambassadors, other public Ministers and Consuls;—to all Cases of admiralty and maritime Jurisdiction;—to Controversies to which the United States shall be a Party;—to Controversies between two or more States;—between a State and Citizens of another State; [7]— between Citizens of different States;—between Citizens of the same State claiming Lands under Grants of different States, and between a State, or the Citizens thereof, and foreign States, Citizens or Subjects.

[2.] In all Cases affecting Ambassadors, other public Ministers and Consuls, and those in which a State shall be Party, the supreme Court shall have original Jurisdiction. In all the other Cases before mentioned, the supreme Court shall have appellate

[7] Restricted by the Eleventh Amendment.

Jurisdiction, both as to Law and Fact, with such Exceptions, and under such Regulations as the Congress shall make.

[3.] The Trial of all Crimes, except in Cases of impeachment, shall be by Jury; and such Trial shall be held in the State where the said Crimes shall have been committed; but when not committed within any State, the Trial shall be at such Place or Places as the Congress may by Law have directed.

SECTION 3. [1.] Treason against the United States, shall consist only in levying War against them, or in adhering to their Enemies, giving them Aid and Comfort. No Person shall be convicted of Treason unless on the Testimony of two Witnesses to the same overt Act, or on Confession in open Court.

[2.] The Congress shall have Power to declare the Punishment of Treason, but no Attainder of Treason shall work Corruption of Blood, or Forfeiture except during the Life of the Person attainted.

Article IV

SECTION 1. Full Faith and Credit shall be given in each State to the public Acts, Records, and judicial Proceedings of every other State. And the Congress may by general Laws prescribe the Manner in which such Acts, Records and Proceedings shall be proved, and the Effect thereof.

SECTION 2. [1.] The Citizens of each State shall be entitled to all Privileges and Immunities of Citizens in the several States.

[2.] A Person charged in any State with Treason, Felony, or other Crime, who shall flee from Justice, and be found in another State, shall on Demand of the executive Authority of the State from which he fled, be delivered up, to be removed to the State having Jurisdiction of the Crime.

[3.] No Person held to Service or Labour in one State, under the Laws thereof, escaping into another, shall, in Consequence of any Law or Regulation therein, be discharged from such Service or Labour, but shall be delivered up on Claim of the Party to whom such Service or Labour may be due.

SECTION 3. [1.] New States may be admitted by the Congress into this Union; but no new State shall be formed or erected within the Jurisdiction of any other States; nor any State be formed by the Junction of two or more States, or Parts of States, without the Consent of the Legislatures of the States concerned as well as of the Congress.

[2.] The Congress shall have Power to dispose of and make all needful Rules and Regulations respecting the Territory or other Property belonging to the United States; and nothing in this Constitution shall be so construed as to Prejudice any Claims of the United States, or of any particular State.

SECTION 4. The United States shall guarantee to every State in this Union a Republican Form of Government, and shall protect each of them against Invasion; and on Application of the Legislature, or of the Executive (when the Legislature cannot be convened) against domestic Violence.

Article V

The Congress, whenever two thirds of both Houses shall deem it necessary, shall propose Amendments to this Constitution, or, on the Application of the Legislatures of two thirds of the several States, shall call a Convention for proposing Amendments, which, in either Case, shall be valid to all Intents and Purposes, as Part of this Constitution, when ratified by the Legislatures of three fourths of the several States, or by Conventions in three fourths thereof, as the one or the other Mode of Ratification may be proposed by the Congress; Provided that no Amendment which may be made prior to the Year One thousand eight hundred and eight shall in any Manner affect the first and fourth Clauses in the Ninth Section of the first Article; and that no State, without its Consent, shall be deprived of its equal Suffrage in the Senate.

Article VI

[1.] All Debts contracted and Engagements entered into, before the Adoption of this Constitution, shall be as valid against the United States under this Constitution, as under the Confederation.

[2.] This Constitution, and the Laws of the United States which shall be made in Pursuance thereof; and all Treaties made, or which shall be made, under the Authority of the United Sttaes, shall be the supreme Law of the Land; and the Judges in every State shall be bound thereby, any Thing in the Constitution or Laws of any State to the Contrary notwithstanding.

[3.] The Senators and Representatives before mentioned, and the Members of the several State Legislatures, and all executive and judicial Officers, both of the United States and of the several States, shall be bound by Oath or Affirmation, to support this Constitution; but no religious Test shall ever be required as a Qualification to any Office or public Trust under the United States.

Article VII

The Ratification of the Conventions of nine States, shall be sufficient for the Establishment of this Constitution between the States so ratifying the Same.

AMENDMENTS

Amendment I

Congress shall make no law respecting an establishment of religion, or prohibiting the free exercise thereof; or abridging the freedom of speech, or of the press; or the right of the people peaceably to assemble, and to petition the Government for a redress of grievances.

Amendment II

A well regulated Militia, being necessary to the security of a free State, the right of the people to keep and bear Arms, shall not be infringed.

Amendment III

No Soldier shall, in time of peace be quartered in any house, without the consent of the Owner, nor in time of war, but in a manner to be prescribed by law.

Amendment IV

The right of the people to be secure in their persons, houses, papers, and effects, against unreasonable searches and seizures, shall not be violated, and no Warrants shall issue, but upon probable cause, supported by Oath or affirmation, and particularly describing the place to be searched, and the persons or things to be seized.

Amendment V

No person shall be held to answer for a capital, or otherwise infamous crime, unless on a presentment or indictment of a Grand Jury, except in cases arising in the land or naval forces, or in the Militia, when in actual service in time of War or public danger; nor shall any person be subject for the same offence to be twice put in jeopardy of life or limb; nor shall be compelled in any criminal case to be a witness against himself, nor be deprived of life, liberty, or property, without due process of law; nor shall private property be taken for public use, without just compensation.

Amendment VI

In all criminal prosecutions the accused shall enjoy the right to a speedy and public trial, by an impartial jury of the State and district wherein the crime shall have been committed, which district shall have been previously ascertained by law, and to be informed of the nature and cause of the accusation; to be confronted with the witnesses against him; to have compulsory process for obtaining witnesses in his favor, and to have the Assistance of Counsel for his defence.

Amendment VII

In suits at common law, where the value in controversy shall exceed twenty dollars, the right of trial by jury shall be preserved, and no fact tried by a jury shall be otherwise re-examined in any Court of the United States, than according to the rules of the common law.

Amendment VIII

Excessive bail shall not be required, nor excessive fines imposed, nor cruel and unusual punishments inflicted.

Amendment IX

The enumeration in the Constitution, of certain rights, shall not be construed to deny or disparage others retained by the people.

Amendment X

The powers not delegated to the United States by the Constitution, nor prohibited by it to the States, are reserved to the States respectively, or to the people.
[The first ten Amendments were adopted in 1791.]

Amendment XI

The Judicial power of the United States shall not be construed to extend to any suit in law or equity, commenced or prosecuted against one of the United States by Citizens of another State, or by Citizens or Subjects of any Foreign State. [Adopted in 1798.]

Amendment XII

The Electors shall meet in their respective states, and vote by ballot for President and Vice-President, one of whom, at least, shall not be an inhabitant of the same state with themselves; they shall name in their ballots the person voted for as President, and in distinct ballots the person voted for as Vice-President, and they shall make distinct lists of all persons voted for as President, and of all persons voted for as Vice-President, and of the number of votes for each, which lists they shall sign and certify, and transmit sealed to the seat of the government of the United States, directed to the President of the Senate;—The President of the Senate shall, in the presence of the Senate and House of Representatives, open all the certificates and the votes shall then be counted;—The person having the greatest number of votes for President, shall be the President, if such number be a majority of the whole number of Electors appointed; and if no person have such majority, then from the persons having the highest numbers not exceeding three on the list of those voted for as President, the House of Representatives shall choose immediately, by ballot, the President. But in choosing the President, the votes shall be taken by states, the representation from each state having one vote; a quorum for this purpose shall consist of a member or members from two-thirds of the states, and a majority of all the states shall be necessary to a choice. And if the House of Representatives shall not choose a President whenever the right of choice shall devolve upon them, before the fourth day of March next following, then the Vice-President shall act as President, as in the case of the death or other constitutional disability of the President.—The person having the greatest number of votes as Vice-President, shall be the Vice-President, if such number be a majority of the whole number of Electors appointed, and if no person have a majority, then from the two highest numbers on the list, the Senate shall choose the Vice-President; a quorum for the purpose shall consist of two-thirds of the whole number of Senators, and a majority of the whole number shall be necessary to a choice. But no person constitutionally ineligible to the office of President shall be eligible to that of Vice-President of the United States. [Adopted in 1804.]

Amendment XIII

SECTION 1. Neither slavery nor involuntary servitude, except as a punishment for crime whereof the party shall have been duly convicted, shall exist within the United States, or any place subject to their jurisdiction.

SECTION 2. Congress shall have power to enforce this article by appropriate legislation. [Adopted in 1865.]

Amendment XIV

SECTION 1. All persons born or naturalized in the United States, and subject to the jurisdiction thereof, are citizens of the United States and of the State wherein they reside. No State shall make or enforce any law which shall abridge the privileges or immunities of citizens of the United States; nor shall any State deprive any person of life, liberty, or property, without due process of law; nor deny to any person within its jurisdiction the equal protection of the laws.

SECTION 2. Representatives shall be apportioned among the several States according to their respective numbers, counting the whole number of persons in each State, excluding Indians not taxed. But when the right to vote at any election for the choice of electors for President and Vice President of the United States, Representatives in Congress, the Executive and Judicial officers of a State, or the members of the Legislature thereof, is denied to any of the male inhabitants of such State, being twenty-one years of age, and citizens of the United States, or in any way abridged, except for participation in rebellion, or other crime, the basis of representation therein shall be reduced in the proportion which the number of such male citizens shall bear to the whole number of male citizens twenty-one years of age in such State.

SECTION 3. No person shall be a Senator or Representative in Congress, or elector of President and Vice President, or hold any office, civil or military, under the United States, or under any State, who, having previously taken an oath, as a member of Congress, or as an officer of the United States, or as a member of any State legislature, or as an executive or judicial officer of any State, to support the Constitution of the United States, shall have engaged in insurrection or rebellion against the same, or given aid or comfort to the enemies thereof. But Congress may by a vote of two-thirds of each House, remove such disability.

SECTION 4. The validity of the public debt of the United States, authorized by law, including debts incurred for payment of pensions and bounties for services in suppressing insurrection or rebellion, shall not be questioned. But neither the United States nor any State shall assume or pay any debt or obligation incurred in aid of insurrection or rebellion against the United States, or any claim for the loss or emancipation of any slave; but all such debts, obligations and claims shall be held illegal and void.

SECTION 5. The Congress shall have power to enforce, by appropriate legislation, the provisions of this article. [Adopted in 1868.]

Amendment XV

SECTION 1. The right of citizens of the United States to vote shall not be denied or abridged by the United States or by any State on account of race, color, or previous condition of servitude.

SECTION 2. The Congress shall have power to enforce this article by appropriate legislation. [Adopted in 1870.]

Amendment XVI

The Congress shall have power to lay and collect taxes on incomes, from whatever source derived, without apportionment among the several States, and without regard to any census or enumeration. [Adopted in 1913.]

Amendment XVII

The Senate of the United States shall be composed of two Senators from each State, elected by the people thereof, for six years; and each Senator shall have one vote. The electors in each State shall have the qualifications requisite for electors of the most numerous branch of the State legislatures.

When vacancies happen in the representation of any State in the Senate, the executive authority of such State shall issue writs of election to fill such vacancies: *Provided,* That the legislature of any State may empower the executive thereof to make temporary appointments until the people fill the vacancies by election as the legislature may direct.

This amendment shall not be so construed as to affect the election or term of any Senator chosen before it becomes valid as part of the Constitution. [Adopted in 1913.]

Amendment XVIII

SECTION 1. After one year from the ratification of this article the manufacture, sale, or transportation of intoxicating liquors within, the importation thereof into, or the exportation thereof from the United States and all territory subject to the jurisdiction thereof for beverage purposes is hereby prohibited.

SECTION 2. The Congress and the several States shall have concurrent power to enforce this article by appropriate legislation.

SECTION 3. This article shall be inoperative unless it shall have been ratified as an amendment to the Constitution by the legislatures of the several States, as provided in the Constitution, within seven years from the date of the submission hereof to the States by the Congress. [Adopted in 1919.]

Amendment XIX

The right of citizens of the United States to vote shall not be denied or abridged by the United States or by any State on account of sex.

Congress shall have power to enforce this article by appropriate legislation. [Adopted in 1920.]

Amendment XX

SECTION 1. The terms of the President and Vice President shall end at noon on the 20th day of January, and the terms of Senators and Representatives at noon on the 3d day of January, of the years in which such terms would have ended if this article had not been ratified; and the terms of their successors shall then begin.

SECTION 2. The Congress shall assemble at least once in every year, and such meeting shall begin at noon on the 3d day of January, unless they shall by law appoint a different day.

SECTION 3. If, at the time fixed for the beginning of the term of the President, the President elect shall have died, the Vice President elect shall become President. If a President shall not have been chosen before the time fixed for the beginning of his term, or if the President elect shall have failed to qualify, then the Vice President elect shall act as President until a President shall have qualified; and the Congress may by law provide for the case wherein neither a President elect nor a Vice President elect shall have qualified, declaring who shall then act as President, or the manner in which one who is to act shall be selected, and such person shall act accordingly until a President or Vice President shall have qualified.

SECTION 4. The Congress may by law provide for the case of the death of any of the persons from whom the House of Representatives may choose a President whenever the right of choice shall have devolved upon them, and for the case of the death of any of the persons from whom the Senate may choose a Vice President whenever the right of choice shall have devolved upon them.

SECTION 5. Sections 1 and 2 shall take effect on the 15th day of October following the ratification of this article.

SECTION 6. This article shall be inoperative unless it shall have been ratified as an amendment to the Constitution by the legislatures of three-fourths of the several States within seven years from the date of its submission. [Adopted in 1933.]

Amendment XXI

SECTION 1. The eighteenth article of amendment to the Constitution of the United States is hereby repealed.

SECTION 2. The transportation or importation into any State, Territory, or possession of the United States for delivery or use therein of intoxicating liquors, in violation of the laws thereof, is hereby prohibited.

SECTION 3. This article shall be inoperative unless it shall have been ratified as an amendment to the Constitution by conventions in the several States, as provided in the Constitution, within seven years from the date of the submission hereof to the States by the Congress. [Adopted in 1933.]

Amendment XXII

SECTION 1. No person shall be elected to the office of the President more than twice, and no person who has held the office of President, or acted as President, for more than two years of a term to which some other person was elected President shall be elected to the office of the President more than once. But this Article shall not apply to any person holding the office of President when this Article was proposed by the Congress, and shall not prevent any person who may be holding the office of President, or acting as President, during the term within which this Article becomes operative from holding the office of President or acting as President during the remainder of such term.

SECTION 2. This Article shall be inoperative unless it shall have been ratified as an amendment to the Constitution by the legislatures of three-fourths of the several States within seven years from the date of its submission to the states by the Congress. [Adopted in 1951.]

Amendment XXIII

SECTION 1. The District constituting the seat of Government of the United States shall appoint in such manner as the Congress may direct:

A number of electors of President and Vice President equal to the whole number of Senators and Representatives in Congress to which the District would be entitled if it were a State, but in no event more than the least populous State; they shall be in addition to those appointed by the States, but they shall be considered, for the purposes of the election of President and Vice President, to be electors appointed by a State; and they shall meet in the District and perform such duties as provided by the twelfth article of amendment.

SECTION 2. The Congress shall have power to enforce this article by appropriate legislation. [Adopted in 1961.]

LIST OF CASES

Cases shown in italic type are those reprinted in the text

Abbate v. United States, 359 U.S. 187 (1959), 393

Abel v. United States, 362 U.S. 217 (1960), 372

Ableman v. Booth, 21, How. 506 (1859), 201

Abrams v. United States, 250 U.S. 616 (1919), 226–231

Adair v. United States, 208 U.S. 161 (1908), 423

Adamson v. California, 332 U.S. 46 (1947), 363–370

Adkins v. Children's Hospital, 261 U.S. 525 (1923), 422

Adler v. Board of Education of City of New York, 342 U.S. 485 (1952), 295, 297–301

Alabama Power Co. v. Ickes, 302 U.S. 464 (1938), 112

Alberts v. California, 354 U.S. 476 (1957), 271–278

Allen-Bradley Local No. 1111 v. Wisconsin Employment Relations Board, 315 U.S. 740 (1942), 142

Allgeyer v. Louisiana, 165 U.S. 578 (1897), 416

Amalgamated Assn. v. Wisconsin Employment Relations Board, 340 U.S. 383 (1951), 142

American Communications Association v. Douds, 339 U.S. 382 (1950), 294

American Insurance Co. v. Canter, 1 Pet. 511 (1828), 3

Anastaplo, In re, 366 U.S. 82 (1961), 296

Anderson v. Dunn, 6 Wheat. 204 (1821), 94

Ashcraft v. Tennessee, 322 U.S. 143 (1944), 386

Ashwander v. TVA, 297 U.S. 288 (1936), 25

Associated Press v. NLRB, 301 U.S. 103 (1937), 233

Associated Press v. United States, 326 U.S. 1 (1945), 233

Austin v. Tennessee, 179 U.S. 343 (1900), 418

Baker v. Carr, 369 U.S. 186 (1962), 40, 62–76

Ballard v. United States, 329 U.S. 187 (1946), 409

Barenblatt v. United States, 360 U.S. 109 (1959), 96–102

Barron v. Baltimore, 7 Pet. 243 (1833), 222, 361

Barrows v. Jackson, 346 U.S. 249 (1953), 433

Bartkus v. Illinois, 359 U.S. 121 (1959), 393–399

Bates v. City of Little Rock, 361 U.S. 516 (1960), 297

Beauharnais v. Illinois, 343 U.S. 250 (1952), 224, 262–269

Beilan v. Board of Public Education, 357 U.S. 399 (1958), 295

Benanti v. United States, 355 U.S. 96 (1957), 373

Berman v. Parker, 348 U.S. 26 (1954), 418–419

Betts v. Brady, 316 U.S. 455 (1942), 402–407

Bibb v. Navajo Freight Lines, 359 U.S. 520 (1959), 141–142

Bob-Lo Excursion Co. v. Michigan, 333 U.S. 28 (1948), 141

Bolling v. Sharpe, 347 U.S. 497 (1954), 435, 440

Bowles v. Willingham, 321 U.S. 503 (1944), 88, 184

Braden v. United States, 365 U.S. 431 (1961), 96

Breard v. Alexandria, 341 U.S. 622 (1951), 244

Ribnik v. McBride, 277 U.S. 350 (1928), 425

Rice v. Elmore, 333 U.S. 875 (1948), 60

Rochin v. California, 342 U.S. 165 (1952), 374

Roth v. *United States,* 354 U.S. 476 (1957), 271–278

Saia v. New York, 334 U.S. 558 (1948), 243

Scales v. *United States,* 355 U.S. 1 (1957), 311; 367 U.S. 203 (1961), 311, 324–328

Schechter Poultry Corp. v. United States, 295 U.S. 495 (1935), 87–88, 122

Schenck v. United States, 249 U.S. 47 (1919), 225

Schneider v. State (Town of Irvington), 308 U.S. 147 (1939), 233–234

Schneiderman v. United States, 320 U.S. 118 (1943), 308

Schware v. New Mexico Board of Bar Examiners, 353 U.S. 232 (1957), 296

Selective Draft Law Cases, 245 U.S. 366 (1918), 184

Semler v. Oregon State Board of Dental Examiners, 294 U.S. 608 (1935), 416

Senn v. Tile Layers' Protective Union, 301 U.S. 468 (1937), 424

Shelley v. Kraemer, 334 U.S. 1 (1946), 433

Shelton v. *Tucker,* 364 U.S. 479 (1960), 296, 301–306

Shreveport Rate Case, 234 U.S. 342 (1914), 122

Shuttlesworth v. Birmingham Board of Education, 358 U.S. 101 (1958), 436

Siebold, Ex parte, 100 U.S. 371 (1880), 58

Silverman v. United States, 365 U.S. 505 (1961), 373

Skinner v. Oklahoma, 316 U.S. 535 (1942), 417

Slaughter-House Cases, 16 Wall. 36 (1873), 359, 360, 415

Slochower v. Board of Higher Education of New York City, 350 U.S. 551 (1956), 295

Smith v. Allwright, 321 U.S. 649 (1914), 60

Smith v. California, 361 U.S. 147 (1959), 271

Snyder v. Massachusetts, 291 U.S. 97 (1934), 358

Sonzinsky v. United States, 300 U.S. 506 (1937), 106

South Carolina v. United States, 199 U.S. 437 (1905), 104

South Carolina Highway Department v. Barnwell Brothers, 303 U.S. 177 (1938), 141

Southern Pacific Co. v. *Arizona,* 325 U.S. 761 (1945), 141, 143–149

Springer v. United States, 102 U.S. 586 (1881), 103

Stettler v. O'Hara, 243 U.S. 629 (1917), 422

Steward Machine Co. v. Davis, 301 U.S. 548 (1937), 113

Strauder v. West Virginia, 100 U.S. 303 (1880), 409

Stromberg v. California, 283 U.S. 359 (1931), 307

Sunday Closing Cases, 366 U.S. 420 (1961), 342, 347–355

Sweatt v. Painter, 339 U.S. 629 (1950), 435

Sweezy v. New Hampshire, 354 U.S. 234 (1957), 95

Swift & Co. v. United States, 196 U.S. 375 (1905), 122

Talley v. California, 362 U.S. 60 (1960), 234

Tennessee Electric Power Co. v. TVA, 306 U.S. 118 (1939), 112

Terminiello v. *Chicago,* 337 U.S. 1 (1949), 253–261

Terry v. Adams, 345 U.S. 461 (1953), 60–61

Texas v. White, 7 Wall. 700 (1869), 199

Thomas v. Collins, 323 U.S. 516 (1945), 226

Thornhill v. Alabama, 310 U.S. 88 (1940), 245

Times Film Corp. v. *Chicago,* 365 U.S. 43 (1961), 280, 286–292

Toolson v. New York Yankees, 346 U.S. 356 (1953), 123

Torcaso v. Watkins, 367 U.S. 488 (1961), 332

Trop v. *Dulles,* 356 U.S. 86 (1958), 445–451

Truax v. Corrigan, 257 U.S. 312 (1921), 423

Tucker v. Texas, 326 U.S. 517 (1946), 244

Twining v. New Jersey, 211 U.S. 78 (1908), 361, 386

Tyson and Brother v. Banton, 273 U.S. 418 (1927), 424

Ullmann v. *United States,* 350 U.S. 422 (1956), 384, 387–390

United Public Workers v. Mitchell, 330 U.S. 75 (1947), 244

DATE DUE

03. 83	
FEB 6 '91	
MAR 6 '91	